DISCARD

PEARL HARBOR COUNTDOWN

Admiral James O. Richardson

SKIPPER STEELY

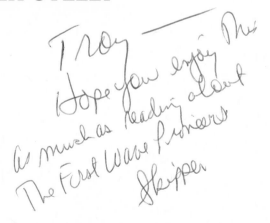

Troy —
Hope you enjoy this
as much as reading about
The First Wave Pioneers
Skipper

PELICAN PUBLISHING COMPANY

GRETNA 2008

*The word "Pelican" and the depiction of a pelican
are trademarks of Pelican Publishing Company, Inc.,
and are registered in the U.S. Patent and Trademark Office.*

Library of Congress Cataloging-in-Publication Data

Steely, Skipper.
  Pearl Harbor Countdown : Admiral James O. Richardson / by Skipper
Steely.
    p. cm.
  Includes bibliographical references and index.
  ISBN 978-1-58980-592-7 (hardcover : alk. paper)
1. Richardson, James O. (James Otto), 1878-1974. 2. Admirals—United
States—Biography. 3. United States. Navy—Biography. 4. Pearl Harbor
(Hawaii), Attack on, 1941. 5. World War, 1939-1945—Naval operations,
American. 6. United States—History, Naval—20th century. I. Title.
  E746.R53S74 2008
  359.0092—dc22
  [B]

                                2008002455

*Front-jacket photograph: James O. Richardson, from the Photo
Collection at The Naval Historical Center, Washington Navy Yard,
Washington, D.C.*

Printed in the United States of America

Published by Pelican Publishing Company, Inc.
1000 Burmaster Street, Gretna, Louisiana 70053

Contents

Preface

For several years as I wrote local articles for my father's weekly Texas newspaper, the *Lamar County Echo,* and later for the *Paris News,* Retired Army Lieutenant Colonel Henry Lee Somerville related that the most famous alumnus of Paris, Texas, was Admiral Otto Richardson. "He was fired by the president," he would tell me, "because he wanted to move the [U.S.] Fleet away from Hawaii."

Surely, I thought, if Richardson, the valedictorian of the Paris High School Class of 1894, was that smart, he would have avoided a presidential conflict and run the fleet as in the past. But, then, as I began to read about his career, the problems became clear. No commander in chief of the U.S. Fleet (CinCUS) had ever faced this predicament. With war closing in from both sides of the United States, civilians began to believe that the fleet, with most of its ships in the Pacific, could serve as a deterrent to the Japanese.

Admirals in charge in 1940 knew differently. For two decades after Charles Evans Hughes chaired the Washington Treaty of 1921, the U.S. Navy had been hindered in its growth by an inventory ratio derived from that conference.[1] However, as much as this blueprint for nations disgruntled Great Britain and the United States naval world, it had the Japanese fuming. They were made second-class by the treaty, though they thought they were equal.

Richardson was a big man, and looked even larger when I saw him renewing his subscription on one late 1950's day in my father's newspaper. Being just a fifteen-year-old with no extensive World War II study other than Sunday-night Walter Cronkite *20th Century* television programs, he meant nothing much to me. My father had been an officer in the Mediterranean during World War II, but was not a storyteller.

The admiral, however, though he wrote a book on his career,

left few personal materials behind.[2] His relatives in Paris are gone now. A sister married a widower, to which family Somerville belonged. She had no children, but some of her husband's family took an interest and provided stories, materials, and literature. The admiral had a son of his own, who was a rather prolific screenwriter. He wrote many episodes of *The Lone Ranger* radio show. However, the son, Joe Fenet Richardson, had no children, though he and his wife adopted a daughter. Unfortunately, she stated that she knew little of the admiral and did now allow me to sift through materials in her father's Beverly Hills home.

Richardson and his editor, Admiral George C. Dyer, wrote more than a few times that Richardson destroyed parts of his diary pertaining to 1940 and the constant argument about the fleet's location. In the 1970 movie *Tora! Tora! Tora!* Richardson is portrayed flying over Pearl Harbor in a PBY flying boat, talking with Admiral Husband E. Kimmel, his replacement.[3] This movie is still a very good look at what led up to the attack, mainly because its producers used as consultants Ladislas Farago, author of *The Broken Seal,* and Gordon Prange, author of *At Dawn We Slept.* However, Richardson is only called Jim in the movie and is not really identified to the audience as the outgoing commander. My research reveals that only Richardson's wife called him Jim. His old Paris friends always called him Otto, and Navy personnel just shortened it all by calling him Joe, or JO. The sailors fondly called him Uncle Joe.

When the new look at the Pearl Harbor attack came at the sixtieth anniversary in 2001, that movie left him and most of 1940 out completely. However, what that movie did uncover through the curious researchers, and the anti-government critics, was Richardson's two meetings with President Franklin D. Roosevelt and the argument between them about placing the fleet unprepared in harm's way at Hawaii. The Internet began to be pasted with much of the testimony in the eight subsequent hearings conducted on this subject. Each time the Kimmel family made one more move to soften the history of their father and grandfather, who was blamed for the disaster at Pearl Harbor,

Richardson's career was placed out in the open also. In 2006 an episode of Oliver North's *War Stories* finally revealed more about Richardson and his part in the story.

Therefore, the timing to write Richardson's life and thoughts seemed to be proper, especially with the seventieth anniversary fast approaching. For, without knowing what Richardson was thinking, and doing, an understanding of the Pearl Harbor debacle cannot be attained. Hopefully, this book will guide the reader through the days of his life and the years of his career to help explain why he managed the Navy fleet as he did in those crucial times leading up to America's dramatic entry into World War II.

PEARL HARBOR COUNTDOWN

CHAPTER ONE

The Greatest "I Told You So" in U.S. History

Extensive Navy Career Taught Many Lessons

On December 7, 1941, Admiral James Otto Richardson slipped into the kitchen of his Georgetown home where his wife May was cooking breakfast. Normally Richardson was the chef, but this time he sat and read the Sunday newspapers. After a few minutes of quiet, he mentioned his War College thesis on Japanese policy. He told May he was going to reread it that day.[1] He also told her he thought the United States was on the verge of war, nothing new to May, since she had heard that comment for the past three years.[2]

Back in Paris, Texas, the previous Friday afternoon the couple's hometown newspaper had bannered the headline "Japan Delivers Fateful Answer to United States." The subhead declared: "Question of War or Peace May Be Settled This Week." The Associated Press story summarized what was happening. Japanese Special Envoy Saburo Kurusu and Richardson friend Japanese Ambassador Kichisaburo Nomura delivered to American Secretary of State Cordell Hull a fateful answer to the question of war or peace in the Pacific.[3] So, even in the remote area of northeast Texas, citizens were aware of the impending chances of war with Japan.

It was a year and two months to the day from the time that Richardson had stood in the White House, tired after an overnight trip from the West Coast, and told President Franklin D. Roosevelt that the Navy did not trust the civilian leadership.[4] For this outburst, three months later Richardson was relieved from his post as commander in chief of the United States Fleet. The acronym fit the situation—CinCUS (Sink Us)! His protests to FDR were not new. This time, however, it was his aggressiveness that proved fatal. As a result, Richardson's career seemed to be "sunk."

However, ten months after being detached and replaced by Admiral Husband E. Kimmel, Richardson was still an employee

15

of the U.S. Navy. After breakfast he found the 1934 paper he had planned to review that day.[5] The weather was warmer than normal, so he sat on his semi-enclosed porch as he did almost every morning.

He completed reading the paper before noon.[6] It was a typical military study paper, one of two he did at the War College, and much like the book he wrote in the 1950s explaining his side of the story of Pearl Harbor. His thesis was about the relationship in war of naval strategy, tactics, and command, sometimes versus policy. Even then, as early as 1934, he felt that the ability to discuss what American naval plans should be in case of war depended upon a good knowledge of the country's foreign policy. "But, the form of our Government is such that no one can state what the American foreign policies are," he wrote then, and probably still felt in 1941.[7]

He thought that a nation should have the right to remain neutral, if it wanted to do so, and that this right should be spelled out during peace times. However, at that time the United States struggled to remain neutral. He was firm in his belief that it would be impossible for the United States to be neutral in any future war in which a strong naval power was engaged.[8]

Like Roosevelt, Richardson was miffed that the American people were so unalterably opposed to entanglement in European affairs and assumed they would also be so when it came to Asiatic difficulties with Japan. "The American people are primarily concerned with domestic affairs, have no desire to participate in World politics . . . beyond expressing moral sentiments and altruistic aims which they like to talk about and wish for, but are unwilling to support by force," he wrote eight years before the attack on Pearl Harbor.

He wrote that the Hawaiian Islands should be prepared as an outpost defending the West Coast rather than a stepping-off place for any westward movement across the Pacific. In that regard, he and Roosevelt somewhat agreed, but Richardson was stubborn in his belief that the U.S. Fleet was not prepared for permanent placement in or near Pearl Harbor. Richardson did expect that the citizens would demand that the Navy take some aggressive stroke in response to Japanese overt actions. But, he had no confidence that enough study on the situation had been done by the leaders of the government or the Navy.

In his final paper at the War College, Richardson discussed the future battle in the Pacific. It would come from aircraft carriers. He knew then that it would be hard to locate and attack such ships, which might be separated by fifty or more miles. Since searching for and attacking carriers would be difficult even by air, he suggested that heavy cruisers be added to the U.S. naval force to supplement intelligence gathering. "Yet, we have devoted little time and effort to develop the proper method of utilizing these vessels in scouting," he wrote.[9]

Richardson felt that World War I forced reorganization of the U.S. War Department into a war-making mode. However, since the Navy was mainly administrative and supply during that conflict, it had not undergone such change. He agreed that the Navy was very conservative and would resist change anyway. He laid much of the blame for that situation on the civilians who staffed the strongly entrenched bureaus, some on the officers, and a bit on Congress. Ironically, because of his dismissal in early 1941 by Roosevelt, Richardson was selected later to be on boards and commissions that did initiate reorganization, some of it slightly too much for Richardson.[10] On that morning of December 7, 1941, his ideas concerning the lack of prewar planning were about to be proven correct.

Richardson still believed much of what he had written in 1934, and as a member of the 1941 Navy General Board he knew well that administrative duties still overwhelmed officers. "All hands are so busy keeping their desks clear of papers that they have no time to think about how the whole service might be improved," he wrote. Because of his unexpected release as U.S. Fleet commander eleven months earlier, Richardson had little chance to enact his own management style into the Navy Fleet.

At 1:30 P.M., the phone rang. Unlike other admirals, his duties as a special assignee to rework regulations and study promotions did not entail Sunday overtime at the office. And, he loved golf, planning a trip to the Army-Navy Country Club if the temperature remained steady and the rain held off. "Joe, turn on your radio," a voice on the phone said. "When this was done," he wrote later, "the report of the Japanese attack on Pearl Harbor was heard." The greatest "I Told You So" in U.S. history had just occurred.

From January 6, 1940, until his detachment from CinCUS on February 1, 1941, Richardson had steadfastly told all who would listen or read his messages that the Navy could not stand up to a war mode in one ocean, much less in two. After Richardson realized that the April 1940 docking of the fleet at Pearl Harbor was becoming permanent, a steady stream of conversation and messages went from his office to Washington, DC. Remaining at Pearl Harbor, to him, was an enticement to force the Japanese hand. To FDR, at least outwardly, it simply told Japan that the United States was not only determined to hold what it owned, but was willing to move westward if necessary.

Richardson had an Oriental mind-set, having served a dozen assignments in the Pacific. He studied what Japan did to Russia in early years of the twentieth century, and he knew well what was happening at the moment as the Land of the Rising Sun expanded its horizon. He had only informal intelligence lines, but he knew just from his associations that the Japanese were capable of capturing all the lands they desired in the Pacific Rim. However, his pleadings for awareness and action were ignored, or so he thought.

Loving the Navy as he did, it was only natural to him to spread his perception. He was not a cocky person, nor was he overwhelmed with his own knowledge. His background was education. His father and stepmother were the backbone of the teaching world in his small northeast Texas hometown. However, there was military experience in his family history. His father had served some eighteen months as a Civil War Confederate prisoner on Johnson's Island. Richardson's cousin, Wilds Preston Richardson, attended the U.S. Military Academy at West Point. He later created most of the early highway systems of Alaska. In the Great War, Otto's cousin

Dick Richardson gained some fame when he was ordered by President Woodrow Wilson and General John J. Pershing to evacuate the American Expeditionary Forces in North Russia.

Therefore, Admiral Richardson was keenly aware that his influence could create a foundation for leaders to follow when war began. To him, it was not a matter of *whether* the United States and Japan would clash, but *when.* His belief was so strong that until ordered to cease by Chief of Naval Operations (CNO) Harold R. "Betty" Stark, while commander of the U.S. Fleet, Richardson sent out patrol planes each day to check the ocean for signs of an attack on Pearl Harbor.

In a more subtle way, however, CinCUS Richardson began to prepare his younger Navy officers. He talked personally with the ones he noticed had potential to be war leaders. Robert B. Carney, for example, was startled one day in the summer of 1940 when Captain Harold M. Bemis told him that he was to go over and talk with Richardson. "I wondered what I had been caught at," Carney wrote years later after he was a retired admiral himself.[11]

Still with dark hair, wearing wire-rimmed glasses, and knocking his pipe clean while standing over his desk, Richardson broke right into his speech with no long summary of why he had called Carney to his office. "I am sure that a war with Japan is inevitable," he began, and proceeded to tell Carney that it would be a long one. "He wanted to talk to some of my age bracket, those he considered would be wartime leaders," Carney wrote.

Flattered, but still naïve and confident, the Naval Academy graduate was sure that he knew what to do if a war arrived. Richardson painted the scene. "To me, what he said was shattering," Carney remembered. The admiral outlined the lack of advanced bases. He probably told Carney what he later wrote in his book, "The pre-World War II development of Guam as a naval base was defeated in Congress by the pacifists and isolationists, who as predicted, argued that any such work would be an aggressive act conducive to war with Japan."[12]

Not one to emotionally hammer upon his table with the end of his pipe, or to raise his voice, Richardson simply continued to tell

Extracted Americans from Russia: Wilds Preston "Dick" Richardson was both a stepbrother and cousin to Admiral J. O. Richardson. Since there were seventeen years difference in their ages, the pair probably never knew each other well, though the Army officer came back to Paris, Texas, several times to visit the family. W. P. Richardson guided the building of the Alaska highway system, and after World War I followed the orders of President Woodrow Wilson and General John J. Pershing, organizing the departure of American troops from Northern Russia. He died in 1929. (From U.S. Army Register 1913, copy at Alaska State Library—Historical Collections)

Carney that the Navy was lacking in both offensive and defensive capabilities; short on ammunition, fuel, and spare parts; and had only a few ships to support the fleet as it advanced. Basically, the warships needed to return to the West Coast to be properly prepared for war. For example, wooden decks should be removed and replaced with steel, portholes closed and sealed, and outdated guns replaced by more powerful ones.

Carney listened to each point the sixty-one-year-old admiral administered to the young commander. "He dismantled my confident belief that the U.S. Navy could win a quick decision." Instead, Richardson told him that it was his firm belief that it would take the United States two years to build up an offensive strength. The country would have to hang on while that strength was developed.

In Richardson's mind, following the entry into war, there would be at least one year and probably two of hard fighting. It would most likely be a four-year war. This pronouncement stunned Carney. "I considered myself a competent professional, versed in all the experiences and skills required for advancement. At least I had so considered myself." But, when Richardson finished, Carney later wrote, "I was sure of nothing!"

Staggering from the flagship USS *Pennsylvania,* Carney went back to the battleship *California,* almost physically sick. "Sleep would not come. My tight little professional world had collapsed." Carney accepted, however, what Richardson conveyed to him that day, and started reexamining his naval views from scratch. From that moment on, Carney changed. "No matter what the conventional wisdom held on any given subject, from then on I would challenge it, disregard it, and make my own evaluation."

For one officer, at least, the CinCUS had made a lasting impression, sending him off to carry the word throughout the lower ranks. "I later expressed my gratitude," Carney wrote. Not many did so, and especially not Richardson's superiors President Franklin Roosevelt, Chief of Naval Operations Harold Stark, or Secretary of the Navy Frank Knox. However, many small statements recorded in print during the following years remind readers and researchers that Richardson warned many times about the lack of preparedness in the Navy.

On Monday, December 8, 1941, the day after the Japanese attack on Pearl Harbor, Richardson quietly walked into the General Board room. Sitting around were his peers, all giving out their individual viewpoints.[13] Each tried to explain why, and how, the surprise attack had happened. In his book, *On the Treadmill to Pearl Harbor,* Richardson does not name those present, but most likely few there knew of the intelligence capabilities of the Navy, that messages had been read for months indicating that such a fate awaited some American site in the Pacific.

The president of the General Board, Vice-Admiral William R. Sexton, finally said, "Joe. You haven't said a word up to now. What are your views?" Fully aware that his thoughts were already in numerous correspondences to his superiors, friends, and family, Richardson simply replied, "All I have to say is that every day, from now on, I am going to pray for two things. The first is for the success of our arms; the second is that I may keep my lips sealed!"[14]

Richardson almost immediately made a plan to burn his personal notes. He did not want to be accused of disobeying his commander in chief, or of saying disparaging words about the president. He knew he would be called to testify sometime, somewhere about the Pearl Harbor attack. In the meantime, he did as he said. However, as he wrote, "I did not lay down the bricks" and retire from the Navy or society. He had been busy as a member of the General Board since March 25, and though he did remain quiet about his past thoughts, Richardson began what was perhaps his highest call to duty. He served for six more years, working on several projects that would formulate life for the future of others. As he feared, in 1945 he was finally called to give extensive testimony before Congress. But, true to his promise to the Navy Board, he remained fairly quiet during the war years.

Finally, in 1956 his former aide, Admiral George Carroll Dyer, and the Naval History Division, convinced Richardson to reconstruct his career and thoughts. Apparently the pair worked biweekly for months on the drafts as Richardson slipped toward eighty years of age. "I can attest," wrote Dyer later, "that . . . Admiral Richardson had an inexhaustible memory for facts, figures and personalities." Though completed, the work remained dormant until a year before his death in 1974 at the age of ninety-five. He had requested, because of the frankness of his manuscript, and the long working relationship between the two, that it not be published until after Stark's death.[15]

In the end, Richardson expressed regret that he had burned many of his diary pages. However, he wrote, "Since in the diary I expressed frank and sometimes offhand opinions (some of them highly critical) of various officers of the Navy, and of officials of the Government for their actions or inactions during the 1939-1941 period, I thought it best that the diary be burned. So, I burned it, after extracting some non-critical parts. I also burned some of my personal letters and various naval communications carrying my pithy comments."

Today, those comments do not rank in the menial category. They are essential to supplement history's view of Pearl Harbor, and to evaluate Richardson's importance to the string of events that preceded it.

CHAPTER TWO

"At Home They Called Me Otto"
Youth in Paris, Texas

The noticeable wise demeanor and likeable personality that Otto Richardson carried throughout his life came basically from his father. Though his family all originated from the Spartanburg, South Carolina, area, John James "J. J." Richardson was a DeKalb County, Alabama, native. He was born there in 1837, but moved to Providence, then to Pickens County, where his mother's four brothers lived.[1] He obtained a degree from the University of Alabama in 1861.[2]

The six-foot, two-inch, gray-eyed, and dark-haired J. J. Richardson was at the Battle of Shiloh in April of 1862, participated in Confederate General Braxton Bragg's campaign up through Kentucky the following fall, and at the turn of the year fought near Murfreesboro, Tennessee. Federals captured the twenty-six-year-old at the Battle of Missionary Ridge near Chattanooga on November 25, 1863.[3]

After the Civil War, Richardson went west to Texas to teach. Why he landed in Paris is unknown, but his uncle Oliver Perry Richardson was a teacher forty miles away in the small Hunt County farming community of Ladonia.[4] J. J. Richardson returned to Alabama to marry Frances Goodlett Foster.[5] She was a native of South Carolina.[6] The couple constructed a house on the northwest side of Paris.[7]

The Richardsons soon had a daughter, Jessie, born on February 12, 1871. They lost a son, John P., when he died after sixteen days in March of 1873. Then a second daughter was born in September of 1874; she was named Mary Moss. A third daughter was added to the family in mid-1876, and named Fannie. Finally, a healthy boy survived. James Otto Richardson was born on September 18, 1878.

In addition to private teaching, Professor Richardson's duties as the acting county superintendent for the judge and commissioners court expanded.[8] To supplement his salary, he went to work for the Paris Female Institute in 1870, which had been recently acquired by the Methodist church.[9] In March of 1875, as the agent for the county, he took a huge step for the local educational world by purchasing Graham School, four blocks from his family home.[10]

T. H. Hadden was an early student enrolled in classes taught by Professor Richardson. "While he was the laziest man in Lamar County," Hadden told his friend and newspaper editor A. W. Neville, Professor Richardson "could, when not chewing tobacco, do a fine job of instructing."[11] Rail traffic to and through Paris was bustling.[12] Thus, more traffic brought more students for the Richardsons. They finally just leased Graham School from the county in August of 1878.[13] But their idyllic life shattered in less than a year.

When Otto Richardson was only thirteen months old, his mother died, probably in another childbirth. He later wrote, "After my mother died, her sister [Laura] took me in. So, she had two babies about the same time to care for."[14] William Anderson Wingo and Laura Pattillo Foster Wingo settled near Ladonia, Texas, in 1872.[15] Here they lived and worked on a farm near Oliver P. Richardson, whose late wife had been Anderson Wingo's sister. By 1879, the Wingos not only had their own baby, Augusta, but they also had a two-year old son, Clifford Earl.[16]

Oliver Richardson's wife Hester left him two children to raise, Lula and Wilds Preston. However, the house was not wifeless for long, for on December 15, 1864, he married a fellow teacher, twenty-year-old Susan Ann Neilson. She was a native of North Carolina, schooled in her mountain home of Asheville. She was the oldest of a family of seven, but was twenty-three years junior to her husband.

The couple had a child of their own in 1869, naming her Sarah. However, eventually she took the name O. P.—"just the initials," as she would tell everyone all her life.[17] Some, however, spelled her name Opie.

A few months after Otto lost his mother, Oliver Richardson

unexpectedly died. By then Susan was a respected Ladonia teacher, Lula was married to Memory H. Turner, and Dick was preparing to enter an Army career, applying to attend West Point. In the meantime, during the late spring of 1880, he boarded in nearby Paris and tutored with his father's nephew, J. J. Richardson, Even though he was nineteen, Dick was still taking academic lessons.[18] He entered the academy that fall.

Susan Richardson was boarding with the William W. Swafford family in the southwest portion of Lamar County, north and east of Ladonia. Opie was with her, eleven years old at that time.[19] Teaching jobs were more plentiful in Paris, so Susan moved to the larger town. In the late summer of 1883, she and Professor Richardson married.[20] The children on both sides left no trace that this marriage upset them in any way. In fact, the connected families seemed to socialize and even study together as one. The widely traveled Dick Richardson referred to Paris, Texas, as home many times as he served in the United States for the Army. Lula remained in Ladonia for some years. In later years, Opie received as much attention from Otto as did his two sisters.

Admiral Richardson said in later interviews that he moved back to the Paris home when he was about five years old, after his father remarried.[21] Otto began to learn games from his father, an expert chess player who was also good at dominoes. Professor Richardson began taking his son on rabbit hunts and fishing and camping trips into the Indian Territory, fifteen miles to the north of Paris across the Red River.

Opie stayed in Paris for some time where she was active in the local theater.[22] Then, on a trip to visit her half-brother Dick at St. Michaels, Alaska Territory, she was traveling down the Yukon River when the ship docked. On the way to shore, the ferry capsized in the rough waves. A man she just met saved her life. He was William Ogilvie, the just-resigned commissioner of the Yukon Territory for Canada. The couple married three years later.[23]

No matter where the Richardson children went in town, they were likely to be taught by their father or some of his associates. Even at the Methodist church, Otto ran into his father's educational influence. Professor Richardson and neighbors taught Sunday school.[24]

Another lifelong influence on the Richardson youth was the Paris attitude toward liquor. However, Richardson's "niece" Clareda Purser claims that efforts to impress upon Paris citizens and youth the negatives of a tainted drink did not take with the admiral. "Once in my twenties a friend of mine and I visited him in Georgetown. After a 'royal' tour of D.C., he sat with us on the sun porch. He had the colored woman who worked for him bring us a beer! This really impressed me because my grandmother, his sister Jessie, was so anti-alcohol . . . so, having a beer with the Admiral was a secret I never revealed to my relatives."[25]

The Paris Centenary Methodist Church began construction of a brick building southwest of the Lamar County courthouse in 1885, four blocks from the Richardson home. As a member of the church, Professor Richardson was given a chance to purchase lumber from the old facility as it was torn down.[26] With this material, he built a larger home next to the site of the old Richardson house. He was then able to use it to conduct a private school during the day, and house his family during the evenings.

As Otto Richardson approached his eleventh birthday the sheltered world around him felt good, but the education he was receiving broadened his mind. Letters from and visits home by Dick must have given Otto a desire to see the world too. When Dick returned to Paris one Christmas, a large dinner-dance was given in his honor. It was unusually cold, but Dick and his sister Lula stayed out until a late hour. Sue Richardson heard the gate latch click as the two came into the yard. She quickly arose from bed to stir the coals in the fireplace, hoping to start a blaze to warm the living room. Earlier, young Otto had left a "35-shooter" Roman candle in the wood basket. In the dark Sue took it, thinking she had a broomstick. In a moment the three in the room were greeted with a shower of colored balls and sparks shooting about the house.

When the excitement subsided, Dick commented, "All Paris has united to do me honor, but only Momma thought to set off a pyrotechnic display." He was a large, round-chested, mustached man, with a good sense of humor. The family would not have too many times in the future when they would all be together.[27]

At first, Otto Richardson attended grade school in the one-story frame building on Graham Street. His stepmother was teaching there too, as well as his father. In 1889, however, Paris erected a two-story brick facility on that location. On January 2, 1890, the pupils assembled, thanking the school board and city for the "commodious" building erected in the third ward. They resolved to take care of it and the contents, and hoped that "the boys and girls may develop into honorable, useful men and women."[28]

In Paris, the 1890s saw a furious onslaught of religious fervor against the saloons. Still, all-around growth was apparent in this county seat of 9,358. An engineer named Walter C. Dean would become a major part of the city planning, and his daughter a small part of Richardson's later life.

When Otto Richardson began his first year at Paris High School, the building was imposing, with round-topped windows and a mansard roof. There was plenty of airflow to keep the students fairly cool during the hot weather of summer, but the heating system was well taxed to keep them warm that winter. When one norther hit, ducks were knocked to the ground like chunks of wood, and the river froze.[29] School was still held.

Despite the weather interruptions, students at Paris High

Otto and his sisters: In a photo taken by Hudson Photography Studio about 1894, Richardson posed with his sisters, Moss, Jessie, and Fannie. On the far right is O.P., his stepsister/cousin. Moss became a college teacher in West Texas. Jessie lived most of her life in or near Paris, Texas. Fannie died in 1901. O. P. married a Canadian and lived in Ottawa. (Photo from Elizabeth Wingo Banks Papers, Duncan, Oklahoma)

School were taught astronomy, botany, history, algebra, trigonometry, reading, writing, and arithmetic. Each Friday botany classes gathered flowers from the countryside, background for Otto's later interest in gardening. The day began at 8:00 A.M., ending at 4:00 P.M.[30]

If they were ambitious, the fifteen graduates of Paris High School in 1894 had little in career opportunities locally. By then most of them were indoctrinated into the wider-thinking world of their first-year superintendent, J. G. Wooten. This graduate of Bethel College, Kentucky, also had a law degree from the University of Virginia. After five previous years as superintendent at Oxford, Mississippi, he introduced many innovations to the classrooms in Paris.[31]

Their well-educated principal, University of Texas graduate E. L. Dohoney, Jr., also stimulated the undergraduates. He guided the some 130 high school students, 51 more than the previous year. He was the son of the anti-secessionist who wrote, "It is worth more to a child to be properly begotten, borne, and born, than a thousand years of education."[32] However, despite this statement, the elder Dohoney strongly supported public education. Free education for all was quickly replacing the private school effort, though Sue and J. J. Richardson still held classes at certain times for sixteen years in their home.[33] With so many always traipsing through his boyhood house, Otto Richardson could later adapt quickly to the confined space of a ship.

The Paris newspaper reported the spring graduation, noting, "The valedictory of '94 could not have been entrusted to an abler orator than Mr. Otto Richardson. Otto is a close student and although the youngest member of the class, was selected as valedictorian and right well did he do his part. He is a chip from the old block, and has pursued a course the result of which is creditable to the school, himself and his parents."[34]

Only three of Otto Richardson's fifteen classmates were remaining in Paris by the time the group reached the age of fifty, with the rest stretched from California to Washington, DC.[35] Like Dick, Otto applied to attend West Point. On the test, he finished in the top three.[36] However, another nominee was chosen. So, at age sixteen Otto went to work at the Lion Drugstore on the northwest corner of the public square. He became a "jack of all trades," formulating a lifetime friendship with older fellow clerk, D. Williams.

The days in Paris between 1894 and 1898 were not exactly dull, however. Years later Williams would tell big-city newsmen craving information about the new fleet commander's background, "Otto was very popular with members of the younger set here. He was an excellent dancer, and went to a dance every Friday night in the old Peterson Hotel."

Though riding bicycles was popular in that era, Williams said Richardson "was a bookworm like his father." After two years at the Lion Drugstore, he became "frontman" at the Greiner-Kelly Drugstore. There he made acquaintance with one of the silent partners in the concern, Mayor Ed McCuistion. "Otto was a likeable boy," the amateur historian and banker said of his young friend. "He was always courteous. I have never heard anyone say an unkind word of him."

Early in 1898, Richardson again took the required examination for West Point. However, on March 19 a letter arrived from the War Department's Adjutant General's Office. It revealed that Richardson had passed all the various parts of the exam, but that the regularly appointed candidate had also been successful. "There is no vacancy from your Congressional district," it concluded.[37]

Then, *Paris News* editor Neville spotted a notice one day. It announced that a Naval Academy exam was being held in Dallas. With some financial assistance for travel, Otto took the test. He passed with flying colors. A happy day came when Senator John Sheppard's letter arrived appointing Richardson to Annapolis. He had also been nominated by Fourth Congressional District Representative John W. Cranford of Sulphur Springs as an alternate cadet candidate.[38]

In the summer of 1898, Otto received his appointment. He and the new superintendent, fifty-nine-year-old Rear Admiral Frederick V. McNair, both arrived in Annapolis in the fall. What a world the twenty-year-old from Paris, Texas, must have viewed on the way. Paris had no cars, but now he was near the hub of industrial activity. Paris had a golf course, but it was reserved for the well-to-do citizens. Now the young man would be in a world where playing a course would be common, accessible for all ranks, and most acceptable. He would seldom see Paris again, but would become the city's most traveled alumnus, and its most important citizen to serve the country in a military position.[39] For sure, his mind was molded from a small-town atmosphere, but with a broad look at surroundings.

In the big world, the Spanish-American War was raging. The United States had just severely damaged opposition ships outside Santiago Harbor in Cuba. The war with Spain was heated. Spanish officers were held in Naval Academy buildings and treated more like guests than prisoners. Consequently, Otto would have a clear view of the dangers of the seas when he graduated four years later. After four years of waiting, he also had an appreciation of the opportunity afforded him.

CHAPTER THREE

"At the Academy They Called Me Ritchie"
Tall Texan Fits In

When brown-eyed Otto Richardson was packing to leave Paris for Annapolis, his father was seriously concerned about his son's loose, low-key attitude. He could exhibit a slight gruffness at times, but was lovable and popular among his peers. His slow-speaking, moderately high voice was relaxed, but authoritative. Classmates at the Naval Academy described it as "big and loud."[1] Professor Richardson had some doubts that a Texan could keep up with all those Northeasterners.

"Son," he said, "you can't hope to compete with those Northern fellows at the Naval Academy. There's something about this Texas sunshine and Texas wind that dries up your brain!"[2] The beginning would be a bouncy start. By the summer, when the ninety-four members of the Naval Academy Class of 1902 reported, the Spanish-American War was intense. The June members were sent back home on leave.[3] They would miss their first summer cruise. Back in Paris, Otto Richardson awaited orders to return to Annapolis.

Finally, the time came. He was entering into that awful nightmare called "Plebe September" at the Naval Academy. "I was determined to do well," he told an interviewer years later.[4] He was the oldest student in his class, although several had been in attendance at universities before appointments. Actually, because of the delay in entrance, he was three days over the limiting age of nineteen.[5]

In the first few weeks three of the class fell by the wayside. By February of 1899, the resignation of seventeen more followed. In a letter to his friend Birch Mahaffey at West Point, Richardson wrote, "On the semi-annual exams we bilged [washed out] fifteen plebes. There were thirteen plebes held over who were unsat[isfactory]. They bilged three second classmen."[6] Faces came and went, and the pressure was immense.

A bit of hazing was thrown in between the activities of the day. Richardson wrote Mahaffey, "We do not have any class organization while we are plebes. We do not rate going to hops, or doing anything else but breathing and answering fool questions."

Mahaffey was in the middle of a hazing investigation at West Point that would cost him dearly.[7] Richardson wrote him of the similar investigation at the academy, "and the upper class men have been afraid to fight any of us" since. "Several plebes have offered to fight, but the upper class men are all afraid of being caught."

Still signing his letters with Otto or OR, Richardson had defied his father's fears. While there was no hot sun in Annapolis in the fall and winter, there was a harried schedule. He admitted to Mahaffey, "the Texas men here do not stand very well as a rule," but added that Sinclair Gannon of Columbia in south Texas, who entered in 1896, "was a captain of one of the companies."[8] Richardson was impressed with Ohio men, "about the savviest men in the school," but said Kentucky represented smart men in each class.

Richardson amazed his fellow midshipmen by working math problems as a form of relaxation. But, after all, his stepmother had been a mathematics instructor during his childhood.[9] It may have also helped that a Texan, Lieutenant (j.g.) Daniel Wilbert Wurtsbaugh of the Naval Academy Class of 1896, was one of his instructors in mathematics and clearly understood Texanese.

The group began packing, not for home but for the summer cruise. Otto Richardson carefully crammed twenty cubic feet of belongings into the allowed ten cubic feet of space. The summer cruise class of 1899 thought they were on a tub, but actually it was the USS *Monongahela*. This 1863 ship served as the tool for practice cruises at the academy from 1894 to 1899.[10]

The cruise landed first at Plymouth Harbor in Massachusetts.[11] It was quickly transported "by special train" to bigger game— London. When docked there, the American trainees hit the town for a quick five days of fun. The occasion was "not dampened even by being at times mistaken for messenger boys or guides by agitated old ladies."

Upon return to Plymouth, the group set out to Madeira,

Portugal, the next day. Two nights of rough weather were spent in the Bay of Biscay. Some realized that their sea legs were not yet fully developed. A thirteen-knot "breeze" shook the old vessel, and all its pegs. In a few days they moved over to Funchal, where the remainder of the small funds available were spent on shore.

The executive officer of the *Monongahela* was the original Bill "Bull" Halsey. "The elder Halsey would stand on the bridge . . . and, in a strong wind, roar so loudly that the midshipmen on the royal yards would hear the command," wrote Richardson.[12]

The trip home was slow and full of dragging time. The sun bore down "in relentless fury, and water was at a premium." It was here that the midshipmen apparently learned to "appreciate" the "vile yarns" that Otto would tell to anyone who listened.[13] For five weeks this misery continued until they struck a "slant o' wind." Three days later the cadets hurriedly walked down the plank and spread out across the United States on leave. In early September, Otto Richardson was in his hometown, visiting his parents and friends for a short two weeks until he was to report for his second year at Annapolis.[14]

The remaining group of sixty-seven could then be called "Mr." by the 1899 arrivals. Some of the 1903 group would become the highest-ranking Navy officials during World War II, men such as Stark, Samuel M. Robinson, and Walter S. Anderson.[15]

Of Richardson's class, only twenty-one could master the required 2.5 grade in the Drawing Department. Spring came, however, and passed on. Construction began on the first building for the planned campus. It was called Dahlgren Hall. The June ball ended the second year.

The summer of 1900 was to be spent on board the USS *Newport,* and the USS *Chesapeake.* However, the exciting voyage of the first year was not repeated. Given early leave, the cadets dispersed on Sunday, August 26, to homes throughout the United States. So eager was the class to leave that the supper was not eaten that evening.

Campus construction progress allowed the class to live away from main quarters. With housing in the safety of the annex, the class gathered in early October for the third year. They thought the facility was as fine as the Waldorf-Astoria. It had a fireplace, bookcases, and other "luxuries." New plebes forming the Naval Academy Class of 1904 included future World War II admirals W. F. "Bull" Halsey, Jr., and Husband E. Kimmel.

Disturbed by reveille inspection now and then, the members of the Class of 1902 improved on their social opportunities. "Some of us . . . so neglected our books that we could not even have passed a West Point examination," Otto Richardson recalled. He plugged on, however, taking advantage of the social offerings. He was on the Hop Committee, but was careful to hit the books when necessary. The yearbook says he never inflicted "gold bricks." The cadets had use of the newly arrived USS *Holland,* a submarine to be used for training and testing.

In March of 1900, McNair completed his stint as superintendent and was replaced by Richard "Uncle Dick" Wainwright, a member of the Class of 1868. He was the executive officer of the USS *Maine* when it was destroyed two and half-years earlier during the Spanish-American War.

Classmates considered Otto as basically strong-minded when it came to arguments with professors, a trait that would both gain him an admiralty and lose him a job in the future. "He has the temerity to sometimes question the text-book[s]" and the audacity to try to understand them. Some thought that what Otto said was just determination, but others thought it was actually obstinacy. He was often heard saying after a problem was solved, "Gee! That was a cinch."[16]

Aboard the practice ships that June, the Atlantic coast was more enjoyable. The USS *Chesapeake* was back. Time on shore was more involved, however. One-half of the trip was spent in the instruction of old-time reefing, furling, and maneuvering. The second half was spent on the man-of-war where knowledge was absorbed despite all the midshipmen's efforts to the contrary.[17] Otto Richardson suffered martyrdom, said the yearbook *Lucky Bag,* when he acted as spokesman for his classmates on the practice cruise.[18]

Richardson began June 10 on the USS *Indiana* with Naval

Cadet M. G. Cook serving as head of the expedition for the First Class. Thirty-one of the Class of 1902 went along, while the others were out with the *Chesapeake*. This was the first chance Richardson had to formulate working relationships with lower classmen such as Robinson, H. B. Fairchild, Royal E. Ingersoll, and others who would eventually reach high rank. William V. Pratt was a lieutenant (j.g.) on board the ship, serving as the watch officer and instructor of seamanship.

When this "voyage" was over, Richardson and his group, on July 20, transferred to the *Chesapeake*. They were out ten days before docking at Gardiners Bay, New York, and Newport, Rhode Island. On August 6 they departed Newport for Portland, Maine. On August 16 the ship left for a slow trip to Annapolis, and the end of the summer cruise eleven days later.[19]

Richardson received the rank of cadet ensign as his last year in the academy began on October 1. He ranked fifth in his class order of general merit.[20] Emory "Jerry" Land was the cadet lieutenant commander, the hero of the 1900 Army-Navy football game when he scored the only touchdown.[21]

Richardson joined *Lucky Bag* editor Harold David Childs' staff as an associate. The anticipation of being in the fourth year at the academy was more important than the reality. The men took charge of the annex and slept on the second floor according to rank. They thought they were to be the envy of every first class for years. Plebes that year included several who would later influence Richardson decisions. Chester W. Nimitz was present.[22]

The sixty-one-member Class of 1902 was forming a bond that would lead them to the time when thirteen of them would become flag officers in the 1930s. And, along with the friendships, many earned nicknames that stuck with them for the duration of life. All are listed in the *Lucky Bag* edition of 1902, and some were not so flattering. However, it was all in fun and compassion. Almost immediately Richardson was called Jo, for his initials J. O. Some called him Ritchie.

The class was graduated officially on May 2, a month earlier than normal. The Navy needed them quickly.[23] Richardson held his fifth ranking of the fifty-nine graduates. The members were the last class to be called "naval cadets." From then on "midshipman" was the title to be used. It was up anchor and go out on the high seas to adventure. What these graduates would see and experience in the next forty-five years or more would be awesome.

The graduates were out into a world that at that time had no radios on ships, no gyro compasses, no internal combustion engines, no steam turbines, no oil-burning boilers, no range finders, few telescopic sights, no directors, no semaphores, no damage control, no radar, no large-scale War College attendance, no "P.G." (post-graduate) school, no specialization, and no promotion by selection. Before Otto Richardson took over the fleet, great naval changes were made.[24]

CHAPTER FOUR

"On Duty They Began to Call Me Joe"
Around the World Training Begins

Within a month or two, forty-one of the Class of 1902's members were in the Asiatic Station (Far East). In June, Richardson and a number of his class boarded the USS *Solace,* a hospital ship. The trip took them from San Francisco through Pearl Harbor and on to Manila in the Philippines. Richardson's first glimpse of the Hawaiian stop was as the Navy was busy purchasing land around the protected inlet.[1]

At Manila, Richardson boarded the USS *Quiros,* a 350-ton gunboat built for the Spanish Navy at Hong Kong in 1895. It was captured at Manila in 1898, and commissioned by the U.S. Navy in March of 1900.[2]

The 137-foot-long, steel-framed, wooden-hulled and copper-sheathed vessel had a complement of one lieutenant, two midshipmen, and forty enlisted men—a number that ballooned to sixty at most times. Winter and summer cots were on the forecastle, shielded from the cold winds only by canvas curtains. A stove did little to ward off the frost.[3] The *Quiros* had no electricity, no refrigeration, and only one dry compass. Most inconvenient for Richardson was the fact that his bunk was eight inches short.

However, roaming the southern Philippines off the coast of Mindanao in the Moro Group of the Sulu Islands was sometimes a bit exciting. Four commanders were on board the *Quiros* during the fifteen months that Richardson served it. Due to the slow promotion of that era, one was a forty-year-old lieutenant named William Bartlett Fletcher. The next three lieutenants were not as comfortable with the passed midshipmen as was Fletcher. They thought the only way to convert them into worthwhile ensigns was to "give 'em hell." Richardson wrote that this harassment lasted "every minute of the day, and a fair share of the night."[4] Despite this ordeal, Richardson commented later that he felt he learned one valuable lesson: how to get along with seniors, particularly what were called "sundowners." From this experience he wrote, "I learned the importance of being able to handle sailormen." In addition, he learned to read extensively on board and gained an appreciation of the "tranquilizing" effect a man-of-war can have on a disturbed political arena.[5]

He also learned that most requests for transfer would not be granted.[6] Mainly because of the inadequacies of equipment on board the *Quiros,* Richardson wanted to be on a battleship. One commanding officer attempted to soothe Richardson. He told him that no assignment in the Navy offered a better opportunity to learn how to handle enlisted men than on board a small ship. Richardson concluded faster than most that "a man likes to serve under a taut officer who is always fair."[7]

Richardson's request for transfer to a battleship was not accepted. Instead, at Chefoo, China, on August 3, 1903, Richardson became a watch and division officer to the protected cruiser USS *New Orleans.*[8] There his ranking officer was Gottfried Blocklinger, an 1868 Naval Academy graduate who was only at the commander rank.[9]

The first sail a month later was to Tsingtao on the China coast, where the new German port was viewed. Then the *New Orleans* moved on to Nagasaki, Japan. Finally, it was on to Kobe and then Yokohama, twenty miles from Tokyo.[10]

Cable orders came on December 3 for cruisers to make a hasty trip to Honolulu in lieu of planned winter work in the Manila Bay region. Two days out of Midway the battleships joined. To Richardson, it was a sight to behold.[11]

After the *New Orleans* returned to the Philippines, Richardson became ill. He was put on the *Kumano Maru* for Hong Kong. This Japanese ship would soon become a troop-carrying vessel after the Russo-Japanese War began on February 8, 1904.[12] Richardson was sick enough to be transferred to the Naval Hospital at Yokohama in mid-morning of February 4. It was some time before he returned to action.

The successful surprise Japanese attack on the Russian fleet at

Tsushima on May 27, 1904, influenced Richardson's thinking for a lifetime. "It was a shock to my susceptible mind," he wrote years later. He thought perhaps he was too conditioned to the Naval Academy code of honor. He called the actions of the Japanese Navy "foul blows that stuck in my 'craw' all thru pre-Pearl Harbor . . . and showed up in some of my letters on our War Plans."[13]

Richardson read of these events, first while in the hospital and later while traveling in mid-May from Yakohama to Woosung to catch up with his ship.[14] On July 4, at Shanghai, he was transferred to a rebuilt 1863 monitor named the USS *Monadnock*. She spent time firing her ten-inch guns at target practice in Nimrod

First sea duty: As all new midshipmen, one of the first things done when they hit cities of the Far East was to have a photo taken. Richardson was in Shanghai during the first years of service. (Photo from Elizabeth Wingo Banks Papers, Duncan, Oklahoma)

Sound in March of 1904, spent that summer in Shanghai, visited Nanking in November, and steamed down the Whangpoo River for the last time on January 15, 1905.[15]

The commander, Dennis H. Mahan, was basically in charge of the gunboats operating in the Yangtze River and its tributaries, guarding properties owned by the Chinese and British.[16] Though it was an outdated ship, Midshipman Richardson found some liking in his duty as the officer of the number one turret. His first target practice was off Flake Island from November 9 to 19.[17]

Richardson observed keenly the leadership of Admiral Robley Evans, who based his thinking on one point—that wherever the Chinese government allowed American citizens to reside, he claimed the right to send proper force to defend them in case of necessity. Though the American minister to China, Edwin Hurd Conger, somewhat disagreed, Evans and Secretary of State John Hay based this direction upon "the most favored nation" clause in the Sino-foreign treaties. They said in essence, and to the interpretation of Evans and Hay, that whatever the other foreign gunboats did, the American ships could do also.

The older officers were not highly supportive of gunnery practice. It, and other types of realistic battle drills desired by Richardson, was highly disliked, mainly because the drills tended to spoil the paint and brass work of the ships. Therefore, sail training was considered of more value, even when it no longer had practical value. But, things were changing.[18]

During 1904 and 1905, the number one turret on the *Monadnock* stood first among all the monitors in the Navy.[19] Again, in February of 1905, newly commissioned Ensign Richardson's turret did well in the competition.[20]

The effort was not easy. The *Monadnock* was still using the old brown-powder ammunition, not the new smokeless powder. There was no gas ejection system. Richardson wrote later, "We rigged canvas bags on the guns and secured them to the front armor plate of the turret, closed the access to the handling room with a rugged wooden door, and to the door connected the discharge of a powerful electric blower." Some of these modifications he may have learned on summer cruises at the Naval Academy, some he read about, and some he learned from older sailors on the exercise.

"With the blower running at full speed," he explained, "the handling room, turret chamber, and turret were put under air pressure, so that when the breech plugs were opened, everything except the molten brown powder was blown out of the gun. Within my knowledge, this was the first instance of providing a means of clearing the bore of a gun of hot gases after firing the gun."[21]

Loading the powder rapidly was rather dangerous. Thus, Richardson's crew rigged wet blankets over the openings of the ammunition hoists, "so that the burning grains of powder, which frequently fell back into the turret as the breech was opened, would not get into the ammunition hoist where the next powder charge was exposed."

On May 15, 1905, Richardson left Cavite in the Philippines, scribbling in his diary, "for home." Evans had left in March of 1904, his replacement lasting only until July. At that time, P. H. Cooper was replaced by Yates Stirling. Thus, Richardson closely observed the leadership of three admirals of distinction during this tour of duty. He went home via the collier USS *Zafiro*.

The trip gave him a week to visit Myanoshita and Tokyo in Japan before heading out to sea and Bremerton, Washington.[22] After arrival on the West Coast, Richardson took five days to travel home to Paris, but stayed with his parents and friends five weeks. The town was prosperous, in the midst of a religious revival about to rid the community of taverns, and many large homes lined the major streets leading to the two rail depots. He could tell, again, that his parents were frail, but he had his own life by that time, and it was not inland.

While in Paris he received a letter from the Navy informing him that his request to be placed with an armored cruiser squadron was filed. He wanted to be on duty with the USS *Maryland*.[23] Instead, Richardson was assigned to the USS *Nashville*. He was its new watch and division officer. Richardson left home on July 26 for Boston, taking a route that led him through Toronto to see Opie and her husband.

In mid-1905, the ship had been placed in dry dock at Boston, and was going back into commission at the Navy Yard there, to be assigned to the Atlantic Fleet. He officially requested again that he be transferred to the *Maryland,* but was denied.

The *Nashville,* with Richardson aboard, went to New York, and left there on September 8 for Monte Cristi in the Dominican Republic. The crew worked the waters around the port of Santo Domingo as part of the Sixth Division of the fleet during the latter part of 1905 until June of 1906, arriving back at Boston on June 26 for Independence Day celebrations.[24] Two days later Richardson applied for a month's leave to go to Paris. This request sat in files, also, and was not granted. Then, the ship was placed out of commission again on July 23. Richardson went to Ottawa for a week, then on August 2 reported at League Island in the Philadelphia Naval Yard for a pleasant tour on board the new armored cruiser USS *Tennessee.*[25] He was assigned as watch and division officer, and commanded the number one turret. Gunnery, efficiency, and accuracy grew that year to record heights. Competition between ships was considered a highlight.

The *Tennessee* was big, fast, and brand new. However, the ship was not in the same class with the vessels the Japanese were building at the same time.[26] The commander was Captain Albert O. Berry. Assigned with Richardson were also future flag officers Ashley H. Robertson and Samuel M. Robinson.

The armored cruiser finally left League Island for Hampton Roads, Virginia, and departed for Piney Point, Maryland, on November 8, 1906. Three days later, the *Tennessee* was an escort for the USS *Louisiana* in which President Theodore Roosevelt had embarked for a cruise to Panama to check on the progress of work constructing the Panama Canal. The warships arrived back at Hampton Roads on November 26.[27]

From that date through April, the *Tennessee* was at League Island. Richardson fell sick again in February, and even asked if he could go to Asheville, North Carolina, for his health, maybe to visit his stepmother's folks.[28] On May 27, he was promoted to lieutenant (j.g.), and two weeks later had taken leave and was in New York.[29]

After summer duty in Europe, Richardson received his first command. Because of the shortage of officers, on October 3 he was assigned to command the twin-screw torpedo boat USS *Tingey*. She was fast, at twenty-six knots, and had been commissioned for only three years, being earlier placed into the reserve fleet. She was recommissioned on December 11, and for almost two years was home for Richardson.[30] She stayed at dock much of the time.

On June 23, 1908, the *Tingey* experienced a small fire. Someone set a lighted oil lamp down in the wrong place.[31] However, after some letters of reprimand, and an admonishment to "exercise greater care in the future," the situation settled down. Richardson did protest, however.[32] He received a letter for efficiency in March of 1909, informing him that his vessel "attained the highest night battle efficiency of any vessel of her class."[33] But, not all news was good.

In late March of 1909 Richardson received notice that his father had died on the twenty-sixth of the month. Services were held in the Centenary Methodist Church where he had voluntarily served for so many years. The *Paris Advocate* stated that almost everyone in town attended the ceremony.[34]

In the northeast corner of the Old City Graveyard the professor was laid to rest. Jessie came from Detroit, Texas, Moss from her teaching post at New Boston, and Otto from his command on the USS *Tingey*. Fannie had died in 1901. The stepchildren, Dick and Lula, were apparently unable to attend. Opie was most likely already in town, preparing for what would become a third unsuccessful childbirth.[35]

The Navy lieutenant returned to duty at the Navy Yard in Pensacola, Florida.[36] He was notified in early April that he was being considered for a marine engineering teaching post at the Naval Academy. He had no engineering assignments to date, and begged off, requesting instead postgraduate instruction at the Massachusetts Institute of Technology. On April 12, 1909, he wrote the Bureau of Navigation of his desire. However, the squadron commander forwarded the request with a notation,

"Disapproved. This officer is too valuable to waste his time going to school."[37] This response did not upset Richardson, for he would rather stay at sea.

On April 26, Richardson wrote another letter hoping he could stall off going ashore at all. He asked that once the *Tingey* reached Charleston, South Carolina, he be assigned to the USS *Minnesota,* or a ship of her class.[38] And, since a recent memorandum had suggested that it was not good to keep an officer from a fleet assignment for more than three years, he thought he had a chance to be assigned to duty on a battleship.[39]

Again, he struck out. Instead, he was transferred to command the torpedo boat USS *Stockton,* and the Third Division of the Atlantic Torpedo Boat Flotilla. His future boss, Harold R. Stark, was a commander of one division, and Stark's 1903 classmate Charles A. Blakely of the other. The three considered it quite fun to slip through the sea at twenty knots in a wedge formation so close they could throw a pack of cigarettes from the bow of the wing boats to the fantail of the lead craft. "I was most reluctant to go to shore duty," Richardson later wrote of those times.[40]

Despite his desire to remain on the ocean, his reputation led him to be chosen as one of ten officers for the first postgraduate marine engineering class at the Naval Academy.[41] He reported there on September 29, 1909. In the second year of school, he was interrupted by sad news. His stepmother was deathly ill. On March 29 he applied for leave and headed home.[42]

Less than three months since she was noted as being at the fiftieth wedding anniversary party of Captain and Mrs. William Bell, which was held two blocks from her home, Sue Richardson was dead.[43] Just three weeks earlier she had reported to the *Paris Advocate* that her stepson, Dick, had received promotion to the rank of lieutenant colonel. He was stationed at that time in Washington, DC, where he was testifying on Alaskan affairs to Congress, but was soon to be in Seattle with his regiment.[44]

"She will always be remembered in Paris as one of our noblest and truest Christian women," the newspaper editor wrote. With assumption, perhaps, Otto Richardson met May Fenet while in

Paris. On April 10, he telegraphed a request to Annapolis asking for extension of his leave by five days, but soon he was on his way back East.

In mid-1911, Richardson went on board the USS *Delaware* as assistant engineer officer, which led later to a promotion to senior engineer officer.[45] The *Delaware* was the first battleship to run on oil as well as coal. Richardson joined her at Boston in May, just before surprise orders arrived. The *Delaware* was to sail at full power for twenty-four hours as soon as she could coal up. On June 4, she headed for Portsmouth, England. From June 19 to 28 she took part in the fleet review accompanying the coronation of King George V.

The U.S. Navy had doubled in size during Richardson's service. He was thirty-three years old and single. He thought the quality of enlisted personnel had improved, and noted that fewer foreign-born sailors were on board ships. Despite the fact that 14 percent of Americans were foreign-born in 1910, the Navy Department explained that it wanted "the boy from the farm" rather than foreign-born sailors with Old World allegiances.[46] Richardson fit that image perfectly. The future of a Navy career still looked appealing and enjoyable for him. Still, he was thinking about that girl back in Paris, Texas. He was led to believe that he would soon be appointed as a naval attaché in Italy, and would like to take her along with him on his new assignment.[47]

In May, Richardson asked to be assigned to Babcock & Wilcox boilermakers to be assistant to the inspector of machinery for the Navy after his May 5 graduation from the engineering class.[48] This assignment would fulfill an earlier assessment of abilities. He was recommended for assignment at a Navy Yard or at the torpedo manufacturing plant where he could observe shop methods.[49] He was given the billet in Bayonne, New Jersey. First, important things were on the calendar. He took leave to go to Paris, asking not to return until the twenty-sixth.[50] He spent the summer in New Jersey, but then returned to Paris in early fall.

Weddings of the early part of the twentieth century were always news in Paris, and were written up in detail in the local newspapers, the *Paris Morning News* and *Paris Advocate.* The Richardson and Fenet merger was no exception. On Wednesday, September 20, 1911, Lieutenant Otto Richardson lost his bachelor status; but after all, he had seen much of the world, and it was possibly the right time to marry. The Presbyterian ceremony was held in the Fenet home. The decorations were elegant and refined, the ceremony formal.

After the wedding, the couple left within the week for Brooklyn, New York, where Richardson would await new orders at the shipyard there. He would receive his battleship assignment. Moss moved on to the University of Texas to study and work in Austin. Jessie returned to New Boston. Home was not the same to them now. Jessie was the only one to return semi-permanently.

That fun honeymoon the Richardsons planned was cut a bit short by a continuous series of sea duty assignments, not one of which was to Italy as he had foreseen.[51] Still, May was determined to be close to him when possible, and spent her part of the Navy career crisscrossing the world. For the next thirty years, she would never know a home with the admiral for much more than two years at a time. She would travel the China coast in small steamboats and live through typhoons in Chinese inns and hotels. She would even have a house with ten Chinese servants, not a one of whom spoke English. She would fly from Estonia to Finland, from Norway to Germany, from Panama to Los Angeles. More than once she would arrive at a port only to find that her husband's orders had changed.[52]

When May was pregnant, and while Jim was sent to sea on the *Delaware,* she went inland to Opie's home in Ottawa.[53] Though for several years he had been in private surveying practice in Ottawa, Ogilvie was now on an extended trip to the western interior of Canada working for the country's Department of the Interior.

In the spring of 1912, gunnery practice was held, and most of the summer Richardson was in and out of harbor. However, on July 27, he requested a ten-day leave to travel to Ottawa.[54] Joe Fenet Richardson was born on July 30. Joe was destined to be schooled all over the globe—in China, Japan, and the Philippines in the Far East, and in Long Beach, Washington, DC, Annapolis, and Newport in the United States.[55]

The *Delaware* took part in a fleet review by President William H. Taft in the Hudson River off New York City on October 14, 1912, and received a visit from the chief executive that day. That event was exciting, but Richardson was soon gone on a long trip while his bride began motherhood.

News also came in November that Oglivie had died. He contracted pneumonia near James Bay while exploring options on three million acres of land on the Saskatchewan and Nelson Rivers. For several weeks he was confined to bed, but he died at age sixty-six in the Winnipeg General Hospital in Manitoba.[56] Opie and her stepson Paul made it in time to be at his side.[57]

Richardson was not on land at the time, but on a trip with President Taft. He was taken to the Panama Canal Zone for an inspection of the unfinished isthmian waterway. The *Delaware* was along on the trip, and Paris, Texas, was also represented in the Zone by thousands of shovel handles made by the Ames Tool Company. After putting the inspection party ashore, the ships sailed to Cuban waters for shakedown training, then returned to the Canal Zone on December 26 to escort President Taft to Key West, Florida.

The *Delaware* joined in exercises, drills, and torpedo practice at Rockport and Provincetown, Massachusetts. She then engaged in special experimental firing and target practice at Lynnhaven Roads, Virginia, trained in Cuban waters, and participated in fleet exercises from February through March of 1913. She engaged in the war games off Block Island, on the coast of southern Rhode Island, from May 7 to 24, then quickly headed back to New York for the monumental festivities honoring the battleship USS *Maine* from May 28 through 31. May was sick with the aftermath of "milk leg," but most likely she and the baby watched the festivities from shore.

That summer the *Delaware* served as training for midshipmen. This was an experiment by the academy to place midshipmen of the first and second classes upon a battleship rather than among a few selected ships forming a special training squadron.

In October, Richardson had thoughts of resigning and going to work in industry. He was still a lieutenant at the time.[58] However, he experienced a version of the modern-day "stop-loss" phenomenon when the Navy told him it disapproved. It cited that too much investment had been placed in Richardson's education, including his engineer schooling, to allow him to resign from the service. Also, in the note to him was a speech Josephus Daniels had given to the graduating class at the Naval Academy, expressing his views in regard to resignations of graduates. Richardson apparently never officially submitted the application.[59]

From November 8 to 30, 1913, the *Delaware* visited Villefranche, France, while on a cruise. Early in 1914, tension heightened between the United States and factions in Mexico. American ships arrived off Veracruz, on the Gulf of Mexico, on February 16, 1914, remaining there during the ensuing occupation.

Most of the Atlantic Fleet participated in exercises in Caribbean waters between January 26 and March 15, and then that spring off the Virginia capes to Tangier Sound off the Maryland coast in the southern drill grounds. During this assignment, the Richardsons made their home in Newport, Rhode Island.[60]

In the second fleet review, which occurred in 1912 while Richardson was aboard the *Delaware,* he was pleased that President Taft was quoted as saying:

"A Navy is for fighting, and if its management is not efficiently directed to that end, the people of this country have a right to complain."[61]

Richardson thought that this statement should be carved over the door of the offices of all civilian secretaries of the Navy and their assistants. He kept it as a theme he would hammer time and again into anyone who would listen.

Observed first hand, Richardson exercised his "right" to discuss matters by writing what he thought. After experimenting for two summers, the new plan for Naval Academy midshipman serving aboard battleships was working well. He even wrote an article about its good and bad points.[62] He felt it most important that the young potential officers see that the fleet operated well even with them as part of the process. "They learn that officers are not of a superior class, but are really older brothers."

At the same time, Richardson chastised any officer who felt like doing nothing but "try not to step on them." He called for a special order to be given to a particular division officer to manage the program. Being one who would not criticize if he did not have an answer, he recommended that the senior assistant engineer officer of the battleship involved be "relieved from watch-standing during the summer and be given the additional duty of instructor of the second class in engineering."

Lieutenant Richardson himself received his chance to deal first-hand with the managers of the Navy when, on May 11, 1914, he reported to the Bureau of Steam Engineering in Washington, DC. May and Jim could finally settle into a civilian routine, seeing each other for extended periods of time. This assignment and the personalities he would meet would mold Richardson's thought patterns as a leader. The couple also would begin to seriously consider Washington as a permanent place to settle. In July Richardson learned that he was appointed as a lieutenant commander.[63]

In 1914, a reorganization of the Navy was caused by the frustrations brought upon traditional operators who opposed Secretary of the Navy Josephus Daniels and his ideas. Richardson saw firsthand the creation of the office of Chief of Naval Operations. Though at first adamantly opposed by the secretary, Daniels later enthusiastically endorsed legislation that strengthened the position.[64]

It was in Washington, as aide to the chief and only one of twelve officers in the entire Bureau of Steam Engineering, that Richardson met a young assistant to Daniels. His name was Franklin Delano Roosevelt. The two would have a long, up-and-down relationship for the next twenty-seven years.

CHAPTER FIVE

"Roosevelt Insisted on Calling Me Joe"
Desk Job Brings Contact with Future Leaders

On Woodrow Wilson's inauguration in January of 1914, New York State Senator Franklin D. Roosevelt ran into newly appointed Secretary of the Navy Josephus Daniels of North Carolina.[1] The two could not have been from worlds farther apart, but Daniels thought Roosevelt could balance out his Navy office. Thus, right away he asked FDR if he would move to Washington as his assistant. The agreement was struck and the appointment made.[2] It was from this position that Roosevelt's cousin, Theodore, had jump-started a political career fifteen years earlier.

Chief of the Bureau of Steam Engineering was 1878 Naval Academy graduate Robert Stanislaus Griffin. He was part of the Cuban blockade in 1898, serving on the gunboat USS *Mayflower.* He rose from fleet engineer, North Atlantic Fleet, in 1904, to the bureau job in 1913. His tenure was full of fuel problems.

The USS *Nevada* was the first Navy ship to run entirely on fuel oil. It was built at Quincy, Massachusetts, between 1912 and 1916 as a 27,500-ton battleship, and was the first to have triple turrets.[3] A vast fuel change was coming to the military, and Daniels hoped that petroleum owned by the United States government would be used exclusively to run the Navy. These reserves had been created in 1912 under the William Howard Taft administration, to be used in case of national emergency for the Navy.

Richardson was to learn from Griffin's assistants, Samuel S. Robison and Arthur J. Hepburn. In addition to his normal duties as aide, Richardson served as personnel officer and the bureau representative. He found his role dealing with fuel contracts the most important duty, and his actions there sent a ripple effect as far as 1996 when Naval Petroleum Reserve sites began to be sold.

On that very first day he arrived in May of 1914, Richardson was assigned to represent Daniels in the compliance of the Navy to a congressional resolution requiring that both the Navy and the Department of Interior investigate the idea of creating a Naval Petroleum Reserve pipeline.[4] The immediate report to be studied and made to Congress dealt with the proposition of laying a pipeline from the mid-continent fields to the West Coast.

On May 19, in the company of Commissioner of Indian Affairs Cato Sells, Richardson traveled to view these fields. Daniels wrote in his 1913 annual report that he hoped Congress would give immediate consideration to the idea. He wanted the Navy to refine its own oil from its own wells. "The recent trial test of the USS *Nevada* . . . emphasizes the growing need of a large supply of oil for the Navy."[5]

Richardson and Sells roamed the public lands of Wyoming and California for several weeks, and a few months later reported to Secretary of Interior Franklin K. Lane that the pipeline idea was feasible and desirable. The secretary reported likewise to Congress, but Daniels only felt that the project was doable, but not yet desirable. Thus, Congress did nothing on the idea at that time.

Still, Richardson felt that the report should be kept alive, and submitted it to Dr. George Otis Smith, director of the Geological Survey. Smith had been the director since 1907 and most likely knew Richardson's cousin, Dick, then an Army colonel.

Richardson prepared a letter for Daniels to present to the president on the matter. With Smith's notations that there were large deposits available, Richardson had convinced Daniels of the project. On April 30, 1915, Wilson, by executive order, and thus bypassing Congress, created "naval petroleum reserve Number 3."[6] It contained 9,481 acres of land with great oil-bearing capability.

The California fields at Elk Hills Reserve #1 and Buena Vista Hills Reserve #2 were also developed as a result. The one in Salt Creek, Wyoming, mentioned as #3, became widely known during the Warren G. Harding administration in 1921 as Teapot Dome.

Daniels was adamant that these lands be kept in reserve in case of war, which came closer when, off the Irish coast on August 19, a German submarine sank the British White Star passenger liner

Arabic. She was headed for New York with no contraband. Roosevelt had admirals shaking their heads in September when he advocated a Naval Reserve of 50,000 citizens and squadrons of private powerboats. After all, a similar system was in place in the Army. Daniels approved, but did urge that it not become a seagoing club for Roosevelt's yachtsmen.

It was time for extended leave for the Richardsons. After a two-day visit to Annapolis, Richardson left his office on December 20 for thirty-four days, most of it to be spent in Texas. He had taken only seventeen total days of leave in three years. He listed his address to be at the Fenet home in Paris.[7] What he saw then was gone by March, however, when 1,440 structures burned to the ground. Luckily, the Fenet home survived for future visits.

Richardson became adroit at appearances on Capitol Hill before Committees on Public Lands of both the House and the Senate. The experience was immense for a young officer, and his service for men who wanted expansion of the Navy was invaluable. He acquired from Daniels a great interest in the common man. He, however, was a bit skeptical of the Daniels practice of taking a hundred sailors annually from the fleet and making them eligible for entrance into the Naval Academy. But, under the Daniels leadership the Navy expanded greatly. He changed the image of the sailor from one who joined to see the naked women of the South Sea Islands to one who was not shiftless and had purpose. He began the recruiting spin that once a sailor was on board, he would be educated by the Navy with classroom studies. Daniels, and FDR, did not think much of judges who used the Navy as a reformatory for wayward youth who were offenders of the law.

Daniels may have ruffled Richardson and career officers a bit by abolishing the officer's wine mess, but the ban went into effect while Roosevelt was out of town. Therefore, the officers spared FDR the immediate wrath.[8] The officers of course thought little of a peer who could not control his drinking habits, but felt that problem's root came from the liquors kept in the personal rooms. Both Captain Joseph K. Taussig and Richardson stated later that they and other naval officers were also most resentful toward Daniels that the news organizations first announced the policy. The secretary did please many when he installed laundries on board, and by 1914, many ships had electric ice cream makers. He encouraged fleets and squadrons to make frequent visits to foreign port to give recruitment more ammunition.

However, his unrealistic approach to the venereal disease problem in the Navy brought on various comments. He banned the distribution of contraceptives, thinking rather simply that he could urge sailors to keep their ships free from "loathsome diseases."[9] It did not work. Carney was the recipient in those days of several letters from Daniels discussing the dregs and scourges of the Navy. He became very resentful of the Daniels moral structure, and the reluctance to use social disease medicines and preventive measures. In the meantime, the Navy was dealing with rampant cases.[10] Daniels then turned heads when he allowed the introduction of women into the service

The association with Daniels gave Richardson many lessons about how to work with Congress, procedures that he would need years later. He believed that at his lieutenant commander rank he was fortunate. "I greatly profited from the experience." He added, "I learned that, to be effective, a witness must be honest and forthright."[11]

After two years at that rank, and most of it on shore, Richardson was anxious to return to sea, especially since a war was going on in Europe, and it seemed likely the United States would soon become involved. When Woodrow Wilson won over a strong Republican campaign by Charles Evans Hughes in the fall of 1916 election by only twenty-three electoral votes, the civilian appointees planned for another four years.

John Hood obtained flag rank, and consulted the list of people he wanted to serve with him on the USS *Alabama* in the Atlantic Fleet. He first reached out to invite Richardson, despite knowing "you were doing something special with the Secretary."[12] Daniels found Richardson's assistance too valuable, and held him over six months until June of 1917. This extension was quite a compliment, for

Daniels held a substantial mistrust of Navy officers, especially the "dead wood" he considered to be at the top. Expecting to retire soon, Griffin even told Richardson that though he was young, he felt that the lieutenant commander should take over as bureau chief. Richardson, not mincing words, said, "I will refuse the assignment. I just am not qualified."[13]

Daniels wanted Richardson to transfer from the line of the Navy, to be an Engineering Duty Only officer. This was a "new breed of cats," as Richardson notated, just created by Congress. Despite having a wife and a five-year-old son, Richardson "hankered" for sea duty.

Richardson kept at his interest in the Petroleum Reserve Sites #1 and #2. In a long article, he outlined the nation's need for more oil production, and the Navy's desire to switch all ships to fuel oil after the success of the USS *Nevada.* His warning about eventually having to purchase oil on a foreign market went basically unheeded.[14]

In the meantime, Roosevelt was gaining a host of contacts while in his naval position. He actually was working hard to make himself personally agreeable in transactions of the day. However, he clashed at times with Daniels and Navy officers like Richardson and Taussig. Many of the top officers in the Navy mistrusted Roosevelt, but kept quiet about it. After all, Roosevelt did advocate a big Navy and an active foreign policy.

To Roosevelt's detriment, however, his actions and excited emotions put him on dubious grounds. For instance, he maintained relations with Wilson critics, and even passed on naval intelligence information to Republicans, hoping they would budge Daniels from his lack of war preparedness.[15] Nevertheless, in the process Roosevelt learned that there was some wisdom in compromise, and he gained substantial administrative experience in the years as assistant secretary.[16] In addition, his discovery that a president could lend-lease machinery and supplies was to be most valuable prior to World War II.

Roosevelt's ideas at times were rather grandiose. Richardson liked to tell about the time, before World War I, when Congress authorized construction of some subchasers. After the Navy decided that the wooden-hulled vessels should be 110 feet in length, Roosevelt argued for a 65-foot subchaser. Being the yachtsman he was, he loved the woodwork, and was adamant for the shorter length. Richardson and his fellow officers believed it was simpler than that. They thought that since a Roosevelt friend produced an engine that would power a 65-foot ship, the contract was better suited for the friend.

Richardson's classmate, J. O. Fisher, was in charge of the internal combustion desk in the Bureau of Engineering at the time of the discussion. He squashed the idea. Several days later Roosevelt ran into Richardson and muttered, "J. O., I am going to have your friend Joe Fisher ordered to Guam!" Richardson replied, "Surely, Mr. Secretary, you are not going to establish Guam as a penal colony or punish an officer for doing what he believed to be his duty?"[17]

The skirmish did not die at that. The idea went before the Navy General Board. Captain Hugh Rodman was a member of the board. He told Richardson one evening that FDR's civilian aide, Louis McHenry Howe, sternly said, "It would be to your [Rodman's] advantage to recommend this program be adopted." Rodman said he quickly growled back, "You dirty little SOB. I will not make any recommendation unless I think it to the advantage of the Navy." The subchasers were built at 110 feet, without the FDR engine.

Richardson knew well most of the officers below flag rank who dealt with Roosevelt. "FDR had great personal charm, and attracted people to him," Richardson wrote in the mid-1950s. He pointed out also that these particular officers carried a special bond of association with them for the next dozen or so years. They were all moving up in the Navy ranks while Roosevelt was away from Washington. They became captains and flag officers. As president in 1933, Roosevelt greeted them as friends, and took pleasure, according to Richardson, in creating opportunities for that group.[18] Roosevelt by then was an expert at dealing out favors, expecting them to be a form of control, to be reciprocated later.

CHAPTER SIX

Away from Washington
Back to Sea

A month before Richardson was released from his Washington assignment by Daniels and Griffin, President Woodrow Wilson addressed the American public and Congress in special session on April 2, 1917. He explained that the Imperial German Government, as most knew, had announced it would sink any and every vessel that sought to approach either the ports of Great Britain and Ireland or those on the western coasts of Europe.[1]

Especially upsetting to Americans was a statement released by the United States government on February 28. It made public a communication from Germany to Mexico proposing an alliance, and offering as a reward the return of Mexico's lost territory in Texas, New Mexico, and Arizona.[2] Wilson, the idealistic academician, told the American leaders that he had given up on appeasement, and that war was declared.

This was a valuable lesson for Roosevelt. Wilson had told him earlier, "I don't want the United States to do anything in a military way, by way of war preparations, that would allow the definitive historian in later days . . . to say that the United States had committed an unfriendly act against the central powers." Roosevelt would not let this happen two decades later. He would react differently. Even though he would face an isolationist American citizenry as Wilson had done, careful plans and decisive preparedness would be made before war came.[3]

Richardson's career ladder was brighter now. On June 27 he reported to the battleship USS *Nevada* as navigator. However, over the next seventeen months he would find too few opportunities to get back to see May and Joe.

Joseph Strauss, the first of four commanders Richardson would serve under during the next two years, captained the *Nevada*. Strauss soon received other orders, being given the assignment to lay a string of mines from Norway to Scotland. This was a Roosevelt-supported idea, called the North Sea Mine Barrage, a plan designed to keep German submarines out of the North Sea by "belting" together a string of mines. It was an idea Roosevelt would again desire to implement in the Pacific in 1940. Daniels opposed the plan, but FDR appealed directly to Wilson, and it was approved. The laying began in the spring of 1918, but it was never actually finished. It did contribute, however, to limited success.

When Richardson reported to the *Nevada*, William D. Leahy met him as the executive officer. The two officers had much in common. That October of 1917, Richardson was promoted to the position of temporary commander.[4] When Leahy left in April of 1918, Richardson was elevated to executive officer.[5] Finally, in August of 1918, the *Nevada* moved toward Europe as part of Battleship Division Six. Vice-Admiral William S. Sims, Commander of U.S. Naval forces in European Waters, operating from headquarters in London, summoned more assistance. In the process Richardson again ran into his classmate, Jerry Land, who had been assigned to the Sims staff in July.

Sims was a Richardson-type person, having gained some fame for not following traditional paths at times. He once became highly frustrated when Navy officials scorned his ideas on gunnery. He wrote personally to President Theodore Roosevelt about the problem. Surprisingly, but not so to Sims, the president listened to the lieutenant. Roosevelt placed Sims in charge of target practice, first for the Asiatic Station and later for the entire U.S. Fleet. He was blunt and outspoken, but had brilliant ideas and observation.[6] He had been president of the Naval War College in 1917 before called to war duty.[7]

The dreadnoughts USS *Nevada*, USS *Oklahoma,* and USS *Utah* were under the command of Rear Admiral Thomas S. Rodgers when ordered from the United States to the port at Berehaven, Ireland. The *Nevada,* captained at that time by A. T. Long, served as the flagship for Rodgers when the contingent left Hampton Roads on August 13 for Bantry Bay.[8] The three ships arrived on August 23.[9] The immediate duty assignment was to guard

American transports, which by that time were moving 300,000 troops per month across the Atlantic.[10]

However, duty was rather mundane, much of the time was spent in port. The *Nevada* received the mail from home, and had the responsibility of distributing it to other ships. There was some excitement, however. One evening about midnight, a small fire was discovered in the *Nevada's* 5-inch gun compartment #17.[11] A hot smoldering iron had fallen among some clothes, not too unlike Richardson's experience ten years earlier on the USS *Tingey*.

At times Rodgers would send a "deputation" of U.S. Naval officers by train and ferry to visit the Grand Fleet at Scapa Flow in the Orkney Islands of Scotland. He wanted a liaison between the two fleets in case they should be called upon to merge and work together.[12]

The great "War to End All Wars" was a mess by November of 1918. Sponsored by German money, Vladimir Ilich Ulyanov, known later as V. I. or Nikolai Lenin, and Leon Bronstein, who took the name Trotzsky, seized Petrograd and deposed of the Russian government leader Alexander Kerensky. It had been only two months since Kerensky had declared the country a republic. Lenin became premier. At the same time Georges Clemenceau took the same title in France.

The end of the Great War did not come as quickly as those in the Navy might have thought—but it was rather sudden. On November 18, Long, Richardson, and crew departed with the USS *Nevada* toward Roysth, Scotland.[13] The trip went through Scapa Flow before the American ships arrived at Roysth on November 23, five days after leaving Berehaven.[14] Two days earlier Richardson and his fellow crewmembers had received news of the surrender of the German High Seas Fleet near the entrance to the Firth of Forth, an estuary in Scotland that flows into the North Sea.[15]

The stay at Rosyth was too short to enjoy much. On December 1, just before noon, Division Nine with the USS *Nevada* left for Portland, England, to join U.S. Battleship Division Six. It had moved over to the southern coast of England from Berehaven. Three days later the two divisions were together.[16]

By that time it seemed that almost all the countries of the world were turning on Germany, including those in Central and South America. In addition, a flu epidemic added to the misery of soldiers and some sailors.

While basing around the British Isles, others Richardson knew became involved with the European experience. In the late summer of 1918, Roosevelt made a visit to the Western Front. By that time some twenty-seven divisions of the American Army had arrived in France. What he saw there gave him material for a public speech eighteen years later, when he said, "I have seen war . . . on land and sea." He visited the Verdun battlefield and the ruins of Fleury, and his party was shelled on the way to Fort Douaumont. He then visited Rome before he departed for the United States.[17]

About a week before Roosevelt set sail from Brest on September 12, 1918, Dick Richardson arrived at the French port with the Seventy-eighth Infantry Brigade, Thirty-ninth Army Division. By that time he had the rank of brigadier general and was just out of training the command in Louisiana. He worked under General John J. Pershing's American Expeditionary Forces on the Western Front in the closing months of the war. That experience, along with his cold-weather heartiness, would place him a few months later in a strange, dangerous, and short-lived assignment in northern Russia.

On December 12 the fleet sailed from Portland.[18] The following morning, the battleships rendezvoused with President Wilson on the transport USS *George W. Washington* and its escort, the USS *Pennsylvania*.[19] Wilson was to attend the Paris Peace Conference. He was hoping to strike a unique treaty. French and American ships boomed their salutes as the converted liner steamed into the Brest harbor at 12:30 P.M. Observing, Pershing said of Wilson, "He has been a good President to me, but he has his hands full now."[20]

On December 14, all the American ships but the USS *Wyoming* were underway for the United States.[21] In the mid-afternoon of Christmas Day, Richardson and friends anchored off Ambrose Light, New York. The next day the ships entered New York Bay to be reviewed by the secretary of the Navy and other dignitaries sitting on board the USS *Mayflower*.[22] Nineteen guns boomed their arrival. They moored in the North River for the next month. Richardson was glad to be back to the United States. The days away from May and Joe had been long enough.[23]

After January 30, Richardson spent some of the winter off Hampton Roads in gunnery and maneuver exercises, and went with Battleship Force Two to near Guantanamo Bay, in Cuba.[24] Fleet training lasted nearly two months with the USS *Nevada* finally arriving back in New York City on April 14.

Time at home was short. May was perhaps second-guessing her marriage to a Navy man, but she knew that ships were made to be on the seas. However, on June 14 the USS *Nevada* left Hampton Roads en route for the Philadelphia Navy Yard. Finally the Richardson family could settle into a home on one site for a few months.

Richardson left duty on the USS *Nevada*.[25] He then was assigned to nine years of what he called "leadership training." It did allow for more time with his family, though it was not exactly at one spot. First, he served as head of the Department of Steam Engineering at the Naval Academy, then as commander of the South China Patrol as the commanding officer of the gunboat USS *Asheville* of the Asiatic Fleet. He then returned to Washington as chief of the Bureau of Ordnance. Richardson went to sea after that duty, serving as Commander Destroyers, United States Naval Forces in Europe, and later as Commander Destroyer Division 38. These were most formative years for Richardson, especially the China and Asiatic positions.

He would then be prepared for the duties that met the rank of captain. For Roosevelt it was on to politics. He could play fifty-four holes of golf on a summer day. He was what sportswriter Walter Camp called a "beautifully built man, with the long muscles of the athlete." Camp had come to Washington to set up a physical fitness program for the Navy while FDR was assistant secretary. Two fit men—Richardson and Roosevelt—went temporarily in different directions, both to learn their craft.

CHAPTER SEVEN

Left Alone at Times to Make Decisions
Another Assignment to China

On January 8, 1919, the United States Fleet was formed, and that following summer it was organized into two divisions: the Atlantic under command of Admiral Henry B. Wilson and the Pacific led by Rodman. Half the Atlantic forces were detached to make up a Pacific effort designed to puzzle Japan.[1] The U.S. Navy was expanding dramatically, but still it was second in size to the British Fleet. Richardson noted that the conversion of the collier USS *Jupiter* to an aircraft carrier named the USS *Langley* was an important step forward. It would provide for development of aviation in the Navy.[2]

The 1922 Treaty of Washington called for the nations of the world to hold down construction of most new war machines. Funds were low anyway. The U.S. Navy did not even hold combined American maneuvers "on account of lack of appropriations."[3] At the end of 1924, Secretary of the Navy Edwin Denby reported that "due to inadequacy of funds" the material condition of the fleet had not improved during the past twelve months.[4] Fuel oil was so short that the training of personnel in seagoing duties was highly limited.

However, for Richardson a respite would soon come from his academy teaching assignment. He was assigned in the spring of 1922 to be commander of the USS *Asheville*.[5] This patrol gunboat was a single-screw, steel-hulled craft laid down at Charleston, South Carolina, in June of 1918.[6]

In early 1922 the ship was detached from the Special Service Squadron, and for the next few months underwent conversion from a coal-burning vessel to an oil-burner. She was the first of her type ship to be altered, though her galley still remained coal burning for many more years.[7] Richardson was headed for another tour of duty in the Asiatic Fleet.

On June 5, the *Asheville* departed Charleston. Though he would not see May or Joe for months, Richardson was back in his favorite element—at sea. The ship and its crew sailed toward its destination, but by going first across the Atlantic. She stopped at Bermuda and the Azores, and reached Gibraltar on July 2. On through the Mediterranean she went, stopping at Valetta, Malta, eight days later. She steamed on to Alexandria, Egypt, where the crew took a week off to visit the ancient land. Adventurous as any of the sailors, Richardson took a camel ride out to see the sights, being photographed at the Sphinx with Lieutenants William B. Young and Roy W. Hayworth. All three were in business suits; Richardson and Hayworth wearing long ties while Young opted for a bow tie.[8]

They passed through the Suez Canal on July 24, and after clearing, visited places such as: Aden, Arabia; Bombay, India; Colombo, Ceylon; Singapore; and the Straits Settlements. News came in August that the ship had won the engineer award with a score of 82.75, and the next month a message arrived saying she had also won gunnery competition for the previous year which had ended on June 1922.[9] She reached Cavite, in the Philippines, in September, a four-month tour of more than one-half of the world. The commander of the Asiatic Fleet, Admiral Edwin A. Anderson, was also new to the assignment, having arrived in late August. The *Asheville* conducted short-range battle practice off Corregidor at the end of the Bataan Peninsula until unrest in China sent her in late October to a position near the coastal Fukien Province.

Uprisings affected the business of the treaty powers operating out of Foochow and Amoy. Thus, American assistance was needed to protect both the businessmen and the missionaries.[10] At that time there were 8,000 Protestant and about 4,000 Catholic workers in some 1,149 locations in China.[11]

To reflect a concern that Chinese military and political leader Chiang Kai-shek would unite China against the West, a few more Marines were placed on board the Asiatic Fleet.[12] The majority of them were young, and had less than four years of service. Richardson had only to look around to see that only 3 percent of his naval enlisted force had served more than twelve years. He probably had no one on the ship his age.[13]

Richardson debarked Marines of the Fifteenth Infantry while anchored in the mouth of the Ming River near Foochow. The leathernecks went upriver where they would be quartered at the American consulate. For the next six weeks the *Asheville* would remain at Pagoda Anchorage. This was one of at least five times between April 1922 and November 1923 that U.S. Marines were landed to protect Americans during periods of unrest. Of his experience, Richardson wrote about Amoy and Swatow, "I saw these cities change hands one or more times, and met several of the contending warlords."[14]

Some in the Navy resented protecting the missionaries. Rodman was retiring in 1923, but he was not through with his thoughts on China. He wrote in his biography that he thought the China resident "has a perfect right to his own religion in his own country." He had little patience with the missionaries who wanted to preach on board his ship, but would not let the "rough class" of Navy men go on land and attend services.[15]

He wrote that personally he was later not sorry to see missionaries expelled from China.[16] But, as Navy commanders, he and Richardson did the job assigned to them. "I doubt that, after he reached the grade of lieutenant, he ever read a professional book," Richardson wrote. However, Rodman was a top ship handler, and according to Richardson, "the best cribbage player that I ever saw."[17]

On December 5, Richardson up anchored the *Asheville* and headed for Tsingtao, ready to be present for the transfer of the former German-leased territory of Kiaochow from Japanese authority to China.[18] On the last day of 1922, the *Asheville* sailed for Shanghai where she took on supplies and fuel, and finally gave her crew a few days of recreation. However, the Chinese revolutionary movement under American-educated Chinese leader, Dr. Sun Yat-sen, was turning its attention to Canton. The previous month, Richardson and other Americans had received news that the South China leader was about to seize the customs at Canton, at that time under international control.

In response, during the first week of 1923 the Asiatic Fleet destroyers were ordered to join other navies off Canton to assist in the protection of foreign lives and property.

On January 27, the *Asheville* was sent to Swatow. The United States and other nations also sent six destroyers. The *Asheville* reached that port in three days, remaining anchored for almost a month. "Sun Yat-sen's proposed action was a serious threat to all the Treaty Powers, whose loans to China were serviced by the revenues of the Chinese Maritime Customs," Richardson said of the crisis.[19] He thought that the firm stand shown by the naval forces influenced Sun Yat-sen to withdraw his threat. Customs management remained the same for the moment.

Recently commissioned Ensign Henri Smith-Hutton told more. He related that on a Saturday morning in Manila orders came to ships there to abandon plans for the weekend, refuel to capacity, and proceed at "best speed" to Hong Kong. Bad weather elongated the six-hundred-mile trip to three days. Then, "We stayed in Hong Kong three days," he remembered. He said Richardson, then in Canton Harbor, surveyed the situation with the British, and the decision was made that two ships were enough in the crowded area. He did not initially want all six ships there at the same time.[20]

The Chinese were "excited" about the concentration of foreign ships, and threatened to sink those headed to Canton when they neared the Boca Tigris fort and its battery of 10-inch guns. Richardson ignored the danger, and ordered his other ships toward him. Commander John S. Abbott took the lead. They went through the mouth of the river at twenty-five knots, reminisced Smith-Hutton.

"The Chinese soldiers near the batteries stood at attention and waved at us as we went by, but no shots were fired," he continued. The harbor was indeed congested, he said, and in a "seamanlike manner each United States vessel went right to their buoys." He said, "I think Commander Richardson was pleased, and I recall later that the British and the French officers at the Canton Club said they were much impressed with the way in which our captains had handled the destroyers on arrival at Canton." Smith-Hutton's group stayed two weeks before being relieved by two other ships.

The *Asheville* then went to Hong Kong for drydocking to take care of minor repairs, and so Richardson could spend some time with May and Joe. On March 27, however, the *Asheville* and the crew were back at Swatow. By that time, Sun Yat-sen had firm control at Canton, and was upsetting the trade contracts.

On April 10, 1923, the *Asheville* left Swatow for Cavite, arriving three days later. It then conducted day spotting, long-range battle, and night battle practice in Philippine waters.[21] Soon the *Asheville* was back to patrol off the coast of South China. She reached Hong Kong on May 4, where she transferred new enlisted men. In the ensuing months Richardson and crew used Hong Kong for recreation, and stood by ports of Swatow, Canton, Foochow, Amoy, and Yeung Kong. The wives and children did their best to find their loved ones. The naval forces witnessed three changes of government at Swatow, sending Marines ashore at times to protect American lives and property.

At Yeung Kong, the bluejacket landing party carried bacon, rice, and flour to the foreigners. At Canton the *Asheville* lay in the waters while warlord Chen Chiung-Ming made repeated attempts to take the town from the Sun Yat-sen party.

By late summer of 1923, May and Joe were in Tokyo staying at the Frank Lloyd Wright-designed Imperial Hotel.[22] Most Americans were still in conversation about the unexpected death of President Harding a month earlier. On September 1, at five minutes before noon, the building began rocking, chairs and beds sliding around the rooms. For almost seven minutes a 7.9-magnitude earthquake shook the entire southern Kanto region. Though everything around was highly damaged, the hotel building survived, and no following fire destroyed it. However, with water lines cut in all directions, fires began to eat up Tokyo and Yokohama. Hundreds of aftershocks followed for several days.

The huge Ueno Public Park offered some safety and activity for the youth, so days were spent there. May and Joe, and the other military families, spent the nights on mattresses thrown on the Imperial Hotel grounds. Those registered at the hotel could eat some of the small amount of food the staff could muster. The water wells began to fail from overuse.

A steamer in Yokohama Bay had been able to send an immediate message to the U.S. Asiatic Fleet, so Richardson and his patrol knew of the disaster.[23] Goods began to arrive from the U.S. Navy and from other ships. Some from the Asiatic Fleet, under orders from Anderson, broke routine with a voyage to Yokosuka, Japan, to relieve victims.

The USS *Tracy* left anchor at Dairen, Manchuria, immediately for Yokohama. Upon arrival, she participated in the initial relief work there and carried refugees from Yokohama over to Tokyo. She sent repair parties ashore to assist in laying fresh water lines and remained in the Yokohama area for two weeks before heading for Shanghai. After September 5, much of the Asiatic Fleet's Destroyer Division 38 had arrived to assist. Admiral Charles A. Pownall said he never could look again at kimonos. The ship had to plow through bodies of women and children floating dead in the water, all wearing beautiful clothing.[24]

Its facility destroyed, the U.S. Embassy staff set up a temporary office at the hotel on the third day. In Japan to learn its language, Ellis M. Zacharias was assigned to the embassy, but lived down the coast in a house. It was partially damaged by the small tidal wave caused by the shift in the surface. When the quake hit, Zacharias was on a pier at Yokohama to see off some friends leaving on the *Empress of Australia*. The pier partially sank, and the ship rammed against others in the harbor. Before it was over, Zacharias said he looked up and saw that the city was in flames.[25]

By September 5, some at the Imperial Hotel were sleeping in their rooms again.[26] The next day three trucks took trunks to a barge to be placed on the destroyer USS *Whipple*. May and young Joe, along with U.S. citizens and other foreigners, walked the three miles to the dock that early morning. They were then taken a short distance to the Osanbashi Pier at Yokohama, where they were transferred to a disabled French ship, the *André Lebon*. For the time being it could hold up to 1,000 refugees.

The meals were very simple, coffee and crackers for breakfast, but sustainable food for lunch and dinner. Hopefully, the group was told, the SS *President Pierce* would come into harbor soon. Cables could not yet be sent to loved ones to ease their minds.

The passengers had the option of taking a liner to Kobe, or awaiting the *President Pierce* and returning to America. News was just coming in that the quake's current was even the partial cause of a U.S. Navy disaster off Honda Point in California. The majority of the Navy families opted to continue their normal quest to follow their officers in the South China Patrol and Asiatic Fleet. On September 10, most of the Americans with this group left Japan. It was some story to tell for many years.

The *Asheville* sailed in late October to visit Hong Kong for nearly two weeks. However, a diplomatic crisis arose at Canton when Sun Yat-sen threatened to seize customs. After offering assistance there, Richardson returned to Canton at the end of the first week of November.

Each evening Richardson would report by radio to his new commander in chief of the Asiatic Fleet, Admiral Thomas Washington, who had replaced Anderson on October 11. The two were friends, so they knew each other's capabilities well. Richardson worked in conjunction with vessels of other nations present. He also reported each night to Jacob Gould Schumann, American minister to China. A teacher of Christian ethics and moral philosophy, and former president of Cornell University for twenty-eight years, the sixty-nine-year-old Schumann had been in China for two years.[27]

After explanation of the day's events, Richardson would close with the statement, "In the absence of other instructions, I propose to . . ." He would carry on to explain his own thought process. However, Richardson received no great guidance from either direction. "Every day I anticipated receiving a statement of policy from Washington. I scanned the radio operator's log of the Cavite broadcast schedule several times each day," he later told

Dyer. "After ten days, I found that the USS *Asheville* had copied
. . . a coded dispatch . . . in a code not held by me." When it was
decoded, he sent it on to Admiral Washington, but received back
a message that said: "Concentrate necessary forces at Canton
and prevent Sun's seizure of customs by all measures short of
war."[28] A wrong move could lead to war and disaster for the Navy.

The tense weeks turned into calm, however. The assembled
forces disbursed. Richardson had been in command of by far the
largest naval group present with no daily instructions. Admiral
Washington was in the southern Philippines at the start of the
incident. He told his chief of staff simply, "Richardson knows
more about this than I do. There is no need for me to go to
Canton and stick my neck out!"[29] Richardson said that "he
loved" the power of decision dumped in his lap, far more than
usual for his rank. "I believe that it was conducive to my development," he later wrote.[30]

During his time in the China patrol, more than once did
Richardson receive calls of help from the American consul, only
to find that the area to which the gunboats were dispatched
needed no assistance. Frustrated, he reported to Washington
once that in all the locations to which he had rushed expecting
an incident, the consul would just say, "Well, the grave crisis has
passed, but there remains strong possibilities of trouble, and I
think USS *Asheville* should remain here for sometime."[31]

Anne Briscoe Pye, wife of William S. Pye and good friend of the
Richardsons, cowrote a book with Nancy Shea in 1942 describing life for Navy wives. "In the good old days, everyone looked
forward to duty on the Asiatic Station."[32] Except, on this particular tour Richardson was rarely in port long.

Paychecks were in gold, so the barter system existed for each
sailor and his wife. An ensign's pay could even go a pretty long
way. In the autumn, most wives and children would migrate back
to Manila where there were old frame buildings. The Army and
Navy annex housed many of the junior officers' wives. The Army
welcomed the return of the Navy, for it brought signs of cooler air
and more social life.[33]

Though Richardson protested to Admiral Washington about a minor problem on an inspection report, his duties were well done as the commander of the South China Patrol (ComSoPat).[34] He applied for duty at the Naval War College. By that time Henry Wilson was the superintendent of the Naval Academy, and he told Richardson that he was to come there.[35] However, at the same time Claude C. Bloch asked that Richardson join him at the Bureau of Ordnance. All the same, by radio Richardson was ordered to proceed to Washington, DC, using the first available transportation. Either assignment would have been fine with May and young Joe. Wilson mumbled that Richardson would be much happier in Annapolis than "in what I call a rather unsatisfactory job in Washington!"

On February 28, 1924, Admiral Washington wrote to Richardson in Canton saying that he regretted to see him go. "I have been much pleased with your excellent work during the time that I have been here." Richardson wrote William H. Gale at the Hong Kong American Consular Service that his classmate, Commander James P. Lannon of the USS *Helena,* would take over the South China Patrol. Like the others, Gale expressed thanks for a job well done.[36] Ernest B. Price of the consulate in Foochow also wrote, thanking Richardson for maintaining the high standards of the Navy.[37] Schumann wrote of his "desire to record my admiration for the efficient manner he [Richardson] had discharged the duties of that difficult post."[38]

Richardson was allowed no leave on the way back to the States, having taken only nineteen days in the preceding nine years. Surprisingly to him, he learned upon arrival that he had been brought home quickly to work for Assistant Secretary of the Navy Theodore Douglas Robinson in connection with the impending congressional investigation of the Naval Petroleum Reserves—which came to be known as the Tea Pot Dome scandal. However, Bloch won over the assignment argument. Richardson went to work at the Bureau of Ordnance.[39]

CHAPTER EIGHT

A Little of This, A Little of That
Washington Duty before Back to Sea, 1924-34

It was time for the Richardsons to purchase a home. The couple located a lot in Massachusetts Avenue Heights, just up one block from the Naval Observatory Circle. It was a quiet, beautiful setting, not too far from the new Bureau of Ordnance office. May took the project in hand that fall of 1924, and a house began to be built in view of the huge Washington Cathedral construction project.

Richardson returned to the Washington scene to find that Bloch, for one, felt that there was a concerted effort to operate the Navy under too much economy.[1] Richardson was not totally against economizing. He contributed an article that called for improvement of the report of fitness of officers.[2] He was always calling for less expensive paperwork, and in this case, wanted a report that was more realistic and honest.

Richardson's salary would bump up to $7,200, helpful in the quest to pay for the new home. Richardson was fond of saying that this period away from sea was a part of the process in preparation for higher assignments. What he learned at Ordnance about ammunition, fire control, degaussing (eliminating an unwanted magnetic field), torpedoes, and nets and booms he would later draw upon in 1940 at Pearl Harbor. His attitudes about the possibilities of aviation warfare were highly formulated at Ordnance.[3] What Richardson learned working with Bloch, who was replaced by Leahy in 1927, was invaluable. His working association with Leahy would gain him a few more opportunities to be assigned to this senior officer.

In October of 1926, Richardson requested sea duty. He had been a regular captain since February, and wanted to carry that rank into the ocean. Near the end of the spring of 1927, Richardson received orders approving his request.[4] He was to command Destroyer Division 38 of the Scouting Fleet in the

Atlantic, spending some time in European waters. His command ship was to be the USS *Whipple*.[5]

Richardson left Norfolk May 26, and joined the division. Departure was from Boston toward various northern European ports. The naval forces were operating in cooperation with the State Department, showing the American flag at stops along the European and North African coasts. It would not be the last time the movements of ships involving Richardson would be controlled by the desires of the State Department.

In the late spring of 1927, the USS *Whipple* followed the USS *Detroit* as it transported U.S. Secretary of State Frank Billings Kellogg between Ireland and France for peace talks. Spurred on by an earlier German-U.S.S.R. agreement, fifteen nations came up with a multilateral treaty for the renunciation of war. It was called the Pact of Paris, but more commonly referred to in history as the Kellogg-Briand Peace Pact. This assignment gave Richardson an early chance to view one of many such conferences and plans that came up with a statement, but provided no mode of enforcement.

In the latter part of 1927, Richardson was invited to a function in Danzig—now called Gdansk—Poland. To travel there, the destroyers left from Helsingfors (Helsinki), Finland. Immediately the division encountered severe headwinds. It appeared that the scheduled 8:00 A.M. arrival would not be possible. Richardson radioed the consul that most likely the arrival would not be on time. A "reply with tears dripping on it" came back. But, the weather moderated. At twenty-five-knot speed, the party arrived in the entrance to the harbor on time. Four men in a small boat met Richardson. "They had on long-tailed coats and silk hats at 8:00 o'clock in the morning," Richardson told a crowd years later.

One of the men represented the consul, another the high commissioner, one the Polish commissioner, and the fourth the Senate of Danzig. "I was given a single spaced, letter-sized paper with the upcoming schedule," recalled Richardson. There was little time for rest after the tough trip.

The Polish representative asked for a copy of the speech

Richardson had prepared for that night's dinner. The official wanted to translate it into German and Polish so he could repeat it after Richardson. "That was the first I had heard that I would attend a dinner, and I had no idea of making a speech at any time," he wrote humorously.

But, at that time the issue was serious. Luckily, when the consul came to the dock, he told Richardson, "I have prepared a speech." Richardson immediately handed it over to the insistent interpreter. Then, after the transcriber was gone, Richardson was told that it was the only copy. He had not even glanced at its contents.

That night, "somewhat assisted by light wines and other stimulants, I got up and delivered an address. The interpreter delivered the written address in German and in Polish. I have frequently wondered what the people there, who could speak the two languages, thought about the interpreter!"[6] In his career, Richardson survived all his speeches but one.

That winter saw some 210 ships of the Pacific and Atlantic hold joint maneuvers. A civil war in Nicaragua was part of the reason. May returned to Norfolk. A good decision it was too. The next orders, which arrived aboard the ship on March 9, were for the division to proceed to San Francisco.[7] The course was set on March 26. In late April, the entire fleet was to gather at Lahaina Roads in Hawaii for fleet exercises.

However, Richardson personally would miss the 1928 Fleet Problem. He did obtain, however, some view of the way the fleet was being managed on the West Coast. Economic restraints had frustrated William V. Pratt since he became CinCUS in 1928. In fact, the fleet had become accustomed to being in port at dark each day, but despite the cost, Pratt arranged an all-week-out schedule. He thought it also reduced the artificial strain that came with the rush of the sailors and officers to get home every evening after target practice.[8] But, Richardson would next view this monetary crunch in Washington. In a few years, he would be behind the desk arranging the Navy budget.

Meanwhile he was not happy about leaving sea duty. The chief of the Bureau of Navigation, Admiral Richard Henry Leigh, knew it, and was a bit shy about telling Richardson what he had planned. He let his assistant, the current Officer Personnel Director Thomas Richardson Kurtz, do the duty. Kurtz wrote Richardson that "it seems important to get the best man possible for the duty," even though the bureau realized it was pulling a candidate from sea duty prematurely.[9]

Richardson admitted the decision to work for Navigation was "a distinct shock to me." He thought taking him away from sea duty, coupled with his inability to garner a place at the War College, would practically put an end to his naval career. He figured he had just a small chance anyway for promotion to flag rank. In a note to Kurtz and Leigh, he explained that most in his class on average were nearly two years ahead of him in sea time.[10]

Richardson noted another problem. His house and all his household effects except silver were leased to J. P. Jackson until August of 1929. He recommended others for the job, saying that J. C. Townsend was an excellent choice. Worse than that, he had on board a trunk full of May's clothes and "some junk" acquired in Europe, "and I do not want to leave them on the West Coast." The pleading did not work, however. Richardson and the trunk detached in San Francisco on April 13, 1928. As a concession, Leigh promised him that the next cruise for Richardson would be a long one.[11]

At the age of fifty, Richardson was 125th in grade among 243 captains. The CNO at that time was Admiral Charles F. Hughes. Richardson soon considered his navigation billet as fine as a captain could have. It called for knowledge of many facets of the Navy, as well as its officers and their talents and interests. It gave him some testimony time before congressional committees, explaining promotions and Navy details of assignments.

Near the end of three years as director of officer personnel, Richardson received what was promised. He was slated to command the new cruiser USS *Augusta*. She was sleek, loaded with guns, and had four aircraft. In addition, she could slide through 9,300 tons of displaced water at a maximum of thirty-two knots. She had a crew of 621 when fully complemented, and nine 8-inch guns.

After a forty-five-day leave in between assignments, Richardson reported on October 30 as the first commander. The *Augusta* was commissioned at the Norfolk Navy Yard in Portsmouth, Virginia, on January 30, 1931. Richardson began his trend of having neither civilians nor ladies on board for ceremonies. Far from being anti-social, he just believed that such occasions represented an opportunity for the commanding officer to impress his ideas upon the officers and men.

He said to the sailors:

> "Today we take over a new ship of the Navy just delivered by the builders. Now she is an inanimate thing, without life, without spirit, without record and without reputation; what she becomes depends upon us."[12]

By May, Richardson and the crew had the *Augusta* ready to become the flagship for Commander Scouting Force Vice-Admiral Arthur L. Willard. That summer, she and the force carried out tactical duties off the New England coast. Then, in August of 1931, the *Augusta* was reclassified as a heavy cruiser.

When the Scouting Force disbanded, the USS *Augusta* came home to the Norfolk Navy Yard. For the Richardsons, living there was quite a slower pace. May and Jim had quality time together until the beginning of 1932. When Pratt had taken over as CNO in September of 1930, he had definite ideas on the organization of the fleet. He wanted more command with the CinCUS rather than the share of authority with the Battle, Scouting, and Asiatic Forces. Battle Force became a single entity consisting of battleships, aircraft carriers, and destroyers, stationed on the West Coast. Scouting Force would be on the East Coast, joined by a small training force and some old destroyers. Submarines would answer to a Base Force. Pratt then designated "type" commanders to be responsible for training and readiness of the specific types of ships.[13]

Pratt also broke down the carriers into two divisions, placing the *Langley* with the Scouting Force as the sole carrier in Division 1. The *Saratoga* and the *Lexington* were Division 2.

Another big change came for the Navy. Georgian Carl Vinson took over as chairman of the House Naval Affairs Committee. He immediately secured funding for eight destroyers that gained congressional approval in 1916, but were never ordered.[14] Under his leadership, the Navy began to build.

The cruisers of the Scouting Force assembled in Hampton Roads, and departed on January 8, 1932, headed to Guantanamo Bay. Joe was at Princeton, so May was free to follow the fleet again when she received word to join her husband.

For a month, training was held near Cuba, but on February 18, the force moved to the Panama Canal on its way to the eastern Pacific for Fleet Problem XIII. Arriving in San Pedro, California, on March 7, the USS *Augusta* took off only three days later to simulate attacks against the Battle Force at widely separated points or "atolls" on the West Coast.

Just before the Scouting Force arrived, Admiral Harry Yarnell had taken the carriers *Lexington* and *Saratoga,* along with two destroyer divisions, on a simulated attack of Oahu and bases at Pearl Harbor.[15] This "raid" would later be a subject discussed at length by the 1945 Congressional Pearl Harbor Hearings. It was very successful.[16]

The *Augusta* also practiced strategic scouting and both defense of and attack upon a convoy. At the completion of the problem on March 18, Richardson experienced firsthand the power of politics over the fleet. Instead of returning to the Atlantic, the Scouting Force was told to remain on the West Coast throughout 1932. Most thought this order was a Hoover administration attempt to restrain the Japanese from more aggression upon China, begun with the invasion of Manchuria in 1931. The blame most likely fell on Secretary of State Henry L. Stimson, who apparently thought he could bluff the Japanese by keeping a larger force on the West Coast. Sending the fleet to Pearl Harbor at that time was not feasible. The facility was not yet ready for such traffic. But, the idea was brewing.

In mid-April 1932, Admiral William Harrison Standley watched a fleet review from Point Fermin off the coast of San Pedro. He would be named as the CNO to take over from Pratt in July of 1933. He later told President Roosevelt that though the fleet parade was impressive, he feared that it simply deceived the American public into a safe-mode thought pattern. Standley felt the fleet was not prepared and lacked manpower to maintain full power for more than four hours.[17]

From a firsthand position, Richardson saw the effect upon the sailors, and realized how difficult it was to move wives and families to a temporary assignment where housing was not financed by the government.[18] He could afford for May to come out and live in the rather "elegant" Villa Riviera, and still keep the house in Washington.[19] However, others were not as financially able. A 15 percent pay cut stung both officers and enlisted men.[20] Each year Congress attempted to reduce the commissions from the academy graduating class. They even forbade graduates to marry during a probationary period.

The ruse to "muscle up" on Japan did work to some extent. Japanese ambassador Katsuji Debuchi protested the fact that so many U.S. ships were stationed on the Pacific Coast. Stimson was mindful that at that time the combined U.S. Fleet was larger than anything the Japanese could float.[21]

Frederick A. Edwards was ordered to the USS *Augusta* after he asked to be assigned to a heavy cruiser. He arrived there about the same time that Richardson did. "In the ward room, we'd say if we have a war, we want Joe to run it," he commented about Richardson. "He was a down-to-earth guy, levelheaded around the clock." He thought that at that time Richardson was a bit apprehensive about air power, but explained mostly that was because at shooting practice the spot planes hardly ever arrived on time.[22]

Ensign Joseph Caldwell Wylie, Jr., was aboard with six or seven of his 1932 Navy classmates. "He was very kind to his JO's [junior officers]," commented Wylie about Richardson in his oral interview. Once Richardson came in and watched Wylie observing the navigator. Richardson told the navigator, "You're relieved for forty-eight hours. I want this young man to do it." Though he viewed Richardson as a no-nonsense leader, "I was, in a very, very distant way, quite fond of him," added Wylie.[23]

Ensign Lloyd M. Mustin was there with Wylie, also on his first duty assignment. He got off on the wrong foot when one morning about dawn the *Augusta* got underway. Edwards told the story. "As we got underway, we saw a shore boat coming toward the ship, hell-bent." Up came Mustin, apologizing for oversleeping. Eventually he reported to Richardson, who simply said, "Well, now, I want you to stay aboard until you feel you're rested up." After about a week, Mustin gathered enough courage to tell Richardson that he thought he was rested up enough.

Mustin gained Richardson's confidence when he drew out an explanation of why the *Augusta*'s main hydraulic ram would fall when the Healey-Shaw motor lost pressure. This occurrence was causing the rudder to go all the way right, twisting off a mechanical follow-up gear. Mustin attacked the problem as if he was in mechanical drawing class at the Naval Academy, only to find out that his drawing was more technical than Richardson desired. "So, I learned in a fairly loud voice to reorient my thinking," recalled Mustin. Richardson knew the cause of the problem—a defective design in a spring-loaded relief valve. A correction was made, and that problem was solved. Despite overcomplicating the task, Mustin did impress Richardson.[24]

Richardson and Nimitz taught Mustin the technique called "10 turn minus 100 rule." This rule taught the crew when to start turning the ship in a channel by taking the number of degrees in the turn and multiplying it by ten and subtracting one hundred. "That tells you how far back from the intersection of those two track lines you should put your rudder over to start the turn," Mustin told an interviewer years later. For example, a ninety-degree turn began eight hundred yards short of the new channel, about half a nautical mile. "Richardson and Nimitz were magnificent, magnificent ship handlers."[25]

Mustin also explained the man overboard drill taught by Richardson. It revealed how to most quickly return the ship to a point on its wake, for example, where a man might have fallen. He used 270 degrees as an example, explaining the speed of the ship, and the backing up maneuver involved. It had to be precise in total darkness or fog. Each ship differed.

Richardson was in the second year of what was to become the longest command cruise of a large ship in his memory. Willard left, and was replaced by Frank H. Clark, Jr. Standley came on board, using the USS *Augusta* as his flagship while he was Commander Cruisers Scouting Force.[26]

Again, in the 1933 Fleet Problem the Scouting Force was designated as *Black,* and this time it was simulating a strike at Oahu by a carrier's aircraft. Yarnell learned from this exercise that there was a need for planes and three additional 18,000-ton carriers, which were permitted under existing treaties. All, even the battleship advocates, were becoming aware of the emerging potential of naval air power. It was difficult, however, to move the thinking ahead and consider the carriers as the future of the U.S. Fleet.

Before leaving the West Coast, Richardson and May experienced another earthquake. Although not as horrible as the one in Japan in 1923, it nonetheless was devastating to the Long Beach area. It hit a few minutes before 6:00 P.M. on March 10, killing 120 and injuring hundreds more. Property damage was extensive. The Roosevelt administration took office in March, and kept the Scouting Force in the Pacific, but on May 20, Richardson, with thirty-one years service, finally was on his way to the Naval War College.

In 1930, Richardson was told by CNO Hughes that if an officer never went to the Naval War College, it would not be a negative upon his career. Richardson had applied many times, but had never been approved. Indeed, a "vigorous" minority of senior officers felt that a course at the Naval War College tended to create a merely theoretical officer. Richardson knew it was quite a jibe when a senior captain was sent to the college. Still, he was excited to be selected.

School in Newport was a natural for Richardson. It included lectures and a reading list of nearly seventy books, with much information on strategy and a bit on tactics. A third of the reading list dealt with Japan. The next year, eight of eleven books had Japan as the subject. These were "not for simply a higher education of the Naval officer, but a series of mental exercises in the preparation for war."[27]

Students wrote four essays annually. The subjects were about command, strategy, tactics, and policy. For each essay, officers were given sets of themes. It became rather deep and confusing.[28] As a result, many of the student writings were poorly researched, but the thought process put into them was reasonable, at least with Richardson. Academic statements abounded among those who wrote. Many were critical of the civilian population around them. Richardson believed at that time that the United States held vital no external interests.[29]

Even then, Richardson was espousing his thoughts on fleet unpreparedness. He wrote that in the event the American people wanted war with Japan, the fleet was incapable of any western movement across the Pacific. "If war came," wrote Richardson, "the Navy would be impotent to bring it to a successful end."[30] He wrote this message as Vinson was ending the long downward funding trend for the Navy, and knowing that in the fall of 1933 the Japanese had held its combined fleet exercises as close to Hawaii as the Caroline and Marshall Islands, provoking some nervousness among Navy leaders.

Even five years before he would be called upon to write *War Plan Orange* (the color chosen to represent Japan), and seven years before he took over as CinCUS, Richardson's mind was formulated with the opinion that the mind-set of the American public might never be anything other than isolationist. He already knew that the population as a whole was anti-interference when it came to European matters. He wrote in a gloomy, but at that time, realistic manner:

> The Open Door policy is essentially a kind of intervention policy, and since the American people are unalterably opposed to entanglement in European affairs, they will not support entanglement in Asiatic affairs. . . . The American Government has made such intervention impossible. . . . An American Naval strategy that would be in keeping with present public opinion would be a purely defensive strategy.[31]

With this viewpoint in mind, Richardson also had his thoughts made up on Hawaii's position. "The Hawaiian Islands would be a defensive outpost rather than a stepping off place for our westward movement across the Pacific."

Richardson wrote much of what he would speak a few years later:

> The Navy is primarily maintained for war purposes, but during long periods of peace administration, the less combatant function of command acquires a dominant position. The Navy becomes material minded, and officers become admininstrators rather than leaders.[32]

Again and again, he preached this message to those who would listen and even to those who ignored. By 1934, he had seen much of both ends of the Navy, and knew the problem. He feared that "the failure to indoctrinate subordinates during peace may give us future leaders who will fail under the trial of war." He added, "The only time during the past 20 years when I have been conscious of any effort to so indoctrinate me has been at the Naval War College."

So, Richardson came to understand the value of the college, and recognized its other positive—getting to know and work beside his peers. From the 1934 class, its juniors, and its teachers, Richardson and at least eighteen others reached flag rank.[33] Richardson thought the college did an acceptable job, and the Bureau of Navigation was commended by him for its selection of these students.

It was Richardson's opinion that his real preparation for flag rank began in 1933 when he went to Newport. His promotion was attained in December of 1933, though it did not become effective for another year.[34] On the last day at Newport, as the senior member of his class, he arose to speak. No one else had done so. He said, "Today an ambition of long standing is being realized. I am completing the course at the War College for which I have applied periodically during the past 15 years." He pointed out that his idea of what to expect never changed, and it was fulfilled in the eleven months of instruction.[35] "I think that the course makes a good officer a better officer, but that it tends to convert a fool into a damn fool!"[36] He thought that many of his statements during the year 1933-34 were correct, but several years later he pointed to one that converted him to the "fool" status:

> It would probably be safe to assume that our Navy will not, in our lifetime, be employed in escorting large troop movements across the Atlantic.[37]

Before 1941 he truthfully just never could believe that the American public would allow such a thing to happen.

CHAPTER NINE

Quick Training for High Rank
1934-37 Full of Duties

When Richardson was director of officer personnel during 1928-30, he and Standley discussed the difficult process of selecting properly qualified officers for high command. These were the positions of CNO, CinCUS, commanders of Asiatic Fleet, Battle Fleet, Scouting Fleet, and other commands that carry with them the higher temporary rank of admiral or vice-admiral. Standley and Richardson took an idea to CNO Hughes, who was getting beat up just trying to compose a trim budget each year. The plan called for the Bureau of Navigation to place flag officers in such duties, from the time of their selection to flag rank, that would qualify them for a certain job to which it might be expected they would be assigned later.

That way those doing the selection could pull from several qualified names. Richardson made up a "training slate" for the various officers involved, and it seemed to work. In several years he believed that even he was a recipient of the plan's success. He had six details in six years after leaving the Navy War College.

In the summer of 1934, Richardson was assigned to Washington as director of Naval Communications in Naval Operations. But, Bloch found an unexpected opening as Judge Advocate General, and left his post as the Navy's budget officer. He suggested that Richardson relieve him. The change of orders came just as Richardson left Newport. By December 12, he would be a rear admiral in charge of the Navy finances.

Richardson would work for Secretary of the Navy Claude A. Swanson, his assistant Henry Latrobe Roosevelt, and CNO Standley. Swanson and Richardson worked well together, but in the spring of 1935, Leahy was to leave the Bureau of Navigation. When told he would be selected to replace Leahy as chief, Richardson quickly said he did not want the job, but would take it if pressed, and do it to the best of his ability. However, shortly afterward Admiral Joseph Mason "Bull" Reeves came to Washington to discuss Fleet Problem XVI, which was to begin on May 5. Reeves, the first CinCUS from aviation, wanted to maneuver the ships to an area covering five million square miles of the North Central Pacific between Midway, Hawaii, and the Aleutian Islands.[1] He wanted the 321 ships and 70,000 men to make an impression upon Japan.

The Reeves announcement of this maneuver was ill timed, for it came the same day that Japan declared it was pulling out of the Washington and London Treaties. Letters poured in from citizens thinking that Reeves had provoked the Japanese decision.

The scope of the Fleet Problem was limited to some extent, but was to be covered by more than thirty correspondents to the consternation of Reeves. This problem was solved when the Navy Department required that anything written be reviewed first. Most editors balked at this control of the press. Only five writers then remained to witness the sixteenth fleet exercise.

Before Reeves left Washington, he solved Richardson's problem by obtaining the Bureau of Navigation billet for his chief of staff, Adolphus Andrews. At the end of May, however, Admiral Frederick J. Horne was relieved as Commander Cruiser Division 6, and Richardson quickly asked Swanson if he could have his permission to fill that vacancy. Swanson had asked "Joe" months earlier to stay with him until he left office, but he knew the tug of the sea was strong for a Navy admiral.

Richardson helped Swanson find a "wholly satisfactory" replacement. It was Kimmel. Standley and Leahy approved. May began to pack. The assignment would take a quick twist after they again became settled in their apartment at Long Beach.

First, the admiral caught the Cruiser Division 6 contingent at Bremerton, Washington, in June of 1935. It left there on the last day of August, arriving in Long Beach twenty-four hours before the Labor Day holiday began. Richardson went ashore to the apartment at the Villa Riviera to see May. But, he was surprised at what she said: "Did you know that you are going to be ordered as chief of staff to 'Bull' Reeves?" Irritated, partially because he did not know and she did, Richardson exclaimed to his longtime partner and best friend, "Not if I can help it!" It did not matter to Richardson that he would work for a *Time* magazine cover subject.[2] Richardson was skeptical about the assignment. He quickly went to Leahy the next morning, despite it being a holiday. By that time Leahy was Commander Battle Force.

"Joe," Leahy said, "I recommended you for this job, and you cannot refuse, because you are now under Reeves' command and you must take the job."[3] The CinCUS barge came alongside at that moment. An aide boarded, and said that Reeves wanted to see Richardson. "I went over in the barge," wrote Richardson, giving no summary of the discussion with Reeves. On September 16, he was relieved as Commander Cruiser Division 6, and became chief of staff.[4]

Though Reeves used the USS *New Mexico* as his flagship until 1936, aboard the USS *Pennsylvania* Richardson may have noticed some young officers who were very impressive and were in favor with Reeves. Lieutenants Joseph J. Rochefort, Arthur H. McCollum, and Edwin T. Layton would miss working much for Richardson in the future, but they were energetic and knowledgeable about Japanese habits and culture. So were their friends. Layton had been on the *Pennsylvania* since June of 1933. He was a division officer in charge of turret four. Tommy Dyer, his classmate, who was also interested in intelligence, manned turret three. Wesley A. "Ham" Wright came on board the *Pennsylvania* in 1936 shortly before Rochefort, and fresh from cryptanalytic training at OP-20-G.[5] Just five years into the future these would be the backbone of intelligence gathering and decoding for World War II.

Reeves impressed Richardson with his tireless work, preparation, and fleet readiness. A former chemistry and physics teacher at the academy, Reeves had a mind Richardson enjoyed. His experience in civil and naval matters was broad. He would tell Richardson and others why he worked so hard. "No Naval commander wants to leave the issue of victory to the Lord. If he's an able commander, he must control all the factors of victory."[6]

All through the fall and winter the fleet exercised and trained. Whether in port or at sea, naval life basically followed a regular routine, but Reeves would upset that routine at times.[7] For instance, on Friday, March 20, 1936, he played a realistic game with the sailors, who were in the process of preparing for liberty. In fact, some were already on shore. At a few minutes before 3:00 P.M., a fleet-wide dispatch was sent, ordering all units to get under way at 4:00 P.M. It ruined a good day of golf for some, but some never got on board in time.[8] It was a valuable exercise, and all came back into port in a matter of twenty-four hours.[9]

For the first time Richardson would be in on both the planning and the actual Fleet Problem exercise. This one would begin in April with the fleet sortied around Panama. The seventeenth problem was designed to practice scouting.

On September 25, 1936, the day after Reeves boarded his barge for shore and the end of his seagoing days, Richardson took over as Commander Destroyers Scouting Force.[10] Being around Reeves left him with so many thoughts about fleet command. Reality in the performing of exercises was one. A second was the fact that the CinCUS continually tussles with the CNO. Reeves and Standley were not close anyway, but during the months as chief of staff to Reeves, Richardson helped draft many letters to Washington for his boss.

Someone from the fleet tipped off Standley that Reeves was not following the CNO's objectives. It upset Richardson that the fleet staff would go directly to Reeves with their concerns, and it upset Reeves that someone would go directly to Standley and not through the CinCUS. Richardson could only watch and learn as the messages flew between the fleet and the CNO's office.

Reeves was probably right, as proven in World War II, that task forces in war conditions would come and go, depending upon missions. He thought an organization around types with type commanders was more suitable. His successor, Arthur J. Hepburn, thought basically the same. The open opposition came from Tommy Hart and Charles Peck Snyder, the former on the

General Board after being in the fleet, and the latter president of the Naval War College. Snyder had no desire to make the radical change to the college curriculum.

Whatever the organization of the fleet would be, at the moment Richardson's new command put him in charge of thirty-eight destroyers, the light cruiser flagship USS *Richmond,* and two destroyer tenders. Since naval aircraft were not yet equipped with radar units, the force under Richardson was involved with antisubmarine work and was charged with the responsibility for night search and torpedo attack.

The period included the last crisis-free months of Richardson's move up to commander of the U.S. Fleet. He took it easy and experimented in different ways of management. One of the favorite stories Dyer told of Richardson involved events that happened during the first week of duty in June of 1936. Richardson sent out the traditional first order. It named the staff and gave some basic data. A second order, however, confused the young Dyer. It said that one of the problems on board destroyers was a lack of attention to the chores at hand. It appeared to Richardson that there was too much leave and liberty, and too many special privileges.

At the first staff conference the first order was discussed, and approved. Richardson moved to the second memo, and asked Arthur S. "Chips" Carpender what he thought. He said that it had some merit, some good points. Then Richardson asked the rest, one by one, and each only expressed some limited doubts, if any at all. "What do you think of it, Mr. Dyer?" Richardson asked. "I think it stinks," Dyer blurted, and quickly tried to sensibly explain.

"Admiral. If you had been here for three months and made up your mind that that was what was happening with the force . . . and wanted to take remedial action which you have proposed, this . . . would be quite all right." He then added, "But, you are absolutely a new broom." He explained that Richardson was casting aspersions without any evidence. "None of this staff know because none of us have served in the Destroyer Force recently. I just think that it's a terrible order."

"I had no more gotten to my Flag Secretary's office when there was a buzz from the Admiral," Dyer recalled. "I went down toward his cabin dying a thousand deaths." There he was on his first staff job, and he was being called in for what he had said.

Dyer thought he probably deserved a dressing down. Upon arrival he faced Richardson across the desk. The admiral said, "Look," pointing to the wastepaper basket. "There were the pieces of paper, all torn up, of the order which he had written," said Dyer.

"I wrote that order knowing that it stank," Richardson said as he puffed on his pipe. "I wanted to find out from whom in my staff I could get an honest opinion." He went on to explain that a flag officer rarely obtains an honest thought, and needs more eyes. "He can't hear everything, or be at every place," Richardson explained.

"I now know that I have one person on my staff who will tell me just how it is," he went on. "I won't always agree with you," he added, but "I will know at least that I'm getting an honest opinion from you." Dyer said it was a "wonderful lesson to me," and he used it in his own command billets more than once.[11]

Dyer was given many duties by Richardson, one of which was operation of the mooring board. "I was the Flag Secretary, not an operations officer, but I could handle the mooring board." In fleet exercises, with the destroyers tagging behind, Dyer said it was difficult to visualize them from the lead ship. But, he could turn a formation with talent. Whenever the admiral would want to move from here to there, "I would give [him] the course and speed to go," said Dyer. Richardson built up faith in Dyer's methods, which seemed to work each time.[12]

This talent dragged Dyer along three years later when Richardson went to command the Battle Force for Admiral Bloch. Richardson told Dyer, "You relieved me of so much worry during the last cruise. I know I can sleep well if I've got you there doing that old 'is-was' thing of yours."

On December 31, orders came for Richardson to report to Washington to sit on the Selection Board. The previous year the board had passed over Laurance F. Safford, and Richardson felt this decision was made simply because so little was known of his intelligence work. "I understood it as my mission to inform the board . . . of the great future value . . . of Safford's continued promotion in the Navy," wrote Richardson in the last section of his book. He told the other eight men:

"Should the United States become involved in the war, in the Pacific, what this officer has done and can do will probably contribute more to bring victory to our Navy than the efforts of any or all of us who are serving on this Board."[13]

Safford gained his promotion, being selected by all nine voters. In view of what was later disclosed at the Pearl Harbor hearings, Richardson wrote that he felt his statement was borne out by the events.

When he returned west, in Fleet Problem XVIII, Richardson's command tested the individual ship and composite-type capabilities. There was a considerable amount of night work involved, revealing various flaws. In late April of 1937, the problem began in the northern Pacific. Then, the USS *Richmond* was supposed to lead a quick swoop down upon French Frigate Shoals, an atoll in the Hawaiian Islands. This atoll was five hundred miles northwest of Oahu, and covered a space of only twenty miles, two to four miles wide. The games called for an enemy force to be anchored there, conducting air searches. "We were supposed to wipe out the sea plane tender," said Dyer. The area, in all reality, was rather dangerous, and always avoided by shipping vessels.

"We had to approach it by night," said Dyer, explaining the hazard of the maneuver, which took place on May 6. "From 300 miles away we were running at speeds between 25-38 knots, moving down from the north. There were no lights at Frigate Shoals, or bell buoys—your navigating had to be darn accurate."

In the late afternoon, Dyer took some sun lines[14] before starting the approach. Of course those on the *Richmond* were most interested because they were leading the group. Dyer found that his readings were far different from those of the ship's navigator. The force was supposed to arrive forty-five minutes after first light. It was a nervous time for Dyer. He had located the force farther away. He hoped he was right.

Luckily, the attack went as planned. Richardson called for top speed until the last minute, and it worked.[15] Dyer was correct with his readings. The *Richmond's* navigator "got the dickens from his captain, S. F. Heim," said Dyer, relieved that he was correct rather than the navigator.[16]

The friendly force in Fleet Problem XVIII was supposed to hold Hilo, Hawaii, for a week against a *Black* invasion. This did not work, however, and the Big Island was taken, an enemy base established, and a successful attack followed on Oahu. Once again, having the large U.S. Fleet exercise in the Pacific had little effect on Japan's plans. It invaded China in a few months, causing much headache for the Asiatic Fleet, and for Richardson in Washington, when an American ship was sunk.

Fleet Problem XVIII gave Richardson another view of the carrier. One analysis that came out of that experiment held that a carrier could not operate effectively and safely if held down by slower moving vessels in a main body. That maneuver would allow an enemy carrier and its force to come within striking distance, which would result in a slugfest until one of the combatants was destroyed. The other view from the problem was that carriers should be an integral part of the main body. The faster USS *Ranger,* built in 1934, could at that time handle some of the scouting duties, especially as soon as the larger carriers *Yorktown* (1937) and *Enterprise* (1938) joined the fleet.[17]

Bloch was Commander Battle Force (*Black*) for Problem XVIII, and firmly believed that carriers were best employed in formation with the battle line, receiving protection from the surface combatants and their antiaircraft guns. However, the aviators contested this "old fashioned" contention, saying that command of the air should be achieved before the opposing fleets engaged. During the problem, Bloch restricted the carriers to flying patrols over the battleships, and to covering the fleet's landing force. In the process, the *Langley* was "sunk," and the *Saratoga* and *Lexington* heavily damaged. In the heat of the debate, Horne, commander of all carriers, put out a paper calling for independent carrier operations. Bloch had him recall all copies.[18]

All this conversation and discussion came out at the critique held in the Submarine Base Motion Picture Pavilion at Pearl Harbor on May 18 and 19. Operations Officer Captain R. L. Ghormley spoke twenty minutes, Bloch seventeen minutes, Commander White Fleet W. T. Tarrant ten minutes, and others like Richardson from five to ten minutes each.[19]

One of the last things Richardson did before he went back to Washington was suggest to Tarrant that Dyer was the man he needed to "clean up" his flagship, the USS *Indianapolis*. While riding back to their respective ships on a barge, having attended a fleet conference in San Pedro Harbor, Tarrant said he would be "wholly happy" to find such an officer. So, Dyer again obtained a billet at the suggestion of Richardson. He became the housekeeper of the ship as damage control officer.[20]

Richardson went again to Washington, this time to housekeep for CNO Leahy.

CHAPTER TEN

A Most Interesting Year
In 1937-38 Richardson Serves as Assistant to Leahy

In June of 1937, Richardson reported for service as the assistant chief of Naval Operations. Dyer thought that since his "boss" was still a junior rear admiral, it was a bit early for the assignment.[1]

For most of 1937 through 1939, and many times before, Richardson and Leahy had lunch together. "He was a successful student of human nature," Richardson wrote years later, and "was astute in regard to the 'Washington Scene.'" He found Leahy to be a skilled negotiator in naval matters. On rare occasion, however, Richardson felt that Leahy yielded to opposition rather than risk defeat. Nonetheless, Richardson believed that Leahy "did more to advance my interests than any other officer in the Navy, and I am grateful."[2]

Richardson always thought the CNO should ask Congress for 100 percent of the men and ships needed. Once, when Richardson was chief of the Bureau of Navigation in 1939, he asked his personnel section head to produce the numbers of enlisted men for each unit that were necessary to carry out full duties. When then-Budget Officer Kimmel showed it to Leahy, the CNO sent for Richardson.

"You can't do this," Leahy exclaimed, having succumbed to the congressional habit of underfunding the Navy to about 75 percent of its needs. "I would be stultifying myself if I were to ask for one hundred percent of the men needed by the Navy." Richardson wrote later that the readiness of the Navy was the more important of the choices available to the CNO. This instance may have been a partial reason why Richardson was not chosen to succeed Leahy later in 1939.[3]

Leahy followed the tough job held by Standley, finding that he was to be even more responsible for the Navy since Swanson had been sick for so long. The seventy-five-year-old had been secretary since Roosevelt took office in 1933. He fought for a strong Navy, and by 1937 knew many of the officers personally. As assistant CNO, however, Richardson had little contact and did not form a bond with Swanson until the next year.

Whatever the difference in the feelings about management, Leahy and Richardson apparently coordinated well while Richardson was the assistant from June 21, 1937, to June 10, 1938.[4] For Richardson, Leahy was just hard to decipher entirely. For Leahy, his loyalty lay with the president.

In 1937, there was no vice or deputy chief of Naval Operations, and only one billet for an assistant chief. Richardson and May took two weeks off to move back to their Georgetown home. The Navy Department in the middle of what can be hot and humid Washington, DC, weather was not as uncomfortable as conceived. Olaf Hustvedt, head of the CNO's Central Division, said that air-conditioning was not really missed, especially since it had never been there in the first place. The CNO office was on the front corridor, he said, and was on the north side, second floor. "Probably the most comfortable part of the building physically. I just don't remember being uncomfortable. We had our fans and we had awnings."[5]

It was a pleasing assignment, or so Richardson originally believed. However, it would be a more exciting and stressful first year than envisioned: the search for the missing American aviator Amelia Earhart would be followed by the Japanese attack on the USS *Panay,* sent to protect American interests in China, and that incident was followed by Richardson's assignment with an Army representative to come up with a compromise to *War Plan Orange.*

Earhart was reported missing somewhere near Howland Island in the South Pacific.[6] The publicity was enormous, and the pressure to find the famous aviator immense. For sixteen days following the disappearance of the Lockheed Electra 10E she was flying, Richardson would help coordinate from Washington the $4.5 million South Seas search.

Richardson considered the Earhart event a "headache" to

the Navy budget. "It put a heavy strain on our aviation funds," he wrote.[7]

On July 18, Richardson released the USS *Lexington* from the search. July 19 was the last front-page article in the *Paris News*. "Mystery of Amelia Left as Unsolved," editor Neville placed above the Honolulu story by the Associated Press. "Four naval vessels manned by more than 1,500 heat-plagued men sailed away empty handed . . . where they completed the greatest ocean hunt ever launched," the story informed Parisians.[8]

For Richardson, only a few days of normal duties and paperwork followed the end of the Earhart search. On July 29, 1937, word came that fighting between the Japanese and Chinese taking place west of Peiping (Peking) had spread to Tientsin. This old main port of northern China was bombed and occupied on August 11. Roosevelt changed his mind against sending over bombers, and ordered Leahy to ship them. They left on the USS *Wichita* from Baltimore on August 29, but word came of a Japanese blockade on goods going to China. The planes were then unloaded at San Pedro.[9]

On the light side, from the West Coast, Bloch wrote Richardson about the upcoming slate he was trying to organize, once again depending upon his friend for ideas. He mentioned the huge rain that he read had fallen in Washington. "I hope your flowers were not washed away and the cellar drained properly!" He also commended Richardson for building on a rock foundation and on the side of a hill. He said that young Joe was welcome to visit if he got tired of the whirl of Hollywood, where he was becoming a screenwriter. Bloch concluded, "You must be a busy man with all of the fireworks in the Far East and in Spain [a reference to the ongoing Spanish civil war], especially with Leahy on leave."[10]

The next incident was war threatening. On November 8, the Chinese Army evacuated Shanghai. Chiang Kai-shek's representatives notified the American embassy on November 21 that it should prepare to leave Nanking. The ambassador and most personnel exited that day. On December 12 Hankow, four hundred miles upriver, was established as the new capital of the central government of China.

The senior Japanese officer explained that he had orders to "fire on every ship on the river."[11] Japanese pilot Masatake Okumiya wrote, "An advance army unit had reported seven large merchant ships and three smaller ones fleeing the capital [Nanking], loaded to capacity with Chinese troops."[12] A catastrophe was in the works. That day, the United States Navy Department phones and message centers began to receive word that the USS *Panay* had been sunk in the Yangtze River by Japanese bombers.[13]

Richardson determined that this was the sixth event since 1931 by Japan that was proving the death knell to the experiment in naval limitations begun in 1922. In 1931 Japan occupied Manchuria, renaming it Manchukuo. A year later Japan sent troops into its district and into Hongkew and even into greater Shanghai. In 1934 Japan gave notice of her termination in the Washington Naval Treaty, effective December 31, 1936. Then, in 1936 Japan withdrew from the London Naval Treaty Conference. The 1937 launching of the China campaign should have opened eyes in the coffee shops and barbershops of even small-town America.

Leahy was out of Washington when news of the sinking of the *Panay* came through, thrusting Richardson into the CNO's hot seat. At meetings, the thinking among various civilian and naval officials was going in many directions. Some contemplated that this latest aggression was the unannounced blow common to the way Japan began her modern wars. Others leaned toward the accidental angle, and believed it had no future significance. The latter thought that pattern prevailed.

In September, Richardson had attempted to meet Asiatic Fleet Commander Yarnell's request for more assistance. Though not very successful, Richardson was instrumental in sending the Sixth Regiment of Marines to China, but was unable in December to launch the requested division of heavy cruisers. Only the 7,500-ton light cruiser USS *Marblehead* was finally ordered out after the sinking of the *Panay*.[14]

After the Japanese attack on the *Panay,* a call came from Congress and citizens to remove the Asiatic Fleet and the 2,300 servicemen who were mostly on seven gunboats, one heavy cruiser, a light cruiser, thirteen destroyers, a converted yacht, six larger gunboats, three minesweepers, an oil tanker, a cargo ship, and a naval transport. The sailors were more or less helpless to guard U.S. interests in the area.

However, Roosevelt was of Richardson's mode of thinking, wanting to send in more than a token military force. He felt that the United States could not abandon Chiang Kai-shek. The president wanted to quietly, without knowledge of the press, send U.S. bombers to give assistance to the Chinese. But, he knew that when the Senate discovered this action, the strict application of the Neutrality Act would be demanded. His attempts to rally the public to join an effort to quarantine Japan fell on deaf ears.

The United States ambassador to Japan, Joseph Grew, warned Washington of the futility of "moral thunderbolts" toward Japan. Those, and the resolutions by the weak League of Nations, went unheeded in Japan. He said the United States had to summon to Washington the nine powers that just sixteen years earlier had sworn to protect China. A conference was finally held in November, but it was full of disunity and further angered the Japanese.

Though Richardson thought the outcry in the United States and in the world to be soft, the headlines were large, even on the front page of the *Paris News.* At 12:30 P.M. on December 13, Secretary of State Hull was handed a message from President Roosevelt. It listed three things for Hull to tell the Japanese ambassador, Hirosi Saito, when the pair met in thirty minutes: (1) that Roosevelt was deeply shocked over the USS *Panay* event; (2) that facts were being assembled; and (3) that he expected the Japanese government to be preparing full expressions of regret and planning full compensation for losses.[15]

Roosevelt also wanted to know what methods would be implemented to prevent another such incident.[16] The Japanese in Tokyo quickly began drawing up notes of apology. Fearing a reprisal, U.S. Ambassador Grew, remembering what the sinking of the USS *Maine* had done to attitudes in America in 1898, began to pack. But Japan of 1937 was no Spain of 1898.

Sick and frail, Swanson was wheeled into the first cabinet meeting after the attack. In a hoarse voice, he called for war. Leahy returned to Washington where he pronounced that he thought maybe it was time to take on Japan in China.[17]

On December 14, the Rising Sun flag of Japan flew at each corner of the walls of Nanking.[18] Japanese Foreign Minister Koki Hirota handed the letter of agreement and apology over to Grew.[19] Even though new statistics revealed that some sixty-six Chinese who were on the oil vessels *Meian, Meishia,* and *Meiping,* and fifteen who were on the mother ship, the USS *Panay,* were missing, the public seemed to accept the event as over.[20] In the meantime, a million Japanese citizens marched in Tokyo to celebrate the occupation of Nanking.

A week after the attack, Roosevelt read what the naval court of inquiry report said, condensed from its interviews after convening on board the USS *Oahu* when it came into the Whangpoo River and docked across from Shanghai at Pootung.[21] The complete report would arrive by airmail later. It was released to the press representatives on Christmas Eve.

Roosevelt also viewed the Universal Studios film of the attack, and, ironically fearing too much of an outcry, had it censored before it was released to the local theaters. The close-ups of the pilots' faces were removed, giving some impression that the attack was an accident. Though Roosevelt might later long for such an attack that would afford him the chance to build his naval and military forces, he lost the chance in the fall of 1937. He eventually accepted Japan's check for $2,214,007.36 in reparations.[22]

The day after the attack began a time of horror in China. Nanking residents were brutalized and raped for a period of four weeks. More than 50,000 Chinese solders were killed by various methods, and 42,000 civilians in Nanking met the same fate.[23] Eventually, some quarter of a million Chinese were brutally tortured and killed.

When the USS *Augusta* arrived at Manila, Charles Speed

Adams wrote to his brother, George L. Adams, on January 9: "I was on the *Panay* when she was bombed . . . and believe me . . . I don't care for any more of that!" He said that the Japanese planes tried to drop a bomb on one small boat heading to shore, and did machine gun one of the men in the chest. He thought that the boat crews were under more fire than those on the *Panay*. Speed said he was struck by several pieces of shrapnel, but that his worst wounds "were three blistered toes on that three days out in the interior of China" after surviving the attack.

He was angry. "I don't see why the U.S. is taking that apology from those Jap monkeys, for although the U.S. is not ready for war, our shooting is so much superior to theirs," he wrote his brother.[24]

On January 13, 1938, Prime Minister Neville Chamberlain of Britain cabled to Roosevelt, suggesting that the president should hold any action for a while. There were no British warships to spare. The chance to check Japan was lost, or really was never feasibly there. A poll of American citizens revealed that almost 70 percent wanted the United States to withdraw its military forces from China.

Yarnell's chief of staff Riley F. McConnell wrote a long letter on January 27, 1938, apprising Richardson of his thoughts and of events in the Asiatic region.[25] It confirmed Richardson's thoughts. "What the Japanese really want is political domination with all that that implies in the Oriental mind," McConnell wrote in an eight-page treatise. "We need to always understand," he continued, "that contradictions of policy and actions render it quite impossible for an Occidental to understand the mental processes of an Oriental." He warned that this significant fact should always be kept in mind when dealing with the Japanese. Richardson took heed.

McConnell warned that the Japanese Army could be highly disciplined, but at many times it refused orders from higher commands. "The colonels are running the show," he wrote. In the meantime, neither the Japanese Army nor Navy was concerned about orders from civil officials in Japan. He said the general thought was that even the Japanese war minister did not know of actions in the field, nor did military commanders in the field have control over their subordinates. "Press representatives are denied going anywhere near front lines," he explained, "lest they paint a too vivid picture of the murder, rape and arson that goes on in the wake of the Japanese Army."

Japan had to buy materials from many foreign firms or countries. McConnell said the diplomatic feeling as observed by the major powers gave him the impression that the Japanese "will never be fit to live within the family of nations unless and until they are defeated in war so thoroughly that they will be unable to salvage a diplomatic victory." This was a gruesome thought to Richardson, but one he knew was true.

McConnell closed his statements by listing observations of Japanese personnel, reasons the United States should be wary of the future. Two struck home to Richardson: skill of seamanship in night operations in the Yangtze River without casualties; and vast activity in ocean and river transport indicating the great value of Japan's large reserve of seamen.

Richardson wrote in the 1950s that he began to clearly see that in 1937 the desire of the American people for a quiet and pleasurable life was even more powerful than the "counsels of prudence and restraint exhibited by the Roosevelt Administration." The president was merely reacting to this desire by being conciliatory.[26] After all, in the United States, an election rolled around each four years. Even at the CNO complex of offices, the USS *Panay* incident was not viewed by some as extremely critical. Hustvedt said later, "I don't remember that there was any crisis atmosphere during the time I was there. I don't remember that [the sinking of the *Panay*] was anything earth-shaking."[27]

Stephen Jurika said in an oral interview, "It didn't cause much of a ripple on the social life or even on the official life." He added that there was little reaction in the carrier squadrons to which he was attached, or in the general area of Coronado, California, where those attached to the squadrons lived and shopped.[28] He did say that after that incident Ernest J. King, Commander Aircraft Battle Force, did require more night flight training, instrument flying, and changes in work times. Nothing was to be regular.

The USS *Panay* incident did not leave Richardson's desk completely for many months, and even as chief of the Bureau of Navigation in 1939 he was dealing with the event. He coordinated many of the medal applications and approvals for those involved.[29] He watched as the Japanese agitated the situation by balking at payments of restitution to those who lost goods when the ship sank.[30]

The Chinese-constructed USS *Panay* was designed for the U.S. Navy to use as protection for American merchant vessels from river pirates on the Yangtze River. Its demise revealed an enlarged inadequacy of the U.S. Navy. Richardson wrote later that the incident greatly deepened his interest in Navy war plans. "It made me realize that our Navy was most inadequate in size to wage war successfully against the Japanese Navy of that period."[31]

As Richardson promised himself, after the USS *Panay* incident he did become more active in the preparation of war plans.[32] He had been quite involved in the planning changes when he was chief of staff for Reeves. He was aware of the work and thoughts of fellow Texan David F. Sellers in 1934, when that admiral reported that the Navy had to arrive in the Philippines before *Orange* (Japan) could securely garrison that area.[33]

Since 1914, in conjunction with the Army, the Navy had developed a series of war plans using colors to depict certain countries or fleets. By 1924, the plans were more detailed and were more than statements of intention. They were sophisticated outlines of what would be done in case of war. The British were called *Red*. The Germans were *Black*. Mexico was *Green*, and Japan was designated *Orange*. Since Britain was an ally, Germany was defeated, and Mexico was not viewed as a threat, between the years 1924 to 1938 war planners concentrated upon a conflict with Japan. Therefore, *War Plan Orange* was updated almost each year.[34]

Socially, Richardson reported to Bloch that he was on the "water-wagon" since dropping off the past July. "Furthermore," and this was a shocker, "I have not smoked this year." He added that his golf was terrible since he only played on Saturdays now and then. Time was too short for much of anything but work.

On January 19, 1938, Richardson and Army Major General Stanley D. Embick were directed to make a joint study of the Pacific Theater. They were to take the current *Orange* plan and develop compromises satisfactory to both services, and to suggest realistic plans in case of war. The pair was given only a few weeks to present ideas.[35]

Embick firmly believed that in the Pacific, the United States should concentrate upon holding a line along a strategic triangle of Alaska, Hawaii, and Panama.[36] Trying to save the Philippines was not an option he or the Army wanted to consider. He cited the Philippine Independence Act (Tydings-McDuffie Bill) that was passed in 1934.[37] Even though the act did not allow Philippine independence for at least ten years, it convinced the Army that the risk should not be run nor should the obligation be accepted to fight the Japanese in the western Pacific.

The thought pattern of Embick, Chief of the Army War Plans Division, and his counterparts was that the Navy would be better equipped to operate if the Alaska-Hawaii-Panama line were held in peacetime. Then, in case of war, there would be less chance of a disaster. Embick wrote time and again that reliance upon a base that was inadequately defended was an invitation to disaster.[38]

In July of 1937, in between hours spent managing the Earhart search, the CNO's office altered plans for a western base concept. Three new possible base facilities were added: the Marshall Islands, the Carolines or Palau, and one to be added later.[39] Then in the fall of 1937, when Japan embarked upon its thrust into China, the Joint Army-Navy Board ordered a reexamination of plans, basically in four volumes of print totaling some eight hundred pages. And, that did not include the Navy Fleet plan of similar length.[40]

The Joint Planning Committee, the senior Army-Navy advisory body assigned to coordinate and improve working plans between the services, admitted that it had reached no agreement. For months, the Navy had viewed the Army ideas as unacceptable. It did not want to simply patrol a triangle. Peacetime Navy planners thought the fleet had to be ready to take the offensive if war broke out. It was almost unthinkable for the Navy to give up operations west of Hawaii. For some time this point had been hotly argued, but most of those involved in the debate were fearful to bring the question up to Roosevelt for decision.

Back in May of 1936, the planners submitted separate reports on Far East possibilities. The Army recommended that when the Philippines became independent, the United States should withdraw from both it and China. The Navy felt that a complete reexamination of *War Plan Orange* should be on the agenda before making such profound decisions on America's future in the Far East.

Of course this indecision did not sit well with the Joint Board. The planners went back to work, submitting a revised *Orange* plan that did not require holding the Manila Bay area, but just the entrance to the bay—basically Corregidor and nearby islands. The Navy still wanted a progressive movement through the Japanese Mandates, a group of islands in the South Pacific administered by Japan after the defeat of Germany in World War I. There was a revision of the plan in regard to the Hawaiian garrison, however. It stated that Oahu would be held as a main naval base for seventy days. By that time the fleet should have arrived there.

If the guide for war fell short of being offensive, the Navy wanted no part of the plan. Richardson and many of his peers were convinced that once war began, production would be quickly on the increase. While forces were being assembled, the Navy was ready to move westward into Japanese territory. Richardson also knew that all this activity was improbable because the Navy was not manned properly, nor were the vessels being produced in the mid-1930s at the rate of those being constructed by Japan. Legislation had been enacted in late 1937 authorizing construction of six auxiliary vessels, though funds were only available for two. Still, Richardson and Leahy thought that increase was a move forward.[41]

On December 7, 1937, the Joint Board directed the planners to find a compromise, giving a small edge to the Navy. The consequential plan should emphasize the defeat of Japan but with an initial temporary position of readiness for the Pacific Coast and the strategic triangle envisioned. The Army was to protect the designated onshore assignments while the Navy was eventually to mount offensive operations against *Orange* armed forces, and to interrupt Japan's vital sea communications. The planners were to produce the recommended forces and materiel necessary.

In the midst of unreality, based upon what was actually happening in Japan, the Army felt able to protect the United States and its possessions in a defensive mode, while the Navy thought that it could overpower Japan's Navy, and thus bring its will to fight to a halt. All of this action was being considered even though intelligence reports from Japan about its activities and construction were almost nil.

Thus, the Joint Board faced a stone wall. Since it could not reach a decision on how to proceed, it chose Embick and Richardson to sit down together and come up with a solution. The two men were experienced military leaders, but both had doubts about the plans and had offered criticisms of them for many years.[42] Embick's ideas were almost on opposite poles from those of Richardson.[43]

Backed by Leahy, Richardson held on to the plan to take the offensive. He was the preservationist of a plan that a year and a half later he would begin to take apart when given the opportunity. His years of experience in Washington had given him the practical knowledge, however, that the plan was always there for budget purposes.[44]

Richardson's work on the plan was interrupted when his brother-in-law and best man at his wedding, Joe Porter Fenet of Paris, died on February 2. The admiral and May traveled to the funeral of the fifty-eight-year-old owner of extensive real estate and farm holdings.[45]

When Richardson got back to Washington, he and Embick agreed to reduce the Army forces to a barely operable number able to carry out the campaign in the Marshalls and to make an advance to Truk in the Caroline Islands. The Air Corps' portion of the opening campaign dropped from 600 to 150.[46] As a result, the meat of the force was gone. Under this plan, there would be no quick movement to the Japanese Mandates.[47]

Despite the antagonism against *War Plan Orange* by both the officers, the pair came up with figures needed to meet readiness for offensive operations, but only after guaranteeing the safety of the continental United States. Then, assuming the Atlantic Theater was in control, the Navy could proceed to take the offensive, directing efforts toward the Mandated Islands, and then steadily across the vast ocean toward Japan. It sounded a bit too simple. It was. Some history writers thought the two avoided most of the important issues.[48] The Philippines were not mentioned when it came to reinforcement or relief issues.

On February 18, the Embick-Richardson staff submitted a revised and compromised *Orange* (Japan) versus *Blue* (United States) plan.[49] The Army agreed that operations emerging by it, west of the Hawaiian Islands, would not require direct presidential authorization. The Navy took out its references to conducting an offensive war, the destruction of Japanese forces, and even the early movement of the fleet west. A broad statement was inserted into the plan noting that the initial goal was to deal with pressure both militarily and economically upon Japan. Then, when the severity of the national objective became critical, the defeat of Japan would be the next step. The first measures were to be naval, but were designed to ensure the safety of the United States, Alaska, Oahu, and Panama.

The principles of each service held tight. The Joint Board approved the plan on February 21. A week later, both secretaries had passed on it. Based upon the contents, Roosevelt recommended a higher budget to Congress. In May 1938, Congress did approve the Navy's request for a 20 percent boost in funds. There were even five advanced fleet air bases added to the logistic planning requirements: Unalaska and Adak in Alaska, and Midway, Johnston Island, and Wake Island in the Pacific.[50] The admission in 1938 was that the reinforcement of the Philippine garrison would be based upon the amount of time that the fleet would take to advance across the Pacific. This admission by the planners, Richardson and Embick, revealed they did not believe the islands could be held.

However, changes were forever coming, and Richardson's trust in the plan was not full-hearted. The planners of 1938 did expect a surprise attack, just as in all other *Orange* presentations since 1904. But, no one expected a successful annihilation of a huge portion of the U.S. Fleet before there were Japanese attacks upon U.S. possessions such as the Philippines. Plus, so much depended upon the time it took to prepare for an offensive after war began.

If Richardson's theory that war plans were constructed with budget making in mind was correct, it succeeded in 1938. That May, Congress adopted an increase in composition of the U.S. Navy, strengthened the inventory of naval aircraft, and addressed pay issues. For Richardson, he did not carry on through the spring in the assistant CNO position. On April 8, 1938, he was appointed to be the chief of the Bureau of Navigation.

CHAPTER ELEVEN

"Don't Go While I'm Here"
1938-39 Bureau of Navigation Assignment

In early 1938, the pressure was once again put on Richardson to be chief of BuNav (the Bureau of Navigation). "My civilian or military seniors, including the President, talked to me 16 different times" about the position, Richardson wrote later.[1] He verified this number by checking his diary. On January 20, Swanson, Richardson, Leahy, and Andrews gathered in the secretary's office. "I had hoped that this job would not be offered to me," Richardson replied, but added that if he were promoted to the assignment, he would give it the best possible effort. On March 22, the White House called. Richardson was informed that Andrews had arranged through Roosevelt's secretary, Marvin McIntyre, for an appointment at 11:15 A.M.[2]

When he arrived at the White House, Richardson was told he had only ten minutes. "I don't care how long I wait," he said, "but I must have ten minutes." He figured he could talk his way out of the assignment in that time. Thirty minutes after the due time, he was called in. "Joe, I have decided to ask you to take on the duties as head of navigation," the president said.

Roosevelt started out lecturing about the actions of "white-haired" boys in the Navy. "At times, BuNav has been the worst offender." Leahy had warned Richardson that he better cut in as soon as possible, and he did. "I want to talk to you for five minutes," he said, "because I do not want this assignment."

He then began to present his three reasons.

First, he felt the chief should be in the job at BuNav for two, and maybe three years. "On July 1, I will have but four years and three months before retirement." He wanted another sea duty. The assignment to the head of BuNav would destroy the chance of returning to sea.

Second, Richardson said that, like Roosevelt, he believed that officers should not repeat. "But, the billet of chief of BuNav is difficult." It would be very hard to manage with assistants who had no previous experience. "I would not expect to have many repeaters, but I would count upon having a few in key positions."

Last, Richardson said he could not support the impending Naval Line Promotion Bill in Congress because it would allow a large number of officers into the upper grades. As chief of BuNav, he would be called to give his opinion before the House Naval Committee. Without complete study of the proposition, Richardson said he would not be a good witness for the Navy.

Roosevelt quickly discounted two of the problems, and promised that he would release Richardson from the job for sea duty in proper time. Richardson replied that if given the job, it was his temperament to stick with it until done properly. He did not expect to be in the position in a year or two, and then to be released. He left the White House office rather discouraged, the last six words of the president ringing in his head: "Now remember, no repeaters in Washington."[3]

What he did remember was that a friend once got shingles during a long wait for Roosevelt to make up his mind. Richardson expected it would be two or three months before the announcement. He was surprised when the Navy Department received the word of the assignment on April 8.[4]

By then Swanson was gravely ill, and Leahy was directing the Navy with some help from the secretary's assistant, Charles Edison. A few days after Richardson's appointment, and with no consultation with the admiral, Roosevelt made the personnel bill easy to pass by agreeing to some requested changes in the controversial portions. It was sent to him for signature. But, on a Sunday from his home at Hyde Park, New York, Roosevelt sent a telegram to the Richardson home. He wanted to know whether the bill should be signed.

"From my point of view the bill is unacceptable," replied Richardson. But, he added that the president's letter to Committee Chairman Senator David I. Walsh committed him to sign it after the changes were made. So, it was signed. Richardson had to deal with the assignment and promotion problems it presented.

Of course Richardson knew that Roosevelt would continually tinker with assignments of senior officer personnel. Since BuNav's official function was personnel, Richardson had a close-up relationship with the president during the next year. Despite this working condition, which included nine meetings in the president's White House office—five with just the president and the admiral alone—Richardson never became comfortable with the quick changes of mind.[5]

The Roosevelt idea of "no repeaters" was fairly popular among naval officers. Only 7 percent, about 520 officers, were in the Navy Department in the late 1930s. A large number of officers had never had Washington duty, and they resented the fact that some of the better sea duties came from those who served near the top echelon. It seemed to them, also, that "repeaters" to Washington reached flag rank quicker and more often.

However, the policy never got off the ground. Within the first week of duty, Richardson received a call from McIntyre. "The President wants Lieutenant Commander Walter R. Jones detailed to command the USS *Potomac*." Stunned, but probably grinning, Richardson quickly retorted, "Why, Jones had that detail once before. The President just told me he wanted no repeaters." The assignment would not be fair to Jones's rank either. McIntyre backed off, but called the next day. "We want Jones," he said. Richardson wrote later. "The no-repeater policy hadn't lasted a week!"

Richardson wrote Bloch on June 4, eating crow about taking the BuNav position. Coming west to east at that time was Joe Richardson, taking a break from his Hollywood studio writing assignments and visiting in Washington until July 3. "He is looking fine," Richardson wrote Bloch.[6]

Bloch replied, chiding Richardson for playing in a golf match between a team from BuNav and the Bureau of Construction. Bloch immediately told his office after hearing of this game, "J. O. has the job licked—he is out playing golf and winning cups!" Bloch was already preparing the fleet for its move to the East

Coast and Fleet Problem XX. Richardson immediately replied that he only won because of his thirty handicap. Actually, he shot ninety-six on the tough Army-Navy Country Club course. He then needled Bloch by seriously writing, "I have been able to get away for golf only three afternoons during the week since I have reported for duty." He knew Bloch would be jealous of the supposed "spare time" in Washington for golf.[7]

By August of 1938, Richardson was fed up with fitness reports that came in from the fleet. He wrote Bloch, "Chief: The whole officer personnel, if reports are to be believed, are all Launcelots and Sir Galahads combined!" He reiterated his long line of thinking. The selection boards about to meet in the late fall could not make any discrimination between officers solely on the basis of the reports before them. They needed more guidance, more honesty in the process. "This is nothing new," Richardson told his good friend, "just a little bit worse than before, perhaps."[8] He never won this battle for a more objective selection process, but he admitted that perhaps the heat of August in Washington was raising his ire.

Back on April 25, 1938, Swanson, Andrews, Leahy, and Richardson met with Roosevelt at noon. It would be the last White House meeting for Richardson until October. The summer would be full of personnel assignments and requirements. There Richardson's thoughts about planning and having the proper numbers became more solidified.

Another huge problem Richardson noted was that there were 280 captains with only 66 sea billets. He explained to Bloch that this discrepancy was the reason some officers had to be changed prior to the Fleet Problem, in order to get as many in sea duties as possible, though the times were shorter than in the past.[9] Bloch was disappointed, but Richardson did not like the situation either.

On October 26, 1938, Richardson met with Roosevelt in the White House. They met again two months later, on December 20, and then two days later.[10] Roosevelt kept no notes of his meetings, and since Richardson destroyed his diary in the late 1950s or early 1960s, speculation only leads to the conclusion that the last two meetings were in preparation for Fleet Problem XX.

Roosevelt planned to attend it, traveling to the Caribbean on board the USS *Houston.* Leahy and his aide, Lieutenant Commander W. L. Freseman, would be on the trip, but not Richardson.

Richardson did write to Bloch, who was at Balboa, Canal Zone, in early January, explaining that the second December meeting was a long one, with discussion mostly about the flag officer slate. "I urged him to give early consideration of who would be CNO and CinCUS after June 1."[11]

Later in January 1939, Roosevelt told Richardson that the decision would be made while he was with the fleet, but that he would not release the answers until after his return. Richardson agreed, but asked that no public announcement be made until after the Fleet Problem XX critique. He knew that delay would keep the focus of newly named officers on the matter at hand.

In early 1939, Swanson asked his former aide and then assistant chief of the Bureau of Navigation, Frank Jack Fletcher, and Richardson, to meet with him at the former President Hoover summer home and camp at Rapidan, Virginia. Leahy had made it clear to Richardson that he would not recommend his own replacement. "J. O., when I leave this job, I am going to completely sever my connections with the Navy," said Leahy, an odd statement Richardson thought.

While at the meeting with Swanson, Richardson told the secretary it would help if he would name the new CNO for him. Leahy planned to retire in May. He said, "J. O., did Leahy say to you he would make no recommendation? Huh. He doesn't have to—he has already recommended."[12] It was Harold R. Stark. That announcement was quite a shock. Though Richardson believed Stark to be very capable and well liked, he did not think he was equal to the requirements currently needed under existing conditions. Richardson left Rapidan Camp and the Shenandoah Valley thinking he would be asked for more possibilities later.

Some historians write that there was speculation that Roosevelt would take along with him to the fleet exercises several Navy officers in line to replace Leahy as CNO. Richardson wrote that he and Leahy did meet with Roosevelt in early February to discuss the presidential trip. "I asked . . . if he had made up his mind about the 'new slate,'" wrote Richardson. Roosevelt indicated he would know more after watching the performance of the fleet. The president then picked up his copy of the 1938 *Naval Register* and began asking the admirals about specific possibilities. He mentioned that Andrews was a fine officer, but not CNO caliber. He then told Richardson that he should not worry. "You aren't going to go to sea this year." Repeating just what Richardson had told him the previous year, he added, "I think that the Chief of the Bureau should be in his job at least two years." Richardson still agreed, feeling that he was just becoming familiar with the position after seven months of service in it.[13]

Before the meeting was over, Richardson managed to get in some positive comments about Hart and Snyder. "Admiral Hart is too able, too young and too capable to be overlooked for a billet at sea," he told Roosevelt, "and Snyder should be given serious consideration for one of the top billets." Roosevelt did not solicit a recommendation to replace Leahy. If asked, Richardson would have given the nod to Bloch. "He had no peer in the handling of committees of Congress," thought Richardson.

Richardson was not going to Fleet Problem XX. Before the president left, Richardson and Roosevelt had one more meeting, on January 19, 1939. The entourage took off in mid-February.

From Culebra, Puerto Rico, on March 1, Presidential Aide Commander Daniel J. Callaghan issued a telegram for the press to use. "All Fleet officers present . . . of the rank of rear admiral and above called on the President during the early afternoon."[14] Arleigh Burke and the other admirals had the view that this whole affair was "sort of a pass-in-review" to aid Roosevelt with the decisions on how to fill the forthcoming open positions.

As for the problem, Jerald Wright reported in mid-March that fleet members met for the critique of the exercise. It "was not as colorful as I had expected," he wrote his wife Phyllis. After explaining that the reports were full of reasons for this and that, he said, "The real information is learned at the officer's club bar on the night before."[15] The fleet officers were in Haiti.

On March 9, Roosevelt met in his office at lunch with Richardson and Leahy to discuss apparently the Fleet Problem trip and the Navy operations.[16] He already knew that the CNO recommendation from Swanson was Stark.[17] Swanson and Roosevelt had narrowed down the personnel choices to five combinations. One scenario had Richardson as CNO. This recommendation process was being carried out when Swanson was ill and no longer at work. Edison sent over the final letter, recommending Stark, and saying that Swanson approved.[18]

Leahy, Richardson, and the president, nonetheless, discussed the upcoming slate of changes in personnel. Roosevelt then presented a typed slip of paper entitled, "President's Slate." It was three columns across, the first column listing the office, the middle column the current office holder, and the third the proposed relief. Stark was to be CNO. Richardson would replace Edward C. Kalbfus as Commander Battle Force, and then be promoted to CinCUS when Bloch retired in the winter.[19]

Hart would take Yarnell's place in the Asiatic. Andrews would remain in the Scouting Force.[20] J. W. Greenslade in Battleships would be replaced by Snyder, and after some discussion, Nimitz would replace Richardson at BuNav.[21] Nimitz had not been on Roosevelt's list, but after Richardson said that the president's choices did not hold the confidence and respect of the mature officers, the three prospects were marked off, and Richardson's recommendation inserted.[22] Richardson would make a similar *confidence* statement to Roosevelt in 1940, but it would not receive a positive reaction. Hart, when he heard of the results, wrote in his diary that he thought, all in all, the solutions looked very good indeed.[23]

Richardson walked out of the White House, the sun brightly shining on him. Roosevelt had lived up to his word in this one instance, releasing him for sea duty beginning that summer. He was proud to be an important part of the "new slate."[24] He informed Hart of the new slate in person, since he was in

Washington, and then the others by confidential mail. When Stark arrived, he came into Richardson's office, rather "flabbergasted" at his selection.[25] "Where are Kimmel and King going to be detailed?" he asked. Then he added, "In my opinion, and with present company excepted, they are the two best Flag officers in the Navy today."[26]

Kimmel was to relieve Stark as Commander Cruisers Battle Force. King would be coming to the General Board. Richardson wrote later that he shared Stark's view of Kimmel and King, but that King was overdue for shore duty. Richardson did not view the General Board as a dead end as many others concluded, but as a billet in which an admiral could be quietly placed, and still be available for important duties.[27]

The lower portion of the slate was not easy to complete, as indicated from Richardson, Bloch, and Stark correspondence. Shuffling many officers around, allowing certain captains to get in the necessary sea duty to qualify for flag rank promotion later, and even to make sure that Alan G. Kirk stayed in the United States until his daughters graduated from school were part of the various determining factors.

When the announcement of the upper part of the slate came on March 15, Burke was delighted with the choice of Stark and Richardson. He figured the USS *Honolulu* would be crowded with Stark well-wishers, so he crafted the idea that he could pass along his congratulations by word through Stark's friend and personal aide, Lieutenant Commander Hal Krick. It worked, with Stark saying later that the effort to get the message through rated nothing short of a 4.0+.[28] Krick said that Burke was right; Stark was very busy with "everyone and his brother coming by to make their numbers."

Lieutenant W. R. Smedberg and Commander Charles Wellborn went ahead of Stark to Washington as his flag lieutenant and flag secretary, respectively. Smedberg said Stark "could hardly believe it. But, he had quite a bit of ego and it didn't take him very long to feel they'd made a good choice." He added that Stark "was a dear old man and I loved him very much, but it's not the man that I would have chosen as Chief of Naval Operations."[29]

Richardson was still wrestling with many other assignments late in March. He called the chore a "maze," and changed it again and again. He did set Bloch up by saying that the Navy had too often chosen passed-over captains as head of the districts, when in fact, "the day will come when the CNO will find that he will need one of his ablest and most energetic assistants as director of the Naval districts."[30]

In his diary, Hart expressed his thoughts about Stark and Richardson. "Stark is to become CNO. He is good, very good," he wrote, but then added, "but, I fear not enough so to justify taking a man with such a paucity of sea experience." He added that Richardson would be replacing Bloch in six months. "That was the other place in which I might have been put—but it's all right, for I believe very much in Richardson."

On May 3, Roosevelt gathered together at the White House Vinson, Leahy, Richardson, and McIntyre. Vinson and Richardson had known each other since 1914. He had been on the Naval Committee for years, and as Richardson wrote, at that time "he probably knew more about the Navy than any single officer in the Naval Service."[31]

Richardson thought highly of the congressman, co-author of the Vinson-Trammel Naval Bill of 1934. Vinson almost alone "forced" the construction of carriers, telling the Navy Department he would not support one new battleship unless the plan included a commensurate number of carriers. The result was that, even though the United States was behind Japan in numbers of carriers, several were under construction when Pearl Harbor was attacked.

More than likely during this noontime meeting, the five discussed the upcoming development act before Congress. The 1938 Naval Expansion Act authorized gradual growth over the next ten years. Though it was called the "Navy Second to None" act, no funds were provided. The Depression had returned, and money was extremely tight.[32] In the act that was passed on April 20, 1939, the proposal going into 1940 was to raise the naval tonnage

25 percent, but that increase was not to be. That 1940 bill wasted away for months, the additional tonnage reduced to only 11 percent.

It was Richardson's belief, and that of most of his peers, that by 1939 the limitation agreements had caused a substantial loss of naval power for the United States as compared to that which existed in 1922. Japan had been angry about its restrictions for the entire period, and had dropped out of agreements in 1936. Like Roosevelt, Richardson felt that though other nations like Japan, Germany, and the Soviet Union had reversed this trend by internal action, the United States would not react until there came "real hurt which another nation would inflict upon us."[33]

Before sea duty, Richardson had one last important detail to perform in Washington. The king and queen of England were coming to visit Canada and the United States. Roosevelt asked if Richardson would perform the responsibilities of naval aide to the royal couple during their time in the United States.[34] The high temperatures in Washington were almost unbearable, but all excursions and parties were held.

After four days of activities in Niagara Falls, Washington, New York City, and at the president's home, a tired Richardson left Hyde Park after the king and queen had departed, caught a train at 12:50 A.M., and arrived back in Massachusetts Avenue Heights at 7:10 A.M. on June 12. He took home two leather-framed photos of the king and queen. May, who was part of some of the ceremonies, found a good location for the photos on the table next to the admiral's favorite chair at their apartment when they moved to Long Beach a few weeks later. He was not happy that the royal visit had knocked off the front page the significance of the May 7 signing of the Pact of Steel between Germany and Italy, but "being aide to the King and Queen was a very pleasant chore," he wrote about the whirlwind experience.

On June 15, 1939, Richardson walked over to the White House to meet with the president for a 1:00 P.M. lunch. It would be the pair's last White House office meeting before J. O. left for the fleet. Richardson was happy that in most instances during his year as manager of personnel, he had done his legally defined job. "A real effort was made by all of those subordinates of the President to assure that the President should not substitute his arbitrary judgment or his personal likes and dislikes for that of normal Naval process in picking officers for high command," Richardson wrote of the time in BuNav. But, he quickly added, "These efforts were far from being 100 percent successful!"[35]

He and May began the process of renting the house and moving once again. May knew the territory and once again chose the Villa Riviera.[36] The world situation was grim. Just since March, when Richardson was told he would be the next CinCUS, Japan had moved farther south and even annexed the French-claimed oil-rich Spratly Islands in the South China Sea, seven hundred miles southwest of Manila, between the southern Philippines and Indochina. Despite the feeling by Richardson that the U.S. Fleet had no real capability to stop any of this Japanese movement, Roosevelt felt it could be a deterrent. This idea had come from presidents since Woodrow Wilson had agreed to the creation of a separate Pacific battle fleet in June of 1919.[37]

In mid-April of 1939, the fleet unexpectedly went back to the Pacific where it would hold its next exercises. The plan had originally been for the ships to move from Fleet Problem XX to New York to celebrate the initial opening of the World's Fair.[38] However, some felt that Australia's fears would be eased a bit if the fleet were quickly returned to the Pacific.[39] More than 300,000 people watched the ships anchor on the West Coast at 7:00 A.M. on May 12. Newsreels took the scene to the world, hopefully giving notice of American sea power.[40]

Richardson would be in Los Angeles Harbor shortly thereafter to assist Bloch. But, as he left Washington, instead of news of the open border fighting between Soviet and Japanese troops, front pages were full of stories about the German and Italian alliance. Richardson felt that he was ahead of everyone with the idea of urgency to upgrade the Navy for war. However, he felt that this act could be better done personally if he were on the seas working with those in the fleet who were more in line with his thinking.

The annual report completed in June, Edison said that the Navy was prepared to bring the enemy to "our terms" quickly, and at the same time keep him at a safe distance from American shores. "I had heard no responsible Naval officer voice such an opinion," wrote Richardson. He again listed the problems: ships under strength; too few auxiliary ships to allow movement away from American shores; and not enough ships. He viewed such statements otherwise to be a disservice to the country.[41]

CHAPTER TWELVE

Off to Sea Again—1939
Preparation for CinCUS Assignment Begins

Though Richardson felt he should have stayed on as chief of the Bureau of Navigation because of the many personnel problems facing the Navy, he was anxious to float on the sea, to deal with the real reasons the Navy existed.[1]

Roughly, Richardson figured he had 40 more ships, 130 more aircraft, 1,000 more marines, and 6,000 more naval personnel than in 1938-39. He considered this number "piddling" compared to the enemy buildup in Europe, not to mention in Japan.[2] "If there is any blame to be assigned," he wrote, "it belongs to the Congress."[3]

One month into Richardson's time with the fleet, Swanson finally succumbed to his ailments, dying away at Rapidan Camp on July 7. Richardson and others on the West Coast attended a memorial service held in San Francisco. The handsome old Virginian was buried in Richmond.[4] Edison was named acting secretary. He had long been a Roosevelt friend, and was also politically ambitious, so there would be little change in the operation of the Navy Department.[5]

However, Edison did not get along particularly well with Leahy, and told future admiral Robert "Mick" Carney that line officers had little else to do but push ships around. Needless to say, this was not the attitude Navy officers thought should be a part of the mission. Years later in his oral interview, Carney, whose daughter married Joe Taussig, Jr., said that Edison had "all the latent liking for the unusual," but did not have the work habits of his famous father.[6] He was also a bit deaf, and not very "ship wise."[7] However, Edison seemed to enjoy the company of Richardson, the two mathematical minds perhaps finding conversation challenging.

Later in July, Edison advised Roosevelt that the status of the naval auxiliaries was very satisfactory. But, Richardson expressed confusion at Roosevelt's plan to use merchant marine for the duty.

"President Roosevelt always had it in his mind that, by and large, our merchant marine overnight could become our Fleet Base Force or Fleet Train, and be available immediately for an overseas movement of combatant and expeditionary forces." Though he had confidence in his friend, Jerry Land, assigned to make that vision become a reality, Richardson did not believe the idea would have the time to work. Plus, there still had to be a merchant fleet.[8]

Though passenger-carrying ships could be converted for dock-to-dock transportation, they could not feasibly be converted to land troops upon shores. "Though President Roosevelt did marvelous things in building up the combatant Navy during the period 1933-1939, he just could not or would not do much about providing the Fleet with the necessary ships for amphibious operations and for the Fleet Train," wrote Richardson. This was especially not done in advance of the need.[9] However, Land guided the construction of 179 maritime ship starts, with 84 launching by December of 1940, with more than 50 in service by the time Richardson left Honolulu.[10]

Even if the Navy ships could be constructed at a faster pace, the worry then shifted to the training of personnel to man the vessels. John Lowrey of Paris, Texas, a sailor aboard the USS *Pennsylvania* in 1936, said in conversation in 2002 that it was very obvious the crew was not 100 percent. "It felt like only half of the assigned men were on the ship," he said.[11] Richardson said that at least one advantage was that every man trained in a little better billet than if the top level of assigned personnel were approved.[12]

Though he did not reenlist, Lowrey thought morale was fine, saying that when he left most enlisted men were enjoying the experience. He even enjoyed Pearl Harbor, though it was not geared up for many sailors to visit. He was a triggerman on a three-barrel turret. He described the thrill of the exercises, the roar of the three guns, the shaking of the ship, the force so hard that it seemed the vessel slid sideways. A photograph in *Life* magazine in the fall of 1940 shows the barrels, two lowered and one up firing a shell, the fire exploding outward, and then the smoke covering the turret.[13] Lowrey said the middle shell came out in a tumble, destined to do the most damage. Firing could be so violent that sometimes the ship's light bulbs would break, and periodically some pipes would spring leaks. Everything in the photo is just as described by Lowrey a few moments before he teed off for another round of golf against "kids" almost half his age, but not with the solid game he still had at that time.

Not only was there a shortage of enlisted men, but officers were not in abundance. On June 30, 1939, the officers were 700 below the allowed total of 7,562. Richardson, however, viewed this shortage of officers as less of a problem than a shortage of enlisted personnel. He felt that a good four-year college graduate could learn the Navy management ways in four months. Then six months later he would know a subordinate billet, and within a year he would be adapted to seagoing life. On the other hand, he felt that it took four to six years to graduate a high schooler into a leading petty officer. He was right about the officers, but lucky for the United States, in the war effort thousands of high school graduates, once in the Navy, picked up the skills at a much faster rate than envisioned.

Richardson also thought that the junior officer ranks could be filled quickly from the leading petty officer list. He thought it might take two or three civilians in uniform to do one young officer's regular job, "but it could be done."[14] So, with war on the horizon, those were his thoughts and challenges as he came to the Villa Riviera in the summer of 1939. His salary was then $15,000.[15]

Richardson missed some gunnery practice held after the fleet returned from the Atlantic in May of 1939. For years everyone noticed that event. Back in the 1920s the ships would return each evening after practice, having shattered Long Beach windows with their firing. Besides changing the fleet schedule, Pratt did not allow target practice within thirty miles off shore.

The practice itself was not totally safe among the ships and participants. Once the USS New Mexico, towing the targets, fell accidentally into jeopardy when the spotter almost placed the USS California's guns into the unsuspecting battleship's path. In late 1931, an antiaircraft gun exploded aboard the USS Colorado, killing five sailors. Charles F. Kepper, aboard the USS *Salt Lake City,* said that during the rare nighttime practice, towing of targets could be a big thrill. "We would be some distance from the target, but the hot shells were clearly visible and actually pretty to watch, almost like they were in slow motion."[16]

Lowrey explained just how dangerous firing could be. Powder bags of about a hundred pounds each were made up of numerous smaller explosive packages, and sometimes the larger containers broke open during loading, spilling out the small pellets. The pellets would then jam the door. "We all would scramble away when it happened," he nervously laughed.[17]

Richardson expected a good relationship with the citizens and leaders of Long Beach, San Pedro, and Los Angeles. Arguments of the past had somewhat been settled, such as lack of adequate housing, housing discrimination, and unfair treatment of the sailors when in town. By 1939 the community had evolved into a host town with a more receptive attitude. Monies from the New Deal projects were being funneled into the shore facilities. City-owned properties were deeded to the Federal government, streets were improved and new ones planned, new berths were constructed, and at San Pedro a target repair base was built. The Chambers of Commerce, the cities, and the Navy were proud of the new recreational facilities being finished, and were planning a long-term partnership.

After some political setbacks, but with the emerging Japanese threat, construction flowed rapidly after the Vinson-Trammell Act of 1938. Even Reeves Air Field was upgraded to the status of a Fleet Air Base. But, an argument over transfer of the land to the Navy, so that appropriations might be easier to garner from Congress, carried on into late 1939. The Navy also met resistance in its attempt to increase its shore activities in San Pedro's Outer Harbor. These discussions went on well into the 1940s when the fleet was "temporarily" settled in at Pearl Harbor.

Back in 1923, before being selected as the Navy's third CNO, native Texan Admiral Edward W. Eberle made his Pacific Fleet headquarters in the waters off San Pedro. However, when the second breakwater neared completion, the flagship USS *Pennsylvania* began to anchor closer to Long Beach. Admiral Bloch followed this habit, and later Admiral Richardson parked the USS *California* nearby.

On June 24, 1939, wearing his ever-familiar wire-rimmed glasses, Richardson stood on board the *California*. He was in his dress formal blues, with fore-and-aft hat and elaborate shoulder boards, or epaulets, upon his large frame, watching the ceremonies installing him as Commander Battle Force, U.S. Fleet. Three seventeen-gun salutes were fired: the first from the *California* when the Kalbfus flag was taken down; the second on the same ship when the Richardson flag was raised; and in response, a third from the *Pennsylvania*.

One of the first things Richardson did when assigned to Battle Force was to ask Dyer if he would go with him. Dyer had been tagging along in Richardson's career since the two were on a summer cruise aboard the USS *Nevada* near the end of World War I. He had been ordered by Richardson down from Philadelphia in January of 1939 to work on the planning staff of BuNav. "It was a very interesting detail," he discussed in 1973. Richardson gave him congressional experience too, sending him over to the House Naval Affairs Committee once to answer personnel questions. He survived the Carl Vinson barrage, and was most impressed with the congressman's knowledge of the Navy.[18]

Dyer was in the office when Richardson came back from the March 9 meeting with Roosevelt. "He was all smiles," he remembered. The admiral was going to sea. Later that afternoon, Richardson called in Dyer, and said: "I'm going to do something that Adaline will hate me for. I'm going to ask you to go to sea with me . . . in June." Since Dyer had just come from a sea duty, rented a place in Chevy Chase, Maryland, and bought a house full of furniture for the first time ever, he was financially in a tight bind. "Anyhow, I said, 'I'd be delighted.'" He would later deal with his wife about the opportunity.

That night Mary Adaline Dyer told her husband she was not keen on moving to Long Beach. "But, she was really wonderful, really the light of my life," Dyer explained. She told him if it was good for him, it was good for her.[19]

Richardson already knew who would be part of his staff the latter half of 1939 and on into the time when he would be promoted to CinCUS. He told Dyer five days later that Sherwood Taffinder would be his chief of staff and that Bernard H. Bieri would be the operations officer. "I knew Captain Taffinder," said Dyer, but did not know Bieri well. However, Bieri had served with Richardson as a passed midshipman on the USS *Delaware* in 1911.[20] And, he could play cribbage. Richardson trusted and knew Dyer so well that he then said, "I want you to pick out the rest—the line officers. The Bureau will pick out the doctor, the paymaster and the Naval constructer," he said. It did not exactly work out that way, but almost.[21]

The staff had a head start of six months before it would operate the U.S. Fleet when Richardson moved up to CinCUS. This procedure was mostly the norm, but this staff was even more highly experienced by the time it was in charge. In the meantime, back in Washington, that summer and fall the Joint Planning Board was working on a new series of war plans called *Rainbow*. It surmised that war would be against a coalition of enemies, and most likely fought in two oceans.[22]

Out on the ocean, there was much to do before given the plans. Dyer said that during 1939 the fleet began, for the first time, to experiment with task groups placing carriers in the center. Richardson and Bieri took that initiative and more. "He [Richardson] was a very remarkable man in many ways," said Bieri years later. "He knew everybody, every officer in the Navy, practically." Of course, that was possible for Richardson because of his stints in BuNav, and as Bieri said, "He not only knew their names, but their records."[23]

Bieri learned by working with Richardson that the admiral's abilities to interact with naval personnel carried over into his work with civilians. "He was a very forceful man, and very likeable," said Bieri. He knew that Richardson had a background of service in foreign countries, and "and was one of our ablest officers."

Before Richardson and Bieri arrived, the fleet had experimented with alongside-refueling of a carrier at sea, the USS *Saratoga,* as instructed by Leahy. The CNO also wanted CinCUS to practice refueling battleships and other heavy ships. As a result, the refueling report came to Richardson when he became Commander Battle Force a few days after the experiment.

In mid-August, Richardson directed the type commanders to revise their procedures for fueling destroyers at sea, and have them to him by December 18. On October 13, the CNO approved the purchase of necessary refueling gear. Detailed instructions were then printed and given to all destroyers. This procedure, for the first time, would permit them to receive fuel from any type of large combatant ship. However, it took another nine months to manufacture and install the gear in order to conduct the tests.[24]

Richardson and Bieri incorporated more of this refueling effort to be a part of the upcoming Fleet Problem XXI.[25] Though Dyer was impressed with Richardson's command abilities, he always stressed that the long, tall Texan was full of funny stories and had a human touch with everything. But, "he had a really sort of fundamental dislike for newspaper people," he told an interviewer. However, he never dropped his hometown subscription to the *Lamar County Echo.* For relaxation and companionship, "He played golf anytime that he could."[26] On the West Coast, Richardson's choices of golf courses were wide.

"If there were people who didn't like him, I've yet to find a person," Dyer explained of his former boss, who at the time of his own oral interview in 1969 was ninety-one. Dyer did not have the same thing to say about another subject discussed in the interview and an object of another book—Richmond Kelly Turner. He was not as well-liked. In comparison, Dyer said that Richardson just had a "tremendous galaxy of friends."

When he took over as Commander Battle Force, Richardson honestly was far more interested in activity in the Asiatic and Pacific Ocean areas than in what was happening in the Atlantic. He and ages of classes from the academy were of like mind—that Japan was to be the sea enemy. He was aware from conversations with Roosevelt that the president was more detailed daily with Atlantic and European events. To be realistic, events in Europe were becoming more serious. Richardson admitted that he had no foresight in March of 1939 to the swift shift of the Soviet Union to the side of Hitler, even though it was temporary, or to the Poland attack by Germany in September. "I left Washington fearing that war in the Pacific would come upon the United States before the Navy could be prepared for it, but not expecting the war in Europe to occur as soon as it did," he wrote.[27]

Richardson explained his working relationship with Snyder. Having a senior as his subordinate was not distasteful in this case for Richardson or Snyder. From the beginning, Richardson thought they made a good team, and after the first six months, when Richardson moved up to CinCUS and Snyder to Commander Battle Force, the proof was revealed. "He might have gone farther had the President known him," Richardson wrote of his friend.

In the last half of 1939, there was work on high-speed target set-ups, and the scouting force had been strengthened. The training squadron was removed from it and made an independent detachment. Some night battle had been inaugurated during the past few years, so heavy cruisers investigated night aircraft spotting, using flares in the night firing, though some earlier, like Hepburn, reported it was rather hazardous, however, to land and recover planes at night during peacetime exercises.[28]

Antiaircraft firing was atrocious. In 1938, for instance, the .50-caliber machine gun could hit almost nothing at 600 yards. Eleven heavy cruisers fired 5,824 rounds in the summer, scoring only three hits. Even with cash rewards, few gunners could score. The 1.1-inch "Pom-Pom" was not much more reliable in 1939 when five destroyers shot off 623 rounds, and missed them all. Fortunately, the idea that it took a plane to intercept a plane was prevalent.[29]

Turnover in personnel was a constant worry. Delays in construction emphasized the shortage in destroyers, and train vessels were overage. Increased time was taken each year to address new demands for developing measures for attacks against aircraft and submarines. The use of carriers was always in development, and the new radio and telephone equipment brought in innovative tactics. The problems went on and on. Richardson again mentioned that each report noted the shortage of personnel. Bloch wrote specifically that Fleet Exercise Number 5 in 1939 revealed the need of an aircraft weapon, such as a depth charge, to attack submarines.[30]

As for any international tension involved with the work, Hustvedt was there as Bloch's operations officer. He said in his oral interview, "We weren't sitting on the edges of our chairs waiting for the storm to break." However, he said the officers were very aware that there were tensions.[31] "The war in Europe, of course, had come on and that was of great interest."

Richardson was anxious to address many of these problems during the six-month period before the change of command, and not be a "crown prince just waiting for the mantle to fall around my shoulders."[32] He was determined to avoid the problems suffered when he was chief of staff for Reeves. He wanted his staff, plus fleet commanders and their staffs, to work in harmony, to avoid friction. He met with them in the first weeks of the summer, and set forth his policy. Then, he set his "eagle eye" to scanning dozens of letters going out each day over the signatures of subordinate members. He wanted to check for any violation of his decree. It was tedious, but the readings taught him much about the way his fleet managers operated.

He told his staff that he viewed the problems of the fleet to be wider than the number of ships. He wanted to attack the training schedule, to study the cruising dispositions and how the fleet was going to carry out the early days of an *Orange* war. He wanted to work on usefulness of the Pacific island bases, improve the logistic support, train the officers to be in tune with those requirements essential for successful war-making, reduce letter and report writing time given the fleet, and hold the Battle Force personnel to a very high standard of discipline and effort.[33] With his background, this work schedule sounded uncharacteristically tough. However, he wanted everyone in the Battle Force to be ready for the transition to his promotion, and to be in the frame of mind for war. He wanted his feelings of urgency to expand among the fleet.

Richardson despised reports designed to follow the expenditure of each dollar. He and his staff took forty-five standing orders in the Battle Force and reduced them to a dozen. A new edition of the *Battle Force Instructions* manual streamlined reports and outlined indoctrination. He was pleased when, at the end of his command in Battle Force, even the Navy Department reduced reports, discontinuing fifty-eight of them.

To watch him, Richardson exuded a relaxed state of life, and was humorous during the day. However, he was serious about running a taut ship. On June 28, he disappointed many officers and their wives when he issued a letter about future dress at change-of-command ceremonies, and who could attend. He pointed out that the service uniform was worn by many, and that in the future U.S. Navy Uniform Regulations "are specific as to the uniform to be worn . . . and will be strictly complied with, within this command." He added, "Ladies will not be present when the ceremonies take place on board ship." He was not being an old fogy, but felt that with war on the horizon, thoughts should be only upon work, not ceremony.[34]

To Richardson the base situation was even more serious. He knew that work on Guam and Wake Island was not funded by Congress in fiscal year 1939-40. However, work was appropriated for Midway, Johnston Island, and Palmyra Island in the Pacific; San Juan in Puerto Rico; Pensacola and Jacksonville in Florida; Kodiak and Sitka in Alaska; Tongue Point in Oregon; and Pearl Harbor and Kaneohi Bay in Hawaii. The fleet would need these bases if it went across the Pacific in the near future because of war.

Patrol planes had not been funded accordingly to operate out of these new bases. It had taken three years to budge Congress to accept the bases, but without the planes, problems would occur quickly.

Two problems during the fall of 1939 especially received Richardson's notice—the Reserve Fleet and the Hawaiian

Detachment. Decisions were being made that gradually stepped up the tempo of war preparations. One was the recommissioning of Reserve Fleet destroyers, long stored in "mothballs." He felt that they could be properly modernized and were essential to the patrol mission protecting merchant shipping, and to assist in overseas movements provided by the *War Plan Orange*.[35]

The Reserve Fleet also included out-of-commission submarines, tenders, oil tankers, and other ships of the Fleet Train. Richardson told anyone who would listen while he was chief of BuNav that it was fine to recommission the ships, but that the Navy had better have a plan to hire and train more personnel to be ready to quickly operate the old vessels. Roosevelt thought that such action would alarm the public, but this situation changed in September of 1939.

Two days after the president's neutrality proclamations, Edison sent a message to all Navy stations, asking for preparation of active service and recommissioning of priority one destroyers, light mine layers, and the USS *Patoka,* a 16,000-ton oiler constructed in 1919. It would be converted to a seaplane tender. He went on to detail what would happen in stages with the Reserve Fleet, as the funds were available. The next day, September 8, Roosevelt proclaimed a state of "limited emergency" and increased the naval enlisted strength cap to 145,000.[36]

This act disappointed Richardson, who knew the president had been advised to put the level at 191,000, a number he could legally supply at the time. Richardson also knew that ordering personnel increases did not mean they would come. He watched as his fears came true. The extra officers needed to man the ships removed from mothball status came from postgraduate school and the Naval War College. They were ordered to sea before completion of their study assignments. The same happened with enlisted men. More than 1,700 petty officers to man the upgraded old ships were to come from the U.S. Fleet.

In addition, in the plans were retired officers. More than 1,000 were to be recalled, as were 670 reserve officers, 3,000 enlisted Fleet Reservists, and 2,750 enlisted reserves.[37] Nimitz was finding the BuNav job most incredible as the world situation changed so rapidly.[38] Those who later thought the United States was caught totally unprepared for war did little research.

This approach, however, chagrined Richardson, who thought instead of cutting back on education and training, the Navy should be expanding those functions. The Navy Department also found out that the Reserve Fleet could not be simply recommissioned in thirty days as planned, but that it would take sixty to ninety days for those destroyers parked at San Diego to be upgraded. Once again, Richardson blamed most of this situation on the reluctance of Congress to fund the expansion of the personnel needed to man the vessels. To him, it was a twenty-year-old problem. He concluded that in the future, ships in the Reserve Fleet should never be part of a war plan if not continually kept in reasonable condition. He stressed, also, that numbers of personnel aboard the Active Fleet should be high enough at all times to quickly supply personnel for Reserve Fleet vessels when needed. Waiting until the ships were ready for sea was too late to start.[39]

These worries did not deter Richardson from experimenting with new ideas, nor having fun. In between work, he fell into a lake fishing in Tacoma, visited Seattle, and fished again, went to a large dance in honor of the fleet and Canadians, and even met the chairman of the Securities and Exchange Commission, William O. Douglas, nominee to the Supreme Court.[40]

A tactical exercise was held in late September of 1939, with Richardson serving as commander of the *White* Fleet. This was the first time that a carrier, in this instance the USS *Enterprise,* occupied the key spot in a cruising formation. Also, he put all the antiaircraft resources in position to protect the carrier. While this action was common later and during World War II, at that time it was highly experimental.

The USS *Cummings* and the USS *Tucker* were at the center with the carrier, while Richardson located four battleships ahead. On a second circle, he spaced out seven cruisers, and on a third circle were eighteen destroyers. The spacing between circles was one mile. This exercise gained approval from Bloch, even though he thought that leaving the carrier at a distance from the main body left it vulnerable. This experiment revealed the basic principles used by the task groups of the fast carrier forces operating after 1941.[41]

On September 22, 1939, Bloch received a dispatch from the Navy Department saying that the following units would be "temporarily" transferred to Hawaii: two heavy cruiser divisions, one flotilla flagship carrying flotilla commander, two destroyer squadrons, one destroyer tender, one aircraft carrier, and such base force units necessary for servicing the task group. Who went was left up to Bloch and Richardson.[42]

The Hawaiian Detachment was officially formed on October 5. At first the USS *Indianapolis* served Andrews as the flagship. The USS *Houston* was in her overhaul phase after the Fleet Problem XX assignment, but was given the duty as flagship for the detachment beginning in December.

Kepper had come to Los Angeles Harbor in August with the USS *Salt Lake City*. "In October of 1939, our ship was notified that we were to be permanently assigned to a group titled Hawaiian Detachment," he wrote in his memoirs.[43] The new aircraft carrier, USS *Enterprise,* would be the centerpiece, under command of Captain Charles A. Pownall. He reported to William Halsey, who, after his stint as a student naval observer at Pensacola in 1934, began the path to aircraft carriers from his previous expertise with destroyers. At that time Halsey was simply called "Bill" by Richardson and his peers.[44]

Newspaper editorials across the United States seemed to support the idea that a stronger presence at Pearl Harbor would deter Japanese thoughts of attack. Some cautioned there might be reprisal. For instance, the *Charlotte News* published these thoughts:

Pearl Harbor
It Is 2,000 Miles Nearer the Orient Than San Pedro

The sending of "a pretty fair-sized detachment" of U.S. warships from the fleet's base at San Pedro, Calif., to Pearl Harbor, H. I., is only for training purposes, the Navy Department announces. The transfer has been contemplated for years and has no connection at all with defense in Europe and Asia.

We are prepared to believe as much and to absolve the Navy of any intent to move out into the Pacific for reasons other than those expressed. But the Japs and the Russians may not be so credulous. After all, the Navy's moves, unrelated as they may be to world events, have happened to counter moves elsewhere as though in a checker game.

After basing in the Pacific these last years, the fleet early in 1939 was ordered to try the Atlantic for awhile. Then the Japs began to take a high hand in Shanghai and Tientsin, which Britain, being otherwise very much engaged, could only endure.

Promptly the American fleet called off its Atlantic visit and hastened back through the [Panama] Canal.

This present shifting of the fleet may or may not be as a result of any Russo-Japanese understanding in the Orient, an understanding which could very seriously jeopardize British influence and possessions. But it is indisputable that the Hawaiian Islands are 2,000 miles closer than San Pedro to the theater of operations in the Pacific, a geographical fact which interested nations know better than we.[45]

Such wording horrified Richardson, Bloch, and others. In no way would the Navy train in this manner, and in no way did the Navy leaders believe the small numbers of ships would deter any aggressive country. The editorial never mentioned that Roosevelt, not the Navy, called off the World's Fair appearance and ordered the fleet back into the Pacific.

Long Beach and San Pedro quickly began to feel the initial changes that war would bring to those businesses and local citizens. Until then, families could rely upon seeing each other on a fairly regular basis. "I saw my family on weekends," related Hustvedt. His job on Bloch's staff did not allow him time for any golf. He did not ever recreate or exercise, saying, "I saw little enough of my family as it was."[46]

Andrews sailed for the new Hawaiian assignment on October 5, 1939. The civilians around Roosevelt were influencing the fleet position, believed Richardson. To him, this action was the forerunner to the control Washington politics would have over management of the Pacific Fleet. Richardson thought that it was also the beginning of messages to Bloch, and then to him, that were double talk. "It was obvious to every 'polly wog' in the Fleet that the stationing of a major portion of the Fleet in Hawaii would not facilitate training," he later wrote. What he penned to Navy officials was not so blunt, but to the point.

"Tongues were set to speculating," he thought, when the true reasons for movement of the fleet were not presented. He felt that this situation was like the camel putting his nose under the tent. The U.S. Fleet was quite unprepared to undertake war operations in the western Pacific at its current level of strength. By placing a good portion of it in Hawaii, it would weaken rather than strengthen the deterrent power expected by the president and the State Department. Or, so thought Richardson.[47]

This move of the fleet toward permanent station at Pearl Harbor was unstoppable by that time, and Richardson thought that even when the Washington hierarchies realized its "deleterious" effect upon naval readiness, it would be too late to turn back. Roosevelt and his advisors did not consider any possible loss of face if the decision was later forced to be reversed. They would not retreat to the West Coast. Richardson warned in his book that he would advise future Navy planners to make sure the difference in peacetime operations versus war time readiness never have too much of a gap.

In the meantime, the world became more prepared for an Atlantic disruption. The United States and twenty other Western Hemisphere nations met in late September in Panama. Sumner Welles, Under Secretary of State, represented the interests of the United States. On October 2, this Congress of Nations declared that no warlike act could be committed within 300 miles along the Atlantic coastline. The decree did not last long. The chase of the German battleship *Graf Spee* off the coast of Uruguay in December soon exposed the weakness of the so-called security belt.

During November, Richardson quietly entered the upper half of rear admirals when Yarnell retired.[48] At work, Richardson and Bloch experimented further with carrier formations. This time the USS *Saratoga* was in the center. Richardson placed the battleships on circle three this time, and the cruisers on circles four and five. Destroyers were on circles five and six, stretching out the force extensively. Carrier commanders were slow to accept the advantages of such position in the middle, but his younger staff members prodded Richardson on with the idea.[49] They were convinced the carrier should be the nerve center in the next war. They were sure that tactical command would be more effective if coming from a carrier.

During that fall of 1939, short-term aims of the unnatural alliance of Germany and the Soviet Union were disclosed. On September 17, in an agreement with Adolph Hitler, the Soviet Union invaded Poland. Warsaw surrendered twelve days later. The blitz to conquer that country took only twenty-nine days. It was thus divided between Germany and the Soviet Union. Estonia, Latvia, and Lithuania disappeared as independent countries. On November 30, Finland was attacked by the Soviet Union. The confusion in America reigned. Who could tell who was with whom? Headlines each day held new theories.

In the midst of all this confusion, Leahy did not stay retired long, just from August 1 to September 11. He took office as the governor of Puerto Rico, with goals of relaxing far away from Washington, DC. In a matter of weeks, he would break his oath to Richardson when he said, after leaving as CNO, he wanted to get far away from the Navy and government.

In the United States, Richardson felt the public apathy problem lay with the president's reluctance to arouse the country. Not truly understanding politics, and being a bit too much of an idealist, Richardson felt that personal popularity and a political party's continuance were subordinate to the vital interest of the country.

Richardson, on the eve of his greatest challenge, believed that only "an uninformed or misinformed people clamor for peace at the price of future well-being." Armed with all these ingredients, he was determined to tighten up his end of the world. He would do his best to prepare the fleet for any attack.[50]

CHAPTER THIRTEEN

Choosing the Final CinCUS Staff
Past Experience with Reeves Valuable

In his book, Admiral Richardson explained the importance of staff appointees. "Every officer in command in the Navy is anxious to have competent subordinates," he wrote.[1] Richardson did not mind a wayward comment or varied opinion now and then, as Dyer pointed out, but he knew that teamwork and mutual respect drove the successful commander. Richardson knew he would not be able to appoint to the staff only those he knew personally. Therefore, he sought suggestions.

However, he took the Reeves experience and tried to remedy the problem for himself as he began ascending toward the assignment Reeves had held in 1935-36. Richardson was also convinced it took only one "bad apple" on a staff to cause much "eyebrow raising" by subordinates. So, he attempted to study carefully who would be on his own staff for the next two or more years. In this situation his BuNav experience was invaluable.

For assistance and recommendations he went to the Bureaus of Supplies, Aeronautics, Engineering, Construction and Repair, and the Commandant of the Marine Corps. He carefully reviewed the nominations, and made some choices: Force Paymaster Captain William N. Hughes, Aviation Aide Commander Osborne B. Hardison, Force Engineer Commander Thorvald A. Solberg, Force Constructor Commander Sidney E. Dudley, and Force Marine Officer Lieutenant Colonel LeRoy P. Hunt. These men he did not know personally, and of these, only Hardison was still on the staff when a photo was taken in late 1940.[2]

Lieutenant (j.g.) Harry B. Stark and four ensigns were nominated as communication watch officers. They were chosen by commanding officers of battle force ships on which they were serving. The four ensigns were Earl W. Cassidy, Joseph A. Dodson, Jr., Newell E. Thomas, and John C. Patty, Jr. All were Naval Academy graduates of 1937. Stark graduated one class ahead of them. In late 1940, only Stark remained on the staff, the other four being replaced by Ensign Robert G. Bidwell, Lieutenant (j.g.) Walter J. East, Lieutenant (j.g.) Laurence H. Marks, and Lieutenant Allan L. Reed. Ensigns Leslie J. O'Brien, R. H. Burgess, and C. R. Johnson joined the staff of communication officers later.

Richardson chose as aerologist Lieutenant Commander Thomas J. Raftery, a 1922 academy graduate serving already on the staff of Commander Battle Force. The Bureau of Aeronautics desired that he stay, and Richardson agreed. Apparently the admiral approved of his work, for Raftery was still a staff member in late 1940 when the photo was taken.

A friend and coworker for some time, Commander Dyer was chosen as aide and flag secretary. Dyer recommended several staff choices: Force Gunnery Officer Commander Ernest E. Herrmann, Assistant Operations Officer Commander Marcy M. Dupre, and Force Communications Officer Maurice E. Curts. In addition, the huge Navy tackle off the 1926 national championship football team, Lieutenant Daniel T. Eddy, was picked to be an aide and the flag lieutenant.[3] Of these choices, in late 1940 only Curts, who had worked as officer in charge of the Naval Research Laboratory from 1936 to 1938 on a radar project, had moved on to another assignment.

Richardson did his own picking next. He chose Taffinder as the chief of staff, feeling that the captain had all the traits necessary—he knew how to manage details with sound judgment; was a self-starter; and though some disagreed, had a likeable personality. He was able to compromise without losing "the meat of new ideas."[4]

As force operations officer, Richardson continued with Captain Bieri. By that time Richardson knew Bieri had a conservative, loyal, and keen mind. "He had an extremely broad professional knowledge and training, as well as a very fine grasp of naval operations," Richardson later dictated to Dyer when they wrote together. "He had a wonderful sense of what was practical and what was not." Richardson observed that young officers had an almost adoration for Bieri. In late 1940,

Taffinder, Bieri, and Dyer were still serving with Richardson.

For his last staff appointment, Richardson's compassion for his fellow man brought him to ask the Navy Surgeon General Percy S. Rossiter if Dr. Joel T. Boone could be the force surgeon. A World War I Congressional Medal of Honor recipient, Dr. Boone was a pall-bearer at the ceremony for the unknown solder.[5] He had been assistant White House physician for Presidents Warren G. Harding and Calvin Coolidge, and the physician for President Herbert Hoover.[6]

However, the doctor had just undergone a very serious stomach operation, and Richardson thought he deserved a more appropriate and less mobile position. After some discussion, Richardson and Rossiter come to agreement on Captain Kent C. Melhorn, a fifty-six-year-old native of Ohio. Richardson liked him, and the two had been friends since 1909. "I would have asked him in the first place except for the desire to help Boone," Richardson wrote.[7] Melhorn had served as fleet surgeon with Reeves.

"I received a dispatch," from Richardson, Melhorn said several years after World War II. "He wanted me to join his staff. I was on the *Dixie* when I first met him. Of course, my reply was 'Aye, Aye, Sir!'" Therefore, Melhorn began a second tour as fleet medical officer, Pacific.[8] He thought the utmost of Richardson, saying he was beloved by both enlisted men and officers, but had very firm ideas about keeping the battleships "enmasse." Melhorn was not with the staff, however, in late 1940.

As staff left in the next year and a half, these were added: as aide, Commander Vincent R. Murphy; and as engineering officer, Captain Robert R. Thompson. Others in the 1940 photo who were not with Richardson when he was Commander Battle Force in 1939 were Lieutenant Commander Wilfred B. Goulett, and Ensign Ralph W. Cousins.

Richardson took great pride in noting that of these men he chose on the 1939 staff, seven became flag officers of the rank of two stars or above: Taffinder, Bieri, Hardison, Solberg, Herrmann, Dyer, and Curts. Dupre became a rear admiral, and Hunt rose to the rank of four-star general. Cousins became a rear admiral. Of course, it is only reasonable that the top-notch players in any unit rise to prominence later, but this group was an extraordinary assemblage of talent. Their work after leaving Richardson's wings was impressive.

Richardson knew that he had a staff far superior to the one he had directed under Reeves. Of those who served Reeves, among the nine seasoned line officers, lieutenant commander and above, only three later became flag officers with two stars and above.[9]

Richardson knew that his selection as CinCUS over Snyder was not in accordance with tradition. Snyder graduated two years before Richardson, was smart, a good talker, and had much experience at the Naval War College. But, Richardson felt that since Roosevelt did not know Snyder, it was a detriment to future appointment to CinCUS. "Snyder said from the first," reported Richardson, "that he would serve me loyally and he did."[10]

The other new "principal" subordinates chosen by or for Richardson were admirals: Charles A. Blakely, Commander Aircraft Battle Force, soon relieved by Bill Halsey; William S. Pye, Commander Destroyers Battle Force; Edward J. Marquart, a Navy classmate with Richardson who would be Commander Minecraft Battle Force; and the figure of the future, Husband E. Kimmel, Commander Cruisers Battle Force. G. J. Meyers was Commander of the Base Force, but died suddenly in December of 1939. Richardson asked F. H. Sadler, but he refused. Thus, W. L. "Bill" Calhoun was chosen.[11] Other force commanders remained the same as those who had served under Bloch.

Richardson highly admired Kimmel and had been with Blakely in the Third Torpedo Boat Flotilla in 1908-9. Pye, a natural senior to Richardson, was a great writer of strategy and tactics. He was a better thinker than doer, said Richardson, but he was pleased to have him serving under him. Marquart was an expert in materiel administration and logistics. "He was not an outstanding leader," Richardson later wrote, "but . . . he was one of my most loyal classmates. I valued highly his support."[12]

Thus, the fleet was set for action in mid-1939 with leadership Richardson expected to carry on into 1940 during his tenure as CinCUS.

CHAPTER FOURTEEN

Fleet Problem XXI—The Last One
Richardson Attempts Realistic Exercises

On a late February 1939 day in Washington, DC, May Richardson received a call from Carolyn Hawkins Edison. Like May, she played well the part of caring and socializing wife. The couples seemed to like each other, enjoying an evening of dinner and bridge now and then. Admiral Richardson always said there was not enough time for him to be "excellent" at bridge or poker, but that did not mean he was a slouch.[1] Roosevelt and Charles Edison, of course, were rather close, but the secretary was not going with the president on the USS *Houston* to observe the Fleet Problem XX exercises in the Caribbean.

Edison was twelve years younger than Richardson, but the admiral admitted more than once a fondness for the third son of famed inventor Thomas A. Edison. That did not mean they thought the same way about the Navy's future. Leahy constantly annoyed Edison, said Carney years later.[2] However, the thin and narrow-faced CNO was becoming a close advisor to the president, and Edison wanted to play politics too. Therefore, Leahy and Edison attempted a working relationship. The clash between the pair in the naval offices may have eventually moved Edison on into a political career a bit earlier than he planned.

None of this opposite-pole attitude with Navy leaders ruined a good game of bridge. Richardson and May enjoyed the conversation when they dined, treating all events as learning experiences. On that cold Washington, DC, night in early 1939, the sometimes naïve admiral was asked by Edison, "Joe, if you had your choice of details, would you prefer to be the CNO or command the fleet?" Richardson replied that of course all good Navy officers would prefer sea duty. "I certainly would," he concluded.[3]

On the way home, May chided him a bit, saying she thought that Edison was sounding out her husband for a future detail. "I scoffed at the idea, saying that he was just asking a question normal to the conversation, trying to obtain viewpoints." As it turned out, May was probably correct. Swanson died on July 7, 1939, and Edison was thrust into the position of acting secretary of the Navy. The dinner conversation and choice Richardson expressed more than likely was conveyed to Roosevelt at some time. When the president was choosing who would replace Leahy as CNO, and Admiral Bloch as CinCUS, Richardson fell into the latter's slot.

Richardson wrote years later that he still had no regrets that he received the fleet billet. However, he quietly placed in a short paragraph in his book an indication of his decision-making process had he been chosen as CNO. "I do believe that the United States Fleet would not have been in Pearl Harbor on December 7, 1941, had I been the Chief of Naval Operations at that time."

On December 9, 1939, it was announced officially that Richardson would be assigned the highest sea command, the third Texan in a decade to hold that position.[4] The *Paris News* and Editor Neville proudly announced, "Parisian Heads Fleet."

John E. King, Washington staff correspondent for the *Dallas Morning News,* noted that the "big, round faced, snub-nosed Admiral, gruff in manner but kindly at heart, retains a happy outlook on life and can find fun in everything." He went on to describe nicely what so many of those who stood before Richardson's desk encountered: "Peering over his glasses, he may greet a subordinate with a gruffness that would startle one who didn't know him. But, the merry twinkle in his eye will belie the gruff voice, and if the time and occasion permit—and they usually do—there follows a joke and a hearty laugh."[5] The next few months would test that personality to the utmost.

But, for the present, the moment was his. Looking for more background, members of the press went to Paris. Richardson's life-long friend, fellow drugstore clerk, D. Williams, then had a son of his own who could claim a degree from Annapolis. Williams said of his fellow worker, "He was unselfish, always considerate of others and very popular with members of the young set here," he told writer Robert E. Hicks, whose article was printed in other places.[6] Williams said that Professor Richardson accused his son, however, of being a "regular bookworm." Most in Paris said he had never changed from the human qualities learned through his father.

No Parisian was at the change of command ceremonies on Saturday, January 6, 1940. After all, it was a long trip to Long Beach, California. Early that morning, Richardson piddled around at the apartment, and before the 9:30 A.M. event began, ran down to the market for his wife. Joe, then twenty-eight, was there to observe his father's finest hour. Joe had recently been hired to work for the Metro-Goldwyn-Mayer Corporation.[7] He was much amused seeing his father, in command of 144,000 officers and enlisted men, come home with a sack of beets, carrots, and apples less than an hour before the ceremony began.[8] Joe gained admission to the event through a press pass. May listened to the broadcast over the radio.

The Richardson sisters read with pride of the event. Jessie, who lost her first husband in a gun accident, was married to David Chambers and lived in Detroit, Texas. Moss was an "old maid" English teacher at West Texas State Teachers College in Canyon. Stepsister and cousin Opie was retired and still living in Ottawa, Canada. May's sister-in-law lived in Paris, and they corresponded often.

Four months past the age of sixty-one, Richardson was not old in that era of the Navy. As he later pointed out in his writings, "Only the unknowing and the brash would assert that age handicapped."

He considered carefully his remarks to be presented in Los Angeles Harbor on board the USS *Pennsylvania*. He knew that if he mentioned fleet readiness, the press would want to know what he thought. That would not only cause controversy, it would also embarrass Bloch.

Richardson was correct. As he stood to Bloch's right, almost directly under the turret, the outgoing commander told the audience that "the Fleet was ready to fight."[9] And, to be fair, many strides had been made in the two years since Bloch had come to the same quarterdeck, relieving Hepburn. But, ready to fight? Richardson did not agree.

Richardson took his friend's place at the stand. "In these serious and disturbed times, the people of the United States confidently rely upon the Navy as their first line of defense," he began. "We cannot honorably discharge our obligation to our country unless each of us voluntarily contributes the last bit to his assigned task."[10]

Richardson praised Bloch's leadership, and noted that he knew him more intimately than any other officer in the Navy. But, he warned that the fleet could not remain in a static condition. "It must either improve or deteriorate," he said. Seconds after his rather short remarks, he said, "Admiral Bloch, I relieve you." Seventeen guns roared, and the four-star admiral's flag was raised to the main-mast.[11] His desire as expressed to Edison eleven months earlier came true. "I became the Commander-in-chief of the largest Navy in the world not currently at war," he wrote later.[12] In the rain and under an awning on the deck, he then opened a press conference after most of the force commanders and their staffs had left the ship.

He immediately told writers that, despite his long friendship and assistance gained from his relationship with *Paris News* editor Sandy Neville, "I have learned to distrust and fear the press." He quickly told them that he realized that "you make your living by informing the American public of what is happening." And, he agreed that the public had a perfect right to know. "I shall be happy to give you any information, that is not, in my opinion, inimical to national security." Though most had to run to their dictionaries later to understand the meaning of "inimical," nearly all the press knew Richardson well by then. He was a good interviewee.

But, to make his point clear, Richardson said something that went over their heads completely—all of them except young Joe. The admiral threatened the fourth estate. "*Personally,* I do not care what the press says about me," he began. "The only people on earth who care anything about me are three old ladies. If you should say anything favorable about me, they would think [simply] 'the press is learning what we have always known.' And, if you should say anything unfavorable, they would think that 'this is an example of the lying press!'" It was a sly way to tell May, Moss, and Jessie (and perhaps Opie) that he was thinking of them.

However, the ladies may not have appreciated being called "old."[13]

He then made another dig at the corps present, saying, "*Officially,* I am most anxious to receive favorable press attention because the officers and men of the Fleet like to feel that their Commander-in-chief is worthy of the position he occupies. The extent to which you can give me favorable press notice will assist me in the discharge of my duties." There was more than one chuckle from the audience. Richardson smugly bragged years later that he diverted the press from that question about fleet readiness. Most of the press, instead, wanted him to explain which events had made him suspicious of the news industry. When one newspaper reported that Richardson said the fleet was ready for war, the admiral's attitude toward reporters stiffened even more.[14]

Bloch proceeded to Washington for conferences before he was to report for work as the commander of the Fourteenth Naval District in Hawaii. Fleet work was continued, but Richardson began to tighten the rules. He instigated additional security measures. These included more strict movement of visitors on board ships, a more guarded use of confidential and secret papers, and a scrutiny of packages brought with sailors to the vessels.

He tried to cease photographing of the ships and movements; he wanted reports on the travels of nearby foreign ships and placed more protection around powder magazines. A "mild hysteria" followed, especially when alarms were given. However, after so many false warnings, the inefficiency was reduced. The citizens of the Long Beach area thought that all of this activity brought adverse effects, the crews being more tense and overworked. The eventual numbers of small "cries of wolf" created an unreceptive attitude toward security orders. Some of these instructions causing fear were of Richardson's making, but others came from Washington.[15]

First on the sea agenda was the Joint Army-Navy Exercise that would cost planner Harry W. Hill his position. Richardson planned the joint amphibious exercise off Monterey, California, the previous fall. He worked on details with Lieutenant Colonel Mark Wayne Clark of Fort Lewis.[16] Richardson arrived by automobile at Presidio about dusk on January 29. "It was a miniature

Admiral Richardson at desk: With a photo of former Secretary of Navy Claude A. Swanson on the wall and a call button to his left, James Otto Richardson begins his U.S. Fleet duties on his flagship, the USS Pennsylvania *in January 1940. Swanson had been dead since July 7, 1939, and was only replaced by Acting Secretary Charles Edison on January 2, 1940. New photos had yet to be distributed.* (From the Papers of David Tweed Ferrier, Richardson's staff radio officer in 1940)

Teakwood decks in 1940: One of the important reasons J. O. Richardson wanted the fleet back on the West Coast was to change the decks from teak-wood to metal. He is standing here on the battleship USS Pennsylvania *with Captain Sherwood A. Taffinder, the chief of staff and aide for the commander in chief U.S. Fleet. Later photographs taken during World War II in the Pacific reveal the wood decks went to war.* (From the Papers of David Tweed Ferrier, Richardson's staff radio officer in 1940)

edition," he wrote in his book, "in many respects, of the amphibious operations of World War II."[17] During this joint venture, on January 18, Richardson held a replica of the attack on the German pocket-battleship, the *Graf Spee*.[18]

There was time for deck duty during February, a type of "slavery," according to Seaman Second Class John Rampley from North Carolina. "We'd scrub the teakwood, and when it dried it was a brilliant white. Sure made the beans and cornbread taste wonderful." He and his buddies lived on the ship, arising at 5:00 A.M. to swab the decks.[19]

Richardson announced in the ship's newspaper, *The Keystone,* that all hands could worship according to their individual convictions. He directed that during the Lenten Season, regular and additional services would be held in each ship as permitted by the number of chaplains available. It was announced in the paper that the *Pennsylvania* would be represented on the airwaves on February 10, when Lieutenant Eddy and others were to be part of the *CBS Sports Review* program broadcast from Hollywood.[20]

In mid-February, Richardson received a dispatch from Andrews, explaining that public information about the change of homeport for that part of the fleet would help the housing problem in Honolulu. Richardson agreed, and pointed out to Stark that information about the detachment had already run in the Honolulu, Los Angeles, Long Beach, and San Diego newspapers. He knew Stark was in a delicate political position, but the restriction of publicity and the housing problem were about to affect the "contentment and morale" of the sailors.[21]

On February 26, 1940, the U.S. ships in the Atlantic began Fleet Landing Exercise VI.[22] The so-called Atlantic Neutrality Patrol, however, reduced the numbers participating in that Caribbean training. Another West Coast landing and base defense exercise was held in late May, prompting Richardson to realize that aerial photography before attacking had to be available. Techniques were developed at an accelerated rate during that year and the next.

In addition to these landing exercises, two advanced light force practices were held in the San Diego-San Pedro region in the weeks before the fleet left on April 1 for its annual problem studies.[23]

Richardson suspended the usual peacetime practice, allowing the ships maneuverability to avoid the incoming practice torpedoes. However, the reality took a back seat when the screening destroyers went out to recover the expensive torpedoes. This action limited the use of smoke as a cover. The submarine hits were determined by sound.[24] During this time, one confirmation of a foreign submarine periscope was made. Richardson said that this event was a precursor of things to come from the Japanese as the fleet held more training exercises. Some experimentation with mines was held; then in April the fleet went on to the big show.

The various commanders and planners had worked for months to map out Fleet Problem XXI.[25] Richardson wanted this one to be the most realistic of all the annual exercises involving the entire fleet. He was so focused upon reality that he politely told Stark and the Navy General Board that he would not exactly follow their recommendations for portions of the Fleet Problem experiments.[26] This disclosure may have been the initial clue back to Washington that Richardson was going to be a bit more independent with fleet management than those before him, Reeves not withstanding.

Perhaps the most realistic problem for Richardson was the warning he received in January from the Naval Attaché in Tokyo. "According to information I have, the Japanese Navy is making plans, which are unusually elaborate, to cover our Fleet problem."[27] He added that tankers, submarines, and Japanese destroyers would be in the area. However, the fleet already was aware of the Japanese efforts to view their training.

Richardson's main worry was the communications system, and how the U.S. Fleet could disguise the radio orders. He knew that, in the hurry to send messages, the cryptographic systems would occasionally reveal a mistake, and thus offer the Japanese an audio look at the fleet's operation. Plain language would be a necessity in the close-in training.

Despite the potential problems presented by Japanese presence, Richardson still issued the message on January 14, 1940, that all U.S. ships involved were to assemble at normal bases by March 31. Problem XXI would last until May 17, and then the fleet would return to standard locations, most on the West Coast.

Edison wanted to become more active. On January 2, 1940, he officially stepped into the position of secretary of the Navy. He asked to be present for part of the fleet exercise. The request was naturally granted. It gave Richardson and the staff a chance to dine and converse casually about Navy business and thought patterns. When Edison arrived, they first had lunch at MGM's filming lot facility, most likely arranged by Joe Richardson.[28] Arthur Walsh, vice president of Thomas A. Edison Inc., and his actor son were in attendance, as well as others from the studio and Washington, DC.[29]

When the time arrived to eat on board ship, disaster hit when Richardson lost his steward to double pneumonia. He was to be in the hospital for some time. Fortunately, Calhoun sent over his steward. He was "a fine and talented man," wrote Richardson a few weeks later in a letter to Stark. When Edison arrived on board, everything was in order, and he was greeted by the flag officers. At 2:45 P.M., the group went ashore to inspect several Long Beach and San Pedro facilities with Edison and the mayor of the town. The members of the Harbor Commission met the secretary, and agreements were made to expand some recreational facilities.[30] This agreement was one indication that Edison had no notion of any Washington orders set to keep the ships at Hawaii permanently.

Before returning to the ship, Richardson took "the whole party" to his "apartment." May entertained the men on short notice. At seven thirty that evening, all the flag officers dined with Edison on the USS *Pennsylvania.* On April 1, the battleships and cruisers left their anchorages in two main bodies, sailing toward the Hawaiian Islands for the games.[31]

For the duration of time in which Edison observed the Fleet Problem, he dined with different partners each evening. He was talkative, and asked many questions. Most tried to convince him to abandon his ideas on the reorganization of the Navy, but his interests did not wane, according to what Richardson wrote to Stark.[32] It was a moot argument anyway, for on April 3, unknown to Richardson and Edison, the president sent a memorandum saying that he did not want many changes made.[33]

Edison saw the entire ship, and viewed various functions at work, such as loading of the turret guns, seaplanes being catapulted, smoke screens set, air attacks launched, and all of the third phase of the planned action. He even saw a forced landing while he was on board the USS *Saratoga*. It was quite a dose of realism. The plane sank, and with it a good bit of investment.[34]

Along with Edison was Admiral Ernest J. King.[35] Richardson was a bit uneasy that the senior officer was there, being quite aware that he may have borne resentment that he was not chosen to be the CinCUS. But, Richardson later told Stark, "The presence of King in the party was far more pleasant than I anticipated. King brought along his two aides, Captain Morton L. Deyo and Lieutenant R. H. Rice."[36] Walsh, a longtime friend and officer in the many Thomas Alva Edison enterprises, and later a senator from New Jersey, also accompanied Edison in the fleet exercises.[37] Though Edison wrote Richardson afterward that he thought the trip was one of happy "remembrance," he did not "shower down accolades upon either the Fleet or its boss."[38]

Richardson may not have impressed Edison highly with the fleet maneuvers, but those who had been in the Fleet Problems before found his departures "from the restrictions of the goddess of safety . . . a refreshing break from the past."[39] King's tactics with the carriers in Problem XX had been innovative and futuristic, and then a year later Richardson's emphasis on realism was a deep training ground for the upcoming war. Though he kept an eye on safety, even agreeing that night landings were still too dangerous in training, Richardson tried as many wartime actions as possible.[40]

On April 2, Burke said that his new ship, the USS *Mugford,* was part of an antisubmarine screen in what was called the "*White* Fleet," representing an American force. About all he and "mere" destroyer commanders knew was that a "*Black* Fleet," the enemy, would attempt to attack Hawaii.[41] As Lowrey would say, as a previous member of the crew of the USS *Pennsylvania,* few knew what the overall plan was during exercises. Each portion of the fleet would react to orders, assuming they were the correct instructions under certain conditions.

Fleet Problem XXI was conducted in two phases, as Richardson noted. Both phases would follow possible *Orange War Plans.* Probably, Richardson was attempting to prove some of them obsolete, especially if he had a fleet that was not up to full steam. Two teams or forces were created in each phase. Richardson would be the umpire and observer.[42] A four-day period of special exercise would be held in between the two phases.

Implementing what the commanders learned in tactical exercises during late 1939 and into January, February, and March of 1940, the Fleet Problem Phase One began in the Eastern Pacific Ocean area with the first group concentrated. The other was divided into detachments with considerable spacing. The second phase involved a fleet movement with Marines, the seizure of an island and the defense of the base thus created. Richardson wrote later that the exercise was very similar to what the U.S. Fleet carried out during World War II in massive style at the western Gilbert Islands atoll of Tarawa, at other Pacific islands, and even against the Philippines by the Japanese.

Seventeen carriers would amass to attack Tarawa in late November 1943, but in 1940, with only three carriers available in the Pacific, the training was not under positive, maximum, or desired conditions. However, Richardson did what was possible. Messages were sent from Richardson's command center. Commander of the *White* Fleet, Pye, was informed at Long Beach that during the latter part of March, *Black* was sending a raiding force to destroy *White* shipping. *Black* had with it one carrier and several heavy cruisers and destroyers. If possible, *Black* would try to bomb shore objectives in the Hawaiian area.[43] Simultaneously, *Black* had also advanced a covering force toward the San Francisco area.

After *Black* theoretically bombed the Hawaiian sites, the *White* force moved west across the Pacific trying to intercept *Black* as it retreated. However, a *Black* submarine reported the movement of the *White* force. In the meantime, a *White* submarine, operating from Hawaii, torpedoed the simulated *Black* carrier. Being without the protection of a carrier, the *Black* raiding force thus sought the *Black* covering force for protection. By that time the covering force was nearing San Francisco. The *White*'s Navy Department intercepted the coded message about the *Black* rendezvous. The *White* commander received the information on April 3. The two opposing forces were to attempt, according to the problem's design, to obtain control of the North Pacific, east of longitude 160 west.[44]

Black Fleet commander, Snyder, knew he had an inferior covering force. He knew it was natural that the *White* Fleet would try to attack it first before the merger of the two *Black* forces. One problem to Richardson was that under budget constraints, speed was limited. Only the carriers could go faster, and only when they were launching or recovering aircraft. Thus, a bit of this exercise was foggy when compared to just what would happen in actual combat.

Pye decided to organize his *White* Fleet into three task forces: one with carriers as a striking force; one force of old cruisers and twenty-three destroyers to attack at night; and the main body, with battleships, light cruisers, and eight new destroyers. He planned to find the *Black* covering force, attack it with bombs, hoping to slow down *Black*'s speed, and make repeated night attacks. Then he would advance his main body to attack before the two *Black* forces connected.

But, Snyder also knew it would be difficult for his Hawaiian force to reach the San Francisco covering force before *White* approached and engaged. He had been given only five hours to merge the two, which was possible only if the two forces went directly toward each other, had good weather, and exerted maximum speed. Therefore, the only hope to save the *Black* covering force being chased by Pye was bad weather. It would affect *White*'s ability to attack from behind. Thus, keeping his five-hour leeway restriction in mind, Snyder took the *Black* covering force on a detour as far to the north as feasible; then steamed directly to the rendezvous, hoping the bad weather had slowed down the chase.

Snyder planned to let his *Black* carrier ride to the far side of the covering force, fifty to seventy-five miles away and on the opposite side from where he perceived the *White* fleet would arrive. When the battle engaged, he would then send in the aircraft from there to assist the covering force. However, the weather was unseasonably good. Near the end of the second day, *White* search planes located the *Black* covering force churning south. Pye's force damaged the *Black* covering force carrier and slowed down the *Black* battle line. He maneuvered into a position between the two *Black* merging forces, allowing him to defeat both *Black* contingents.

What was learned? Mainly that it is folly, as Richardson wrote, to put a carrier in a position where it can not receive maximum protection from the task force. That was a tactical problem that might have a remedy. The strategic problem learned from Phase One was tough. How can a fleet's parts be united? Many variables existed there.

Then came the time for Fleet Joint Air Exercises 114 and 114A. The first compared patrol plane attacks on surface units, using planes in high-altitude tracking. This exercise met with good success. However, the second did not. It tried to underscore a greater cooperation between Army and Navy in the defense of Hawaii.[45] Richardson ran this exercise as a single tactical unit of the main fleet. He tried various defensive formations, and let the types of ships and aircraft attack each other. He included night destroyer attacks, trained in fueling destroyers at sea, and the shifting from various formations to another for defense.

On April 10 several ships anchored at Lahaina Roadstead off Maui.[46] The April 6 edition of *The Keystone* had primed the sailors for the liberty parties for those who could depart the fleet for Mala Wharf, a mile from Lahaina. The paper made many suggestions about how to spend shore time, including golf at the Maui Country Club at Sprecklesville and the West Maui Golf Club at Honolua Mountain. A municipal course was located at Waiehu. Not many of the sailors could afford a round, so they took trips about the sparsely populated island. Its "unspoiled" atmosphere soon bored them.[47]

After lunch, on April 10, Edison left the fleet with Bloch, King, Deyo, Rice, Walsh, and Andrews on the USS *Indianapolis,* headed for Honolulu. Edison was the third secretary of the Navy to visit the islands. Daniels was there in 1919 and Swanson in 1933.[48] Edison discussed with officials and the press various Navy subjects, including the new PT (patrol torpedo) boats. Meanwhile, preparations at Lahaina were made with the thought in mind that the fleet would be "attacked" while at anchor, a test of the vulnerabilities.[49]

There was no plan for any of the fleet's 159 ships, including 12 battleships, 3 carriers, and 23 cruisers, to enter Pearl Harbor at that time and enjoy Honolulu, although many Navy wives were already there.[50] Jim Vlach on the USS *Arizona* took time to write his new bride the next morning. "The sea is really choppy. All the fellows who went over last night came back, soaked both ways!" he wrote. "I don't intend to go over at Lahaina. It is a small place, and I saw it once."[51]

The sailors fretted about the time it took for letters from the West Coast to reach the fleet. However, when mail came, it was voluminous. On April 10, at least 101 pouches and 500 sacks of parcel post came in on the SS *Matsonia.* It would be flown to Lahaina for distribution.[52] Vlach said that if Jeanne did not mark "air mail" on her letter mailed April 8, it would not reach San Francisco quickly enough to be on the clipper that left there three days before he was writing his letter. "It would then lay there for a whole week." He expected the *Arizona* to be out on exercises when it arrived. He did not anticipate her letter reaching him until April 27. This delay was a big deal to a lonely, just-married seaman.[53]

Fleet Problem XXI then moved, starting on Sunday, April 15, to the Central Pacific Ocean. J. M. Loutt wrote a detailed description of how the Hawaiian Detachment Flagship USS *Indianapolis* joined the exercise from Pearl Harbor. Printed in the newspaper two weeks later, it gave the citizens a clear look at what the exercise was like for participants.[54]

"Sailing orders were for midnight. At 8 p.m., sailors started to drift toward the Army and Navy YMCA in Honolulu, where a great fleet of taxis made ready to transport them back to Pearl Harbor to their ships." The fleet sailors envied their counterparts in the detachment who were permanently assigned to Hawaii and could party or live in the big city. "Gradually the crowd of sailors grew. Some of them had just downed their last beer. Others had just seen a movie, still others had just kissed the kiddies goodbye and left a waiting wife at the door."

Loutt explained what happened when all duties had been performed from midnight to early light. "Morning found smoke pouring from the stacks of the various ships. Suddenly the routine noises of the morning were disturbed by the whine of a siren, followed by the deep blast of a ship's whistle. Mooring lines were cast off bollards. Screws started churning the water. Ships slid away from docks and moorings. Fleet Problem XXI had started Phase Two."

"We were now divided into two fleets," wrote Loutt. The two foes had different names. *Maroon* and *Purple* were at war. "The former was defending, the latter were the aggressors," explained the sailor. The *Indianapolis* was part of the *Maroon* force, being the Americans or friendly force. The enemy was labeled *Purple*.

The game began. *Maroon* was divided into a force near Unalaska, Alaska, with the other standing at five hundred miles north of the equator. The southern detachment was the main force. The plan was to merge the two for a day fight against *Purple* in an area where *Maroon* could utilize carrier planes and shore fields.

As the watch went on from the USS *Indianapolis,* Loutt explained that good sleep patterns were essential. "One could not see the enemy if he looked for him with sleepy eyes." He said that when the ship was sealed up for wartime cruising, it was too hot to sleep below. Sailors were on the main deck aft and on the communications deck sleeping in the fresh and cooler sea air. Some slept soundly, he wrote, but others stared off into the sky, never noticing the moon or stars, only seeing a "vision of a blue-eyed girl with a flashing smile."

Initially, the days drug on with common drills, awaiting the clash, which could come at any time. The *Indianapolis* refueled a destroyer, a process described by Loutt. "The quartermasters skillfully guide the two ships on steady courses. The destroyer then pulls away. She has had her drink, and is ready for battle." Then, from the loft lookout comes word that two planes have been spotted. "Suddenly, from nowhere, they dive. Tiny specks in the sun, roaring down on the floating fortress, to zoom away, only to be followed by another, and another. Banking, turning, climbing, diving, all in a mad mass of man and machinery." Then, Loutt writes, from the opposite direction come the defenders. "The attackers become the attacked. Dog fights take place, and then the planes steal away."

In the problem's theory, *Purple*'s expeditionary force departed for the mid-Pacific from the Far East. By April 15, detachments occupied Samoa, and a day later, Wake Island. A strong *Maroon* force was headed west, located at latitude 8 degrees north and longitude 119 degrees west. Richardson's staff radioed both forces that *Purple* intended to seize a *Maroon* Fleet advanced base in the Hawaiian Islands. It was to be at Lahaina Roadsted. This attack called for obtaining the base, and then *Purple* was to destroy the local defenses that *Maroon* had established in the Hawaiian area.

Speed restrictions were lifted, or substantially eased by Richardson. Not only were the sailors made a part of the realism of battle, this increased realism affected the thinking of the more junior officers. They could see actual potential of tactics applied from an array of means.[55] Richardson did not let patrol planes take much risk, however. He thought it a waste to send them in the wrong directions during a fleet exercise. Snyder commanded *Purple*, but this time the U.S. Fleet was led by Andrews on the USS *Indianapolis*. His *Maroon* force was far below the strength of *Purple*'s, and in addition, he would not have the Marines and Army stationed at Oahu to help defend Maui.[56]

Snyder had his troubles with his split *Purple* Fleet, one at Samoa and one in reality at Wake. He had only a small minesweeping force, and his transports were vulnerable. He had a deadline, and it would be toughened by the constant, but necessary, zigzagging. On the other hand, *Maroon* had a strong submarine force, mines, and an advantage in patrol planes. Andrews also had the

Oahu area well defended. The mission would be eerily similar to some World War II efforts by the United States when attempting to seize bases in the Gilberts, the Marshalls, and the Marianas.[57]

Snyder finally concentrated the *Purple* main body and the raiding force; then took a detour on the way to Lahaina, hoping to avoid the *Maroon* patrol planes. He hoped to establish his own patrol base in the smooth waters at French Frigate Shoals, 480 miles west of Maui, and also expected to deny *Maroon* the Johnston Island area 717 miles to the southwest of Hawaii. Snyder would make early air attacks on the *Maroon* local naval defense units and base facilities in the Hawaiian area. *Purple* would then destroy any of Andrews' main body that happened to be in the way.

As described by Loutt, the day fight did not materialize for Andrews. Instead, an accidental night fleet engagement took place. At first, "All is quiet," Loutt wrote about the experience. "Ships are darkened. Suddenly the clanging of bells signals that the attack has arrived. The battle is on!"

This engagement was the first experience of this type for Richardson. He had seen a planned night landing earlier as part of Fleet Problem XII in 1931, but not a fight that just fell together spontaneously.[58] The men hurried to stations, and Loutt described it in detail. "Searchlights are manned . . . suddenly a blinding light is flashed. The ship is being attacked. Lights fade in return. Soon the whole area is alive with light. Ships can be seen darting here and there. Battleships plow in the distance. Destroyers dart in, attack, and then vanish. Cruisers turn and zigzag. Then, it is over."

Burke's description agreed. He said the exercise went on long past sunset and culminated in an unplanned and confused night engagement, with near collisions and missed gunnery and torpedo opportunities. He felt this exercise hastened the adoption of radar. He and other officers were forced to devise tactical measures later employed in nighttime war operations.[59]

This clash, guided by Richardson, further strengthened his opinion that this was an area that needed much training. Kimmel agreed in his report later. He felt that in nighttime action, fire had to continue during the melee, even as the enemy was heavily hitting a ship. Richardson wrote fifteen years later on the subject, saying that he and Kimmel should have put more corrective effort into night fighting. Its success was the key to the first major U.S. naval offensive in World War II, the Battle of Savo Island.[60]

The destroyers USS *Benham* and USS *Craven,* along with the USS *Shaw,* were damaged in heavy seas during the early part of the last half of the Fleet Problem XXI exercises. All three went back to Pearl Harbor for repair.[61] The *Craven* and the *Shaw* received minor hull damage during refueling operations.[62]

Loutt described the scene after the stressful battle exercises. "Down in the compartments and throughout the ship, the men are drinking coffee. They are tired, but satisfied. They will be able to sleep through a full night without getting up to stand some watch." That would not be the case in just a year and a half, but at least they had a short taste of war and its relentless conditions.

Then the ships reorganized, the fleet separated, and all of the vessels headed back to their prospective anchorages and into port. "By dawn the ship is shining and spotless," Loutt wrote. "The crew is full of horseplay now, not silent and grim awaiting an attack. After two weeks, they are coming into port soon. The second night brings into view the outline of Diamond Head and the lights of the city. Suddenly, the search light drill is on." Honolulu was ready for a big party.

The USS *Pennsylvania*'s print shop was busy printing up rules and suggestions for those going ashore. Time limits were also in print, and Ensign E. L. Schwab, the "managing editor," was preparing to distribute some 1,300 copies. More than 40,000 sailors were told to read the instructions before heading into the crowd in search of recreation.[63] Honolulu's 179,326 inhabitants thought they were ready too.

Richardson completed his written summary of Fleet Problem XXI, again noting that the fleet, and especially the commander, should be knowledgeable in regard to all aspects of radio intelligence, including cryptanalysis. In addition, the experiment with camouflage schemes during Fleet Problem XXI would receive further study.

Also, one of the additional exercises conducted outside the two phases proved once again that Hawaii was a sitting duck. Like other commanders before him, Richardson tested out the Hawaiian defenses. Between the Fleet Problem phases, on April 9, Richardson sent Andrews with a raiding force to simulate an air attack against Pearl Harbor. He reported to Stark that he was hoping the force would serve as an object for attack by the Navy patrol planes and Army bombers there. However, Andrews reported seeing Navy patrol planes, but no Army bombers.

The next day, the fleet was picked up by Navy patrol planes at 6:30 A.M., but "we did not see any Army bombers," Richardson reported to Stark. This was quite a disappointment to those who felt that the Army should be ready for any attack. After all, the Army at Pearl Harbor knew of the Navy's presence and practice, unlike months later when surprised by the Japanese. On April 10, even the submarines slipped in unnoticed on several attempts from short distances. Richardson did concede "white caps and heavy swells made it difficult to see the submarines."[64]

In the past, Pearl Harbor had been "bombed" at least four times. The most controversial was in 1932 when Richardson was in his second year as commander of the new heavy cruiser USS *Augusta*.[65] In Fleet Problem XIV, the next year, Oahu was again attacked by carrier. Admiral Frank Schofield was CinCUS. The exercise revealed that Oahu could be captured and the West Coast defenses were too weak. The Japanese espionage watched it all.[66]

Ellis M. Zacharias participated in both those Fleet Problems. He was in command of the destroyer USS *Dorsey*. After that assignment, he took his knowledge later in 1933 to the senior course at the United States Naval War College. At Newport, he and Richardson wrote similar papers on relationships with the Japanese. Zacharias thought even from 1932 on that there would be a progression of events leading up to a surprise air attack on the U.S. Fleet. He listed them as happenings: noncombatant shipping would be withdrawn by Japan; a marked increase in radio traffic would be heard; there would be an appearance of a Japanese submarine in the Hawaiian area; and he really believed that when three diplomatic envoys converged in Washington, DC, that event meant war.[67] Like what happened to Richardson, few listened to his warnings.

Again, during 1937, in Fleet Problem XVIII, the exercise challenged Hawaiian waters. Unimpressed, Japan invaded China less than four months later. In 1938's Fleet Problem XIX, the first phase was almost an identical movement to the one in 1932. With the *Lexington* out of the game because of sickness on board, King took the *Saratoga* northwest of Oahu. There he hid in a squall system, away from patrol aircraft, for three days. He then launched a successful attack on Pearl Harbor.[68] For good measure, he then took his fleet on a planned San Francisco attack, but a deceptive course gave him free rein to conquer Mare Island Naval Yard. Not fair, maybe, but successful. There was little doubt that a carrier fleet could sneak in for an attack. The question of fuel, torpedo accuracy, and exact target kept Navy officers content that Japan could not bring over many carriers, especially not six.

Unknown to all, Richardson's Fleet Problem XXI would be the last such huge training exercise by the Navy until 1947. The next time Pearl Harbor was attacked, it was by the real enemy.

CHAPTER FIFTEEN

"Remain at Pearl Harbor Until . . ."
Surprise Orders Cause Problems

If Admiral Richardson read the April 23 and 24, 1940, morning editions of the *Honolulu Advertiser,* he gained some insight into what faced him in the last half of 1940. In fact, the newspapers on the island would tell him more at times during his stay than he would learn from Washington.

On April 23, news that educated citizens and naval personnel normally considered mundane and acceptable flashed around the United States as drastic and caustic. The headlines stated that Admiral Joe Taussig had "stripped the curtains of camouflage" from isolationist thinking and boldly told the Senate Committee on Naval Affairs that a war with Japan was inevitable.[1] Bloch wrote Stark, saying, "It occurs to me that he might have taken the precaution of making this statement in executive session, thereby saving a great deal of adverse criticism to the Navy, to saber rattlers, and to himself."[2] That was not Taussig's style, however.

In May of 1933, Taussig had been called to Washington as an assistant to CNO William Harrison Standley. The Chief of Navigation at that time, William D. Leahy, was very aware of an old rift between Taussig and Roosevelt, and warned his Navy friend that maybe he should not bring his family to Washington. Things might change. Louis McHenry Howe, a friend and confidant of Roosevelt since 1911, told Leahy that he spotted Taussig's name and that he had better get rid of him. Howe was a former newsman. He was a powerful, behind-the-scenes coordinator of the Roosevelt mystique. Though very disheveled in appearance, he had the complete trust of the president. Not wanting Howe to control his life, Taussig talked with Roosevelt's naval aide, Walter N. Vernou.[3] As a result, Taussig got word from Roosevelt that everything was okay.

Now and then, Taussig would make the news, but as a whole

the next few years were uneventful between him and Roosevelt. Taussig left Washington in June of 1936 to command Battleship Division Three, and the next year Cruisers Scouting Force and Cruiser Division Five. In May of 1938, he took his father's old Norfolk command to become commandant of the Fifth Naval District and the Naval Operating Base.

Taussig said he was not even finished with his spring of 1940 prepared statement when the bulletins began going out over the wires. He was not aware that any statement he made clearly said there would be war soon, but it was surely interpreted that way.[4] He had said basically the same thing many times before, but on this occasion it irked the presidential staff and even Roosevelt, who was at Warm Springs, Georgia. Without reading the testimony, the president called Stark, demanding Taussig's dismissal. Ironically, General George F. Eliott was in the room with Stark and heard the conversation. He had said something similar after Taussig finished, but it did not draw the same, if any, press reaction. For twenty minutes, Stark listened and argued the point. He subsequently wrote a simple letter of reprimand, but Taussig said it was not placed in his file.[5]

Columnists Drew Pearson and Robert S. Allen wrote that Taussig even left out some of his prepared remarks, trying to tone down the message. After Taussig told the committee that modern warfare could bring even the overthrow of the American form of government, he was to have said a few words about the current financial public debt.[6] However, he skipped over this dig at Roosevelt's New Deal. The *Honolulu Advertiser* did not agree with Taussig, saying that the Japanese might be fed up "with what they have on hand," and might be misled by "jingoistic" war lords, but they were like any other country. A Japanese spokesman summed it up as just annual budget talk. He was quoted as saying, "Other interests are using Japan's naval program in connection with Congressional appropriations."[7] Richardson's incoming fleet to Hawaii did not bring such press coverage. He surprised residents by arriving at Lahaina Roads at 7:30 A.M. on April 24.[8] In the morning paper, next to the story about the three destroyers damaged in heavy weather during the end of the Fleet Problem, there was a photo of Senator Bennett Champ Clark, a Democrat from Missouri. The legislator was so angry with Admiral Taussig that he was demanding a court martial.[9]

"Taussig's statement is the type of militaristic sword-swinging that has brought Japan itself into its present deplorable situation," he was quoted. "The fact that the Japanese allow naval officers to dictate domestic policies is precisely what is responsible for all the trouble in the Far East."[10] He was the leader of a Senate isolationist bloc, and an opponent of a larger U.S. Navy.

Far away, Richardson was busy arranging several days to enjoy in Hawaii until the fleet would depart on May 8. As if he were a part of the festivities, back in Washington Stark played a rare round of golf. "Maybe I can repeat it in another eight months," he humorously wrote Bloch.[11]

May Richardson was in Hawaii at the time, as were many other officers' wives. The next night, the ships gave a spectacular sea review highlighted by a massive show of searchlights.[12] The main portion of more than a hundred ships of the fleet had been anchored at first in Lahaina Roads, though earlier some forty vessels of Edward J. Marquart's Mine Craft Force, Wilhelm Lee Friedell's Submarine Force, and Bill Calhoun's Base Force had eased into Pearl Harbor. Then, that afternoon Richardson had the larger ships up-anchor and move toward Pearl for the night review.[13]

That morning the newspaper printed the names of all the officers who were there.[14] Before relaxing, however, the fleet had to be protected while anchored in Pearl Harbor and in Lahaina Roads. An antitorpedo boat boom was set across the entrance of the harbor channel, extending three miles seaward. Rigid restrictions were placed upon land and water movements. A patrol plane schedule was formulated.

The ships arrived off the entrance to Pearl Harbor, and at 5:30 A.M. on Friday, April 26, the first vessel began moving inside. With Richardson on board, the USS *Pennsylvania* went in an hour or so later. It moored at 10-10 Dock, originally opened in 1911 as a 1,010-foot drydock. Pye put the USS *California* next door.[15] The carrier *Yorktown* moved to moorings at the Ford Island Naval Air Station. The aircraft carriers *Lexington* and *Saratoga* remained off Honolulu and Waikiki Beach, dropping anchor near Kewalo Basin immediately after the searchlight review was over the evening before.[16] With some 20,000 anxious sailors ready to see the city that day, and 20,000 more set to disembark twenty-four hours later at Pier 19, the next few hours were busy.[17]

After cleanup, sailors and officers could be seen streaming down gangplanks into the arms of waiting relatives and friends. Taxis and buses were quickly filled.[18] Bloch immediately came aboard the flagship to greet his successor. Snyder came over, and all greeted Honolulu Mayor Charles Crane when he called.[19] The schedule awaiting Richardson and officers would be enough to make them very happy to be leaving in a couple of weeks. First, Richardson went to the capitol to see Governor Joseph Boyd Poindexter. He then received a seventeen-gun salute at Fort Shafter that morning when he called on General Charles D. Herron, commander of the Army Hawaiian Department.[20]

A tea dance was set from 4:00 to 6:00 P.M. for all officers at the Pearl Harbor Officers Club, with a 9:00 P.M. dance. A dinner was set at Washington Place in honor of Richardson and senior officers. It began at 7:30 P.M. and was held by the governor and his daughter, Helen. May Richardson and Navy wives were there also. In the meantime, the YMCA was the scene of eight hours of entertainment for sailors, starting at 1:00 P.M. Various live shows and movies were on schedule.[21] Some ship baseball teams began to play and drill at the local facility.

The Hawaii Tourist Bureau arranged a car for the week for some of the flag officers.[22] After Friday's onslaught, Saturday's newspaper gasped, "Today another 20,000 will do it all over again."[23]

Richardson appeared in a front-page photo with Bloch. Adjoining was a large one-column headline stating, "Navy Will Shift Posts of Admirals." Assistant Secretary of the Navy Louis Compton was quoted, saying that twenty admirals, mostly involved with flight assignments, would be shuffled to different commands during the summer and early fall.[24] These changes were no doubt noted while Richardson and his staff met during the next days, discussing and assessing the just completed fleet exercises.

At a news conference, Richardson outlined the Fleet Problem to the press and public. The newspaper said the gathering was informal, but wrote that Richardson at one time during the questions and answers adjusted his sword belt and took his white dress gloves from a Marine orderly. He was, however, called "genial" by the press.[25] He told them that the *Lexington* would remain to replace the carrier *Enterprise,* at that time on the West Coast undergoing overhaul.

He explained that the mooring of the fleet was done much as in the past and as it would be if in a wartime mode. He told the group the fleet looked forward to leaving on May 9 for the Southern West Coast home facilities. He said plans were for the fleet to remain at

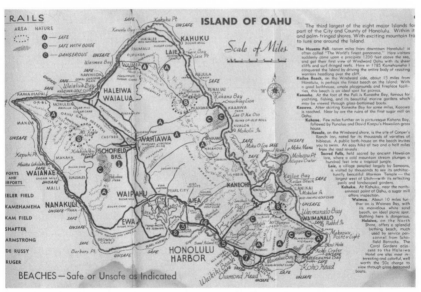

Tourism guide map: One of the better maps of 1940 comes from a brochure produced by the Army and Navy YMCA. The Richardsons kept a place near Black Point on the other side of Diamond Head from Pearl Harbor. So did several other officers, but it is doubtful that in 1940 the men spent too much time at the houses. However, there were numerous social gatherings. Some of the women, with children, lived together at various times. Only a few owned a home at Honolulu. (Steely Collection, James G. Gee Library, Commerce, Texas)

the bases there until July 1, when it would move to San Francisco. The battleships would go on to Portland, Oregon, and Puget Sound with some submarines and destroyers visiting Alaska.[26] He mentioned that another phase of Fleet Problem XXI would be held on the way back from Hawaii to the West Coast.

Meanwhile, the sailors took over the city and countryside, climbing coconut trees and hunting for grass skirts. They photographed everything. Some expressed the opinion that the hulas needed a bit more "umph!"[27] A daily schedule was printed with the planned events to be carried out through May 7, when Richardson would host a dinner on board the USS *Pennsylvania.* A big party was held for the Richardsons. At the end of the column of events the last two paragraphs caught Richardson's interest:

> The officers' golf tournament will be held April 29 at Waialae Golf Club for 300 officers.[28]

Perhaps Richardson later found that playing at Maui Country Club's nine-hole course was less eventful and quieter. He discovered this course by accident when invited to play there by Elliott R. Thorpe, commander of the Maui Military District at that time. It was near Wailuku, a quiet town of less than 5,000, which the sailors visited only once before finding it too docile. It was informal when playing at that country club. Thorpe wrote, "A foursome might include a plantation manager, a carpenter, a bank clerk and someone from the cannery."[29]

Thorpe went to Lahaina village dock the day the fleet first arrived. He wanted to make his own courtesy call on Richardson, but it was too breezy to ride in a small boat. Therefore, the next day before the fleet went over to Pearl Harbor he tried again, and made it. After the visit, he went back on the admiral's barge.

On Sunday night at Pearl Harbor, another brilliant display of ship lights filled the sky for those on land. Anchored off Waikiki, the *Lexington* participated.[30] The days on shore had been filled with excitement and social gatherings. The Saturday night formal dinner with the mayor and board of supervisors was over, and the admiral and his lady were beginning to get to know each other again after weeks away from their place in Long Beach.[31] It was not a long separation by Navy standards, and not the least bit bothersome to May to once again follow her husband. She was feted on the island; she and the admiral also went to a reception Sunday afternoon held by Admiral and Mrs. Andrews.[32]

A small story in the *Honolulu Advertiser* back pages foretold the future, however. "P.H. Will Take Whole US Fleet," it quietly noted.[33] The story, quoting Admiral Orin G. Murfin, was short, and discussed the possibility that Pearl Harbor would soon be able to meet the needs of the U.S. Fleet as a base. Murfin added that the island of Oahu was "impregnable." He would be reminded in the future of that overconfidence.

On Monday, April 29, while Richardson slept, expecting to be up early for the Navy Golf Tourney, Roosevelt was preparing to arrive back in Washington from eight days in Warm Springs, Georgia. The newspaper accounts said he was to meet with only Hull that afternoon. The vacation was supposed to last two more days, so rumors were spreading around the capital city. He also met with Stark, Compton, and Nimitz in the White House. The decision made in that meeting would change the worlds of everyday workers, Navy personnel, and the citizens of both Hawaii and those bases along the West Coast. A dispatch was proposed to be sent from Stark to Richardson, delaying the departure of the fleet at least two weeks.[34]

Roosevelt later called Stark, and the wording was constructed. The president and Stark told Richardson that because of the possibility of Italy becoming "an active belligerent" in May, instructions might come to keep the fleet in Hawaiian waters. Any changes in movement of ships made before May 9 "may not be contemplated." Stark urged that the utmost secrecy be kept.[35] The message was most probably given to Richardson by O'Brien, although as a young communications officer he took many messages back and forth. It was placed upon Richardson's desk.

Unaware of the incoming wire, Richardson and 213 other officers arrived for the tournament organized by Lieutenant Eddy, who also carried the title of Fleet Athletic Director.[36] Richardson's group teed off at 8:25 A.M., the sixth foursome on the course. He was playing this day with William Pye, W. R. Munroe, and Harold Bemis. Behind them teed off Taffinder, Bieri, Hardison, and Eddy. Because of afternoon duties, the staff apparently played early and together. The last group finally teed off at 2:00 P.M., about the time Richardson was completing the round. No list of scores was posted in the newspapers, but Lieutenant R. K. Johnston of the *Yorktown* fired a 76 in a match play with par format.

What was a deliciously happy break from planning and war exercises was converted into a nightmare when the Washington message was read.

Working while at sea: Chief of Staff Captain Sherwood A. Taffinder, Aide and Flag Secretary Lieutenant George C. Dyer, Fleet Commander Admiral James Otto Richardson, and Flag Lieutenant Daniel T. Eddy meet on board the USS Pennsylvania. *They may be planning recreational activities for the sailors after they came into Honolulu in late May 1940. Richardson was an avid golfer whenever he found time to hit the courses. Eddy was the fleet's athletic director. (From the Papers of David Tweed Ferrier, Richardson's staff radio officer in 1940)*

Richardson quietly kept the information secret all day, knowing that the sailors were going to attend, among other things, the Hawdet Variety Show on board the *Yorktown*. It was to be performed by the Hawaiian Detachment. A luncheon was held for the Navy Class of 1907, and a tea dance for younger officers was set for that evening on the USS *California*. It might have been Tuesday for the working force of citizen Hawaii, but the plans to party continued for the fleet. The city's Chinese even planned a large dinner for the next Monday evening, honoring Admiral and Mrs. Richardson.[37] The planners of the Chinese dinner expected twenty-one admirals and the wives who were currently visiting the islands. Richardson had to keep a steady face while dealing with this drastic new change of plans.

Wednesday, a huge festive Lei Day on the islands came and went, but brought no public news of the change of plans. The newspaper published an article relating that without permission, no one could photograph or sketch the fleet while in port. A $1,000 fine awaited any violation.[38] Richardson, in between various duties and planning for the exercise summary, wrote Stark:

> As soon as practicable after I arrive on the Coast, I want orders for Commander Murphy and myself to proceed to Washington on temporary duty for a few days in order that I may talk to you, and the President, if you approve, about the present war situation, the possibility of our being drawn in, and our existing war plans.[39]

Richardson did not want any misinterpretation, and sensed that he was not in the decision-making loop. Fresh off the Fleet Problem, he knew the weaknesses of his command. He was worried about the basic war plans as drawn by him and others. He added that a firm reestimation of the situation should keep the United States out of the conflicts in Europe and Asia until the Navy could be primed for war. "I hope that nothing will delay the arrival of the Fleet at its normal bases on the Pacific Coast." He had little idea of the seriousness of Roosevelt's mind-set on the matter.

Meanwhile, work and play continued. The cruiser USS *Detroit* was undergoing repair work, and the *Lexington* sailed from

Waikiki anchorage on a scouting exercise, contacting a theoretical enemy, but came back in before nightfall. The *Saratoga* was planning similar drills.[40] The battleship USS *New Mexico* was due into port from Puget Sound by Saturday. She was set to sail back to the West Coast on May 9 with the fleet.

The *Lexington* was scheduled to remain with the Hawaiian Detachment until replaced by the *Yorktown* in August. However, all plans were about to be abruptly rearranged. In Washington, Edison was putting his new knowledge of the fleet and Pearl Harbor before Congress. He gained some headlines, but fewer than Taussig, when he said the large Navy ships were improperly armored and vulnerable to air attack. He also mentioned a key element at Pearl Harbor—the above-ground fuel tanks. He wanted them to be placed underground in bombproof shelters.[41] The editors at the *Honolulu Advertiser* wrote that it was no surprise to them that the tanks were sitting ducks.[42]

With Richardson's fleet were two hundred reserve officers, most called to active duty for the period of a year.[43] Seamen were interviewed each day for a newspaper column called "The Fleet's In!" Most were on their first duty, and especially enjoying the entrance into the month of May as celebrated by Hawaiians. The Navy had hardly ever seemed such a glamorous assignment. In the small print among all this news of various parties hid the announcement that Pearl Harbor dock projects were speeding up.[44] Edison had alerted the Chamber of Commerce about that development, and noted that it was beginning to happen.

The SS *Lurline,* the popular liner that ran back and forth from the mainland to Hawaii, set sail on Saturday, May 4. Few if any of the admirals' wives embarked at this time.[45] Most planned to depart at or after May 9 to be on the West Coast about the same time as their husbands. The front-page clues from Washington were not sinking in.

Some of the messages taken by O'Brien, Chris Johnson, and others in the communications shack were of transfers and promotions. Most Richardson knew about, especially on Saturday, May 4, when it was announced that Bill Halsey would become

Commander Aircraft Battle Force, with the additional duty as Commander Carrier Division Two.[46] Admiral Arthur A. Bristol took command of Division One of the Aircraft Battle Force, succeeded in the Patrol Wing Two office by Admiral Aubrey W. Fitch.[47] Fitch had little clue about how he would take only sixty planes and search every day, but Richardson would insist that it be done.[48] There were constant movements of personnel about to be caught up in the vague orders coming down that day.

A May 4 dispatch came to Richardson in Pearl Harbor from Stark, dashing any faint hopes that the fleet would move out on the ninth. "It looks probable, but not final, that the Fleet will remain in Hawaiian waters for a short time after May 9th. Will expect to appraise you further Monday or Tuesday next."[49] That message made for a long weekend of apprehension and silence for Richardson.

The fleet social program, however, continued unabated. Officers were to be entertained that night with a buffet dinner dance at the Pearl Harbor Officers Club.[50] Almost any group available was preparing a party for the last weekend the fleet was scheduled to be in the region. The Richardsons must have been "dinnered out" by that time.[51]

Richardson and the officers kept at the plan to critique Fleet Problem XXI on Monday and Tuesday. About 650 gathered at the Pearl Harbor Submarine Base at 8:15 A.M., on May 6.[52] The problems were discussed with Richardson directing. The USS *New Mexico* arrived about an hour earlier, just in time to watch the program. The newspaper still headlined the news that the fleet would begin departure on Thursday. Some tankers and members of the Train were said to be already "departing."[53]

With aircraft on a three-hundred-mile offshore patrol to protect the fleet, and with destroyers on constant exercise, the officers went deeply into the Fleet Problem XXI phases. The press caught wind that extensive use of warplanes had been a major part of the drills. Reporters told their audiences that the *Saratoga* had been "theoretically" sunk while at Johnston Island, a tender was "destroyed," and the *Yorktown* lost fifteen of its planes and suffered deck damage when attacked by aircraft from the *Lexington*. Much fun was had trying to discover the contents of Richardson's upcoming report.[54]

That evening, Admiral and May Richardson, along with other fleet flag officers, went to the Americans of Chinese Ancestry gathering at Waikiki Lau Yee Chai.[55] About the same time, Roosevelt suddenly returned to Washington from a brief visit to Hyde Park, eight hours ahead of schedule. Richardson lauded the Chinese contributions to the American scene, while the press in the nation's capital conjured up many reasons for the hurried return of the president. Richardson reminisced with the Chinese about Hawaii. "This is the fourth or fifth visit I've made here," he told them. "The most delightful Christmas I ever spent was in 1903 when the Young Hotel was just completed," he added. May perhaps later asked him some pertinent questions![56]

The next day—May 7—more than 770 Marines landed in the troop transport USS *Chaumont*. That reinforcement doubled the Marine strength in the islands.[57] Finished with the two-day fleet exercise critique, Richardson took a break to host a dinner on board the *Pennsylvania*. He thought it would crown the visit to Hawaii. However, during that day he received another upsetting message from Stark.

CinCUS make immediate press release in substance as follows: "I have requested permission to remain in Hawaiian waters to accomplish some things I wanted to do while here. The Department has approved this request."[58]

The "CinCUS" barely saw the next paragraph. He had not "requested" to stay, nor was there in his mind any logical reason to make such a request. He read on:

Delay Fleet departure Hawaiian area for about two weeks, prior to end of which time you will be further advised regarding future movements. Carry out regularly scheduled overhauls of individual units, movements of base force units at your discretion.[59]

What a monumental task Richardson then faced. How was he going to tell the sailors that they were to stay? How was he going to request that the Hawaiian citizens drape their arms around the young men for two more weeks, or more? How could he carry on training when facilities and tools were not available? How was he to budget fuel and supplies? Most of all, Richardson could not bring himself to announce a false message to the public and his fleet. He did not request that the fleet stay. May was set to leave for their home on Friday with the civilian liner SS *Matsonia*. At least she was there to consult with her husband about the abrupt and unusual orders.

In a May 7 letter Richardson received later, Stark said that he had just hung up the telephone after speaking with Roosevelt. "By the time this reaches you, you will have received word to remain in Hawaiian waters for a couple of weeks." He continued to say that the Italian situation was extremely delicate.[60]

"I did not resent being told to do something," Richardson later wrote, "but I did resent being told how to do it, particularly when that 'how' made a perfect 'nitwit' out of me!"[61] He analyzed the situation, feeling he could not train fundamentals to officers and men without services available. He was in high gear at the moment and resisted an abrupt change in his schedule. Many more exercises were planned, especially as part of the trip back home. There were no tugs, targets, target rafts, target planes, towing planes, or large enough repair ships at Hawaii. Remaining there two more weeks did not upset him too much, but the possibility of a longer stay was a logistical nightmare.

"I was concerned that I might start all those [training services] toward Hawaii at towing speed, and then before or about the time they arrived 16-20 days later, the Fleet would be ordered to return home," he wrote. This was a problem never before faced by a CinCUS. He was especially insistent that the mid-May gunnery competition not be interrupted. He read more messages sent to him from his boss.

When the Fleet returns to the Coast (and I trust the delay will not be over two weeks, but I cannot tell) the President has asked that the Fleet schedule be so arranged that on extremely short notice the Fleet [will] be able to return, concentrated to Hawaiian Waters.[62]

Richardson finally broke the news to his staff, and did announce publicly that the fleet would remain, but he did not issue the requested news release. Still, what he did say gave the citizenry the impression that he alone was responsible for the decision. The *New York Times* wrote that the Navy Department and Richardson requested the stay in order to hold "tactical exercises."[63] The announcement seemed to them no big deal, and was printed on page eight at the bottom. The big-city editors assumed that since Edison had been with the spring exercises, he was responsible for greatly influencing the decision. Whatever really happened, news editors always said in the coming weeks that the decision to keep the fleet at Hawaii had been requested by Richardson.[64] The admiral had little control over what the public perception was becoming.

Roosevelt and Stark were not a part of the news. Instead, Edison made the *Honolulu Advertiser* headline on Wednesday, May 8. In seventy-two-point boldface type it declared:

FLEET WILL REMAIN INDEFINITELY, EDISON REVEALS.

In addition, a subheading stated: "White House Secretary Stephen Early said Secretary of the Navy Charles Edison informed President Roosevelt the Fleet would stay in Hawaii indefinitely." So, Early and Edison were the "nitwits"![65]

The Army was to place its 23,000 troops in Hawaii on wartime status starting the next Monday, planning a twenty-minute "blackout exercise" for the islands on May 23. Actually, this annual event had been announced weeks earlier.[66] Richardson continued shore liberty until Sunday night. To move the fleet out of the way, it was announced that 150 ships would sail for Lahaina Roads "next week." There, the news report said, the fleet would remain "indefinitely." Still, Richardson hoped not. His mug shot was placed on the front page in an awkward position, within an article of speculation about why the fleet was remaining.

The headlines suggested that perhaps the fleet's stay was linked to problems in the East Indies. Below Richardson's seemingly "smirking" photo was a small subheading, "Diplomatic Observers In Washington See Implied Warning To Japan By United States."[67] By no means did Richardson believe that story. The official line was that the fleet wanted to train more in the Hawaiian waters, but Richardson and every other admiral knew that Roosevelt was attempting to show a facade of force to the Japanese. Few Navy officers believed it would accomplish anything.

The Navy still tried to tie the responsibility for the action to remain to a request from Richardson. A naval spokesman, unnamed by the newspapers, said, "Lack of any 'particular need' for the Fleet in coastal [U.S.] waters contributed to the Navy Department's willingness to acquiesce to Admiral James O. Richardson's request." No report is extant to indicate how the admiral reacted when he read that report, but surely it was not with a positive demeanor. As hard as he resisted, he was becoming the focus, the reason and center of the decision.

With the possibility of 42,500 officers and men based out in Lahaina Roads, Richardson was faced with a major overhaul of plans. On May 9, the fleet began some of its movement over to near Maui.[68] The Japanese announced, "We are not greatly concerned, although we feel it constitutes another indication of America's anti-Japanese feeling." The consul-general for Japan in Hawaii, Gunji Kiichi, said that "to have the Fleet remain in Hawaii might not make a favorable impression on the Japanese people."[69]

The following day, the bulk of the fleet was still in Pearl Harbor, but it was leaving after eighteen days in town. As a cautionary measure, submarines joined in the three-hundred-mile daily security patrol.[70] About 150 ships, including those of the Hawaiian Detachment under Andrews, cleared out to sea. Good fortune came the way of sailors on the USS *California,* USS *Louisville,* USS *McCall,* USS *Maury,* USS *Balch,* and USS *Moffett.* Those vessels headed back to the West Coast for various overhauls.[71]

Richardson bade farewell to May, who boarded with 250 Shriners returning home from a ten-day pilgrimage to Hawaii. Mrs. Pye and several of the officers' wives who had come out for the festivities of the post-Fleet Problem joined them. Fortunately they did not know of the seriousness of the Washington messages to Richardson, nor did they have a clue of the next time they would see their husbands.[72] Elliott Thorpe writes in his book that Richardson sent May home as an example for the officers.[73] Richardson knew that he would not be able to allow too many leaves, even for the officers. The fleet should be ready for movement at all times. Several other wives left on the following departure of the SS *Lurline*.[74]

On May 11, the Saturday newspaper accounts stated that the stay off Maui by the fleet would last until probably June 15, and maybe longer. The editors apparently were more cognizant of the length of the stay than Richardson was. They found out by simply talking to the Fourteenth Naval District supply personnel, who were directing Maui suppliers to be ready for a month-long "bag of business."[75]

During the first week after the new orders, Richardson and his fleet kept hope that they would start back at the end of the two weeks mentioned, but that belief was crushed on May 15 when another dispatch arrived from Stark:

> Some British authorities feel that Italy may join Germany in active participation in immediate future . . . our state department inclined to disagree. Regarding the Dutch East Indies, Japan has made two statements which if taken at their face value state they wish status quo preserved . . . present indications are that Fleet will remain Hawaiian waters for some time. Hope to advise you more definitely next week.[76]

This message tantalized Richardson. There was always a reason to wait a bit longer. Three days earlier, *Collier's* magazine writer Jim Marshall, arriving at Honolulu with his wife after a four-month swing through the Orient, summed it up: "The Japanese don't understand Latin very well." He explained that statement further:

"When they say 'status quo' that means they desire to take over the Indies." He added, "It's all a matter of oil."[77]

As he prepared for the USS *Pennsylvania*'s Tuesday departure out of Pearl Harbor, Richardson appeared on the Monday morning edition of the *Advertiser*, thanking the citizens of Honolulu. "Now that the period of official entertainment of the Fleet has ended, on behalf of the officers and men . . . I wish to express . . . our appreciation." The locals could then catch their breath, but for how long?[78] The story stated that some of the ships would return at intervals to allow shore duty.[79]

In Washington, Roosevelt announced that in two days' time he would ask Congress for "a large sum" to bolster national defense. He said he might even call a special session. Even at that, he banned the topic of a "two ocean Navy" at his news conference, saying that label was "stupid and dumb."[80] The story was buried at the bottom of page one, but most likely did not escape Richardson's view.

By Thursday, the fleet was all anchored off Maui. The next day residents of that island watched as planes from the *Saratoga* "attacked" their cities. Puunene Airport there was busy, especially when all the 155 flight officers involved dropped in to eat their box lunches.[81] Thirty ships anchored at Lahaina Roads left for sea drills. "I believed strongly in keeping the Fleet at sea, and so kept two-thirds of it operating at sea as a routine measure," Richardson explained.[82] He kept the crews as busy as possible.

However, there was time for play. On Fridays the men were given short shore leaves to coincide with their weekend liberty. Navy families were already arriving on Maui looking for housing, some mentioning rentals for six months or longer. The quiet life on Maui was about to change somewhat, but not for long. Richardson would not allow it. Thorpe said, "The merchants had visions of a windfall . . . but to the intense annoyance of the Honolulu shopkeepers as well as the wives who had followed the Fleet from the West Coast, the Admiral had definite ideas about where his ships would spend their time—and this did not include very often Pearl Harbor" or Maui.[83]

So, the ships were between Maui and Lanai, with the small island of Kahoolawe giving shelter from the stormy southwest winds. The wives soon caught on that since Richardson did not allow May to remain, that they too would not be staying until this whole mess was untangled and the base was officially moved to Hawaii.[84] Still, some tried their best to see their husbands.

Thorpe and his wife would on occasion invite Richardson and his staff to his home on the Haleakala side of Maui, and no doubt conversation turned often to surveillance of the fleet by Japanese spies. Though he was officially an instructor for the National Guard, Thorpe said his principal reason for being on Maui was for intelligence purposes. Richardson tried to keep the press and any spies off guard with constant ship movements. But, the newspapers pretty well kept everyone informed of any changes in the fleet schedule anyway. The CinCUS was determined, however, to train the members of the fleet, even with a lack of facilities and supplies.

On May 22, another message arrived stating that there was nothing more definite to report.[85] However, the newspapers stated that the fleet would remain until June 9. The report said that sources had revealed that some sixty ships would join others already based in Pearl Harbor.[86] Richardson never got over the snub, not being told by Stark fully why the fleet was being retained, and thus not given the opportunity of formulating plans. Perhaps Stark could not interpret Roosevelt. Richardson surely knew that communication with the chief executive was a problem, but did not outwardly reveal it in his writings or testimonies.

Also, in the newspaper headlines were stories about Japan's growing tendency to join Germany and Italy. Dr. Brooks Emeny was in the Orient while the U.S. Fleet was on exercises. The author and authority on foreign affairs said that while in Japan, he was aware that the maneuvers at sea by the U.S. Fleet caused much comment. He added that many Japanese approved of a movement into the Dutch East Indies by their country because of the strain on local resources.[87] Offsetting that news was the release of $6.1 million in Navy funds to be spent in Hawaii. This action told the Hawaiians at least, and must have alerted Richardson and the Japanese, that the fleet would be in Hawaii permanently. More than $1 million was to be used for housing at Pearl Harbor, and other monies were for wharf and channel work. Even bombproof berms were to be constructed to protect the fuel tanks.[88] The underground tanks desired by Edison were not mentioned.

The first days following the delay of the fleet's departure were filled with decisions on how to treat the sets of detachment orders for those who were to leave the Navy upon the once-planned arrival on the West Coast. Richardson received permission to "hold in abeyance" the detachment of all officers except those whose departure was authorized by the CinCUS. Exceptions were those taking passage back to the West Coast on the USS *California,* the USS *San Francisco,* and the USS *Louisville.* He ordered no detachment of any officer from the carriers unless relief had arrived, and the new officer was fully qualified in the required duties. This plan did not work with the aviators who had instructional abilities. They were soon ordered by the Navy Department to Pensacola, even if reliefs had not yet arrived at the fleet.[89] This order highly offended Richardson, who assumed that the Navy Department thought more of training aviators than of maintaining the fighting efficiency of the air arm of the fleet. He considered, since this transfer information was public, that the Japanese would know that the presence of the fleet in Hawaii was just a bluff.

After devoting attention to the transfer issue, he then had to turn to the real problems—overhaul of ships, interim docking, target practice, and mobilization of loads of ammunition and oil. He listed the problems to Stark in numerous dispatches. Perhaps he was trying to overwhelm Roosevelt and Stark with the enormity of the new base needs, and change their minds. His duties seemed to be of a leader who knew the fleet was not returning to Long Beach and other facilities in the United States. Though his plans to return some ships, prepare them better for combat, fill them up with essentials, and return them to Hawaii were accepted, he could see that the department was playing "a game of blind man's bluff" with the Japanese. He sent a message to Washington in which he suggested the preparation of a news release regarding the return of those ships that had left for West Coast docking. The department replied that it wanted no publicity about the returns. "We plan to say that overhauls and dockings of vessels will be continued in the customary manner," as if the Japanese spy network did not see a difference.[90]

Ammunition was so short there was no way the fleet could move west of Hawaii. The Navy only had two ammunition ships, and they were controlled by the CNO's office. Stark said the *Pyro* would be on its way quickly to remedy part of the problem. The problem was, it would not arrive in Hawaii until mid-August.

A May 13 letter to Stark was probably the most definitive that Richardson sent at this point. His hopes to go to Washington immediately had been dashed. At the end of the personal letter, Richardson wrote, "Rest assured that although I am entirely without information, I realize your position . . . and if the situation becomes such that higher authority decides we should go west, all of us are ready to give all we have."[91] Nine days later Stark wrote, saying that he felt the quick changes in Europe had dampened any thoughts of the fleet's movement.[92]

Pearl Harbor was not entirely void of information. On May 13, the Fourteenth Naval District surmised from plain radio intercepts of three days earlier that the Japanese Fourth Fleet had been ordered to the Mandated Islands. It was to proceed to or base in the vicinity of Palau. This seemed like a quick decision by the Japanese, perhaps in response to the announcement that the U.S. Fleet was staying at Hawaii indefinitely. This was the force that had just returned to Yokosuka, Japan, about May 1 from the Mandated Islands area after watching the United States Fleet Problem XXI.[93] Richardson does not make it clear whether he saw this message, or the subsequent one from Washington instructing the intelligence office at Fourteenth Naval District headquarters to follow all the Fourth Fleet's movements. The note mentioned, however, the Navy Department's thoughts that this move endangered the Dutch East Indies, not Hawaii.

With Fleet future plans in mind, Richardson sat down to write another message, this time clearly asking Stark to outline why the fleet was there in Hawaii. "Are we here primarily to influence the actions of other nations by our presence?" or "Are we here as a stepping off place for belligerent activity?" He added that if it was the latter, "we should devote all of our time and energies to preparing for war."[94] He suggested that returning to the West Coast, accomplishing the changes, and then returning to Hawaii could better achieve this goal.

His three pages of thoughts and questions concluded by saying that if the fleet were there to develop Hawaii as a peacetime base, then the considerations should be about the efficiency of the fleet, and the morale of its servicemen and a few nurses aboard the USS *Relief.* He was worried about inadequate anchorages, airfields, recreational venues, and other necessary facilities to care for thousands of sailors.[95] He said he was returning to Pearl Harbor in two days, with plans to remain until June 10 for upkeep. Other ships of the fleet still on the West Coast were coming out in June. He reiterated that he was in the dark about "the Department's purposes and intentions," and as a result, "I feel we may work at cross purposes."

While most of his sailors were returning to Pearl Harbor after two weeks, and flocking into town on Thursday, May 24, Richardson fretted. More than 120 ships crowded the harbor, minus those sent to the West Coast for repair.[96] The local merchants, and the Chamber of Commerce, were happy. Those several hundred tourists arriving on Tuesday aboard the SS *Lurline,* set for a vacation, may not have been as content as the merchants. Fighting that crowd was most likely not on their agenda.[97]

The answer to Richardson's queries about "how long we'll stay and why are we here?" came in a May 27 letter from Stark.[98] It was precise. "You are there as a deterrent effect which it is thought your presence may have on the Japs going into the East Indies." Stark explained his earlier connection with Italy's entrance into the war. "With Italy in, it is thought the Japs might feel just that much freer to take independent action . . . with a free hand in the Dutch East Indies." Stark could not tell Richardson how long the fleet would be in Hawaii. "Rest assured that the minute I get this information I will communicate it to you." Stark told the Pearl Harbor Hearings in 1945 that it was strictly Roosevelt's decision that the fleet remain in Hawaii.

Stark seemed to answer the next question, "What does the Navy do if Japan invades the East Indies?" He put it as a caution to Richardson. "Even if the decision here were for the U.S. to take no decisive action if the Japs should decide to go into the Dutch East Indies, we must not breathe it to a soul," adding "if we do it would completely nullify the reason for your presence in the Hawaiian area." He said that as long as the Japs were ignorant of what the U.S. would do, they might hesitate, or be deterred. This was a bunch of mumbo jumbo to Richardson.

It was a long letter, but it contained a nice caveat.[99] Stark told Richardson, "You have the authority for returning ships to the Coast for docking, taking on ammunition, stores, etc., and this should help in any case." At least it would assist the sinking morale. Stark gave Richardson wide rein on other matters, such as leasing auxiliary air fields, placement of the carriers, splitting the Hawaiian Detachment back into the normal type commands and training plans.

Stark gave a lame excuse to Richardson regarding the facilities and developing the base. It was a long, tiring, worn-out story about how tough it was when he was young. "I wish I could help you," he wrote. "I spent some of my first years out of the Naval Academy in the West Indies. I remember the last port I was in after a 22 month stay, and where we did not move for six months." This attitude toward service members was not workable even in early 1940.

He then suggested an elementary solution that Richardson had probably taught Stark. "The great antidote I know is WORK and homemade recreation such as sailing, fishing, athletics, smokers, etc." There was no mention of family or social life. It was almost as if Stark was so out of touch he knew little of the fine facilities just completed at bases back home, nor of the lack of mobility for 43,000 men in small Honolulu. He concluded, "We will solve the oil situation for you."

Richardson's problems grew on May 28 when the commanding officer of the USS *Saratoga*, Captain Robert P. Molten, only fifty-three, died of a heart attack.[100] Halsey rushed out a message to Stark and the chief of the Bureau of Construction and Repair, A. H. Van Keuren, in Washington. "Bobby was stricken at 2:30 P.M.," Halsey wrote. "I have suffered a very deep loss," adding that he was glad that if it had to happen, it was over quickly.[101] Molten was replaced temporarily by Commander James M. Shoemaker. A week later Captain Archibald Douglas of the USS *Enterprise* took command. He had been on the "Big E" as its CO only four hours before receiving his message from Richardson to replace Shoemaker.[102]

Richardson wrote Stark, the mood of the comments being serious and reflective, and even futuristic. Business-wise, he said he did not approve of a plan to place a naval representative in the Long Beach-Los Angeles area. There was simply not enough work, he said. Reflectively, he wrote to his friend that the United States needed to stress preparation and training upon "our people." He thought everyone should be liable for compulsory military service, for that time spent would assist in a program of understanding. People would then realize the cost, sweat, privation, and hardship involved in defense of the country.[103]

In the meantime, and in the real world, all Richardson could do was cut back on training programs. The four-week gunnery time was reduced to one and one-half weeks for carriers. For heavy cruisers, it was only two weeks.[104] Richardson continued to stump for a return to the mainland, but settled down into the task of keeping the fleet war ready. In later years he was asked if he ever wrote Stark that the fleet would be more secure on the West Coast. He hunted for any such correspondence in vain. However, he assured in testimony before Congress in 1945 that being on the West Coast was of greater security, but not of absolute security. He said, "The Japanese . . . would quite likely have been able to deliver the same attack on Puget Sound."[105]

Richardson later put much blame for the change of fleet operations to Hawaii on Roosevelt's Far Eastern Policy advisor, Stanley Kuyl Hornbeck. Once a teacher in Chinese universities, he was a New Yorker like the president. Hornbeck fancied that he was a friend of admirals. In June of 1935, he sailed to Hawaii on the USS *Memphis* with Standley to gather information on the Japanese.[106]

Richardson based his Hornbeck opinion upon a July 2, 1940, luncheon held in Hawaii with Clarence E. Gauss. Gauss was consul-general at Shanghai, just coming from Washington on his way to his new post as minister to Australia.[107] Bloch was also at the luncheon with Richardson when Gauss stated that disposition of the fleet was determined more by Hornbeck than the Navy leaders.[108] It was Hornbeck's opinion that the U.S. Navy was far superior to the Japanese Navy. That may have been true in 1937, but Hornbeck's mind had not been updated into 1940, or so it seemed to Richardson.

For the rest of his life, Richardson was irritated that the senior leaders of the Navy, in which he included himself, were not consulted on the positioning of the fleet in May of 1940. He concluded that Japan was a military government in the first place, that Grew never talked with Japanese military officers, and that the supposition by Hull, FDR, Hornbeck, and other civilians that simply placing the fleet in Hawaii would form a deterrent, was wrong. He agreed with Smith-Hutton that it did give the Japanese press a good excuse, however, to write anti-American propaganda.[109]

But after all, the Japanese military government knew that the fleet was undermanned, unprepared, and without a Fleet Train, though as Richardson said in the congressional hearings, the force was never in want of food.[110] Richardson often told the story of the small man versus the big man. The small man was better equipped in the art of fisticuffs. He moved in closer, then closer, and then served a quick punch to the larger man's jaw. Richardson viewed the U.S. Fleet as getting in too close and being too ill equipped to take on the smaller opponent.[111] In addition, this smaller enemy was close to becoming larger.

"It seems to me," wrote Richardson, "that President Roosevelt and Secretary Hull evaluated the Japanese leaders in terms of themselves [as] elected representatives. In the United States, military moves . . . valueless from the hard realities of war, and just window dressings, were assigned great weight" by the civilians. The Japanese civilians really knew little about their military posture until it happened.

A long summer awaited Richardson.

CHAPTER SIXTEEN

"The Fleet Is Here—So Let's Go to Work"

Slowly, Grudgingly, Pearl Becomes Home

A huge congregation of naval rank assembled for a Hawaiian review at Schofield Barracks on Friday afternoon, May 30, 1940.[1] The meeting was held in honor of Admiral J. O. Richardson, said the newspaper report. The general public gathered with sixteen admirals of the fleet.[2]

More than 6,000 people watched the two-hour ceremony and full-dress parade. In addition, sixty airplanes flew above. At 2:30 P.M., Hawaiian Army Division Major General William H. Wilson presented his command to Richardson, who inspected the troops before taking the reviewing stand. Fifteen bombers came in at low altitude, noisily concluding the glamour for the CinCUS, the governor of Hawaii, and the Honolulu mayor.

The carrier USS *Lexington* had left for sea the day before the event, and the cruiser USS *Pensacola* exited for Guam to serve as a guard ship for fifteen naval patrol bombers going from Oahu to Manila. Richardson announced that the Hawaiian Detachment would be under CinCUS command while the fleet was at Pearl Harbor, and that Admiral Adolphus Andrews would be in his regular post as Commander Scouting Force. The fleet expected to go to sea on June 9.[3] Richardson read the papers each day to learn his schedule!

Meanwhile, the Roosevelt administration announced an embargo on exports of machine tools from the United States. While it affected all countries, this move stunned Japan, which depended largely upon the United States for such materials.[4] Fletcher was coming to the fleet to take over Cruiser Division Six, replacing Ingersoll, who would go to work with Stark as his assistant. Captain Robert "Fuzzy" Theobald was coming out to the fleet from the General Board to command Cruiser Division Three. The Navy assignments were always in a state of flux, so these were just common everyday changes for Richardson to manage.[5]

Richardson's effort to thwart wives from living in Honolulu was going downhill. The weekly arrival lists included vast numbers of wives who were hoping the fleet would stay in one place long enough for some reunion with their loved ones. Dinner parties were regular events.[6] Some family, like Mrs. Friedell and her daughter, were coming back. Even Eddy had installed his wife in a Kahala home.[7] Richardson tried hard to set the example, but few were following. Ordinary sailors had no extra money to bring out their wives, so the grumbling from below would eventually grow loud.

Richardson radioed Washington requesting orders to allow him to travel there to discuss the situation.[8] The fleet was in the last phase of leaving Pearl Harbor. Some of the vessels went directly to Lahaina Roads, while others went on out to sea for maneuvers. That evening, Richardson listened to Roosevelt's University of Virginia commencement speech delivered two days earlier.[9] The admiral was concerned when he heard the president all but declare war on the Axis powers of Germany and Italy. Guessing that the fleet would not return to the West Coast before September, Richardson was worried that between then and June, Roosevelt would take the Navy to war unprepared. Three days later the CinCUS sent a radio dispatch to Stark again, suggesting that he and Murphy come to Washington. He wanted to depart by air on June 18.[10] This request was approved the following day.

The common thought on the islands was that the fleet would drill a couple of days past June 28. If anyone, including Richardson, seriously thought the fleet was not going to use the islands as a major base, the news each day quickly dispelled that illusion. More federal money coming to Hawaii was announced nearly each day in June. Complementing this development was terrible news from Europe, the explanations pitched on front pages in 36- to 84-point boldface type. In the middle of June, the Germans were only thirty-four miles from Paris, France, and on June 10, Italy finally did declare war against the Allies. Four days later the Nazis entered France. This event probably took place after Stark had scratched out a reply to Richardson about coming to DC. While operating off Lahaina Roads on June 14, Richardson received the quick reply to his earlier message asking to go to the States. Finally, Richardson's chance to voice his views was coming.[11]

On June 15, a very small article was featured on page 2 of the *Honolulu Advertiser,* quoting newspaper publisher and former GOP vice-presidential candidate Frank Knox. From the old nineteenth-century school of politics, Knox encouraged people to call him "colonel, a reserve Army title he was given years after serving with Teddy Roosevelt in the Spanish-American War and in France during the 'Great War.' He would be called 'Mr. Secretary' in just weeks when Edison left" the Navy Department.[12]

The carrier *Yorktown* left the fleet in Lahaina Roads, just a day after arriving from the mainland. Some forty vessels remained anchored as Richardson and Murphy packed and planned for their trip east. Continuing the implementation of various ideas, Richardson had three Torpedo Squadron Five (VT-5) Douglas Devastators on the aft end of the fight deck painted in various camouflage colors, continuing this experiment with aircraft colors begun during the earlier Fleet Problem exercises.[13]

On Monday, June 17, Richardson switched his flag to the USS *Colorado* and started toward Pearl Harbor, anxious to get in the air for the trip to Washington. However, radio news arrived just at that moment stating that France had capitulated to the Germans.[14] If Hitler subsequently took the French Fleet, then the U.S. Fleet would have to quickly move some of its ships from the Pacific to the Atlantic to assist Great Britain in its war against Germany and to protect the Western Hemisphere. Soon a message from Stark arrived, canceling the trip.[15] Stark and Hull had met at length that day, apparently discussing how to enforce the Monroe Doctrine, which held that the United States would consider an attack against any nation in the Western Hemisphere as an attack on America.[16] Stark informed Richardson that redistribution of the fleet between the Pacific and Atlantic might come soon.

At the same time, Army Chief of staff George C. Marshall sent out an "alert" to General Charles D. Herron, commander of the U.S. Army, Pacific, headquartered in Hawaii:

> Immediately alert complete defensive organization to deal with possible trans-Pacific raid comma [sic] to greatest extent possible without creating public hysteria or provoking undue curiosity of newspapers or alien agents. Suggest maneuver basis. Maintain alert until further orders. Instructions for secret communication direct with Chief-of-staff will be furnished you shortly. Acknowledge.[17]

The war-ready status would last six weeks.[18] The citizens and the newspapers treated it as if it was just another "wolf" cry, the announcements being just as Marshall said—maneuvers for an indefinite period.

The Navy Department again issued a statement placing the fleet's position directly at Richardson's deck. It stated that the CinCUS had full powers to reach any decisions, but that Richardson was apparently pursuing his earlier request to keep the fleet indefinitely based in Hawaii.

One smoking pipe may have been thrown against the wall when Richardson read words he would never utter. The writer then quoted "informed sources," who said that Richardson had even emphasized the importance of the fleet in the mid-Pacific, especially in the view of "recent intimations of Japanese participation in disposal of France's Far Eastern colonies."[19] Someone in Washington was playing a morbid game of chicken, using Richardson as the bait.

The good news from Washington was that the House Committee on Naval Affairs voted 17-0 to increase the Navy's fighting tonnage 70 percent. The bad news coming across the news wires was that Japan expected, when the empire of France was put on the carving block in Munich, it would have permission to take over Indo-China. The aid still being given to the Chinese by the remaining French leadership was cited as the reason for the action taken by Japan. It warned one last time against further assistance to Chiang Kai-shek from the French colony, later to be called Viet Nam.[20] Japan also noted that the two-ocean U.S. Navy idea was of grave concern.[21] What was left of political stability in the Pacific was coming apart.

"By in large [sic] the people of the Hawaiian Islands welcomed the prolonged stay," Richardson wrote in his book. They "took many steps to make off-duty hours more pleasant for officers and men alike." He did mention that fishermen were not of the same mind. The large number of ships, the gunnery practice, and the simulated bombing raids interfered with business and drew complaints.[22]

Richardson heard about the June 17 Army alert the day after its transmission to Herron. Andrews told him that Bloch understood that the alert had special emphasis on possible enemy carrier and plane attacks. In keeping with Richardson's pre-established plan, Bloch and Andrews had already ordered Calhoun to fly an inner air patrol from Pearl Harbor. The outer radius patrol, initiated by Richardson on April 10, had been flying out of Lahaina Roads.[23] It normally covered 220-335 degrees at a 180-mile radius.[24] Andrews asked Richardson if there should be a patrol from the base covering the north through the west, to the south, at a distance of 300 miles. Though Andrews could have initiated this patrol on his own, Richardson told him of his approval.[25] There were not enough planes to inspect a full 360 degrees.[26]

Of course, Richardson wondered why the Navy Department had not sent a similar alert message to him. Thus, a quick evening message was sent over to Bloch, asking if this was simply an Army exercise. Bloch responded at 9:45 A.M. the next day, June 19, "Request of commandeering general was based upon a directive from the War Department. He has no information as to whether or not it is an exercise."[27]

The next Navy message, arriving also on June 19, was more perplexing.[28] Stark, who was being quoted often after his speeches on naval efficiency and budgets, asked that the fleet leave Pearl Harbor on June 24 as a "test" to see what would happen. The CinCUS was ordered to leak the information that the fleet was headed toward the Panama Canal.[29] He would maintain radio silence. Then, Stark finished up by writing, "Anticipate ordering you to Washington for conference on your return."[30]

That day, Richardson also received a more detailed response from Bloch. "Herron received a dispatch from the War Department the other day." Bloch said that Herron then asked if the Navy "could see its way clear to have an off-shore patrol." Bloch added that for two days he had sent out the Fleet Marine Force and their antiaircraft guns, with ammunition. They were in the Navy Yard proper, and Bloch was not comfortable with the safety of that position, so he planned to place them the next Monday "on a distant station somewhere near the Army guns."[31]

It was the proper time to confer face to face. At 7:45 a.m. the next day, Richardson flew over to Pearl Harbor to confer with Bloch and Herron. The general admitted that he did not even know if the alert was real or just a drill. Richardson knew that it was a drill based simply on the fact that the Navy had not been alerted. He was certain the two departments, even though in competition daily, would not be that far out of step with each other during a real wartime alert.[32]

Still, Richardson sent off a message the next morning to Stark, asking about the Army alert. The answer was interesting. It came on Saturday, June 22, at 5:00 P.M. by radio, as a priority dispatch. However, if read at all, it was basically forgotten until much later by Richardson. Andrews and Bloch never remembered it. Stark suggested that Richardson, Bloch, and Andrews cooperate with the Army alert, and said that it had been a part of consultation with the Navy before it was given. "War Department directive concerning alert issued as precautionary measure. Request you continue cooperation." Again it appears that someone thought they knew more than Richardson and Herron.[33] That day Stark also wrote, "Tentatively, decision has been made for the Fleet to remain . . . where it is. This decision can be changed at any time."[34]

When Herron asked for more specifics, Marshall told him there was suspected to be an impending agreement between the Japanese and Russians, and added that the War Department felt that once the U.S. Fleet left Hawaii, there would perhaps be a raid of the islands by the Japanese. This event would pull the fleet back to the Pacific arena, keeping it from reinforcing the Atlantic contingent. None of these reasons made much sense to those on the "front line."[35]

"I thought it was a poor way to run a railroad," mused Richardson in his book. He never accepted the Navy line on the matter. He sent a terse letter to Stark, recommending that in the future the commanders of both the Army and Navy be jointly informed.[36] Ironically, when part of the fleet was ordered out in late November 1941, Hawaii was actually attacked.

Richardson was not alone in his opinions in 1940 about unorganized orders or the plight of the fleet. That month he received a report from Atlantic Squadron Commander H. E. Ellis which stated: "Destroyers of the Squadron are not ready for war . . . the present composition of the Squadron is quite inadequate . . . the battleships . . . of Division Five are not ready for war." From the viewpoint of those on the seas, the situation was bleak.[37]

Twenty ships in Lahaina Roads were scheduled on Wednesday, June 26, to begin entrance into Pearl Harbor for a two-week stay. There were some long faces on board when the announcement was made that the fleet was leaving for points away from Hawaii on Monday. At least several thousand sailors on vessels anchored in Pearl Harbor had been able to enjoy liberty over the weekend. This latest announcement came on the heels of an official announcement made the previous week that the scheduled trip to San Francisco, Portland, Seattle, and Puget Sound during the latter part of July was cancelled.[38]

With some unsuspecting officers, wives, and children coming in from Los Angeles on the SS *Lurline* two days later, part of the fleet moved as quietly as possible in front of thousands of eyes out of Pearl Harbor, Honolulu, and Lahaina Roads all day on June 24.[39] Newspaper editors this time were baffled, and reported that the fleet was most likely headed to California. Disappointed merchants and vendors were left with tourists and base complements for customers—which meant a quiet week compared to what had been contemplated. Only the USS *Relief* and one destroyer were anchored at Lahaina, but both were steaming up on Tuesday to leave. It was obvious to even the most relaxed citizen that the news of the French collapse was serious.

There was no mention that the fleet was heading toward Panama and the canal. In fact, Bloch stated that he would not deny that the destination was California. Richardson issued no statement.

At the time, the Navy had no secretary, Edison having left office and Knox not yet confirmed by the Senate. It was an editor's nightmare. After conferring with Roosevelt, Welles, and Marshall, Stark said he had no comment either. The possibility that the fleet might be headed for the Orient came up. Most believed the heading was not toward Panama, so the secret was with the fleet and the higher-ups at that point.

Hawaii was not totally without Navy presence. The recently overhauled carrier USS *Enterprise* came in after the fleet had departed. In fact, more than forty ships were still operating around the Hawaiian area, including the carrier *Lexington*.[40]

Richardson was actually racing toward Panama with five battleships, seven cruisers, and seventeen destroyers.[41] The newspapers, Hawaiian citizens, and Japanese spies could easily tell that the fleet exiting was not especially huge. The newspapers even ran the names and numbers of most of the remaining ships! It actually was an ideal time for Japan to launch a sneak attack.

Just the same, Richardson did his duty by attempting to fool the Japanese. The fleet communications crew began dummy radio traffic with Panama, beginning on June 19, when the initial order came for the movement. Panama's commander of the Fifteenth Naval District sent them back as if the fleet was serious. This sham communication reached a peak on June 23. Then there was radio silence.

On June 27, naval operations requested of Richardson to explain all the radio silence. "I don't know if we fooled the Japanese," Richardson later wrote, "but we did fool at least one office in our Navy Department." Dyer actually did the tip-off to newsmen, as ordered by Stark. Richardson thought it received distribution, but the news pages imply otherwise. For once, the fleet had confused the public into pure speculation. When he listened to news broadcasts, Richardson realized even more that the Navy Department was out of step with the CNO. The Navy press officer said the fleet was still in Hawaii. And, in his defense, Richardson was not in the loop of information,[42] which was an understatement.

By broadcast one day, Richardson heard news that Stark had told newsmen if they wanted to know more about the fleet location, ask Welles. This alarmed Richardson; then he heard that Hull had no official information.

Somehow, Richardson found out that the Japanese consul at Honolulu reported to Tokyo about the seaward movement of the U.S. Fleet. The radio intercepters at Pearl Harbor reported that Tokyo issued long orders to the main Japanese Fleet and others. This information did help the analysts locate the Japanese ships at that moment. Richardson simply made the comment in his diary, "This monkey business may involve us in a war." At that time the Japanese Fleet was at Saipan, with eighteen cruisers, and a carrier at Palau practicing landing attacks.[43]

Stark sent a message saying that if Richardson could keep the U.S. Fleet's location a secret, then he was not to return until June 30. He did so. During this adventure, important news arrived. The Bureau of Navigation cut new orders, again authorizing Richardson's trip to Washington.[44]

Abruptly, the fleet began coming into Lahaina Roads at 8:00 A.M. on Sunday, June 30, and were anchored by 9:30. Dyer informed the newsman from the Associated Press that there was no sabotage at the Panama Canal, so the fleet had returned to Hawaii.[45] He read a Richardson statement.[46] Some reports thought the fleet had returned because of grave news from Hong Kong. Some writers thought the fleet had not gone beyond Hawaiian waters.[47] Behind the public scene, Richardson viewed the exercise as faulty because the fleet was only out six days. Normally it would be at least an eighteen-day trip to Panama and back. But, Washington was happy, and sent a message of "well done."[48]

As perhaps a reason, or merely a coincidence, while the fleet was out, Japan suddenly began to clamp down on traffic out of Hong Kong toward interior China. Some two thousand troops were moved into position to cut off the British colony. Evacuation of the city was underway. The U.S. Fleet went one way, but the Japanese went the other.[49] Perhaps *Orange* knew where the American Fleet was located, and felt comfortable to begin more aggression in its own region.[50] All non-Chinese women and children were told to leave Hong Kong on July 3. Some 1,600 arrived that day at Manila.

Congress and the various military departments were wide-eyed. The United States stepped up promotions for officers, eliminating the written portion of the Navy exam. It was announced that naval construction would hasten, and contracts for forty-nine warships would be issued, complementing the nineteen underway. Americans reading daily news reports were very aware that war was near.

Richardson put the flagship *Pennsylania* into dry dock to have her hull scraped and painted. The fleet would probably be in town for about two weeks. He read that day that the confirmation of Knox as secretary of the Navy had been approved.

In late July, in a meeting with the officers, Richardson explained that one of the purposes of the fleet movement toward the Panama Canal was to prepare everyone to learn the importance of secrecy. He told them he believed the administrative line, that the rumors were strong, that if the fleet went through the canal it would be sabotaged. If such people were preparing at that time to inflict harm upon the fleet, perhaps they would be apprehended. "It would have destroyed the purpose of the movement entirely had it been generally reported here that the Fleet had gone out to sea and would return in four or five days."[51] It is doubtful whether he really believed what he was telling his men, but the secrecy point was well taken. What Reeves had taught earlier was rubbing off on Richardson.

Marshall was not as forward with Herron and his men, nor was his reasoning the same. He told Herron:

You have no doubt wondered as to the alert instructions sent to you on the 17th. Briefly, the combination of information from a number of sources led to the deduction that recent Japanese-Russian agreement to compose their differences [in] the Far East was arrived at and so timed as to permit Japan to undertake a trans-Pacific raid against Oahu, following the departure of the U. S. Fleet from Hawaii. Presumably such a raid would be in the interest of Germany and Italy, to force the United States to pull the Fleet back to Hawaii. Whether the information or deductions were correct, I cannot say. Even if they were, the precautions you have taken may keep us from knowing they were by discouraging any overt act.[52]

Richardson returned to Hawaii where he observed that his "no wives" wish was basically no longer being heeded. Three days earlier Snyder's wife had come in on the SS *Monterey* from Los Angeles. His daughter, wife of Captain W. M. Collins, was with her. On the same voyage was the wife of Captain C. C. Baughman. However, Richardson would have expected no less of the families and understood their efforts to be together. He later told the officers that they were clearly within their rights to advise their family, but not to do so based upon secret information they had received which would jeopardize the fleet.[53] Then, he had to pack to travel to Washington. With luck, he would be with May for some time in the next two weeks.

CHAPTER SEVENTEEN

Great Persuader Versus Great Politician
At Least Richardson Had Hope

Murphy had the Bureau of Navigation reserve airplane seats on the California Clipper for a man named George Mandley and one named John McCleary. They left on Friday, July 5, at 2:30 P.M., on a plane damaged the week before when it landed on a coral at Midway.[1] Though it needed repair work done in San Francisco, it was deemed safe.[2] Mandley and McCleary, listed only as naval personnel with no rank given, arrived in Washington on Sunday after an exhausting trip.[3]

While the two travelers were flying "incognito" with a "gal and her husband," Roosevelt invoked the Export Control Act.[4] Taussig took some of the heat off Richardson that Saturday as he spoke at the Naval Institute's proceedings, saying that when the Japanese finished with China, the Philippines would be attacked next. He added that it would be cowardly for the United States not to go to the aid of the Philippines. "With the Dutch East Indies as bait for aggression . . . ," he continued, "we may be forced into a Far Eastern war willy-nilly." He warned that the Navy did not have sufficient ships for such a venture, and it could end in failure.[5]

In addition, the retired Yarnell wrote a United Press article that was printed across the nation on July 7. He condemned any accord between the United States and Japan.[6]

When Richardson and Murphy landed at Washington-Hoover Airport on the Potomac, they were greeted by Nimitz and Smedberg. Stark and Compton were out of town.[7] Rest was on the agenda before Richardson had a Monday lunch with Roosevelt. Though given no particular reason why, Richardson and Murphy had gone from Hawaii to Washington in complete secrecy. In fact, the *New York Times* and others thought that Richardson arrived on Monday, July 8.[8] The writer called it an "unheralded" flight by naval plane. The *Honolulu Advertiser* snooped around and determined that the pair left on Friday's Pan-American Clipper. The newspaper writers noticed the strange names of two naval officers, and surmised the plan.[9]

Rest was short for the pair. As soon as the doors to the Navy Department opened, Richardson and Murphy were there. During the early morning, Richardson spent his time talking with Stark and Nimitz. Both promised to produce adequate enlisted personnel plans.

Then, Richardson walked the short distance to the White House for the 1:00 P.M. luncheon.[10] The hour and a half was pleasant, and the thoughts of the CinCUS on personnel and inadequacies of the fleet were assured, somewhat, when the president said he had no foreseeable plans to send the fleet to the Far East.[11] Richardson stressed the need for more personnel, and made it plain that the fleet could not fight so far from its bases. He reminded the president that ships were being constructed faster than personnel could be trained to serve them. If war came, Roosevelt said he planned to draft or enlist men of mechanical trades.

Richardson added to what Roosevelt already knew, that a war with Japan would be long and expensive. But, it must have been difficult for Roosevelt to place much emphasis on the Pacific. The Atlantic and European events were far more overwhelming at the time.

Both the president and Richardson met with the press, and both insisted that the visit was to discuss routine matters, that it was normal for a CinCUS to return now and then to Washington. The pundits did not take this claim seriously, especially since several days earlier the writers had interviewed Leahy. He had told the scribes that the fleet's place right then was in the Atlantic and Caribbean. However, Richardson and Roosevelt said there was no plan to shift a part of the fleet from the Pacific.[12] Richardson explained that his visit was good timing, since most of the ships were in Pearl Harbor for upkeep.[13]

The evening was spent at Stark's home at the Naval Observatory, with Admiral and Mrs. Nimitz present. The men talked until nearly midnight. Statistics and desires were pitched around for all to sleep on.

On Tuesday, July 9, Richardson met with Hull and Welles, noting, "I fully stressed to them that the *Orange War Plan* was useless." Welles said that he felt there was little danger of attack at Hawaii, and his statements were partially backed by comments from Grew, though the ambassador was never directly asked about the fleet basing at Pearl Harbor in 1940. However, the two were diplomats with little feel for the logistics of island-hopping across the Pacific.[14] To Richardson, it seemed that Hull wanted to take a strong stand in response to each Japanese move. Welles was a bit more experienced, and was less inclined to this view. "I wanted to know what was back of this whole thing," Richardson testified in 1945, saying that he desired to understand why it was publicized that the CinCUS made the request for the fleet to say in Hawaiian waters.[15] "Hull gave me his view fully," Richardson wrote in his diary. However, Richardson got the impression that he had Welles in agreement with his side of the discussion, but not Hull.[16]

At mid-morning on July 10, Richardson saw Senator James Byrnes, a man the CinCUS thought wielded great political power over the size of the Navy. Again, Richardson stressed the case of more personnel.[17]

An interesting lunch with Marshall followed, and a deep conversation on the "alert" took up some of the time.[18] "Oh, that was simply an exercise," said Marshall, according to Richardson. "I thought if I did not state that it was an exercise, the exercise would be carried out more completely." So, maybe Richardson had guessed rightly.[19] However, Marshall did not mention what he later revealed to Congress—that the Army had "information . . . regarding diplomatic affairs."[20]

At 5:00 P.M., Richardson made a short call on Knox.[21] The next day the Battle of Britain began, as Germany launched a relentless aerial attack on that island nation. As a result, Richardson began to see where the view of Washington was focused—toward the plight of the British.

July 11 found Richardson finally with the source he believed most responsible for Roosevelt's tendency to keep the fleet at Hawaii. At 10:30 A.M., he and Hornbeck met for an hour and a half. In his diary, Richardson wrote, "He is a strongman on Far East, cause of our stay in Hawaii where he will hold us as long as he can."[22] It always miffed Richardson that Hornbeck was not called before the Congressional Pearl Harbor Hearings in 1945-46, for he felt that the Far East "expert" was full of answers about the fleet's repositioning.[23]

Hornbeck may have been a Richardson suspect in the fleet assignment question, but the two kept up study and correspondence on the situation not only into the fall, but also during World War II. Each would attempt to persuade the other of certain points. The discussions picked up as the fall of 1940 rolled around. Richardson naturally presented the problems of the fleet being in the Pacific, and Hornbeck countered with ideas that the fleet really did offer a deterrent.[24]

At noon, after the Hornbeck meeting, Richardson met a few minutes with the president.[25] Not even Richardson mentioned in his book this second meeting between the two, but it was not over lunch. He did tell General Counsel William D. Mitchell, in 1945 at the Congressional Hearings, that no subjects "of any moment" were discussed at this second meeting with Roosevelt.[26] Still, in notes taken from his diary, Richardson wrote that Roosevelt was an "extremely dangerous man fully determined to put us into war if G.B. [Great Britain] can hold out until he is re-elected."[27]

It was a whirlwind visit. At 6:00 P.M. Richardson and Murphy began the trip back from Washington to the Territory of Hawaii.[28] Stark dropped Bloch a note, adding at the end, "We thoroughly enjoyed having J.O.R. with us and I only wish he could have been around here longer." He said he hoped Richardson got something out of the visit.[29]

Five days were spent on the West Coast in business and pleasure, and seeing May for a short while.[30] Somewhere in this time period, Richardson called his sister Jessie, in Detroit, Texas. He alerted her that the meeting with Roosevelt had not gone well. She related some of what she was told to the Chambers family, and Lee Somerville's father called his son at college in Huntsville. The family always thought the July meeting did not go as smoothly as was recorded.[31]

By 5:00 P.M., Wednesday, July 16, "Mandley and McLeary" were off the ground at San Francisco. Richardson and Murphy were back with the fleet the next day at noon, settled near Maui.[32] The CinCUS hoped that he had accomplished his mission and desired to stress to the leadership the danger of keeping the fleet in

Richardson's sisters pose: Jessie, sitting, and Moss Richardson pose for a photo when together in Canyon, Texas. Moss taught English at West Texas State Teachers College for decades after leaving Paris. Jessie lived eighteen miles to the east of Paris, Texas, in Detroit until her husband died. She then lived for some time in Canyon. When visiting his sister in West Texas, Otto and Moss Richardson would travel to see cousins in Tulia. Moss never married. She donated her home and furnishings to the Methodist church there, but it was removed, replaced by a parking lot. (Photo from Elizabeth Wingo Banks Papers, Duncan, Oklahoma)

harm's way, while at the same time not bringing the complements up to date.[33] It particularly bothered Richardson that the sailors were not being psychologically prepared for war. On the contrary, they were continually being told the United States would not be involved, even though they were educated and could read the front pages each day. Even the fleet newspaper printed some of the European results now and then.

"I was told the Fleet would remain at Hawaii indefinitely, and to move out any necessary services," Richardson wrote later. His best summary of the problems he faced were expressed five years later before Congress, where he concluded, "To take the Fleet in and out of Pearl Harbor wasted time," not to mention other problems involved. But, he was told that all his fears as to personnel and billets were to be soothed and solved. "I came away with the impression . . . the President was fully determined to put the United States into the war." Richardson could understand that determination, but he did not appreciate the contrary talk from Roosevelt.

The fleet moved out of Pearl Harbor for an indefinite time on July 15, as Richardson was on the way back from the mainland. Seven days later, Richardson would temporarily lose the *Lexington,* which was heading back to Puget Sound for an overhaul.[34] He gained the battleship USS *Maryland,* which returned to Lahaina Roads from her repair and refit.

On the way back from Washington, DC, Richardson composed in his mind a letter to Stark. On July 20, three days later, he wrote a confidential note to his old friend and boss. He again stated that he felt the exchange of views among the Departments of State, War, and Navy were not strong enough. Again, he said the State Department was in charge of the fleet's position. He suggested how it should have been done. He expressed the fear that as war came near, the contact between the Army, the Navy, and the president was not close enough. Being an "outsider," visiting after a year's assignment outside of the capital, and interviewing with all those involved, he could see the various paths being taken by each, and they were not on the same page, he thought.[35]

He added that despite the assurances from Stark and Nimitz,

it did not seem that Roosevelt and Byrnes were on the same thought pattern. This was one of Richardson's better letters, well organized and not personally critical of anyone. However, he never sent it! On July 26, Roosevelt sealed any further possibility of an amicable settlement with Japan when he placed aviation gasoline and certain classes of scrap iron on the control list.[36]

Japanese Navy Captain Yuzuru Okuma lashed out in the newspapers, saying that if the United States continued along such lines she was certain to cause international repercussions.[37] The political portion of the leadership was intent on war with Japan, Richardson thought, but was not preparing the military or the people for this contingency. Roosevelt may have misjudged the hardship he placed upon U.S. companies dealing with China and Japan. A loud cry came from Far East American businessmen when they found that the embargo actually cost them their businesses.[38]

The people of Hawaii could see the seriousness of the expenditures coming their way since the fleet had arrived three months earlier. Construction and transformation of housing was everywhere, even at the Maui airport at Wailuku. More than two hundred officers and men were to be calling it home soon. Those on the incoming SS *Lurline* got a thrill and a dose of what was happening when they came in on July 24. The bulk of the fleet showed up at the same time off Honolulu Harbor, in from a trip across the equator.[39] One of the carriers sent her turret guns into action, startling the liner passengers. To the sailors' enjoyment, the *Lurline* carried 4,705 bags of mail.

The fleet arrival was not a surprise. Spies and others could more than figure that the fleet was coming in soon, for the newspaper pointed out that Mrs. Taffinder and her two daughters were arriving Wednesday on the SS *Matsonia*.[40] Much of the fleet came into Honolulu for liberty on Thursday. The Scouting Force was mostly still at sea, but there was plenty to enliven the town for three days.[41] The enlisted men told a newspaper writer that the islands were tops for nature attractions, but nightlife was "deadly and dull." There were not enough nice girls, they claimed, so the only things to do were drink and see movies. Roomy dance halls were needed, they said, and maybe an amusement area with rides, concessions, and "stuff." No one mentioned the women on Hotel Street! The males were young, energetic, lonely, and wanting for recreation. Their admiral knew it.[42] It was also extremely hot, and very humid even for Hawaii.

On July 31, Richardson received an airmail letter from Stark. It discussed an embargo on high-octane gas, still being sold to the Japanese, and other items. Richardson noted, "In my opinion, we seem intent on war with Japan unless she backs down, but [at the same time] the [American] people are not being prepared nor the men provided."[43] He planned to do his part to call attention to that dangerous situation.

On August 3, Richardson assembled all the squadron, division, and commanding ship and unit officers, and the admirals, for a morning meeting at the Submarine Base Theater at Pearl Harbor. He gave a long, but well-organized speech, summarizing his trip to Washington, DC, and what he had learned. He stressed that what he said was not for general dissemination among anyone other than the men of the Navy. He explained the personnel items, and told the men they would begin to accept into the Navy aviators from other sources than the Naval Academy. "I found that everybody in Washington was not as concerned about enlisted personnel as I am. I hope that everybody . . . is more concerned about it now," he said to the crowd.

He threw out statistics about the growing Navy, and he warned of the probability of training draftees and permanent Navy side by side. About the training, he expressed probably the most profound and farsighted idea he had mentioned to that date. "It is essential . . . that every one of these men leave the service with a kindly feeling towards the Navy," for a very important reason. "Many of them may be influential later in national affairs, and it would be unfortunate for the Navy if they were embittered with their short experience in it."

He stressed that the officers should be cheerful, and work hard, and that their attitude and actions would filter down to the men. He knew the enlisted men were becoming restless, and those with wives and family far away were lonesome. He was aware that some families were finding permanent abodes on the islands.[44] He then became critical of his officers, saying that too many times they were reluctant to instill disciplinary action. "No leader that is so chicken-hearted that he fails to take appropriate disciplinary action through fear of hurting an officer's records can be expected to direct operations in war that will surely result in loss of life."

He referred to what he had observed. Many times officers moved a disciplinary problem to the USS *Relief* for fear the sailor would commit suicide. "We are in a profession where many people are going to be killed. Why not do your own job and why try to wish upon the USS *Relief* a job that she is not prepared to do?" The room was quiet. He chastised those who shipped problems ashore for courts martial. "You cannot have discipline until you do your part to maintain it."

He added that he was not "crying war," but that if the fleet did not prepare, "we may be sorry. If we do get ready and we have no war, we will not have wasted one stroke of work." This time he made a mistake. He mailed the speech to Stark, who was not happy with the personnel statements. He too had worked hard and felt that Richardson still did not understand the impossibilities of some of his desires.[45]

Young at the time, Lieutenant Commander Raymond D. Tarbuck, Commander of the USS *Worden,* said that he and others got the message, "that the pot was boiling—something was going to happen." He got from Richardson's speech that Roosevelt had turned down all requests, from more personnel to allowing the battleships to return to the West Coast. "Of course, when Pearl Harbor was attacked, it didn't sound too well for President Roosevelt, in our minds."[46]

In an August 6 detailed letter to Nimitz, Richardson expressed his concern about what the public was being told and what the figures actually were. In mid-July, Senator Walsh made a statement placed in the *Congressional Record* that said the Navy had ample supply of enlisted personnel for the next fiscal year. Richardson wanted Nimitz to point out to Congress, soon, that the 170,000 number for 1941 was inadequate to supply the ships in commission already, much less for those new ships under construction. "Every force and type commander in the U.S. Fleet . . . have brought to my attention the inadequate numbers of enlisted personnel now available," he wrote. He went on to give advice as to what Nimitz should tell the president and Congress. Nimitz sent the entire letter to Callaghan, who made sure Roosevelt had it on his desk to read.

Despite his efforts, fleet morale began to wane quickly as sailors realized that the gap between Hawaii and home would not narrow any time soon. Only 10 percent of the enlisted men who were married had their wives in Honolulu. While it seemed higher, officers with wives there only numbered at that time about 45 percent. As Richardson explained to Congress in 1945, "Americans are perfectly willing to go anywhere, stay anywhere, do anything when there is a job . . . and they can see a reason for their being there, but to keep the Fleet, during what the men considered normal peacetimes, away from the coast and away from their families, away from recreation, rendered it difficult to maintain a high state of morale that is essential to successful training."[47]

Hot or not, bad news or not, May Richardson returned for an "indefinite" time to be with her husband. On the *Lurline,* she traveled the first week in August to Hawaii with such "famous" people as opera star Lily Pons and Hollywood producer Jack Warner, who most likely knew the Richardsons' son, Joe.[48] May and Warner were interviewed and photographed separately for the "Port and Off Port" column in the *Honolulu Advertiser.* May was categorized as both an "islander" and a "comebacker" by the newspaper writers.

The scorching Hawaiian temperatures of July continued to break records into August, the hottest period of time in fifty-one years. It was nothing like Jim and May had experienced while growing up in northeast Texas, where not only would the temperature soar between 100 and 110 in the late summer, but where at times it was very humid. In Texas, there often were no winds to keep collars from wilting.[49] Still, by Hawaiian standards, the heat was uncomfortable for everyone.

On Friday, August 11, the USS *Tennessee* joined the fleet in Pearl Harbor, in from the West Coast. It was surmised that the USS *Pennsylvania* would leave in twenty days for work and over-haul at Puget Sound in Bremerton, Washington. It was thought that Richardson would move his flag to the newly arrived battle-ship.[50] Shore leave was also granted those on the *Yorktown* and the twenty-five cruisers floating in Lahaina Roads for that Sunday afternoon, and some of the next two weeks. May and the admiral would have plenty of time to "house" shop and visit with friends and associates. The newspaper again ran the photo of May print-ed in early May before she left for Long Beach. It was much more flattering than the one taken when she stepped on shore from the *Lurline* four days earlier.[51]

More than ever, secrecy surrounded the fleet movements. The newspapers would only discover tidbits of information about the location of various types of ships, but they still printed what was known from conversations and the few press releases. What the press did know was that Asiatic Fleet Commander Hart was in Shanghai predicting that a showdown would come between Japan and the United States over defense in that international city.[52] It was proposed that Marines patrol the seven-block Bund business water-front. With the fall of France and the hold on China by the Japanese, it was not likely that a U.S. Marine presence would matter.

According to letters between Herron and Marshall, Hawaiian coordination and a working relationship between the Army and Navy was smooth. "Rich [Joe Richardson] is the salt of the earth, and I am devoted to him," Herron wrote, adding that Bloch was "never narrow minded or stupid."[53]

On board the USS *Pennsylvania*, writers for *The Keystone* reminded the crew that it was sporting season, that Uncle Sam was supplying free guns and ammunition, and that there was even a "lovely bonus for men who can best keep the cross-hairs on. What could be sweeter?"[54] The print shop was busy preparing and taking orders for a booklet called *Crossing the Line*, an album depicting a recent trip across the equator. In addition, that day Richardson issued general security orders in the Fleet Letter 31-

40, which ironically was still on the books until 1942.[55]

Richardson planned intensive training until October 1, and he also noted that Knox was taking a trip to visit every naval base and facility possible.[56] He would be in Hawaii in mid-September, more than likely. The fleet, however, would come back to Pearl Harbor for the weekends. There were always what seemed to be an unusual number of ships going to Puget Sound now and then for repairs and normal maintenance.[57] It was highly probable that Richardson used the decision-making latitudes granted to him by Stark to get his men back to the West Coast as often as possible.

Accidents, always a part of realistic training, continued to happen.[58] The sailors did take note of the permanency of their assignment when the floating dry dock came in from New Orleans on August 23. It had left for the 6,100-mile voyage on March 18. Naval authorities allowed no photographs of it.[59]

Bloch reported to Stark that a housing project had poured some of its foundations, and a subterranean oil storage facility was progressing. But, it was two to three months away from full construction. The arrival of more than 1,000 civilian workmen was "quite a jolt," thought Bloch. It was hard to find housing, and finances were awkward. Three Greek ships were anchored with scrap iron bound for Japan. Bloch was told that six to eight more were coming in. He mentioned the possibility that they would be sunk in a surprise raid and cause major problems. "I wonder," he asked Stark, "if somebody can't get them sent somewhere else?"[60]

Weekend liberty for the celebration of Labor Day brought the fleet to Honolulu beginning on Friday, August 30. The crews would "blow it out" for three days, and then go to sea again until September 16. Richardson did not transfer to the USS *Tennessee*, but rather on August 31 to the USS *Enterprise* for the time being.[61] A large cage within his cabin was constructed for Richardson, to be used as an office.[62] The ship's exective commander, John L. McCrea, managed the transfer of records.[63]

James D. Ramage was an aviator on the carrier, just a year out of the Naval Academy. "Well, it was hate at first sight," he said. "It was a big staff . . . must have had 60 or 70 people. They immediately took over everything."[64] Captain Pownall, commander of the *Enterprise,* knew Richardson. He was on the USS *Huron* when it assisted Americans, including May and Joe Richardson, to safety after the Japan earthquake in 1923. "I kept a box of cigars for Richardson in my own cabin," Pownall said.

Ramage explained that the junior officers were housed in the wardroom with the young fliers. "We just got along like cats and dogs," he humorously told the interviewer.

Other than overhaul, it was probably time for the *Pennsylvania* to return to the West Coast for the sanity of the sailors. Though no written report is extant, it seems there were rumors enough about discourtesy to officers by enlisted men to warrant a Richardson note to his units. Dyer investigated and submitted a report to Richardson, and then drafted a letter on August 20, 1940, to distribute.

Apparently, at a ship movie, some malcontent was mouthing at officers present. Richardson wrote that the rumors had no foundation in fact. "The conduct of the PENNSYLVANIA has been exemplary at all times," he flatly stated. He blamed the persistence of the rumors on a subversive element in the Hawaiian area. He labeled it as just malicious gossip. He asked everyone to report the sources of such rumors.[65]

These gripes made a slow journey to a Drew Pearson and Robert Allen column almost a year later, on June 21, 1941. When he first became aware of the circulating story, Richardson immediately dropped a letter of detail and denial to Knox. He explained that in July of 1940, a story circulated that problems had arisen during movie scenes when Long Beach and Los Angeles came upon the screen. Sailors were said to have become rambunctious, yelling and creating disorder. They were said to have even thrown benches overboard, and hooted at the chief of staff. Richardson continued his note to Knox, saying, "No incident could have occurred of the character alleged without its having been brought to my attention. I made every effort to ascertain how this story was started, but was never able to find its source." No one on board could even remember such a movie being shown.

Officers and sailors, Richardson said, resented this malicious rumor. He wrote also that when they were repeated to petty officers on shore, a couple of them became involved in a fight for the reputation of the ship. Knox dropped a line to Richardson via the General Board, where he was assigned at that time. Knox felt that the column writers had a reputation for unreliability, and that he had no plans to follow up on the issue.[66]

Though numerous interviews have not uncovered substantial proof of wide discontent, hints now and then indicate that those with families back on the West Coast were going through a definite hardship. A good example was Jim Vlach and his wife Jeanne. He was luckier than most of the sailors stuck in Hawaii, however, for after six months near Pearl Harbor, the ship went back to the West Coast for a brief time. The couple enjoyed two weeks at San Pedro. Then she followed him to Bremerton. Finally, well into 1941, the couple decided that Jeanne should come out to Honolulu. The cost they would bear.[67] He says that though some came in the early summer, most wives of enlisted men did not move out in great numbers until after September of 1941. Housing was still scarce then.

Kleber S. Masterson's wife Charlotte always made a concentrated effort to follow her husband. Like Vlach, he was on the USS *Arizona*. She packed up their two boys and arrived in Honolulu on the *Matsonia* on April 24, 1940, for a ten-day stay. But, the fleet was out. She stayed, and the couple found some times to be together between training exercises. When the *Arizona* returned to the West Coast six months later, she came back long enough to turn in the rental house there, store the furniture, and head back across the Pacific. Even for a higher-ranking graduate of the Naval Academy, this move was expensive. "Charlotte and I lived all over Hawaii for a year and a half," Masterson explained. "She was one of the few wives out there . . . rents were high." He added that since the fleet was on TDY (temporary duty), the government paid no moving expenses.

"We'd rent a house in Honolulu, then the USS *Arizona* would go out on maneuvers and end up at Lahaina Roads," he continued.

Richardson, however, had warned everyone of the hardships. Charlotte and the boys more than once came over to the Grand Hotel on Maui to see Masterson. "Many times I was the only officer leaving the USS *Arizona* to go ashore at night, because there wasn't another thing to do on the island unless you could see your family."[68]

Masterson pointed out that the alerts were only treated as cries of "wolf" by many of the officers and crews. "You can't just keep anyone on alert—especially when most of them can't be with their families—for two years without paying the price." He always assumed that Richardson was later relieved of his positon as CinCUS for political reasons; for it was not that the fleet was unprepared. "We were really well trained," he said. But, he also added that the old antiaircraft equipment was terrible. "We couldn't hit the side of a barn," he said. New equipment was coming, but in reality, as he stated, the fleet was more afraid of submarine torpedoes.

Bernard Max Strean, a native of Big Cabin, Oklahoma, not too far north of Paris, Texas, agreed. "We were thinking about war all the time. The same warning was always: 'beware of wide-spread sabotage and such things as that.'" He added in an oral interview, "I think that what happened [in 1941] is that they cried wolf just too long and too often."[69] Finding the cost of living in Pearl Harbor "a little beyond me," he was fortunate enough to gain assignment in December of 1940 as instructor at Jacksonville Naval Air Station, and was not a part of the Pearl Harbor attack.

After the Fleet Problem, the members of Felix L. Johnson's USS *Lang* went back to the West Coast as an escort for the USS *Philadelphia*, which was headed to Bremerton for overhaul. Johnson thought the destroyer was sent alongside the cruiser for protection. "They were a bit nervous in those days about sending off their cruisers alone," he mentioned. The *Lang* then returned to the San Diego/San Pedro area for coast duty.[70]

The crew of the USS *Balch* was also "fortunate." Their ship left the Fleet Problem XXI exercises in the late spring of 1940 to undergo work at Mare Island Navy Yard. After that time, like many other ships, she made alternate trips back and forth from the West Coast to Hawaii.[71]

The USS *Altair* was sent to Hawaii in March of 1940 to service the destroyers of the Hawaiian Detachment; thus its crew was more settled than others. They could bring out family and be assured that the ship would be based there for some time. However, the permanent assignments away from the West Coast, in addition to the fleet being held at Hawaii, caused quite a stir and congested the Pearl Harbor area to a great extent.[72]

The destroyer USS *Wilson* guarded the carrier *Saratoga* out to Hawaii for the Fleet Problem, arriving off Lahaina Roads on April 10. She then worked with the *Lexington* during the exercises. After the orders to stay, she operated off Honolulu, but the crew was fortunate that she returned to the Puget Sound Navy Yard for a brief overhaul in late May. She then operated near San Diego beginning on June 28. However, she almost immediately began escorting the battleship USS *Maryland* to Hawaii, arriving there on July 12. Any visits with family by that crew were short-lived. She remained in Hawaii, conducting tactical operations in the nearby waters, until late November. The *Wilson* left for San Diego on December 2, spent Christmas there, and then went a few miles to San Pedro's Bethlehem Steel Company's yard for an overhaul. As Richardson was later detached from Hawaii, the *Wilson* returned in late January of 1941.[73]

Members of the crew on the USS *Shaw* were not happy about the change in assignment either. Eventually, those who could afford to bring out families made arrangements. For those who could not fetch loved ones, November brought some excitement when they were told the ship was returning to the West Coast for overhaul. For those who still had wives and children on the mainland, this was a nice reunion. For those who had their families moved to Honolulu, it was again a long two and half months of isolation.

Honolulu was accessible only with a liberty pass. Life there was maddening for sailors. Captain Forrest Biard said he more than once saw lines of men in front of brothels. "They were told that because the action would be so quick, not to even take off their shoes!" he said in 2002 at the age of ninety from his home in Dallas, Texas.[74] Films of the lines indicated that business was brisk, even in the daytime.[75]

The streets were full of shore patrol sailors, and the Hawaiian citizens were not happy with the quick influx of so many personnel. In some cases, the ship captains assisted. The commander of the USS *Shaw* eventually followed suit of the commander of the USS *Case*, hiring a flatbed truck to carry the sailors away from the bustle of town to beach houses on the far, windward side of the island.[76] Members of the *Case* received thirty-day leaves when the ship went to Mare Island Naval Shipyard for three months of overhaul.

One dread for all officers was a congressional "inquiry" into a complaint by a constituent. Some sailors became frustrated with life in and near Hawaii, and would write their representatives.[77] With wages of twenty-one dollars per month for a seaman, not much social life was possible when liberty was granted. An ensign made $1,500 a year.

The USS *Case* made a cruise to Midway, Johnston Island, and Palmyra Island during late July of 1940. Richardson wanted it to survey the anchorages and facilities of these islands for possible military bases. The USS *Saury* was a part of this exercise. Her crew returned to the West Coast in September for a ship overhaul at Mare Island.

Family separations were becoming a large problem, one that Richardson was attempting to solve with his idea of sending back groups of ships. He announced on August 16 that commencing about October 1, groups would visit the West Coast bases for two-week leaves with full liberty periods. All but Submarine Squadron 4 and some mine craft were scheduled to make the trip. Some vessels, like the USS *Pensacola*, had been away from the West Coast since October of 1939.[78]

In Washington, Stimson was adamant about the placement of the fleet at Hawaii. This had been his aim since Japan's invasion of Shanghai in January of 1932.[79] Japanese ambassador to the United States, Katsuji Debuchi, protested about the large numbers of ships in the Pacific. Stimson simply said that the reasons were obvious to the ambassador. In addition, the Navy found resistance to its expansion plan in San Pedro's Outer Harbor. The argument with the city commissioners over use of the entire Outer Harbor, south of 22nd Street, drug on from 1939 into 1940. This argument and crusty stance by San Pedro may have hastened the decision to send more funding to Pearl Harbor.

Congressman Lee E. Geyer sensed that the disagreement was near to a disaster for San Pedro, and wrote Los Angeles Mayor Fletcher Bowron. A strong proponent of the naval expansion, Congressman Geyer said, "Unless the Navy can purchase Pier One at a low figure" San Pedro would lose the fleet and all the harbor improvements to Long Beach. To the surprise of both Geyer and Bowron, not only Long Beach but the entire West Coast lost when the fleet permanently, and so quickly, moved its operations to Hawaii.[80]

After terminating a problem involving Admiral Forde A. Todd, which eventually brought H. Kent Hewitt to Hawaii, CinCUS efforts turned to the fleet again. Richardson may or may not have been aware of the various factors in the decision to keep the fleet away from the West Coast. He was aware, however, that Admiral Ghormley was not coming out to the fleet to be Commander Cruiser Division 9. Formerly the director of the Navy War Plans Division and assistant to Stark, Ghormley had already chosen his flag lieutenant to work with in the fleet when the president ordered him to London to serve as Special Naval Observer.[81] His war plans expertise would have assisted the fleet's efforts. Richardson did know he was not receiving enough background from Stark to understand some of the reasons for the decisions being made, but he did assume heavily that Stimson and others were very much in control of everything that involved the Navy.

This situation disturbed Richardson almost to the point of resignation. He wrote in his daily notes that he was "uncertain as whether or not I should remain in command under existing conditions." At that point in his long naval career, all the years of preparation for CinCUS seemed to be unraveling.[82]

He was about to meet with one of the powerful forces that would continue to be in the mix of decisions on the fleet's location and movements.

CHAPTER EIGHTEEN

New Secretary Inspects Fleet
Richardson's Attempt to Educate Flops

Not often did a CinCUS have the duty of escorting two secretaries of the Navy through maneuvers in the span of just six months. Nevertheless, Richardson welcomed the visit by Knox and his mentor, William J. "Wild Bill" Donovan, the future director of the Office of Strategic Services (OSS), forerunner to the Central Intelligence Agency (CIA). Knox called Donovan in Wyoming, insisting that he meet the party at Treasure Island in San Francisco. Donovan was reeling from the tragic death of his daughter in a Virginia car accident, and needed to stay busy. Plus, it was a good chance for him to get to know the fleet admirals.[1] Captain Deyo, then naval aide to Knox instead of King, was coming back. John O'Keefe, special assistant to Knox, would be part of the group.[2] With them was also Captain Charles M. "Savvy" Cooke.[3]

The officers of the fleet were skittish about what they were to meet in Knox. Bieri said that just before he came out to the islands, Knox gave a speech on the mainland, saying rather roughly that he challenged the Japanese to cause trouble. In the speech, Bieri was of the understanding that Knox said, "Just let the Japs start anything, if they feel like it. We'll knock their ears back so quickly that they won't know what happened to them," or words to that effect, added Bieri.[4]

Therefore, Richardson welcomed the visit as a chance to get to know Knox better, to explain the fleet's limitations. "All too frequently they forget that the reason for the existence of the Navy Department is to assist in ensuring that the Fleet is ready," Richardson wrote years later about the visit.[5]

Richardson and Knox should have easily been friends, or at least pipe-smoking buddies.[6] Even for a military mind, it was simple to guess that Roosevelt would win the third or "emergency" term in the next election.[7] The two could work together for some time.

*Photo of Knox personally signed to Admiral Kimmel: Newspaperman Frank J.
Knox took over as secretary of Navy in July 1940. Richardson met him that
week while in Washington, DC, and two months later when Knox came to
visit the fleet. Though Knox irritated the senior officers, Richardson, Stark,
and Kimmel all thought he was a favorable secretary. Knox thought the leaders of the Navy were not war-minded enough. Despite their disagreements,
Knox and Richardson worked on several small projects from 1941 to 1944.
The secretary died of a heart attack, but his replacement, James V. Forrestal,
kept Richardson busy through 1946.* (From the Papers of Tom Kimmel, Jr.,
grandson of Husband E. Kimmel)

A PBY took the Knox group from the Golden Gate to Hawaii. It was so heavily loaded with fuel, it barely cleared the San Francisco Bridge. This was the first such flight for the new plane. It was cold in the cabin, but when a crewman attempted to fix the heating system, a fire broke out. Once the flames were doused with an extinguisher, everyone on board was safe.[8]

Part of the fleet, after enjoying the holiday, moved out to Lahaina Roads beginning early Tuesday. Others went southward of Oahu, and some toward Barbers Point.[9] Halsey took Army General Maxwell Murray on the USS *Lexington* to observe a day of operations.[10] Marines prepared for a nineteen-gun salute as Knox exited his plane.

On Friday, September 6, Knox arrived at Naval Air Station, Pearl Harbor at 5:32 in the afternoon. The travelers said they saw almost all the guard ships along the way. Knox arrived in Admiral Arthur B. Cook's Consolidated "bomber" in good time.[11] Public information said he was late because of bad weather.[12] Knox and Richardson posed for a photograph, with Knox appearing pretty silly in his aviation gear. Richardson took him into the Fourteenth Naval District offices to meet General Herron; General William H. Wilson, commander of the Hawaiian Army Division; and Admiral Marquart. Mayor Crane was present, along with several other dignitaries.

Eddy and Richardson had dinner with Knox at the Royal Hawaiian Hotel. After a night's rest, Knox met Saturday morning with Governor Poindexter, then with Bloch and other naval officials of the district. A noon luncheon was held for him by the Chamber of Commerce at the Royal Hawaiian, following about the same ceremonies offered Edison earlier. That afternoon Knox and Bloch toured the Kaneohe Naval Air Station, which was in the building stages.

The secretary pleased the press with his outspoken comments about the conscription bill and other wartime subjects.[13] He expounded at length on studies he and Donovan had done recently on Nazi subversive movements in the States.

Sunday morning, Richardson took Knox to the *Enterprise* for a day's tour and evening dinner while anchored in Lahaina.[14] Richardson thought that Knox was "intensely" interested, and gained insight from talking with the flag officers present. Standing before them in a reception room, Knox told the officers he was strongly in favor of the destroyers for British bases deal in the making.[15] In conversation, Knox told the officers that war would be upon them before March of 1941, even though the daily news noted that twenty Japanese warships were anchored off Do Son, south of Haiphong, Indo-China.[16] Richardson knew this was not what the secretary nor the administration was telling the public, and did not approve. However, the public could read, and should have been well informed each day by the headlines and stories being published in the media.[17]

Richardson had written his own thoughts three days earlier in his diary. He surmised that Great Britain desired the destroyers as evidence that the United States would form an alliance against the Axis Powers. He added, fretfully, "We are likely to follow the road trod by France because our people are not informed and united."[18] He was referring to the way the French government glazed over what was actually happening, both on the ground and diplomatically.

On September 9, the *Enterprise* and the rest of the fleet embarked for a sample exercise with Knox and Donovan on board. The Navy laid down a busy schedule for the visitors, shifting them to other ships, large and small.[19] Planes took off and landed on the carrier twice. The fleet demonstrated submarine attacks, and worked even into the evening with simulated destroyer attacks. In one night exercise, Knox became the first secretary of the Navy to be "sunk." He was aboard the destroyer USS *Clark* when it and a flotilla tried to attack the main body. The drill went awry when the guns of the big ships "hit" several of the attackers. That evening Knox and Richardson discussed at length the subjects of personnel and six-year enlistments.[20]

The next day, adding to the reality of the exercises, Knox and each of his party took off individually in four aircraft from the *Enterprise,* with Donovan unprepared for the gusts of wind. He lost his wallet, watch, and four hundred dollars when his coat blew out of the cockpit.[21] Knox said the takeoff and hundred-mile trip back to Pearl Harbor for him was so smooth he did not know when the plane left the deck. The fleet gave the secretary a nineteen-gun salute while he was above looking down upon the impressive sight.[22] He saw Kaneohe and Oahu before landing. Donovan looked ahead and commented, "If we can do this, the Japs can do it too!"[23]

"I made a real effort to see that Secretary Knox had the opportunity to talk to all the Flag officers in the Fleet," wrote Richardson. After all, one-fourth of the eighty admirals of the line were in Hawaii. Richardson especially made sure Knox had time to talk with Snyder, Andrews, Kimmel, and Commander T. H. Binford, a young officer whom Richardson held in high regard.[24] For four days, the fleet hosted and performed for Knox, returning him to Pearl Harbor on September 13. By that time he was filled with Richardson's thoughts and fears that the fleet was not prepared for a quick decision to go to war.

Before he left Hawaii, Knox inspected more shore facilities, including the Army's Schofield Barracks.[25] Knox spoke before a huge Chamber of Commerce crowd on Saturday, September 14, with all the admirals present. He stressed the fear of sabotage as a danger across the nation, not only to the fleet or Army bases. Richardson noted that the secretary made an excellent speech. His feelings toward Knox were warming up considerably.

A reception for Knox was held on Saturday night in Honolulu, but one admiral did not make that event. Fletcher was in a car wreck, but emerged unscathed. Not so lucky in that same pileup was Commander Harvey E. Overesch who was too badly injured to continue to the party. That day had also seen a key change of command on the USS *Astoria*. Captain Kelly Turner was going to Washington to become Director of War Plans for Stark.[26]

On Sunday morning, Knox went aboard the submarine *Sea Dragon*, christened by May Richardson in April 1939, for a short dive. Richardson and Knox even played golf together that day, along with Bloch and Andrews. "My game is terrible," Richardson noted, not saying that his time on the course was fairly limited.[27] Knox lifted off at 4:00 P.M. It was a cram-packed visit for him, and one that the Navy was relieved to finish.[28]

Bieri said he understood that one session between Richardson and Knox was quite "stormy." At the dinner Knox held for only the younger flag officers—he did not invite Richardson or Pye— Knox told them he found a lack of fighting spirit in the Navy. He also told the group, according to Bieri, "What the Navy needed more than anything else was younger officers in charge of the Fleet, and in positions of responsibility." Bieri concluded that there was a serious clash between Knox and Richardson.[29]

On September 14, Richardson prepared a six-page memo on the various points that had been discussed during the secretary's visit, giving it to Knox the next day as he departed.[30] In it he stressed that if factors other than purely naval matters were influencing the decision about the placement of the fleet, it would be proper to include Navy input, especially of the readiness of the fleet at that time. He feared the State Department was still of the opinion the fleet was mobilized and could embark on a campaign directly from Hawaii. He pointed out that training at Lahaina Roads was perilous. After all, the fleet was 2,000 miles closer to enemy submarines than it would be if it were positioned on the West Coast.[31]

However, Richardson knew he was not getting his points across, nor winning the discussions. Knox mentioned that the president had no funds to completely ready the fleet with requested personnel. Richardson simply pointed out that a huge base in Jacksonville, Florida, was being constructed at the president's order, and that more personnel could be enlisted without even legislative approval.

Later, Richardson talked with his officers, and his friends. They related that they understood Knox to say that Richardson put undue stress on the personnel issue. Knox later told other Richardson friends that the fleet lacked "war-mindedness." Bloch echoed to Richardson these comments from Knox. In Bloch, however, Richardson may have not had as much of a like-minded friend as he thought. Being close to fleet happenings, the former CinCUS did not take kindly to the "Johnnies-come-lately" who assumed control when he stepped down earlier in the year. Curts remarked years later that Bloch "kept a rather jealous eye on the situation in the Pacific Fleet." Bloch, who according to later letters was a true friend with Richardson, was so far behind that he was still of the mind-set that ordnance was much more important than naval aviation.[32]

Strangely, Knox even told others that Richardson was too social-minded. It was stated so after Bloch and Richardson held a reception for Knox and Donovan. Richardson was simply trying to relax the participants, and let the new-to-the-Navy secretary get to know the leaders. He did nothing more than was normal in the military.[33] Knox later wrote Ghormley, "There was too little appreciation of how near war was in the Fleet, as I found it."[34] How ironic. Correspondence back and forth from Stark and Richardson gave the opposite impression, stressing that the administration did not understand the seriousness of disallowing the fleet to prepare for war.

Donovan commented, "I . . . never knew there were so many admirals in our country!"[35] Still, Richardson's efforts soaked into Knox more than Richardson realized. After arriving in Washington, Knox almost immediately took a tour of Army training in Louisiana. After this tour, he voiced the opinion, "We are not equipped to go to war."[36] He became very outspoken to very influential people, backing up much of what Richardson had conveyed to him.

On the other hand, it would take a bit longer to bring the secretary further around. Knox, in Richardson's view, did not take full advantage of the chance to meet so many officers at one gathering. Knox viewed such a social assembly as proof the fleet did not have war-readiness on its mind. Later called "Mr. Right-Winger" by the press, Knox more than likely took offense to the Richardson memorandum, especially the part that almost challenged him and the administration to plan out what was to come.[37]

Richardson sent a copy of the memo to Stark, and even one to

Hornbeck. He stressed that telling the public that the fleet was ready was not proper, and that it was dangerous to lull the public to sleep thinking they were safe. While Richardson was dealing with this issue, much of the fleet came into Pearl Harbor on Friday, September 13, for two weeks of upkeep.

Richardson was most displeased that Knox did not immediately send him a personal letter about the visit. Aide Deyo penned a canned message, and wrote to others.[38] Knox did send a note to Bloch afterward.[39] Stark explained it to Richardson, saying that he was sorry, but that normally that duty fell to an aide.[40] That was not the case in Richardson's world, however.

Stark knew it to be true, apparently hinting to the secretary, and the next day Knox penned a long letter to Richardson. He expressed his deep appreciation for the "painstaking efforts" to make the visit for the secretary and his entourage enjoyable. He especially thanked Lieutenant Eddy for his contributions, and sent word through Richardson to tell May thanks for the gracious hospitality she showed him at the Richardson's Black Point home. He invited the Richardsons to dine someday at the Knox house in Washington. It was late, but with the prodding of Stark, Knox perhaps learned that personal notes were very helpful.[41]

Knox apparently did let one specific comment from Richardson stick with him. "I told him the President had two hobbies—stamp collecting and playing with the Navy," Richardson wrote in the mid-1950s. From his personal experience he knew how Roosevelt operated. The president would send for a subordinate officer, and talk with him about official Navy business. He would not go through the secretary of the Navy first. Richardson had experienced this behavior many times, when he was budget officer, assistant chief of Naval Operations, and chief of the Bureau of Navigation. He told Knox that personally, he always reported back to the secretary, but that not everyone did so. Frequently, the secretaries learned of news long after their subordinates did. News filtered back to Richardson later that after returning to Washington, Knox issued an order "providing that the procedures [Knox] had followed be compulsory in all cases of Presidential beckoning."[42]

Richardson was fighting a losing battle. He had tried to change the mind of a man who just six months earlier had written in his newspaper, "It is simply unthinkable that we will ever again send overseas a great expeditionary force of armed men."[43] He would be the same man who said on December 4, 1941, "No matter what happens, the U.S. Navy is not going to be caught napping."

Richardson was not getting his "get ready" message across to his fleet, nor to his bosses.

CHAPTER NINETEEN

Time to Visit Washington Again
Fleet Begins Rotations Home

Almost the moment Knox flew off the deck of the *Enterprise,* the fleet began preparation to visit the West Coast in shifts. On September 17, about thirty ships were busy, preparing to head for San Diego to begin the three waves of liberty worked out by Richardson and his staff.[1] The newspaper said that Richardson was on board the *Enterprise* with the rest of the fleet that put out to sea the same day for maneuvers. Actually, Richardson shifted to the USS *New Mexico.*[2] The USS *California* was back from West Coast repairs, so Pye moved his flag over to it from the *New Mexico.* He and Richardson planned to assume a "normal" schedule.

Knox had mentioned during his visit that he wanted Richardson to come to Washington in early October, maybe when he arrived with the sailors for their West Coast liberty. Richardson had planned to be with the first wave, but stayed back for a couple of days.

Richardson quickly wrote Stark and expressed surprise at another Washington trip, and said he had nothing to take up with the State Department, or others, adding, "I do not know of any benefit to the Navy that would accrue from my coming to Washington."[3] He thought that response would end the invitation.[4]

The fleet was becoming more rigid, laying down photography rules that more or less restricted even the American sailors from taking snapshots anywhere.[5] This was no joke. Four months earlier, four men were arrested by the FBI at the outside entrance to Pearl Harbor, one a forty-six-year-old photographer of Japanese descent. Then, two Japanese nationals were questioned in late July for taking photographs from Pier 27.[6] Their cameras were confiscated. Both were longtime residents of Hawaii, and may have meant no harm, but the Navy was determined not to have its movements too well recorded. It was a losing battle.

As Isabel Short wrote years later about her husband's efforts to deny a photograph of the beautiful place, the rules were impossible to police. "It was like trying to seal off the Hudson River from New York to West Point."[7] The island influx of people still drifted along though, with visitors coming over daily from the mainland to work for periods of time or just to relax.

Richardson moved his flag to the USS *New Mexico* on September 20. Ramage said, "There wasn't anything about it [the time the staff was on the *Big E*] that was pleasant, so when they left the ship, it was good riddance." Ramage said the *New Mexico* was a beautifully turned-out ship while the *Enterprise* "was kind of dirty and noisy!"

Richardson struck out for California three days later.[8] The day before, the Japanese began to move on Dong Dang near the French Indo-China border. Two days later, they were entering in great numbers. In just a few days, on a short Richardson trip, the world would change even more toward war. Despite the photo ban, *Life* magazine cameraman Carl Mydans was allowed to make the trip to the West Coast with the USS *Idaho.* He and writer J. G. Underhill had been with the fleet almost a month.[9]

Despite the rules, Richardson ordered more fun for the sailors. Mayor Crane and the Navy Hostess House had viewed the survey taken of sailors, and noted that they wanted more dances. Richardson put Snyder in charge of arrangements. About three hundred men would attend the informal dances two Wednesdays per month from 8:00 to 11:00 P.M. The first would be at Ala Moana Park's pavilion.[10] This diversion would help, but there was a scarcity of girls who signed up to attend. The trips to the coast were worth more.

The almost ghost towns of Long Beach and San Pedro would be accepting one-third of the fleet back, but for just two weeks. As the ships came into the Long Beach docks the morning of September 30, the *Saratoga* fired a seventeen-gun salute to the USS *New Mexico,* which returned a like salvo. But, basically, the community did as the CinCUS requested—kept the visit all rather low key so the sailors could have the maximum time with

Written histories of Admiral Richardson: Because of his loyalty to Admiral Harold R. "Betty" Stark, Richardson did not approve the publishing of his own book, On the Treadmill to Pearl Harbor, *until 1973. Thus, little was known of his thoughts about Pearl Harbor. Until then, quotes from him were not included in other books that covered the Japanese attack. However, up until the time he was "detached" by Franklin Roosevelt in January 1941, Richardson was a well-known figure. He appeared in special issues of* Life *magazine twice and on the cover of* Time *magazine, was featured in* Holland's Magazine of the South, *and in numerous newspapers, even the* Fort Worth Star-Telegram. (Photo by Skipper Steely in 2007, Steely Collection, James G. Gee Library, Commerce, Texas)*

families. The first day, one-half of the 6,000 aboard the twenty-four ships that stopped there were given permission to go ashore first.[11] One citizen noted the faces of the returning were more "stern" than when they left. However, an unmarried bluejacket blurted out that he had cursed "this place" months earlier, but "I had to get away to appreciate it."[12]

On October 3, news hit the papers that Richardson would visit with Knox in Washington, even though the CinCUS had not definitely stated that he would go. News of the Burma Road reopening was screaming across headlines around the United States. In the summer of 1940 Great Britain told Japan it would hold ship-ments of munitions over the Burma Road for three months. The reasoning was slim, but the British hoped this act would stimu-late successful peace discussions between the Chinese and Japanese. Many thought it was the beginning of the end for British appeasement to Japan's actions in the Far East. The next two weeks would be nervous for the United Kingdom and the United States.

In his October 2 press conference Knox said that Richardson was coming to Washington to discuss "nothing specific." Also, the Navy announced that it would merge 125 vessels in the Atlantic into a patrol force. It would be under Richardson's control, but under direct command of Ellis. Knox denied that any decisions were being made to send U.S. warships on a trip to Australia, nor were there plans in the making to use the British naval base at Singapore. He mentioned that the base personnel situation in the Pacific could be improved.[13]

Gradually other admirals were beginning to express opinions about the Japanese risk. Then retired, Admiral Yates Stirling gained national press when he wrote that the United States should ignore what was happening in the Far East and prepare to go to the support of England.[14] He pointed out that Japan could not be appeased, and that "our important naval task is to prevent a British . . . defeat."

Though Knox's announcement of a meeting came before Richardson decided upon the trip, negotiations had been ongoing since he left Hawaii. On September 24, Stark wired Richardson that he agreed there was no need for the CinCUS to visit Washington, but that he would take the matter up with Knox.[15] At the same time, Stark wrote Richardson about his three-hour meeting with Hull, Welles, and Hornbeck at the State Department. He cautioned that an embargo on scrap iron might be next. He said he strongly opposed a restriction on fuel oil, and it seemed for the time being that the three State Department rep-resentatives agreed. This report only built on Richardson's fear that the Navy was not determining its own placement.[16]

Three days later, Stark wrote again, stating that "the Secretary just rushed in for a minute . . . and asked me to tell you he would like to have you come East at your convenience."[17] When the *New Mexico* docked at Long Beach six days later, Richardson, accompanied by Murphy, still did not know the disposition of the proposed eastern visit.

On October 1, Richardson again received a dispatch from Stark. Knox wanted to talk about a detachment being sent to the Far East. "It is being urged here by some," Stark penned.[18] He added that he and Ingersoll had opposed this desire, but "your thoughts are likely to be determinative." Apologizing for having a "full complement" staying at the Stark abode, he then said he was tentatively setting up a dinner at his house for the next Tuesday, October 8.[19] However, Stark said the feminine part of the family would retire upstairs so that the evenings would be clear for "stag get-togethers." That bit of information told Richardson he was going.[20]

So, at noon on Sunday, October 6, Murphy and Richardson left the Los Angeles airport on American Airlines.[21] They arrived eighteen hours later at Washington-Hoover Airport, just as the sun was rising over the capital's impressive monuments.[22] Immediately they met with Knox, Stark, Yarnell, Ingersoll, and Nimitz. Also present were Under Secretary of the Navy James Forrestal and Compton.[23] Most strongly suggested sending cruisers to augment Hart's Asiatic Fleet, to base eventually at Singapore, if necessary.

With a long day of work behind him, Richardson may have been a bit tired, and for sure he was not prepared well enough to discuss any of the upcoming civilian ideas about protecting American interests in the Pacific. Still, he had prepared some thoughts. Thus, he arrived on October 8 at 1:00 P.M. for lunch with Roosevelt.[24] To his mild surprise, he found Leahy there.

Small talk about Leahy's duties as governor covered the initial conversation, Richardson wrote years later. In 1945, he told the participants at the Congressional Pearl Harbor Hearings of the meeting.[25] He said the trio talked about giving strength to Hart.

Leahy assured Roosevelt that all sent out there would be lost. He recommended distributing only "the least combatant ships we have, the 7,500 ton cruisers."[26] A decision to send nothing was reached. Richardson noted in his diary, "I strongly and repeatedly disagreed with F.D.R. as to the influence on action of Japan resulting from retention of the Fleet in Hawaii."[27]

In 1945, Richardson tried, in the quiet of his home of so many years, to reconstruct the conversation as it went on October 8, 1940. Before Congress in a crowded committee room, five years after the second visit to Washington, he explained what he remembered of his conversation with the president. He spoke to the audience in his slow drawl, emphasized even more with the echo in the large room. Luckily for posterity, some of it is on tape to be watched and heard as if there.[28]

He began with the discussion that he and Roosevelt had on the retention of the fleet at Hawaii. Richardson was no political dummy. He knew the election was near, and that any move now would flip votes one way or another. Still, he told FDR once again that if it was a civilian government running Japan, the president's idea might work, but it was a militarily run process there, and those leaders knew the U.S. Fleet was not prepared for what Japan could throw out. Intelligence had more than once revealed the possibility of much Japanese ship construction, and of bases being built in the Mandated Islands. He reiterated that the Japanese would pay more attention if a Train was assembled and the fleet returned to the West Coast.[29] The ships would then be filled with the complements, fully supplied with ammunition, fuel, and war necessities. The teakwood decks would be replaced with metal, and stripped otherwise for war operations. Portholes needed to be welded. All these things Roosevelt already knew. Stark had told him many times.

"No," replied Roosevelt, convinced that his actions to date had exerted a restraining effect on Japan.[30] "I still do not believe it," Richardson replied, "and I know that our fleet is disadvantageously disposed for preparing for or initiating war operations."[31] Richardson became more stern, and said he did not believe the restraint angle was true. Some were of the impression that Richardson called Pearl Harbor a "godd—n mousetrap," but there is no evidence of that statement.[32]

The president then challenged anyone to come up with a good statement to release to the press, one that would convince the Japanese and the American people that returning the fleet was "not stepping backward."[33] Votes and embarrassment seemed to be the top-shelf elements in the fleet decision at the moment. This information was all Richardson revealed to the congressmen about the meeting.

At 4:05 P.M., Roosevelt took questions from the press in the White House. He told them that Leahy, Richardson, and he had simply studied maps. He answered that way four times. Then questions turned toward domestic housing for a while before drifting back to the Navy's possibility of establishing a two-ocean fleet. However, Roosevelt said there weren't enough ships.

It was clear listening to tapes of the conference that Roosevelt was not in the normal, jovial mood he exhibited at other taped press conferences in his office. That evening, after the gathering of the writers had left, still on tape, he did lighten up a bit, talking about a far-fetched proposal from the chief of the Japanese press association. It called for the United States to withdraw militaries from all over the East, including Hawaii. This proposal brought Roosevelt's ire up, and he even cursed the idea that the Japanese would tell America to leave Hawaii.[34]

In his next press conference, a week later on October 15, just before adjournment at 4:33 P.M., one reporter nearly clipped the truth hiding in Roosevelt's emotions. "A great many reports have been floating around about a possible shakeup of the Navy high command. Any basis for those reports?" Roosevelt said simply, "No. No basis." Another question was posed, "Admiral Richardson and Admiral Stark to be replaced?" Again, Roosevelt claimed to have never heard of such talk.[35]

Richardson did not tell Congress what followed in the October 8 meeting, and he may have never heard of the later press conference question about his future as CinCUS. But, he did mention in his 1945 statement that the president said several times the Japanese would sooner or later make a mistake, and the United States would enter into a war with them. However, that would be after they had attacked Thailand, the Kra Peninsula, the Dutch East Indies, or perhaps even the Philippines.[36]

Roosevelt just did not think he could order any movements backward with the fleet that would keep him from losing November votes. In fact, the president would still tell audiences that he would not take the country into a foreign war unless attacked.[37] Leahy later followed Richardson to the microphone at the early portion of the Congressional Pearl Harbor Hearings, saying that he did not remember the president saying an attack on the Philippines would be without retaliation. "In all my dealings with the President on the subject of war, I never got the indication he would not come to the aid of the Philippines if attacked," he said to Senator Alben W. Barkley's committee while Richardson and May sat in the audience.[38] Perhaps Leahy never read the contents of the last war plans, and especially that of *Rainbow Five*, which Roosevelt approved.

In the October 8 conversation, Richardson was irked that he could not make the president understand that a seasick civilian garage mechanic drafted into the Navy would be of no use. Training had to be done earlier. Roosevelt stuck by his belief that civilians would perform well, a point eventually proved correct. This discussion, according to Richardson's words, "waxed hot and heavy" for some time. Richardson detected, he admitted, that reelection season political considerations were controlling the decisions. Everyone, however, was in a new territory—a third term for a president was unprecedented, and the fleet had never been told to stay at Hawaii.

For years, Richardson did not reveal to the public the meat of the presidential meeting. Some, like Betty Carney Taussig, heard through her father that the president wanted to send the fleet to Indonesia, and in response to that idea Richardson told Roosevelt it would be sheer folly.[39] However, the conversation was deep and blistering. As the exchange between the two old acquaintances heated up, the frustrated Richardson blurted out words he felt were true, but which dealt his job and future on the sea the final blow:

> "Mr. President. I feel that I must tell you that the senior officers of the Navy do not have the trust and confidence in the civilian leadership of this country that is essential for the successful prosecution of a war in the Pacific."[40]

As Kemp Tolley would later say in his oral interview, "That was a tremendously impertinent thing for a commander in chief to tell a president!"[41]

Roosevelt had a pained look on his face, and replied:

> "Joe. You just don't understand that this is an election year, and there are certain things that can't be done, no matter what, until the election is over and won."[42]

Ironically, Leahy described Roosevelt's style and fears as being just what Richardson had pointed out. The president, Leahy wrote later of his one-time friend and boss, "had little confidence in some of his executive departments, and, therefore, took detailed action with his own hands."[43] Leahy had chemistry with Roosevelt, and could stroke him smoothly at times, or just remain quiet. Historians still discuss whether Richardson meant that those advisors around the president were not trusted, or whether he also included Roosevelt in the statement.

Richardson said his own statement was not just blurted out devoid of thought. It had been prepared while on the USS *New Mexico*. He was doing what Stark thought had to be done, and could be accomplished only by Richardson. Stark, Richardson surmised, was not succeeding in bringing Roosevelt around to the naval point of view. Possibly, Stark was very aware of this fact, and thought that perhaps Richardson could talk some sense into Roosevelt. If he did not, then the consequences would fall upon the CinCUS, not the CNO.

In July Richardson had discussed with Vinson the inability of Stark to convince Roosevelt. Richardson also believed that the president had been a part of the Navy for so long that he believed his decision-making process to be on the level of professional Navy leadership. Richardson thought that it was time to risk his neck to make the point with Roosevelt that more official naval input should be given to decisions of the fleet. "I thought I had but this one chance," he wrote seventeen years later.

"I thought what I believed to be the true opinion of many senior Naval officers, and that . . . this would be a real shock to the President." Trouble was, sitting right there in the meeting was one admiral who thought that perhaps Roosevelt was right, and he wanted to remain in his job. Five years later Leahy would tell Congress that some of the Richardson comments about the meeting he did not recall as being said. Leahy did emphasize that he was surprised when Richardson told Roosevelt that the fleet was not war ready.

Richardson realized after his comments that the president was truly shocked. As long as the two had worked together, Richardson may have missed the boat, and actually did not know FDR well enough to be that blunt. Within twenty-four to thirty-six hours after Richardson left Washington, Roosevelt called Stark, saying, "I want J. O. relieved."[44] Somebody most likely pointed out to Roosevelt that it might be highly politically damaging to his campaign to fire Richardson a week or so before the fleet coverage was due on the stands in *Life* magazine.[45] It was only three and one-half months since Richardson had appeared on the cover of *Time* magazine. Therefore, Richardson's tour was extended, but only by three months.[46] Perhaps Richardson fell for the old Roosevelt personality as he left the meeting, actually thinking that maybe, just maybe, he had gotten his point across. However, Eleanor Roosevelt said on occasion, "I'm afraid that my husband had a habit of letting people leave his office thinking that he had agreed with them."[47]

Richardson presented to Stark a partial summary of what was said in the White House.[48] It mentioned that the president did agree to go ahead and assemble a Train of auxiliary vessels, transports, repair ships, and supply ships for Hawaiian use. The two agreed that this act would indicate to the Japanese true U.S. preparation for war. The president, said the memorandum, asked if enough fuel was in Samoa for four old light cruisers. Richardson told him no, but included this portion of the conversation in the memo so Stark would be on the alert that such a request might be coming. In Richardson's mind, this was perhaps a Roosevelt plan to sacrifice old ships in a Japanese attack, which would be, conceivably, reason enough to declare war.

Though he did not agree with Roosevelt about moving the fleet farther than Hawaii, in the memo Richardson asked Stark to provide him with a chart of British and French bases in islands of the Pacific east of the international dateline. Richardson also noted to Stark that the president might approve, as a gesture of U.S. seriousness, sending a division of old light cruisers to visit Mindinao in the Philippines.[49] "He did not appear favorably disposed toward sending a stronger force."

In the remaining hours in Washington, Richardson worked on war plans and talked again with Hornbeck.[50] Richardson later told congressional members of the Pearl Harbor Hearings that he continued to be of the impression that Hornbeck was unwilling to accept responsibility for the fleet's placement. "I doubt whether I told him that he was completely wrong," Richardson said in the hearing, "but I expressed my view fully."[51]

Despite Leahy's earlier advice, more naval conversation was held on the possibility of beefing up Hart in the Asiatic Fleet. All knew that a string of ships across the Pacific had been a longtime presidential consideration. Roosevelt was certain that a policy of encirclement and strangulation was superior to military war plans. However, he did not instruct that such a blockade plan be devised by the Navy when he brought it up in 1938. Then, in 1940, he thought that his third alternative was to place the fleet in a position threatening to Japanese expansion.[52]

In addition to the many conversations, Richardson was kept busy in Washington making phone calls and sending messages to Long Beach, arranging just how nearly 5,000 sailors could travel to Hawaii in a week. For some reason, Richardson had not been told of the new recruits, and the first day in Washington was given the news that they had landed on the West Coast, awaiting his direction.[53]

Before leaving in the late day of October 11, Richardson, Nimitz, and Stark discussed looking ahead a year. Experience told Richardson it was time to begin thoughts of his replacement for that date. It was "normal" for a CinCUS to serve about two years. In fact, he told Nimitz and Stark that names should begin to be suggested for all the officers who would come up for relief in early 1942. He felt that any of the senior flag officers might find reason for earlier detachment, and that it was good to have names in the book to replace them quickly. They agreed, then said that Richardson could submit his ideas. He submitted a list, which included King or Kimmel as possibilities to take his place. On October 29, he received a note from Nimitz, agreeing to shift up King if anything happened.[54] However, Nimitz informed Richardson as he left Washington that there was no plan to replace the CinCUS position until the two years of service was up. Nimitz had no inkling about the presidential anger developed from the Richardson meeting.

Knox assured Richardson in one of their conversations during the visit that "we have never been ready [for war], but we have always won." Richardson gathered that Knox actually believed there was a "lack of war mindedness in the Fleet."[55] Richardson was of the impression that most in Washington thought the CinCUS a "nut" on personnel. Most knew he was accurate, but it was a slow process to convince every entity to move quickly.[56]

In 1945, Representative J. Bayard Clark asked Richardson if he really thought the Pearl Harbor debacle would have been a bit different in conclusion had the fleet been up to 100 percent manned. "Yes," Richardson said in reply. "I think the difference would have been infinitesimal." The legislator did not ask for more detail.[57]

CHAPTER TWENTY

Fleet Remains, Supplies Begin Arriving
Congress Opens Bank Account to Help Hawaii

Richardson's all-night flight back to Los Angeles gave him much time to contemplate matters. He arrived at 8:00 A.M., and had a couple of days to spend on shore. He told Friedell, Russell Willson, Kimmel, Baughman, John H. Carson, and the staff that he "was positive that the U.S. would be at war soon."[1] On October 14, he reboarded the USS *New Mexico* with many recruits assembled on the *Saratoga* and in among the crews of the other ships at Long Beach. Roosevelt told the press that these new men would be used to build up the crews of the ships to 100 percent, "whereas they now are only at 82 percent."[2] The first fleet group to visit "home" was heading back to Hawaii, but Richardson and his flagship remained to be around the next two groups.[3]

Good-byes for the veterans of the fleet were extremely difficult, especially for seamen like Robert E. Patterson. He was leaving his wife and his three-month-old baby he had just met fifteen days earlier.[4] At about the same time, a second group with 10,000 sailors was leaving Honolulu to replace the first. The third group would finally arrive to see kinfolks and friends in time for Thanksgiving. For many on the mainland, this was a final glimpse of many of the ships.[5] Almost all of the sailors would leave for the last time, never setting foot again onto the facilities that had housed the fleet for so many years.

Before Richardson could depart, Zacharias approached him at Long Beach. He was the Eleventh Naval District intelligence officer headquartered in San Diego, his office charged with curtailing foreign spy networks in the aircraft production region. His staff began to realize that a Japanese espionage system was real, and somewhat large. Of course, just like the United States, Japan sent over "students" to learn the American ways and language. Employees of consulates were also trained to spy on the United

States, even if it just involved reading local newspapers.

The Japanese fishing fleets were always suspects. With the information they had, Japan would easily have the ability to know every inch of the West Coast. Though he was about to take sea duty again, on the USS *Salt Lake City*, Zacharias wanted to investigate an alleged plot that involved destruction of four battleships.

An agent told the intelligence office that suicide planes would accomplish the deed. It was an incredible notion, but the date set was October 17, and deserved some action, Zacharias thought.[6] Of course, Richardson had three battleships with him, so Zacharias arranged a meeting with the CinCUS. He and Richardson had possibly known each other since the early 1920s, and for sure since their 1934 days at the Naval Senior War College. Both had served with Reeves in the mid-1930s, and had spent an evening together earlier in 1939 at a Long Beach dinner where they laughed at the antics of ventriloquist Edgar Bergen and his wooden partner Charlie McCarthy.[7]

They decided to shift the battleships and a cruiser up to San Francisco. Richardson posted alerts, and moved the ships out in a fog before daylight. Nothing happened.[8] However, the importance of intelligence, and the knowledge that U.S. surveillance action was occurring, impressed Richardson. He took the ships on to Bremerton, where he corresponded with Stark on October 22 about his Washington visit and war plans.[9]

Richardson summarized the difference in the two trips to meet with leadership in Washington. The first time he came away in July knowing three things: (1) the fleet was retained in Hawaii to support diplomatic representations and as a deterrent to Japanese aggressive action; (2) there was no intention of embarking on actual hostilities against Japan; and, (3) the immediate mission of the fleet was accelerated training and absorption of new personnel. This time, when he left Washington, he felt that a heavier atmosphere existed. He acknowledged that much of this somber mood was due to a closer identification with the fate of Great Britain. However, he sensed that more active, open steps aimed at Japan were in serious contemplation. These steps, if taken, he wrote Stark, might lead to active hostilities.[10]

In the duration of just two months, much had changed in regard to the Pacific. Fueled by continual rumors of the reopening of the Burma Road, which might bring retaliation by the Japanese, Hart stopped the advance bookings for Navy families coming to join their loved ones in the Far East. While Richardson was gone, a subcommittee of the Naval Affairs Committee visited the Hawaiian installations and fleet for a few days.[11] The Navy ordered reservists to active duty, bringing the number of active personnel up to 235,492. Little news filtered to the press in Hawaii about Richardson's Washington meetings.[12]

However, some of the press sensed a higher assignment for Leahy, and asked the president later if the former CNO was being called to duty again. In his "famous" reply, Roosevelt reiterated that when he met with Leahy and Richardson, they simply studied maps during the long meeting.[13] Strong rumors, perhaps begun because Stark was not at the White House, were that Leahy would again be appointed CNO and Stark would be reassigned. Reports were circulating all over Washington that Leahy had urged Roosevelt to revise the entire naval leadership.[14] It was unprecedented for a retired officer to make such recommendations, but the relationship between Leahy and the president was very close. Leahy returned to Puerto Rico a few days later.

In the meantime, Stirling was hammering away through his columns. He finally hit the nail on the head, predicting that the Japanese would more than likely hit the U.S. Fleet without a formal declaration of war. This surprise attack would give the Japanese, he wrote, more time to capture Singapore, bases in the Dutch East Indies, and Hong Kong. He said that carrier and submarine raids could be expected on the West Coast and at Pearl Harbor. He assumed, not knowing what the president had told Richardson, that the surviving portions of the fleet would then head west for twenty-seven days to Singapore and encase Japan in a blockade. He made this assumption based upon a scenario in which Britain was not defeated.[15]

The fleet in Hawaii anchored for the October 12 weekend. A

new Navy order required that only service dress blue and whites be worn, the dress uniforms being put into mothballs for the time being. White dress for Navy enlisted personnel was discontinued. Richardson boosted morale by ordering a trial period of wearing a white "shorts" uniform.[16] He received good reports from Halsey, even participating in the test himself. So, on October 26, he authorized the uniform throughout the fleet.[17]

Halsey wrote Richardson to tell May that Mrs. Halsey expected to sail for the West Coast on November 1. Their daughter Jane and children had left the previous Friday. He said he told his "entourage" that if and when Task Force 3 returned, "I consider that affairs will be so uncertain from then on that probably it would be wiser for all hands not to have anything on their minds except their business." All commanders were expecting something to happen in the remaining days of 1940. It would surprise them that no war in the Pacific would start for more than thirteen months.

News of the Army draft for men between the ages of twenty-one and thirty-five was beginning to fill pages, and even though its decision might negatively affect Roosevelt's reelection campaign, it was put into action.[18] Word from Manila was that families of Navy men were put on notice, and told to be packed for a quick departure.[19]

Richardson was asked by Stark to send out to Hart the assumptions and tentative fleet disposition drawn up in Washington while the CinCUS was there. Captain Jesse B. Oldendorf, traveling there on board the USS *Houston,* took the paperwork personally.[20] The subject was basically "reinforcement of the Asiatic Fleet" and the international situation.[21] The plan was never implemented, even though Richardson said in the Congressional Hearing that it did influence future strategy. He told Senator Homer Ferguson that he never told Knox he would not put a proposed patrol line plan into effect if ordered. "I could have tried it," he said.[22] Its implementation was contingent upon retaliation by Japan upon the opening of the Burma Road.[23]

Richardson added that he told Knox in most likelihood "we would lose the ships" sent out under the blockade-like plan, which included an effort to stop trade between Japan and South

America. He told Knox it would just mean trouble not only between the United States and Japan, but also with countries of South America, who felt free to trade with anyone they desired. Knox insisted that there would come a time when the fleet would have to stop the trade.

Richardson told Hart that he understood there would be no Army forces available to assist those in the Asiatic region. He also reminded Hart that the U.S. Fleet was not to go too far out into the Pacific. It might receive quick orders to assist in the Atlantic. Many assumptions were clothed with many problems, many alternatives. He told Hart that there was even a tentative plan for a western movement. A dress rehearsal might be held after January 1.[24] A Train would assemble in West Coast ports with transports, utilizing Christmas Island as a site. Despite thinking the idea rather fantastic, Richardson wrote five pages on its positives and negatives. Enforcing the Asiatic Fleet might "coincidentally" be taken with the exercise. The idea was that this evidence of determination by the United States to protect its American interests would impress Japan.[25]

One more sensible plan was being devised by Stark to bring the fleet back to the various West Coast bases by Christmas.[26] Apparently, discussions almost brought Roosevelt and his advisors to the point that they would allow a return home, much on the basis Richardson had recommended. "As I recall," Stark told the joint congressional hearings, "we had about come to the conclusion we might bring the Fleet back in the fall or for Christmas. . . . and that later we decided not to do it, but keep them there. After that time, about the last of 1940, it just became a fixed policy to retain the Fleet" in Hawaii.

Ghormley had been in England about six weeks observing the European situation. He wrote Knox that London was not in the shambles that some in America perceived, but that there was damage there. Knox focused much of his work and opinion upon what Hitler might do to England and in the Mediterranean. Ghormley, however, related that in talks with the British Admiralty, he still emphasized that the U.S. Navy should keep its eyes to the west. He noted that the Japanese Navy "has suffered little" in the Chinese conflict. He emphasized that not only did he think that situation had spurned them on to action elsewhere, he also thought that in the eyes of the Japanese citizens, the Navy was inferior to the Army. The Japanese Navy, therefore, felt that it needed to set and fulfill commitments. He told Knox that Europe was "a war laboratory" for the United States, "and we must take every advantage . . . for applying it practically to our own Navy."[27]

In Long Beach, Richardson could tell from the news that his points were not well taken. Compton told a Philadelphia audience that the Navy "is ready to give a damned good account of itself in the Pacific if it has to."[28] That may have been news to Hart. He received a note from Stark on October 22 saying, "I am delighted over the prospect of getting our women and children out of the Far East." He also stated that he was glad Hart was in Manila.[29]

In Hawaii, most of the fleet was able to enjoy a bit of time off on land to celebrate the October 27 Navy Day. A large portion of the local newspaper space was given to Navy articles, many written by admirals. The *Honolulu Advertiser* even printed an old story Richardson had written on the history of the Bureau of Navigation.[30] Photos throughout the editions gave a tourist or outsider a clear view of the fleet's ships and participants.

Richardson, who enjoyed just a short time at Long Beach before he went to Bremerton, was made aware on October 28 that his position was tenuous. Washington residents, for some reason, put strong credence in a roughly typed newsletter published by the Kiplinger Agency. It consisted of hundreds of crudely constructed paragraphs with generous underlining of key phrases or words. Readers often found new information in it that the newspaper world felt not yet credible and ready for print. The October 19 edition included, at the bottom of the newsletter's first page, two paragraphs that friends brought to Richardson's attention.[31]

> Our Naval officers are divided on Japan. Many want to fight, thinking we could smash Japan quickly, do it now, get it over with. Others insist it would be a long war of attrition, taking years, costly, leading

to permanent policing of the Orient, "not worth it even if we win." Admiral Stark, top man in the Navy, is inclined to go along with White House suggestions. Admiral Richardson, commanding the Fleet, is less pro-war. If he should be shifted, it would be a war sign.[32]

The next day Richardson received a note from Nimitz that King would be his replacement "if I had to be taken out."[33] For the first time, as Richardson wrote later, he realized that someone was packing his bags for him. Still, Richardson said he did not have any feelings of foreboding of a blow about to be dropped on him. "I looked forward to the year 1941 with the great hope that it would be a year of fast-improving readiness of the Navy for war." It was ironic that he was being labeled by outsiders as the one who was most against war. He was the highest ranking Navy leader most apt to believe there was to be an attack on his command, the one professing that the ships needed to be converted to war-time conditions, and the one most placing his career on the line to get this point across. Richardson's decision to be quieter would cost him this time.

Word began to sift into Hawaii that on November 2 the SS *President Pierce* was boarding the first Americans to evacuate the Far East. More than 2,000 Shanghailanders were present to bid farewell when the ship sailed at 1:30 P.M. with more than two hundred passengers, mostly women and children. Nine Japanese planes increased tension when they flew over the American consulate and embarkation jetty. On the Whampoo River, the ship's passengers saw Japanese warships and the last of the American gunboats, most of the Asiatic Fleet being concentrated in the Philippines.[34] The SS *Mariposa* was in Hawaii, about to depart for the mainland, but transferred its two hundred passengers to sail on the SS *Lurline* to California, and turned back toward Shanghai to assist the evacuation.[35]

Also on the *Lurline* were the wives of Admirals Pye, Snyder, Halsey, and Marquart. The ladies may have been simply traveling back to Long Beach to close out quarters there, with immediate plans to return to Honolulu. However, it may have been noted by Japanese spies that even the wives of admirals were leaving the

Pacific, maybe encouraged by their husbands who knew of the threat. Some of the wives would reconnect with their husbands who went with part of the fleet to the West Coast for liberty. Halsey had just come back to San Diego from a trip to Washington, DC, and Annapolis to attend the Army-Navy game.[36] Some things were important!

Mrs. LeRoy Hunt, who lived in the Gill Apartments in Honolulu for seven months, went to the mainland in November while her husband remained in his assignment with the USS *California*.[37] Mrs. Bemis, Mrs. Calhoun, and Mrs. Binford followed two and three weeks later.[38] However, arriving on the SS *Matsonia* a few days later was Mrs. Chester W. Nimitz, Jr., and her four-month-old daughter. If the Bureau of Navigation's daughter-in-law was in Hawaii, some reasoned, there must be no fear of imminent danger.[39]

Ironically, arriving at the same time aboard the USAT *Leonard Wood* was General Frederick L. Martin and his wife. He was to be commander of the Army's newly designated Hawaiian Air Force and of Wheeler Air Base's Fourteenth Pursuit Wing. He was considered quite an expert on aviation and would team up later with the Navy's Patrick L. Bellinger to plan patrol security for Pearl Harbor.[40]

What an oxymoron life was. At the same time wives were being discouraged to come out to Hawaii, the Navy announced the construction there of its largest recreation center to be a part of a new housing project. They would be completed by the latter part of the next summer.[41] Not counting the fleet, more than 5,700 Navy personnel worked out of Pearl Harbor. There were another 5,000 Navy civilian workers. So, if Hawaii was not considered ready yet for the fleet base, it would be in 1941.[42]

On November 6, headlines around the world reported that Roosevelt had carried thirty-nine states on his way to a landslide victory in the presidential election. The Democrat vote even carried Lester Petrie to an upset over Honolulu Mayor Charles Crane. Speculation nationally then perceived Roosevelt with a mandate to expand overseas influence by the United States. Fleet news still was almost nil, as if editors had been ordered to cease daily stories on its location. Now and then, small articles would appear, but they were about accidents.[43]

An editorial appeared on November 10, saying that Hawaiians "could not see the forest for the trees." The finest naval fleet in the world sat outside their door, but little attention was paid to it. That was fine with Richardson. The editorial noted that the recent October 28 issue of *Life* magazine, and recommended that islanders read it.[44] Apparently the November through Christmas liberty break did not include many sea maneuvers since the fleet was divided. Richardson received orders to send some assistance to the Asiatic Station. Immediately he sent the submarine USS *Shark* to Manila.[45]

Still on the West Coast, Richardson departed Bremerton on November 15 for Long Beach. At 3:00 P.M., he received a dispatch from Stark instructing him to return to Pearl Harbor as planned. The hopes of bluffing Japan were to continue, while at the same time European events were heating up. German, Russian, and Italian talks were just being completed in Berlin. Still, there was the observation by Richardson that Great Britain might ask the assistance of the United States to protect her Asian interests.[46]

From his location, on November 24, Richardson ordered the USS *Augusta* to quietly check out waters north of the Hawaiian chain. Reports had been received that *Orange* tankers were in the vicinity. The *Augusta* was on its way back from the Asiatic Fleet, being replaced by the *Houston*. She hit terrible weather, making impractical any air search. At 35 degrees north latitude, 165 degrees west longitude, she darkened the ship. Captain John H. Magruder, Jr., estimated they swept a belt about twenty-five miles wide, maintaining radio silence. They saw nothing.[47]

Optimistic faces were difficult to find as the Free World watched its possessions crumble.[48] Maine's Senator Owen Brewster was spending time touring the Hawaiian facilities. He stated that, in simple terms, he felt that Hawaii "is a billion dollar filing station for the Navy." In his mind, he had not yet come to the conclusion it should be a permanent base for the fleet.[49]

On Saturday, December 2, the three light cruisers, USS *Trenton,* USS *Concord,* and USS *Drayton* slipped into Pearl Harbor, the first of the third group sent on liberty to return. They left Long Beach almost unnoticed after Thanksgiving Day. Richardson noted that he left on November 29.[50] The annual Navy reports were beginning to be made public, but were very outdated since they discontinued data at the end of June. However, it was overwhelming to the public to read that taxpayers would eventually have 185 submarines, 325 destroyers, 91 cruisers, and 18 aircraft carriers roaming the seas and perhaps stationed in or near Pearl Harbor. Navy leaders knew that these were wishful figures, but many of the vessels were already under construction.[51]

Even another islands visit from a congressman came when the chairman of the House Military Affairs Committee, Dow W. Harter, arrived on the SS *Lurline* on December 5. Other congressmen were arriving on the USAT *Hunter Liggett* five days later for a study of the Army needs.[52] They were in time to view 772 family evacuees landing from a trip on the liner SS *Monterey.* The ship's crew had been on a six-week, 31,000-mile roundabout trip to gather in women and children from Korea to the East Indies. The wife of Admiral William A. Glassford, commander of the Yangtze U.S. Patrol, was among the group.[53] Captain Duane L. Whitlock wrote years later that the pain of losing loved ones from the Philippines was compounded by the costs, taken from "our meager pay." But, it was worth it since families would then be safe.[54]

All of this movement of families Richardson saw as he returned from the West Coast on December 6.[55] Dr. Melhorn was on the quarterdeck when Richardson returned. "As [Richardson] came up on deck, he saw me and gave me the high sign to follow him. I went down to his cabin, and he said, 'Well, Melhorn, my days are numbered.'"

Already Richardson felt that a detachment was coming as a result of his meeting with Roosevelt and Knox. He told Melhorn, "I've had a very strenuous time talking to the President, and he doesn't agree with my views about the battleships. I'm being detached." He told his fleet doctor that he recommended Kimmel as his replacement. The news was straightforward, but the results would not come in December.

Still, Richardson kept at his job, hoping for the best. He planned to move the fleet out of Pearl Harbor soon, and anchor in Lahaina Roads for a brief time, but he would keep the fleet moving about. The naval population swelled with 8,000 more sailors. There was still a considerable number of the fleet in Bremerton, but most, including the USS *Pennsylvania,* were about finished with overhaul in the Puget Sound Naval Yard. The USS *New Mexico* had completed an overhaul while there earlier with Richardson in tow. Then, there were some fifteen ships in San Diego that sailed the day Richardson arrived in Hawaii. Soon, the fleet would be combined again in full strength, just in time for Christmas.[56]

Still, Richardson lost ships here and there to the Asiatic Fleet and sometimes to the Atlantic Patrol. The sailors on the USS *William B. Preston,* for example, were leisurely listening to the Army-Navy football game by radio when she was ordered to proceed to the Asiatic Fleet. She first returned to Pearl Harbor for supplies. Then, on December 6, she left for a fixed war zone with no idea of a return time. "We tried to explain to our daughter I may be away for two years," wrote Lester A. Wood. It was a tough change for a couple to make, especially on such short notice.[57]

A patrol squadron left to eventually settle in Manila. Hart complained to Stark that if more ships were coming, it would be sensible to bunch them in larger groups. He had to provide guard ships from Guam, as did Richardson from Honolulu to Guam. "I have to get out so many ships," he wrote.[58]

Early December news articles speculated that a strong U.S. Fleet base in the Far East was being contemplated, and that the fleet supply Train was being rapidly expanded, which was news to Richardson and those in the middle. It was noted that the Philippine army and air forces were being strengthened, but from what was seen and heard coming through Hawaii, these were small increases in comparison to expected needs. Richardson viewed with skepticism the various Navy announcements from Washington.[59]

However, these thoughts were footnoted when the chairman of the Senate Appropriations Committee, Elmer Thomas of Oklahoma, landed with the USAT *Hunter Liggett* to join Brewster and the others on a four-day look at military facilities.[60] Harter told the Hawaiian press that first-line planes were to come to Hawaii "as soon as production . . . is stepped up." He mentioned they would come before "foreign attack."[61]

Roosevelt placed exports on virtually all iron and steel products under rigid licensing control to begin December 31. Administration officials said this action was mainly to "keep iron and steel under proper control so there will be ample supplies for the defense program." A total embargo was not yet in the plan. At that time, Japan obtained 32 percent of her imports of these products from the United States. The embargo the United States had placed earlier on iron and steel scraps simply was skirted by Japan. She began to legally purchase rods, bars, and ingots to make up the difference.[62]

December news also was affecting nineteen divisions of the fleet reserves, now ordered to duty. This activation would only boost the numbers by 65 officers and 1,540 enlisted men. Judging by the numbers of housing units being purchased, constructed, or upgraded, inhabitants of Hawaii could tell anyone that more Army and Navy servicemen were coming. On December 16, the "Naval high command" officially announced that the fleet would remain in Hawaiian waters.[63]

That same day the announcement was made, Richardson received a report that an unidentified submarine had most likely been discovered in the restricted area right off the entrance to Pearl Harbor.[64] He fell back on his intuition and knowledge, and disbelieved the reports from the commander of the destroyer, the commander of destroyers, and about three-fourths of his staff. This was not the first such report.[65]

Tarbuck thought that at times his ship observed submarines, and went so far as to say, "We tracked those Jap submarines, but we weren't allowed to attack them." More than likely he confused events in 1941 with 1940.[66]

Melhorn was walking on the deck of the USS *Pennsylvania* with Taffinder one day when the chief of staff said, "One of our destroyers picked up a foreign submarine that was passing up and down in front of the Pearl Harbor entrance." He explained that sounding equipment was dropped, and even one of the fleet's submarines went ahead of the destroyer to see if the suspicion was legitimate. From this information, Melhorn sensed there was going to be eventual trouble, but was not aware that "those things were discussed openly." He added, however, "I knew it wouldn't be long before we were going to get into a war."[67]

Only two other staff officers shared Richardson's skepticism. At first, however, Richardson ordered depth charges dropped on any such contacts, but later noted that "without being influenced by any superior authority, I rescinded that order." Richardson told the Joint Congressional Hearing members in 1945 that Stark later said he wished the CinCUS had followed the contact for a longer period. However, Richardson was not sure that Stark was referring to this December 16 incident.[68]

Weather in early December near Hawaii caused some accidents and problems in fleet training.[69] The bulk of the fleet was out on maneuvers, leaving Pearl Harbor uncommonly empty. Newspapers reported that the intensified fleet activities were called by Richardson. He wanted to "waste no time lying idly at anchor in Pearl Harbor." Maybe he wanted to be gone when the senators were in town. However, some wives like Mrs. R. A. Theobald, were arriving from the mainland, indicating to most that the fleet's time out would be short.[70] This impression was solidified when it was announced in the Matson Line release that a passenger on the December 18 landing of the SS *Lurline*, was Mrs. James O. Richardson.[71] A photo pictured her, naturally in a hat, but she had a tired, firm-mouthed expression.

Mrs. Hewitt was also on board, ready to visit with her husband. They would stay at the old Waikiki Beach Halekulani Hotel for the Christmas season. Her husband was Commander Cruiser Division 8, stationed on the USS *Philadelphia*.[72] In his notes, Hewitt mentioned the long and strenuous schedule of training under simulated war conditions. "All ships were kept at a maximum state of readiness and full up with fuel, provisions and other necessary supplies," he wrote.[73]

While passenger ships were loaded to the brim most of the time, traveling from Hawaii to the mainland and back, ships normally full headed to the Orient unloaded light loads on brief stops at Pearl Harbor. On Christmas Eve one of the *President Cleveland*'s passengers, a journalist leaving the Far East, told the *Honolulu Advertiser*, "No news can be sent out of Japan any longer . . . assignment in Tokyo is the next thing to being in jail."

But, for the fleet it was Christmas, and mostly lonely. Arrangements were made with radio station KGU and the NBC Blue Network to broadcast messages to a party of wives and family gathered in Long Beach and San Diego. This was done on Christmas Eve, with men representing each of the various units speaking at noontime in Honolulu to their loved ones. Richardson appointed Admiral G. J. Rowcliffe, commander of Cruisers Scouting Force, to be in charge of the operation. Rowcliffe started the broadcast by talking with his wife and three children in Long Beach. Then men of various ranks talked over the microphone. It was fun, but not anything that would create a Merry Christmas to everyone.[74] In Stark's Christmas message to Navy personnel, he said that a great buildup was in progress.[75]

For Richardson, the boom would fall in just two weeks, after all the celebrations and golf rounds while the fleet was in for the break.

CHAPTER TWENTY-ONE

War Plans Unrealistic
Hard to Address That Point

Richardson and Vince Murphy began a lifetime friendship in 1939. Until 1937 no CinCUS staff had included a Fleet War Plans Director.[1] Murphy was tabbed by Richardson to fill that slot on his staff. He and the admiral would work hand in hand for a year, fruitlessly telling their thoughts to anyone who would listen—war plans are necessary, but are of no good to the U.S. Fleet if it is not fully manned and supplied with the correct materials.

"When I left Washington for the Pacific in June of 1939, this unreality of our Naval War Plans was one of my major items of concern," wrote Richardson in 1957. He explained that though he had never had a billet exclusively responsible for war plans, he had held a number of assignments in and around the planning process.

As a commander, Murphy was assigned to Richardson's staff from his duties at Op-12, the Navy's War Plans Division.[2] He was a native of Norfolk, Virginia, and a graduate of the Naval Academy in 1917. After tours on surface ships, he was instructed in submarines.[3]

Though more than a dozen years in age separated the pair, they worked together well. In fact, a friendship grew to such an extent that Murphy was a witness to the admiral's will in 1968.[4] In November of 1945, he assisted the admiral with preparation for his appearance before the Joint Congressional Hearings on Pearl Harbor.[5] The two lived only a mile apart in retirement, and apparently spoke often.

Within three weeks after taking command of the fleet, Richardson wrote to Stark detailing his thoughts on the *Orange War Plan* and its future.[6] The January 26, 1940, letter covered in detail what he considered to be the unrealistic aspects of the current plan.[7] He stressed that the administration had to know fully the cost and possible duration of the plan if implemented. He used "for instances," like "What if we really do take Truk? What would we have? A secure anchorage, and nothing else." The fleet would still be several thousand miles from the nearest dry dock. He could not quite see the huge picture Nimitz would control just two years later, nor conceive how fast America could build.

He fussed that he did not know what Stark was telling Roosevelt, nor did the CinCUS know the meaning of the diplomatic moves he so often read about in the newspapers. "You need to tell the boss that he cannot just sail away, lick *Orange* and be back at home in a year or so."

He continued, "It has always been a source of great concern to me, lest President Roosevelt, blithely inspired by his own impetuosity and urged on by the clamor of the American people to 'do something,' might ignore the restraints written into the *Orange War Plan* over a period of 15 years, and order the Fleet to proceed to the Western Pacific without the benefit of the necessary preparations or consideration for the necessity of having superior strength over the Japanese Navy." He wrote the secret letter by longhand, and sent it by "custody of an officer of my staff." Stark never directly replied to this correspondence, according to Richardson.

Harry Hill, Admiral Bloch's war plans officer, came to the fleet at San Pedro in June of 1938. He finished his courses at the War College that spring, and served in temporary assignment a couple of weeks in Washington, being briefed on developments and policies.[8] When he went to work for Bloch, Hill was following the work done by Cooke, known for his ability to quickly understand discussions and plans. For some confusing reason—maybe he had something better in mind—Richardson had not agreed with the selection of Cooke in 1936 when Hepburn chose the commander for the fleet planning berth.[9] Cooke, an academy graduate of 1910, and Richardson were two among thirteen of the 1934 graduates of the Naval War College to become admirals.[10] Hill felt that Cooke was "a brilliant submariner," noting that he finished number one in his academy class.[11] Cooke created his reputation by being cool and calm when his submarine sank during training off the East Coast in September of 1920.[12] He and the crew managed to cut a small hole in its aft section, which was bobbing above water. The men then waved flags on a stick at passing vessels.

The effort to find a practical fleet solution for the *Orange War Plan* was a set of "devious and frustrating" attempts, Hill said. His greatest supporter was Admiral Fairfax Leary, chief of staff to Bloch. Leary, though admitting the deficiencies of materials, was aggressive and believed the plan could be made effective. Along with Richardson, Hill, and others, Leary did not flow with the tendency to discount the strength of Japan in the Mandated Islands.[13]

Hill agreed it was discouraging to "have so few tools to work with," citing the lack of amphibious landing equipment to effectuate a Pacific war plan.[14] "Our Fleet planning had to be devoted to studies and tests of what we could do with what we had, in event war came tomorrow," he said in an oral interview years later.[15] Also, poor intelligence about the Japanese construction in the Mandated Islands left the Navy in the dark. Still, he said, "many of us had faith that an aggressive attack, supported by powerful gunfire and air bombardment, could succeed against outlying and unsupported Jap positions." Here he clashed in some regards with Richardson. Hill agreed there was doubt to the extent the Japanese had fortified targets the Navy would be attempting to hit.

Hill would work on a master plan with supplements from the subordinate type commanders, their operations officers, and Richardson. "Many of the type commanders disagreed with this plan," Hill said, "and thought this category of development was a waste of time."[16] He then explained that the opposition did not think the Navy had enough strength to attack a shore position. They thought landing troops and material would be almost impossible, especially in rough seas. "We, the planners, thought we could go in . . . where there was smooth water around an atoll . . . or beaches," explained Hill. He again reiterated that the opposition came mainly from senior officers of the fleet.[17]

Bloch was not so much agreeable with the plan, but interested in its maximum development. He continued to urge Leahy and later Stark to expedite the development and construction of large and effective amphibious landing craft. Hill lost his strong supporters when they were reassigned in late 1939, but he was held over to his staff after the change of command, according to Richardson, "to assist in the tremendous workload in the CinCUS war plans section."[18] Hill's vision of a successful landing operation was bolstered by the January 1940 exercise eighty miles south of San Francisco on the beaches of Camp Ord, near Monterey Bay, California.[19] As he watched from the USAT *Leonard Wood*, "the whole landing exercise went off remarkably well," he thought. Not so apparently in the minds of his bosses.

"I reported to Admiral Richardson my conclusion that the *Orange Plan* could be made effective against lightly held enemy based under smooth sea conditions." Asked what the reaction was, Hill said, "I think the future events showed what he thought." Shortly after this exercise, Hill found himself detached from the staff.[20]

Taffinder apparently was not completely satisfied. Like Richardson, he was stern on the theory that the exercises had to be done under real conditions. Theobald was not on board with what was planned. "He proved to be an extremely hard and disagreeable man to work with," Hill said.[21] Theobald had fixed ideas and resented any new suggestions. Even at that, however, Hill said, "He had no use whatsoever for the *Orange Plan*." Hill's woes would expand quickly. "I soon found out that Admiral Richardson had serious doubts about [it] . . . and showed a definite unwillingness to accept [*Orange*] as a basis for Fleet action in the event of war." He did point out that Richardson maintained pressure on the Navy Department to expedite the amphibious building programs.

In late January or early February 1940, Hill left for Washington and his new assignment in the CNO's office, carrying with him some of Richardson's "highly classified letters" for the Navy Department, including a tentative *Rainbow Two* draft.[22] Hill would again replace Cooke, this time in the War Plans Division. His boss there was Captain Russell S. Crenshaw. However, the rather lackadaisical approach to planning quickly changed when Crenshaw was replaced soon afterward by Turner. Ironically, the fiery and many times constant-drinking Turner and Hill hit it off well.

Even though he liked working for Turner, Hill found out that there was another senior officer who did not especially care for the old *Orange Plan*, nor for what was being created in the new *Rainbow Plans*. Turner best summarized his feelings at the Hart Pearl Harbor Attack Inquiry on April 3, 1944: "I shared the opinion with many others that the war plans which were in existence during 1940 [*Rainbow One* and *Rainbow Four*] were defective in the extreme. They were not realistic; they were highly theoretical. They set up forces to be ready for use at the outbreak of war, or shortly after, which could not possibly have been made available."[23]

Most of the ideas Hill carried back to Washington from Hawaii, formulated by Bloch's staff under scrutiny of Richardson, were meant to serve as a start. It was thought that Op-12 would develop from that draft basic assumptions to be then sent back to Richardson as his guide in making the fleet's portion of the operating plans.

On May 11, Richardson received a dispatch from the Navy Department saying that the plan, plus his distribution of forces outline, had arrived, and was tentatively approved. The minor exceptions would be sent back to Richardson.[24]

When preparing for his congressional testimony, and later when arranging the subjects to be placed in his book, Richardson discovered a digest of a conference held on May 1, 1940. The meeting had been held in Stark's office. Richardson thought that it best summarized the thinking of the Navy's senior officers during that time period.[25] At the time of the conference, Richardson and the fleet were in the midst of its Fleet Problem XXI.

Present with Stark were six other admirals, six captains, and Commander Forrest Sherman, a member of the War Plans Division. Four General Board members were there along with the directors of Naval Intelligence, Fleet Training, and War Plans. In addition, present were the assistant chief of Naval Operations, a member of the Fleet Training Division, and three more members of the War Plans Division. A total of fourteen officers sat and discussed their feelings about a plan called 0-1. This was their second gathering on the subject.[26]

Hill was there, along with Cooke, C. J. Moore, and Crenshaw. With Sherman, they were basically the War Plans Division.

Stark spoke, saying he was open-minded about the subject, but understood that many of the senior officers felt that it put the fleet too far west of Hawaii. Crenshaw went over what he felt was the basic objective of war planning. He said the plans were primarily completed so the logistical and other support missions would provide the fleet's commander with adequate forces. Then, the commander would have the freedom to act as he moved westward.

Cooke then pointed out that there had been a lack of practicality in the plan since its first writing in 1927. He said, however, many benefits had come from the almost annual versions of the plan down through the years. He insisted that the entire basis was concocted upon assumptions. In reality, operations might require a very different movement of the fleet. He recommended specifically that future Fleet Problems provide for the actual capture of an island base. He wanted a permanent Task Force in the fleet, especially for the duty of establishing the advanced base upon its capture.

Hill then assisted Cooke, describing some of the proposed features. It called for movement from the West Coast and hoped that early help would come from England and Holland. Details included a decision on the capture of the Marshalls or Carolines to be dependent upon submarine and air reconnaissance there as the fleet moved west. The assumption was that Japan had already taken the Philippine Islands and Guam, and might be stretched thin to hold the Marshalls and Carolines. Capture of a base there would supposedly isolate the islands to the east, causing their eventual fall. This would protect the American trade to and from Hawaii.

The plan did call for the capture of Truk, and along with the seizure of the Marshalls, would cut the enemy's lines of communication and safeguard that of the U.S. Fleet.

It was stressed to the group that Richardson considered it futile to attempt to make operating plans lasting for more than sixty days. An emphasis was made that it was imperative that materials and facilities for advanced bases be readied in peacetime, not waiting until war broke out. A list of ten immediate needs was submitted, and Stark asked that they be more detailed for later referral.[27]

Discussion then began. Director of Intelligence Walter S. Anderson wanted inserted into the plan consideration that the Navy would initiate cruiser warfare against any Japanese trade routes in the world, forgetting again that the ships were spread thin even at the moment. General Board members Greenslade and King did not think the plan offensive enough.

Chairman of the General Board Sexton, and Leary, said there was not enough time given nor staff currently available to the senior officers afloat to do adequate war planning. Hill could quickly second that thought, having worked tiring hours during his last few months with the fleet. The officers and the fleet commander needed to be more "war plan conscious," noted the two admirals.[28]

So, although Richardson thought he was openly defying the *Orange Plan* by himself, he had plenty of support from his peers and the War Plans Division. He personally dated his "harping" on the unrealistic aspects of the *Orange Plan* back to his assignment as assistant to Leahy. But, he felt seriously that his efforts were no small factor in the establishment of a new series of war plans. In fourteen months, *Orange* would be scrapped for the *Rainbow* proposals, which were already in the making during the spring of 1940.

In fact, work on *Rainbow One,* a plan based on the assumption that the United States would be at war with a number of nations instead of just a single government, began in 1938 when Richardson was chief of the Bureau of Navigation.[29] It was approved on October 14, 1939, and then revised greatly in April of 1940. The Joint Army and Navy Board, the predecessor to the Joint Chiefs of Staff, approved it on May 6.[30]

By the time Turner took over the War Plans Division in the fall of 1940, there were five *Rainbow* plans in different stages of completion.[31] The first plan was approved during a time that Germany was overrunning Belgium, the Netherlands, and France. Richardson believed it was "promulgated on a crisis basis," and it mainly dealt with protection of the Western Hemisphere as covered under the Monroe Doctrine.[32]

Richardson was not happy that the Navy part of the plan had only one mission of offensive nature: "To destroy enemy sea forces operating in the Atlantic or in the Western Hemisphere."[33] This mission seemed to him far removed from reality. Much had changed since he sent Hill back in January, but some of it was agreeable to Richardson. In a May 13, 1940, letter to Stark, he tried to express his view that protecting the Western Hemisphere would be severely hindered if the fleet was moved anywhere west, and that such a move would mean hostilities with Japan.[34] "I feel that at this time it would be a grave mistake to become involved in the West where our interests, although important, are not vital, and thereby reduce our ability to maintain the security of the Western Hemisphere, which is vital."

Stark wrote a reply nine days later, telling Richardson to keep in mind that a complete Allied collapse could occur, including the fleets. "A very probable development of such a catastrophe is visualized in the *Rainbow One Plan.*"[35]

Richardson, Murphy, and Hill hardly had time to prepare a Fleet Operating Plan for support of *Rainbow One* when in came more urgent versions. Richardson wrote in his book that no matter what *Rainbow One* accomplished, it did stir up the naval districts under his command. It got them thinking about plans for a two-ocean Navy for war operations.

In May, with the Richardson staff recommendations mostly included, *Rainbow Two*'s Joint Plan was nearly complete. Stark wrote Richardson that a copy was about on its way to him, with attachments of the studies supporting the decisions.[36] He warned a knowing Richardson that he should assume the present strength and disposition of the fleet as a developmental basis. Stark urged that the tentative Fleet Operating Plan be quickly prepared.

The goal of *Rainbow Two* was basically to accomplish what *Rainbow One* set out, and in addition sustain the Allied powers' influence in the Pacific. The European war gained little notice.[37] Richardson said it called for immediate "projection of U.S. forces into the Western Pacific." It assumed that the British Navy was still operating and helpful, and that the Netherlands was an accommodating ally. *Rainbow Two* lost its validity as European fortunes continued to fall, and Japan made more moves to its south.

While Richardson was talking with Roosevelt and other Navy and governmental officers in early October of 1940, about the fleet being stuck in Hawaii, Murphy met with the War Plans Division. They discussed at length the world's current and future political and military posture, and the useable plans for war. Events were changing daily.

At dinner on the evening of Tuesday, October 9, 1940, a day after the rugged visit with the president, Richardson visited in Stark's home with Knox and seven admirals: Sexton; Nimitz; Bureau of Ordnance Chief William R. Furlong; Bureau of Yards and Docks Chief Ben Moreell; and Bureau of Aeronautics Admiral John H. Towers. Also there in place of Bureau of Ships Chief Samuel M. Robinson was Captain James M. Irish. Cooke was also present. Commandant of the Marines General Thomas Holcomb had been invited, but was not present.

It was a bit odd that the secretary was there. It was he, after all, who had after his visit to Hawaii said that Richardson was a bit too social. Maybe he felt that a small dinner was different, and a chance to grill the officers too much to resist. Knox was a newspaperman, and did enjoy a good interview. During conversation, he asked about war plans against Japan. Richardson said, "We had better have a plan, or ideas for one, or some cockeyed plan [will] be forced on us from above."[38]

Late the next day, October 10, after his visits with Hornbeck, Vinson, and Stark, a call came from Knox.[39] The secretary wanted Stark and Richardson to come over. Richardson and Murphy originally had air tickets to leave that day, but were still working with the war plans staff. The 5:00 P.M. meeting also included Murphy, Cooke, and Ingersoll.

Knox had just been in contact with Roosevelt, and the two were concerned about the reopening of the Burma Road, closed by the British in July under Japanese pressure. The road was the main highway for war materials to be sent to China. How would Japan react on October 17 when traffic resumed, the two wanted to know. If the Japanese responded with attacks on the road, the president was considering shutting off all South American trade with Japan, and was contemplating the patrol line idea—placement of light ships in two lines. One would extend from Hawaii westward to the Philippines, the other from Samoa toward the Dutch East Indies.[40] Stark thought this to be another Roosevelt spontaneous idea, and remained relatively quiet.

The group did not know that Knox, the day after he dined with the Navy leaders at Stark's home, sent over to Roosevelt a memorandum outlining measures in case the Burma Road opening caused a Japanese military response.[41] The memo included three measures to be taken at once: (1) call up the Naval and Marine Reserves, (2) call up the Fleet Reserves on a selective basis, and (3) lay nets and booms for drill purposes. In addition, Knox said, "The following steps in preparation for war can be taken to impress the Japanese with the seriousness of our preparations." He went on to list various options: reinforce the Army in Hawaii; fill up garrisons in the Fourteenth Naval District's outlying bases; withdraw nationals from China; plan to evacuate families out of Hawaii and Panama as well as secure the canal; prepare to seize Japanese merchant ships in ports or near the U.S. coasts; prepare plans for concentration camps; call volunteer reserves; withdraw Marines from North China and close the embassy there; assist the Netherlands East Indies in materials; freeze Japan's credits and assets; assist Chinese credit; and alert the Asiatic Station at once to remove ships other than river gunboats from China. He recommended the last to be the first step.

The sweeping plan may have overwhelmed even Roosevelt, or maybe he agreed. Perhaps that was the real reason Richardson was called to Washington by Knox. The president's question about stored fuel at Somoa was more sensible at that time. It had a relation to the establishment of this patrol.[42] Whatever, before Stark, his staff, Richardson and Murphy arrived to meet with Knox, the president sent over a memorandum saying, "In relations to the secret memorandum . . . covering measures to be taken in preparation for war, I approve the first three. Please do not put any of the others into effect without speaking to me about them."[43] Later the two apparently spoke by phone, prompting the idea that since Richardson was in town, they should have him and the others discuss the possibilities in Knox's office.

Richardson said that in the Knox meeting, the question was quickly raised whether stopping Japanese shipping was an act of war.[44] Amazed at the proposal, Richardson said that the fleet was not prepared for such a plan. Certainly not ready for a war! "We would certainly lose many of the ships," he added. He then asked if the president was considering an act of war.[45] He was not aware that the new British Prime Minister Winston Churchill had asked for a squadron of U.S. ships to visit Singapore at the same time.[46] Richardson was, unknowingly, supported by Army Chief of Staff Marshall, who said such a Churchill proposal was at the least, "provocative." If Knox had clued in the group of the Churchill proposal, Richardson's reaction would have been extremely negative.

Seeing this "line of ships" idea tried, but failing in war plans and subsequent exercises, Richardson thought little enough of that idea, much less of taking a large portion of the fleet to Singapore. "I was amazed at the proposal," Richardson later wrote.[47] It was discussed with Knox that a simpler way to accomplish the goal was to control the source of trade with a patrol off the relatively few ports involved.[48] But, this was dangerous and would be confrontational to the Japanese, as well as to countries in South America.

Knox was displeased with the general reaction, and specifically with Richardson's quick disapproval. Richardson wrote later, "He seemed incensed when I said we were not prepared for such a plan or for the resulting war."[49] Knox quickly responded, in a Roosevelt way, "If you don't like the plan, then draw up one of your own to accomplish the purpose." This suggestion was just what Richardson wanted to do in order to squash what at least one writer called down through the subsequent years "a plan from a reckless amateur Naval strategist [Roosevelt] who thought that ships could be disposed about the oceans in the way that a child places dominoes on a board."[50]

Stark, Richardson, and the war plans staff were asked for an outline to be ready the next day. It was formulated with ten assumptions. The eighth one Richardson must have written: "The United States is prepared to accept war if the measures taken cause Japan to declare war."[51] This was a statement he had been unable to pull from the president.

If the Japanese reacted militarily to the Burma Road reopening, the U.S. Fleet would quickly take ten steps. Mobilization would follow the old *Orange Plan*. A long list followed, detailing that some patrol planes would be withdrawn from the Atlantic as well as two carriers, numerous old and new destroyers, and maybe a cruiser or two. The west coast of both South and North America would be then covered.

A detachment was considered to reinforce the Asiatic Fleet, which would have been withdrawn to the East Indies area. It would operate with the British and Dutch naval forces. A detachment from Hawaii toward Alaska was proposed, with the duty of stopping Japanese commerce. A Train would be assembled at the same time on the West Coast, with Marines boarding. The plan called for reinforcement of Midway, Wake, Johnston Island, Canton Island, and Samoa. Submarines were to go to the Carolines and the Marshalls for some preliminary reconnaissance there to see what was going on. Finally, upon completion of the mobilization, the fleet was to assemble in Hawaii, "prepared to initiate further measures as the situation requires." Nowhere in the outline did it mention time frames.

The plan's outline was completed on time per the Knox orders, but then it was discovered that both the president and Knox had left town.[52] Roosevelt, feeling the election pressure, left on a two-state tour. The attitudes of Richardson, Murphy, Cooke, Moore, and Hill were pretty sour after working all night, thinking the plan was wanted immediately. "Mr. Knox was really incensed with me," remembered Richardson seventeen years later. In two days, the secretary of the Navy and the president lost the remaining patience they had toward Richardson.[53]

Actually, Richardson said he liked Knox, and thought the news-paperman worked well and hard for the Navy. However, "he was impatient and given to snap judgments."[54] Though Knox would later become more astute, he was still ignorant of naval opera-tions. Richardson still had Stark's confidence, or so he thought.[55]

The senior officers who wished the battle to be fought in the Pacific with 100 percent effort were on the wrong track. Events in Europe were dangling constantly on the edge of disaster. When Stark sent the ideas over to Reeves for his thoughts, the view that the Atlantic was more important was mostly sealed.

"Should we wage war against Japan and enable Japan to fight, and furthermore, to fight in an area to her own advantage, it seems to me to be extremely poor strategy," Reeves replied three weeks after the Knox meeting with Stark's staff.

The influential old admiral, the same one so aware that Pearl Harbor could be attacked, threw a real monkey wrench into any Richardson hopes of an offensive movement in the Pacific by telling Stark he believed the soundest and safest course involved three things. First, he thought the United States should protect the Americas. Second, he thought the United States should aid Britain "with our whole strength." That would hopefully ensure victory in the Atlantic and Europe. Then the third step could be taken. It would be dealing with Japan and any other questions in the Far East.[56] The Reeves letter to Stark ended up in the Roosevelt Library, so at some time it was sent over for the pres-ident to review. Surely, it weighed heavily on Roosevelt's deter-mination that he could not have a CinCUS so out of tune with the prevailing Washington philosophy.

Nothing official came of this planning memorandum, but it stirred up ideas and emotions. Richardson thought it pointed out well the administration's careless proposals and attitudes that could quickly lead his fleet into war, unprepared. Therefore, he still was disgusted that the civilian leaders would step so close to causing war. It grated upon his nerves that whenever the military minds mentioned the word "war," tempers flared and harsh words flowed. He felt that the administration thought with so many ships deployed all over the Pacific, perhaps Japan would make a mistake, attack one of them, and provoke America into war despite the isolationist mood in the States. In reality, Richardson was not in real tune with the Navy thought pattern coming from Washington, which was influenced so heavily from the constant daily pressure of European news. In addition, the American public was still not emotionally or mentally prepared for another world war.

When Richardson flew in from Washington on October 11 to see May at their Long Beach home, and to operate his headquarters from the USS *New Mexico,* he was worried. But unlike his actions after his July meeting with Roosevelt, he did not call his sisters in Detroit or Canyon, Texas.[57] Back in Washington, Pan American Airways Chairman C. V. Whitley was meeting with Roosevelt. Use of the Pan Am route facilities could assist any movement west.[58]

Everyone held their breath when midnight, October 17, came. Not much happened, but supplies began to make their way along the 712-mile Burma Road. The aim was to keep the Chinese strong enough to hold the Japanese ground forces concentrating in that war-torn area. This maneuver worked until five days after the attack on Pearl Harbor when Japan clamped down on the use of the road. But, as far as the autumn of 1940, the alarm was falsely ringing.

When Richardson wrote Stark from Bremerton, Washington, on October 22, 1940, he said that neither of the *Rainbow* plans was valid at that point in time.[59] *Rainbow Two* was never issued.[60] Richardson wrote a long summary to his naval boss, often referred to as "that letter," expressing again his views of the present situation, especially in the Pacific.[61] Under current conditions, he cautioned against any movement west by the fleet.

The fear that the British Isles would be invaded by German forces had subsided to an extent, which meant that any future plans would not place the British Fleet into the management realm of the U.S. Navy. The Lend-Lease program positioned the United States in close identification with the British cause, expressed Richardson. The Japanese aggressions had sifted south into Indo-China. There was much expectation that the Japanese would eventually take the Dutch East Indies, the source of 86 percent of the crude rubber supply for the United States.[62]

Richardson and Murphy did notice a more active effort in the planning division aimed at Japan. The admiral felt that, if an aggressive step west were taken in the fall of 1940, it would bring about more active hostilities between the two countries. If the *Orange Plan* was to be used as the guideline of response, its demands were beyond what the U.S. Navy had in strength and resources, said Richardson in "that" letter.[63]

Writing as if he knew something more than those in Washington, Richardson told Stark that even if the British Fleet took over the U.S. positions in the Atlantic, "we cannot . . . denude that ocean of sufficient forces to protect our coastal trade and safeguard interests in South America." He felt that after those commitments were given, there still would not be a large enough U.S. Fleet in the Pacific to advance westward. As he pointed out in the Tokyo War Crimes Trial six years later, the U.S. Fleet was losing in numbers as the Lend-Lease agreement grew. The fleet lost fifty of its ships to the program, though most were of the World War I era.[64] In exchange, the United States received the right to establish bases on British possessions in the Western Hemisphere, including Newfoundland, the Bahamas, Bermuda, Trinidad, British Guiana, St. Lucia, Antigua, and Jamaica.[65]

Richardson not only brought up in "that" letter the deficiencies of the Navy, but he explained that the Marines and Army were not equipped to advance in case of Japanese hostilities toward an Allied position. He wrote on in detail what it would take just to establish the first base. He was alarmed that these moves would come without detailed knowledge of the area being captured. In addition, he made clear that he was not aware of any material yet assembled to accomplish this objective.

Richardson was muddled in a game of his need of preciseness versus the war plan generalities. He noted that only tentative ideas based upon unsupported assumptions had advanced from the forces afloat, and not much more from the Navy

Department. He and Murphy viewed the time limit of sixty to ninety days envisioned to set up the first western base as extremely unrealistic. He wrote that even with much energy, it would be more like six months to a year.

"I know of no flag officer who wholeheartedly endorses the present *Orange Plan*," he wrote Stark, knowing that he might be the loudest voice, but that many others were saying the same things.[65] Even after Turner took over the Navy War Plans Division, Army planners did not change their minds. They felt there was a lack of realistic capacity in the Far East and were reluctant to make any major commitments there.[66]

With *Rainbow One* in front of him, and the tentative draft of the second version there for approval and corrections, Richardson was even more frustrated. "The assumptions of neither of these plans are applicable," he commented. He apologized to Stark for the length of "that" letter, but said that he felt with the lack of good national policy, his position as fleet commander was simply to supply security and defense. He would try to accelerate the preparation for further eventualities as he could.

He listed four things necessary for a *Rainbow Three* effort: security and defense of the Western Hemisphere; long-range interdiction of enemy commerce; threats and raids against the enemy; and extension of operations based upon the real Navy strength, and that of any Allies surviving and able to assist. Richardson closed the letter by once again asking that he be better informed by the Navy Department, meaning Stark.

Richardson felt the letter could not quickly reach Stark if he waited for the next officer courier, so even though he felt it of secret classification, he sent it by registered mail. Turner testified at the Naval Court of Inquiry that when he saw Richardson's letter, "I immediately started preparation" of the plan.[67] McCrea verified this fact years later in an oral history. He was assigned in September of 1940 to the CNO. In Washington his office was next to Turner's.[68] "One day Turner came charging through the door, saying 'The *Orange War Plan* is in a hell of a shape . . . I'm locking my door,'" and added not to disturb him until after 5:00 P.M.[69]

Two weeks later, Stark dropped a personal letter to Richardson. He had done about the same. He sat down one morning in his office in the Old Main Navy Building, and worked until 2:00 A.M. the next day in an effort to "clear my own mind."[70] After a bit of rest, Stark gathered with Turner, Cooke, Wellborn, Sherman, Hill, Sexton, Moore, and Oscar Badger. Apparently this group spent ten days, including a weekend, producing *Rainbow Three*. As of November 12, it was in Roosevelt's office for perusal. Stark referred back to the Richardson July meeting in Washington. He warned Richardson, despite *Rainbow Three*'s inclination to fight in the Pacific, that the feelings that the first vital theater was the Atlantic had not changed.

Even though the Richardson and Murphy ideas were included in places, it was not a good plan. It assumed that the Philippines and northern Indies were lost and that Japan was closing in on Singapore. The United States would deny the enemy, however, the oil in Borneo. This campaign would begin with a Hawaiian gathering of the fleet and troops. Though the move westward would have intermediate objectives along the way, it would not stretch as far as Singapore.[71] Planners had a hard time "dreaming" that any moves by Japan would first include an attack on the U.S. Fleet at Pearl Harbor.

After he arrived back in the Hawaiian area on December 6, Richardson was antsy to hear more about the completion of *Rainbow Three,* often referred to as WPL-44.[72] Murphy returned from Washington on December 21 with four advance copies, plus some revisions done on *Rainbow One*.[73] Richardson was told to prepare fleet operational plans quickly for a war such as envisioned by the assumptions in *Rainbow Three*.[74]

Stark continued in his directive to Richardson, saying that the changing world military situation could affect the policy at any time. He added that two studies were currently being made: one would involve the defense of the entire Western Hemisphere from attacks from the east and west, later called *Rainbow Four;* and one would assume the principal portion of the effort would first move to the eastward, to be called *Rainbow Five*.[75]

Stark made reference to Richardson's complaint about being ill-informed, saying that in the past as well as the future, the CNO had been and would be advising the fleet commander of all he knew. Stark also said that the *Orange Plan* was drawn up under circumstances that no longer existed. He thought his letter would calm Richardson's worries a bit. It did not.

The *Orange Plan* continued to be the only one available to the fleet in the Eastern Pacific for another seven months while war planners drew up *Rainbow Five*. That situation was not good.[76] The two previous *Rainbow* plans would crash and burn along the way as Japan moved south and Germany filled up Europe and North Africa with its troops.

Stark later testified at the Naval Court of Inquiry that he was "delighted to receive" the October 22, 1940, letter from his CinCUS. However, Richardson thought by the mid-1950s that perhaps that was not true. What he wrote had been too direct. Stark's official reply, which did not come for nearly two months, was "very terse."[77] But, Stark said that he was in much agreement with Richardson's thoughts. *Rainbow Three's* planned thrust west probably proved his point. It was the last plan to put heavy offensive action into the Pacific before the war in the Atlantic was over. Stark did claim, however, that Pacific plans of some offensive extent were placed in *Rainbow Five* because of Richardson's summary.

Rainbow Three's completion and delay in delivery to Hawaii dragged on. Stark finally pulled McCrea, now a captain, into his office in early December. He knew little about war plans, but Turner and Stark wanted him to be the messenger to the Pacific, taking the changes in the war plans to Richardson and others. McCrea had been told of this possible trip in the middle of November.[78]

There is no explanation why Murphy had not been given copies when he was in town. He had just left Washington to return to Pearl Harbor. He sat in on meetings about *Rainbow Three,* and conferences held by Turner. McCrea was also at the meetings, and said in testimony later that he felt a relief that Murphy could take back the proceedings and explain them to Richardson. McCrea was taking a crash course in war plans, and still did not feel comfortable with explaining the details.[79]

It would be a long and grueling trip for both men.[80] McCrea left on December 13 from Washington, originally by plane, but was grounded in Kansas City. He then went by train to Albuquerque, where he boarded a plane for Los Angeles. There he chartered a single-engine plane to San Pedro so he could catch a Pan American Clipper to Hawaii.[81]

Halfway there, the Clipper turned back because of terrible weather conditions. After more than twenty-two hours in the air, McCrea found himself in San Francisco with the important papers! At night, they were under his mattress. At the movies they were in his lap; but on the fifth day he was on a plane in the afternoon under orders of the Postmaster General. Enough mail had been removed to accommodate him for the trip.

Murphy was having the same trouble returning to Hawaii, but he was in Long Beach. McCrea knew where Murphy was, and obtained orders to have the Clipper fly to San Pedro. In the plane, they moved around mailbags until comfort was obtained. By 8:00 A.M. the next day, they were at Pearl Harbor.

During his six-day stay, McCrea worked with Richardson and Murphy on the USS *New Mexico*. In the future Richardson planned to establish a headquarters on land, most likely at the submarine base. Though Turner's staff had briefed him on war plans for only two weeks, McCrea fielded many questions from Richardson and his staff. McCrea said this experience helped him better prepare for the reception he would receive when he took the plans to Hart in the Orient.

McCrea was in the dark about Stark's orders coming down the pike relieving Richardson. On January 1, 1941, McCrea went on into the Pacific for three weeks, briefing Hart and even General Douglas MacArthur. He spent ten days talking with Hart, after suffering through a rough six-day trip out.[82] The one-day delay in arrival at Manila was more than that since Hart left twenty-four hours before McCrea set down on January 6 at the Navy Yard, Cavite. McCrea used the time to discuss *Rainbow Three* with Admiral W. R. Purnell, who was leaving soon for a conference at Batavia in the Dutch East Indies.[83]

While on board the USS *Nashville* near Olongapo in the Philippines on January 10, Hart received word of Richardson's dismissal.[84] Hart noted in his diary that Richardson hauling down his flag was unimaginable. At first he assumed a larger duty was awaiting the CinCUS, but then he penned, "Or, is Richardson being fired? I just don't understand anything about it all."

McCrea met up with Hart on January 11 at Olongapo. He sent a message to Turner saying, "Rest assured, I shall get back [to Washington] as promptly as possible—besides, I'm running out of money!" Almost immediately, a dispatch came to McCrea from Stark. It said to contact Kimmel, the new CinCUS, on the way back through Honolulu. Hart was perplexed that Stark should have to ask such a common protocol task of his envoy.[85]

Most of Saturday and Sunday, January 11 and 12, Hart met with Commander (Captain) A. M. R. Allen, a naval observer at the American-Dutch-British conversations in late 1940 and April 1941, and McCrea. He noted that he did not like the outlook of being in the prospective war, and was beginning to believe that perhaps the "keep America out of the war cult" attitude was tending to grow positively with him.[86]

On January 13, Hart received a dispatch from Purnell that all was going well with the Dutch conference. The war planning meetings kept Hart from much time on the bridge. He wrote his comments about *Rainbow Three* in longhand, so his notes that evening were short. On January 13, Hart started his seventeenth diary volume, stating that it might be the last before retirement. He was sixty-five that day. His birthday gifts were smoking accessories.[87]

Instructed by Stark to wait for Purnell's report, McCrea paid a visit to U.S. High Commissioner of the Philippines Francis B. Sayre. After the talks and the receipt of the report, McCrea left Manila on January 20.[88] Along with him was a letter from Hart to Stark with thoughts on *Rainbow Three*, and a memo from Hart to Richardson.[89]

When McCrea arrived two days later at Pearl Harbor, he wrote, "I met with Admiral Richardson. I didn't get any impression from him that he was bitter over his sudden relief."[90] Holding in his feelings, Richardson fooled most everyone. "I had gotten to know and like him greatly," said McCrea. He presented Richardson and Kimmel a twelve-page memo of notes and thoughts as a result of his conversations with Hart and others in the Asiatic Fleet.

Hart had plans in all directions, if worse came to worse. Through McCrea, Hart related to Richardson some thoughts that might be insightful later when dealing with MacArthur. Feeling that the general "knows many things that are not so," Hart warned that if it weren't for the salary, MacArthur would "duck out." Hart felt that MacArthur was not too happy in the job. On the other hand, MacArthur knew that if attacked by the Japanese, he would receive little or no help.

In his memo, McCrea reported to Richardson and Kimmel that there were 10,000 Americans in the Philippines and 4,000 U.S. troops. The report on other facets of strength there was dim. Hart, unlike Richardson at Pearl Harbor, was ready to net and boom (put nets and floating objects to stop entry to the bay) at the "front door," Manila Bay. Outside that area, and from the "back door" of Luzon, Hart felt little could be done to stop a landing and cross-country attack.

"The best thing the 16th Naval District has," added McCrea in the memo, "is the underground development of Corregidor." The Shanghai security unit was moved there. The location was then ready for use as a main radio receiving station. However, as at Pearl Harbor, the air patrol was puzzling. "The air people don't understand me, and I evidently don't understand them," Hart told McCrea. Hart felt they were not going "full out."

Again, McCrea went over *Rainbow Three* with both Richardson and Kimmel. Taffinder; Captain W. W. Smith, to be Kimmel's chief of staff; Captain W. S. DeLany; Captain C. H. "Soc" McMorris; and Murphy were in attendance.[91] All agreed that the antiaircraft defenses of Pearl Harbor left much to be desired. Richardson commented that they were "wholly and completely inadequate."[92] He gave out a long list of what he felt needed attention, then Kimmel chimed in with his thoughts too.

McCrea pointed out what Hart said about his situation, "I doubt Washington will be able to do anything in time and that all that will be accomplished must be done locally." In early 1941, Hart still had the feeling that Japan might leave the Philippines out of its immediate plans of invasion. He had no confidence in the U.S. Army, saying it "just doesn't think we should be fighting out here." This attitude was not new. Richardson had experienced the same thing in 1938 when he worked with Embick.

As for Pearl Harbor, Richardson went on to tell McCrea, "The army must realize that the protection of this base is their paramount consideration of the Pacific." He must have thought that he would have been more able to bring that purpose to fruition with the newly assigned Army commander in Hawaii, General Walter C. Short.

Richardson even had an idea of specifics for the Army duties and munitions. Kimmel suggested that a balloon barrage in and near Pearl Harbor was needed, as well as additional planes. McCrea said that Richardson was not a fan of the balloons, thinking them a nuisance to his own forces. Torpedo nets were discussed, but the group thought the technical difficulties involved were insurmountable. No one at Pearl Harbor envisioned that torpedoes could be altered to fall into the water from planes, and then run shallow. The common experience was that, before leveling off, they initially went farther down than the depth of Pearl Harbor.

Hart said he accepted all the *Rainbow Three* assumptions, but added, "It does not appear to me that they have been thought out all the way through." He noted that Japan could initially hit the Philippines, at the same time go down the east coast of the Philippines and roll up to the Netherland East Indies, and/or stay west and attack the British possessions first, including North Borneo. He almost had it pegged, but still said, "I think they will hope to the last to keep us out of it."[93]

Hart completed his remarks, given to Richardson by McCrea. "This is the front line trench," and added that above all, he wanted priority of attention from the Navy Department. He disliked follow-up dispatches to Washington, and considered answers altogether too slow. He was frustrated, and fearful. He seriously thought that Admiral John M. Smeallie's December 1940 break-down as commander of the Sixteenth District was due to too much worry over war plans. "The average Naval officer gets lost in the maze of details," he added. He thought that if the leaders expected another year of peace, then they should tear apart the plans and simplify them.[94]

Though delivery of war plans was his mission, both Richardson and Kimmel knew that McCrea would give a long report to Stark upon his return, about all subjects. Bunking on the USS *Brooklyn* and then the USS *Houston,* during the days McCrea sat in on the meetings of the two staffs, one incoming and one outgoing.[95] A few Richardson staff members would be mingled into Kimmel's. Concerns by the new CinCUS were about the same as those expressed by Richardson, naturally.

McCrea left four days before the change of command cere-monies were held on board the USS *Pennsylvania.* In fifty-two hours he returned to Stark loaded down with notes he had col-lected during the seven weeks.[96] The work impressed Stark, and gained McCrea the job of drafting most of Stark's letters to Kimmel in 1941.

As for Richardson, the *Rainbow Three* mentality ended when on January 22, 1941, he received a dispatch from Stark. It stated that the international situation had deteriorated so rapidly that he suggested that a new plan follow *Rainbow Three* mobilization with some modifications. Stark called it *"Plan Dog,"* which came from Section D in a memorandum he had prepared for Knox. It called for a much stronger British Isles reinforcement, most coming from the Pacific Fleet. The kicker was at the end. "Asiatic Fleet can not expect early re-enforcement. Carry out tasks according to circum-stances." Hart's forces were basically left to improvise.[97]

The door was rattling. Despite signing use accords with the pro-Axis Vichy Indo-China government, within hours on September 22, the Japanese Fifth Infantry, withdrawing from China, crossed the Indochina border near a rail junction at Lang Son. The road to Hanoi was opened. The local brigade was no match for the 30,000 Japanese troops. Japan joined German and Italy on September 27 with a treaty of alliance, signing a Tripartite Pact. Richardson learned about this pact on the way to the West Coast, and wrote in his notes, "Only a question of time until we are in the war in both oceans."[98] The three Axis countries pledged to help the one attacked by the United States or Britain.[99] Rather quietly, the U.S. Marines landed at Midway Island to begin construction of defenses. Knox placed organized Naval Reserves on short notice to report for duty. On October 9, while Richardson and Murphy were in Washington, DC, the United States discontinued subsidies on wheat previously shipped into the Far East.[100]

On October 25, Japanese planes attacked Chungking, China, and toyed with the Americans in the gunboat *Tutuila* and those in the American embassy by dropping bombs nearby. Other bad news was weather. A typhoon destroyed U.S. Navy Yard facilities at Guam on November 3. Though Richardson thrived in his job and would not have liked to be a member of the General Board, at times he may have wished that he was in Greenslade's shoes. He was on orders from Knox, touring the new bases acquired from the British.

Richardson would not want Leahy's new job—ambassador to the shaky pro-Nazi Vichy government in France. Leahy was notified by Roosevelt in mid-November 1940 that his cushy job as governor of Puerto Rico was over. The president felt that Leahy was perfect for the assignment in Europe. He wanted Leahy to stop the French from becoming an ally of Germany and an enemy of the British.[101]

By January of 1941, Japan was feeling the effect of the lack of certain commodities it had been buying from the United States. These included arms, ammunition, aviation gasoline, petroleum products, machine tools, scrap iron, pig iron, copper, lead, zinc, aluminum, and other elements vital to a war effort.[102] The United States would no longer provide these parts of the equation; thus, Japan would look elsewhere, and quickly.

Richardson saw all this news in the daily papers. So did the

American citizens who were still stubbornly hoping to remain aloof from the foreign troubles. The Japanese also noted that on January 9, the first increment of American workmen arrived at Wake Island aboard the transport *William Ward Burrows*. A new Naval Air Station was to be constructed. Tensions grew higher.

With a *Rainbow Five* draft in hand, as delivered by McCrea, and in collaboration with Kimmel, Richardson wrote Stark on January 25, 1941.[103] He said the CinCUS war planning staff would do no more work on *Rainbow Three* and would move on to the fifth in the series. Murphy was dizzy by then, and Richardson knew at that point it was futile to hold on to the Western Pacific as a priority. The European war was number one on the agenda.[104]

Rainbow Five actually began in writing as a memorandum from Stark's office after his late-night formulation of an outline.[105] Its thoughts came as a result of a September London meeting of military and naval officers of Great Britain and the United States, and from the urgings of Richardson to use more reality. The memo was dated November 12, 1940, and incorporated Stark's subparagraph D that dealt with a strong offensive in the Atlantic, and defensive posture in the Pacific.[106] After a second meeting, this time held in Washington between the British and American military staffs, it became "the chosen vehicle" for the *Rainbow Five* war plan.

Thus, it was the plan that went into effect in basic form after December 7, 1941.

In summary, Richardson listed three ingredients of necessity for war plans: (1) the strategic plan had to be within the capabilities of the logistical plan; (2) the time in preparation should be considered; and (3) the plans had to be in place prior to the period of strained relations or war. Old plans can always be readjusted, but new ones are difficult to prepare.[107]

When he wrote his book, Richardson was still confused about why the planners omitted some obvious points. He felt the assumption that Japan would be in a war with the United States without notice should be in the plan. Neither *Rainbow Five* nor the Fleet Operating Plan assumed this scenario, even though from 1923 until 1940 the old *Orange Plans* did. Nowhere in *Rainbow Three* nor in *Five* was it written that a period of strained relations, and hostilities, would precede the formal declaration of war, though to Richardson that seemed sensible and probable. After all, that was exactly what was happening as the plans were being constructed.

He also felt strongly that it was disastrous that the warning Pearl Harbor could be a Japanese objective was not in the *Rainbow* plans. It was placed into the *Orange Plan* on March 26, 1937.[108] Perhaps the planning staffs were just not aware of the content changes, or the many times the Fleet Problems addressed an attack on Hawaii. Perhaps the many intercepted messages in late 1940 and all of 1941 indicated a southern movement by the Japanese, and that information was believed. Or, perhaps the decrypted messages were not shared with the planners often enough.

For leaving this possibility out, Richardson aimed his perplexity and the blame toward Stark. In his book, Richardson reminded readers that in his last letter to Stark, his sixth assumption about fleet action addressed that possibility. On January 25, 1941, he wrote: "Japanese attacks may be expected . . . surprise raids on Pearl Harbor, or attempts to block the channel, are possible."[109]

Richardson also took Kimmel to task for placing into his fleet's War Operating Plan a change in that assumption. Kimmel's war plans staff included as its head Captain Charles H. "Soc" McMorris, assisted by Murphy, Commander L. D. McCormick, and Lieutenant F. R. DuBorg. They wrote that the fleet should expect "possibly raids or stronger attacks on Wake, Midway and other outlying United States positions . . . raiding and observation forces widely distributed in the Pacific, and submarines in the Hawaiian area."[110] Down in the list of tasks to subordinates, Kimmel listed as number thirteen, "Guard against attacks by Japan."[111] Sadly, there are no records of comments Richardson and Murphy may have had in casual conversation during their retirements. It seems strange, however, that Murphy would have been a part of such omissions.

Still, Richardson put the ultimate blame upon Stark and his

staff for not ordering a change to the plan, reflecting a possible attack on Pearl Harbor. He absolved himself of any blame, saying, "Any influence I might have had on our War Plans ceased when, on June 11, 1941, the *Orange Plan, Rainbow One* and *Rainbow Three* were placed inactive." Concentration was then on *Rainbow Five,* a plan on which Richardson did not directly work, though his persistence prodded its creation.

In the January 25, 1941, letter that McCrea took to Stark, Richardson pulled no punches on how he felt about the contents of *Rainbow Three.* He said that plan fell short "under the new situation," and that with emphasis toward the Atlantic war, if Japan struck in the Pacific, the fleet would be in a "waiting attitude," primarily defensive. However, he reserved the option that the fleet then seize opportunities to damage Japan as the situations present themselves, or could be created. That was exactly what happened after the attack on Pearl Harbor. The United States military fired back at Japan with the Doolittle raid in April of 1942, and as the Navy rebuilt and the Army grew, slowly drove across the wide Pacific.

The Doolittle raid by Army bombers was one of the "created" opportunities. After the attack on Pearl Harbor, the Navy was in action several times west of Hawaii, but military and civilian leaders wanted a message sent home to Japan that there would be retaliation. For months the pilots practiced a takeoff on the ground, then loaded up on the new carrier USS *Hornet.* When 600 miles from Japan the planes took off the deck for the first time, all successfully. They flew over various areas of Japan, dropped bombs, and then hoped they had enough fuel to reach stations awaiting them in China. Some crashed, and eight were kept prisoner, including one who had gone to Paris Junior College in Richardson's hometown. He and two others were executed. The bombing did little damage, but the surprise to the Japanese and the upshot of morale to the United States made it all worthwhile. It was all portrayed in a book and movie called *Thirty Seconds Over Tokyo.*

Richardson thought a Stark-ordered change to the Fleet

Operating Plan's non-assumption of an attack on Hawaii would have brought a different action to the November 27, 1941, "War Warning" dispatch drawn up by Turner and approved by Stark. "Pearl Harbor," felt Richardson, at that time "would have been protected by an adequate seaplane patrol to the full limit of the resources available."[112]

CHAPTER TWENTY-TWO

Patrol and Security of Fleet
Focus Is Intense, Results Weak

Seaplane patrol headaches were a constant with Richardson and the fleet in 1940. From the time of docking at Pearl Harbor in May, the impossible had been attempted.

A little rearranging and changes in assignments were on the agenda during October of 1940, especially in the leadership position of Patrol Wing Two. Fitch was moved to Commander Carrier Division One. His son Jack had been visiting him at his quarters on Ford Island that summer. "There was talk even then of a Jap attack," he said. "DD's [destroyers] patrolled off Pearl Harbor, along with the Pat Wing Patrols. There was always talk of Jap spies on the Island."[1] Then, in came Bellinger with his family on the SS *Lurline*.[2] He would take over the difficult assignment of fulfilling Richardson's wishes that patrols be sent out each day. The Army's mission was to protect the Navy, but according to agreement, the Navy would provide offshore scouting by air. Pat Wing Two was assigned that task, and it was Bellinger's responsibility to command.[3]

In late 1940, Richardson and Stark hardly exchanged ideas on moving the fleet back to the West Coast. In fact, perhaps the last time they mentioned it in correspondence was on November 12 when Stark wrote, "It does not now appear that we can withdraw . . . without some good pretext."[4] It was Richardson's feeling that Stark became of the same opinion as Roosevelt as early as the October CinCUS visit to Washington, DC. However, Stark later testified that all discussion or mention of moving the fleet back did not disappear until about the time of command change on February 1, 1941.[5]

Nonetheless, the Navy Department did not change homeports so sailors could bring out their families. "I am sure it will come as something of a shock to the Honolulu Chamber of Commerce,"

Richardson wrote later, quoting from the Commander Destroyers Battle Force May 17, 1940, report, "[but] . . . in 1940 . . . enlisted men, on the whole, did not desire duty in the Hawaiian area."[6]

Still, Richardson thought that bringing the families would be money well spent, but the idea was bucked by Moreell. By then, Richardson expressed his displeasure at the recommendation to bar families, but to little success. Some families were still coming out on their own budgets. Richardson had a well-learned theory about this scenario, and also the reason the Atlantic Patrol had more submarines there than he had in the Pacific. It was simple to him. "It was a matter of life that its [Washington's] principal officers could drop in on the Department any day . . . and air their needs and views. For the rest of the U.S. Fleet . . . talking matters over with the 'powers that be' in Washington was quite more difficult a matter."[7]

It was also difficult to place mid-Pacific island base construction on anything near moderate priority. The Atlantic bases gained through the trade for destroyers agreement with Britain positioned the allocation of funds toward the maintenance and improvement of them.[8]

Thus, the CinCUS had to plug on, attempting as best he could to train the fleet and provide security for the ships and facilities. This task required some cooperation with the Army, but Richardson and Snyder thought the two worked together fairly well. There were, of course, complaints about fleet maneuvers clashing with Army plans. There was no single air commander for the forces assigned to Herron and Richardson.

The November aerial attack by the British against Italian ships in Taranto, Italy, impressed Richardson and his staff, and perhaps they studied the earlier British attack on French vessels after France's surrender. The staff had what was believed set into place a decent plan of security around the fleet, with patrol planes searching each day to some extent. But, the ease with which Britain had destroyed a large part of the Italian Fleet using old biplanes was unnerving. In Washington, Knox was impressed, and was awaiting more details, "especially to what extent aerial torpedoes were used."[9] Knox, after a few months on the job, was convinced that the cautious and precise attitude at the Navy Department was actually defeatist. Like Edison's lack of understanding that men live on a ship and on off hours sleep or play, Knox seemed unable to comprehend that if a U.S. ship sank, it was difficult to win the battle.

Richardson was becoming cautious. Pownall was not sure when it was ordered, but pressed into his mind when interviewed in 1989 was that Richardson ordered at least the USS *Enterprise* to man batteries early every morning and in the evenings.[10]

Bellinger came to the Naval Academy the year after Richardson left, and had spent two stints as commander of the Naval Air Station in Norfolk, Virginia. He had been encouraged in 1920 by Roosevelt to stay in the Navy, and was called Pat by the president two decades later when Bellinger rode him around Norfolk. Many of the pilots Bellinger would meet in Hawaii he had trained. He was fifty-five years old and had participated in mock attacks on Pearl Harbor. About his only drawback was that his eyesight was too poor to allow him to fly alone.[11]

He wore five hats in Hawaii: commander of Pat Wing Two; Task Force 9; Fleet Air Detachment; Task Force 4; and liaison with Bloch. His responsibilities stretched from Ford Island to Wake Island, and he took orders from both Richardson and Bloch. He conferred with Towers, Forrestal, and Stark before coming out to Hawaii, and was told by Towers to take his family with him. Stark agreed, saying, "If there is any case of trouble, there will be plenty of time to get them out."

When he was sworn in and took over for Fitch on November 11, Bellinger was a captain. Roosevelt promoted him to rear admiral a month later. Bellinger was disappointed with the defenses of Oahu. He was even more concerned when the Navy began to study what happened at Taranto.

As far back as 1928, predictions had flown around the fleet that a continuous offshore search would be needed to protect Pearl Harbor from carrier attack.[12] To prevent this kind of attack from happening, a patrol would need to be on a search of three hundred miles out. Planes had to be spaced at about thirty to forty miles in order to spot ships, especially submarines. Dyer said in an interview that Pat Wing Two never could search even 180 degrees.[13]

In 1938, an estimate was made that to search 360 degrees in the Hawaiian area would require 159 aircraft. If war were launched as according to the then current *Orange War Plan,* 199 planes would be necessary. Stark could only provide 110 for 1939, and not many of those were in Hawaii. When Richardson was removed in January 1941, Bellinger told Kimmel that he had only fifty-seven old PBY-3s, with eight awaiting spare parts. Pearl Harbor Hearing statistics in 1945 revealed that when Richardson took over the fleet in January of 1940, some sixty-seven "VPB" planes were at Pat Wing Two. A year later four fewer were at Pearl Harbor, the only aircraft capable of flying a long distance.[14] Bellinger's planes had flown 5,145 hours since October 16, 1940. He compiled a strong letter to Stark in mid-January 1941, running it through Richardson's lame-duck staff for ideas.[15]

Bellinger wote that Pat Wing Two operated on a shoestring, was not ready to assist, was not slated for upgrades until last, and listed the steps he would take to present a decent security patrol for installations and ships at Pearl Harbor.[16] Although Andrews echoed these thoughts, Bellinger found out that local sabotage was more on the minds of both Navy and Army leadership.

Still, early on, Richardson insisted that Pat Wing Two search seven days a week, even though he knew the distance was limited. It was feasible to search out to about 150-250 miles from the carriers, and up to 700-800 miles in distance from shore by patrol aircraft. The pilots were never aware of their assignment until they reported to work at 5:30 a.m. each day. Richardson met great resistance from the crews.

Dyer said that about every three months the Pat Wing Two "people" would come up through Commander Scouting Force with a "tremendous beef on this tiresome search."[17] The aircraft were simply wearing out, and the pilots were drained. George van Deurs was one such pilot. He said a 360-degree search was tried, at six or seven hundred miles, "but after three days of that [activity] every engine in the wing needed an overhaul."[18]

There were no spare mechanics. To cover just nine degrees required forty planes. The U.S. Fleet and the Asiatic Fleet had all the aircraft assigned to patrol, but the numbers were not credible. Staff aviation expert Arthur C. Davis, and before him, Hardison, presented the wing's argument, while Bieri and Dyer were strong to keep the search. Taffinder would ride the fence. Richardson was left to decide, and each time he kept them flying to some extent. Dyer said the premise was that if you could not know 100 percent about what was on the sea around Hawaii, then it was at least sensible to know 50 percent of the activity.

Van Deurs commented that the thinking among pilots was that 700 miles was not far enough. Such a search would not reveal a Japanese carrier, for it would still be over the horizon. "A carrier could start a run-in after we left, and be at launching point by daylight the next morning."[19] The fourteen-hour patrols took a tremendous toll.

Strean worked for Van Deurs. He remembered patrolling out to 500 miles or so. He said, "I understood that Admiral Richardson was always aware of the fact that planes were not plentiful, and that the kind of constant patrols he wanted to maintain were not quite possible because the burden was too great." When Strean left in late 1940 to teach flight school students, "there were patrols sent out in certain sectors, but there were other sectors that were left blank." He was "just a young pilot who was carrying out orders," Strean added.[20]

The patrols actually began simply as part of Fleet Problem XXI when it temporarily anchored at or near Pearl Harbor on April 10. Richardson had planned this activity as early as January 12, 1940.[21] In early March, he instructed Calhoun to execute security plans for the fleet when it came into the Pearl Harbor area. Calhoun was to work with the Fourteenth Naval District, which had some responsibilities along that line. The published assumption of the exercise was that a foreign power *might* execute an attack. The May 22, 1940, Base Force report from Calhoun had not ignored an enemy attack on ships, but it naturally assumed it would be outside Pearl Harbor and off Honolulu since that was where the fleet was then located.[22]

At first, it was an inner patrol covering out to 30 miles radius from Ahua Point Lighthouse. It was complemented by an antisubmarine patrol of all the entrances to Lahaina Roads. The outer patrol would stretch to 180 miles radius, centered at Ahua Point near Hickam Field.[23] Twelve aircraft daily were to fly from daylight to dark.[24] It was then solely an exercise, not adequate in number of planes or distance covered to truly protect the fleet, Richardson later said in testimony. However, he emphasized at that time, though he gave the assumption of an attack, he felt no fear of a Japanese fleet assault. Still, he said, "I flew this patrol so it could not be said of me after the thing [attack] happened that I was warned and did nothing about it." Stark had implied in messages that there could be an attack somewhere, and though Richardson did not think it imminent, he used the patrols as a "personal defensive device" as well as a training exercise.[25]

As commander of the Aircraft Scouting Force, Bristol created a chart in June. It visualized certain patrol areas. Richardson later wrote that what Bristol perceived was basically used after December 7, 1941, when necessary patrol plane resources became available.[26] In 1940, it took only six months to build a PBY, but twenty-four months to train a pilot. So, assistance to Pearl Harbor was slow in coming. Bloch called for more planes before Richardson did. Pilots were required to have fewer and fewer hours before flying in the fleet. Of course, this change did not sit well with leaders of the Air Scouting Force who saw their time dwindle in gunnery, navigation, bombing, and radio training. Several times between the fall of 1940 and December 7, 1941, patrols were called off. "Train some spare crews," Van Deurs recalled being told. "Well, fine, but we had no people to train for spare crews."[27] A well-qualified aviator needed to know many things. This need for pilot preparation put much pressure on Richardson, who continued the reconnaissance though constant reports were given to him by Davis about the wear and tear on machinery and personnel.[28]

Dyer said the staff continued to have dogfights in conference on the matter. Richardson would patiently listen, and then make the decision to continue the patrols.[29]

In June, Richardson did not believe a "responsible" country would provoke war by attacking the fleet or base. He focused security possibilities upon sabotage from small craft. He thought this sabotage would come in the form of a blockage of the channel entrance to Pearl Harbor, or that mines would be laid in the approaches to the docking complex.[30] When the June 17 alert was placed upon the Army, Andrews was the fleet's senior officer present in Pearl Harbor. He modified the patrols to a distance of 300 miles. The arc changed from 220-235 degrees to 180 miles through west to north, Richardson told the congressmen in 1945.[31]

In July, Fitch sent a note to Bristol, saying that the daily security patrol consisted of six planes, each flying 8.5 hours on average, or 1,500 hours per month, 50 percent over normal.[32] The Navy Department priority list for the Hawaiian area patrol was low, and it was mid-December before word came that PBY-5s would be shipped to assist. At that time these craft were mostly assigned to the Atlantic, or sold to the British and other future allies.[33]

Richardson finally modified the patrol to cover periodically an arc between 170 degrees and 350 degrees. He attempted to confuse anyone watching each day from shore. Sectors were rotated, but most of the time the search was in the same basic direction.

Bellinger continued to dispatch unhappy thoughts to Richardson about the daily reconnaissance. Dyer called them "long-winded" letters. Bellinger pointed out that it took fifty naval patrol planes to search an 800-mile, 360-degree area from Pearl Harbor. He had only about sixty VPB planes in total, when all were in good repair. Planes and crews could fly only every second day on the 922-mile journey. Bellinger was conservative in his estimates compared to an Army report that it would take seventy-two B-17D types.[34] At the same time, Bellinger believed that the shorter, 300-mile route by six to twelve planes was so unacceptable it was nothing but a burden on patrol plane resources. Sometimes Bellinger was not able to put six planes in operation.

He would improvise now and then, allowing planes flying other missions to search while they were en route.[35] Richardson later pointed out in his book that the flying was unnecessary every day—for when the fleet was out, the patrols flew from it.[36]

Thomas H. Moorer, later to become a CNO, was with the patrol planes in 1939-41. He agreed with the six-plane availability statement of Bellinger, and confirmed that the sectors flown each day were chosen at random.[37]

While Richardson was still away from Hawaii and on the West Coast, he and Stark corresponded about the patrols and security of the fleet. Richardson was in draft form on his new effort to tighten up external security, and continued to prescribe the long-range air reconnaissance. However, that was not in the final form issued. Before he published the final rules, he wrote to Stark from Long Beach on November 28, and stated that "wartime measures" of security had to be carried out. He thus sent a tentative draft of the proposals to the CNO office for suggestions.[38] Murphy was in Washington as an official courier for the fleet, and to work on war plans. He told Richardson by letter that Stark felt that wartime security measures were not necessary, nor was the continuous use of air patrols. That information was stricken from Richardson's December 5 order.[39] It proved to be a serious, costly decision that the Japanese found advantageous one year later.[40]

At this time while Richardson was hammering Stark for help, and Stark was attempting to relay the CinCUS thoughts to Knox and the president, Grew wrote a long letter to Roosevelt on December 14 appraising the situation. He summarized that unless the United States was prepared to withdraw entirely from the entire sphere of Greater East Asia and the South Seas, "we are bound eventually to come to a head-on clash with Japan."[41]

Stark did not reply to Richardson's November 28 letter until December 23, having received it only nine days earlier. He knew from Murphy's comments that it was coming, however, and strained to locate its whereabouts in the confines of letter bins in Washington. However, Stark told Congress in 1945 that, unknown to Richardson, it was mailed from the USS *New Mexico* after the arrival back in Pearl Harbor on December 6.

Most of Richardson's questions, however, Stark and Murphy had discussed, and the answers were presented to Richardson when his war plans officer returned to Hawaii. Stark, however, went into detail in his December 23 reply, stating, "As I discussed with Murphy, there will be an advantage in making occasional sweeps by aircraft and surface craft, but it is not yet necessary to make these continuous."[42] Incredulously, Richardson had no great support from the CNO on patrols out of Pearl Harbor, even though Stark constantly reminded him that war could be near.

The bulk of the letter replied to Richardson's plans for a large exercise that would train for beach landings. Richardson had mentioned that maybe San Clemente would be perfect for the final scale, but Stark nixed that idea. Surely knowing that Richardson's time as CinCUS was very short, Stark still went on to discuss such training. Any such exercises were not to be held until most likely mid-1941.

Amazingly, Stark began his letter to Richardson by stating, "Though security measures should be prosecuted . . . it has not yet reached the demands of full war time" status. However, he ended it by noting, "Every 24 hours past is just one day nearer to actual hostilities . . . be completely in the frame of mind that we will be in the fighting business most any time, and purely as a guess on my own part, I would say at any time after the next 90 days." That statement seemed drastic to Richardson, who would be on the attacked end of such warnings, while at the same time not afforded the patrol elements to prevent such a calamity.

So, Richardson had in his hand the letter from Stark of December 23, essentially ordering him to cut back the patrols. Thus, a turning point in the Pearl Harbor attack saga was reached.[43] Richardson discontinued the long-range patrols, and held coverage to just the fleet operating areas. He never changed his view about patrols, but he did alter his previous actions. Two weeks after the change of command, Kimmel's security orders were released, basically written by Richardson's staff, and basically the same as the one issued on December 5. Richardson wrote later that, though Bellinger was very influential, he put most of the blame upon Stark for discontinuing long-range reconnaissance.[44] Part he put upon himself. "Once stopped, my successor found it unnecessary to restart them," he wrote. "Perhaps if I had kept them going, and he had kept them going, despite CNO's disbelief of their necessity, they would have served a very useful purpose on December 7, 1941."[45]

Bloch brought it to Richardson's attention that he was convinced the Army's means to defend the fleet were "insufficient." As Murphy described to the Hart Pearl Harbor Inquiry in 1944, even "telephone communications with the Army were almost non-existent."[46] After discussing the figures, Richardson decided to see for himself what was there.[47] He toured all the Army facilities in December, with the guidance of Herron, and then sent a memo to Bloch.[48] Bloch released a report, partially drafted, and then approved by Richardson, of the views of the Fourteenth Naval District on patrols and security of the harbor and other nearby bases.[49]

By mid-December of 1940, the idea had begun to develop that a Japanese carrier attack was highly feasible. In their study, Bloch and Richardson gave bleak conclusions.[50] Right out of the box, Bloch addressed the issue of an aircraft carrier attack on Pearl Harbor. There were two ways to defend against such aggression: locate and destroy the carrier before launching of its aircraft; or, if that effort failed, to drive off the bombing planes after they had left the mother ship. First, however, everyone involved had to be convinced that plans needed to include a coordinated defense effort.

Navy pilot Van Deurs said that no matter how much discussion went on between Navy and Army Air Corps staff, even basic rules of responsibility were impossible to put in writing. He remembered one conversation about carrier attack, probably after Richardson left, when a colonel stated, "You know it couldn't happen. We'd have two weeks to get ready and decide what we're going to do." When Van Deurs asked how that could be, the colonel said that intelligence would "let us know." Van Deurs, who later attained flag rank, told him how simple it was to lose a fleet. "We can't tell if the Japs are going to head this way instead of China," and related a recent incident in which the press tried to find out what had happened to two cruisers that did not return with the U.S. fleet after exercises.[51]

Frustrated, Van Deurs even drew up a report describing two possible routes of attack the Japanese carriers could take to surprise Pearl Harbor, and presented it to Bellinger. The possibility report was observed by the Army Air Corps, signed and placed in a file, and never put into effect. Van Deurs' second scenario proved to be correct. It was another chink in the defensive armor, another system-wide failure poking its face above the distant horizon. But, Richardson was working on some coordination and knowledge that would possibly correct the situation, and he expected to be able to convince the incoming Short to react to the facts.

Quickly, he pulled ideas together. In full agreement that the Army could not protect Pearl Harbor with its current abilities, on January 4, 1941, Richardson sent what would be his final report to Stark. Items other than air patrol were discussed, such as the feasibility and problems of placing torpedo nets to protect moored vessels.

The report's contents floated around Washington, and by its repeated reference in the 1945-46 Congressional Pearl Harbor Hearings, Richardson surmised that it did bring to Pearl Harbor a small number of additional ships, aircraft, guns, and equipment.[52]

Another resounding change Richardson made in the fleet, which would be discussed again and again in the future, was to move the ships into Pearl Harbor. Richardson openly took the blame for this mistake.[53] At that time, however, his staff carefully studied what meager facts they had on Taranto, especially the torpedo effectiveness. In Washington, staff studies simply came to the conclusion that torpedoes would not run in Pearl Harbor because of its shallow depth.[54]

The result was that the staff felt that Lahaina Roads, though safer than anchorage outside Honolulu, was a vulnerable position, both to submarine attack and to aircraft dropping torpedoes. Therefore, Richardson reduced anchorage there beginning even before he returned to Hawaii from the West Coast. After the middle of November, the number of ships in those waters was practically zero, Richardson later wrote. The fleet either was underway at sea or berthed inside Pearl Harbor.

Settling into Pearl Harbor on a habitual basis was the best of the worst choices for Richardson, who, as Charles Julian Wheeler later said, was one of the few who anticipated an attack by air. "He was tremendously exercised about the safety of the Fleet," said Wheeler, who was on the USS *Astoria* during 1940. Mary Taylor Alger Smith, wife of Commander Roy C. Smith, Jr., said that her husband saw the danger of an air attack each day, and continually commented that not only were the ships in peril there, but the big oil tanks were inviting targets. "He said this would be the easiest place in the world to bomb." She heard Richardson's comments at parties when he fretted in polite terms over the bottled-up fleet.[55]

But, this knowledge was nothing new, and Richardson was not uttering secret information to those at the parties. Back in May, when Edison visited the fleet, the headlines of the *Honolulu Star-Bulletin* screamed in 72-point type,

Edison Finds P.H. Vulnerable.

The kicker below warned, "Says Exposed Oil Tanks Are Easy Targets."[56]

On November 28, Richardson also dismissed for good the conversations on torpedo threat from aircraft. He thought later, however, that if his staff had more detailed information about the Taranto attack sixteen days earlier, and the July British attacks on the French ships at Mers-el-Kebir, near Oran in Algeria, and the French battleship *Richelieu* at Dakar in Senegal, the decision would have been different. His son Joe wrote to author John Toland, after the publication of Toland's book *Infamy: Pearl Harbor and Its Aftermath,* emphasizing this point. He thought the significance of Taranto was not covered well by any writer as of the early 1980s, and that "this most vital link in this whole chain of disaster has never been sufficiently stressed." He thought that if a reader understood more clearly the immunity leaders felt toward an aerial torpedo attack, the more they would understand the decisions not to alert the Hawaiian command at or before December 7, 1941.[57]

Admiral Richardson also did not think that torpedo nets in the confined Pearl Harbor were practicable. Additionally, he thought that the ships were safe from submarine torpedoes because they were moored too far from the opening into the harbor.[58] The same data produced the same decisions by Kimmel in 1941.

By mid-December of 1940, Richardson later told Congress, there were more ships in Pearl Harbor than on December 7, 1941.[59] Of course, by 1945, Richardson knew more about the Taranto attack, and knew that even the balloon-stretched cables, powerful lights, a formidable array of antiaircraft weapons, and guns on the ships at that harbor had failed to foil the successful British attack. He knew also by then that the British torpedoes could operate in shallow depths. Had he understood all that in 1940, perhaps other arrangements for docking would have been created.

There were many things Richardson did not know about activities in and around Pearl Harbor. The future would surprise him, as well as others, as the facts came out during the next four years.

CHAPTER TWENTY-THREE

Just What Did Richardson Know?

He Knew He Was Being Left Out

After eighteen months of effort, the Japanese secret diplomatic code, *Purple,* was broken in August of 1940. The first decoding of an entire text was accomplished on September 25.

The ninety-seven intercepts during late 1940 were eventually gathered from all the message traffic traveling between the foreign office in Tokyo to its embassy personnel abroad. Besides breaking *Purple,* the effort began to read lower-grade "J" codes.[1] Director of Naval Intelligence W. S. Anderson began to call the decrypts, *"MAGIC."*[2] The name stuck.

Still, as Anderson said in June of 1940, naval intelligence gathering was meek. "We have at present no intelligence network abroad other than the Naval attachés." These representatives gathered information about strength, disposition, and probable intentions of foreign naval forces.

On October 4, 1940, senior assistant CNO Ingersoll sent a letter to both Richardson and Hart. It said the Navy was tracking Japan's naval radio system.[3] However, the fleet leaders were left out of the loop. Richardson had been complaining about this lack of intelligence sharing since the fleet training exercise ended in May.[4]

During those months of late 1940 and early 1941, Hart and Richardson had no idea of the Washington power grab that War Plans Director Turner was attempting to pull over the functions of the ONI. Turner would tell Hart that it was likely the Japanese would attack Russia before going south, while Alan Kirk, the new Director of Naval Intelligence, would attempt to show the Asiatic Fleet commander that intercepted messages said otherwise. This conflict became much worse in the middle of 1941 when Turner was prompted in anger to write on a Kirk summary, "I don't think the Japs are going to jump now or ever!"[5]

"Terrible" Turner angered many, but he had the confidence of

Stark and Ingersoll. When Kimmel later traveled to Washington in June of 1941, neither Kirk nor Turner briefed him on the *"MAGIC"* operation, nor was he given more intelligence staff as requested. Layton says that much of this intercept information was even hidden from Congress in the 1945-46 Pearl Harbor Hearings. There is no indication that Richardson was aware of the *Purple* intercepts even after he left Hawaii and worked in Washington during World War II.

Layton was told by the Navy Department not to discuss at the Joint Congressional Hearings intelligence information dating before July of 1941. In *Treadmill,* Richardson indicates he knew a bit, but says he could not say much about Safford's duties, for instance, because, "What is accomplished in his field [signals intelligence] is a closely guarded secret within the Naval Service, and there is a galaxy of regulations and laws against public disclosure . . . so I write guardedly."[6]

There was also another problem looming—Japanese intelligence gathering near the fleet. Neither Richardson, nor Hart, nor Ingersoll had a full grasp of the Japanese knowledge gained simply from watching American fleet movements in Hawaii. For example, a Japanese career intelligence officer named Kanji Ogawa sent a message to Admiral Isoroku Yamamoto on December 29, 1940, detailing the December 1 decision Richardson made to more permanently locate the fleet inside Pearl Harbor.[7]

Richardson realized as common knowledge that the Hawaiian inhabitants of Japanese ancestry, one-third of them aliens, had among them some spies, but he had not received any spy messages. Knowledge that the American fleet had moved permanently into Pearl Harbor indicated to Yamamoto that this was the only site in the Hawaiian Islands to attack.[8] At that time, he asked Ogawa to shift intelligence efforts to Hawaii rather than the West Coast of the United States.[9]

That fall Consul General Kiichi, a veteran diplomat with a distaste for spying, was recalled by Foreign Minister Yosuke Matsuoka, and replaced in Honolulu by Otojiro Okuda.[10] Immediately, Okuda enlarged a crew of spies.[11] They would provide

Tokyo with information on ship arrivals, departures, berth locations, and other facts. On December 2, 1940, Okuda notified Tokyo of ship movements; twenty days later he said there was no traffic in Pearl Harbor on the nineteenth; and four days later, on Christmas Eve, he reported to Gaimudaijin (Foreign Minister Tokyo) that the ships returned on the twentieth, with plans to stay until January 4.[12] Some of this information he had learned from simply reading the newspapers.

Richardson was troubled about spies watching the movement of the ships, but was more worried about the newspaper accounts of fleet locations. Bloch wrote Stark asking that the CNO's office deal with the news services. Stark refused to do anything at the time. Richardson went further with his thoughts, and was sure that the State Department, especially Hornbeck, had released some information to the news media. He assumed that Hornbeck thought this action pressured the Japanese to remain less aggressive.[13]

Zacharias sailed to Hawaii by Matson Liner on November 9, 1940, not really sure of any orders other than he was to be commander of the heavy cruiser USS *Salt Lake City*.[14] He was surprised to learn his future from a passenger on board. The passenger, the father of a Honolulu tailor, said his son knew that two fleet ships were coming to Long Beach soon: the *Salt Lake City* and the *Pensacola*. Richardson had for some time attempted to surround the fleet in secrecy of movement, but it was almost impossible to do so.[15]

Richardson had earlier assigned Captain W. K. Kilpatrick to complete a survey of fleet intelligence work and facilities. Kilpatrick asked Zacharias to assist him.[16] In his limited time, Zacharias visited with the Fourteenth District intelligence staff. He was appalled. On the following morning he called upon Bloch, who was not totally unfamiliar with the problem. He had already requested twenty-one billets to expand the district's communications intelligence function.[17] Despite this perceived problem, Zacharias convinced the district commander that he could organize the office similarly to the one on the West Coast. After return from his subsequent trip to the West Coast, Zacharias assisted

Richardson with the newly created office for the fleet. He had even recommended an officer for the job—Layton.[18]

On December 7, Layton arrived to serve on the Richardson staff as fleet intelligence officer. He found "Uncle Joe" to be "forthright and direct. I liked him very much."[19] Layton was surprised that he was the first to perform these duties full time. He was rather taken aback when he saw the eighteen haphazard files in the safe of the USS *Pennsylvania*.[20]

Layton's two tours in Japan gave him knowledge that the Japanese Navy was a formidable adversary. He had extensive study of the Mandated Islands and their use by the Japanese military. After his arrival at the CinCUS staff, he too visited the Fourteenth Naval District's communications intelligence office. Layton's offer to help was quickly accepted, and he soon recovered enough values to begin a plot of Japanese military buildup in the Mandated Islands. While Layton and the officers receiving messages at Hawaii's Station HYPO did not have the ability to decode, they did study ship placements.

By late December, Layton presented some of his findings to Richardson. The admiral was skeptical at first, but soon began to realize the importance of Layton's work.[21] He exclaimed that it had taken twenty years, but "now we know that the Japs are secretly violating their directive for administering those islands." Layton was impressed with Richardson's quick grasp, calling him "the rangy admiral from Texas." But, the two did not have many more days to work together.

In mid-December of 1940, Richardson received notice that Anderson was coming to his command.[22] There is no evidence that Anderson ever took part in any Layton-Richardson staff discussions. In fact, he did not arrive in Hawaii until a few days before Richardson was relieved in February of 1941. It is possible that neither Layton nor Richardson wanted Anderson's assistance. He seemed to be unpopular with both men.

Richardson mentions in his book that Anderson may have spent valuable time with the new radar and radio work being done on the fleet.[23] If Richardson saw or met with Anderson, it would have been in a gathering after Anderson arrived on the SS *Lurline* on January 29.[24] About Anderson, Stark was in step with Richardson. He knew his 1903 classmate well. Stark even apologized to Kimmel in February of 1941 for sending Anderson to the fleet. "The appointment was forced on us by the White House . . . don't promise Anderson a promotion. He's always looking ahead for a new job."[25]

In early 1941, Anderson may have been the only person in the fleet to know about *Purple* and especially about *"MAGIC."* He probably knew that only eight intercepts were in the processing stage, and only another five had been actually translated.[26] Anderson tried to bring an even more experienced intelligence officer to the fleet with him—McCollum.[27] His eventual notoriety came from actions as head of the Far East desk of the ONI. McCollum wrote a memorandum for President Roosevelt in October of 1940, one day before the last meeting between the president and Richardson. Even today, the McCollum suggestions still garner attention.[28]

If Richardson had seen this McCollum memorandum, he would have understood the Roosevelt and Knox interest in placing the U.S. Fleet into higher profile in the Far East. The suggestions McCollum made were surely repugnant toward the Japanese-American relationship. He recommended that the United States use Singapore as a base; use the Dutch East Indies bases; aid Chiang Kai-shek even more; send a division of heavy cruisers to the Philippines or Singapore; send two divisions of submarines to the Orient; keep the U.S. Fleet at Hawaii; insist that the Dutch refuse Japanese demands for economic concessions; and completely embargo all trade with Japan.[29]

Despite Anderson's efforts, Ingersoll personally cancelled McCollum's orders to go to sea. McCollum became even more "famous" later for drafting a letter from Stark to Kimmel saying that there was no Japanese attack on Pearl Harbor planned for the foreseeable future.[30]

It is still a mystery why Anderson did not tell Richardson, or especially Kimmel, about *Purple.* Some of the original interceptions came from Station HYPO in Pearl Harbor's old administration building, and more from the Army's Station Five at Fort Shafter. It is also indicative of Layton's attitude toward Anderson, that nowhere in his book is Anderson mentioned.

After December of 1940, Richardson and then Kimmel were physically very near to some of the top intelligence officers in the Navy. Besides Layton and Anderson, Rochefort was there, in charge of what was called the Communications Intelligence Unit at Pearl Harbor.[31] What Richardson would have done with these abilities can only be left to conjecture. After the announcement of his early detachment, Richardson spent the month of January more focused on preparing Kimmel to take the command.

Not completely understanding how close he came to seeing the results of decoding efforts going on in Washington, Richardson also had little suspicion of anything secret passing through Pearl Harbor during the third week of January 1941. Stark sent a message directing Richardson and Hart to escort the USS *Chaumont* from Honolulu to Guam, and then on to Manila. This was a strange request, for up to that time no escorts had been given for transports in the Pacific.

If Richardson had mentioned the Stark dispatch to Layton, perhaps a bit of light would have been shed on the subject. But, it is likely Layton had no clue that a version of a new decoding machine was possibly on board. Only eight *Purple/*"MAGIC" analog machines had been constructed.[32] One was headed for new quarters in the new caves located on Corregidor Island.[33]

Though he writes that Hart later told him a cryptographic decoding device was on the ship, Richardson still thought it was a "professional military lapse" for Stark not to reveal to him the reason for the escort request. The CinCUS was kept in the dark for some unknown reason.[34]

By late January, Layton had spent considerable study time at Rochefort's office. It became apparent that something unusual was happening in the Mandated Islands. The traffic of ships there was vastly increasing. Messages captured, mainly by the U.S. Station *George* at Guam and forwarded to both Rochefort's

Hawaiian unit and Op-20-G in Washington, included subjects of ammunition storage, radio stations being constructed, and barracks and defense attachments at many places within the islands. Rochefort, through Layton, reported all this to Richardson and Kimmel.[35] Later he found that Washington had filed the originals and never read them.[36]

On January 31, stopping off at Pearl Harbor on his way to his diplomatic post in Washington was Admiral Nomura.[37] Richardson sent out two destroyers to meet him two hundred miles from port.[38] He remained at Honolulu for fourteen busy hours. Nomura and Richardson had known each other since the two had been in Washington, DC, during the World War I years. The men were both tall, imposing, and had equally friendly smiles. There was little evidence that Nomura had lost sight in one eye in 1932.[39]

In photos, the men appear to genuinely like each other. Nomura was a naval attaché when Roosevelt was assistant secretary of the Navy. When Richardson was director of officer personnel in 1928, Nomura brought a Japanese midshipmen's training squadron to tour the East Coast. Richardson provided Nomura with a liaison officer, William Joseph Sebald, who knew the Japanese well and had met Nomura earlier while living in Japan.[40] Nomura was a delegate at the Washington Naval Conference of 1921, and commanded the Japanese Third Fleet in 1932. He retired from the Navy in 1937.

In Honolulu that late January morning, the atmosphere was cordial, though back in Japan Prime Minister Fumimaro Konoye laid out the situation as "an emergency unparalleled in her long history" as he talked before the Seventy-Sixth Session of the Imperial Diet.[41] Layton had known Nomura, so he was given the duty to meet the ship as it arrived at Honolulu. He was then Nomura's naval honorary aide while on land that day.[42]

Nomura interviewed with the press before he visited with Okuda and members of his staff. Richardson and Herron met him at the dock, and the three lifted glasses of spirits in the ship's envoy suite. Nomura then went to see Governor Poindexter. After his visit to the Japanese consulate, he called on Bloch and Herron. Nomura then went on board the USS *Pennsylvania* to talk again with Richardson.[43]

The Honolulu Chamber of Commerce held a luncheon for Nomura, followed by a tea, and then he was a guest of the United Japanese Society at the Shunchoro Teahouse.[44] At this large dinner, introduced by Honolulu Chamber President George S. Waterhouse, Richardson spoke before the mostly Japanese crowd assembled, saying that the officers of the U.S. Navy were pleased that Nomura had been appointed to the highest diplomatic post in Washington.[45]

"It gives me great pleasure," Richardson told the crowd, "to be the first official to extend greetings and welcome to this man." Nomura said, in his speech, that he would work for good relations.[46] The irony that many American evacuees accompanied him on his ship from Tokyo was not lost on the press. However, the passengers were impressed by Nomura's sincerity, but also stated that his selection had been highly opposed by the more nationalistic groups in Japan.

Nomura left for San Francisco at 10:00 P.M. It was not in Richardson's past experience to suspect that Nomura would participate in the espionage charge later leveled at him by Tokyo. In fact, Nomura at first had turned down the request from Foreign Minister Matsuoka. But, under pressure and with hope that he could ease tensions between the countries, Nomura accepted the post in early November of 1940.

Zacharias was still with the *Salt Lake City* at Mare Island when Nomura passed through San Francisco at the end of the first week of February 1941. The two had known each other since 1920 when Nomura was chief of Japan's naval intelligence.[47] Zacharias asked Richardson if there was any objection to a confidential talk with Nomura. Richardson had none, and asked that Zacharias report to him later about the ambassador's mission. Of course, by the February 8, hour-long meeting in the Fairmont Hotel, Kimmel was in charge, not Richardson. The frank, private conversation was then reported to Stark, with a copy sent to Kimmel at Pearl Harbor.[48] The Nomura meeting convinced

Zacharias that war with Japan was near, but he still did not view the ambassador as one of the extremists. In fact, Nomura apologized to Zacharias for the strong Japanese movement to oppose the United States.[49]

Japanese intelligence gathering was being highly organized during Richardson's last days as CinCUS. Ship information was sent on January 6, 7, 9, 16, 21 and 28.[50] Richardson knew none of this, and he did not see a January 27, 1941, message from Tokyo to Washington from Grew. It said, " . . . heard that a surprise mass attack on Pearl Harbor was planned by the Japanese military forces." He attributed the knowledge to a Peruvian colleague. Grew called it a rather fantastic notion.[51] ONI did pass the message on to Kimmel's office on February 1.[52] It is possible that Richardson then saw it, or was notified of its contents by Kimmel.

Richardson was not the only high leader to be ignored. There is some evidence that neither Roosevelt nor Hull knew about the *Purple/"MAGIC"* secret until January 23, 1941. FBI Director J. Edgar Hoover, while given summaries, did not see original intercepts.[53]

On January 30, Corregidor's decoded messages were given to Roosevelt.[54] These messages informed the president that there was a large buildup of Japanese warships in the South China Sea off French Indochina.[55] Knox had written Ghormley of this expectation back in mid-November of 1940. "Rumor is that she [Japan] will move her forces . . . to Saigon as the first step on the march to the Dutch East Indies," he revealed.[56] Knox said he and the president decided to send five additional submarines to reinforce the twelve already there, hoping "this may have a certain deterrent value."[57]

Many field leaders remained fuzzy about the existence and use of intercepted messages; even General MacArthur, who, when questioned about *"MAGIC"* after the war, was vague about its operation.[58] At that time, most of the commanders thought the diplomatic messages were better interpreted by those in Washington.

Two of the messages captured on January 30 would have put

Richardson on notice that a huge change in Japanese direction was made. One said to the Japan's foreign office secretary, " . . . for the purpose of being prepared for the worst, we have decided to alter . . ." the publicity and propaganda of the past and install more intelligence work.[59] A second message followed that day, outlining in more detail what Tokyo wanted to know.[60]

Five days after the fleet command was turned over to Kimmel, even before May and Jim Richardson left Hawaii, the Japanese began the serious intelligence work. On February 5, Matsuoka wrote to his Washington office, wanting an employee named Koshi to proceed with a program involving aid from Japanese businessmen working in the United States.[61] Also, on February 5, Ogawa instructed the Hawaiian consul general to shift emphasis from any propaganda to intelligence work.

In Washington, these messages were read, and a memorandum was sent to Stark on February 12, urging him to bring the information to the immediate attention of the president.[62] Ten days later Ogawa told Okuda exactly what to observe and feed to Tokyo.[63] In a few days Okuda received word that Nagao Kita would leave his post at Canton, and become consul general in Hawaii. By March, Takeo Yoshikawa arrived in Honolulu, but he checked in as Vice Counsul Tadashi Morimura. He moved freely about, sending back messages using Okuda's name. From Aiea Heights he simply watched Pearl Harbor with his binoculars.[64] Admiral Richardson would know much of this operation by the time he was the Navy witness in the Tokyo Crimes Trials.

Kimmel was only aware that reports of submarine activity by the Japanese picked up the day he took command. Books and articles have been compiled since, revealing what Washington knew about the consulate messages from Honolulu to Tokyo. As CinCUS, Richardson knew nothing, and Kimmel would not know of the word *"MAGIC"* for months.

Often Layton realized the diplomatic messages he knew were being read in Washington would be of great assistance in Hawaii, so he asked for a decryption machine. McCollum said he agreed, but that matters of security, "et cetra," made it impossible. "I appreciate that all this leaves you in rather a spot, as naturally people are interested in current developments," he concluded to Layton.[65]

From then on, Kimmel's letters to Stark became alarmingly similar to those Richardson had sent in 1940.[66] No commander wanted to be in the dark, especially when so far from home base.

CHAPTER TWENTY-FOUR

"They Can't Do That to Me!"
What a Way to Ruin a Good Round of Golf

How Richardson lost his command early confused everyone but the admiral. On the golf course with Bieri and two other officers, in Hawaii on Sunday, January 5, at 11:45 A.M., Dyer approached him.[1] Richardson was in the middle of a lively game. He normally shot in the mid-80s on the courses around Pearl Harbor. He had tried to put most of the business formats of the week out of his mind and relax for a few hours. His son Joe had arrived on the SS *Lurline* three days earlier to visit his parents.[2]

Dyer had a great love for Richardson. He was always impressed at Richardson's amount of energy, his good looks, great determination, and character. "He had a human touch, even though he called things the way they were," Dyer said, even when Richardson was ninety-three. "He was always full of funny stories, and he loved golf, playing anytime that he could." Dyer always stated that if there was anyone who did not like Richardson, "I've yet to find [that] person."

However, there was at least one person in the chain of command who did not like Richardson. It was the president. "I think that he [Richardson] misjudged Roosevelt in how much criticism of himself he would take," said Dyer. Therefore, when the dispatch came in, Dyer was on duty, and was dismayed. "I got on my horse and buggy, and went out to the golf links. I delivered this dispatch to him, and his remark was: 'My God. They can't do that to me.'"[3] Many who knew Richardson could not comprehend such an outburst from the normally confident, low-keyed commander. It is highly possible that this was not the time nor place to present him with the news. But, as Smedberg said years later, it was quite a shock to everyone. "He was told he was staying on another year, then, bingo!"[4] Bieri said he could not remember just exactly what Richardson said, but that it "was a terrific shock to us all."

Just a few days earlier, the announcement had been again made by the Navy Department that the fleet was to remain in the Pearl Harbor area. And, by that time Richardson did not push the issue. The local newspapers hardly noticed the fleet anymore, and the sailors apparently were behaving themselves, for no negative news of their activities reached the press. More and more wives were coming out to Hawaii, or were extending their Christmas vacations. Fleet Problem XXII was being cancelled, and it was a bit perplexing to plan just what training was to be done on a limited basis in a confined area.[5] Facilities were improving, however.

May did express her uneasiness about living in Hawaii. She told Gerry Wheeler that she didn't like the idea of settling down in a Honolulu home. She was concerned not only about the safety of the fleet, but of those in Hawaii.[6]

The best news was that May's cousin Isabel, and her husband Walter C. Short, were coming to Hawaii. It was announced on December 18 that he was replacing Herron.[7] This was quite a surprise to the Shorts and Richardsons. Never before had the wives been assigned to the same place. The first cousins had not seen each other very often since the Dean family moved from Paris, Texas, north to Oklahoma thirty-four years earlier.

Within a week after Christmas, the Shorts left the Fourth Army in Columbia, South Carolina, for West Point to see their son Dean, a cadet there. They visited with families on the trip west, and in St. Louis picked up their niece, Mary Elizabeth Short. The three boarded the SS *Matsonia* at San Francisco for what they hoped would be a relaxing trip.[8] Isabel was seasick all the way, "and too miserable to enjoy our luxurious cabin and the many parties we were invited to," she wrote after her husband's death in 1949.

Roosevelt had been working since the 1940 campaign to prepare the public to accept an expanded lend-lease plan. On January 1, he conversed with reporters about aiding the Allies. Two days later he told Senators Barkley, Harrison, and Byrnes that he would submit a comprehensive plan for all-out aid to Great Britain. That day, he told the press he was sending Harry Hopkins, one of his closest advisors, to London. Then, on January

6, Roosevelt gave his annual message to Congress, saying that he had a design to furnish enormous quantities of arms, munitions, implements of war, and other commodities to the Allies to fight against the Axis Powers. This was one of those Roosevelt turnarounds loathed by the military who knew they were not ready for the resultant war the aid would cause.[9] Roosevelt made no mention of the change in CinCUS.

For four days, news of the detachment of Richardson was kept from public knowledge. A large portion of the fleet left anchorage on January 6, including the USS *New Mexico*. A Japanese dispatch to Tokyo said the vessels were going on training exercises, but would be back on January 12.[10] On January 9, it was announced that the less senior Kimmel would take over the newly formed Pacific Fleet. Richardson was ordered to report to Knox, who was the official explaining Roosevelt's decisions. Some other changes of command were within the story, throwing a smoke shield over the unexpected detachment of the CinCUS after only one year at duty. A name change came for the Atlantic Patrol, now in a fleet of its own, to be commanded by King.[11] If the three fleets—Asiatic, Atlantic, and Pacific—were in operations together, Kimmel would wear the hat of CinCUS. However, the main group, the Pacific Fleet, would remain chained to Hawaii for the time being.[12]

The Richardson staff was told about the changes. Some under his command were receiving January orders to other jobs anyway. In all, fifteen changes were announced on January 9.[13] The next day was enough of an event for Richardson to note in his diary that he came into Pearl Harbor for the last time, on the USS *Pennsylvania*, around Ford Island. The reality perhaps was finally sinking in.[14]

Richardson wrote later that he was shocked at the orders from Roosevelt. "I was deeply disappointed in my detachment, yet there was some feeling of prospective relief. I had never liked to work with people whom I did not trust, and I did not trust Franklin D. Roosevelt."[15] A most profound letter from Richardson's sixty-seven-year-old sister, Moss, arrived the third week in January 1941. This put some perspective on the situation. He thought it was "remarkable insight and wisdom."[16] Only an English professor could have inserted an old 1901 story into the current events, and made the point:

> Dear Brother:
> One Sunday morning, forty years ago, I came down to breakfast to find the sitting room empty and the *Paris Morning News* spread on the table.
> We had been eagerly watching to see the publication of the Paris public school teaching staff, which had been delayed.
> When I saw that, I read it and found my name omitted. At the foot, the notice said, "Miss M. Moss Richardson, on account of poor health and in recognition of her excellent service as a teacher, has been granted a leave of absence."
> I was stunned, but I went on into the dining room quietly. Momma [stepmother Susan] said, "Moss, did you see the paper?"
> "Yes."
> "Did you ask for a leave of absence?"
> "No."
> "Had anyone ever said anything about a leave of absence for you?"
> "No."
> Papa said, "Well, Moss, Mr. Wooten [the school superintendent] has not done anything to you that you would not have done to him. You never have approved of him, and I suppose he knows it. If you could, you would have dropped him."[17]

Moss wrote more to her brother, saying that her release moved her to do work where she "can have approval." A devoutly religious lady, she suggested that God would use Otto effectively during the rest of his life. Richardson was so proud of this letter that for years he showed it to friends, and passed out copies to those he thought would benefit later from the words of such a wise "old-maid school teacher."[18] Four years later, he used a version of it to answer a question posed to him by the Congressional Pearl Harbor Committee.

When the shock of the abrupt detachment orders wore off, decisions were made. Other lives were drastically changed by the presidential decision. Forever in the right place, Anderson became commander of Battleships Battle Force to the chagrin of Kimmel and Stark.[19] Taffinder's world would change dramatically.

For the year, Richardson operated mostly through him. The two thought alike, but according to L. J. O'Brien, Taffinder was more outwardly spoken against Roosevelt. "I found him tough to work with," commented Chris Johnson in 2002. Like O'Brien, Johnson was also a communications ensign at that time.[20] Taffinder remained in Hawaii, moving into John H. Newton's position as Commander Cruiser Division Five. Newton replaced Rowcliff as Commander Cruisers Scouting Force. The public was too dizzy by the changes to read on.

From Richardson's staff, Murphy remained to serve with Kimmel. He worked for War Plans Officer Captain McMorris. Curts was Kimmel's communications officer, and East remained with him as an assistant, as did O'Brien. "Curts was my favorite staff officer," said O'Brien at the age of eighty-seven in 2002. "He, Allan Reed and I played cards often." Reed remained as security officer. Davis was also Kimmel's aviation officer. Layton would continue as fleet intelligence officer. Pye stayed on as commander of what was called Task Force One, or Commander Battle Force. Dyer went over to the USS *Indianapolis* to serve as its executive officer.

Bieri had been working on a plan for the fleet to protect itself with its own guns while in Pearl Harbor. "That was supposed to be the Army's duty," he said, "but it had nothing; they had no equipment for that purpose." So, he stayed on with Kimmel for two months, working with the new operations officer, DeLany, on perfecting the plan.[21] In March, Bieri became commander of the heavy cruiser USS *Chicago*.

Snyder quietly said he enjoyed working for the younger Richardson, but would not do the same with Kimmel, who was four years his junior. Thus, Pye took Snyder's place, and faced the decision in December of 1941, after Kimmel was released, whether or not to raid the Marshall Islands. Others were assigned back into the Pacific Fleet or to the mainland. Kimmel asked Melhorn to stay, but the physician begged off. "After thanking him, I said I had been at sea for almost three years, and wanted to command a Naval hospital."[22] Outside the Richardson staff, Bellinger remained in charge of patrol security, Halsey was commander of Task Force Two, and Bloch was still commander of the Fourteenth Naval District. Base Force Commander Calhoun remained.

Officially, changes were due to take place on February 1. In the meantime, Richardson, in office again on the USS *Pennsylvania,* saw a rash of stories and releases from Washington attempting to soothe thoughts that the Pacific was about to erupt into war, and that the American forces could combine with British, Dutch, and what was left of the French and thwart any Far Eastern movement by the Japanese. Again, the assumptions did not include an attack on the U.S. Fleet first, followed quickly by other various Japanese attacks in the Pacific. The thought pattern by the Navy, as given to writers, was that the Asiatic Fleet could harass and delay Japanese ships. The official public line was that the Asiatic Fleet would not be a suicide squadron. The Japanese would not venture far from their homeland, the U.S. Fleet at Hawaii acting as a deterrent to such a movement. Or so thought Washington.

Before Kimmel took over, Richardson had a month to wrap up various reports and duties, write many letters, and complete his thoughts on the war plans. He brought in Kimmel and his senior staff to witness and discuss everything pending.[23] While he did so, the five-foot, ten-inch, 180-pound Kimmel held his first press conference on Friday, January 10. He pointed out quickly, however, that he was not yet in charge, and earlier expressed to friends some great surprise at his appointment.

The beginning of the conference with the writers was delayed as Bloch adjusted one of Kimmel's breast buttons. This movement quickly caught a photographer's lens. In close-ups taken, Kimmel's eye sockets were dark, as if he had not slept in some hours. He dangled a cigarette from his mouth and fingers. If Roosevelt thought Richardson looked like an old man after the long trip to Washington in October, photos of Kimmel are not of a young, energetic fleet commander either.[24] He exuded much properness, however, not the relaxed looseness that Richardson gave audiences when he was in a gathering. No funny stories emerged from this admiral. Kimmel admitted, "This is all new to me," looking around at the lights and flash bulbs, "and you've got to let me get my bearings." When a flash bulb exploded, he jumped, signifying his nervous manner before the civilians.

The son-in-law of the late Rear Admiral Thomas Wright Kinkaid, Kimmel told the press that the less published about the fleet the better, and that he hoped there would be no more such conferences. His and Richardson's antagonism, or more fairly called skepticism, toward the news media would prove a grand negative at the end of each admiral's career. Curts's son, Bob, noted that "Richardson was 8,000 miles ahead of Kimmel in intellect . . . several levels above." After all, Kimmel replaced a man who was a card shark, who mesmerized everyone with his shuffling of the stack, and one who liked to play math games for relaxation. However, Kimmel was "an uncompromising, but very honest man."[25] Curts added, "Kimmel exhibited a confidence that fit Roosevelt's personality."

At the press conference, Kimmel put an end to the rumors flying about that he knew the president well. He reiterated that he had not had a discussion with Roosevelt since 1918.

O'Brien would later call Nimitz, who permanently replaced Kimmel after the Pearl Harbor attack, a "breath of fresh air." Obie laughed at the atmosphere Richardson would portray around his men. "He would even let you into his quarters when he was in his night gown," he said.[26] "We got to attend every staff meeting," Johnson said. "We were quiet, but we got to listen to high up talk. I faced him personally with almost every message I took. He was very pleasant."[27] Kimmel was more reserved, but had behind him the confidence of Richardson and Stark. However, he did not gain any fleet popularity when he discouraged wives from coming out with families to live in Hawaii.[28] While Richardson thought the government should allow funds to bring out families, Kimmel thought wives being there offered excuses not to make difficult decisions. It was a hard call either way.

Devastating war headlines coming from Europe simmered a bit during the winter, but new daily revelations came from Knox's office. He was constantly telling Congress that he had no fear of an attack unless Great Britain fell. The public, and the enemy, could tell things were getting serious when Nimitz announced that henceforth Naval Academy graduates would go straight to ships.[29]

Far away from "home," the changes of command began on the respective ships at 8:15 A.M. on Friday, February 1.[30] At 8:30 Saturday morning, the rest of the nine ceremony rites began. At 10:05, Richardson emerged from the companionway to the salutes of assembled staff officers and crew. A simple ceremony on the quarterdeck, under the guns of the just-returned USS *Pennsylvania,* began with Kimmel and Richardson.[31]

The old and new staffs stood at the base of the guns, the old staff depleted a bit without the members who had moved to Kimmel's group, or who had left on Friday. Richardson was on their right, Kimmel on their left. The press and invited guests were more to the front of the battleship.[32] The Navy erected a "press bridge" so reporters and photographers could better view the ceremony held on the polished, still teakwood deck. They did have a close-up view of the plugged guns. On top of the turret, to Richardson's back, CBS had set up its equipment and microphones, for the world to hear what was happening.[33]

Richardson turned over the command with these words:

> On taking command of the Fleet over a year ago, I called on you to join me in working together as a team. I asked that each member be imbued with a cooperative spirit, mutual respect, good will, understanding, and a determination to voluntarily contribute the last bit to his assigned task.

> That you have done.

> All of you can take pride in the work accomplished under trying conditions. The path ahead is not easy. There is much to be done. My regret in leaving you is tempered by the fact that I turn over this command to Admiral Kimmel, a friend of long standing, a forthright man, an officer of marked ability and a successor of whom I am proud. Under his leadership I know that you will continue to so perform your duties as to justify the confidence with which the nation places its security in your hands.[34]

It was an unusual ceremony. No seventeen-gun salute could be fired, since the ships were moored to the dock. The Marine band did not even play when Kimmel came on board the *Pennsylvania* because of what the press described as "the existing emergency."[35] With 1,600 of the *Pennsylvania* crew nearby, and those watching from the cruiser *Honolulu,* Richardson read the orders. The reporter for the *Honolulu Advertiser* said there was utter silence, and then "the elderly, distinguished CinCUS, with a nod and a murmured order, instructed his flag to be hauled down."[36] A few minutes later, the more than one hundred ships in Pearl Harbor saw Kimmel's flag rise.

Afterward, as was tradition following all such ceremonies, the new commander and his staff invited the former commander and his staff into the new commander's quarters as a courtesy.[37] In the meantime, in Washington, Roosevelt celebrated his birthday.

It was all over now, at least officially. Kimmel paid a last visit to Herron at Fort Shafter.[38] There were a few meetings, and several social functions remained for the Richardsons. Hans L'Orange, manager of the Oahu Sugar Plantation, and his wife threw an aloha cocktail party at their Waipahu home on Sunday afternoon.[39] The Chamber of Commerce gave a going away party at the Royal Hawaiian Hotel, as did the wardroom and junior officers of the *Pennsylvania,* held in the officer's club at Pearl Harbor.[40] At the Chamber of Commerce party, the newspaper described Mrs. Richardson as wearing a black gown complemented by a white hat and pikake leis. She went few places without her hats.

The Richardsons could have attended a showing of the new movie, *Flight Command,* at the air-conditioned Waikiki Theater. The production used much of the U.S. Fleet off the West Coast as a background for stars Robert Taylor, Ruth Hussey, and Walter Pidgeon.[41]

Before heading back east, the Richardsons awaited the Wednesday, February 5, landing of the Shorts. It was quite a surprise to the passengers on board the SS *Matsonia* when they learned that the general was aboard. The guests had been buzzing all the way from California about the most famous couple on board. It was not the Shorts, but Mrs. and Mrs. Ernest Hemingway.

Few of the 550 passengers on the liner knew of General Short's rank until a review of twenty-four B-18 bombers flew over the *Matsonia* near Diamond Head. Orginally, he had signed in as Mr. Short, but that cover was blown when the aircraft from Hickam Field roared over the liner as she rounded Diamond Head shortly after sunrise.[42] A temporary aide, Major Hobert Hewett, met the Shorts at Pier 11.[43] He informed the couple, and the general's niece, that the 9:00 A.M. Friday change of command ceremonies would have bleachers that would hold more than two hundred civilians. Herron would sail for the mainland at noon, following the ceremonies, on the returning SS *Matsonia*.

For some reason, Herron had not planned to be in Hawaii long after Short was to officially replace him. Herron should have been in no hurry, except to retire. He told the press that he was going back to his home in Maryland, "open up my house and keep my mouth shut." Several days later, after he had left, the newspapers printed that the Herrons were going to tour the southern United States for three months before heading to Bethesda.[44] He seemed like a person who wanted to quickly get out of the hot seat of Hawaii, where he had been since March of 1938, but he promised to come back to visit someday.[45]

On the other hand, there is no mention by Isabel Short in her manuscript that explains why they did not leave for Hawaii earlier. To catch Short up on operations, Herron sent to San Francisco a briefing book, an agenda, and exhibits for discussion when the two met in Hawaii. The five days at sea would have given Short plenty of time to study the packet, but Isabel's seasickness made that task difficult. Herron was of the impression, also, that it was more than any outside influence that kept Short from study of the briefings. In fact, Herron later told special Pearl Harbor investigator Henry Clausen that Short indicated he did not give them much reading en route, and spent the time with a novel.[46]

Isabel wrote in her manuscript that, despite the fact that her father was seriously ill, the couple was excited about the new position, though it was far from friends and family. They were career military and not unfamiliar with the problems of being far away. However, Herron was convinced from what he saw of his replacement between landing on February 5 and his own departure on February 7 that Short was more than indifferent about the assignment. In the barely two-day indoctrination, Herron said that Short did not ask him any questions nor did he ever correspond about information later.[47]

One of the few times the public was made aware that Isabel Short and May Richardson were related was printed in the "Port and Off Port" column in the *Honolulu Advertiser* as the Shorts arrived. It told the readers that Short was a personal friend of Admiral James O. Richardson.[48]

The Shorts received the bad news of Richardson's replacement as they settled in and met with May and the admiral. "I had been especially happy over the new assignment because my first cousin's husband was in command of the Pacific Fleet. We had been like sisters since our childhood days," Isabel wrote in her unpublished manuscript. The Dean family had eventually moved to Oklahoma City where Isabel's father worked and served as mayor. Therefore, as a teenager, she finished growing up there. Along with other young ladies, she would take the Frisco Railroad eighty-five miles to Fort Sill for parties with Army personnel.

She was engaged to another, but when she met Short, plans were changed. The two quickly became a couple and married in 1914, honeymooned in Cuba, and set up a career together.[49] So, in Hawaii there was to be much to talk about between the two women. "Both of us were thrilled, because we thought we could be near each other for the first time in many years." Before she came out to Hawaii, Isabel laughingly wrote May that the two of them might soon get tired of each other since one would be on the right of the hosts, and the other on the left at many social functions.[50]

The day after arrival, the Shorts were honored with the Herrons at a reception held at the Waialae Golf Club, sponsored by the Honolulu Chamber of Commerce. Isabel came in a light figured sable brown print gown, and wearing a white hat.[51] The early Friday morning, twenty-minute change of command was not as "glamorous" or staged as well as that of the Navy, nor was it seen by as many observers, but it was impressive, and more public. It was covered well by the press. In fact, Short had to plow his way through the cameramen once he left his car.[52] The pass in review was extensive. Three hours after taking command, the rank of lieutenant general was pinned upon Short by Isabel, making him one of only six in the U.S. Army to wear that rank.[53] The photo made the front pages of many newspapers, and is shown in several books.[54]

At one point, Kimmel paid a visit on the Shorts, who were staying with the Richardsons before they moved into their Army quarters at Fort Shafter.[55] Isabel had already received the Richardson detachment news. She wrote, "I did not know he was taking over the Navy command and remarked, 'I am just sick about Admiral Richardson being relieved.'" He smiled and informed her that he was the new Pacific Fleet commander in chief, and said he hoped to do as well as Richardson. "I said, I was still sorry . . . about the change."[56] On February 9 Short paid a visit to Kimmel's domain and headquarters in Pearl Harbor.[57] The new leadership officially was underway.

What Richardson would do next was anyone's guess. Herron was convinced that "there is something of overwhelming importance to be done in Washington or they would not be taking you back there."[58] Most of Richardson's peers were jockeying into important wartime positions while he, Snyder, and Rowcliff were headed for the "bone yard," the General Board. Bristol was going to be also close by in the Navy Department. Several admirals who knew much about the fleet's tribulations in 1940 would be sitting around in Washington trying to keep quiet. With Herron up the road in retirement, and staying mum, this waste of knowledge and experience left a void in the operation of forces formulating the road toward the Pearl Harbor attack.

The newspapers speculated that Richardson would perhaps undertake a special assignment in the Navy Department or maybe a London ambassadorship.[59] His 1939 duty with the king and queen of England made that a perfect assumption.[60] After what happened, however, that was not an alternative. Those who heard the quick answer on January 17 to a question put to the president at a press conference realized it was not an option. "Mr. President," a writer asked after several domestic questions, "will you have any special assignment for Admiral Richardson on his return?" As he often did, Roosevelt short-answered by saying, "I think he was ordered to report to the Secretary [of Navy]. I don't know." There were no follow-ups.

When all the Short festivities calmed down, the Richardsons were taken on an "illegal" but "delightful" cruise aboard the USS *Oglala*. Richardson's 1902 classmate, Commander Minecraft Battle Force Marquart, did the honors. The departing couple left on board the SS *Lurline* at noon on Valentine's Day.[61] They had more than a month before the admiral had to report to Washington, but some of that time was required to shut down their apartment in Long Beach. Richardson was again a rear-admiral; his pay and lifestyle would be somewhat stressed to live again in Washington.

Richardson and May left Hawaii, arrived at the Matson line dock at San Pedro on February 21, gathered belongings, made arrangements to ship goods, and left by car on March 1. Richardson called it a "leisurely trip across the continent."[62] They briefly stopped to see Moss in Canyon, Texas. In Paris not even the kinfolks or close friends were told the true story of 1940, or why their loved one had been relieved. For years Clareda Purser believed what she was told when young. "Uncle Otto and the President became angry with each other because when the Fleet had the Japanese ships surrounded, Richardson wired the President for permission to wipe them out, but the President said no."[63]

CHAPTER TWENTY-FIVE

Duties Back in Washington
Richardson Spends No Idle Hours

About all Parisians understood was that its famous native and his wife were at the Fenet home in early March 1941. Notice of Richardson's release did make the front page of the local daily newspaper on February 2, but it was short.[1]

Paris was a getaway from the real world. Richardson could walk through Bywaters Park and admire the beautiful peristyle, use the library across the street, sit quietly reading, walk the Italian-like plaza to talk with old friends, or just rest. Commanding the fleet had been a tiring and stressful assignment, with an unbelievable ending.

But, Richardson was not retiring back to home. He was full of Navy and full of desire to stay active. Just as Roosevelt had said, it was in the orders for Richardson to report to Knox on March 24, 1941, not to Stark or to the president.[2] May and Jim Richardson pulled into Washington at 4:00 P.M. the day before he was due to report. The next day, he arrived to speak to Knox.[3] He did not take long to tell his civilian superior, "I have never known a Commander-in-chief to be detached in such a summary manner as I have been. I feel that I owe it to myself to inquire as to the reason for my peremptory detachment."

Looking surprised, Knox replied, "Why Richardson. When you were here in Washington last October, you hurt the President's feelings by what you said to him." He could tell that Richardson was not so clear about what he was being told. "You should realize that. But, I'm sure that someday soon, the President will send for you and have a talk."[4] Of course, he did not. In fact, Richardson never saw Roosevelt in person again in any scenario.[5]

"I did not believe that the President would send for me, because it had been my observation that Franklin D. Roosevelt took pains to avoid personal meetings and discussions with those

Fenet dining room in Paris, Texas: When visiting Texas, the Richardsons spent their evenings at the Joe Fenet home on the tree-lined Church Street. After May Richardson's brother died in 1936, the house was still the center of a visit to the hometown. Mrs. Fenet left the entire room and furnishings to Paris Junior College, where it is used as a dinner facility and meeting room for the board of regents and other groups. No photo of the admiral and Mrs. Richardson hangs on the walls, however. (Steely Collection, James G. Gee Library, Commerce, Texas)

with whom he had differed sharply—or had dropped from his team." Richardson never asked Stark why the detachment was ordered. Stark had not written to Richardson from January 5 to February 1 about the change in assignments, which spoke millions of words. "This I thought was strange, very strange," Richardson penned later. The two did cross each other's paths many times in the next fifteen years, but Richardson said neither of them ever brought up the subject.[6]

However, Richardson well understood his release. He told Congress at the end of his 1945 testimony, basically repeating what Moss had written:

> Mr. Chairman:
>
> I thank you for this opportunity to state that I never bore any resentment toward President Roosevelt because of my detachment from command of the United States Fleet.
>
> He was the constitutional Commander-in-Chief of the Army and Navy. I was one of his senior subordinates; there was a difference of opinion; each of us frankly expressed his views; neither could induce the other to change his opinion; I was relieved of command of the Fleet. Had I been constitutional Commander-in-Chief of the Army and Navy, I would have taken the same action.[7]

In addition, Richardson told the committee that he sent to Stark on January 28, 1941, a message that read:

> The day I was made Commander-in-Chief, I realized then and thereafter that the same power which made me Commander-in-Chief could unmake me at any time. When I arrive in Washington I shall keep my lips sealed and my eyes in the boat, and put my weight on the oar in any duty assigned.[8]

Richardson was putting his career on the line and hoping it would continue. The day after meeting with Knox, he was assigned to the General Board.[9]

Richardson incredulously saw headlines on April 9 that added Jerry Land to the list of Richardson and Taussig. There were then three admirals calling for more aggressive preparation and action when the United States dealt with potential enemies. Land, iron-ically a cousin to isolationist Charles Lindbergh, was serving as chairman of the Maritime Commission and was a good friend with Roosevelt. Still, in a radio address Land called for the coun-try to lick the German menace "at its source" instead of merely feeding it more supply and passenger ships to devour. "Bomb the repair and rest stations where the submarines go when not at sea," he said.[10] Richardson must have questioned why Roosevelt allowed this strong talk to go unpunished. But, Land also had known Roosevelt since the Woodrow Wilson administration, and met with him often from 1927 through 1941. He simply felt him out better than Richardson.[11]

Sexton was the chairman of the General Board when Richardson arrived. Others in this assignment were: Rear Admirals Horne, Greenslade, R. S. Holmes, Ellis, Rowcliffe, and A. P. Fairfield. Commander J. J. Mahoney was the board's secretary. Richardson's physical exam revealed that he was still fit, but with the ailments of a sixty-three-year-old: a hypertrophic osteo arthritic spine, which must have made the golf swing difficult; eyes that were 16/20, corrected to 20/20; and myopia. He was, however, only sick one day in 1940, for rhinitis. His teeth were not good, with eight missing and three removable bridges. He had shrunk to seventy-two inches in height, and weighed 189 pounds. Still, he stood erect and looked taller than his actual height.[12]

Snyder did not officially report until April 1, and two weeks later Greenslade was detached to become commandant of the Twelfth Naval District in San Francisco Bay. Several others came and went during the thirteen months that Richardson had duty on the board, but there was no new assignment for the former CinCUS.

Bloch left Hawaii in the spring of 1942, reporting to the board on May 11. After the Pearl Harbor attack, he suggested to Stark that a "young and robust" officer, willing to continue the post through the end of the war, should be chosen to replace him. He estimated that replacement to be three to four years in the future.[13] Therefore, during the year that Richardson served on the board, four figures (Rowcliffe, Snyder, Fairfield, and Bloch) from the 1940 argument over the fleet being placed at Pearl Harbor joined with Richardson to make major Navy suggestions and reports.

After the attack on Pearl Harbor, on December 16, 1941, Roosevelt signed an executive order that placed operational control of the Navy under a separate title, taking that duty from the CNO position. King was selected as commander in chief of the U.S. Fleet (COMINCH), but after taking office on December 31, he operated in Washington side by side with Stark, whose duties by that time were mainly preparation of long-range war plans. King's responsibilities were ill defined.[14] The situation was awkward, to say the least, and King's strong personality was taking over. He had the president's attention, and the public's too. He hoisted his commander in chief U.S. Fleet flag at noon, December 30, 1941, on board the USS *Vixen* at the Washington Naval Yard.[15] The fleet would be managed from a Washington desk! However, Nimitz was sent to Hawaii to replace Pye, who had been acting as CinCPAC (Commander in Chief Pacific) since Kimmel's release on December 17, 1941. To his credit, Stark maintained a harmonious office relationship with King.[16]

In February 1941, Knox sent Richardson out to Pasadena, California, to talk at the Lincoln Club dinner. Robert A. Milliken, a member who was chairman of the executive council at the California Institute of Technology, wrote Knox, "We at first hoped that you might be the speaker . . . [but] Richardson as a substitute lent just the atmosphere that we needed." He thought the speech was "a very fine one."[17]

On February 18, six days after the dinner, Richardson wrote Bloch a long letter, the first correspondence he had sent his former "chief" and close friend since leaving Hawaii a year earlier. He said that he had run into a mutual friend in Los Angeles, John McWilliams, who mentioned that Bloch hoped Richardson would "not rock the boat" too much. He assured Bloch that so far he had "loyally pulled my oar" and at least kept "my mouth shut." The journey west afforded a chance for Richardson to drill Standley, his old friend and member of the Roberts Commission, the group that first studied the Pearl Harbor attack. The two were on the same trip.

"It was most interesting," was all Richardson noted at that time.[18]

Two weeks after Richardson returned, on the first Sunday in March of 1942, Richardson and Sexton were in the General Board section when King came by. He asked the pair to draft a presidential executive order to reorganize the Navy again.[19] He and Roosevelt wanted one officer to serve jointly as CinCUS and CNO. Sexton, being five years senior to Richardson and perhaps wanting no hand in this change of longtime management, turned the job over to Richardson.[20]

The draft Richardson wrote gave King "supreme command" over the operating forces, as well as control for their readiness and logistic support. Most important, thought Richardson, the new position's job description meant that one person could coordinate and direct the efforts of bureaus and offices of the Navy Department. This change rankled some, like Forrestal, who did not like King's interference into the procurement functions.

Richardson must have agreed with the formula, or he would not have taken the assignment. Had events been different, he might have been in King's place, and desired the new powers. He had high respect for King, despite the man's impulsive personality. Stark felt the same toward King. He knew of King's disappointment three years earlier when he was not chosen as CNO. Neither of the two knew that perhaps Richardson's statement to Edison that he preferred sea duty may have opened the door for both of them to rise to such important places in history.

Richardson's draft was accepted in total, with two words added later from his own suggestion. However, he was highly disappointed that Stark was not cognizant of the change. Richardson thought this lack of communication was unfair, and another example of the way Roosevelt treated those who ceased to be useful to him.

"When King first asked Sexton and me to draft the Executive Order . . . I asked him what was to become of Stark?" The answer was cruel and rough. "The President said that he did not give a damn what happened to Stark, so long as he was gotten out of Washington as soon as practicable."[21] The next question was predicted. Richardson asked, "Does Stark know?" King said, "No." But, he agreed that in all decency, he should be informed.

King's aide, Ruthven E. Libby, said years later that King was outraged "by the filthy deal that Admiral Stark got over Pearl Harbor." Neither Libby nor King, however, thought Stark was any "ball of fire as CNO." Libby stated that he thought Stark was too much of a hound for detail and did not turn enough over to "his hired help," a description with which Richardson would more or less agree, and a position that is again and again revealed in Stark's letters. Still, Libby said that King had high regard for and loyalty to Stark.[22]

It is likely that Stark already knew he was being replaced. He apparently had suggested such a move in a February 9, 1942, letter to Roosevelt.[23] On March 7, Stark met with the president for two hours. He resigned as CNO, but Roosevelt did not disregard Stark's talents as he did Richardson's. Stark was given the title of Commander U.S. Navy Forces Europe. He liked the idea, and the president and Knox knew that Stark would be most influential over there. Stark formally was relieved by King on March 26, becoming the fourth man out in the Pearl Harbor blame game.[24] He and his family moved from the Naval Observatory to their nearby house, then he reported to London.

In mid-1942, Richardson was appointed by the chief of the new Bureau of Naval Personnel (BuPERS) Randall Jacobs to be the senior member on a board to draft regulations for the president to approve. They dealt with the temporary promotion of all naval officers during the war. Actually, he had first served at the beckon of Knox on this board on July 14, 1941.[25] He carried to the meetings his old feelings that those working in Washington should not have advantage of promotion opportunities over those performing the actual operations in the Navy. He did not believe, either, that reserve officers should be promoted faster than regular officers. Though they naturally were not as qualified as fulltime officers, he would have a tough time derailing this structure for the war period.[26]

He drafted regulations that allowed promotions only one grade at a time, and unless there were unusual circumstances, only to be made in accordance to contemporaries. He sent the ideas up the line to Knox, which went then to Roosevelt. The president surely knew early on who was drafting the regulations, and the previous job description for King. Maybe he remembered Richardson's abilities and was quietly using him.

The scheme backfired on Roosevelt. He realized that the proposal was a problem. "Richardson has hamstrung you and me so that we can't promote whom we want to," he told Knox. Therefore, the draft was returned to the Navy Department. Richardson had a chuckle, and participated in the change that allowed reserve officers to be appointed from civilian life into the Navy in the highest permissible grade, which was lieutenant commander, on one day, and then immediately be bumped upward the next day. "This was done for the favored few by the Secretary," said Richardson.[27]

CHAPTER TWENTY-SIX

A Permanent Job or Two for Richardson
Navy Relief Society and Creating Defense Future

On May 27, 1942, Richardson walked into a job he never dreamed of taking two years earlier.[1] He knew that a wartime sea duty was beyond hope at that point, and was anxious for a domain of his own. It came in the form of the Navy Relief Society. He was named by Knox to be the organization's executive vice-president. It was no fluff job, especially during wartime when families were out of funds and the society was assigned the awful duty of relaying messages of death to loved ones across the country.

One sure thing about living in Washington is that there will be special assignments, parties, and gatherings of old friends, and that the talk will gravitate toward events and rumors. In September, Richardson received extra duty from the Navy, serving as president of the Naval Retiring Board.[2] The next month, Standley was in town. He was at that time American ambassador to Russia. He and Richardson had an in-depth conversation about the prewar disposition toward Japan.[3]

Leahy had said in his speeches and talks about town that as CNO he had favored a strong position with Japan early in the Chinese incident. Hull was perturbed about any assertion that the State Department's attitude during that time was one of appeasement. Perhaps Hull had not read history too well, or even newspapers during the middle 1930s. Standley thought Hull should talk with Richardson. Hull expressed some hesitancy to Standley about any views Richardson might express. Even so, Standley told Richardson he insisted that Hull meet with the former assistant CNO who had experienced many of those times and events almost first hand.

Richardson told Standley that he had little to add, but that he would call on Hull if invited to do so. Weeks went by before a January 3, 1943, State Department publication was announced.

It was called *Peace and War: United States Foreign Policy 1931-1941*.[4] Three days later Hull's office phoned Richardson, arranging an appointment between the two in the late morning of January 8.

Hull had not seen Richardson since their July meeting in 1940, but was of the impression he had talked with the admiral during his second Washington trip that year. Hull insisted that he was at the White House and saw Richardson in conference with Roosevelt. A later check of Richardson's diary proved he had not seen the secretary that day. After that strange badger, the conversation continued about the State Department "paper."

Richardson had obtained a copy only the day before, so he had not read through its some nine hundred pages. Hull set Richardson back a bit when he complained that the press had exaggerated the importance of Grew's January 27, 1941, report on the danger of a Japanese surprise attack on Pearl Harbor. Hull thought that what Grew wrote was not nearly as specific as a warning that the Navy Department (Knox) sent to the War Department (Stimson) on January 24, 1941. If this was so, why was the Navy warning not in the "paper"?

Richardson explained that he was instrumental in drafting the contents of that Navy warning, though Turner indicated in his book and in his congressional testimony that he drafted the Washington version.[5] Hull said he did not see that the letter favored a stronger position toward Japan. Also, he had been studying earlier reports and speeches given by naval officers for any feeling that the Navy was ready to support a more aggressive course of action.

Hull wanted Richardson to show him examples, if he could. "I was extremely busy as vice-president of the Navy Relief Society," Richardson told Hull " . . . but that there were several Naval officers of high rank, long experience and some personal knowledge of the subject."[6] He specifically mentioned Hart and Bloch. Again, Richardson explained his position, saying that for several years he held the opinion that the State Department stance on the Japan matter had been stronger than the power of the Navy to support such a position.

During the course of their conversation, Richardson discussed his ironic rereading of his Naval War College thesis on the day of the Pearl Harbor attack, and presented Hull with a copy of its conclusions. His point, as summarized succinctly by a friend in 1948, was that if the United States had no policy on where it wanted to go, and its strategy was only to "beat the other fellow to a pulp, then you are in a bit of a jam."[7]

Later that day, Richardson examined *Peace and War*. He thought it was simply an alibi for the State Department.[8]

Richardson then ran into Hart, who told him that in a recent White House meeting with Roosevelt, the president had mentioned, "Why, I could have stalled the Japs off for about one year longer."[9] Hart felt the same as Richardson about this "paper." He wanted some sort of explanation made public that removed the possible implication that the records of other departments were not as good. Stark was in town on a visit from London, and Richardson suggested that Hart ask the former CNO to speak to Knox and Hull. Hart did not.

On the last day of 1943, Richardson was at the Sellers' home, and ran into Dr. Hornbeck. "I spoke to him about the White Paper," wrote Richardson. Hornbeck said the "paper" was written to show the gradual turn in public opinion away from isolationism and how the State Department encouraged that change. In one of those rare times, Richardson sounded like a member of the press. He said he was of the opinion, also, that the January 27, 1941, Grew report was the most newsworthy part of the White Paper's contents. Hornbeck took Hull's side of the issue, saying that the Navy (Richardson/Kimmel/Bloch/Turner/Knox) report was much more comprehensive. After all, he said, many warnings like the one Grew presented were received weekly. No one was going to change the State Department effort to establish a prepared demeanor.

At this time, and in many other instances, Richardson fell back on his late stepmother's words uttered to him as he left Texas in 1898 for the Naval Academy:

The wise man seeks to outshine himself. The fool seeks to outshine others.[10]

So, Richardson let the matter drop, and let historians battle it out in future publications.

Despite his efforts to keep a low-key lifestyle and to continue to work diligently for the Relief Society, the press still believed that Richardson was destined for a higher call. John O'Donnell, a New York columnist, wrote on December 8, 1942, that Congress was about to throw around its anti-New Deal weight since the mid-term elections were over, and predicted, along with it would go Knox. Word was that Richardson would replace him. The reports were fueled on the fact that Richardson was perceived to be such a close friend of Roosevelt and Leahy, and that Richardson backed Halsey's tough actions in the Pacific. A photo of Richardson talking with Knox, taken in 1940, was printed along with the column.[11] It was a source of amusement to Richardson, but certainly pure fantasy.

In 1944, the sixty-six-year-old Richardson was named chairman of the Special Joint Chiefs of Staff Committee for Re-organization of National Defense.[12] Office space was found in the Munitions Building. Colonel H. Jordan Theis was assigned as manager.[13]

The committee is somehow ignored in most studies of the reorganization and unification of the national defense structure. Richardson's team included: former assistant Secretary of War for Air Colonel F. Trubee Davison; Assistant Chief of Navy Operations Rear Admiral Malcolm F. Schoeffel; an expert on demobilization, Major General William Fraser Tompkins; and General Harold Lee George. Davison related later that the first Navy officer on the committee was a reluctant Admiral Arthur W. Radford, but that with some pull, Malcolm F. "Red" Schoeffel replaced Radford.

The 1944 Joint Chiefs-of-Staff (JCS) established Richardson's group as a congressional committee on the subject disbanded. It was hoped the JCS committee would come up with acceptable recommendations to "unify" the Army and Navy, and with the thought of creating a single Department of Defense whose "commander" would serve as chief of staff to the president.[14] The committee was also to study a separate air force department.

Richardson worked tirelessly, attending every meeting, participating in interviews, and calling on his friends around the world.[15] "We had frequent hearings," added Davison.[16] Schoeffel said each of the members had a Webster's unabridged dictionary in front of him, "to make sure we were all talking the same language."[17] One day Richardson asked, "Are we getting anywhere, Schoeffel?" He replied, "Well, Admiral, I'm having a wonderful course in semantics!" Richardson chuckled, asking, "What's that?"

In the late fall of 1944, the Richardson committee traveled to England. The pilot was Lieutenant Henry Myers. Alive in 2005, eighty-seven-year-old co-pilot Elmer F. Smith confirmed that in addition to him and Myers, the crew included five others. They left on October 30. After picking up passengers in New York, on board were Generals George, Tompkins, Richard C. Lindsay, and Howard A. Craig, as well as Admirals Richardson, Schoeffel, Gilbert C. Hoover, and J. M. Steele.[18] Davison and perhaps another passenger were also there.[19]

On November 1, the group landed near Newquay, England.[20] The committee spent a day with Stark and his deputy, Glassford.[21] They then flew to Paris, France, for a week's stay. General Dwight D. Eisenhower had moved the Supreme Headquarters Allied Expeditionary Force to Versailles.[22] His naval aide, reserve Captain Harry C. Butcher, assisted with many of the committee arrangements.[23]

In a glassed-in sunroom, Eisenhower repeatedly told the Richardson committee that it should actually be talking with General Elwood R. Quesada of the Ninth Tactical Air Command which supported the First Army.[24] After returning to Paris for a couple of days, the committee was "shepherded" to General Omar Bradley's Luxembourg headquarters on November 7.[25] The weather was distinctly worse; plus in the air at night could be heard German flying bombs and rockets heading to Allied targets.[26] Schoeffel said, looking back on it, "There we were, a whole bunch of flag officers, captains and colonels, and not a cap pistol among us. We could have gotten gathered up by the Nazis in nothing flat."[27]

Bradley's aide, Chester B. Hansen, noted that the question of unification was critically important. Bradley surmised that much of the Pearl Harbor problem had been born from the interservice reluctance to cooperate. Another reason to unify, wrote Bradley, was to avoid such chaotic war production planning.

Hansen said the talk was from all sides. The Navy wanted to retain its air force and the Marine Corps. "Army," Hansen wrote, "basically disapproves the formation and retention in strength of the Marine Corps—it simply duplicates functions usually performed more ably by army personnel."[28] Bradley thought the roots of the separation predated World War II.

Hansen wrote that the committee's naval representatives related that history and tradition favored the retention of its functions. "Still, they all seem sincere in the motive to establish a satisfactory system of national defense."

Eisenhower then arrived. After a short additional discussion, the committee went on its way to talk with Walter Bedell Smith and Quesada. Richardson was rather "knocked down" when Smith, Eisenhower's chief of staff, said that the air function was not a coequal with the Army and Navy, but that "they are the most important of the three." Richardson slowly drew out his Texanese, drawling "You know, General, we've always been kind of brought up to believe that it's the doughboy who wins these wars." Smith said, "Well, let me rephrase my answer. The G.I. may conclude a war, but air is the key to victory."

Kirk, then naval assistant to Eisenhower, "gave a brilliant piece of testimony," said Davison.[29] He felt that the problems could be solved. "He was the only exception that I can recall," said Davison, in reference to Navy personnel who testified there.[30]

The committee flew out of Paris on November 10 to Naples. There they met with naval officials of the Eighth Fleet. The headquarters of the Fifth Army under General Mark Clark was above Rome by then, at or near Mount Belmonte. The committee traveled by C-47 from Naples to near Florence, then by vehicle through the mud to visit Clark. He, too, was near the action.

Despite the bad weather during the previous days, it was clear but cold. The committee met with Clark and his chief of staff,

General Alfred M. Gruenther. Present also were Steele, Hoover, Captain William L. Reese, Colonel Phillip Cole, Theis, and Lieutenant Colonel Hamilton Robinson.[31] Richardson first threw out questions based upon the various proposals on the table.

Clark replied that he favored both the single department proposal and a separate air force, but insisted that in war conditions the air operations staff should remain with the ground commander. Clark mentioned that if there were three services, run by one department or person, the staff should remain small.

Clark and Gruenther thought that continuing the joint chief of staff would facilitate proper working conditions. All agreed that the chief of staff should be responsible directly to the president rather than reporting through a cabinet officer. "I think that would be better for the armed forces," replied Clark, but looked at it more realistically. "The American people would not like such an arrangement."

It was amazing that so many questions were answered, for during the conference a spark from the fireplace hit the camouflage net over the hut. A small fire ensued.[32] Schoeffel said he became unpopular with Clark by letting loose some dogs to get them out of the way. "They went tearing off and had to be rounded up later," he remembered.[33]

After lunch the committee left the command post. That one-day visit with the Army was followed with three days in Rome. President Roosevelt's representative to the Vatican, Myron C. Taylor, hosted the group. Since some in the party were Catholic, while there they had an audience with Pope Pius XII.[34]

In Rome, the committee discussed ideas with a pioneer of Navy flight, John Lansing Callan. When Richardson's group met him, Callan was chief staff officer in Italy.[35] The committee met also with Commodore Charles M. Yates and Colonel J. M. McDonnell.[36] Yates commanded the Naval Operating Base, Oran, Algeria.

Extra time was spent in Naples with Deputy Supreme Allied Commander of the Mediterranean Theater General Joseph T. McNarney. The members left there on November 16 for Casablanca, Morocco. Expecting to head smoothly back to the

States, the Richardson committee departed the next day. However, after nearly eight hours in the air, they began a return. Schoeffel said the weather near the Azores was bad, and that a block of fighters coming in from Newfoundland was given priority. "No bunch of old crocks like us was going to interfere with this," Schoeffel said.

Finally, near midnight on November 19, the committee arrived in Washington. More interviews were scheduled. The Army air personnel found the unification question still difficult. Therefore, Marshall brought into his office the Army committee members and gave an inspiring talk on unification. It sounded great, but then the group gathered to work out the details. "The more we worked on it, the less sense it made," said a discouraged Davison.[37]

Admiral Marc "Pete" Mitscher wired in his answer, immediately stating, "I don't know what the whole shooting [match] is all about." His chief of staff, Burke, was asked why air operation was not an irritant to the Navy. Burke explained. Living on board a ship, and the nature of naval operations, lessened the problem for the Navy. Army flyers began to think they could win a war with enough strategic bombing. "We solved that problem in the Navy by sending senior officers to go to school in Pensacola for flight training." They were not fine aviators, he thought, but the experience turned them into enthusiastic supporters of aviation. "The Army did not do that," said Burke.[38]

For the trip west, the Richardson committee and the same four extra passengers flew in the president's aircraft, *Sacred Cow*. The pilot again was Myers, assisted by Smith. "Golly, it was nicely fitted up," said Schoeffel.[39] Richardson used the State Room, or what Schoeffel referred to as the den.[40] One area had a large conference table, fitted on one side with maps. Here the card games went on for hours. "Richardson was damn good at cribbage," said Smith. "He was one of those who could know what you had after one card was put down." He added, "Now, I could whip Schoeffel . . . pretty regular."[41]

The committee left Washington on November 26. In San Francisco, it interviewed Mitscher, just weeks after being in the

Battle for Leyte Gulf. He surprised the fact-finders by coming out for unification. "That was just the beginning," said a taken-aback Davison.

Interviews were held in Honolulu while awaiting takeoff for a grueling Pacific trip filled with talk and more cribbage. Richardson had promised May at Washington National Airport that he would not drink more than one alcoholic beverage per evening. "He complied faithfully," laughed Smith, "by slowly drinking one full glass of bourbon minus any water or soda!"

The committee arrived at Leyte, Philippine Islands, on December 3. "By golly," said Schoeffel, "the airfield there was certainly a disaster waiting to happen."[42] The October monsoon rains spread into late fall. When Davison stepped onto land, his cane sank into the mud at times as much as two feet.

The conditions were not confined to the airfield. "At one street intersection," Schoeffel continued, "there was a big mud puddle where the upper part of the steering wheel of a jeep appeared! The jeep was down there . . . in the hole." MacArthur had set up headquarters in Tacloban City in the Joseph Price Mansion. It was so impressive that Davison called it a hotel. However, Schoeffel's memoirs paint an entirely different picture. He said that headquarters was in an old masonry warehouse, once used by the Japanese as an officers' club. Nearby were corrugated metal buildings where officers billeted.[43]

It was possible that MacArthur was using the warehouse as deception. Perhaps, however, Davison did not get to this warehouse meeting. He was separated from the group at one time when the participants got lost.[44] He "bummed a ride with a jeep," and arrived at what he thought was MacArthur's headquarters—the home. "I got out of the jeep and walked in. MacArthur was sitting there having lunch with the rest of the gang," Davison said.[45]

The lunch "wasn't bad," said Schoeffel. "It wasn't K-rations." Afterward, MacArthur took the committee out on a balcony. He gave his speech on the positives of unification, a switch from what Davison said was his original testimony months earlier. The "gang" then talked with others, including Embick's son-in-law,

Albert C. Wedemeyer. He too favored the unification idea. To Davison, it now seemed that all theater commanders had come to the realization it was a necessity.

On December 4, the committee flew to the Carolines; then the next morning the men went a two-hour flight to Ulithi Atoll. The Third Fleet assembled there was "about to make one of its famous strikes," said Davison.[46]

Halsey gathered John McCain, Mitscher, who was back from San Francisco, and various other officers. First, they ate. The Navy lunch there "put MacArthur's to utter shame," Schoeffel related. The Army members were impressed. The afternoon and evening discussions were long and educational.

On December 6, the Richardson party received Commander Harold E. Stassen's opinion. Next they talked with Admiral W. A. Lee, then Carney and McCain.[47] Stassen, a former governor of Minnesota, was for it. He further suggested that it was imperative that civilian control always be maintained, echoing Clark's understanding. Stassen was thinking ahead, and Davison said that for the first time, this civilian control idea was strongly imbedded in the committee's analyzation process.[48]

The "junket" then returned to Honolulu. The group relaxed a bit then, even playing a round of golf. The aircraft had a fuel leak that needed attention, so the committee used the time to interview more of those on its list. This went on for four days before departure.[49] The group arrived back in Washington in the early morning rush hour of December 16. Richardson's notes say that he went directly to work that day.[50]

On January 4, 1945, Richardson explained to JCS chairman Leahy that the committee was still pursuing the single-department angle. Leahy later wrote about his longtime associate, "Richardson had reached a conclusion that a single Secretary of Cabinet rank for the armed forces was desirable."[51]

The committee's draft report then began. Davison was impressed with the chairman's phrase making, and was sure that Richardson was voting for all he was writing down. The group left on February 18 for Miami, Florida, in an effort to obtain a secluded place to work.[52] When they came back to Washington, only a few minor final changes were made. George finally came up with the concluding question: "Now, where do we get this thing printed?"

Richardson pulled the rug out at this point. He announced his disagreement with the proposal. "Well, you could have knocked us over with a feather," said Davison later. "There was nothing we could say to argue with him. He knew just as much as we did."[53]

Schoeffel commented, "This threw a big monkey wrench into the works." Speaking in 1970, he said that if the majority report had been accepted and implemented, "we might very well have avoided this terrific multiplication of bureaucracy that has occurred in the Department of Defense."[54]

Did Richardson abruptly change his mind? Probably not. In September of 1940 he wrote, "With a separate air corps there is bound to develop a loyalty to the Corps rather than to the Navy, a jealousy. . . ." He felt that a higher degree of cooperation would exist if all continued to be intimately bound together in one Navy.[55]

Under what must have been tremendous pressure, Schoeffel stuck to his guns. However, he said, "I made a poor witness in attempting to defend our report. I was very dissatisfied with it myself."[56]

The majority and minority reports came out in April. They touched off heated discussions. The majority report that Richardson basically wrote was shorter than his minority manuscript. It mentioned that the decision to support a single department system was favored by many officers in the field and in Washington.[57] The press and citizens mostly agreed.

The committee urged a separate air force, one that would include aviation that was not inherent to the land or sea forces. The Marines would remain with the Navy. It added that a single defense department, headed by a civilian, should be enacted not more than six months after the end of the war.[58]

Richardson explained that he just could not come to vote for a single department system for the armed forces—at least not yet. At the same time, he wrote, "If those in authority decide to establish a single department system, I can, at this time, conceive of no better plan than that proposed by the Special Committee."[59]

Richardson proposed four actions rather than reorganization. First, he wanted the JCS to be continued after the war. Second, he wanted the organizational gains of the War and Navy Departments made possible by executive order during World War II to be continued. Third, Richardson thought that a study of the reorganization should be continued in the light of war experiences. Finally, he held that a full exploration of the establishment of a joint secretaryship within the present organization should be pursued.[60]

Richardson's part was over, but not the issue. Two more years of study and wrangling followed. Finally, a compromise draft was sent to Congress in February 1947. On July 26, Congress passed the legislation. Appropriately aboard the *Sacred Cow*, President Harry Truman signed the National Security Act of 1947.[61] "The effort wore out many."[62]

Ironically, after the passage of the unification legislation, Forrestal became the first Secretary of Defense. All in all, what evolved in time Richardson surely would have basically approved. At the least, it received much study. The Navy kept its air component. Davison thought that despite the controversy Richardson raised with his last second change of mind, "He was a fine old man."

Midway through 1945, Richardson's third year at the society was over. He retired a bit early on May 10, 1945, a month after his committee handed in its reorganization report on April 11. At the end of that year, the society had a net worth of $12,761,766, with more than $12 million of that sum in investments, all with the United States government. The society hired Vice-Admiral R. M. Brainard as executive vice president.[63]

Richardson had an offer from Dr. William B. Munro to teach in the V-12 candidate program at Caltech, but replied, "I am beginning to feel averse to moving about," even though it meant being near his son.[64] The pace was tiring him. "I've had a spring cold and a lame back," he wrote, "and as a result am below par." Even though he said the special committee was to complete its report that day, he told Munro about his decision not to vote for it, and added another surprise. "I also find that I am not in favor of Universal Military Training as advocated by the Army and Navy."

Richardson also knew he would be called to testify at some time before Congress about his role at Pearl Harbor. It would take some massive study, research, and time to copy documents, and get ready for the questions.

Brainard moved the society offices to Main Navy, where they remained for eighteen years. Brainard lasted only a little more than a year, but to Richardson's delight, Murphy, then a vice-admiral, became the executive vice-president. He served there for sixteen years. Today, there are more than 250 offices ashore and afloat, with the executive complex in Arlington, Virginia. Overhead expenses are covered by proceeds from the Reserve Fund established during World War II.

It was a quiet job done well by Richardson.

CHAPTER TWENTY-SEVEN

All the Many Investigations
Conclusions When Later Facts Arrive

After Richardson commented to the General Board that he hoped he could keep his mouth shut, he made the decision to burn pertinent letters and part of his diary.[1] He was sure that in time he would be called to testify in one of the upcoming investigations, and he did not want to quote passages that criticized the president, the government, or Navy personnel. He was rather horrified at the result of the first Pearl Harbor report that came quickly from the disaster. He had been told that Justice Felix Frankfurter had a strong hand in the creation of what became known as the Roberts Commission. Richardson thought that Justice Harlan F. Stone requested to serve, but was refused. Instead, Justice Owen D. Roberts led military members Standley, Reeves, Major General Frank Ross McCoy, and McNarney during hearings in Washington and Hawaii.

The Army members were naturally close to Marshall, but McCoy had worked for or close to Stimson for years. McNarney was an air expert and aide to Marshall. Standley viewed the retired McCoy as able, but was surprised to see Turner's Army opposite, McNarney, there. He was Major General Leonard T. Gerow's assistant in that service's War Plans Division.

Standley had some preconceived opinions, however, one being that he knew the situation at Pearl Harbor and felt that Kimmel and Short were not the only ones to blame—others deeply involved sat in Washington. He also began to realize why the group was gathered. "In my opinion, our commission was hurriedly ordered by the President on December 16 to forestall just such a Congressional investigation at that time."

The commission first met in Washington in Stimson's office on December 17, about the same time Kimmel and Short were being detached in Hawaii. Knox and Stimson were present, the former

333

having spent two days in Hawaii observing the damage, and the latter having nominated three of the five members. The next morning in the Munitions Building, even though Standley had been delayed in arriving, the group began working. They listened for two days to Marshall, Stark, and other key members of the Washington military staffs. Without being told of the intercepted messages, the group could formulate little thought nor ask pertinent questions.

At the end of the table sat Turner, a witness and soon to be defendant, supporting Stark, who was in the process of testifying before the commission.[2] Out of the Navy loop for some time, Standley felt a bit uncomfortable in what he termed an unusual situation. He protested that the witnesses were not sworn, and this situation quickly changed.[3]

If Knox told them what he wrote to his editor at the *Chicago Daily News* on December 18, the commission was highly prejudiced by the time they were at Pearl Harbor. Knox, even though he had been warned again and again by Richardson, Bloch, Kimmel, Stark, and countless others in the Navy Department, and even though he knew the Navy had attacked Pearl Harbor many times in drills and were successful, told editor Paul Scott Mowrer, "It is simply incredible that both the Army and Navy could have been caught so far off first base. They evidently had convinced themselves that an air attack by carrier born planes was beyond the realm of possibility, because they made no preparation whatever for such an attack." He took no blame. He too thought his being in Hawaii quickly, and the president forming the commission immediately, were both part of an attempt to thwart a nasty congressional investigation.[4]

On December 22, the Roberts Commission flew toward Hawaii. The group met the next morning at Fort Shafter. Short was called in first. Reeves was apparently tough on the general, and felt that Short did not understand the Army's mission to protect the fleet while anchored at Pearl Harbor. The commission kept at the interviews with Army personnel until it moved on December 27 to the wardroom lounge at the submarine base. Kimmel gave his side of the story. Reeves became ill, and missed some of Kimmel's statements. The commission reconvened at the Royal Hawaiian on January 3, 1942.

For the Roberts Commission, Bellinger produced a copy of his January 16, 1941, letter, assembled with the assistance of Richardson and his staff. He called it the "shoestring" letter, which explained the deplorable state of patrol readiness at Pearl Harbor. He would also later testify with the same message in front of the naval inquiry and the congressional hearings.[5]

Of course, Kimmel gained no sympathy from Reeves, who knew it was easy to attack Pearl Harbor. But, since he was not there to hear firsthand testimony, and subsequently read what Kimmel thought were inferior transcripts, Reeves may not have understood the patrol problems. An effort was made to correct the transcripts, but not even Standley would insist that what was already in the record be clarified.[6] The corrections were finally attached as an addendum, but probably not read by anyone on the commission.

On January 9, the commission heard its last Hawaiian testimony, and returned to Washington by ship and then train. Prior to leaving, and fearful that the testimony would be lost if the ship was sunk on the way to the West Coast, Roberts gave the papers to Short's aide, Louis Truman. He told him to take them to Washington by air. Roberts said, "I want you to take this and have it handcuffed to your wrist." Truman described these papers years later in an oral interview. By early 1942, Bedell Smith was secretary to the General Staff for Marshall. His assistant was Maxwell Taylor, who wanted to take the papers in to Marshall. Truman balked at that idea, still with the small mail sack cuffed to his wrist. Finally, Truman agreed to give the reports to Taylor if the two could go into Marshall's office together.[7]

The next morning, Truman met with his cousin, Senator Truman. "What the hell was everybody doing over there [at Pearl Harbor]," the senator bellowed. "All asleep and drunk?" Louis Truman said, "No," not the commanders at least. The senator commented, "I think they are derelict in their duties and they ought to be court-martialed." Then the two kinsmen had "quite a discussion" on the matter.[8]

A bit more Roberts Commission testimony in Washington was taken before the last draft was assembled. The procedure included 127 witnesses. A bitter debate took place between Standley and Reeves, Standley taking the position that Kimmel was not solely to blame. He agreed not to submit a minority report, but only after being persuaded that such language would be divisive during a war effort.[9] Later he wrote a detailed summary of what took place during the commission's existence, and it was printed in Kimmel's 1955 book.[10]

On January 24, the report was presented to Roosevelt. "We took 2,173 printed pages of evidence and exhibits, including that taken in the three days before we left Washington for Pearl Harbor," wrote Standley. He thought that the world situation was so crucial by then that efforts to punish anyone would not go any further. Standley admitted that Kimmel's position with the commission was not as strong as that of his Army counterpart. About this effort, he wrote, "In contrast to General Short, who retained the services of his staff to help him make up his complete and detailed report to the Commission, Admiral Kimmel's staff immediately put to sea with his temporary successor, Admiral Pye." As a result, Kimmel had no one but an aide to help him with his report, nor any fleet records to consult in preparing it, though O'Brien said he did dig through and pull some files for Kimmel.[11] "That was why Kimmel had to make his report to the Commission orally and as factually as he could, answering freely and frankly from memory such questions as we wished to ask," wrote Standley.[12] Standley did not explain why Bloch escaped scrutiny.

Theobald wrote a scathing book in 1954. He said that by placing all the blame on Kimmel and Short, the prestige of the Washington administration was fully preserved in the public mind.

Richardson also felt that Standley was caught in the middle of a difficult decision, and went along with the majority because at that time the nation needed to be united. However, Richardson's sympathy for Standley's position was curtailed a bit. Standley knew Roosevelt and most of the commission, and Richardson felt he should have known the outcome, and avoided serving.

An officer could refuse duty, in some cases, without punishment. When Secretary of Navy Forrestal was unhappy with the Naval Court of Inquiry on Pearl Harbor, and in fact disapproved of all the investigations up to 1944, he asked Richardson to guide another look into the matter. In Texas, a quick way to avoid jury duty was for the prospective juror to tell the inquisitive defense lawyers that he believed in the death penalty. Richardson took this approach, and told Forrestal, "I am sorry, but I am not available for such assignment, because I am prejudiced and I believe that no prejudiced officer should undertake the inquiry."[13]

Forrestal dug deeper. Richardson answered, "I am prejudiced because I believe that any fair and complete investigation will result in placing a part of the blame for the success of the attack [on Pearl Harbor] upon the President." Forrestal said he agreed, but only because Roosevelt had been a poor judge of men. That was not a good reply to Richardson, especially when Forrestal listed those he thought exerted bad judgment, and were retained too long by the president. He did not mention Kimmel, however. Richardson dodged that bullet and was not ordered to conduct the investigation. That unenviable task fell to Hewitt.[14] Kimmel was miffed that any admiral would take the job, and King protested that any individual conducting such an investigation would find it too powerful and too much responsibility for one person.[15]

It rankled Richardson that Kimmel and Short were fired before the Roberts Commission even had its first meeting. But, Reeves was vocal and adamant that a mistake had been made. He thought Pearl Harbor was a disgrace to the Navy.

Richardson was of the firm belief that, after reviewing the horrendous damage at Pearl Harbor, Roosevelt "lost his head" and ordered the Roberts Commission formed.[16] The president thought a focus on Pearl Harbor would divert any discussions of what went on in Washington prior to the attack. At least that was Richardson's assumption.

This is not to say that Richardson desired to keep Kimmel and

Short in their respective commands. On the contrary, Richardson thought they should have been removed, for regardless of who was to blame, "no armed force should remain under the command of a leader under whom it had suffered such a loss." He felt military people understood that principle well.[17] The Roberts Commission just muddied the waters, and he thought it was a sham. "A more disgraceful spectacle has never been presented to this country during my lifetime," he wrote of the commission report a decade and a half later. He felt it inconceivable that the civilian officials failed to show any willingness to take their share of responsibility for the Japanese success at Pearl Harbor.[18]

He reminded readers that Frankfurter wanted a commission that would not be limited by rules of evidence governing either a civilian or military court. Kimmel and Short, thus, were not given a trial, were not permitted to introduce evidence in their behalf, and were not allowed proper counsel. In fact, they could not sit in and watch. Kimmel found that the words he spoke and presented to the Roberts Commission were taken down carelessly, and fought to have them corrected.[19] Short was hesitant to rock the boat and fight for his cause at that time. His granddaughter remembers, "My father always said that my grandfather did not want to disparage Washington during the war." The boom then came down on Kimmel and Short, as it had done earlier on Richardson, and it would be almost four years before the pair could speak before a public forum on the subject.

Meanwhile, the repercussions heaped upon Kimmel and Short were unforgivable. As May and Jim watched, the public was relentless, cruel, and intrusive. Letters threatening the two commanders arrived daily for some time. Their wives were subjected to scorn when out shopping, and even spat upon. Rumors were printed that the pair, while on duty near each other in Hawaii, were not on speaking terms, and that Isabel Short and Dorothy Kimmel were social enemies, so much so that hostesses guarded against inviting them to the same event.

This outrageous rumor was placed into the public by the uninformed. "As a matter of fact," Isabel Short wrote in the 1950s,

"Admiral Kimmel and Walter used to play golf together Sunday mornings, and often the Admiral would stay for lunch and informal talks with Walter."[20] As for the relationship between Isabel and Mrs. Kimmel? They never met. "Mrs. Kimmel hadn't joined her husband at the time of the attack," explained a baffled Isabel in her manuscript. "I never saw her in my life, although we do still exchange Christmas greetings."[21] The shoddy reporting fueled fire to the longtime Richardson mistrust of the press. The fourth estate did a very commendable job of reporting prewar facts and figures, but fell down on the investigative rules of reporting when Pearl Harbor was attacked.

However, the Navy Department's secrecy assisted the ill-reported stories. Richardson was sure that the furor raised by the Roberts Commission prolonged the argument and confused the public. It would not die down. Each side wanted a trial: Kimmel and Short so they could present their facts, and the Republicans because they saw an opportunity to wail away at Roosevelt. Military leaders thought that any trial during the war would be harmful to national interests. Military intelligence gatherers were horrified that as a part of this argument, at any moment the *Purple* decoding secret would emerge.

Isabel Short pointed out her husband's problems, but he was not allowed to make them generally public. "He was given a blank check immediately afterwards for everything he needed," she said of the few days he remained in command after December 7. Before the attack, "General Short begged for radar equipment and appropriate sites for stations. He got three sets and six mobile radar stations," she wrote. "But, the towers . . . were still lying on the docks at Oakland when Pearl Harbor was attacked. In fact, New York, San Francisco and Seattle had modern radar units installed before they were provided for Hawaii."

She also confirmed the basic scene in the movie, *Tora! Tora! Tora!*, relating to troubles placing a radar station on public parkland. The U.S. Interior Department at first refused a permit, but finally agreed with many stipulations upon size, appearance, and location.[22] Two powerful bureaucratic organizations could not come to a quick, sensible solution.

In her manuscript, Isabel also explained the message her husband's good friend Marshall sent that Sunday morning before the attack, but which did not arrive until six hours after the Japanese had come and gone. The cable arrived by telegraph in San Francisco, then was sent on to Honolulu by commercial radio. "It was not marked 'urgent,'" she wrote. "The method of dispatch and delivery, by a little boy, still seems to me to be as ridiculous as the events the message warned about were tragic."[23] She added that it was much later when her husband discovered that the information was in Washington four hours before the Japanese bombs rained down on the harbor.[24]

Why Marshall did not use a phone with a scrambler attached still confused Isabel, as well as those close to the situation like Libby. Isabel mentioned that it was common belief that the message could have easily been sent direct in code or by FBI radio. "Even 90 minutes notice would have enabled him [Short] to disperse the Army planes," she believed. Libby also wondered why Marshall just did not pick up the phone, call, and say, "Look boys, brace yourselves."[25]

When Richardson's book was published, a strong case arose that Marshall was designated as the messenger to Pearl Harbor. Richardson wrote, "I have known Stark well all of his life in the Navy, and I hold him in high esteem. I know that he is an honorable man, and I cannot conceive of how he could have treated Kimmel as he did, unless he was acting under the mistaken impression that he owed no loyalty except upward." Richardson added, "What I think is more likely [is that] his failure to obey his natural impulse was due to influence or possibly direct orders from above." However, as Richardson admitted, "I do not know this to be a fact and I cannot prove it. I believe this because of my knowledge of Stark, and the fact that his means of communication with Kimmel were equal to, if not superior to, those available to Marshall in communication with Short."[26]

Tolley also thought the scenario was ludicrous. He mentioned

Richardson's comments that Marshall had apparently been directed to be the sole person to send a message of warning to Pearl Harbor. He agreed that since Stark did not call Kimmel directly by scrambler phone, it implied that Marshall had been chosen as the official dispatcher.[27]

Isabel also commented that if Kimmel and Short had been given access to all the intelligence that Washington had in its possession several days before the attack, and the freedom to act on it, results would have been different. She wrote that much had been made about the report of planes coming in at 7:02 A.M. on the fateful day, mistaken for the expected arrival of unarmed B-17s from the mainland, and thus ignored. "Even if the radar man's report had been given full credence, and an all out alert sounded, it couldn't have changed the final outcome anything like what it would have been if Washington had given Walter the information it had at hand hours and even days before the attack."[28]

As Richardson knew from correspondence between May and Isabel, Short was told by Knox after the attack that he "had done a wonderful job with what he had." Therefore, Short was "dumbfounded" to hear there was to be an investigation into his state of preparedness. "We first heard of it through a newspaper clipping sent us from the states," wrote Isabel. Then Short was relieved. Isabel wrote about the irony of the detachment message. It was very "unlike the warning message from General Marshall [sent before the attack]. General Marshall rushed out this [detachment] message quickly by not only the phone, but by radio and cable— marked 'urgent.'" Isabel left by airplane for Oklahoma City to stay with her parents while her husband remained behind with Kimmel to report to the Roberts Commission.[29]

Knox was back in Washington, spreading about thoughts that seemed unbelievable for a man who had been secretary of the Navy for thirteen months. In a letter dated December 18 to Colonel Theodore Roosevelt, Knox, said, "The only way to meet a cloud of rumors . . . is to tell the whole truth and put the blame exactly where it belongs [on Kimmel and Short]. The American people always respond to that sort of treatment, and they have in this case."[30] He was right. The diversion of placing sole blame upon the Pearl Harbor commanders had taken pressure off those in Washington.

Knox wrote friend and Chicago businessman Rawleigh Warner, on December 23, saying that the most important job at the moment was to transform the mental attitude of a good deal of the Navy from a defensive to an offensive posture. It was a good thing Richardson was not there in the loop, or he would have quickly pointed out to Knox *Rainbow Five.* Of course, it was a bit difficult to be offensive with a great deal of the Pacific Fleet below water or damaged, and many others dispersed in the Atlantic. Knox thought the admirals needed to think of victory regardless of what happened to the ships. His inexperience was showing badly.[31]

Short was in Oklahoma City when he read in the January 25, 1942, newspaper that he and Kimmel were given the sole blame by the Roberts Commission. "I asked him to call Marshall," wrote Isabel. Confused, but still committed to what was best for the country, he phoned his trusted friend. "Just sit tight," said the chief of staff, "but it might be better to put in a retirement request in case I need it." By airmail, Short sent in the letter, but included a portion that said he did not want to retire. He, like Kimmel, felt worthy of another substantial assignment.

"Walter never received a reply," wrote Isabel. The next day after the phone conversation, Marshall wrote a memorandum to Secretary of War Stimson saying, "I am now of the opinion that we should accept Short's application for retirement today, and to do this quietly without any publicity at the moment."[32] While visiting friends in San Antonio, Short was notified from Washington that he was being retired. No physical was allowed him, though a private physician told him his health called for retirement two years earlier. A smoker like Kimmel, he had emphysema. He was thus not retired with a physical disability.

Kimmel learned of Short's resignation, and took it as a suggestion to do likewise. The *New York Times* reported on Feburary 8 that the two commanders had actually asked for retirement.[33] However, even by late February, Richardson thought Short had not applied for retirement, but he had seen Kimmel's application.[34] Stark praised Kimmel for the nice letter that put the Kimmel career behind consideration of the country.[35] Neither man could seize upon the fact that they would really be retired. Short received his official letter in Oklahoma City on February 18, and the next morning Kimmel found his in the mail. Three days later he received birthday greetings from Stark! On February 28, Knox and Stimson issued statements accepting the retirements.[36]

As Moss Richardson wrote her brother, one life's move leads to other interesting possibilities. The Shorts went to relax at Hot Springs, Arkansas, in the spring of 1942, met a Detroit, Michigan, banker who knew Henry Ford, and a meeting was arranged. The Shorts understood that Ford was upset at the "injustice" given the general, and would have for him a possible job.[37]

Ford offered Short several choices, and the general selected a position of traffic manager for the Jeep assembly plant in Texas. The couple moved to Dallas because of the climate, and because of its location nearer her parents in Oklahoma City. On the way down from Detroit, the Shorts drove east to attend their son's graduation from West Point. McCoy clearly avoided talking with them, but Marshall was cordial and conversed with Short about the early Army days together. "I remember thinking, 'I wished I could be as big a man as my father,'" Walter Dean Short told his mother later. "Dad greeted him pleasantly, and I thought, 'I could never have done it.' I know that Dad did it on my account."[38]

Six hearings followed the Roberts Commission before Congress finally opened up testimony to everyone and to the public eye. Richardson testified in two of them.

The first was called the Naval Court of Inquiry, and was held July 24 to October 19, 1944. The members of the court were: Murfin, president; Kalbfus; and Andrews, all retired. It provided Kimmel a chance to finally be part of a hearing.

Richardson was questioned on September 21, but only slightly. He discussed with the court several items that were in existence in 1940, those overviewed in previous chapters. He was asked if he ever anticipated an air attack on the anchored fleet. "Not so during the period while I was in command," he replied, and emphasized that the primary worry was about a submarine attack.

He was asked if he knew why the fleet was sent to Hawaii. "Yes. For the restraining influence it might exercise on the action of the Japanese nation," he said. He added that he was not fully informed by the Navy Department about any Japanese negotiations. In fact, "I received practically no information along those lines, except what I acquired over the radio or in the public press."

At last he was asked, "Did you have a striking force available which could have been sent out in time" if the patrol craft had spotted a Japanese detachment "standing toward Pearl Harbor?" He answered by first saying that none of the patrol planes were armed, so they could not have helped except to radio back the alarm. "No indeed," he answered to the question, "did [I] have a force to send out toward the enemy fleet." The court then asked whether Richardson could have sent out a force if he had it. "I would have obeyed what I conceived to be the intent of the leadership of the country. I would have done nothing until I was attacked!"

That ended Richardson's testimony in this hearing. Neither Kimmel nor Bloch took advantage of the right to cross-examine Richardson, and he had nothing further to state. He stepped down from the witness stand at 10:30 A.M. Those present knew that the admiral would be a powerful witness in public if, and when, that opportunity was ever presented.

Kimmel learned of forty-three decoded messages during this investigation. Safford told him. He was violating Navy rules by revealing this information, and the JAG (Judge Advocate General) began an investigation to file charges.[39] Still, Kimmel was obstructed from presenting these "MAGIC" messages, but as he left the courtroom one day, he talked loudly about revealing their existence. Magically, the next day the intercepts were in court and being read. Disgusted at what they were hearing, Murfin threw his pencil down so hard that it bounced ten feet up in the air, and Kalbfus shrunk down in his chair. Andrews looked sick.[40] This was the first time Kimmel really received the opportunity to state his case. Though this inquiry aimed no blame toward Washington's leadership, it did release Kimmel from full responsibility and put more on Stark than he expected.

Upon King's orders, Stark had flown from London to testify in late July of 1944. He brought with him a young lawyer named Lieutenant David W. Richmond, who worked for Stark's deputy chief of staff, Commodore Howard A. Flanigan.[41] Stark was the first witness, and was given a week to prepare. Tommy Hart became his counsel, and Richmond assisted. Testimony went on five days. He later returned for more, but Hart felt that Stark did not do a credible job, expanding the subjects too widely at times. His memory was not clear on some points, including where he was the night of December 6, and he needed to review more documents before he appeared before any other hearings. The court found that Stark "failed to display the sound judgment expected of him." King signed an endorsement of approval to the report, and Forrestal agreed.[42]

Hart watched all the proceedings, and had little confidence in the work and knowledge of Murfin and Andrews. He thought Andrews was jealous that he did not receive appointment as CNO in 1939. Hart and Stark respected Kalbfus.[43] Stark returned to Europe, but Richmond stayed behind to dig through files and copy pertinent documents that would be needed in case there was a postwar investigation.

In August, Senator Truman's article on unification of the defense department came out in *Collier's,* and for some reason he brought up the Pearl Harbor argument. He insinuated that Kimmel and Short did not meet enough while stationed in Hawaii, and the disaster happened because the Army and Navy were not totally cooperative. Kimmel broke his long silence, and in public said, "You have made false statements . . . the real story of the Pearl Harbor attack and the events preceding it has never been publicly told." He accused Truman of still relying upon the Roberts Report. He asked for a day in open court and claimed, "It is grossly unjust to repeat false charges against me." He challenged Truman to cease comments of repetition based upon the Roberts evidence

Kimmel son with the father: Ned Kimmel stands in front of a painting of his father, Admiral Husband E. Kimmel. For years Ned, his sons, and his nephews carried on the effort to officially restore the rank and reputation of their family icon. Ned died in 2005, but the process did not. (From the papers of Tom Kimmel, Jr., grandson of Husband E. Kimmel)

that he thought had never met the test of public scrutiny. He predicted the public would be "amazed" at the truth.[44]

The naval court found that Kimmel and Short were working together:

> Based on Finding V, the Court is of the opinion that the relations between Admiral Husband E. Kimmel, USN, and Lieut. General Walter C. Short, U. S. Army, were friendly, cordial and cooperative, that there was no lack of interest, no lack of appreciation of responsibility, and no failure to cooperate on the part of either. And that each was cognizant of the measures being undertaken by the other for the defense of the Pearl Harbor Naval Base to the degree required by the common interest.[45]

Proceedings were secret, but were made public later in the summer of 1945.

King wrote to Stark in early November of 1944, telling him of his endorsement of the Naval Court of Inquiry report, and saying, "You have been found at fault for not keeping Kimmel more informed." He also mentioned that Stark had spent too much concern over protection of the source of secret messages.[46] When Stark saw Roosevelt's condition in January of 1945 at the conference with Winston Churchill in Malta, he knew the president would never be able to defend him, even though Hopkins assured him he would. Roosevelt died on April 12, 1945.

Irony raised its strange head when Hewitt was chosen to replace Stark in Europe. First, Hewitt had to finish up the report of his own Pearl Harbor investigation before traveling across the Atlantic in mid-August. It seemed fitting for this story about Richardson that Stark hauled down his admiral's flag for the last time on board the USS *Augusta*.[47] Stark did not want to leave, but he was past retirement. Given several toasts and going away parties, he left for home on the *Queen Mary*. His wife had not been in Europe with him, so he looked forward to the time again at home. He had no idea what was about to happen to his reputation. Like Richardson in 1941, Stark returned home to little fanfare, arriving in Washington on August 22.

Despite the Army and Navy private inquiries, pressure was on for a public hearing. It came from the press, Congress, and the public. Back in June, Senator Robert A. Taft of Ohio fueled the fire by placing questions relative to Pearl Harbor into the record. They were first brought up by Arthur Krock in the *New York Times* on May 31, 1944.[48] Some were to be answered later by Richardson. But, before that event, some were answered by Republican Representative Hugh D. Scott on September 6. He said before the House that certain questions "were now being freely discussed in Washington."

He said one was: "Did not President Roosevelt remove Admiral Richardson for refusing to keep the American Fleet bottled up in Pearl Harbor and substitute Admiral Kimmel?" He also said, rumor was that Roosevelt asked Richardson to keep the fleet in Pearl Harbor, partially because merchants in Honolulu were upset at the fleet's absence on weekends. He went on to ask several more questions that involved Kimmel and not Richardson. He concluded by asking, "Was not the warning message of December 7 sent by slow 'commercial cable' to the commanders in Hawaii?" And, he added, if these things are not true, then why not have an investigation or court martial promptly and make all facts known?

Short was brought into the fray on September 11 when Representative Forest A. Harness told the House in a long speech that he had access to Short's "documentary files of more than 250 pages." He said this evidence would reveal that Short was denied many requests to beef up the security at Pearl Harbor. He blasted those in charge for not sending the December 6 message by "more rapid direct military means."[49]

Finally came the Joint Congressional Pearl Harbor Hearings. They began on November 15, 1945, and lasted until May 31, 1946, interviewing some thirty-seven figures of importance. Its congressional membership consisted of six Democrats and four Republicans, as follows: Senators Barkley (D), Walter F. George (D), Scott W. Lucas (D), Brewster (R), and Homer Ferguson (R); Representatives Jere Cooper (D), J. Bayard Clark (D), John W. Murphy (D), Bertrand W. Gearhart (R), and Frank B. Keefe (R).

On November 5, a memo went out to potential witnesses

reminding them that what they would say would not later be used against them. It was signed by President Truman.[50] To assist those who would testify, an office directed by Lieutenant Commander John Ford Baecher was set up in the executive office of the secretary of the Navy. Baecher and Assistant JAG O. S. Colclough were liaison officers to the Joint Committee. They provided information both to the witnesses and to the committee from Navy sources.[51]

On Monday, November 19, 1945, newspaper headlines predicted that for the first time President Roosevelt's name might be injected into the Pearl Harbor investigation. The Joint Congressional Hearings would move from questions on what happened on December 7 to events leading up to the attack. The public suspected more than just logistical questions would be asked of the former CinCUS. "Just what Richardson's differences with the late President were has never been published," William T. Peacock wrote in the *New York Daily News.*[52] The writer speculated wrongly about the rift between Roosevelt and Richardson, saying it probably was about moving ships to the Atlantic to aid Great Britain.

Richardson was the third witness of an eventual total of 318 called before the congressmen. A fellow admiral, Thomas Browning Inglis, chief of naval intelligence at that time, was the first witness. He presented a Navy summary of the Pearl Harbor attack, and assured the congressmen that even before the shift of ships to the Atlantic, which took place on Kimmel's watch, the Pacific Fleet was numerically inferior to the Japanese Fleet. But, people wanted to hear from the main source, Richardson, who had remained silent publicly through seven previous hearings.

In a packed room with inadequate acoustics, on Monday, November 19, 1945, he began to tell his story, which has been previously interjected into this book in various chapters. His personal testimony went on for eighty-seven pages, not counting exhibits presented. Before the committee adjourned the next spring, Richardson had appeared on no less than 479 of the 9,754 pages it published. He watched much of the proceedings, many

Richardson gives testimony before Congress: On November 19, 1945, a slim Otto Richardson stood in his fleet admiral's uniform and was sworn in by the Joint Congressional Pearl Harbor Investigation Committee. There was much anticipation in the news about what he would say since he had been quiet after his detachment in January 1940. To prepare for the expected testimony, he resigned on May 10 from the office of executive director for the Navy Relief Society. The next months he researched and made copies of many items, especially the letters between him as CinCUS and Harold Stark as CNO. May Richardson can be seen in the back middle of the photo with one of her familiar hats on her head. (From the photo collection at the Naval Historical Center, Washington Navy Yard, Washington, DC)

times with May by his side in her familiar headwear. In all, from what he learned in his career billets during the years before December 7, 1941, and from what he had learned in the past four years in Washington, Richardson probably knew more about the reasons Pearl Harbor was attacked than anyone.

Richardson did research from Navy Department files as well as from his own possessions. He must have run into Stark's representatives seeking copies of messages and letters. In those days, simply making a copy of a document was a long, expensive process—so those seeking the time of the government to obtain copies met with some resistance. Copying was not easy.

A huge photostatic machine, about seven feet tall, included a "dark" compartment about shoulder high. An operator would place film in a metal 12" x 16" container, about four inches deep. Closed tightly, it was placed inside the compartment; then the door was shut. The door had a rubber sleeve in which the operator's arm slipped through. Inside, in the dark, the hand of the operator would open up the metal container, remove a sheet of film, feel it for the slick side, and place that side against glass, then finger down a metal plate that held the film firmly against the surface.

Outside, in front of the machine, was a tray in which the original letter, photo, document, or whatever was placed between two sheets of glass to smooth it out. A button was then flipped, and powerful lights were turned on to illuminate the original. A button was pushed. The lens would stay open the amount of seconds calculated to transfer the image of the original upon the film. In the dark and by feel, the operator would then remove the film, place it back into the container, close it, remove his arm from the sleeve, and open the door. The container was pulled from the box, and taken to a dark room. There the film was processed in chemicals just as if it were a photograph. Thus, a copy could be made in about fifteen minutes. It could be dried by hanging on a clothesline, or by heating upon a hot drum. This process could only be repeated so many times per day, so time was of the essence for those wanting file copies to study before the November trial began.

Richardson had little or no help, while Stark hired attorney Hugh Obear of Washington to guide a team. Richmond was given full-time assignment to assist. A Stark family friend, James E. Webb, joined the effort. Richmond led the battles with Navy bureaucrats reluctant to release some information. Stark even flew to San Francisco to talk with Turner and Ingersoll, but never consulted with Richardson. Stark's son-in-law, Edwin W. Semans, a lawyer in Philadelphia, also assisted Stark's plight. They even prepared Stark with dry runs.[53] Richardson, on the other had, was on his own.

Still, the initial headlines belonged to Richardson. Much of what he said few had known about before his testimony. In today's context, the comments he made seem meager, but to the citizens of 1945, this was new information. Only close friends and some associates knew that Richardson had been fired for protesting the fleet's location at Pearl Harbor. For the next weeks, cables, telegrams, and letters of support and congratulations came to his address. His friend Adolphus Staton of Silver Spring, Maryland, wrote, "Heartiest congratulations for the courageous stand you took in the trying days before Pearl Harbor." He hoped Richardson had increased his stature in history.[54]

From Joe and Virginia Richardson came a Western Union message that simply said, "Yea Daddy!"[55] Another telegram came from Walter Gordon Roper in Del Ray Beach, Florida. "No one in the Naval service who has ever crossed your path could be surprised that you have lived and are living up to the finest Naval traditions."[56] For years Donald T. Hunter, lieutenant commander (retired), told his neighbors and friends that someday an officer would "let the beans spill where they may" and that everyone would learn about the Pearl Harbor business. He wrote Richardson that his telephone had been ringing off the wall after news of the testimony reached Los Angeles. "Yes," he told the callers, "that is the fella I've been waiting for—and you now have the truth."[57]

Some letters were from cranks, some from Republicans, some from 1902 classmates. Willie Smith wrote from his home in East Orange, New Jersey. "I am proud of you, big boy, but it was as I expected." Smith did not make a career out of the Navy, but spent twenty-six years plus as chief engineer at the Federal Shipbuilding Company.[58] In some cases, old shipmates wrote. John A. Pearson of Brookline, Massachusetts, who served with Richardson on the USS *Nevada,* wrote, "We believed in you during World War I, and we back you up solid now."[59]

Floyd Starr of near Philadelphia said, "I would have given a great deal to have been on hand . . . to hear you testify." He wrote that he did listen to Hull's testimony on radio. He thought the belief that "we could scare the Japs" was an extraordinary one.[60]

Wrote scripts for Lone Ranger *episodes: The Richardsons' son, Joe Fenet, after traveling the world, went to Princeton and in 1938 began work for Metro-Goldwyn-Mayer as a scriptwriter. He served in the Navy during World War II, and then went back to MGM. Joe and his wife lived in Beverly Hills, and with his help, through various celebrity fund-raisers, Admiral Richardson raised a substantial amount of operating capital for the Navy Relief Society during World War II. Joe is credited with thirty-five episodes of both radio and television versions of* The Lone Ranger *and many other popular shows during the 1950s. He inherited more than $800,000 from his parents, most of it in stocks, and their house in Washington, DC.* (Photo from Elizabeth Wingo Banks Papers, Duncan, Oklahoma)

An old Paris friend wrote from New York. "For several days running your picture appeared in the *New York Times* and other papers." He added, "In all but one you seemed to be enjoying yourself!" He wrote that most around him would have been more delighted "if you had hit a little harder." Some admirers, however, did not approve of Richardson's statement that if in the president's shoes, he would have done the same thing. One wrote, "I refuse to believe it!"[61]

Finally, even Clarence Dillon wrote. He had greatly assisted the Naval Relief Society cause, and called the testimony "first class, the sort of straight-forward talk the country likes to hear." He mentioned he was writing the chairman of Loew's, parent company of Metro-Goldwyn-Mayer, to give some assistance to Joe in his quest to return to the script writing business after service in the Navy.

Joe sent his parents a long letter on November 30, most of it discussing his possibilities of rejoining MGM. So many women were hired during the war that positions were all filled, plus the men who did not join a military service were first or second assistant directors. He had some catching up to do, even though he started with the company in 1935. He considered the pay of a script clerk at eighty-five dollars a week not too bad, and was anxious to return, even at that level. He, however, agreed with his father that some outside help, like that of Dillon, would be necessary to convince Louis Mayer to rehire him.

Again, Joe was excited by what his father had done in the Pearl Harbor Hearings. "You were . . . and are . . . wonderful," he wrote.[62] He and Virginia were about to drive across country to Washington, dropping through Texas for a "flying" visit to Aunts Moss and Jessie, and the Fenets. Joe's time with the Navy ended on January 26, 1946, and he reached the rank of lieutenant.

After his testimony ended, Richardson hung around the hearings most days, and listened intently as Leahy testified on Wednesday, November 22. May was with him that day. His former boss was frail, smoked on several cigarettes, and viewed the world in rose-colored glasses compared to the decisive Richardson in his comments before the hearings. To some extent, Leahy adored

Roosevelt, and had an opposite view of the president's management style than other admirals had.[63]

The high point of Richardson's two and one-half days of testimony would change abruptly, however. Leahy stunned the Richardsons when he told the hearings committee that he had no recollection of Roosevelt commenting to Richardson that the United States would not go to war even if Japan attacked the Philippines. Leahy had been called to briefly testify about the October 8, 1940, meeting he had attended with Richardson and the president. "I was exceedingly surprised to learn that the Commander-in-chief did not consider the Fleet prepared for War." It was not revealed to the congressmen that while serving as governor of Puerto Rico, Leahy did not have the opportunity to see all the correspondence going back and forth between Richardson and Stark in 1940, but those exchanges would come out again later when the former CNO testified.

Leahy went on to comment in the crowded room that his knowledge of Roosevelt's thoughts was extensive. "I feel quite sure that if the Japanese had invaded the Philippines . . . the President would have recommended a declaration of war." The camera turned to the audience to show May in her hat and Admiral Richardson with his pipe. He was grinning slyly. Again, Leahy had more than likely not read the five new war plans drawn up in 1940 and early 1941, and signed by Roosevelt. It was apparent that Leahy and Richardson had never discussed the subject after October of 1940.

In the newspapers the next day, the headlines screamed "Leahy Tells of F.D.R.'s Fleet Talks: Doesn't Recall 1940 Statement On Naval Shift." Leahy did explain that Richardson gave the president reasons the fleet was not ready for war. He did not add that before striking out across the ocean, the ships had to undergo preparation for war, and could have done that only back on the West Coast.

Leahy also told Committee Counsel Mitchell that he did not recall Roosevelt saying why the fleet was still at Pearl Harbor, or how long it would remain. Leahy said he rode back to the Navy Department that day with Richardson, expressing a desire that

Richardson correct the fleet deficiencies as quickly as possible, as if he were still the CNO. He was perhaps embarrassed, for he said to Richardson, "I have been telling Congress and the public for some time the Fleet was ready for war." Leahy had listened to Bloch's statement on January 6, 1940, instead of talking with Stark and Richardson. These pre-Pearl Harbor attack public talks by Leahy were just examples of why Richardson insisted the fleet be allowed to convert to a state of war readiness. The public was being fed a line, while the fleet knew it was undermanned and not prepared physically for battle. In 1940, few listened to Richardson's warnings, but in 1945 the desire for blame was still festering, lending more credence to what he was saying.

Brewster drilled Leahy, "You don't question that if Admiral Richardson said he recalled it, that he did recall it?" Leahy quickly replied, "Oh, I haven't a doubt of that" and admitted that he had made no notes of the meeting as did Richardson.

Gearhart asked Leahy if he remembered any talk of going to war if attacked. Leahy said he could not recall such talk, but added that many military men expected that a war with Japan was "inevitable."

Leahy was later asked if he received any information while at Vichy on the danger of a Japanese attack on Pearl Harbor. He said he had not, but a few years later he retracted that statement with the story of an event. In his book, *I Was There,* Leahy claimed he and his wife knew something was up on December 5, 1941, when they dined with eight others at Japanese Ambassador Matsu Kato's apartment in the Hotel Majestic. Kato seemed worried, and Mrs. Leahy mentioned to her husband on the way home, "He was either seriously worried or seriously ill." If all hands had been on the same page, exchanging thoughts, perhaps feedback from Leahy in France to Washington on December 6 would have added to the pile of clues.[64] But, Leahy did not have the realistic thought pattern that was ingrained in Richardson.

Leahy did respond as Richardson and others when asked if he had ever considered Pearl Harbor as a point of attack. "I was always fearful such a thing might happen, and so were many other officers."

Leahy was excused from the testimony shortly before the afternoon session ended. The newspaper accounts say that on his way out he stopped to chat with Richardson. "Both were smiling broadly," the reporter wrote, but most of Richardson's remaining good teeth were most likely grinding. He was too "Navy" to make a negative show of the event.[65]

Confusingly, Leahy told friends and some reporters in later years fairly precise details of the October 1940 meeting. He said that as Richardson was leaving the presidential office, Roosevelt turned to Leahy and said, "What's the matter with Joe? He has got yellow." Leahy wrote that he replied, "Joe is not and never will be yellow. He is dead right." Then Roosevelt said, "I want him fired." Maybe in the congressional hearings, with Richardson present, Leahy did not want such harsh words spoken in front of May and J. O. However, since Leahy and Richardson rode back to the Navy Department that 1940 day in the same automobile, it seems strange that Richardson would have left the White House office ahead of Leahy.[66]

Richardson stuck around Capitol Hill to hear more Pearl Harbor related testimony. Much sidestepping was to follow. A weak and sick Hull followed Leahy, and testified that the cornerstone of American policy at the time was to avoid a break with Japan while the United States strengthened defenses. Welles came up next, and in his baritone voice said, "I do not recall at any time that anybody indicated to me that Pearl Harbor or Hawaii was a probable objective."[67] All the talks and messages of 1940 went unheeded, or else by 1945, most minds were cloudy for some reason.

Richardson reported as ordered for his final physical exam by the Navy, and was declared fit for release from all active duty. On December 15, he received one of those "well done" letters from Forrestal, thinking that he would never serve officially again, but hoping that he was wrong.[68]

Stark took the stand on New Year's Eve 1945. His statement and the documents he placed into public record dealt, naturally, with Kimmel and 1941. He would not attack anyone, and did not place blame, even upon the Army. For almost a month he testified and

End of day's testimony: Admiral Richardson talks with unidentified congress-men after giving testimony at the 1945 Joint Congressional Hearings on the attack of Pearl Harbor. Six Democrats and four Republicans and the commit-tee's officials asked the questions. Richardson's testimony is published on 87 pages, and his name is on 479 of the 9,754 total printed pages. However, he did not completely reveal the total content of his conversation with President Franklin D. Roosevelt in October 1940. (From the Clareda Purser Papers)

answered questions. Still, he could not remember what he did on the night of December 6. Later, when told he and Mrs. Stark dined with friends, Captain and Mrs. Krick, he still could not remember much, and especially not a telephone conversation with the president.[69]

Two months later, Stark retired. The committee would later basically vindicate Stark, and refute what the naval inquiry had reported. Much of that decision rested upon the failure of Safford to prove his point on the so-called winds message. This was an intercepted December 4, 1941, warning that Safford was sure had arrived and was in turn sent out to Hawaii.[70] King even recanted his part of the naval inquiry endorsement two years later, but with

Roosevelt dead, Richardson had no such delusions that anyone would explain why he was fired. Stark never wrote on the matter. On January 24, 1946, May and Jim Richardson cringed as their friend Walter Short was helped to the table and chair by his son Dean. Isabel was there for the first day. Just recovering from pneumonia, Short was not well. However, he spent hours reading his statement. At night he would study more, and then answer questions before the hot lights and pressure of the moment. "Walter opened his testimony with a slashing attack on the War Department's 'buck-passing,' which he said made him the 'scapegoat' of its own errors," wrote Isabel. He said, "My relatively small part in the [Pearl Harbor] transaction was not explained to the American people until this joint Congressional Committee forced revelation of the facts."[71] Isabel wrote, "Walter made these points before the committee:"

1. General Marshall personally supervised the 1940 alert, but failed to follow up in 1941 to see if Short understood the orders.[72]

2. Short was denied information on Japanese intentions that Washington had from decoded messages. However, later a risk was taken that the code secrets would be revealed when Admiral Yamamoto's plane was shot down.

3. Short's *alert* thinking that the danger was sabotage was the wrong one, but he had every reason to believe that he was following the correct Army orders.

4. Short lacked adequate means to defend against a surprise [attack]. The War Department was well aware of the plane and anti-aircraft deficiencies in Hawaii.

5. Marshall's delayed December 7 warning to Hawaii should have been sent by more than one means of communication.

6. Short viewed sabotage as the greatest threat because Admiral Kimmel's staff assured him there was no danger of an air raid on Oahu. Washington did not question Short's decision.[73]

Short concluded in his written testimony, "I do not believe that my estimate of the situation was due to any carelessness on my part, nor on the part of the senior Army and Navy officers with whom I consulted. Nor, do I believe that my error was a substantial factor in causing the damage which our Pacific Fleet suffered during the attack." He pointed to the November 27, 1941, warning that is so popularly used in books and motion pictures.[74] "Marshall's warning ordered precautions, and also instructed me to limit the knowledge of the measures taken to 'minimum essential officers.'"[75]

All of this coming from the Shorts' viewpoint should be conclusive to retract some of the blame from the general. However, there are still others who offer the impression that Short was flippant about the Navy's protection. Short was perhaps not as aware and cooperative as he could have been with the Navy. O'Brien, later an admiral, related a story about the Navy warning message Kimmel asked him to take to Short on November 27, 1941.[76] "I went into his office, gave him the message, and as normal waited for him to read it, sign it and give it back to me. He did neither at first. I insisted that he had to sign it so I could return it to the Navy files. Finally he did," said O'Brien in August of 2002.

However, the story about cooperation continued. Later, when Short was on the Roberts Commission hot seat, word got around that Short said he did not remember the message. "I got a copy out," O'Brien said, to prove that as an ensign he did his part, and that Short signed the message.[77] Short, however, received his own war warning from Marshall.

Dean Short thought that his father did not understand the patrol problems faced by the Navy, but Bellinger and Martin— especially Bellinger—brought out this dilemma again and again, not to mention the various complaints that Kimmel, and earlier Richardson, had sent to the Navy Department about the lack of planes, personnel to fly and take care of them, etc. Dean said later, "I think Dad was sympathetic to Kimmel's problem; so that instead of fighting for himself he was fighting for both of them . . . Dad did not know of these weaknesses in the operation system as he should have. His action might have been different had he known of the Navy's limitations."[78] Dean meant that the Navy did not keep his father up to date on patrol problems, a quandary Short may not have faced had Richardson and May been there in 1941. Richardson's more aggressive nature about the dangers to the fleet at Pearl Harbor would have perhaps flowed over to Short and his dealings with Marshall. For sure, the two would have met more often and discussed key items more frequently.

The love or respect for Marshall died with the Shorts when he told the congressional committee, "I don't know," some thirty-two times. His only excuse for not calling Short was that he was afraid the Japanese would intercept the message. The Shorts wondered, "So, what if they did?" Isabel sat at the hearings watching Marshall talk. A lady next to her said, "Either he is a liar, or the most incompetent person we have had in some time." Marshall also could not recall where he was the night before the attack, or why he was not at his office at 8:00 A.M. after his normal early Sunday horseback ride.[79]

Libby was convinced in his latter years that it was hogwash that Marshall could not be located that morning, while out riding his horse. "They got the warning. General Marshall disappeared . . . and couldn't be found. He was riding at Fort Myer. Now, if the Chief-of-staff of the Army can't be found when he's riding a horse at Fort Myer on a Sunday morning, there's something screwy somewhere." Libby went farther than that with his thoughts. "I will go to my grave convinced that FDR ordered Pearl Harbor to let happen. He must have known." He added that Roosevelt knew of an impending attack, "and all signs pointed it to be at Pearl Harbor."[80]

At some time during the four years, Short began to think like Richardson and some of the admirals. "I don't know when Walter first became convinced or learned what many others knew or strongly suspected—the President was directly responsible for withholding information from the Pearl Harbor commanders," Isabel wrote in the mid-1950s. She lived at that time near Washington. According to her granddaughter, she met often with the Richardsons.

Like Richardson, Short publicly said he held no resentment or ill will toward Roosevelt. But, Isabel said her husband could have felt no differently, because he had no documentary evidence to back up his belief that Roosevelt called the shots that resulted in "Walter's crucifixion."[81]

Isabel's own reluctance to stroke the press may have perpetuated the thought that the Shorts and Kimmels were at odds. During a break at the congressional hearings, being camera shy, she pulled away from Kimmel when the photographer set up. Kimmel later said to her, "Maybe we should have had our pictures taken with my arm around you to show that there was no truth in the rumors about our 'feud.'"[82] It was a good point. The Shorts, Richardsons, and Kimmels never, at least in the early stages, warmed up to dealing with the subject through in-depth interviews by writers.

Richardson watched as Short went through the grueling process, and was noticed by the hearing members at times. When Representative Murphy asked Short a question involving departments that put out fires, the general began to explain about stations controlling the fire of the harbor defense guns. When both finally realized they were on different tracks, Richardson smiled and quietly laughed. "I see Admiral Richardson laughing back there," the congressman said.[83] "I am only a layman and you two are the experts!" Isabel thought it was an honest admission from a congressman who was blindly fumbling "his way toward a goal his Democratic colleagues had pointed out to him." Despite her husband's statement that he felt no ill will toward Roosevelt, all through Isabel's manuscript she made small but negative comments about the New Deal and Democrats.

"Walter died a broken hearted man," Isabel wrote. Even in death she felt he was denied by the Army Department. It would not bury him at the lieutenant general's rank. He was given two gun salutes less than customary because the Army told Dean that since Kimmel was still alive, the higher rank could not be approved. As of 2007, it has never been changed. However, Isabel was paid a higher pension—eighty-seven dollars per month. "I always felt that the Army paid me the pension to keep me from putting my claim before Congress—something I would have had no difficulty in doing," she wrote. Isabel returned to Paris, Texas, twice more—to bury her father in 1952 and her mother in 1958. The aim of the congressional hearings was buried in a mountain of paperwork, awaiting years to be read and digested. The previous seven hearings were attached as part of the forty volumes, but much was not included.[84]

Richardson wrote down his judgment concerning the Japanese and the mistakes made by Roosevelt and his civilian employees:

1. The President and the Secretary of State consistently viewed the Japanese through rose-colored glasses, when they did not actually misread their intentions.
2. The President consistently overestimated his ability to control the actions of other nations whose interests opposed our own.
3. The President's responsibility for our initial defeats in the Pacific was direct, real, and personal.[85]

As his friend Short failed, neither could Richardson back up these opinions with concrete, documented evidence.

However, he did find ways to place his opinion before the public. For instance, Edward Hanify dropped by to interview him for Kimmel's defense. At that time Hanify was a lieutenant (j.g.) who had been added to Kimmel's defense staff. Before the Navy, he had worked for the Boston firm of Ropes Gray, and would leave quite an impressive career behind when he died in 2000. He was daunted with Kimmel's decisiveness, and did not believe this type of man could be guilty of any carelessness.

In his low, long-winded way, Richardson told Hanify that he would just explain it all as a parable. He went on to give Hanify a set of assumptions that he felt were actually true. It was basically a story about how he thought Roosevelt set up an "Incident:"

"You'd want to be sure that whatever the incident, it happened under circumstances where it was perfectly clear that you were not the aggressor, and the resulting incident galvanized your own people to a realization of the terrible threat which they faced from this totalitarian force.

"Now, just think about that. I don't say it's an hypothesis even. It's a fable. You just think about that fable as you study some of this material. And, it's conceivable that it might have some enlightening factors."[86]

If Hanify did not catch on to what Richardson was saying, and where he was placing the blame, it would be repeated in more direct words during Richardson's testimony and in his book.

After the congressional hearings were concluded, Kimmel

continued to pursue a true revelation of what led up the disaster, and wrote a book on the subject in 1955. His son Tom said, "He spent the rest of his life, pure and simple, trying to defend himself, and every step of the way he was obstructed by the government and the U.S. Navy." Kimmel died in 1968, sure that the facts would emerge eventually to prove his theories that Churchill and Roosevelt desired an attack on Pearl Harbor. Into the 1990s and into the twenty-first century Kimmel's sons Thomas and Edward, and then grandson Thomas, Jr., continued an effort to extract a statement from Congress that Kimmel and Short were only part of the blame in the whole picture, hoping to regain their respective ranks.

Even in March of 1999, secretary of defense officials were saying, "posthumous advancement in rank, as a form of an official apology or as a symbolic act, would not be appropriate. The points raised by Admiral Richardson offer only differences of opinion about the significance of the information during the fateful days at Pearl Harbor. Those differences of opinion, while insightful, do not justify absolving either officer of their accountability as commanders—a cornerstone principle that serves as a core value in our armed forces."[87]

Even at that, Congress sent legislation to President Bill Clinton in October of 2000, praising Kimmel and Short and restoring their rank. It added, "Failure to do so serves only to perpetuate the myth that the senior commanders in Hawaii were derelict in their duty."[88] Clinton never signed it before he left office, and neither did George W. Bush.

Books and even another hearing will continue to place forward reanalyzed information. Unbelievably, even six decades after the end of World War II, there are those governmental workers who decide some papers, letters, and orders involved in the attack of Pearl Harbor should still be kept secret.

Standley may have summed up the situation properly when he wrote:

> "As far as Short and Kimmel are concerned, the tragedy of Pearl Harbor was the fact that they were, and had to be, removed from

command without a hearing and that war conditions [*protection of the message interception process*] prevented bringing them to trial by general court-martial before the end of the War. Thus, these two officers were martyred, as it were, for in my opinion, if they had been brought to trial, both would have been cleared of the charge of neglect of duty."[89]

Libby was more pointed and blunt in his thoughts, commenting that Kimmel was not as bright nor as persistent as Richardson. "This [Pearl Harbor] was no place to keep the Fleet," he said, and again alleged that the Army could not, nor did not do anything to protect the ships. He was especially negative about Marshall's part in the event, saying he must have acted under orders to do nothing to clearly warn Short and Kimmel. "If he had not been acting under the direct instructions from the Commander-in-chief [Roosevelt], he could not conceivably have hung onto the job of Chief-of-staff of the Army." He wondered why Stark was detached to Europe while Marshall went "scot free." He did not speculate whether or not Roosevelt had been wise or not during days leading up to Pearl Harbor's attack, but he did say, "He certainly got the country united behind him. Maybe it saved lives in the long run; I don't know." He doubted the public would ever recognize a truth already revealed. "There are certain myths which the American public takes into its bosom and you couldn't shake them loose with a charge of dynamite!"[90]

Carefully observing all this activity in late 1945 and early 1946, Richardson did not care to do battle in the public's eye; he especially did not desire to be viewed as bitter. Still, his expansive desire to learn more kept him at the hearings even to watch Justice Roberts testify. At times, in response to articles about Pearl Harbor, Richardson wrote letters in refute or rebuttal. Some are in files marked, "written but not sent."[91]

He tried, however, not to consume his life with what happened in 1940 and 1941. At home Richardson did his best to carry on with new projects and assignments. His last, and most important, Navy project was coming up later in the year.

CHAPTER TWENTY-EIGHT

The Navy's Last Assignment
Testimony before IMTFE: Tokyo War Crimes Trials

The hours of research set aside in preparation for the Joint Congressional Pearl Harbor Hearings, and all the hours Richardson sat listening to his contemporaries explain the events of 1940 and 1941 paid off in a strange way. In the summer of 1946, the office of the secretary of the Navy called Richardson. Forrestal appointed Richardson to be the Navy's witness at the International Military Tribunal for the Far East (IMTFE), most commonly called the Tokyo War Crimes Trial.[1]

Richardson was the most likely candidate because he had the time. Thus, two months after his release from all active duty on April 23, 1946, he was called back to active service.[2] With a staff, he took a short trip to Japan to gather evidence confiscated from the enemy's possession. Even before the August 15, 1945, Japanese surrender, the military began to organize captured documents in order to prepare for trials. Richardson and his staff had a huge job retrieving useable paperwork that would describe Japan's designs to attack Allied-owned territories. The Allied Translator and Interpreter Section (ATIS) was a part of MacArthur's Southwest Pacific Command. It was given the overwhelming responsibilities for the collection, translation, and exploitation of the records. ATIS and the Washington Document Center (WDC) spent four months in Tokyo during 1945 and 1946 processing and packing over 400,000 documents and diaries, and shipping them to Washington. After the WDC left Japan on March 31, 1946, the ATIS still found and shipped another 58,000 or more documents to be viewed by Richardson's staff and others in DC. In fact, later when Richardson was on the stand in Tokyo, still more documents were being processed for study in the States.

MacArthur, the Supreme Commander Allied Powers (SCAP),

had a strong hand in building Japan into a post-World War II legitimate and contributing citizen. The Tacloban meeting in late 1944 that MacArthur held with Richardson's committee may have played an important part in the choice of the Navy official to appear on the stand. MacArthur knew the pressure from the world would demand a trial of at least some of the Japanese responsible for the upheaval from 1941 through 1945. He wanted credible and dutiful witnesses.

Not one for much negotiation, MacArthur still came to the realization that Japanese Emperor Hirohito would be a positive in the quest for a new order if retained as the head of state. This symbol of historical significance would, he thought, be better suited to assist the Allied cause if he could be rehabilitated rather than be tried and hanged. He was, in MacArthur's mind, the key to the democratization of Japan.[3]

MacArthur ordered the arrest of some thirty-nine suspects just over a week after the surrender. Most were members of Prime Minister Hideki Tojo's war cabinet. On October 8, 1945, MacArthur received Allied approval to proceed with major trials.

The International Prosecution Section (IPS) was formed by December 8 with the mandate to investigate war crimes and the treatment of the Allied prisoners of war. Joseph Barry Keenan, a strong New Dealer and confidant of Roosevelt, and one whom Richardson had known slightly, was chosen by President Truman to head the IPS.[4] He arrived with his first team at the Tokyo airport on December 6, 1945. At the same time, MacArthur issued orders to arrest former Japanese Prime Minister Prince Konoye and Marquis Koichi Kido, Lord Keeper of the Privy Seal and constant advisor to Hirohito during the war period.[5]

Some Japanese took temporary jobs as translators. One, Kazuo Chiba, later wrote of the experience, saying the three Americans with whom he worked "were all good, decent people without a trace of conqueror's arrogance."[6] Those put on trial may have later thought differently as the days dragged on. The language and clerical staff for the trial consisted of 104 Allies and 154 Japanese. Experienced Americans like attorney Roy L. Morgan were sent over by the War Department to assist. He was chief of the investigative division of the IPS.[7]

Keenan was most known for being the author of the Lindbergh kidnapping law, but some suspected Truman gave him this Japanese assignment to move him out of Washington for a time. Keenan led a team of some thirty-nine, which included twenty-two attorneys. At least one of the judges chosen thought Keenan to be "a bit second-rate."[8] Some thought he came to court after drinking a bit.[9]

On January 19, 1946, MacArthur issued a proclamation creating the IMTFE. The rules were drafted by the IPS. There would be eleven judges with no substitutes or alternates. The signatories to the surrender of Japan documents nominated choices, plus representatives from the Philippines and India. Keenan was appointed the single prosecutor, to be aided by several assistants to do much of the questioning.[10]

The defendants were charged with acts that were crimes against peace, conventional war crimes, and crimes against humanity.[11] After MacArthur appointed the judges, he basically let the trial take its own course.[12] As president of the court, MacArthur and the tribunal elected Australian Sir William Webb.[13] He already had worked with investigations of war crimes committed by lower-ranking Japanese in New Guinea. The members of the bench and many of the Americans involved in the trial stayed mainly at the Imperial Hotel.[14]

Initially, chief counsel for the defendants, Beverly Coleman, led the defense. In the whole of the trial, none of the other judges verbally questioned witnesses, only being allowed to pass written notes to Webb.[15]

The tribunal's Soviet prosecutor, Sergei Alexandrovich Glolunsky, a major figure in the Stalin show-trial purges, demanded that two more defendants be named. Thus were included General Yoshijiro Umezu, former commander of the Kwantung Army along the Russian border, and Mamoru Shigemitsu, once an ambassador to Moscow.[16]

At the first meeting of the IMTFE, the indictment was published that day—April 29, 1946. There were fifty-five separate counts for the twenty-eight defendants. On May 31, MacArthur asked that a Navy representative appear as a witness "to present information in regard to documents in the custody of the Navy Department."[17] On July 25, 1946, Forrestal made the request formal.[18] The next day Richardson and his assistants flew again to Japan to prepare for the Navy presentation. They arrived at General Headquarters, U.S. Army Forces, Pacific, on July 31.[19] For once, Richardson aimed not to give his opinion, just to produce evidence that the Japanese had planned for many months an attack on Pearl Harbor.

There were many who felt the entire trial was on show simply as revenge on the Japanese for the attack on Pearl Harbor. Judge B. V. A. Röling of the Netherlands expressed this viewpoint in a later oral history.[20] Whether designed as such or not, the trial did put on show to the world that those in charge of the treachery were held accountable.[21]

Many of those indicted Richardson knew about, or at least had a vague view of their part in the Japanese "aggression." More than half were military men. There were fourteen generals: Sadao Araki, Kenji Doihara, Shunroku Hata, Seishiro Itagaki, Heitaro Kimura, Kuniaki Koiso, Iwane Matsui, Jiro Minami, Akira Muto, Hiroshi Oshima, Kenryo Sato, Teiichi Suzuki, Hideki Tojo, and Yoshijiro Umezu. There were three admirals: Osami Nagano, Takasumi Oka, and Shigetaro Shimada. Richardson would specifically include Osami Nagano and the late Isoroku Yamamoto in his presentation to the court.

Additionally, there was a military propagandist—anti-Western fanatic Colonel Kingoro Hashimoto. Two civilians were included: Toshio Shiratori, a diplomat; and Shumei Okawa, who, while he "did not at any time hold an important responsible government position . . . , was the intellectual leader behind Japan's entire aggressive program."[22]

Top civilian representatives included two prime ministers— Kiichiro Hiranuma and Koki Hirota—and three foreign ministers—Yosuke Matsuoka, Mamoru Shigemitsu, and Shigenori

Togo. Other former cabinet members were Naoki Hoshino (cabinet secretary) and Okinori Kaya (minister of finance). Last was Kido, who in many eyes was indicted as the emperor's proxy. He voluntarily turned over his valuable diary to the prosecution. It became a well-used piece of evidence.[23]

One spring-like morning a crowd began to form at 7:00 A.M. on a hill above Tokyo. In the auditorium of the old Japanese War Ministry building, the trial began with a preliminary hearing on May 3, 1946. If room was available, seats were left open to the public except on rare and announced occasions. There was a concentrated effort to provide liaison with the Allied and Japanese presses.[24]

The often autocratic Webb declared that each defendant should choose his counsel if they wanted to be heard.[25] This announcement caused quite a dispute with Coleman. He thus resigned, followed by the rest of his Navy contingent on the defense team. The result was an individual representation by U.S. counsel, and little coordination of the work of the defense.[26] It was not the last time Webb clashed with the defense.[27]

Each defendant was offered specific representation. Most chose a countryman. The Americans with understanding of legal concepts, cross-examination, and procedures, however, assisted them. Only two of the defense counsel seemed to feel that Richardson's statements needed their cross-examination. Edward P. McDermott spoke for Shimada, and John G. Brannon was American counsel for Nagano.[28]

Richardson worked with his staff at the hotel.[29] The effort had only partially been done, and the days were intense with more building of his testimony. Still, he noted on his book's rough outline that he fished at a place called Chayinzi and had enjoyed MacArthur's food. Though no real courses were yet in Japan, he had played a round of golf with friends in Hawaii on the trip out. He even met with his old friend, Ambassador Nomura, while in Tokyo.[30]

Developing the case chronologically, the prosecution went through ten phases from June 3 to the time Richardson took the huge stand before the judges, press, dignitaries, accused, and visitors in late November 1946. The process for Richardson had been slow. After Keenan estimated that Richardson's part of the trial was still two months away, the admiral left Japan on September 16 for an eight-day trip home, which included a two-day leave in the Los Angeles area. He was thus subject to a two-week notice on recall.[31]

Richardson received notice on October 30 to start back to Japan. Six days later, on November 10, he was again in government quarters in Tokyo, where he would reside for seventeen days.[32] Before he arrived, the defense had complained that Hull, Stimson, Grew, and others had not appeared in person. By the time Richardson returned for testimony, the tribunal had heard of the way Japan was prepared for war, about the Japanese invasion of Manchuria, and the war and atrocities in China from 1937. It heard about Japan's relations with Germany, Italy, France, Thailand, and the USSR. Then it was Richardson's turn to add to that testimony. The defense was beginning to see the uphill battle ahead.

As he entered the 90 x 115 foot, 1,000 seat auditorium, Richardson saw that it had been remodeled carefully both to give some dignity to the proceedings, and to accommodate the photographic needs.[33] Some thought, however, that it exuded a Hollywood aura. Richardson saw the seats for the eleven judges. Across from that area was what was called "the dock," where the defendants sat. The once-powerful figures were no longer so awesome, especially when surrounded by the American MPs. Present were up to 200 members of the press, and some 660 onlookers in the balcony. Richardson would sit to the left of the judges and clerks, in a rather large box.

It and all other seats were wired to the translator's glass-enclosed workroom on a small balcony overlooking what became known as the "stage."[34] It was easy to tell when the cameras started rolling. The courtroom was suddenly illuminated. Large boxed Klieg lights hung from the ceiling, causing Webb to complain about the heat more than a few times. The U.S. Navy's presentation by Richardson and his team, however, escaped the muggy summertime temperatures.

Since October 23, the tribunal had heard about events and documents pertaining to the attack on Pearl Harbor. Then it was time to present materials from the U.S. congressional hearings, and from captured documents, having to do with prior Pearl Harbor planning by the Japanese. It was Richardson's chance to top off this phase of the trials.

Richardson took the stand on Monday, November 25, at 10:45 A.M. as the trials' forty-seventh witness, and would be just one of 419 before the end of the 192-day ordeal.[35] He would admit twenty-two documents or sets of papers. They were almost lost among the 4,336 total exhibits and depositions taken from the 109 witnesses for the prosecution, 310 for the defense who took the stand, and those taken from 779 other individuals who gave written statements.[36] Apparently, only one film was shown in court, unlike the Nuremberg trials of Nazi war criminals.[37] The resulting 49,858 pages were massive amounts of reading for the judges and historians, which may explain why no writings about Richardson, not even in his own book, cover what he did during several months of study, and two days on the witness stand in the fall of 1946.[38]

Before Richardson arrived, Joseph W. Ballantine began the morning proceedings at 9:30 A.M., completing his testimony begun on November 18. Justice Radhabinod Pal of India was not present, nor was defendant Okawa.[39] Richardson watched as S. Okamoto attempted to cross-examine Ballantine, an India-born special assistant to the U.S. secretary of state. He was one of Richardson's 1940 suspects in shaping U.S. policy with Japan. He had directed the Office of Far Eastern Affairs in 1944.[40] Webb hounded Okamoto toward the end of the Ballantine session for making statements and not asking questions.[41] A frustrated defense passed on cross-examination, but by mid-morning, Ballantine's time on the stand was over.

Keenan stood and told Webb that the next witness would be Admiral Richardson, United States Navy, who would be examined by the assistant prosecutor, Navy Captain James J. Robinson. Prosecutor Robinson addressed the tribunal, saying, "It is now proposed to present evidence to show plans and preparations made by the Japanese Navy leading up the naval hostilities which Japan initiated and waged at Pearl Harbor on 7 December, 1941."[42]

Some historians were inclined to conclude that this phase was not worthwhile. And, as the hours ticked by, even Webb seemed to feel that trying to prove the aggression of Japan upon Pearl Harbor was not as clear-cut as Japan's actions against other territories. But, the prosecution plugged on, offering Richardson's narrative and suggested exhibits to file with the court. Before Robinson allowed the admiral to read his statement, a bit of background was presented to the court to reveal the reason Richardson was there.[43] He then gave the court Richardson's statement to be entered as Exhibit #1249.

Brannon, counsel for Nagano, stood. He wanted to know the degree of expertness Richardson had on the subject matter of his affidavit. As they argued about when the expertise of a witness should be introduced, and how, Richardson listened quietly. Finally, with Webb's permission, Robinson asked his witness to proceed with his statement. Richardson quickly cleared the entire matter, saying, "I wish to stress the fact that I am testifying neither as an expert witness stating opinions, nor as a witness stating facts within his own knowledge, but I am simply presenting information contained in official records." He added that he was sticking to the one stated subject.[44]

He said he would omit as he read what few opinions were in his prepared statement. He told the justices that he had been asked by Secretary of the Navy Forrestal, who was responding to a request by General MacArthur during the previous summer, to present information on documents the Navy possessed bearing on the one subject. He then told them how he had proceeded from that point.[45]

He went into detail on each of four departments of concern. He began with the carrier aspect. It was the Navy's feeling that as early as 1934, Yamamoto and Nagano recognized the carrier as the instrument for expansion and aggression. Richardson gave the court several records of statements made by the pair at London's Claridges Hotel in October of 1934, and at the London

Naval Conference of 1935-36.[46] Yamamoto took the position in 1934 at a meeting of the American and Japanese delegations that, "if the Japanese had aggressive designs in the Far East, nothing would be more useful than the retention of aircraft carriers."[47] Because Japan announced on December 29, 1934, that she was withdrawing from the terms of the Washington Conference, effective at the end of 1936, another meeting was planned.[48] Ironically, it began on December 7, 1935.

Nagano was the leader of the Japanese delegation at this gathering in London, when the powers tried to extend the deadline of the Washington Treaty of 1921. The meeting lasted into the spring.

On January 15, 1936, Nagano, according to the U.S. Navy and Richardson, said again, before an official session of the conference, that the Japanese viewed aircraft carriers as the principal type of aggressive naval arms. Japan even felt that to complete a state of nonaggression among nations that the conference participants should agree to abolish carriers. He knew they would not. After a few weeks, Japan withdrew from the conference when not given parity with the United States and Great Britain. Those latter two countries felt that parity meant superiority for Japan.[49]

Richardson noted that Nagano and Yamamoto worked hand in hand a couple of times, once in 1936-37 as Navy minister and vice-minister, and again in 1941-43 as chief of the Japanese Naval General Staff and commander in chief of the Combined Fleet, respectively. The U.S. Navy thought the two took the lead in working out plans and issuing orders for the Pearl Harbor attack. Richardson strongly associated the two with the carrier construction and the abolition of treaty limitations by Japan. This activity went on, Richardson said, until Japan had developed superiority in this category.[50]

Richardson went into detail at this point, summarizing the limitations placed on Japan by the Treaty of 1921. He discussed the times the Japanese tried to change the terms and ratios.[51] After Japan withdrew from the London Conference, she also continued to refuse an exchange of information as was detailed in the London Treaty of 1930.[52] Richardson said, however, that Japan could and did easily obtain information pertaining to construction by the U.S. Navy simply by using the freedom of the society there or by consular espionage.

Richardson rattled off Navy ship numbers, noting that by December 7, 1941, the Japanese had pulled away from an even number of carriers—four, in 1936—to a ten-to-six advantage over the United States in 1941. Only three U.S. carriers, however, were in the Pacific at that time. He suggested in his statement that the Navy believed that captured papers proved the Japanese had as a main objective to destroy those three carriers at Pearl Harbor.

After nearly two hours, the court adjourned for a recess and lunch. It would resume at 1:30 P.M.

Robinson continued the direct examination, and Richardson turned to his second point—evidence that Japan was expanding its naval capacity, using the Mandated Islands.[53] He said the United States protested. The Caroline, Marshall, and Mariana Islands were spread over 1,000 miles between Hawaii and the Philippine Islands.[54] Having control of them meant a country could protect the approaches to Southeast Asia and the passage to the Indian Ocean. The Mandates Treaty between the United States and Japan in 1922 stated that no military or naval bases would be established or fortifications erected in the Mandates.[55]

Control of these atolls and islands could also give Japan one more step toward an invasion of Hawaii, and perhaps the West Coast. The Office of Naval Intelligence (ONI) began to receive reports of Japanese merchantmen offloading materials that were obviously meant for military construction. Richardson presented IPS Document #17 to the court to prove this point. It was found as part of the official files of the Japanese Combined Fleet Headquarters aboard the battleship *Nagato*.[56] Clandestine efforts by the United States to prove violation of the agreements went on for years, but the evidence captured from the Japanese battleship sealed the accusations.

Robinson then said that a certificate signed by Lieutenant Robert I. Curts would then be read into the record. It was a good example of the efforts taken by the military to recover any valuable papers that would give indication of Japanese plans. Curts was the son of former Richardson staff member Maurice "Germany" Curts.

What Robinson read explained how the Japanese ship *Nachi* was sunk in Manila Bay on November 4, 1944. In late March of 1945, the ship was raised. Curts and his intelligence team recovered a bundle of papers from the charthouse.[57] They eventually made their way to McCollum, at that time the Seventh Fleet's intelligence officer. He microfilmed them, and then sent them to ATIS in Brisbane, Australia. Finally, in July of 1945, the papers were in Washington, DC, at the ONI office. There, Curts wrote that he received them into his custody. The originals and the microfilm moved to the Washington Document Center (WDC) a year later, thus explaining where Richardson's team viewed them, and decided to include some of them in the presentation.[58]

Richardson then read a Yamamoto order of November 5, 1941, which referred to a 151-page volume of text, tables, and charts giving outlines for a war beginning with the attack on Pearl Harbor. "The Mandated Islands appear in many places on this order," Richardson told the court. In fact, eight bases were designated. He noted that the pages gave great detail of a concentration of supplies and ammunition. Rations were allotted for 36,000 persons per month at the bases.

The text revealed that the South Seas Japanese Force, commonly called the Mandates Fleet, was ordered to aid "in covering the withdrawal of the Pearl Harbor striking force, allowing it to attack Wake and Guam as quickly as possible, and to cooperate with the striking force in the occupation of strategic areas."[59] Submarines en route from Japan to Pearl Harbor rendezvoused at Kwajalein in the Marshall Islands.

As the newspapers hit the stands the day after Richardson's first hours of testimony, many of the Japanese public were becoming aware for the first time that the war began on a very calculated note, and that they had been deceived by Japanese leaders.

Richardson again said, "It is clear, therefore, that the Japanese Navy, before 7 December 1941, had established naval bases on the Mandated Islands." He, the Navy, and the United States seemed to think this act violated previous treaties, even though the Japanese had five years earlier opted out of the agreements. Still, Robinson and Richardson told the tribunal that many more documents proved an illegal military buildup in the Mandates.

Next, Richardson moved to the third department of his presentation, that of consular spying in the United States and its territories, especially at Pearl Harbor. The openness of the democratic society allowed enemies to easily track the naval building programs. Through Consul General Kita, and his two hundred agents in the Foreign Office at Honolulu, Japan could quickly receive updates about ship movements.[60] While Richardson was CinCUS, the duty fell to Kohichi Seki.[61]

Richardson presented documents to the court proving this point, and showed copies of some of the message intercepts by the U.S. Navy. These particular correspondences were only a portion of the sixty-nine spy messages sent between January 1 and December 7, 1941, between Honolulu and Japan.[62] They were sent via commercial communications companies, said Richardson.[63]

After the submission of several exhibits to the court on the matter, Robinson asked that Richardson continue reading the Navy's statement. A huge chart and wall maps of Pearl Harbor were rolled into place for the participants to follow as Richardson spoke.[64] The admiral presented a message from Tokyo's foreign minister, Admiral Teijiro Toyoda, to his office in Honolulu. The future commander in chief of Japan's Combined Fleet wrote on September 24, 1941, "The waters (of Pearl Harbor) are to be divided into five sub-areas" for the purpose of reporting vessel locations.

Later called the "bomb plot" message by Americans, it also mentioned assignments to spy on waters between Ford Island and the arsenal, waters adjacent to the island south and southwest of Ford Island, and the areas of the east, middle, and west lochs. With regard to warships and carriers Toyoda wrote, "We would like to have you report on those at anchor, tied at wharves, buoys and in docks."[65] He wanted the details. The answers were begun and sent mostly by Takeo Yoshikawa after August.[66] As mentioned in an earlier chapter, he took the identity of a junior diplomat named Morimura.[67]

The court was seeing clear proof of preattack preparation by Japan. With the help of the local Radio Corporation of America (RCA) global office manager in Honolulu, and with orders from the company's president, David Sarnoff, the U.S. Navy had been intercepting some of these messages since Sarnoff's nine-day, November 1941 visit.[68]

However, these intercepts apparently did not work their way back to the fleet at Hawaii, nor into the Tokyo presentation.[69] Richardson did not offer any of the FBI and Navy evidence collected through wiretaps of the consulate at 1742 Nuuanu Avenue. Results found by this method of "spying on the spy" were not relayed to the Navy either, and were ceased on December 2, 1941.[70]

Richardson presented another message, dated November 15, 1941, from the just-appointed Foreign Minister Togo in Tokyo to Agent Riyoji in Honolulu. Togo wanted Honolulu to make the reports "irregular," since the relationship between the United States and Japan was "most critical."[71]

The third message introduced by Richardson emphasized what was being sent to Tokyo a month before the attack. It was from Kita and was sent on November 18. Kida's diary was used extensively to lay the tribunal case for the prosecution. He detailed which ships were in which of the sections. The report was fairly detailed down to just how fast and how far apart the destroyers observed were traveling into the harbor.[72]

Richardson then entered another message from Togo in Tokyo, dated December 2, 1941, but not translated by Americans until December 31. It wanted to know, day by day, where the ships were, if there were any balloons, and if there were anti-mine nets in place. Richardson said, "It raises three important questions preparatory to the Pearl Harbor attack. It likewise bears the name of Foreign Minister Togo."[73]

Richardson told the justices that all this evidence indicated a close liaison between the Japanese Foreign Office and the Japanese Navy. The Japanese prime minister asked that he be told "hereafter, to the utmost of your ability" where the ships were in port. "Wire me in each case whether or not there are any observation balloons above Pearl Harbor, or if there are any indications that they will be sent up." It was a very important point when he also asked to be advised if there were warships provided with anti-mine nets. To Americans, this information indicted Togo, and linked him strongly to the planned attack.

Richardson did not mention that also on December 2 the Japanese embassies in Washington and other locations were ordered to burn various documents. He may not have known of this fact at the time of his testimony. In Washington, two code machines caught the Japanese orders.[74] These intercepts, unlike others, were decrypted in one day, and Kimmel received a paraphrasing. Many felt that had this message been compared with the consul "bomb plot" messages intercepted by RCA, Kimmel and Short would have understood the immediacy of the situation.[75] The "bomb plot" information alone would have sent Kimmel and Short into high alert.

The burn order caught Fletcher Warren's attention. A native of Wolfe City, forty miles from Paris, Texas, Warren was in Washington where he was in charge of a new State Department office called Foreign Correlation. He said that four days before the attack on Pearl Harbor, he received word that the Japanese consulate was preparing to burn papers and codes. He sent a man with binoculars to observe. Frederick B. Lyon, the observer, reported that indeed the Japanese were burning files. Warren promptly relayed this information to Adolf Berle, his superior and a writer of some of President Roosevelt's speeches. Warren thought that Berle alerted Secretary of State Hull.

In addition, but not discussed by Richardson at the trial, and probably not known by Richardson, on December 3, in response to the Japanese message to its embassies, Safford and McCollum sent a quick message to all interception posts. McCollum said the pair asked the naval observers to "burn all their stuff because, we didn't say so, but obviously war was coming." The posts were asked that, when the duty was fulfilled, to simply respond back to Washington with the message, "Gobbledygook." That was Safford's instruction. McCollum said the orders went through the high commanders, and in two days all American posts had responded with the code word. "Our own people had been more or less directed to batten down and get ready for hostilities," explained McCollum. The assumption was that everyone then knew something was up, and would happen soon. The response relay, according to McCollum, came back through the chain of command—giving each office a second chance to study the matter. However, McCollum said in an oral interview he never knew if Stark saw the orders.[76]

Continuing at the Tokyo trial with the spy angle, Robinson then offered into evidence an affidavit by Bernard Julius Otto Kuehn, dated January 1, 1942, and another one dated two days later.[77] Keuhn, probably with help from his wife Friedel, was convicted for spying on Pearl Harbor between November 30 and December 2, 1941. This German couple lived luxuriously on no apparent local income, and had been reported to the FBI as far back as 1939 by anonymous informants. The husband knew the Japanese language well.

As Richardson would tell the tribunal, American intelligence on December 3, 1941, intercepted a message from the Japanese consulate in Honolulu to Tokyo. It was from Ichiro Fujii, allegedly the name used by Kuehn.[78] It detailed an elaborate system of signals that would report U.S. Navy movements at Pearl Harbor.[79] Regrettably, the message was not decoded in Washington until December 11. In the hectic aftermath of the attack, the FBI and G-2 of the Army learned from other sources that signals apparently came from a dormer window at the Kuehn house. On December 8, all the family was arrested except for a son.[80]

After defense counsel William Logan protested to Judge Webb that both documents submitted on the Kuehn subject were copies, and that portions were cut out, Richardson was allowed to continue. He said that Kuehn delivered papers giving full details of the U.S. Navy ships present on December 2, their berthing locations, and a comprehensive code of signals by which information could be communicated to Japanese submarines.[81]

The U.S. Navy professed that Kita transmitted the information to Tokyo the next day. Richardson read the December 3, 1941, letter.[82] It was from Ichiro Fujii, and asked the chief of #3 section of Military Staff Headquarters if he could change the method of communicating by signals. It said a Lanikai Beach house would show lights during the night, and gave the times and number of signals. The lights would come from an attic window. It gave alternative sites for the signals to be transmitted in case of problems.[83] Richardson told the court that the Lanikai Beach house and the Kalama house mentioned in the message were occupied by the Keuhns. Keuhn even confessed so, said Richardson.[84]

Richardson read a message dated December 5, 1941. It was to Tokyo from Honolulu, but not translated until December 10. It gave the location of ships, the numbers and some names. The admiral then stated that a message of December 6 to Tokyo provided direct information for the "surprise attack."[85] It dealt with barrage balloons and torpedo nets. It was translated on December 8. The contents stated that no mooring equipment was in place and no balloons were in sight. It said at its end, "There is considerable opportunity left to take advantage for a surprise attack against these places. In my opinion, the battleships do not have torpedo nets."[86] This message almost alone could have brought Washington to attention if it had been pulled from the intercept stack earlier than December 7.[87]

Also, on December 6, a message to Tokyo, translated by the Army on December 8, said, "It appears that no air reconnaissance is being conducted by the fleet air arm."[88] Again, it was not translated until three days after the Pearl Harbor attack. Both messages were originally captured by Army intercept at San Francisco, forwarded to the War Department in Washington by teletype, and placed in a "to do" basket.[89]

Copies of these last two messages were taken with Colonel Clausen when he investigated the Pearl Harbor debacle for Stimson. Clausen wrote in his book that there was too much pressure upon Rochefort at Station HYPO. This insistent charge to find out what was planned by the Japanese was depicted years later in the movie, *Midway,* when Rochefort was shown talking with the fictional character played by actor Charlton Heston. Rochefort was tired looking, the office was a wreck, and Heston said, "This place stinks!"—an obvious reference to the lack of personal hygiene of Rochefort and his colleagues. Rochefort was commander of the Communications Security Intelligence Unit of the Fourteenth Naval District (Com14). Despite distributing alerting notes from the Honolulu naval intelligence office, he felt that cracking the Japanese Naval Code for flag officers was a higher priority than reading some twenty-seven coded RCA messages. In addition, when he did assign the task, the staff placed the messages in the wrong stack, and did not discover the error until after the Pearl Harbor attack.[90]

Enough said, thought the Navy and Richardson. He concluded this testimony about consular espionage by saying, "The documents. . . . which have been presented have been limited to a few of those dealing with consular espionage in Honolulu." They revealed, he thought, the activities between the Japanese Navy and Foreign Office in planning the espionage as an aid to the Pearl Harbor attack.

He did not present the messages going back and forth while he was CinCUS. With those in mind, and the ones being presented in court, Richardson and the U.S. Navy thought it could amply prove that the Japanese had planned for some time to attack Pearl Harbor.[91]

Richardson then went into a twelve-page summary of the attack, its objectives, its plan, and its execution. He reminded the court that the chief of staff of the Japanese Combined Fleet, Admiral Seiichi Ito, said, "This fleet [at Pearl Harbor] will be utterly crushed with one blow."[92]

Richardson and Robinson introduced an Allied ATIS document that gave the general objectives of the entire Japanese operations. Logan highly protested that it was a SCAP published document, and because MacArthur was the reviewing authority on the case, it should be dismissed, as should be a previous Exhibit, #809. He was overruled.

That previously filed exhibit was IPS Document #1628, which

quoted Nagano as saying that a Pearl Harbor attack would render the U.S. Fleet impotent, giving Japan time to maintain freedom of action in the South Seas, including the Philippines, and in the Mandated Islands.[93] The Soviet prosecutor, when discussing the Japanese policy toward the USSR, had used it weeks earlier. A part of the document dealt with the possibility of Japan attacking Soviet forces at the Manchukuoan border since Germany had the Russians busy in the west.[94]

Exhibit #1265, called also Research Report #132, was very detailed. It stated that Yamamoto conceived the Pearl Harbor plan, according to Nagano, at the same time that Richardson was fired by Roosevelt. It not only accused Nagano and Yamamoto of knowing the entire plan, but also Navy Minister Shimada and chief of the Bureau of Naval Affairs, Admiral Takasumi Oka. It mentioned the preparatory war games held in early September of 1941, and how it was decided that torpedoes could be made effective in shallow waters. Nagano was the ranking officer acting as the umpire.[95]

The document discussed fuel problems, radio silence, the route to be used, and targets to be struck. Every detail was covered. Nagano issued an order on November 5 to Admiral Yamamoto, putting the plan into effect. Two days later Yamamoto issued "Order No. 2," fixing the Japanese date of the attack to be December 8, Japan time.[96] Also on November 7, from the flagship *Nagato,* Yamamoto issued an order for the task force to assemble at Hitokappu Bay at Etorofu (Iturup) Island in the Kuriles, just north of Japan's main islands. Supplies would be boarded until November 22.

Richardson continued by telling the audience, many of whom were Japanese who never knew the details of their country's plans, that on November 25, Yamamoto ordered the force to move out, proceeding the next day without detection along a northern route to the point of rendezvous set for December 3. The 3,000-mile trip began. On December 2, the force received the news that December 8 was the attack date. Yamamoto decided that day to complete the plans.

As almost any American now knows, on the night of December 6 and the morning of December 7, Hawaiian time, the task force came within 230 miles due north of Oahu. Planes were launched at 1:30 A.M. when the six carriers were within two hundred miles of Pearl Harbor, and another wave left at 2:45 A.M. South of the carriers the planes gathered, then went into Pearl Harbor from 7:55 to 8:25 A.M, and again from 8:40 to 9:15 A.M. Dive bombers attacked from 9:15 to 9:45 A.M.

As soon as the task force launched its planes, the ships withdrew at a high speed to the northwest. All the planes but twenty-nine returned to the prescribed location between 10:30 A.M. and 1:30 P.M. Dead aviators numbered fifty-four. Richardson did not mention that the Japanese plan for a third strike was scuttled. The task force eventually proceeded to Kure, located in Chugoku district near Hiroshima, arriving on December 23.

Richardson read out the American casualty list totals, including personnel and equipment. Still thinking in the time period of fair play, even in war, he told the tribunal that he found no document in the governmental files that showed that Japan gave the United States any direct warning that it was about to commence hostilities. He did mention that a notice came to Hull's office sixty-six hours later stating, "There has arisen a state of war" between Japan and the United States.[97]

At 2:45 P.M., the court called a fifteen-minute recess. Already, it was becoming a long day for everyone. But, when Robinson arose after the marshal of the court announced the resumption, he surprised a few by telling Webb that the direct testimony was concluded. The cross-examination was at first to be done by Brannon, and Richardson's experience was on the line.

Defense counsel immediately went back to the expertise of the witness, asking the admiral if he were named specifically in MacArthur's request to Hull to provide a Navy witness. Richardson replied that the SCAP's request for a Navy witness went through the War Department, and then to the Navy. The request asked for Forrestal to designate a senior officer. "My name was not mentioned" at that point, Richardson said.[98]

Brannon continued to drill on the expertise issue, asking Richardson why and how he was selected. "I was designated for the duty by the Secretary of the Navy Forrestal," the admiral replied, explaining that he had little personal contact with the secretary during preparation for the court. "I did not see the Secretary of the Navy within the first two months preceding my first appearance here. I did not see him until a few days before I came for my second visit," Richardson continued. Forrestal apparently had little interest in the trial, or had confidence that Richardson's team would do the proper job. At the time he visited with Forrestal, "All I told him was that I was returning, and he gave me no instructions," added the admiral.

Brannon asked again, "How did you receive the appointment . . . ?" Webb frustratingly jumped in, asking what was Brannon's point. He thought none of the appointment process interested the court. "If you think he is incompetent, well, we will have to determine it. You had better make your grounds clear"[99]

Webb stated that the request came from a neutral authority, and that the supreme commander had not indicted the defendants, thinking that Brannon was trying to prove interference from MacArthur. Webb made a rather bold statement next by saying, "He [MacArthur] is perfectly neutral. I don't know why you bring his name into it." Webb was convinced that MacArthur simply created the court and let it run its course under the justices.

"I don't think any American questions the competency of Admiral Richardson," Brannon said. He added that he just did not want the affidavit's first paragraph to give the impression that MacArthur specifically chose Richardson, and that the SCAP was interfering. Webb countered, "It isn't worthwhile wasting any more time on it."

Richardson was asked if he drafted the report personally. Brannon then was going to get a full dose of the Texanese still deep inside the admiral. He would begin a long series of answers over the remaining testimony that would show his own expertise at being a witness before a governing body.

"Did you draft this report personally?" asked Brannon. "A man of my years and experience seldom does the initial spade work," Richardson answered Brannon. "The project is mine; I supervised its preparation and its final re-write—it is my own work." Brannon learned on the next question that Richardson was sometimes too detailed in his answers.

"Did you bring the records to Japan with you?" he asked. Richardson answered, "I did not personally bring the documents . . . they were in the custody of subordinates of mine who accompanied me in the same plane." Brannon wanted to know if all the evidence presented that day came from the official naval files. Richardson answered, "It did. I repeat. It did."[100]

Brannon again asked Richardson if what he presented represented the Navy view and not the admiral's. Richardson said he had made an earnest effort to state facts only. For Richardson, that was quite a feat, but he added, "In so far as I know, I succeeded and the facts stated are supported by official documents."

Since he represented Nagano, Brannon wanted to know why Richardson included that particular defendant in his testimony that morning. "Because of the statements made in one of the documents," said Richardson. Brannon then made reference to quoting Nagano as of January 1, 1936, saying it should have been 1934. "Is the date a material consideration," Webb asked, "so far back?"[101]

At times Richardson viewed Nagano sitting in the dock. His once rugged, strong look was fading. But, at sixty-six he was sickly, and would die in two months. It was likely that the pair ran across each other in Washington shortly before World War I, after Nagano studied law at Harvard. Nagano was two years younger than Richardson. After becoming a naval officer, he established a strong record in administration. Nagano studied in the United States during the "teens," and was the naval attaché there in 1920-23, most of the time that Richardson was in the South China Patrol.

Webb was not allowing any cross-examination on small issues like the exact date of Nogano's statement, but Brannon said he thought that every error or misstatement in a report was important. Webb warned him to consider substance, and the questioning continued.

Brannon asked why Richardson, in his affidavit, used the words "expansion and aggression," and questioned whether he ever used these terms when referring to Nagano. Richardson said he used the words "non-aggression, non-menace, offensive armament and offensive character," but said, "I see no use of the word 'expansion.'"[102]

Brannon quickly asked if a quotation attributed to Yamamoto was actually a quotation from evidence. Richardson replied that it came from a State Department paper, and he believed it to be an exact quotation. Webb interjected that he felt it to be consistent with anything omitted. Brannon was being thwarted both from the bench and from the witness.

Pointing out that it could not be a quotation since Yamamoto was dead, he called it a "reporter's resume."[103] Brannon then fell game to the admiral's ability to block a line of questioning. Richardson simply agreed with Brannon, "That is correct. That . . . should not appear to be an exact quotation." Webb asked Brannon, "Do you want his exact words? It may be painfully slow to get them from this witness." He pointed out that there might be an exhibit that would help Brannon find the exact Yamamoto words.

Still pounding on the issue, trying to remove Nagano from any exact statement by Yamamoto, Brannon read from an exhibit presented by Robinson. Richardson stated that it was not in his oral presentation. Brannon then asked the admiral if he recognized that what he put in quotes in his affidavit was not what Yamamoto exactly said. Before Richardson could speak, Webb cleared the air by saying, "To set your mind at rest, I think I can tell you the Tribunal will disregard quotation marks." But, he went on to say that the exhibit did have them.

Brannon asked Richardson what Nagano specifically said about the importance of the carriers. Did he only mention carriers? Richardson said that Nagano and Yamamoto referred to carriers, capital ships, and cruisers as offensive. Brannon wanted to know also, what significance was placed on the fact that Nagano and Yamamoto represented Japan at two different times at the naval conferences. Richardson said, "None, except that they were probably considered the best able to present the views of those who selected them."[104]

The defense asked Richardson about his statement that the Japanese abolished the limitations of the 1930 treaty. "Is it a fact that Japan did not abolish the treaty limitations of 1930, but that they expired?"

Richardson agreed with him, basically, but said that "because of Japan's denunciation of the treaty . . . their [the treaty limitations] effectiveness was abolished." Brannon wanted to know if Japan proposed a different proposition in 1934 in regard to naval limitations. Richardson just referred to his statement, saying, "She proposed a treaty limitation based on what she called a *common upper limit.*"[105]

After another comment by Webb, he adjourned quickly at 4:00 P.M. for the day, leaving Brannon hanging in the middle of his cross-examination. Webb spoke many times for the tribunal without discussion with those on the bench. Röling wrote later that he was "a lonely man," adding that the other judges had very little social contact with Webb. "At our daily breakfasts and dinners in the hotel, Webb was always absent."[106]

The early break gave Richardson and his team until the next morning to study and anticipate the next barrage of questions by Brannon. So, on November 26, at 9:30 A.M., the court opened for more proceedings. It was expected that Brannon would continue to carefully pick over the affidavit and the twenty exhibits submitted by the witness and his team. And he did, for some forty-three more pages of transcripts taken by the court.

Pal was still not present, nor was the excused institutionalized Okawa, but the defense and the prosecution teams were the same. Okawa's absence was the result of a strange behavior. He threw the court into an uproar on the first day of the IMTFE proceedings, when the clerk read the twenty-second of the fifty-five counts. He was sitting behind Tojo in the dock. He had been fidgety and nervous. He half-arose from his seat, and whacked Tojo on top of the head. As he hit the former prime minister for a second time, the police jumped on Okawa. He was transferred to a hospital and did not return to the trial.

Unknown to Richardson at that moment, Tojo, and also Kido,

had a link to Paris, Texas, though in a relatively small way. Paris Junior College graduate Dean Edward Hallmark flew the sixth plane off the USS *Hornet* on April 18, 1942, as part of Colonel Jimmy Doolittle's surprise raid on the Japanese homeland. After dropping its bombs, the *Green Hornet* did not make it to the Chinese mainland, ditching about four miles from shore. Hallmark and eight other participants in Doolittle's raid were captured and eventually endured a horrendous period of imprisonment.

After nearly six months of torture, on October 3, Tojo met with Kido at the Imperial Palace to discuss the trial recently held for the Americans, and what to do next. Tojo reported the proceedings and results of the trial. Some or all would be executed. He appealed for leniency. Kido convinced Emperor Hirohito, who agreed that only those found guilty of killing schoolchildren should be executed. A bogus admission of guilt had been presented on paper to Hallmark earlier. In pain, sick, and almost in a state of unconsciousness he signed the document, which was in Japanese. He would be one of three to be shot on October 16.[107] Richardson would read something about it in Ted W. Lawson's 1943 book, *Thirty Seconds Over Tokyo,* and later perhaps see the Van Johnson-Spencer Tracy movie with the same title.

Brannon began Richardson's second day by asking if the admiral's statement in Exhibit #1249 inferred that Nagano led the withdrawal of Japan from the naval treaty in 1935-36. "Was he doing anything other than acting under his country's instruction that led him to leave the conference?" he asked. Robinson objected because he felt the question asked for Richardson's opinion.[108]

"We know well that the Admiral is not aware of the instructions Nagano had unless Nagano told him," added Webb. He then told Brannon that he could ask about the carrier strength and limitations, but that this matter was moot. The charges in this court were against all accused, not just Nagano.

The subsequent questions and answers became very specific and detailed. Brannon wanted to know if tonnage was the first factor to consider in a comparison of the two navies. "I made no statement," answered Richardson. "The statement I made was that the basis in the treaty was . . . tonnage. I used that basis."

Richardson said what he had presented was Navy Department figures on treaty tonnage. He then said he would place comparisons in some conditions on numbers and size of ships. "It depends upon the purposes for which the ships are to be used," he added. Brannon turned to just the attack on Pearl Harbor, asking which was more important there.

Richardson threw him a curve by saying, "In that instance, it would be the total number of planes that could be put in the air." Brannon and Richardson both agreed that size of ship and displacement was important to the number of planes carried. Brannon then presented a list of combat vessels belonging to Japan between 1931 and 1945. It showed the tonnage of the various ships, even those under construction. This list was presented originally on November 1.

Japanese carrier tonnage on December 7, 1941, was 152,970. Brannon asked why Richardson, in his report, referred to tonnage as being 178,070. "When this written statement was prepared, [and given to defense counsel], I relied upon the best information available in the official records of the Navy Department," Richardson explained. Apparently Brannon began a quick question, but the admiral cut him off by saying, "May I complete my reply?"[109]

He was allowed to do so, and expanded on his report, saying that after the termination of Japan's part in the treaty, it built three carriers: the *Hosho, Soryu,* and *Taiyo.* He said after later receiving a list of carrier tonnage also presented on November 1 to the court, he realized that the U.S. Navy tonnage figures were wrong. "Inasmuch as the difference was inconsequential from my point of view, I did not deem it worthwhile to correct the statement that had already been given to the defense staff." It was possible that Richardson was covering for his mistake of not changing the numbers before he read them to the court, or perhaps he was covering for the mistake of his team. Whatever, he fielded Brannon's questions about tonnage for a few more minutes.

Brannon wanted to know if the admiral thought 26,000 tons difference was important. Richardson said the actual gist of his statement was that Japan five years later had doubled her carrier strength. Robinson finally asked the court to stop Brannon's questioning on the tonnage difference, and Webb agreed, with a bit of protest and questions.[110]

As Brannon attempted to show the Japanese strength was not as Richardson presented the day before, Robinson asked the court to remember that "this witness is here to testify as to what the United States Navy records show."[111] He theorized that the inconsistent figures were "merely a tribute to the secrecy with which Japanese Naval construction was being carried on."

Webb chastised Robinson for saying what the witness should have explained. Brannon went on to point out that maybe the U.S. Navy Department's decreasing prewar numbers did not reflect the lending policy with Great Britain "which would account for the decrease in the number of destroyers as stated in your report." Richardson simply answered that he accepted the Navy Department figures as given to him.

Richardson noted, when asked if the number of destroyers given to Great Britain was fifty, "If newspapers can be relied upon, that statement is correct." He did not inquire of the Navy why the numbers had dropped from 225 to 171 as he said in his affidavit, but assumed it was because of the lend-lease agreement.

Asked the names of the U.S. carriers in 1941, Richardson said the *Ranger, Yorktown, Wasp, Saratoga, Lexington,* and *Enterprise.* Brannon wanted to know about the *Hornet.* Richardson said the carrier that lugged Doolittle's B-25 crews far into the Pacific for their attack on Japan was commissioned on October 20, 1941. However, it was not on his list because it had not finished training and did not deploy until December 23, 1941.[112]

Brannon insisted that to be correct, there were seven U.S. carriers fully completed. "I seek to show this Tribunal, Mr. Witness, that the United States possessed seven aircraft carriers, six of which were on the sea ready for use, the seventh of which was fully completed but not yet put to sea." He then asked Richardson if he were correct. Sticking by his guns, Richardson said, "You would not be correct if you were talking to an informed audience." Then Richardson explained.

Taking the side of the defense, and perhaps beating Webb to the punch, the admiral suggested to Brannon that he change his question. "If you would correct your statement to eliminate 'not yet put to sea' and substitute therefore 'not ready for service,' your statement would be correct."[113] Ignoring this response, Brannon went on to the subject of the Japanese carrier *Shoho,* saying that it was commissioned after Pearl Harbor. Richardson agreed, but Brannon said he did not think Richardson stated that fact earlier. "If I failed to state it, it was because my language is not very clear," replied Richardson, playing on the dumb witness slant.

Brannon said that he sometimes had the same trouble, but went on to ask Richardson what the plane-carrying capacity of each carrier was in 1941.[114] The admiral quickly found that information for the six carriers he listed, but did not have that number for the *Hornet.* He took a guess at ninety, however, when pressed. He said the six others could carry a total of 496 aircraft.

Webb asked where the Japanese number was in the exhibits presented, but Brannon did not give them at that moment, saying he was leading up to that point. Strangely, Richardson did not know, saying simply, "I haven't the faintest idea." He did have the displacement of each in tonnage. Brannon asked that Richardson estimate how many planes would be on each carrier.

Though Richardson said he could only give "an absurd" guess, he was asked by Brannon if he could state the comparison to the figure of American carriers. "I would be unwilling to hazard a guess," the admiral replied, saying such figures were not made available to him by the Navy Department. Brannon then asked how Richardson could say 360 at the bottom of page nine of his affidavit, and that the number of the Japanese planes participating in the Pearl Harbor attack could constitute 75 percent of the total Japanese carrier plane strength. Richardson said the estimate was on tonnage, and problems with the estimate were taken care of "by the weasel-word, 'probably.'"[115]

Brannon said the court could be certain that probably Japan had the strength of 500 aircraft. Webb quickly countered, "480," apparently having the numbers before him from Richardson's statement.[116] He told Brannon, "That is in your favor . . . 360 plus 120," figuring 75 percent of 480 was 120 planes at least on the rest of the Japanese carriers.

Brannon dropped that line of interrogation, and asked Richardson the cruising distance of an American carrier. Of course, conditions dictated much of that figure, but Richardson assured Brannon that U.S. Navy ships had maximum cruising radius in comparison with other ships in the world.

Asked if a carrier could have left Hawaii, touched the coast of Japan, and returned without refueling, Richardson, after Robinson objected to the line of questioning, said it depended upon the speed. "But," he added, "the ability to refuel at sea had been so developed that they could have done it twice without a return." It was a confusing attempt by Brannon to compare carrier fleets, and it ended abruptly when Webb called for a fifteen-minute recess at 10:45 A.M.

After the break, Brannon's purpose became clear. He still guided Richardson through some questions about Japanese carriers and their inability to travel to Hawaii without refueling. Therefore, he concluded the carriers were not constructed with an attack on Hawaii in mind. Webb intervened, but agreed that it was a matter for argument. Still, he forbade continuance on that subject.

Brannon then asked Richardson if he was familiar with the three Vinson plans pertaining to shipbuilding. Robinson pointed out to Webb that there was nothing in Richardson's presentation that mentioned Vinson's work and bills supporting ship construction. For the first time since Richardson took the stand, Webb actually conferred for some time with other members on the bench. He returned to the microphone and said the question was allowable.[117]

According to what he wrote in his book later, Richardson was familiar with the Naval Parity Act of March 27, 1934, and the May 17, 1938, Vinson Naval Expansion Act, which authorized a two-ocean U.S. Navy to be constructed over the upcoming decade. In fact, as proved by his meeting in Washington in the summer of 1940, he knew Vinson well enough to have talked confidentially about Stark's relationship with Roosevelt.[118] Vinson and Richardson had conferred many times about naval functions and budgetary needs.

Instead of relating all this to Brannon, Richardson replied, "I am not thoroughly familiar with the proposals and plans for the increase of the Navy."[119] He was then asked about a so-called Stark Plan. "I never heard of the plan until this minute," Richardson said slyly. He knew that Brannon was talking about *Rainbow Five,* of which he assisted in draft form in late 1940. Perhaps if Brannon had pursued and worded the question pertaining to *Orange* Plans and the *Rainbow* Plans, Richardson would have been specific. Along this path, Brannon would have shown the court that the U.S. had also preconceived plans to go through to Japan if attacked.[120]

Richardson told Brannon he would answer as best he could questions on the Vinson plans. After saying he was not really familiar with the subject, Richardson went into detail about the first Vinson plan. He agreed with Brannon that the United States was in a "great shipbuilding program" during 1936 to 1941. Brannon again went to aircraft carrier numbers. "Can you tell me how many were under construction as of December 7, 1941?" Richardson said he did not know, but would search his records. Brannon continued, but Richardson stopped him by saying, "Wait a minute. I was prepared to give you a reply." Brannon said, "Pardon me. I didn't know that you meant at this moment!"

Richardson and his team had been quick to find the figures. The United States had under construction, in all categories, two million tons as compared to 500,000 by Japan. Brannon went back to questions on the number of ships, referring to what the Washington Treaty said about computing a nation's strength. Brannon then asked Richardson, "As of December 7, 1941, which was more powerful, the Japanese Navy or the American Navy?"[121]

Richardson stated the obvious, "In the Pacific Ocean the Japanese Navy was far superior." He guessed maybe 10 to 50 percent stronger. When asked about the percent of the U.S. Fleet being located in the Pacific in 1940, Richardson replied that it was the vast majority of the combat fleet.

For some reason, Brannon brought into the discussion the fuel carrier USS *Langley*. Richardson said she had no combatant use, but had been of "inestimable value" for fight deck training and development. She could only have been used to transport aircraft, he added, thus she was not on the list discussed earlier. "Seaplane tenders" were not included, he said, when pressed further.

Brannon was trying to point out that the Japanese *Hosho* was in about the same position in the Japanese fleet. Its construction had been completed in 1922. Brannon asked that if Richardson had known the *Hosho* was used only for training, would he have left it off the list. "I would not. The exhibit #918 is a Japanese document, and I know nothing about [the *Hosho*]. I would not alter it."[122]

Webb was antsy again, telling Brannon to stop asking Richardson questions whose answers had already been put into record. Apparently, it took some time for Richardson and his team to dig up the answers from their files, and the morning testimony was boring Webb.[123]

Brannon gave up on the subject. He then asked Richardson about his letters to Stark that were presented into evidence a year earlier at the Joint Congressional Hearings. Quickly, Webb asked him to explain his point. Brannon said he hoped to lay a foundation for use of the material. He wanted to show the American attitude in 1940.

Webb thought it a waste of time. "We don't want to get out of the witness what we are going to hear later [or read] when the [U.S. Joint Congressional Hearings] report is tendered." He asked Brannon if he expected Richardson to say anything new. Brannon said not thus far, but wanted to elaborate a minute. "Oh, save time if you can," retorted Webb.[124]

Brannon still wanted to show that the United States had plans in regard to naval preparations against Japan. After some more talk with Webb and the court's monitor about terminology, Brannon admitted he had not read the congressional report and did not know if answers from Richardson would reveal anything new. Webb told him to move on with other questioning until he had read the forty volumes of testimony given in Washington from late 1945 to late spring 1946. Brannon's attempt to show that the United States entertained similar naval preparations as Japan during the prewar period was bogging down.

Richardson told Brannon that even though he was a witness and attended some of the hearings, he had not read all the pages. It was his opinion that the record contained references to American naval war plans, "but only slight references." Brannon then said he would check the hearings report and then come back with questions. He never did.

Moving on to Japan's plan of attack on Pearl Harbor as presented to the court the day before, Brannon pointed out there was no exact copy of the Japanese orders to carry out the plans. Richardson said the plan itself provided for the days of action. Brannon was still worried about the cut-out portions of the documents. He asked Richardson about them, but the admiral said he assumed the translator found the paper in that condition.[125]

Brannon went to prosecution's Exhibit #1265, and back to #809. He asked Richardson if these were the only two documents concerning the actual attack on Pearl Harbor. "I have, among my papers, other documents." But, he thought much of what they said had been taken from those then in front of him, and already submitted to the court. At this point, a noon recess was taken.

When court resumed at 1:30 P.M., Richardson, Robinson, and the witness team had strong reason to believe the cross-examination would continue for at least another day. Brannon wanted to know if Exhibits #809, #1252, and #1265 contained all information then on hand about the Pearl Harbor attack. Richardson answered that those documents did not contain an accurate statement of the results of the attack. Richardson told Brannon that, however, there was no known documentation, which he considered important, withheld from the court.[126]

Brannon then gave a document to Richardson. It was prepared from the recollections of a Japanese warrant officer. In it was the statement, "The Japanese Emperor will declare war on the United

States." Brannon asked Richardson to compare this impression of who could start war with the one presented the previous day placing responsibility on Nagano. The pair then went into a semantically slanted battle about plans until Brannon asked if the U.S. Navy and "the Powers" had an established procedure to prepare prearranged war plans against potential enemies. Richardson said, "Yes, in recent times."

He asked Richardson why it was not considered normal, then, for Japan to have a plan—even to attack another nation. "I think it would be quite normal in the country of Japan," he answered, "but wholly abnormal in the case of the United States, because Japan's success depended upon surprise." He was pointing out that the U.S. plans were more or less defensive or reactionary, while the Japanese plans were offensive, dealing with how and where to attack before being hit first.

Brannon again pointed to where Richardson had referred to Nagano. He wanted to know if Japanese naval officers other than Nagano did not speak these words. Richardson said that his statement contained recollections of Captain Sadatoshi Tomioka.

Tomioka and his Operations Section, Naval General Staff, presented in the summer of 1941 a long list of reasons not to approve the Hawaii plan, protesting to the General Staff and Yamamoto's Combined Fleet Staff. Tomioka feared the risky venture would diminish strength needed in the southern operations, where he thought the major objectives were focused. He felt the Pearl Harbor strike was not necessary, that the Japanese Navy could thwart any U.S. Fleet movement at the Marshall Islands.

The disagreement continued into October on board the *Nagato*. One of the leading arguments involved the number of carriers, Yamamoto wanting four involved, then six. Early that month, the General Staff moved to Yamamoto's thinking. Two new carriers, *Shokaku* and *Zuikaku,* made the decision easier, permitting two other carriers to be released for the southern operations. Yamamoto won out on his desire to use more than three carriers, especially when it became apparent that Japanese Zero fighters could actually make it from Taiwan to the Philippines and back.

This development eliminated use of more carriers for that operation. History accounts give the following scenario: Yamamoto also sent word through Captain Kameto Kuroshima to Tomioka, saying that if the General Staff still disagreed, that Yamamoto and his entire Combined Fleet staff would resign.[127]

Tomioka then took Kuroshima to see his superior, Admiral Shigeru Fukudome. They went up the command line to the vice-chief of the Naval General Staff, Ito, once chief of staff to Yamamoto. He agreed to present the case to Nagano. The threat to resign, and the thought that maybe Yamamoto was right, convinced Nagano. Kuroshima returned to the *Nagato* and Yamamoto with a written affirmation.

On November 5, 1941, Order No. 1 from the Combined Fleet, mentioned a few minutes earlier by Brannon in the trial, briefed senior Japanese officers of the impending war plans. Nagano, commander of the First Air Fleet and overall commander of the Pearl Harbor strike force, received final instructions on November 11.[128] Brannon and Richardson agreed that the general order was for more than just an attack on Pearl Harbor. It also triggered an overall movement against Allied positions in the Pacific.[129]

Brannon hounded again, saying that if the statement was from Tomioka, then "they were not the words of Nagano. Is that true?" Richardson just replied, "They may have been or they may not have been." The admiral finally agreed that he was unable to produce sufficient authority to warrant his attributing a direct statement to Nagano. Brannon finally had won a point.[130]

He moved on to ask Richardson why the U.S. Fleet was moved to Hawaii in 1940. Robinson jumped on this question as being improper cross-examination. Brannon said he had asked this line of questioning earlier in the courtroom to a witness from the State Department. "I would like to be allowed to proceed," he said. Webb thought this procedure was not proper in most of the British Commonwealth, but was in Canada. He overruled Robinson, and Brannon continued.

Richardson told about the fleet exercises. Robinson objected again when Brannon asked why the fleet was retained at Pearl

Harbor. But, the prosecution lost the argument that Richardson was there just to present the Navy case. Brannon wanted to know more. Richardson said the fleet was there upon higher orders, that President Roosevelt had "stated that in his opinion it exercised a restraining influence on the action of Japan."[131]

Surprisingly, Brannon closed his time with Richardson at that point. He gave way to the Japanese counsel for Nagano. However, Webb said the Japanese representative could have put his questions through Brannon, and refused the application.

McDermott then stood, as counsel for Shimada, the Japanese Navy Minister from 1941 to 1944. Before assuming that position he was commander of the China Fleet in 1940 and vice-chief of the Naval General Staff from 1935 to 1937. He was the one who authorized the surprise attack on Pearl Harbor. Later, units under his overall command massacred Allied prisoners of war, transported them aboard "hellships," and killed surviving members of torpedoed Allied ships.

McDermott went to the third part of the Richardson Navy presentation, the one discussing espionage. "Is it not a fact that these same records [presented into evidence earlier] disclose that the United States had established a like system of surveillance, reconnaissance and espionage?" In fact, he thought all nations did likewise.

Richardson agreed to a degree. He answered simply. "The United States has always made it possible for representatives of foreign nations to see more of what we are doing than Japan has ever permitted."[132] McDermott wanted to know more specifically what went on during the decade before Pearl Harbor. Richardson said no records disclosed that the United States ever was successful in a careful and well-defined policy of consular espionage. He did not mention interception of diplomatic messages.

McDermott began to infer that the knowledge of the U.S. Fleet being at Pearl Harbor would be a serious naval concern to the Japanese. Richardson agreed, though he wrote and spoke many times that the fleet represented little threat to Japan's military leadership.

McDermott then tried to ask Richardson more questions about the use of lights as signals, saying that it was a normal practice in modern warfare. Webb did not see the relevance, and ruled in favor of a Robinson objection. McDermott then asked Richardson what a "star boat" was. "I don't mean anything by it," commented the admiral. "I suppose it meant something to the Japanese."

He explained that from the text of the message presented in the affidavit, it meant the boat was to bear a star at the head of the sail.[133] McDermott dropped this confusing direction, and asked Richardson about the percentage of Japanese Navy power over the United States. He seemed confused that the U.S. Fleet would flaunt itself by standing at Hawaii if it was so inferior in power to the Japanese Navy.

"Do the records show why this flash of Naval power [at Hawaii] was made in the face of strained relations between Japan and the United States?" asked McDermott. Richardson had long wanted the answer to that question, but felt it once lay in the laps of Hornbeck, Hopkins, Hull, Stimson, Welles, Knox, Stark, maybe Marshall, and certainly Roosevelt. "In so far as I know, they do not," he answered.[134]

At this point McDermott sat down. Logan told the tribunal there was no further cross-examination. However, Robinson wanted to clean up a couple of points on redirect.

He went over the tonnage figures, and Richardson gave an opinion, explaining why the United States increased construction rapidly beginning in 1939. "My belief is that the United States felt that it was confronted with a serious world situation where she must be prepared to defend herself."[135]

Robinson turned his attention to the USS *Langley* argument. Webb quickly answered the question by saying it was not included in the Richardson figures because it was a tender. Robinson politely asked if Richardson had anything else to say about it.

Richardson told the court that the *Hosho* was built as a carrier, and was the first ship in the world to have electric drive. He called it an experimental ship. On the other hand, the *Langley* was built as the USS *Jupiter,* a collier, commissioned in 1911.

Later she was converted to a carrier. Richardson said he last saw her in 1936, after she became a sea tender.[136] Her forward flight deck had been removed. She had additions, like a boom to pluck planes from the water, but the admiral said if his memory was correct, Japan was informed of the change to the classification.[137]

Robinson then told Webb that he was through, and asked leave for the witness. So, even before the mid-afternoon break of the second day, the Navy presentation was over.[138] Not only was Richardson through, Brigadier Henry Grattan Nolan, prosecutor from Canada, announced to the tribunal that this phase of the trial was over. The court would then hear about matters that occurred after the outbreak of the Pacific War.

On November 28, Richardson packed up for his final trip across the Pacific, leaving a bit after 8:00 P.M. from Tokyo. Flying home had to be both a time of relief and a moment of sadness for Richardson. He had performed his last official duty for his beloved Navy, and would see Pearl Harbor only one more time.[139] For forty-eight years since leaving the drugstore work in Texas, he had enjoyed his career. He took another exit physical and received orders relieving him of all active duty.[140]

Richardson was detached for the last time on January 2, 1947, and received a note from Forrestal, written on a letter to him from Keenan, thanking the Navy for allowing Richardson to testify. "He performed in a forthright and efficient manner," Forrestal wrote at the bottom. "My congratulations to you on another job well-done."[141]

CHAPTER TWENTY-NINE

Richardson Finally Free to Raise Roses
Others Do Not Easily Survive Retirement

One day a lady from down the street walked by the Richardson home. She stopped, admiring the beauty of the roses and the flowerbeds. For some time, she had noticed the same man, dressed in overalls, working in the yard. Otherwise, she had never seen him around the modest home located not too far from the Naval Observatory.

This particular day, she was desperate for help. Her own yard needed some improvement. "Excuse me," she said to the man. It was the admiral. He rose up from his work, still erect in his seventh decade of life. "Yes m'am," he drawled.

"I have been admiring the work you do on this yard," she said. "Would you have time to work on mine too? I am willing to pay your going rate."

The admiral never broke stride. "Well," he said slowly, looking her directly in the eye, pulling out his pipe and not breaking a smile. "I just can't do that. You see, I have an unusual working agreement at this house. I get to sleep with the lady who lives here."

Embarrassed, the neighbor left, but only after he explained the situation a bit more. The neighbors, a few offspring of his peers, and what few Richardson kinfolks exist, still laugh at the story, which more than one says was true.[1]

Next door to the Richardsons lived a former Navy couple, Mr. and Mrs. Charles Carter Anderson. May would send over lilacs at times from her "botanic" gardens. The Andersons lost their only child, a son, at Iwo Jima during World War II. Later, the Andersons befriended sisters Jean and Guinevere Griest, and treated them as part of the family. Guinevere inherited the home, and in 1969 moved into it, observing the Richardsons during the last years of their lives. She says that May was an expert at growing roses, and that one strain May created was even named for her.[2]

Richardson plantings now tall: Jean and Guinevere Griest inherited the house to the northeast of the Richardson home in Washington, DC, and have many fond memories of their next-door neighbors. The azalea they are under was what Guinevere called a "domestic," while May went into nearby woods to dig up the now house-high holly seen behind the sisters. There was an outside, wood-decked sitting area on that side of the Richardson house. "We would look out, and if he was walking on it, one of us would comment, 'The admiral is walking the deck,'" said Jean. It is now an enclosed patio. (Photo by Skipper Steely in 2004, Steely Collection, James G. Gee Library, Commerce, Texas)

The Richardsons enjoyed cooking for friends and guiding them about town. After Isabel Dean Short's mother died in 1958, she moved to Falls Church in northern Virginia to be closer to her son and daughter-in-law. At times, the three and Dean's children would drive over to the Richardson home to eat and visit. "Admiral Richardson was what we called a gourmet cook," said Mrs. Dean Short.[3] "He and May were very warm and welcoming," remembers granddaughter Emily Short Thrasher. "Whenever we three children visited his house, we wanted to see the Venus Fly Trap eat a fly," she added. "He would always take us out in the back yard and try to get a fly for us. We also enjoyed watching him shuffle cards— he was great with a deck of cards and could do lots of tricks.[4]

A cousin from the Ladonia, Texas, side of the family kept in contact through the years. Her family lived at the other end of the world, Tulia, Texas, but when Richardson visited Moss in Canyon, the two would travel over to see the William Howard Wingo family. Their daughter, Elizabeth Banks, remembers seeing Richardson there in the spring of 1946 when she was sixteen.

"I was bold enough to call up the Richardsons on a 1950 visit to Washington," Elizabeth recounted. "They were very hospitable and charming hosts." She said the red-bricked house in Georgetown was very comfortable. "May had a reputation in the family for elegance, which I felt was well borne out by the colored toilet paper in my bathroom!" She stayed two or three nights after "Otto met me at Union Station and dropped me off at the Corcoran Gallery and the Smithsonian. But, he accompanied me to Mount Vernon, which he seemed to enjoy, especially the gardens." She continued, "They were so cordial and put me at ease so. They laughed at some story about their maid's having been up to some voodoo involving their shoe heels."

Elizabeth said that May gave her a two-inch-square carved ivory pendant that has always "been a favorite of mine." She said, "It may have been a bit forward for me just to drop in on the relatives, but I'm glad I did." She was not the first nor last, and the admiral and May seemed to thrive on guests.[5]

On one of the admiral's visits to Tulia with Moss in 1955, the newspaper got wind he was in town. Asked how he spent his time post-Navy, Richardson quickly answered, "Carrying out orders of higher authority," meaning he listened to May and followed her schedule. He admitted that he did much of the family shopping, of course under her direction. He said he seldom listened to the radio or read much anymore.

Moss told the newspaper, "I am justly proud of the accomplishments of my baby brother." She was overwhelmingly Methodist, and more than likely on the drive over and back attempted again to "convert" her sibling.[6] She did not need to. Though in none of his letters or in his book does Richardson indicate he is driven by the guidance of a divine creator, he quoted James Russell Lowell's, "The Present Crisis," at the end of his book. "And behind the dim unknown standeth God within the shadow, keeping watch above His own."[7]

Admiral Eugene H. Farrell and his wife visited the Richardsons during the late 1950s. "He was a Texas gentleman of the old school," Farrell said. Richardson told the Farrells and the two friends with them that this was the darkest day of his life. His ambition to be published by *Reader's Digest* had been dashed by a rejection. It was a military anecdote that, if accepted, would have paid the admiral five dollars!

He read it to the group. It was about an inspection that Hart had made of his flagship, and related to Richardson. Hart had been displeased about the crew's galley in the USS *Augusta*. The pots and pans were not sparkling clean. He expressed his annoyance. When he later arrived in the officers' galley, things were opposite. Everything was spotless. Hart sent for the crew's supply officer to show him how things should look.

The cook was asked to explain how it was done. The Chinese employee revealed his secret:

> "Velly simple, Commander. Cook in tin. Serve in tin. Save pot for Admiral's inspection."

After everyone had finished laughing, Richardson read the magazine editor's reply.

Dear Admiral Richardson:
We regret that your anecdote does not conform to our editorial policy, which is to never publish any material alluding to race, religion, creed or color.[8]

His "charming" sense of humor was not lost on the Farrells or their friends, but went over the heads of the cautious editors.

That maid and live-in caretaker who performed "voodoo" was Azalea Dawson. She was the recipient of cherries the admiral picked from trees down on the tidal basin when stepniece Clareda Purser visited the Richardsons in the 1940s. He may have been imposing looking, "but he never scared me," laughed Clareda when interviewed. "I was in awe of him," she added, especially after he was appointed to be "Admiral of the Fleet." She related that he and May visited Paris several times in her early life, always going to Detroit to see Jessie. She would give long blessings at mealtime, and "he would finally say, 'Sister. The breakfast will get cold before you are through.'"[9]

"He would tell us funny stories," she added. "I remember once he told about a time when he was driven to a meeting. When his car pulled up, a group of sailors were waiting for a cab they had called earlier. Uncle Otto's chauffeur went around and opened the door. The sailors, thinking it was their cab, began to enter! The first, once in the car, saw the Admiral sitting there. Performing the proper military rituals, he excused himself and exited the other side of the car. The next sailor following did likewise. The group filed through Uncle Otto's car and, in fear, disappeared!" Richardson thought it quite amusing.

Clareda stated that May's only concern with her husband's retirement was that he would take command of her domain. She was not accustomed to a regulated schedule. He apparently took orders, and stayed out of the way.

This is the best description of the way the couple lived after the post-World War II and post-Pearl Harbor investigations. Life was full of storytelling, cooking, golfing, some fishing, and much gardening.

Short and Kimmel did not fare as well. Neither did Richardson's friend Safford. While Richardson spent the 1950s growing roses and systematically writing on a book with Dyer, Short died a tired man while working in Dallas in 1949.[10] Kimmel fought on to have their names cleared. Kimmel was so engrossed in the subject that his son Tom mentioned in interviews that his father would drift into the subject almost every time they conversed. Stark lived quietly a few blocks northwest of the Richardsons.

Safford spent the rest of his life trying to prove that one of the "wind" messages, commonly called the *East Wind Rain* message, was actually seen in Washington, and thus sent to Hawaii.[11] He was sure it predicted an attack. Some sources thought it unimportant anyway. Even if it had been received, Hawaii would not have reacted differently. The captured bomb plot intelligence was of more importance.[12] However, Safford was determined to clear his mind and locate the document. He died in 1973 at age seventy-nine. By the end of the hearings, most people viewed him as a crank full of hallucinations. McCollum said that perhaps Safford did see a weather report, but that it was only a bona fide prediction of the conditions. He did not think highly of Safford's abilities, it seems. Safford knew "a smattering of Japanese" from his work with codes and ciphers, McCollum told his oral interviewer in 1973, but "he himself was not a trained linguist." McCollum believed most weather messages were real, and if coded, could mean many things. McCollum said he never saw the message come in, and just thought Safford later had a beef toward the Navy. He added that Safford was not in the office from Friday afternoon until the following Monday after the Pearl Harbor attack.[13]

Safford's many letters to his former translation section chief, Lieutenant Commander Alvin D. Kramer, Kimmel, senior watch officer George W. Linn, and others whom he thought could assist him in the quest to find the *Winds* message are long and full of paranoid statements. In a December 1943 letter, he told Kramer to be guarded with his answers, to just put them next to a corresponding number to the Safford questions; thus, anyone unauthorized would not know exactly what his answer meant. A month later, in another letter, Safford told Kramer, "No one in OpNav can be trusted. Premature action would only tip off the people who framed Adm. Kimmel and Gen. Short."[14] Kramer must have felt the questions were valid. Just a few days after the first letter containing fourteen questions, he sent the answers back.

The January 22, 1944, letter from Safford to Kramer is right out of a Cold War novel, unless Safford was truthful and someone really was holding out the *winds* message, and possessed a different story.[15] Safford claimed that on November 15, 1943, he found proof that Kimmel was framed. On December 2, he confirmed it, and on January 18, 1944, he obtained absolute proof. He continued in the second letter to Kramer with questions numbered 20 through 42. Kramer answered them all in detail. Safford was struggling for clues that might reveal the location of the weather message. The answers do give a clear picture of what Kramer was doing the day prior to the Pearl Harbor attack, much of which is depicted in *Tora! Tora! Tora!*

In 1958, Safford was awarded $100,000 by the government for at least twenty cryptographic systems he devised or helped create.[16] He felt better when Senator Leverett Saltonstall of Massachusetts called him "the man responsible more than any other for keeping American wartime codes safe." If he and Richardson talked during World War II or during the 1950s, no one knows. One of Gordon Prange's editors, Dr. Donald Goldstein, thought Safford was henpecked by his artist wife Ruth, and that the winds execute message was a "red herring."[17]

Dr. John Taylor of the National Archives assisted Safford after 1945 in his continual search for the message. "He was here often. Then, he came in on a Friday one week, healthy and researching, and Monday I found out he had died of a heart attack." Some say he was actually doing research on the Amelia Earhart event. Whatever, unlike Richardson and Murphy, he was not very wealthy in his old age, but he left what he had to an animal clinic.

Hanify was convinced that Safford was not in error about the purported December 4, 1941, message, which the public first heard about on December 14, 1945, when summaries of the Hart Inquiry, the Hewitt Investigation, and the Navy Court of Inquiry were turned over to the Joint Congressional Pearl Harbor

Committee members.[18] A radioman named Ralph Briggs concurred. However, Stark said he never heard of the message, and no Army or Navy file was found.

Richmond "was never euphoric about Safford," wrote Edward R. "Ned" Kimmel about his father's effort to find the truth.[19] "He [Safford] violated Navy regulations and Federal law to come to my father in New York," wrote Kimmel's son about the meeting between the two. Safford disclosed the intercepted messages. However, even in 2001 when contacted, Richmond still felt that Safford was a "loner" who was obsessed. "He had no one who could support him," said the eighty-eight-year-old Richmond. On the other hand, he believed that King exercised much effort to keep information quiet. "There was a lot of Navy stonewalling," added Richmond. "The Navy was run from the White House." He said that in the early testimonies, he and Stark never knew much about *"MAGIC,"* and that the committee did not have that information.[20]

Whatever the perception of Safford by others, Richardson believed in his work. Before Safford was paid for his inventions, Richardson wrote, "His country and his Navy owe him a great debt of gratitude, which neither has fully paid."[21]

Marshall sailed right through all the controversy, surviving six and a half days of congressional testimony. He held his reputation despite many books and movies that contradict his thoughts and answers before committees. He and Stark got away with "amnesia" about their whereabouts on December 6, 1941, and much about what they did the next morning. Marshall was doomed, as Short once said, to never writing his memoirs. His wife did, but they are very mundane.

Because of his remaining respect for his former friend and boss, Richardson would not let his book be published until Stark died. Stark's unofficial biographer was very kind and noncontroversial. Still, Richardson was sure that Stark had a few regrets as to his part in the entire Pearl Harbor matter.[22]

Some of the "senior" admirals always mentioned by Richardson, and a few of his 1940 staff, came to the rescue. Theobald wrote, "The Fleet based in Hawaiian waters was neither powerful enough nor in the necessary strategic position to exert any positive influence upon Japan's plans for Eastern Asia." He thought basing the fleet in the Philippines would have accomplished more, but only if it was adequate. He pointed out that Hawaii to Formosa was farther than from New York City to Gibraltar, evidence that the Pacific Theater was gigantic.[23]

In Texas, the *Dallas Morning News* editorialized on March 31, 1954, about the Theobald book, saying, "It is the first direct charge that President Franklin D. Roosevelt invited the attack at that point." It went on. "The President saw the necessity of entering the war against Germany. He maneuvered Japan into a position where it had to fight." The *News* wrote that Stimson noted, however, "The problem was to get Japan to fire the first shot." The editor said this must have been the reason for the "inexcusable blackout on information to our commanders in the Pacific."

The newspaper added that it was difficult to believe that those in Washington expected the first blow to be Pearl Harbor, as Theobald asserted. "Whether Theobald is right or wrong, the circumstances of December 7, 1941, constitute a sorry story."[24] The editorial concluded, stating that nothing could excuse the raw decision to crucify Kimmel and Short, not as long as the stern words of the Ninth Commandment stand: "Thou shalt not bear false witness [slander] against thy neighbour" (Ex. 20:16 KJV).

The editorial comments eventually filtered to Richardson's mailbox. This time he did not write a letter and file it away—he mailed it to his home state:

> To The Dallas News:
> I am now seventy-five and one-half years old and have never before written to a newspaper, but I can not refrain from writing to commend your paper and the writer for the article, "Why of Pearl Harbor," which appeared March 31.
> I have read thousands of words on this subject. I have listened for days to sworn testimony on the same subject, and with a sound background of personal knowledge. I have thought of it for thirteen years.
> Your editorial is the sanest, most unprejudiced, and comes closest to the truth of all the statements I have read or heard and I especially like the restraint manifest by the last sentence with

respect to the stern admonition of the Ninth Commandment.

A copy of this article was sent to me from the city in which I was born and from which I was appointed to the United States Naval Academy: Paris, Texas.

James O. Richardson

Curious for his thoughts about Theobald's work, Richardson wrote Standley, who was then living at the age of eighty-two in Coronado, California. In the letter, Richardson gave his own opinions; even charting the dates he thought certain individuals became dishonest about the Pearl Harbor event. "I always knew that you wondered why I signed the Roberts Report, because you knew as well as I that it did not present a true picture," Standley wrote back. He added that the Theobald publicity and explanations have "resulted in getting my explanation off my chest."

He mentioned that a friend told him about a Richardson article about to be published in *Newsweek,* and wondered if that were true. He added, "I also agree with you entirely as to the lack of honesty of the individuals" mentioned in Richardson's letter, but said, "I am wondering how you arrived at the dates in question?" Quickly, he extended remarks about the Roosevelt administration, "I assure you that my association with this group was one of the most unpleasant episodes in my entire Naval career." He told newswriters later in life, when he was writing his own book, that he was drawn into the Roberts Commission before realizing that the directive was designed to protect Roosevelt.[25]

Bloch never wrote a book on his memories, but in testimony before Congress he verified all of Richardson's worries about the fleet being stationed at Pearl Harbor. In his letter to Richardson in early March of 1942, before he was detached from Hawaii to the General Board, he said he felt sorry for Kimmel and Short, but understood the logic of the Roberts Commission. "I think both you and I are very lucky, because the same thing might well have happened to either or both of us."[26] He added there were many other things he wished to write, but "it is better to make an endeavor to be discreet for once in my life."

Murphy, who remained a close confidant and friend with

Richardson, became part of a scene later portrayed in the movie, *Tora! Tora! Tora!* When the war warning came in November 27, 1941, he was summoned to a meeting with: Smith, Kimmel's chief of staff; McMorris; DeLany; and probably Layton. They gathered in Kimmel's office and carefully heard him read the dispatch. Then, it was passed around the room for each to look at. Murphy said that he did not really get a complete picture of Kimmel's reaction. "None of us had had time to study the message in any detail." Kimmel said he would hold a conference that afternoon with his principal commanders.[27]

Murphy thought that Calhoun was at the 4:00 P.M. meeting with the same group, and that Captain J. B. Earle, chief of staff for Bloch, was there representing the Fourteenth Naval District. Murphy remembered that the decision was to reinforce Wake Island particularly, with planes and radar gear, and to send some planes to Midway. The carriers were designated for that assignment, and it was done quietly.

When asked in 1944 what his views three years earlier were toward a surprise attack, Murphy said, "I did not think that such an attack would be made." He said he thought such a move by the Japanese would "be utterly stupid." He said he had expressed doubt that the Japanese would attack the Philippines. Even if they attacked Thailand and Malaya, or the Dutch East Indies, at that time he doubted the United States would have declared war. Thus, why attack Pearl Harbor and bring in the enemy immediately? "It was not necessary for them to do so," he explained. If battleships had not been sunk at Pearl Harbor, Murphy did not feel that in December of 1941 the U.S. Fleet could have affected any Japanese movement south. "I thought it was suicide for us to attempt, with an inferior Fleet, to move into the Western Pacific."

When asked if he advocated moving the fleet to the West Coast instead of placing it at Hawaii, Murphy testified that he once did, when he worked for Richardson. "I did not advocate it, as well as I recall, later because I thought the matter had been settled."

Murphy concluded his testimony by stating, "The Commander-in-chief of the Pacific Fleet was confronted with an almost irreconcilable situation in that he had a Fleet which was badly in need of training and materiel improvement. I do not believe that any force can maintain, for a long period, an attitude of complete defensive readiness without severe loss of morale." This was spoken like one who had worked for Richardson for a long time.

Layton became famous when he told Kimmel that he had no idea where the Japanese carriers were. Kimmel said, "You mean, they might be coming around Diamond Head right now?" Layton's 1985 book is a careful, more in-depth study of the decoding and message-processing side of the argument. His remarks before the hearings did emphasize his belief that a large amount of the captured messages held in Washington had not been utilized, or collated, much less disseminated.[28]

Pye testified that reactions in 1940 to the orders to stay at Hawaii were twofold: it was a move toward Japan that would incite the Japanese to take action; it was a very poor time to make such a move because the United States was not prepared. He countered that statement by saying, on the positive side, that most of the admirals thought the advantage of staying in Hawaii would be more funding for the Naval Yard there. "Thus, [the fleet] would be better prepared in the event of a war in the Pacific."[29] He, however, said that it was the general opinion that the fleet could not go past the Marshall Islands. There were no bases. The fleet, he said, could not have carried an offensive as far to the west as the Philippines.

Dyer's book with Turner does not deal with the fleet in depth, only from the point of view of what was happening in Washington in 1940 and 1941. Halsey had his comments, and Taussig tossed in a line or two after his retirement. Carney lived to be ninety-five and displayed many of the traits learned from Richardson and those of that era. He served as CNO, and "found myself unable to change my convictions, which were firmly set."

Many times, this Richardson way of thinking brought problems for Carney. But, before he died in 1990, as he often told his grandsons, "If you can learn to say it on paper, or on your feet, whatever your chosen profession you will be successful."[30] Like Richardson, after retirement he stayed busy with many projects, and wrote articles until his last year of life.

Historian Paolo E. Coletta used Bellinger's unpublished manuscript, written in the late 1950s, for a book in 1987. The background story is sometimes factually wrong, but the comments by Bellinger on various subjects are useful.[31] Bellinger testified before the Joint Congressional Hearings, and emphasized many times that he felt the blame was as much on the president, the Navy Department, and the War Department as it was on Kimmel and Short.

Also with no definitive footnote, Bellinger said the Pearl Harbor attack "was a deep-dyed, deliberate plan to get this country into war with Japan and Germany by needling the Japanese into making the first war move." He based this statement on his own experience—the lack of proper buildup of the patrol force. Also, "in my opinion, Roosevelt and his cohorts criminally failed to keep Admiral Kimmel informed of information that was available—information that the simplest mind would have known was of vital importance to the protection of the Pacific Fleet."

In a complicated set of events after the Japanese attack, Hart scattered his Asiatic command, and took over a combined fleet of American, British, Dutch, and Australian ships called ABD Afloat. This was an unworkable organization, and on February 5, 1942, Hart received word from King that he was relieved. He left Java on February 15, and two weeks later the Japanese annihilated the remaining Allied naval force in the Far East. He returned to Washington, but was only given a menial job, chairman of the Naval Awards Board.

Hart retired in October of 1942. In the first half of 1944, he was back on active duty with the assignment to take Pearl Harbor testimony. He then assisted Stark with his presentation before the Naval Court of Inquiry, and he remained as part of the less important General Board. Then, Hart did every one of his peers one better. Republican Connecticut Governor Raymond E. Baldwin asked him if he wanted to fill the term of Senator Francis T. Maloney, who had died in mid-January. A month later Hart took the oath, and then faced his Navy colleagues from the other side of the desk. But, he only served the remaining two years of the term and retired. He lived until 1971, when at the age of ninety-four he died on, ironically, July 4. He wrote a bit about the 1940 and 1941 events leading up to Pearl Harbor, but mostly he was quiet like Richardson. However, his diary is full of immense opinion.

Dyer received a letter one day in late 1955 from the director of Naval History, Admiral John Heffernan, asking if he would consider compiling a book with Richardson. Heffernan thought that a good publication from Richardson's point of view would restore many of those lost CinCUS files. He offered help from Dr. Edward J. Marolda of the operational archives section.[32]

Dyer was thrilled. However, no one left behind in writing a reason why the admiral agreed to the project. Dyer sat down with the forty volumes of the Joint Congressional Pearl Harbor Hearings and read every page. "It's a major operation," he said later in an oral interview. "I'm sure there probably is not more than 20 people in the United States who have done that!" Not many more since have taken that challenge, though it is now indexed and much is posted on the Internet as of 2008.[33]

Melhorn never wrote a book about 1940, but he did have dinner with May and Admiral Richardson one night while he was in Washington. He had not fulfilled his desire to run a hospital, but during the war he did have the responsibility of overseeing medical supplies going all over the world. He was located in a big plant in New Jersey, but came to the District of Columbia once a week. He mustered up courage to ask Richardson a serious question: "If it's out of order, just consider that I haven't asked the question," he started. Richardson responded, "What is it?"

He knew. But, he listened as Melhorn said, "The whole Navy and whole country was wondering, what was your reaction on the morning of December 7?" Richardson gave him the same two answers he originally gave the General Board. He told Melhorn that after he died, his thoughts would be published.[34] Melhorn always thought that so many things about 1940, in retrospect, were peculiar. He thought it still difficult to understand many years later when interviewed.

Richardson had changed his mind about not placing his career and thoughts in print. At first, he just wanted to be at peace in his Washington, DC, gardens. The first attempt to convince him to write some memoirs failed. That came on September 13, 1948, when he received a letter from Grace G. Tully, former secretary to Roosevelt, and at that time executive secretary of the Roosevelt Memorial Foundation. With much courtesy, she asked if he would prepare a detailed memorandum of his relationship with the U.S. government and the president from 1933 through 1945.[35]

He answered her two weeks later—with two paragraphs. He told her that the drafting of such a memorandum worthy of submission "would require more time and effort than I am willing to devote to this project." He honestly said, "This decision is due to my firm belief that should I succeed in maintaining a purely objective point of view, the product would prove unacceptable to the directors of the Foundation."[36]

Miss Tully wrote again. She told Richardson that the very reasons he stated for not desiring to submit his thoughts were the foundation's reasons for collecting such materials. "Whether it be complimentary or not" was fine with the foundation.[37]

In his reply he gave three reasons he could not comply with the request: "(1) I am too lazy to devote to the undertaking the requisite time and effort; (2) I am too indifferent to care what competent scholars of the future say about Mr. Roosevelt; and (3) I am too modest to believe that what I might record would influence in any way what they may say."[38] The first two were acceptable, but the third, maybe at the age of seventy he really believed. But, at that time, few books had arrived off the presses to stimulate his mind again. The terms *"MAGIC"* and *"Purple"* were just beginning to surface and be explained to the public and to the military. He would change his mind as others began to publish thoughts on the events leading up to the attack on Pearl Harbor.

For some reason, Richardson called Miss Tully on November 15, wanting to know just why she had written to him. She explained that she had asked hundreds of people to complete memorandums for the depository of records on the presidency. He wanted to know if he could come over to her Washington office that afternoon and discuss it some more. He seemed to be genuinely curious about who suggested that he had a story to tell. Still, he did not budge on his objections.

Before he left, he told Miss Tully that Congress thought he had "a great story to unload," but he insisted that he did not. Perhaps he did not read the headlines and stories about his own testimony in 1945. He told her that he was proud that he stuck to his "I'll be damned if I know!" answer when asked why he was fired. He added, also, that too many of the retired naval officers were "bitter old men," and that he had made up his mind, no matter what happened, not to let any disappointments make him that way. He then turned the conversation to cooking! He stated that over a period of thirty-seven years he had collected recipes, and that perhaps if he published a book, it would be a cookbook.[39]

In the last paragraph of her notes from that conversation, Miss Tully said that she felt that the admiral would never provide the foundation with a memorandum. However, she felt that he left knowing that the foundation had a sincere desire to collect friendly or unfriendly materials, and that there was no ulterior motive. For Richardson, it was hard to shake his suspicion of Roosevelt and his associates.[40]

Richardson was more interested in planning the fiftieth anniversary gathering of his Navy Class of 1902, set for May 2, 1952. He was class president. Only fifteen of the twenty-two living members made the function for the class photograph, but an equal number of wives and widows were present.[41]

Dyer suffered two strokes that took him into retirement in February of 1955, but he by no means became less active. His wife and doctor placed him on a strict diet, and he began to write. In January of 1956, Dyer began his interviews at the Richardson residence, and subsequently researched over 70,000 dispatches in the archives and records available near his Annapolis home. Much of the naval material was then located in the old Navy

Department complex on Constitution Avenue. "Admiral Richardson cooperated 100 percent," said Dyer.

The pair started with a detailed outline. Dyer visited the Richardson home every other week. "We would review what I had reduced to draft form," Dyer explained to readers of the book. "Many times, holding the outline in hand, he would relate a further part of his story."[42] Richardson would retain the double-spaced draft at times, scribbling in clarifications, suggested leads, and corrections. When they arrived at the part about his relationship and meetings with Roosevelt, Richardson did the writing himself. Dyer used, now and then, pieces of what was left of the "reduced" diary, but he was given only pages from Richardson's "little black book." Dyer returned the borrowed pages. "I never even saw the diary," he wrote in the preface on December 11, 1972. Dyer completed the manuscript in 1958, and at that time he took payment from the Historical Division of the Navy Department.

At the end of his book, Richardson made note that he had given long consideration to Miss Tully's request ten years earlier, but had declined. "Miss Tully did not yield," he wrote. "But, at the time I stuck to my guns. Now that this document has been prepared, perhaps Miss Tully will consider her polite requests have been fulfilled."[43] Stark died in the late summer of 1972, at the age of ninety-two. Richardson was not as clear mentally at that time, so publication of the book was begun.[44] The next year it was available for sale. Miss Tully died in 1984, having seen her request come to fruition.

Richardson's story was finally out in public.

CHAPTER THIRTY

40-40-20
Blame for Pearl Harbor Attack

Dyer and Richardson hashed over the blame for Pearl Harbor many times during the months they wrote and edited *On the Treadmill to Pearl Harbor*. In the end, Dyer, after discussing for pages of oral interview what he thought Kimmel should have done, apportioned the responsibilities for the attack on Pearl Harbor at 40-40-20. "I think 40% of it belonged to Kimmel, 40% belonged to Stark and 20% to the President."[1]

The interviewer, John T. Mason, Jr., commented to Dyer, "The ultimate decision had to rest with him [Roosevelt] because of his decision vis-à-vis Richardson?" Dyer said simply, "That's right. That's a fact."

Richardson took the accusations and threw them around further, finding it always disgusting that the civilian leadership was never willing to share the huge shame heaped upon Kimmel and Short. Richardson loved his Navy too much to carry on the subject. He always thought that "simple obedience to orders is not enough," but he knew to be true what also was told young sailors. "You should not remain in the Navy if you are not prepared to bear up and carry on under what you conceive to be a grave injustice." Richardson did his best to balance the two suggestions. It was easier said than done.

Richardson was left out of history reports and books up until 1973 because he would not allow his manuscript full of firsthand statements to be published.[2] "I would like to be assured, in writing, that no one except those mentioned [the current CNO, Dyer, and Heffernan] will have access to this record during my lifetime," he wrote before finishing the book. He added that when Dyer delivered the "record of my experiences, the director of Naval History will place it in a sealed envelope which will not be opened, without my consent, during my lifetime."[3]

He eventually reneged on that condition, but only slightly.

Richardson was content with what he had accomplished, and saw no reason to rock the boat while alive. From his origins in the dust of the tree-lined streets of Paris, Texas, and from behind the counter at the local drugstore, he toured the world. He testified before congressional committees about budgets, saw the beginnings of what became the Tea Pot Dome scandal, met with presidents, guided the Amelia Earhart search and the USS *Panay* aftermath, wrote war plans, commanded the U.S. Fleet, managed the Navy Relief Society, helped formulate the future of the U.S. Air Force and Department of Defense, and testified in the Japan War Crimes Trial. He was able to fish at places never known by his hometown friends, and played on golf courses many times more difficult than any in his home state.

Most of all, he did all this with his best friend, the lady of the house—May Fenet Richardson.

Notes

Preface

1. B. H. Lidell Hart, *History of the Second World War* (New York: G. P Putnam's Sons, 1970), 205. Also called the Washington Naval Limitations Treaty of 1921. Hughes also had a Paris, Texas, kinship connection.

2. Library of Congress (LoC) Manuscript Division, George C. Dyer Papers, Box 9 and 10 are many of Richardson's official papers, moved there from the Naval Historical Center. Typed originals of some of *On the Treadmill to Pearl Harbor* are located there with Richardson's editing marks.

3. Directed by Richard Fleischer, Kinji Fukasaku, and Toshio Masuda, it is written by Ladislas Farago, Larry Forrester, Ryuzo Kikushima, Akira Kurosawa, Hideo Oguni, and with references to work by Gordon Prange. It was released on September 3, 1970.

Chapter 1: The Greatest "I Told You So" in U.S. History

1. Admiral James Otto Richardson, *On the Treadmill to Pearl Harbor,* ed. Admiral George C. Dyer (Washington, DC: Department of the Navy: 1973), 451.

2. LoC, Dyer Papers, Box 10, Folder 8.

3. *Paris News,* December 5, 1941.

4. Richardson, *Treadmill,* 435.

5. LoC, Dyer Papers, Box 10, Folder 8, Class of 1934. Thesis dated February 1, 1934.

6. James Otto Richardson, "The Relationship in War of Naval Strategy, Tactics and Command," thesis, Senior Class of 1934 (Newport, RI: Department of Intelligence, Naval War College, May 7, 1934), 4. Also to be found with Richardson notes scribbled on pages in LoC, Dyer Papers, Box 10, Folder 8.

7. Richardson, "Relationship," 4.

8. Ibid., 5-6.

9. Ibid., 9.

10. Ibid., 11.

11. Paul Stillwell, ed., *Air Raid: Pearl Harbor!: Recollections of a Day of Infamy* (Annapolis MD: Naval Institute Press: 1981), 48.

12. Richardson, *Treadmill,* 453.

13. See Richardson *Treadmill,* 279, 441, 459; and Stillwell, 103. See on the Internet: "Hyper War: A Hypertext of the Second World War," in Appendix I: "Principal Civilian Officials and Naval Officers in Command, 7 December 7, 1941-September 2, 1945," at this address in 2001: http://helios.oit.unc.edu/hyperwar/USN/USN-Chron/USN-Chron-I.html.

14. LoC, Dyer Papers, Box 10, Folder 8.

15. Richardson, *Treadmill,* x. The manuscript was completed in 1958, prefaced by Dyer in December of 1972, and sold through the U.S. Government Printing Office to the public in 1972. It cost $8.85 per copy.

Chapter 2: "At Home They Called Me Otto"

1. Steely Collection, research on Hawkins file. Letters back and forth between Captain J. O. Richardson and George L. Hawkins of Hattiesburg, Mississippi, April and May 1931.

2. Mary Reid, *Holland's Magazine of the South,* October 1940, 7.

3. Steely Collection, Betty Dill File. Notes from her genealogy files. Letter from Mrs. Shirley Wagstaff. See also W. P. Howell, *History of the 25th Alabama Infantry Regiment,* ed. Steven L. Driskell (Wilmington, NC: Broadfoot Publishing Company, 1997).

4. Steely Collection, Betty Dill File.

5. Reid, 7. Admiral Richardson thought that his parents were married in South Carolina.

6. Mary Claunch Lane, ed., *The 1870 Lamar County, Texas Federal Census* (Paris, TX: Privately published, 1993), 37.

7. A. W. Neville, *Paris News,* August 6, 1944, 8.

8. This was a free white school, and named W. B. Aikin High School, but was rarely called by that label.

9. Skipper Steely and Frances Ellis, *First Church of Paris* (Wolfe City, TX: Wright Press, 1985), 94. See Alexander White Neville, *History of Lamar County* (Paris, TX: North Texas Publishing Company, 1937), 76.

10. Neville, *History of Lamar County,* 76.

11. A. W. Neville, "Backward Glances" column, *Paris News,* January 19, 1933.

12. Ibid., June 22, 1932.

13. Jake Floyd Swearingen, "History of Public Education in Lamar County" (Austin, TX: University of Texas, master's thesis), 63, or Paris City Council Minutes, August 12, 1878.

14. Steely Collection, Betty Dill File. Notes from her genealogy files. Notes from Elizabeth Moss Wingo Banks letter in 1992. Laura Wingo and Frances Richardson were daughters of Garland and Nancy J. Moss Foster. Also see, Reid, 7.

15. Steely Collection, Betty Dill File. Notes from her genealogy files. Letter in 1992 from Elizabeth Moss Wingo Banks of Duncan, Oklahoma.

16. The 1880 Federal Census, Lamar County, Texas.

17. The 1870 Federal Census of Fannin County, dated November 21, 1870, says that O. P.'s name was actually Sarah. The family lived in Precinct 3.

18. The 1880 Federal Census, Lamar County, Texas, Precinct 6, Ward 3, household 159-165.

19. The 1880 Federal Census, Lamar County, Texas, 67B.

20. Lamar County Marriage License Book, 9-242.

21. Reid, 7.

22. Neville, "Backward Glances," *Paris News,* December 7, 1932. She was in the pageant, "The Crowning of the Queen of Fame," held at the Paris Babcock Opera House in June of 1889.

23. Opie made Ogilvie come to Paris for the ceremony. She spent the rest of her life in Ottawa, coming back to Paris three times for the birth of her babies. Not one of them lived.

24. Steely Collection, J. C. Robinson File.

25. Steely Collection. Letter to Skipper Steely from Clareda Purser, Karnes City, Texas, dated March 10, 1999.

26. Neville, "Backward Glances," opinion page, *Paris News,* December 31, 1931.

27. *Paris News,* August 6, 1944.

28. Neville, "Backward Glances," *Paris News,* November 24, 1931. Also, Paris City Council Minutes, June 1889 through January 1890.

29. Neville, *Paris News,* January 12, 1935.

30. *Paris News,* October 26, 1930, 5.

31. Ibid., September 14, 1984.

32. E. L. Dohoney, Sr., *An Average American* (Paris, TX: Privately published, ca. 1900), 311.

33. *Paris Advocate,* April 1, 1911, obituary for Sue Neilson Richardson. Or, see Skipper Steely, *The Paris, Texas Scrapbook,* Comp. Betsy Mills (Paris, TX: Lamar County Genealogy Society, 1997), 135.

34. *Fort Worth Star-Telegram,* February 18, 1940, 2.

35. The *Owl* Yearbook, Paris High School, 1928, 109.

36. Neville, "Backward Glances," *Paris News,* December 23, 1955.

37. LoC, Dyer Papers, Box 10, Folder 3, Personal Correspondence. Adjutant General to James O. Richardson. Boxes 9 and 10 in the Dyer Papers consist of Admiral Richardson's personal papers.

38. LoC, Dyer Papers, Box 10, Folder 3. Cranford to Secretary of Navy, August 13, 1898.

39. General John P. Jumper actually served at a higher position than Richardson when he was chief of staff of the United States Air Force from 2001 to 2005. He had served as Commander Allied Air Forces Central Europe prior to that position. However, though he was born in Paris, he never lived there for any extensive period of time.

Chapter 3: "At the Academy They Called Me Ritchie"

1. Harold David Childs, ed., "The Class History of 1902," The 1902 *Lucky Bag* Yearbook, Volume IX, 217.

2. Felix R. McKnight, "Sailors from Texas Direct U.S. Warships in Two Oceans," *Dallas Morning News,* April 11, 1942, V-3. Also, Reid, 7. She quotes J. J. Richardson a bit differently.

3. Childs, 59.

4. Reid, 7.

5. Richardson, *Treadmill,* 68. Cited was CHBUNAV (H. C. Taylor), Annual Report, 1902, 21. Enlisted men in the Navy totaled 21,433.

6. Steely Collection, Birchie Mahaffey File. Letter was from Annapolis, dated February 6, 1899.

7. Philip W. Leon, *Bullies and Cowards: The West Point Hazing Scandal, 1898-1901* (Westport, CT: Greenwood Press, 1999).

8. Steely Collection, Birchie Mahaffey File.

9. Swearingen, 43.

10. Department of the Navy, Naval Historical Center, Internet site http://www.history.navy.mil/photos/sh-usn/usnsh-m/monong.htm. The USS *Monongahela* was a 2,078-ton steam screw sloop built at the Philadelphia Navy Yard in Pennsylvania, and was commissioned in January 1863.

11. "Plymouth [England]," Microsoft(r) Encarta(r) Online Encyclopedia 2000. http://encarta.msn.com.

12. Richardson, *Treadmill,* 446.

13. Childs, 217. Richardson was called Richie in this passage.

14. Neville, "Backward Glances," *Paris News,* December 23, 1955. Neville took this information from a September copy of the *Paris News,* but he did not give the exact date.

15. Childs, 73.

16. Ibid., 47.

17. Whitten's full name was Frances Samuel Whitten.

18. Childs, 47, 67.

19. *Annual Register, U.S. Naval Academy, Annapolis, Maryland, 57th Academic Year* (Washington, DC: Government Printing Office, 1901), 22-24.

20. Ibid., 52.

21. LoC Manuscript Division, Emory Land Papers. Admiral Land to *Army and Navy Register* (Washington, DC: Army and Navy Publishing Company, Inc.), November 26, 1934, detail of the game and the one of 1901.

22. Childs, 93. This 1905 class was twice the size of the previous year. It began with 148 members.

23. Richardson, *Treadmill,* 68. Cited was CHBUNAV (H. C. Taylor), Annual Report, 1902, 21.

24. Richardson, *Treadmill,* 72.

Chapter 4: "On Duty They Began to Call Me Joe"

1. Richardson, *Treadmill,* 69.

2. Department of the Navy, Naval Historical Center, Washington Naval Yard. On Line Selection of Photos—Navy Ships, found at http://www.history. navy.mil/photos/sh-usn/usnsh-q/pg40.htm.

3. Kemp Tolley, *Yangtze Patrol: The U.S. Navy in China* (Annapolis, MD: Naval Historical Press, 1971), 116.

4. Richardson, *Treadmill,* 71.

5. Ibid., 72.

6. LoC, Dyer Papers, Box 9, Folder 6. This folder has all of Richardson's orders through 1952. See letters of May 26 and 27, 1903, for examples of transfer denials.

7. Richardson, *Treadmill,* 73.

8. Tolley, *Yangtze Patrol,* 83. The *New Orleans* was part of Cruiser Division One, along with the *Brooklyn* and the *Albany.* LoC, Dyer Papers, Box 10, Folder 6. Richardson Diary 1902-1907, 6. He went on board the USS *New Orleans* on August 7.

9. Richardson, *Treadmill,* 75.

10. LoC, Dyer Papers, Box 10, Folder 6. Richardson Diary 1902-1907, 9. The arrival at Yokohama was on November 11, 1903.

11. Richardson, *Treadmill,* 75.

12. Ibid., 76.

13. Ibid.

14. LoC, Dyer Papers. Richardson Diary 1902-1907, 10. Richardson left the hospital May 5, went to Kobe and Nagasaki via inland sea, and on to Woosung.

15. Tolley, *Yangtze Patrol,* 58. LoC, Dyer Papers. Richardson Diary 1902-1907, 11. On January 19 Richardson noted a trip from Shanghai to Amoy, then on January 31 toward Cavite.

16. Richardson *Treadmill,* 77; also see *Dictionary of American Naval Fighting Ships* [DANFS]. LoC, Dyer Papers. Richardson Diary 1902-1907, 10.

17. LoC, Dyer Papers, Box 9, Folder 6.

18. Edward J. Marolda, ed., *FDR and the U.S. Navy* (New York: Palgrave Macmillan, 1998), 22, from a presentation by Ronald H. Spector titled "Josephus Daniels, Franklin D. Roosevelt, and the Reinvention of the Naval Enlisted Man."

19. LoC, Dyer Papers, Box 9, Folder 6. Chief of Bureau of Navigation to Richardson, August 11, 1905.

20. Richardson, *Treadmill,* 78. Cited was CHBUNAV, August 11, 1905, letter to MIDN [Midshipman] Richardson, "Naval Records Special (NRS)," microfilm file number 1M, NHD. LoC, Dyer Papers. Richardson Diary 1902-1907, 11. The target range was off Manila Bay, with competition from February 15 to February 22, 1905. See Box 9, Folder 6, for Richardson's promotion letters. Richardson was appointed ensign on May 2, 1904, but was not commissioned until February 7, 1905.

21. Richardson, *Treadmill,* 79.

22. LoC, Dyer Papers. Richardson Diary 1902-1907, 11-12. See also Box 9, Folder 6. He asked for two months leave.

23. LoC, Dyer Papers, Box 9, Folder 6.

24. LoC, Dyer Papers. Richardson Diary 1902-1907, 14-15.

25. Ibid., 16.

26. *Jane's Fighting Ships* (London, 1908), 428.

27. LoC, Dyer Papers. Richardson Diary 1902-1907, 116.

28. LoC, Dyer Papers, Box 9, Folder 6. Richardson to Commandant, February 1, 1907. There is no indication of the illness. He had no known relatives in Asheville.

29. LoC, Dyer Papers, Box 9, Folder 6. Richardson was appointed lieutenant (j.g.) on May 2, and commissioned on May 25, 1907. On leave in New York he stayed at the Hotel Breslin for three days, June 10-13, 1907.

30. Richardson, *Treadmill,* 82.

31. LoC, Dyer Papers, Box 9, Folder 6. Acting Secretary of Navy to Richardson, June 23, 1908.

32. LoC, Dyer Papers, Box 9, Folder 6. Richardson on USS *Tingey* at the Navy Yard, Norfolk, Virginia, to Secretary of Navy, June 25, 1908; and Acting Secretary to Richardson, June 28, 1908.

33. LoC, Dyer Papers, Box 9, Folder 6. Secretary of Navy to Richardson, March 16, 1909.

34. *Paris Advocate,* March 27, 1909.

35. Ron Brothers, ed., *Old City Cemetery: Lamar County, Texas* (Paris, TX:

Genealogy Society of Lamar County: 2001), Paris, Texas, records, 41.

36. Richardson, *Treadmill*, 85.

37. Ibid.

38. LoC, Dyer Papers, Box 9, Folder 6.

39. Richardson, *Treadmill*, 87, cited from letter from Lieutenant Richardson dated April 26, 1909.

40. Richardson, *Treadmill*, 87.

41. LoC, Dyer Papers, Box 9, Folder 6.

42. LoC, Dyer Papers, Box 9, Folder 6. Bureau of Navigation to Richardson, April 10, 1911.

43. Steely, *Paris Scrapbook*, 128, taken from *Paris Advocate*, January 10, 1911.

44. Steely, *Paris Scrapbook*, 132, taken from *Paris Advocate*, March 11, 1911.

45. LoC, Dyer Papers, Box 9, Folder 6. Bureau of Navigation to Richardson, May 13, 1911.

46. Marolda, 24-25.

47. Steely Collection, Mary Fenet File. Letter written about family on Scott and White Clinic, Temple, Texas, stationery.

48. LoC, Dyer Papers, Box 9, Folder 6. J. M. Bowyer, superintendent, May 5, 1911.

49. LoC, Dyer Papers, Box 9, Folder 6. Head of School of Marine Engineering to Engineer-in-Chief, May 3, 1911.

50. LoC, Dyer Papers, Box 9, Folder 6. Leave granted on September 1, 1911.

51. Letter from Mary Fenet copied for Skipper Steely.

52. Reid, 7.

53. It is sensible that May went to Ottawa, for though Opie had lost four infants, she was the only one of the family who had the experience of childbirth.

54. LoC, Dyer Papers, Box 9, Folder 6. Leave granted on July 31, with permission to leave the United States. Acting Secretary of Navy to Richardson, July 27, 1912.

55. Reid, 7.

56. See article by Don W. Thompson, "The Yukon and William Ogilvie," provided to Steely Collection, *Ogilvie Notebook,* by Suzanne de Ouden of the Yukon Archives, Whitehorse, Yukon, Canada. Also, see in the notebook an article with no author, "William Ogilvie: Hero and Scapegoat."

57. Message from Gordon Ogilvie to Skipper Steely, May 11, 2000. See Steely Collection, *Ogilvie Notebook.* See Craig Ogilvie, ed., "William Ogilvie: Gentleman of the Yukon," *Ogilvie Kith and Kin,* Volume 19, Number 1 (Batesville, AR, September 2000), 7, or *Manitoba Biography,* Book 5, 5, found in Winnipeg Manitoba Archives. He died on November 13. For his obituary see the *Winnipeg Tribune,* November 15, 1912.

58. LoC, Dyer Papers, Box 9, Folder 6. See letter of October 9, 1913.

59. LoC, Dyer Papers, Box 9, Folder 6. Navy Department to Richardson, October 9, 1913.

60. Lamar County Deed Record, 146-443.

61. Richardson, *Treadmill*, 89, cited from SECNAV, Annual Report, 1910, 18.

62. "The Summer Cruise for Midshipmen of the Second Class," *Proceedings,* Volume 40, 1914, 1685.

63. LoC, Dyer Papers, Box 9, Folder 6. Navy Department to Richardson,

November 11, 1914. He was commissioned on November 7, 1914.

64. Ronald Spector, *Professors of War: The Naval War College and the Development of the Naval Profession* (Newport, RI: 1977; reprint, Honolulu, HI: University Press of the Pacific, 2005), 142.

Chapter 5: "Roosevelt Insisted on Calling Me Joe"

1. Daniels was a businessman who had suffered several failures along with experiencing some newspaper successes.

2. James MacGregor Burns, *Roosevelt: The Lion and the Fox* (New York: 1956; reprint, Harvest Books, 2002), 50.

3. Department of the Navy, Naval Historical Center, Washington Navy Yard.

4. Richardson, *Treadmill*, 90.

5. Ibid., 91, cited from SECNAV (Josephus Daniels), Annual Report, 1913, 6.

6. Ibid., 65.

7. LoC, Dyer Papers, Box 9, Folder 6. Memorandum from H. A. Baldridge, apparently on June 30, 1916.

8. Geoffrey C. Ward, *A First-Class Temperament.* (New York: Harper and Row, 1989), 222.

9. Marolda, 28-29.

10. Betty Carney Taussig to Skipper Steely, November 9, 2001. When Daniels died on January 15, 1948, his family asked that all former CNOs be pall-bearers. Carney was uncomfortable to fill that role because of the many negative letters he had once received from Daniels. However, after finding out that his friend and former CNO Bill Fechteler and others received similar letters from the secretary, they all participated.

11. Richardson, *Treadmill*, 92.

12. LoC, Dyer Papers, Box 10, Folder 3. Rear Admiral John Hood to Lieutenant Commander J. O. Richardson, April 5, 1917.

13. Richardson, *Treadmill*, 92.

14. Lieutenant Commander J. O. Richardson, U.S. Navy, "Naval Petroleum Reserves No. 1 and No. 2," *Proceedings*, Volume 42, Number 1, 1916, 93-123.

15. Burns, 61.

16. Ward, 201.

17. Richardson, *Treadmill*, 438-49.

18. Ibid., 439.

Chapter 6: Away from Washington

1. Woodrow Wilson, War Messages, 65th Congress, 1st Session, Senate Document 5, Serial Number 7264, Washington, DC, 1917, 3-8.

2. Martin Gilbert, *The First World War: A Complete History* (New York: Holt, 1994), 555, Map 3.

3. Burns, 63.

4. LoC, Dyer Papers, Box 9, Folder 6. See letter of January 1, 1918.

5. Richardson, *Treadmill*, 94.

6. Commander L. A. McComas, USN, "Knowing When to Sit Down and Shut Up (and when not to)," found at: http://navyrotc.berkeley.edu/focsle/Spring98/xo.htm.

7. Kenneth J. Hagan, "The Critic Within in Naval History," *Naval History* (Annapolis, December 1998). This is a summary of the career of Admiral Sims.

8. John T. Mason, Jr., Int., *The Reminiscences of Vice Admiral Olaf M. Hustvedt* (Annapolis, MD: U.S. Naval Institute, 1975), 55. This work gives the impression that Rodgers was using the USS *New York*.

9. LoC, Dyer Papers, Box 9, Folder 3.

10. Mason, 57.

11. USS *New Mexico* Log Book, January 1, 1918, to December 31, 1918, September 1 through 14.

12. Mason, 58. The trip was from Bantry Bay to Dublin, across to Holyhead in Wales, then by rail to Crewe, and by train from there to Edinburgh where the contingent joined the Grand Fleet.

13. USS *New Mexico* Log Book, January 1, 1918, to December 31, 1918, September 1 through 14. In addition to Captain Long and Commander Richardson, there were five lieutenant commanders, eleven lieutenants, seven lieutenant (j.g.s), thirty-three ensigns, one Marine captain, one Marine first lieutenant, three members of the medical officer corps, and a chaplain on board. There were 1,286 sailors and eighty members of the Marines attached.

14 Charles Robert Mowbray Fraser Cruttwell, *A History of the Great War 1914-1918* (Oxford: The Clarendon Press, 1936; reprint, Chicago, 1991), 60. LoC, Dyer Papers, Box 9, Folder 3.

15. Rosyth is on the East Coast of Scotland, north of Edinburgh.

16. LoC, Dyer Papers, Box 9, Folder 3.

17. Gilbert, 447-48.

18. LoC, Dyer Papers, Box 9, Folder 3. "Movements of the USS *Nevada* During the Period of When Commander James O. Richardson Was on Board." Division 6: USS *Utah*, USS *Nevada*, USS *Oklahoma*, and USS *Arizona*. Division 9: USS *Wyoming*, USS *New York*, USS *Texas*, USS *Arkansas*, and USS *Florida*.

19. LoC, Dyer Papers, Box 9, Folder 3. "Movements of the USS *Nevada* During the Period of When Commander James O. Richardson Was on Board."

20. S. L. A. Marshall, *The American Heritage History of World War I* (New York: American Heritage Publishing Company, 1964), 362.

21. LoC, Dyer Papers, Box 9, Folder 3. "Movements of the USS *Nevada* During the Period of When Commander James O. Richardson Was on Board."

22. Ibid.

23. Mason, 63.

24. LoC, Dyer Papers, Box 9, Folder 6. Coontz to Richardson, with note from W. C. Cole, commander of the USS *Nevada*, March 26, 1919.

25. The USS *Nevada* was one of the Pearl Harbor-based ships heavily damaged during the December 7, 1941, attack. It was repaired, served the rest of World War II, and then received an unglamorous ending as a target at Bikini Island, sunk by atom bomb testing on July 31, 1948. LoC, Dyer Papers, Box 9, Folder 6. See letter of May 23, 1921. Richardson began duty at Annapolis on October 3, 1919.

Chapter 7: Left Alone at Times to Make Decisions

1. Patrick Abbazia, *Mr. Roosevelt's Navy: The Private War of the U.S. Fleet 1939-1942* (Annapolis, MD: Naval Institute Press, 1975), 23.

2. Secretary of the Navy Edwin Denby, Annual Report 1921, 3.

3. Secretary of the Navy Edwin Denby, Annual Report 1922, 3.

4. Secretary of the Navy Edwin Denby, Annual Report 1924, 12.

5. LoC, Dyer Papers, Box 9, Folder 6. Letter dated March 1, 1922. Box 10, Folder 2. He reported March 16.

6. Walter F. Ashe, Lt. SC, USN (Ret.), resident historian for the city's namesake, found on the Internet in 2002 at: http://toto.lib.unca.edu/findingaids/mss/ashe/history.html. Or, found at the University of North Carolina at Asheville, D. H. Ramsey Library, Special Collections/University Archives, Manuscript Register for Walter Ashe Collection.

7. Navyhistory.com, found on the Internet in 2002 at: http://www.multied.com/Navy/gunboat/asheville.html.

8. Richardson, *Treadmill*, 98. Photo can be found online at Naval Historical Center (NHC) bio on Richardson. Could be seen online in 2007 at: http://www.history.navy.mil/photos/pers-us/uspers-r/j-richdn.htm.

9. LoC, Dyer Papers, Box 9, Folder 7. Letters of August 21 and September 12, 1922.

10. Rose C. Feld, "China Again in Grip of Opium and Morphia," *The New York Times*, August 24, 1924.

11. Barbara W. Tuchman, *Stillwell and the American Experience in China 1911-45* (New York: Macmillan Company, 1971; reprint, New York: Grove Press, 2001), 96.

12. Dennis Noble, *The Eagle and the Dragon: The United States Military in China 1901-1937* (Westport, CT: Greenwood Press, 1990), 32.

13. Ibid., 65.

14. Richardson, *Treadmill*, 101. The photo of the USS *Asheville* is on this page.

15. Hugh Rodman, *Yarns of a Kentucky Admiral* (London: Martin Hopkinson Ltd., 1929), 203.

16. Ibid., 202-3.

17. Richardson, *Treadmill*, 465.

18. Tuchman, 85.

19. Richardson, *Treadmill*, 99; and Secretary of the Navy, Annual Report 1924, 7.

20. NHC Operational Archives, Oral Interviews, Henry Smith-Hutton, #3-39.

21. LoC, Dyer Papers, Box 9, Folder 7. See letter dated August 23, 1923.

22. Reid, 7.

23. Charles D. James, "The 1923 Tokyo Earthquake and Fire," found on the Internet in 2003 at: http://nisee.berkeley.edu/ kanto/tokyo1923.pdf.

24. U.S. Naval Institute (USNI), Annapolis, Oral Interviews, Vice Admiral Charles A. Pownall, #1-50.

25. Maria Wilhelm, *The Man Who Watched the Rising Sun: The Story of Admiral Ellis M. Zacharias* (New York: Franklin Watts Inc., 1967), 30.

26. Charles Blauvelt Diary, found on the Internet in 2003 at: http://www.transpect.com/japan_diary/#a23.

27. Conversation with Dr. William Z. Slany, retired, office of historian, United States Department of State, July 22, 2002; and with current historian, Evan Duncan.

28. Richardson, *Treadmill*, 100, quoted from Admiral Richardson's diary.

29. Richardson, *Treadmill*, 100.

30. Ibid.

31. Noble, 202. This report to Admiral Washington was on February 1, 1923, "Reports of Conditions There for January-March 1923," WA-7, China Conditions, RG 45, Naval Records Collection of the Office of Naval Records and Library, National Archives (NARA), Washington, DC.

32. Anne Briscoe Pye and Nancy Shea, *The Navy Wife* (New York: Harper and Brothers, 1942), 270.

33. Ibid., 273.

34. LoC, Dyer Papers, Box 9, Folder 7. Washington to Richardson, January 9, 1924. Washington was firm, made a decision against the protest, and filed it away in Richardson's Washington records.

35. LoC, Dyer Papers, Box 10, Folder 3. H. B. Wilson to Richardson, February 12, 1924; also see Box 9, Folder 6. Letter of December 21, 1923.

36. LoC, Dyer Papers, Box 10, Folder 3. American Consulate General Gale to Richardson, March 13, 1924.

37. LoC, Dyer Papers, Box 10, Folder 3. American Consul Ernest B. Price to Richardson, March 19, 1924.

38. LoC, Dyer Papers, Box 9, Folder 6. Letter dated April 30, 1924.

39. Richardson, *Treadmill*, 102.

Chapter 8: A Little of This, A Little of That

1. Chief of the Bureau of Ordnance, C. C. Bloch, 1924 Annual Report of the Navy Department, 263.

2. Commander J. O. Richardson, "Report on the Fitness of Officers," *Proceedings*, Volume 50, 1924, 214-18.

3. Mason, 93, 104. He worked on pyrotechnics, propellants, and powders.

4. LoC, Dyer Papers, Box 9, Folder 7. See letters dated February 11, October 8, and March 9, 1926.

5. A description and photo could be found on the Web in 2003 at: http://www.ibiblio.org/hyperwar/USN/ships/AG/AG-117_Whipple.html.

6. James O. Richardson, Assistant to the Chief of Naval Operations, "Organization of the Navy Department," speech given to the Army Industrial College, Washington, DC, December 9, 1937.

7. The USS *Whipple* would again be placed in the Pacific.

8. Harvey M. Beigel, *Battleship Country: The Battle Fleet at San Pedro—Long Beach, California 1919-1940* (Missoula, MN: Pictorial Histories Publishing Company, 1987), 17.

9. LoC, Dyer Papers, Box 10-3. Kurtz to Richardson on the USS *Whipple*, February 21, 1928; March 3, 1928.

10. LoC, Dyer Papers, Box 10-3. Richardson to Kurtz, February 21, 1928.

11. Richardson, *Treadmill*, 102.

12. Ibid., 107.

13. Thomas Wildenberg, *All the Factors of Victory: Adm. Joseph Mason Reeves and the Origins of Carrier Airpower* (Dulles, VA: Brassey's Inc., 2003), 218.

14. James W. Hammond, Jr., *The Treaty Navy: The Story of the U.S. Naval Service Between the World Wars* (Victoria, Canada: Wesley Press, Trafford Publishing, 2001), 88, 98.

15. NARA—College Park, Records of the Pearl Harbor Liaison Office, Box 3, Folder 12. A complete copy of the Schofield Report on Fleet Problem XIII, dated March 23, 1932. The forty-two pages did not mention Yarnell's separate exercise.

16. Hammond, 248.

17. Beigel, 33-34.

18. Steely Collection, USS *Augusta* File, taken from various ship history compilations found in books and on the Internet.

19. Beigel, 33, 41.

20. Hammond, 86. On March 15, 1933, Roosevelt's Economy Act cut the wages of all government employees by 15 percent.

21. Beigel, 33. He cites Thaddeus V. Tuleja, *Statesmen and Admirals: Quest for a Far Eastern Naval Policy* (New York: W. W. Norton & Company, Inc., 1963), 72-73, 77.

22. USNI, Annapolis, Oral Interviews, Frederick A. Edwards, Sr., #3-170.

23. USNI, Annapolis, Oral Interviews, Rear Admiral Joseph Caldwell Wylie, Jr., 1985, 18.

24. USNI, Annapolis, Oral Interviews, Vice-Admiral Lloyd M. Mustin, #3-116.

25. USNI, Annapolis, Oral Interviews, Vice-Admiral Lloyd M. Mustin, #29-1,102.

26. Richardson, *Treadmill,* 108-9.

27. Michael Vlahos, *The Blue Sword: The Naval War College and the American Mission 1919-1941* (Newport, RI: Naval War College Press, 1980), 73.

28. Richardson, "Thesis," 2, also found in Record Group XIII, NHC.

29. Richardson, "Thesis," 6.

30. Ibid., 7.

31. Ibid., 6.

32. Ibid., 14-15.

33. The flag officers were: Milo F. Draemel, Wilson Brown, William R. Furlong, John H. Towers, Harold M. Bemis, James L. Kauffman, Samuel A. Clement, Arthur S. Carpender, Frank T. Leighton, Robert G. Coman, Charles M. "Savvy" Cooke, Augustine H. Gray, Herbert R. Hein, Walton Wiley Smith, Sherwood A. Taffinder, Ralph F. Wood, Ellis M. Zacharias, and Elliot B. Nixon. Of the five line captains in Richardson's class, four became flag officers, and of the thirty-four line commanders, ten became at least rear admirals.

34. LoC, Dyer Papers, Box 10-3. Congratulatory letter from Admiral J. M. Reeves on the Flagship USS *California* to Richardson, December 14, 1933. "It is a satisfaction to be safely over the hurdle, and know it is a matter of time."

35. Richardson, *Treadmill,* 110. More excerpts from Richardson's writings at the Naval War College can be seen on page 111.

36. Richardson, *Treadmill,* 110; Captain Ellis M. Zacharias, *Secret Missions: The Story of an Intelligence Officer* (New York: G. P. Putnam, 1946), 134.

37. Richardson, *Treadmill,* 111.

Chapter 9: Quick Training for High Rank

1. Mason, 143, 148. He was on the heavy cruiser USS *Louisville* during this fleet problem and the one in 1934.

2. *Time,* June 4, 1934, Volume XXIII, Number 23.

3. Richardson, *Treadmill*, 116.

4. LoC, Dyer Papers, Box 10, Folder 2. The orders being cut were dated September 19, 1935.

5. OP-20-G was the section of the Office of the Chief Naval Operations that dealt with intelligence gathering and decoding, or cryptanalysis, before and during World War II. It also intercepted diplomatic messages through the use of high-frequency direction finders at sites in the Pacific and Atlantic and in the United States.

6. "Admiral Reeves Dies at Age 75," *New York Times,* March 26, 1948.

7. Hammond, 255-56. This is a detailed daily schedule.

8. John D. Hayes, "Admiral Joseph Mason Reeves, Part II—1931-1948," *Naval War College Review,* Volume 24, Number 5 (January 1972), 58.

9. Wildenberg, 251.

10. Hayes, "Reeves, Part II," 61. Hayes does not list Richardson as one of the staff who paddled Reeves in the USS *Pennsylvania's* raceboat to the shore. He listed: Commanders (Cary?) W. Magruder, operations; R. M. Griffin, gunnery; F. D. Wagner, aviation; Lieutenant Commanders F. C. Denebrink, flag secretary; W. M. Lockhart, aerology; J. G. Atkins, flag lieutenant; Lieutenants J. J. Rochefort, intelligence; and K. L. Forster, communications; Captain E. E. Larson, USMC; Lieutenants (j.g.) T. J. Hickey, L. S. Howeth, Horatio Rivero; and Ensign W. S. Bobo. LoC Manuscript Division, George C. Dyer Papers, Box 10, Folder 2. Richardson orders dated June 24, 1936.

11. George C. Dyer, "Reminiscences of Vice Admiral George C. Dyer," oral interview done between 1969-73 at Annapolis by John T. Mason, Jr., 161-65.

12. Dyer, "Reminiscences," 168.

13. Richardson, *Treadmill*, 469.

14. Sun lines were used in navigation from the eighteenth century through the 1940s to determine the time.

15. LoC Manuscript Division, Ernest J. King Papers, Box 4, Memoranda 1936-37 Folder, Commander Aircraft, Base Force Critique, 9.

16. Dyer, "Reminiscences," 167-70.

17. Scot MacDonald, "Evolution of Aircraft Carrier: Last of the Fleet Problems," *Naval Aviation News* (Washington, DC: Government Printing Department, 1964). Found on the Internet in 2008 at: http://www.history.navy.mil/branches/cartoc.htm. Neither the *Wasp* (1940) nor the *Hornet* (1941) was ready to be in Richardson's CinCUS command.

18. Andrew Krepinevich, "Transforming to Victory: The U.S. Navy, Carrier Aviation, and Preparing for War in the Pacific" (Olin Institute, 2000). Found on the Internet in 2003 at: http://www.csbaonline.org/4Publications/Archive/A.20000000.Transforming_to_Vi/A.20000000.Transforming_to_Vi.htm.

19. LoC Manuscript Division, Ernest J. King Papers, Box 4, Memoranda 1936-37 Folder. Hepburn to Fleet Present, Hawaiian Area, May 14, 1937.

20. Dyer, "Reminiscences," 173.

Chapter 10: A Most Interesting Year

1. Mason, 152, 158.

2. Richardson, *Treadmill*, 466.

3. NHC Operational Archives, Oral Interviews, William R. Smedberg, #1-122. Richardson, *Treadmill*, 128.

4. Richardson, *Treadmill*, 4-5. Read *Pearl Harbor Attack: Hearings Before The Joint Committee on the Investigation of the Pearl Harbor Attack* (cited hereafter as Pearl Harbor Hearings) (Washington, DC: United States Government Printing Office, 1946). Held before the Congress of the United States, 79th Congress, First Session, Part or Volume 1, 342. Before study of any of the Pearl Harbor hearings, refer to or purchase a copy of the index by Stanley H. Smith, *Investigations of the Attack on Pearl Harbor: Index to Government Hearings* (New York: Greenwood Press, 1990), 251 pages.

5. Mason, 159.

6. *Paris News,* July 19, 1937.

7. Richardson, *Treadmill*, 120.

8. *Paris News,* July 19, 1937.

9. For more on proposed plans to bomb Japan from China bases, see Alan Armstrong, *Preemptive Strike: The Secret Plan That Would Have Prevented the Attack on Pearl Harbor* (Guilford, MA: Lyons Press, 2006).

10. LoC, Bloch Papers, Box 3, Correspondence, Richardson File 1939-42. Bloch on board the USS *California,* U.S. Fleet Battle Force, to Richardson, August 28, 1937.

11. *Washington Post,* December 13, 1937, 1.

12. Masatake Okumiya, with Roger Pineau, "How the *Panay* Was Sunk," *Proceedings,* Volume 79, Number 6, June 1953, 587.

13. *Newsweek,* Volume X, Number 26, December 27, 1937. NARA Downtown DC, Record Group 80, Records of the Department of the Navy 1798-1947, Box 3860, PC-31, Entry 22, General Correspondence 1926-1940, PR4/S3-1 (2) to PR5/S3-1 (1), Folder PR5/L11-1 (371212). Leahy to CinCAF, December 12, 1937, asking for all information available.

14. Richardson, *Treadmill*, 121.

15. *Washington Post,* December 14, 1937, front page. A reproduction of the whole note to Hull is printed here.

16. *Paris News,* December 13, 1937. *Time,* Volume 31, January 10, 1938.

17. Tom Mayock, "FDR: Pacific Warlord." (Unpublished manuscript found on Internet in 2003 at: http://users.erols.com/tomtud/index.html.) Chapter IV, 23.

18. *Paris News,* December 14, 1937.

19. *Washington Post,* December 14, 1937, front page.

20. *Paris News,* December 14, 1937. Front page, 3.

21. *Paris News,* December 17, 1937. Lieutenant Charles J. Whiting was the judge advocate. Members were: Captain Harold V. McKittrick, chairman; Commander Abel C. J. Sabalot; and Commander Morton L. Deyo.

22. *Time,* Volume 31, May 2, 1938, 14. See also *Time,* Volume 30, Part 1, December 27, 1937, 13, or Tuchman, 179.

23. Tuchman, 179.

24. *Time,* Volume 30, Part 1, December 27, 1937, 13.

25. LoC, Dyer Papers, Box 10-3. McConnell to Richardson, January 27, 1938.

26. Richardson, *Treadmill*, 17.

27. Mason, 159.

28. NHC, Operational Archives, Oral Interviews, Stephen Jurika, #9-295.

29. NARA Downtown DC, Record Group 80, Records of the Department of the Navy 1798-1947, Box 3860, PC-31, Entry 22, General Correspondence 1926-1940, PR4/S3-1 (2) to PR5/S3-1 (1), Folder PR5/L11-1 to (380422). Letter of February 4, 1939; (380212) CNO to Secretary of Navy, July 7, 1938, and August 9, 1938 letter from JO Richardson to JAG and various offices, Navy Expeditionary Medal recommended to personnel aboard the USS *Panay*.

30. NARA Downtown DC, Record Group 80, Records of the Department of the Navy 1798-1947, Box 3860, PC-31, Entry 22, General Correspondence 1926-1940, PR4/S3-1 (2) to PR5/S3-1 (1), Folder PR5/L11-1 (380424) to (   ) (*sic*).

31. Richardson, *Treadmill*, 17.

32. Ibid.

33. Ibid., 263.

34. John H. Bradley and Jack W. Dice, *The Second World War: Asia and the Pacific*, ed. Thomas E. Griss (Wayne: NJ: Avery Publishing Group, Inc., 1989), 26.

35. Mark Watson, *Chief-of-staff: Prewar Plans and Preparations,* in subseries, *The War Department,* Office of the Chief of Military History, Department of the Army series *The United States Army in World War II* (Washington, DC: Government Printing Office, 1950), 92. Found online in 2007 at: http://www.ibiblio.org/hyperwar/USA/USA-WD-Plans/USA-WD-Plans-4.html.

36. Ronald H. Spector, *Eagle against the Sun: The American War with Japan* (New York: The Free Press, Macmillan, Inc., 1985), 58. He cites Memo, Embick to CG, Philippine Dept., April 19, 1933, on "U.S. Policy in the Philippines." MS copy in the U.S. Army Center of Military History in Washington, DC.

37. Chan Robles Virtual Law Library, Philippine Law Statutes and Codes, The Philippine Independence Act. It could be found on the Internet in 2002 at: http://www.chanrobles.com/tydingsmcduffieact.htm.

38. Bradley and Dice, 26.

39. Richardson, *Treadmill,* 267.

40. Ibid., 256-57, 263. For a war with Japan, the Joint Board, predecessor to the Joint Chiefs of Staff organization, the distinct war plans were developed between 1923 and 1938. The 1923 plans were in two volumes, the 1929 in four volumes, and the 1938 of similar bulk. The first fleet plan to be widely distributed to unit commanders came from Admiral Sellers in early 1934.

41. Richardson, *Treadmill,* 268.

42. United States Court of Federal Claims, Marcia Fee Achenbach, et al., Plaintiffs, The United States, Defendant. App. 6, 415. See also David Cox, "US prisoners claim Roosevelt left them in Philippines deliberately," found on the Internet in 2003 at: http://why-war.com/news/2002/07/30/prisoner.html. This suit filed in 2002 is based upon the premise that the United States knew for months and years it would abandon those in the Philippines in case of war with Japan. Therefore, the government should have removed all civilians from there at the same time it announced in October of 1940 that American citizens should leave other places in the Far East. Army and Navy personnel were not evacuated, however. App. 10, 209.

43. Thomas Fleming, *The New Dealers' War: FDR and the War within World*

War II (New York: Basic Books, Perseus Books Group, 2001), 6.

44. Edward S. Miller, *War Plan Orange: The U.S. Strategy to Defeat Japan 1897-1945* (Annapolis, MD: Naval Institute Press, 1991), 219-29. He portrays Richardson as a wrench in the works, always bringing about the negatives of the war plans even though during Fleet Problem XXI the admiral brought new realism into the exercises, testing out the facets of the plans. While most readers and historians view Richardson's book as straightforward and honest—even his biographer, George C. Dyer—Miller is of the opinion the comments are from a bitter man who was jealous he was not in the influential loop. Gordon Prange is of a slightly agreeing opinion with Miller in his book, *At Dawn We Slept.*

45. *Paris News,* February 2, 1938.

46. Miller, 228. He cites Joint Board War Plan Orange, February 21, 1938.

47. NHC, Operational Archives, Oral Interviews, Edwin T. Layton, #1-45.

48. Spector, *Eagle against the Sun,* 58-59.

49. Miller, 225. He cites *Joint Basic War Plan Orange,* February 21, 1938, JB 325, ser. 618.

50. Richardson, *Treadmill,* 268.

Chapter 11: "Don't Go While I'm Here"

1. Richardson, *Treadmill,* 121.

2. Franklin D. Roosevelt Presidential Library, Day by Day—The Pare Lorentz Chronology, March 22, 1938. Richardson says in his book, *Treadmill,* 125, that the meeting was on March 23. The time is correct in both sources.

3. Richardson, *Treadmill,* 125.

4. Ibid., 121-22.

5. Ibid., 125.

6. LoC, Bloch Papers, Box 3 Correspondence, Richardson File 1939-42, Richardson to Bloch, June 12, 1938.

7. LoC, Bloch Papers, Box 3 Correspondence, Richardson File 1939-42. Richardson to Bloch, August 6, 1938.

8. LoC, Bloch Papers, Box 3 Correspondence, Richardson File 1939-42. Richardson to Bloch, August 17, 1938.

9. LoC, Bloch Papers, Box 3 Correspondence, Richardson File 1939-42. Richardson to Bloch, August 6, 1938.

10. Day by Day—The Pare Lorentz Chronology.

11. LoC, Bloch Papers, Box 3 Correspondence, Richardson File 1939-42. Richardson to Bloch, January 3, 1939.

12. Richardson, *Treadmill,* 5.

13. Ibid., 3.

14. *New York Times,* March 2, 1939. Steely Collection, Richardson Research, USS *Houston* File. E. B. Potter, *Admiral Arleigh Burke* (New York: Random House, 1990), 50.

15. LoC Manuscript Division, Jerauld Wright Papers, Box 1. Jerry Wright to Phyllis Wright, from Gonaives, Haiti, March 17, 1939.

16. Richardson, *Treadmill,* 2.

17. FDR Library, Secretary's File. Letter from Acting Secretary of the Navy Charles Edison to Roosevelt, dated March 7, 1939.

18. B. Mitchell Simpson III, *Admiral Harold R. Stark: Architect of Victory 1939-1945* (Columbia: University of South Carolina Press, 1989), 2. He cites a letter from Swanson to Roosevelt, January 24, 1939; and a letter from Edison to Roosevelt, March 7, 1939, found in the President's Secretary's File, FDR Library.

19. LoC, Dyer Papers, Box 9, Folder 7, May 3, 1939. Orders from Swanson.

20. Admiral Thomas C. Hart Diary, March 15, 1939. "Andrews stays right where he is; will never get further and that is all to the good," he wrote after hearing of the "flag slate" results. See e-mail from Lynna Kay Shuffield to Skipper Steely, September 12, 2003.

21. Hart Diary, March 15, 1939. "Another case of dipping far down, but he will do a good job," he wrote. See e-mail from Lynna Kay Shuffield to Skipper Steely, September 12, 2003.

22. Richardson, *Treadmill*, 7.

23. Hart Diary, March 15, 1939. See e-mail from Lynna Kay Shuffield to Skipper Steely, September 12, 2003.

24. Richardson, *Treadmill*, 2. LoC, Bloch Papers, Box 3, Richardson File 1939-42. Richardson to Bloch, March 10, 1939. A complete list of proposed slate of changes is here, but tentative. See Bloch to Richardson for the CinCUS changes, March 17, 1939.

25. NHC Operational Archives, Oral Interviews, William R. Smedberg, #1-123.

26. Richardson, *Treadmill*, 8.

27. LoC Manuscript Division, Ernest J. King Papers, Box 4, 1940-42, Orders to Duty Folder. Knox to King, February 12, 1941, and December 20, 1941.

28. Potter, 50.

29. NHC Operational Archives, Oral Interviews, William R. Smedberg, #1-123.

30. LoC, Bloch Papers, Box 3, Richardson File 1939-42. Richardson to Bloch, March 20, 1939.

31. Richardson, *Treadmill*, 463.

32. Fleming, 62.

33. Richardson, *Treadmill*, 36.

34. LoC, Dyer Papers, Box 10, Folder 2. Secretary of Navy to Richardson, May 29, 1939. Richardson worked through George T. Summerlin at the State Department.

35. Richardson, *Treadmill*, 13.

36. Beigel, 41.

37. George Morgenstern, *Pearl Harbor: The Story of the Secret War* (New York: Devin-Adair Company, 1947), 51.

38. Ibid., 52.

39. Beigel, 59. Also see William L. Langer and S. Everett Gleason, *The Challenge of Isolation* (New York: Harper & Brothers Publishers, 1952), 64.

40. Beigel, 59.

41. Richardson, *Treadmill*, 30. SECNAV (Charles Edison, Acting), Annual Report, 1939, 1.

Chapter 12: Off to Sea Again—1939

1. Richardson, *Treadmill*, 55.

2. Ibid., 56.

3. Ibid., 58.

4. LoC, Dyer Papers, Box 10, Folder 7. Notes on Commander Battle Force duty, 1939.

5. Richardson, *Treadmill,* 123.

6. Betty Carney Taussig, *A Warrior for Freedom* (Manhattan, KS: Sunflower University Press, 1995), 55.

7. LoC Manuscript Division, John L. McCrea Papers, Box 1, Folder 5. McCrea to T. E. Chandler, April 11, 1940.

8. Richardson, *Treadmill,* 58.

9. Ibid., 59.

10. LoC Manuscript Division, Emory Land Papers, Box 12, three scrapbooks. He gained the rank of vice-admiral.

11. Interview between Skipper Steely and John Lowry, eighty-six, in the fall of 2002 while waiting to play golf at Paris Golf and Country Club. He left the Navy in 1938, and was thus drafted into the Army for World War II, unable to convince the draft board that he was Navy.

12. Richardson, *Treadmill,* 60.

13. *Life,* October 28, 1940.

14. Richardson, *Treadmill,* 64.

15. Information found at several locations on the Internet in 2003. One is: http://www.villariviera.net/History/HistoryFrameset.html. An apartment at the Villa Riviera can now be purchased in the range of $500,000.

16. Charles Kepper of Tulsa, Oklahoma, telephone conversation with Skipper Steely, February 20, 2003. He was on the USS *Salt Lake City* as a part of the Hawaiian Detachment, and as part of Task Force 8 with the *Enterprise* on December 7, 1941, and with it when escorting the Doolittle raid.

17. Beigel, 17. Also, read Richard L, Schwoebel, *Explosion aboard the IOWA* (Annapolis, MD: Naval Institute Press, 1999).

18. Dyer, "Reminiscences," 181.

19. Ibid., 183.

20. NHC Operational Archives, Oral Interviews, Bernhard Henry Bieri, #2-81.

21. Dyer, "Reminiscences," 184.

22. Bradley and Dice, 26.

23. NHC Operational Archives, Oral Interviews, Bernhard Henry Bieri, #2-82.

24. Richardson, *Treadmill,* 209. He cites CHBUSHIPS, January 17, 1940, letter to Commandant Mare Island Navy Yard, Box 168, CINCUS Files, RG 313, NA.

25. Richardson, *Treadmill,* 209.

26. Dyer, "Reminiscences," 193.

27. Richardson, *Treadmill,* 137.

28. Ibid., 144. He cites CinCUS (A. J. Hepburn), Annual Report, 1937, WW11CF, NHD, 3-17.

29. Abbazia, 14-15.

30. Richardson, *Treadmill,* 147. He cites CinCUS (C. C. Bloch), Annual Report, 1939, 1-11.

31. Mason, 176-77.

32. Richardson, *Treadmill,* 148.

33. Ibid., 149-50.

34. Ibid., 152.

35. Ibid., 159.

36. Ibid., 160.

37. Robert G. Albion and Robert Howe Connery, *Forrestal and the Navy* (New York: Columbia University Press, 1962), 51.

38. Richardson, *Treadmill*, 161.

39. Ibid.

40. LoC, Dyer Papers, Box 10, Folder 7. Notes on Commander Battle Force 1939.

41. Richardson, *Treadmill*, 230. He cites CINCUS, serial 01769 of December 11, 1939, letter to Fleet, Box 103, CINCUS Files, RG 313, NA, 23 (Fleet Tactical Exercises, September, 1939—Report of Exercise No. 207).

42. Richardson, *Treadmill*, 162.

43. Memories from Charles F. Kepper, posted on the Internet in 2003 at: http://sandysq.gcinet.net/uss_salt_lake_city_ca25/kepper.htm.

44. Richardson, *Treadmill*, 446.

45. *Charlotte News*, September 28, 1939.

46. Mason, 180.

47. Richardson, *Treadmill*, 163.

48. LoC, Dyer Papers, Box 9, Folder 7.

49. Richardson, *Treadmill*, 228.

50. LoC, Dyer Papers, Box 9, Folder 7. Orders to CinCUS from Edison, December 13, 1939.

Chapter 13: Choosing the Final CinCUS Staff

1. Richardson, *Treadmill*, 131.

2. Naval Historical Center, On-Line Library of Selected Images, Photo #NH 777082. Taken on board the USS *Pennsylvania*.

3. Dyer, "Reminiscences," 184.

4. Richardson, *Treadmill*, 134.

5. Schuylkill.com Archives, Ethel Manning, "Admiral Boone, Healer of Presidents," found online in 2008 at: http://www.homeofheroes.com/news/archives/2002_1109_boone.html.

6. Milton F. Heller, Jr., *The Presidents' Doctor: An Insider's View of Three First Families* (New York: Vantage Press, 2000).

7. Richardson, *Treadmill*, 134.

8. NHC, Oral Interviews, Kent Melhorn, 60.

9. Richardson, *Treadmill*, 135.

10. Ibid., 142.

11. Ibid., 174.

12. Ibid., 142.

Chapter 14: Fleet Problem XXI—The Last One

1. Reid, 7.

2. Betty Carney Taussig, *A Warrior for Freedom*, 56.

3. Richardson, *Treadmill*, 10.

4. LoC, Dyer Papers, Box 10, Folder 2. Orders from Edison, dated December 8, 1939.

5. John E. King , "Richardson, New Navy Chief, Third Texan to Hold that High Job During the Last Ten Years," *Dallas Morning News*, January 13, 1940.

6. Robert E. Hicks, "All Paris Is Talking about Otto Richardson, Who Grew Up to be Commander-in-Chief of U.S. Fleet," *Fort Worth Star-Telegram*, Sunday, February 18, 1940.

7. *Paris News*, June 25, 1939.

8. Hicks, *Fort Worth Star-Telegram*, Sunday, February 18, 1940.

9. *New York Times*, January 7, 1940. Richardson, *Treadmill*, 170. *The Keystone*, Volume XVI, Number XIII, Long Beach, California, January 6, 1940. The entire Bloch speech is found here.

10. Historic Films, Footage of Admiral James Otto Richardson, Tape #1, assembled for Skipper Steely on October 11, 2002. *New York Times*, January 7, 1940. Richardson, *Treadmill*, 170. *The Keystone*, Volume XVI, Number XIII, January 6, 1940.

11. Reid, 7.

12. Richardson, *Treadmill*, 170.

13. Ibid., 171.

14. LoC, Dyer Papers, Box 10, Folder 7. Notes on chapter in book about CinCUS duty.

15. Beigel, 63.

16. LoC, Dyer Papers, Box 10, Folder 7. Notes on chapter in book about CinCUS duty.

17. Richardson, *Treadmill*, 232. LoC, Dyer Papers, Box 10, Folder 2. Orders stamped October 22. He actually was an observer and attended the critique on January 29-30.

18. "The Battle of the River Plata: The Death of a Commander and a Gentleman," found on the Internet in 2007 at: http://www.history learningsite.co.uk/battle_of_the_river_plate.htm; or it is in movie form. See data at: http://www.imdb.com/title/ tt0048990/.

19. Joy Waldron Jasper, James P. Delgado, and Jim Adams, *The USS Arizona* (New York: Truman Tally Books, St. Martin's Press, 2001), 50.

20. *The Keystone*, Volume XVI, Number XVIII., February 10, 1940.

21. NARA—College Park, Records of the Pearl Harbor Liaison Office, Box 7, Folder 1. February 16, 1940, letter from Richardson at San Pedro to Stark.

22. Richardson, *Treadmill*, 233.

23. Ibid., 235.

24. Ibid.

25. LoC Manuscript Division, John L. McCrea Papers, Box 1, Folder 5, General Correspondence 1940. McCrea to R. R. Adams (Ranney), April 1, 1940.

26. NARA—College Park, Records of the Pearl Harbor Liaison Office, Box 7, Folder 1. Richardson at San Pedro to Stark, dated March 11, 1940, in reply to a February 12 memo.

27. ALSUNA (Naval Attaché) Tokyo to OPNAV (Office of the CNO); or Richardson, *Treadmill*, 237.

28. LoC, Dyer Papers, Box 10, Folder 7. Notes on chapter in book about CinCUS duty.

29. Ibid.

30. Richardson, *Treadmill,* 370-72. Most of this information comes from a letter Richardson sent to Admiral H. R. Stark on May 9, 1940.

31. Beigel, 63.

32. LoC, Dyer Papers, Box 10-3. Stark to Richardson, January 18, 1940.

33. The White House to the Acting Secretary of the Navy, April 3, 1940; or Richardson, *Treadmill,* 374.

34. NARA—College Park, Records of the Pearl Harbor Liaison Office, Box 7, Folder 1. April 10, 1940, letter from Richardson to Stark.

35. LoC Manuscript Division, Ernest J. King Papers, Box 4, 1940-42, Orders to Duty Folder. Chief BuNav to King, March 23, 1940.

36. Deyo served on the staff of CinCUS Harry Yarnell as communications officer in 1936, and later became a flag officer. Rice was the first commander of the USS *Drum* and later the USS *Paddle,* both submarines.

37. Arthur Walsh was a native of New Jersey, and his first job was as a recording violinist for Edison's father. He was in the Army during World War I. See *The Keystone,* Volume XVI, Number XXV, April 6, 1940. On April 1 Edison and his party were "piped" over the side of the USS *Pennsylvania* to observe the Fleet Problem.

38. Richardson, *Treadmill,* 375.

39. Hammond, 227.

40. LoC Manuscript Division, Ernest J. King Papers, Box 4, 1940-42, Orders to Duty Folder. Itemized Schedule of Travel and Other Expenses.

41. Potter, 54-55.

42. Richardson, *Treadmill,* 238.

43. Ibid., 243.

44. Ibid., 244.

45. MacDonald, "Evolution of Aircraft Carriers," could be found on the Internet in 2008 at: http://www.history.navy.mil/ branches/car-toc.htm.

46. Pearl Harbor Hearings, Part I, 255. Richardson said he arrived at 3:00 P.M.

47. *The Keystone,* Volume XVI, Number XXV, April 6, 1940, At Sea.

48. *Honolulu Advertiser,* April 11, 1940, 3, front page.

49. Ibid., 3.

50. Ibid., April 3, 1940, 13; April 11, 3. Large liners like the SS *Lurline* and the SS *Matsonia* brought in passengers every ten days or so.

51. Jim Vlach to Jeanne, Thursday, April 11, 1940, copied by Skipper Steely in January 2003. In Vlach File of Steely Collection, Admiral Richardson Research. See also USS *Arizona* File.

52. *Honolulu Advertiser,* April 11, 1940, 3.

53. Jim Vlach to Jeanne, Thursday, April 12, 1940, copied by Skipper Steely in January 2003. In Vlach File of Steely Collection, Admiral Richardson Research. See also USS *Arizona* File.

54. *Honolulu Advertiser,* April 16, 1940, 1.

55. Hammond, 226.

56. Richardson, *Treadmill,* 248.

57. Ibid., 249.

58. Hammond, 247.

59. Potter, 55.

60. Greg Goebel, "In the Public Domain," could be found on the Internet in

2003 at: http://www.vectorsite.net/index.html.

    61. LoC, Bloch Papers, Box 3, Harold R. Stark File 1939-42.

    62. *Honolulu Advertiser,* April 24, 1940, 1.

    63. Ibid., June 6, 1940.

    64. NARA—College Park, Records of the Pearl Harbor Liaison Office, Box 7, Folder 1. April 10 from Richardson to Stark.

    65. USS *Augusta* (CA-31). Could be found on the Internet in 2003 at: http://www.internet-esq.com/ussaugusta/history/1928-31.htm.

    66. Wilhelm, 62-65.

    67. Captain Ellis M. Zacharias, "Eighteen Words That Bagged Japan," *Saturday Evening Post,* November 17, 1945.

    68. Hammond, 248.

Chapter 15: "Remain at Pearl Harbor Until . . ."

    1. U.S. Senate Committee on Naval Affairs, April 22, 1940, Senator David I. Walsh, chairman. During the first day of hearings Senator Scott W. Lucas of Illinois asked Taussig if he had being saying in public that the United States would be at war with Japan in six months. "If this is true, it does seem to me that the Senate ought to know something about a situation of that kind." Taussig begged off such a discussion at that time.

    2. LoC, Bloch Papers, Box 3, Harold R. Stark File 1939-42. Bloch to Stark, April 23, 1940.

    3. E-mail from Bob Parks, FDR Library, to Skipper Steely, August 6, 2003.

    4. Interview with Vice-Admiral J. K. Taussig, June 7, 1947, found at FDR Library as one of the Frank Freidel interviews. See Construction of Certain Naval Vessels Hearings before the Committee of Naval Affairs, U.S. Senate, 76th Congress, Third Session, H.R. 8026, 187-202.

    5. Betty Carney Taussig, *A Warrior for Freedom,* 56.

    6. Drew Pearson and Robert S. Allen, "Washington Merry-Go-Round," *New York Mirror,* May 1, 1940.

    7. *Honolulu Advertiser,* April 23, 1940, editorial page.

    8. Ibid., April 25, 1940, 2.

    9. Ibid., April 24, 1940, 1.

    10. "Navy Court-Martial Asked for Taussig," *New York World Telegram,* April 24, 1940, United Press article from Washington.

    11. LoC, Bloch Papers, Box 3, Harold R. Stark File 1939-42. Stark to Bloch, May 11, 1940.

    12. *Honolulu Advertiser,* April 26, 1940, 1.

    13. Ibid., 7.

    14. Ibid., 6-7.

    15. Ibid., April 27, 1940, 7.

    16. Ibid., April 26, 1940, 1.

    17. Stillwell, 54.

    18. *Honolulu Advertiser,* April 27, 1940, 7.

    19. Ibid.

    20. Ibid., April 25, 1940, 2.

    21. Ibid., April 26, 1940, 7.

22. LoC Manuscript Division, William F. Halsey Papers, Box 2, General Correspondence 1940 January-June Folder. Halsey to Addison T. Kirk, dated May 11, 1940.

23. *Honolulu Advertiser,* April 27, 1940, 7.

24. Ibid., 1.

25. Ibid.

26. Ibid., 8.

27. Ibid.

28. Ibid.

29. Elliott R. Thorpe, *East Wind, Rain* (Boston: Gambit Incorporated, 1969), 4.

30. *Honolulu Advertiser,* April 29, 1940, 1.

31. Ibid., April 28, 1940, 7. The Saturday night with Mayor Crane was at the Royal Hawaiian Hotel. May stood in the receiving line with Mrs. Charles S. Crane, the mayor's wife.

32. *Honolulu Advertiser,* July 11, 1940, 7. Admiral and Mrs. Andrews lived at 3663 Diamond Head Road.

33. *Honolulu Advertiser,* April 28, 1940, 9.

34. Simpson, 55. Also, *Honolulu Advertiser,* April 29, 1940, 2.

35. Richardson, *Treadmill,* 307; Simpson, 55, 292; Library of Congress, Dyer Papers, Richardson Folder.

36. *Honolulu Advertiser,* April 28, 1940, 12-13.

37. Ibid., April 30, 1940, 2.

38. Ibid., May 1, 1940, 1.

39. Richardson, *Treadmill,* 308.

40. *Honolulu Advertiser,* May 1, 1940, 7.

41. Ibid., May 2, 1940, 2.

42. Ibid., May 3, 1940, editorial page.

43. Ibid., May 3, 1940, 1; Pearl Harbor Hearings, Part I, 260.

44. *Honolulu Advertiser,* May 3, 1940, 7.

45. Ibid., May 4, 1940, 13. A complete passenger list is printed.

46. *Honolulu Advertiser,* May 4, 1940, 1.

47. *New York Times,* April 27, 1940.

48. Dyer, "Reminiscences," 186.

49. Richardson, *Treadmill,* 308. Pearl Harbor Hearings, Part I, 303. LoC, Dyer Papers, Box 9, Folder 6. Original written note brought to Richardson from communications, and a copy.

50. *Honolulu Advertiser,* May 4, 1940, 3.

51. Ibid., May 5, 1940, 2.

52. Ibid., 1.

53. Ibid., 2.

54. Ibid., May 6, 1940, 2.

55. Ibid., May 7, 1940, 1.

56. Ibid., 2.

57. Ibid., 1.

58. Richardson, *Treadmill,* 308-9. Pearl Harbor Hearings, Part I, 260. See received note from communications in the LoC, Dyer Papers, Box 9, Folder 6.

59. Ibid.

60. Pearl Harbor Hearings, Part I, 291.

61. Richardson, *Treadmill,* 309.

62. Pearl Harbor Hearings, Part I, 259. Richardson, *Treadmill,* 310.

63. *New York Times,* May 8, 1940, 8.

64. Ibid., June 18, 1940, 20.

65. *Honolulu Advertiser,* May 8, 1940, 1.

66. Ibid., April 11, 1940, 3.

67. Ibid., May 8, 1940, 1.

68. Ibid., May 9, 1940, 1.

69. Ibid., 2.

70. Ibid., May 10, 1940, 7.

71. Ibid. A complete list of those heading to Lahaina Roads is found on this page.

72. *Honolulu Advertiser,* May 11, 1940, 13.

73. Thorpe, 15.

74. *Honolulu Advertiser,* May 18, 1940, 13.

75. Ibid., May 11, 1940, 1.

76. Richardson, *Treadmill,* 311.

77. *Honolulu Advertiser,* May 12, 1940, 1.

78. Ibid., May 13, 1940, 1.

79. Ibid., May 14, 1940, 1.

80. Ibid., May 15, 1940, 1.

81. Ibid., May 17, 1940, 2.

82. Richardson, *Treadmill,* 228.

83. Thorpe, 14.

84. Ibid., 15.

85. Pearl Harbor Hearings, Part I, 258, 292; Part V, 2106.

86. *Honolulu Advertiser,* May 22, 1940, 2.

87. Ibid., May 24, 1940, 1.

88. Ibid., 6.

89. Richardson, *Treadmill,* 312.

90. Ibid., 316.

91. Pearl Harbor Hearings, Part XIV, 35.

92. Ibid., 292, 935-36.

93. Richardson, *Treadmill,* 331; Naval Dispatch, from ALUSNA, Tokyo, to OPNAV, dated April 23, 1940, in Steely Collection, Fleet Problem XXI.

94. Pearl Harbor Hearings, Part XV, 940; Part I, 259. Richardson, *Treadmill,* 319.

95. NARA—College Park, Records of the Pearl Harbor Liaison Office, Box 7, Folder 1. Richardson to Stark, dated May 22, 1940.

96. *Honolulu Advertiser,* May 25, 1940, 3.

97. Ibid., May 28, 1940, 13.

98. NARA—College Park, Records of the Pearl Harbor Liaison Office, Box 7, Folder 1. Stark to Richardson, May 17, 1940.

99. Pearl Harbor Hearings, Part I, 261; Part V, 2194; Part XIV, 943; Part XXII, 358; Part XXXII, 27, 75; and Part XXXIII, 1186. (Entire letter.) The letter can also be seen at NARA—College Park, Records of the Pearl Harbor Liaison Office,

Box 1, attached to January 20, 1941, letter from CinCUS to CNO.

100. *Honolulu Advertiser,* May 29, 1940, 1. His papers are at the Naval Historical Center in Washington, DC.

101. LoC Manuscript Division, William F. Halsey Papers, Box 2, General Correspondence 1940 Folder January-June. Halsey to Van Keuren, May 29, 1940.

102. *New York Times,* May 28, 1940.

103. LoC, Dyer Papers, Box 10-3. Richardson to Stark, May 28, 1940.

104. First Quarter Fiscal Employment Schedule, CinCUS, serial 1484 of April 30, 1940, Box 20, CinCUS Files, RG 313, NA; First Quarter Fiscal 1941 Employment Schedule, Revised, CinCUS, serial 1770 of May 28, 1940. Richardson, *Treadmill,* 321.

105. Pearl Harbor Hearings, Part I, 300. Richardson, *Treadmill,* 331.

106. For more see Hornbeck Papers, Hoover Institution Library, Stanford, California, Hornbeck Diary, June 1935.

107. *Honolulu Advertiser,* July 2, 1940, 1.

108. Richardson, *Treadmill,* 332. See also LoC, Dyer Papers, Box 9, Folder 6. "Notes Made While CinCUS."

109. NHC, Operational Archives Division, Oral Interviews, Henri Smith-Hutton, #25-283. Smith-Hutton was assigned to Japan at the time, leading an office with assistance from Arthur McCollum, Steve Jurika, Leonard Wagner, and other American Japanese language experts.

110. Pearl Harbor Hearings, Part I, 298; *Honolulu Advertiser,* July 6, 1940, 11. Meal menus are listed here.

111. Richardson, *Treadmill,* 332.

Chapter 16: "The Fleet Is Here—So Let's Go to Work"

1. *Honolulu Advertiser,* June 1, 1940, 7. In attendance were Admirals Snyder, Andrews, Fairfield, Vernou, Rowcliff, Marquart, Holmes, Kimmel, Todd, Halsey, Ingersoll, Newton, Friedell, Calhoun, Willson, Bristol, and Draemel.

2. *Honolulu Advertiser,* May 30, 1940, 2. Another story states that there were eighteen admirals present. See LoC, Dyer Papers, Box 9, Folder 3. Clipped story of event.

3. *Honolulu Advertiser,* May 31, 1940, 5.

4. Ibid., June 5, 1940, 9.

5. Ibid., June 7, 1940, 2.

6. Ibid., June 9, 1940, 3, society section.

7. Ibid., June 9, 1940, 4, society section; June 16, 1940, 5.

8. LoC, Dyer Papers, Box 10, Folder 7. Notes on chapter in book about CinCUS duty.

9. The entire speech could be read on the Internet in 2003 at: http://www.ibiblio.org/pha/7-2-188/188-17.html. The speech was given on June 10, 1940.

10. LoC, Dyer Papers, Box 10, Folder 2. Orders cut on June 14, 1940.

11. Richardson, *Treadmill,* 342.

12. *Honolulu Advertiser,* June 14, 1940, 2.

13. U.S. Navy Patrol Squadrons site, found on the Internet in 2003 at: http://www.vpnavy.com/vt5_history.html.

14. *Honolulu Advertiser,* June 18, 1940, 1.

15. Richardson, *Treadmill,* 342. Pearl Harbor Hearings, Part XIV, 946.

16. *Honolulu Advertiser,* June 18, 1940, 3.

17. In 2003 this message could be found on the Internet at: http://www.ibiblio.org/pha/pha/congress/keefe.html. Also, see War Department, June 17, 1940, dispatch to Commander Hawaiian Department, as cited in Pearl Harbor Hearings, Part I, 271, 288, 312; Part III, 1118, 1378; Part IV, 1884; Part V, 2452; Part XIV, 948; Part XXVI, 22; Part XXVIII, 1038.

18. NARA—College Park, Records of the Pearl Harbor Liaison Office, Box 23, Folder 18. "Herron, Genl., Communications Between War Dept. and Herron, re: 1940 Alert." A twenty-two-page summary of the alert is found here as well as Richardson's letters pertaining to the alert.

19. *Honolulu Advertiser,* June 18, 1940, 7.

20. Ibid., June 19, 1940, 1. NHC, Operational Archives Division, Oral Interviews, Henri Smith-Hutton, #24-278.

21. *Honolulu Advertiser,* June 20, 1940, 1.

22. Richardson, *Treadmill,* 322.

23. Pearl Harbor Hearings, Part XVI, 2341, 2368; Part XXII, 329.

24. Pearl Harbor Hearings, Part I, 271.

25. Richardson, *Treadmill,* 343; copy of letter is located at the NARA—College Park, Records of the Pearl Harbor Liaison Office, Box 7, Folder 1. Adolphus Andrews to Richardson, Tuesday, June 18, 1940.

26. Dyer, "Reminiscences," 186.

27. NARA—College Park, Records of the Pearl Harbor Liaison Office, Box 7, Folder 1. Richardson to Bloch, June 18, 1940.

28. LoC, Dyer Papers, Box 9, Folder 6. In an outline of events, Richardson says on June 19 he received the orders to move part of the fleet toward Panama. See "Notes Made While CinCUS."

29. Pearl Harbor Hearings, Part III, 1536.

30. CNO, June 20, 1940, dispatch to CinCUS. See also Pearl Harbor Hearings, Part III, 1409; Part XIV, 950.

31. NARA—College Park, Records of the Pearl Harbor Liaison Office, Box 7, Folder 1. Bloch to Richardson, June 20, 1940.

32. Richardson, *Treadmill,* 344.

33. Ibid., 345. Pearl Harbor Hearings, Part I, 262, 312; Part III, 1055. Read Roberta Wohlstetter, *Pearl Harbor: Warning and Decision* (Stanford, CA: Stanford University Press, 1962), 96. See LoC, Dyer Papers, Box 10, Folder 3. Letter dated November 28, 1945, from Richardson to William D. Mitchell, general counsel, Joint Committee on the Investigation of the Pearl Harbor Attack. After testifying to the committee, he asked them to hold their thoughts on messages about the June Army alert until he could research further. Richardson was surprised to find that on June 22, 1940, a message came to CinCUS from Stark, explaining the Navy's side of the event. Why it was not read in Hawaii is still unknown. It may have never arrived.

34. Richardson, *Treadmill,* 321. Also see Pearl Harbor Hearings, Part I, 270, 312; Part XIV, 946-47.

35. NARA—College Park, Records of the Pearl Harbor Liaison Office, Box 23, Folder 18. Marshall to Herron, undated letter, ca. June 27, 1940.

36. Richardson, *Treadmill,* 345; Pearl Harbor Hearings, Part I, 262.

37. Richardson, *Treadmill,* 337.

38. *Honolulu Advertiser,* June 23, 1940, 3.

39. Ibid., June 25, 1940. LoC, Dyer Papers, Box 10, Folder 7. Notes on his book's chapter about CinCUS duty. Richardson left with five battleships, three second-line light cruisers, three light cruisers, and seventeen destroyers.

40. *Honolulu Advertiser,* June 27, 1940, 1.

41. Richardson, *Treadmill,* 347.

42. Ibid., 348.

43. LoC, Dyer Papers, Box 9, Folder 6. "Notes Made While CinCUS."

44. Ibid.

45. LoC, Dyer Papers, Box 10, Folder 7. Notes on his book's chapter about CinCUS duty.

46. *New York Times,* July 1, 1940, 1.

47. *Honolulu Advertiser,* July 1, 1940, 1.

48. Richardson, *Treadmill,* 349.

49. *Honolulu Advertiser,* July 1, 1940, 3; July 2, 1940, 1.

50. Ibid., July 2, 1940, 1; July 3, 1940, 1.

51. Richardson, *Treadmill,* 392.

52. Pearl Harbor Hearings, Exhibit 52, 13; Part I, 268; Part III, 1050; Part IV, 1884, 1908.

53. Richardson, *Treadmill,* 392-93.

Chapter 17: Great Persuader Versus Great Politician

1. LoC, Dyer Papers, Box 10, Folder 2. Orders for this second attempt, stamped July 1, 1940. The flight went to San Francisco, then on United Airlines to Cleveland and Washington. Round-trip reimbursement was $233.46. See also in the LoC, Dyer Papers, Box 9, Folder 6. "Notes Made While CinCUS."

2. *Honolulu Advertiser,* July 5, 1940, 13. In 2003 Admiral Leslie J. O'Brien, eighty-seven, said he thought the admiral went under the name of Stanley.

3. Richardson, *Treadmill,* 383.

4. LoC, Dyer Papers, Box 10, Folder 7. Notes on his book's chapter about CinCUS duty. This act was all-comprehensive, but Japan felt it was aimed directly at its purchase of strategic minerals, chemicals, aircraft engines, parts, and equipment.

5. *Honolulu Advertiser,* July 6, 1940, 1.

6. Ibid., July 8, 1940, 1.

7. LoC, Dyer Papers, Box 9, Folder 6. "Notes Made While CinCUS."

8. *New York Times,* July 9, 1940, 1.

9. *Honolulu Advertiser,* July 9, 1940, 1, 5.

10. Day by Day—The Pare Lorentz Chronology, July 8, 1940, at 1300 hours. The source was the stenographer's diary and Miss Tully's appointment diary.

11. Pearl Harbor Hearings, Part I, 268. Richardson thought the meeting went on for two to three hours.

12. *New York Times,* June 9, 1940, 1; *Honolulu Advertiser,* July 10, 1940, 2.

13. Discussions of the July meeting can be found in the Pearl Harbor

Hearings, Part I, 268, 270, 282, 296; Part XX, 4411.

14. Richardson, *Treadmill,* 384-85.

15. Pearl Harbor Hearings, Part I, 258, 270.

16. LoC, Dyer Papers, Box 9, Folder 6. "Notes Made While CinCUS."

17. Pearl Harbor Hearings, Part I, 270.

18. Ibid.

19. Pearl Harbor Hearings, Part I, 290; Part III, 1054, 1118, 1500.

20. Pearl Harbor Hearings, Part III, 1054, 1500. Marshall mentions "magic" messages on both these pages, but no such messages were interpreted until two months later. He is relying on the memory of General George V. Strong, a War Staff member. Marshall even denies that Richardson brought up the alert subject. The general says the lunch was at his house, and that other guests were present.

21. LoC, Dyer Papers, Box 9, Folder 6. "Notes Made While CinCUS."

22. Ibid.

23. Pearl Harbor Hearings, Part I, 264, 268, 270, 296-97; Part XVI, 1987. To the congressmen at the Pearl Harbor hearings in 1945 Richardson said, "I was distinctly of the impression that Dr. Hornbeck was exercising a greater influence over the disposition of the Fleet than I was."

24. Keiichiro Komatsu, *Origins of the Pacific War and the Importance of Magic* (New York: St. Martin's Press, 1999), 146-69. This book provides an in-depth look at the cabinet members and influential persons filing daily opinions with Roosevelt.

25. Day by Day—The Pare Lorentz Chronology, July 11, 1940, at 1200 hours. The source was the stenographer's diary and Miss Tully's appointment diary. Also see LoC, Dyer Papers, Box 9, Folder 6. "Notes Made While CinCUS."

26. Pearl Harbor Hearings, Part I, 270.

27. LoC, Dyer Papers, Box 9, Folder 6. "Notes Made While CinCUS."

28. Ibid. Richardson notes takeoff at 7:30 P.M.

29. LoC, Bloch Papers, Box 3, Harold R. Stark File 1939-42. Stark to Bloch, July 12, 1940.

30. LoC, Dyer Papers, Box 10, Folder 2. Notation at bottom of July 1, 1940, orders.

31. Phone conversation with Lee Somerville, Paris, Texas, September 21, 2001. Asked several times if this call was in the summer or fall, he continually said it was in July, based upon the time when he was going to school at Sam Houston State Teachers College.

32. LoC, Dyer Papers, Box 9, Folder 6. "Notes Made While CinCUS." They arrived in Pearl Harbor at 7:30 A.M.

33. Richardson, *Treadmill,* 386.

34. *Honolulu Advertiser,* July 12, 1940, 2.

35. Richardson, *Treadmill,* 388.

36. LoC, Dyer Papers, Box 10, Folder 7. Notes on his book's chapter about CinCUS duty.

37. *Honolulu Advertiser,* August 1, 1940, 1.

38. Ibid., August 4, 1940. LoC Manuscript Division, John L. McCrea Papers, Box 1, Folder 5. McCrea to all hands on the USS *Pennsylvania,* July 23, 1940.

39. *Honolulu Advertiser,* July 25, 1940, 2. LoC, Dyer Papers, Box 9, Folder 6. "Notes Made While CinCUS." Richardson says they crossed the equator on July 24. They may have not been back at Hawaii until late July 25.

40. *Honolulu Advertiser,* July 26, 1940, 19.

41. Ibid., July 29, 1940, 2.

42. Ibid., July 30, 1940, 1, 8.

43. LoC, Dyer Papers, Box 9, Folder 6. "Notes Made While CinCUS."

44. *Honolulu Advertiser,* July 31, 1940, 19.

45. Richardson, *Treadmill,* 394.

46. USNI, Annapolis, Oral Interviews, Rear Admiral Raymond D. Tarbuck, 1973, #2-65.

47. Pearl Harbor Hearings, Part I, 262-63.

48. *Honolulu Advertiser,* August 2, 1940, 13; August 5, 1940, 11.

49. *Honolulu Advertiser,* August 10, 1940, 2.

50. Ibid., August 11, 1940, 3; August 16, 1940, 3.

51. *Honolulu Advertiser,* August 11, 1940, 5. The good photo was a Murie Ogden Studio work, done earlier apparently.

52. *Honolulu Advertiser,* August 14, 1940, 1.

53. NARA—College Park, Records of the Pearl Harbor Liaison Office, Box 23, Folder 18. Herron to Marshall, August 21, 1940.

54. *The Keystone,* Volume XVI, Number XLIII, August 24, 1940, Lahaina Roads.

55. LoC, Dyer Papers, Box 9, Folder 7. Letter dated August 24, 1940.

56. *Honolulu Advertiser,* August 24, 1940, 7. LoC, Dyer Papers, Box 9, Folder 6. "Notes Made While CinCUS." On August 21, 1940, Richardson received official notice that Knox was coming.

57. *Honolulu Advertiser,* August 20, 1940, 2.

58. Ibid., August 21, 1940, 3.

59. Ibid., August 24, 1940, 2. A photograph does exist, and shows it arriving in Pearl Harbor, but is tagged October 23, 1940. Perhaps another one came later. It could be found on the Internet in 2003 at: http://www.history.navy.mil/photos/images/g410000/g411134.jpg. See also LoC, Bloch Papers, Box 3, Harold R. Stark File 1939-42. Bloch to Stark, November 5, 1940. It sank at first to the bottom of Pearl Harbor.

60. LoC, Bloch Papers, Box 3, Harold R. Stark File 1939-42. Bloch to Stark, November 5, 1940.

61. *Honolulu Advertiser,* August 31, 1940, 1, 15. LoC, Dyer Papers, Box 10, Folder 7, notes on his book's chapter about CinCUS duty.

62. USNI, Annapolis, Oral Interviews, Reminiscences of Vice Admiral Charles A. Pownall, 102.

63. LoC Manuscript Division, John L. McCrea Papers, Box 1, Folder 5. Felix Stump to McCrea, September 1, 1940.

64. USNI, Annapolis, Oral Interviews, Rear Admiral James D. Ramage, #1-38-40.

65. Richardson, *Treadmill,* 366-67. CinCUS, serial 2614 of August 20, 1940, letter to fleet (in Hawaiian area), Box 70, CinCUS Files, RG 313, NA; copies also found in Record Group 80, Records of the Department of the Navy, Office File of Secretary of the Navy Frank Knox, 1940-1944, 49-1-3. See a copy also in the

LoC Manuscript Division, John L. McCrea Papers, Box 1, Folder 5.

66. Record Group 80, Records of the Department of the Navy, Office File of Secretary of the Navy Frank Knox, 1940-1944, 49-1-3. See also Pearl Harbor Hearings, Part XXXV, 430.

67. Interview with Jim Vlach, January 10, 2003. He lives in a retirement home in Riverside, California. Jeannie is dead. Also, see their comments and photos on the Internet in 2003 at http://www.homestead.com/arizonareunion/vlach.html.

68. Stillwell, 171.

69. NHC Operational Archives, Oral Interviews, Bernard Max Strean, #2-58.

70. NHC Operational Archives, Oral Interviews, Felix L. Johnson, #2-111.

71. DANFS, Office of the Chief of Naval Operations, Naval History Division, Washington, USS *Balch II* (DD-363). Located on the Internet in 2003 at: http://www.ibiblio.org/hyperwar/USN/ ships/dafs/DD/dd363.html.

72. DANFS Online. Found on the Internet in 2003 at: http://www.hazegray.org/danfs/auxil/ad11.htm.

73. DANFS Online, Destroyers. Found on the Internet in 2003 at: http://www.hazegray.org/danfs/destroy/dd408txt.htm.

74. Interview by phone in spring of 2002 with Captain Forrest Biard, a native of Bonham, Texas.

75. Beth Bailey and David Farber, *The First Strange Place: Alchemy of Race and Sex in World War II Hawaii* (Baltimore: Johns Hopkins University Press, 1994).

76. USS *Shaw* information site could be found on the Internet in 2003 at: http://www.specwarnet.com/USSShaw/History_prewar.htm. Information on the USS *Case* can be found at: http://mywebpages.comcast.net/wgoffeney/Case/uss-case.htm.

77. Stillwell, 54.

78. Ibid., 55.

79. Beigel, 33.

80. Ibid., 53. See also *San Pedro News Pilot,* June 22, 1940.

81. Truman Library, Oral Interview Section, Rear Admiral Donald J. Mac Donald, August 1970. MacDonald went with Ghormley to England.

82. LoC, Dyer Papers, Box 9, Folder 6. "Notes Made While CinCUS."

Chapter 18: New Secretary Inspects Fleet

1. Anthony Cave Brown, *The Last Hero: Wild Bill Donovan* (New York: Times Books, 1982), 141.

2. *Honolulu Advertiser,* September 6, 1940, 1.

3. Richard Dunlop, *Donovan: America's Master Spy* (New York: Rand McNally and Company, 1982), 226.

4. NHC Operational Archives, Oral Interviews, Bernhard Henry Bieri, #2-84.

5. Richardson, *Treadmill,* 369.

6. *Honolulu Advertiser,* September 7, 1940, 1. Knox sitting with a pipe in his mouth and wire-rim glasses did not look much different from Richardson in the face.

7. *Honolulu Advertiser,* September 1, 1940, society page.

8. Dunlop, 226.

9. *Honolulu Advertiser,* September 4, 1940, 9.

10. LoC Manuscript Division, William F. Halsey Papers, Box 2, General Correspondence, July-December, 1940. Letter dated August 27, 1940.

11. *Honolulu Advertiser,* September 7, 1940, 7. Cook was commander of the aircraft scouting force.

12. *Honolulu Advertiser,* September 6, 1940.

13. The Selective Training and Service Act was instituted on September 14, 1940. Initially, the Navy was not involved.

14. *Honolulu Advertiser,* September 8, 1940, 1. The newspaper says Knox and Richardson left Pearl Harbor at 9:30 on Sunday morning.

15. President Roosevelt, certain the United States would soon be in the European war, designed a program to assist the Allies. He would donate old Navy vessels in exchange for long-term leases at certain locations. This treaty also turned up the volume of American production on newer ships, weapons, and materials. The agreement was struck on September 2, 1940, and fifty destroyers were immediately sent to Great Britain.

16. LoC, Dyer Papers, Box 10, Folder 7. Notes on his book's chapter about CinCUS duty.

17. Zacharias, *Secret Missions,* 266. Headlines droned on for month after month, and became rather mundane, even though revealing.

18. LoC, Dyer Papers, Box 9, Folder 6. "Notes Made While CinCUS."

19. LoC, Dyer Papers, Box 10, Folder 7. Notes on his book's chapter about CinCUS duty.

20. LoC, Dyer Papers, Box 9, Folder 6. "Notes Made While CinCUS." Richardson lists ships Knox visited, but does not include the USS *Clark.* He does list: USS *Boise* with Kimmel; USS *Indianapolis* with Andrews; USS *Binford* with Mayfield; and USS *New Mexico* with Snyder.

21. Mayock, 28.

22. *Honolulu Advertiser,* September 14, 1940, 1, 4.

23. Corey Ford, *Donovan of OSS* (Boston: Little, Brown and Company, 1970), 94.

24. Richardson, *Treadmill,* 378; Pearl Harbor Hearings, Part I, 263.

25. *Honolulu Advertiser,* September 13, 1940, 2.

26. Richmond Kelly Turner, *The Amphibians Came to Conquer: The Story of Admiral Richmond Kelly Turner,* Ed. George C. Dyer (Washington, DC: U.S. Government Printing Office), 154.

27. LoC, Dyer Papers, Box 9, Folder 6. "Notes Made While CinCUS."

28. For more on the visit as appeared in the Pearl Harbor Hearings, see Part I, 260, 338 (memo by Richardson); Part VI, 2562; Part XXXX, 160 (memo).

29. NHC Operational Archives, Oral Interviews, Bernhard Henry Bieri, #2-85.

30. Pearl Harbor Hearings, Part I, 263. He wrote the memorandum on September 12, 1940. A copy can be read at the NARA—College Park, Records of the Pearl Harbor Liaison Office, Box 7, Folder 1. Memorandum to Secretary of State from CinCUS; or at the LoC, Dyer Papers, Box 9, Folder 7.

31. Pearl Harbor Hearings, Part I, 264, taken from memorandum to Knox.

32. Gordon W. Prange in collaboration with Donald M. Goldstein and Katherine V. Dillon, *Pearl Harbor: The Verdict of History* (New York: McGraw-Hill Book Company, 1985), 388.

33. Richardson, *Treadmill*, 380.

34. LoC Manuscript Division, Frank Knox Papers, Box 4, July-December General Correspondence 1940 Folder. Knox to Ghormley, November 16, 1940.

35. Dunlop, 226.

36. Ibid., 228.

37. *Honolulu Advertiser*, September 15, 1940, 7.

38. Richardson, *Treadmill*, 381. Pearl Harbor Hearings, Part XIV, 961. See also the LoC Manuscript Division, M. L. Deyo Papers, Box 1, Correspondence 1940. Deyo to Kimmel, dated September 28, 1940.

39. Prange, *Pearl Harbor: The Verdict of History*, 389.

40. LoC, Dyer Papers, Box 10-3. Stark to Richardson at Long Beach, September 24, 1940.

41. LoC, Dyer Papers, Box 10-3. Knox to Richardson at Long Beach, September 25, 1940.

42. Richardson, *Treadmill*, 382.

43. *Chicago Daily News*, April 3, 1940.

Chapter 19: Time to Visit Washington Again

1. *Honolulu Advertiser*, September 17, 1940, 1.

2. LoC, Dyer Papers, Box 9, Folder 6. "Notes Made While CinCUS."

3. NARA—College Park, Records of the Pearl Harbor Liaison Office, Box 7, Folder 1. Richardson in Honolulu to Stark, September 18, 1940.

4. Richardson, *Treadmill*, 395. Pearl Harbor Hearings, Part XIV, 952-53.

5. *Honolulu Advertiser*, September 19, 1940, 2.

6. Ibid., July 25, 1940, 2.

7. Isabel Dean Short, "The General's Lady" (unpublished manuscript written in the 1950s, perhaps), 000250, located today in the Short Papers, Hoover Archives, Stanford University, Stanford, California. It has rarely if ever been cited as a footnote, mostly because the Short family has been very reluctant to have anything written on the general.

8. *Honolulu Advertiser*, September 21, 1940, 1.

9. Ibid., 2. See the LoC, Bloch Papers, Box 3, Harold R. Stark File 1939-42. Stark to Richardson, August 18, 1940. *Life*, October 28, 1940.

10. *Honolulu Advertiser*, September 20, 1940, 2.

11. Ibid., October 1, 1940, 11.

12. Beigel, 63.

13. *Honolulu Advertiser*, October 3, 1940, 1; *New York Times*, October 3, 1.

14. *Honolulu Advertiser*, October 4, 1940, 1.

15. Pearl Harbor Hearings, Part XIV, 961.

16. LoC, Dyer Papers, Box 10-3. Stark to Richardson on the USS *New Mexico*, Long Beach, September 24, 1940.

17. LoC, Dyer Papers, Box 10-3. Stark to Richardson, September 27, 1940. He asked that Murphy come along, but called him "your war plans officer," giving the impression Stark did not know Murphy well.

18. Pearl Harbor Hearings, Part XIV, 961.

19. LoC, Dyer Papers, Box 10-3. Stark to Richardson, October 1, 1940.

Stark's wife Kit, and their daughter Kewpie, her two children, and a nurse would also be there that week.

20. LoC, Dyer Papers, Box 10, Folder 2. Orders from Stark dated October 7, 1940. See also Richardson's notation on second and third endorsement, October 11, 1940, for exact times.

21. *New York Times,* October 7, 1940, 9. LoC, Dyer Papers, Box 9, Folder 6. "Notes Made While CinCUS."

22. Pearl Harbor Hearings, Part I, 264. LoC, Dyer Papers, Box 9, Folder 6. "Notes Made While CinCUS."

23. *New York Times,* October 8, 1940, 10.

24. Day by Day—The Pare Lorentz Chronology. This says Richardson and Leahy ate with FDR on October 8, 1940, but in the LoC, Dyer Papers, Box 9, Folder 6, "Notes Made While CinCUS," Richardson says it was October 7.

25. Pearl Harbor Hearings, Part I, 265.

26. Ibid.

27. LoC, Dyer Papers, Box 9, Folder 6. "Notes Made While CinCUS."

28. Grinberg Worldwide Images, Gettyimages, Historic Films, and other services can pull clips from various portions of the Congressional Pearl Harbor Hearings.

29. Pearl Harbor Hearings, Part I, 266.

30. Ibid., 265.

31. Morgenstern, 58; Richardson, *Treadmill,* 427; Pearl Harbor Hearings, Part I, 265-68; and LoC, Dyer Papers, Box 9, Folder 6. Notes of testimony before Congressional Joint Hearings on Pearl Harbor, 6.

32. One place this was stated was on the Internet in 2006 at: http://www.microworks.net/pacific/special/history1.htm. It is an essay called "The Alpha: Pearl Harbor, December 1941." It has no listed author. The statement has not been found in a book, letter, or official correspondence. The essay is posted on a Web site created by Tim Lanzendörfer, called The Pacific War: The U.S. Navy.

33. Pearl Harbor Hearings, Part I, 266, 268-69; also in October 9, 1940, memo to Stark, Richardson notes on the meeting sent to CNO Stark, "Points Covered in Talk with the President." Found in CinCUS records held by College Park, Maryland, branch. See Patrick R. Osborn, Modern Military Records, Textual Archives Services Division, to Skipper Steely, dated September 20, 2001. Another memo of what was said in the meeting with FDR is in the LoC, Dyer Papers, Box 9, Folder 6. "Conversation with President 8 Oct. 1940."

34. William Doyle, *Inside the Oval Office: The White House Tapes from FDR to Clinton* (New York: Kodansha International, 2002), 33. To hear these comments, see the whitehousetapes.org site of the University of Virginia Miller Center for History. Go to #19, and the "first time that any damn Jap has told us to get out of Hawaii" comment is at about 11:20 of the 14:25-minute recording.

35. FDR Library, Roosevelt Presidential Press Conference #688, October 8, 1940; Press Conference #689, October 15, 1940. To hear them, go to whitehousetapes.org on the Internet, provided by the University of Virginia Miller Center of History. On tape 18b is October 8. Go to 4:20, and the press conference begins. Maps comments are at about 6:40 of the 11:24-minute recording.

36. Grinberg Worldwide Images. Clips prepared in 2002 for Skipper Steely. This video includes the audio of the exact words uttered by Richardson to the hearing. Alden Hatch portrays the words a bit differently in his book, *Franklin D. Roosevelt: An Informal Biography* (New York: Holt, 1947). See discussion on this subject in Charles A. Beard, *President Roosevelt and the Coming of War 1941* (New Haven, CT: Yale University Press, 1948), 2416.

37. Richardson, *Treadmill,* 427.

38. Grinberg Worldwide Images. Clips prepared in 2002 for Skipper Steely. Date of Leahy's testimony was Wednesday, November 21, 1945. See Pearl Harbor Hearings, Part I, 341-70.

39. Betty Carney Taussig, *A Warrior for Freedom,* 57.

40. Richardson, *Treadmill,* 435.

41. NHC, Operational Archives, Oral Interviews, Kemp Tolley, #4-494.

42. Richardson, *Treadmill,* 435.

43. Marolda, 90.

44. Dyer, "Reminiscences," 196.

45. *Life,* October 28, 1940. The entire issue was given to the Navy, with photos of Richardson directing the exercises from the bridge of the USS *Pennsylvania.* He did look a bit old, but articles gave the impression he ran a good organization.

46. Pearl Harbor Hearings, Part I, 311.

47. Marolda, 174-75.

48. Pearl Harbor Hearings, Part I, 268. October 9, 1940 "Memorandum for the Chief of Naval Operations, Points Covered in Talk with the President." Found in CinCUS records at College Park, Maryland. See Steely Collection, Texas A&M-Commerce Gee Library, Richardson Papers, NARA College Park Files—CINCUS. Richardson had not done a memo after the July presidential meeting. See Pearl Harbor Hearings, Part I, 292.

49. Pearl Harbor Hearings, Part I, 269. October 9, 1940, memo to Stark about the White House meeting the previous day.

50. Pearl Harbor Hearings, Part I, 264, 298. LoC, Dyer Papers, Box 9, Folder 6. "Notes Made While CinCUS."

51. Pearl Harbor Hearings, Part I, 296, 298.

52. Marolda, 54-55.

53. Pearl Harbor Hearings, Part I, 264-65.

54. Pearl Harbor Hearings, Part I, 322. LoC, Dyer Papers, Box 9, Folder 6. "Notes Made While CinCUS."

55. LoC, Dyer Papers, Box 9, Folder 6. Notes of testimony before Congressional Joint Hearings on Pearl Harbor, 6.

56. Pearl Harbor Hearings, Part I, 334-35.

57. Ibid., 335.

Chapter 20: Fleet Remains, Supplies Begin Arriving

1. LoC, Dyer Papers, Box 9, Folder 6. "Notes Made While CinCUS."

2. *Honolulu Advertiser,* October 18, 1940, 5; *New York Times,* October 10, 1940, 1. Some of the new sailors were placed on ships that were heading for Mare Island or Puget Sound for repairs, so they were not immediately taken to Hawaii.

3. LoC Manuscript Division, William F. Halsey Papers, Box 2, General Correspondence, July-December, 1940. J. S. McCain to Commanding Officer, Carrier Division One, dated September 13, 1940.

4. *Honolulu Advertiser,* October 13, 1940, 6.

5. Beigel, 65.

6. Ellis M. Zacharias Papers, in possession of his son, Jerrold Zacharias, on two disks. See PH-0 and PH-00.

7. Richardson, *Treadmill,* 156. This banquet was held in September of 1939 in Long Beach, California, according to Admiral Richardson. However, correspondence with Jerrold Zacharias in 2003 revealed a date of February 3, 1940. Richardson was the guest of honor of newsmen at the University Club.

8. Wilhelm, 99-108. Zacharias, *Secret Missions,* 220.

9. Gordon W. Prange in collaboration with Donald M. Goldstein and Katherine V. Dillon, *At Dawn We Slept: The Untold Story of Pearl Harbor* (New York: McGraw-Hill Book Company, 1981; reprint, New York: Penguin Books, 1983), 40. Pearl Harbor Hearings, Part XIV, 963-64; Part XXXII, 79; Part XXXIII, 1190.

10. NARA—College Park, Records of the Pearl Harbor Liaison Office, Box 7, Folder 1. Richardson to Stark, October 22, 1940; or in the LoC, Dyer Papers, Box 9, Folder 7.

11. *Honolulu Advertiser,* October 5, 1940, 2.

12. Ibid., October 7, 1940, 1.

13. Ibid., October 10, 1940, 9.

14. Ibid., October 17, 1940, 5.

15. Ibid., October 10, 1940, 14.

16. Ibid., October 16, 1940, 8.

17. Richardson, *Treadmill,* 191. LoC, Dyer Papers, Box 10-3. Snyder to Richardson at Navy Yard, Puget Sound, Washington, dated October 21, 1940. Halsey seems to take credit for the shorts idea.

18. *Honolulu Advertiser,* October 17, 1940, 1; October 22, 1940, 2. The first number was drawn by Secretary of War Henry Stimson on October 29.

19. *Honolulu Advertiser,* October 18, 1940, 1.

20. Pearl Harbor Hearings, Part I, 319. Paragraph 8 of the October 16, 1940, letter attached to the plan says that more specific details were being forwarded in a locked box via the Clipper service. NARA—College Park, Records of the Pearl Harbor Liaison Office, Box 7, Folder 11. Richardson to Hart letter dated October 16, 1940. LoC, Dyer Papers, Box 9, Folder 6. "Notes Made While CinCUS."

21. Pearl Harbor Hearings, Part I, 306, 316. The letter is dated October 16, 1940, and should be attached to PH Hearings. See Exhibit 11. It is also mentioned in upcoming war plans chapter. Richardson's cover letter appears on page 318.

22. Pearl Harbor Hearings, Part I, 307, 316-18.

23. Ibid., 318.

24. NARA—College Park, Records of the Pearl Harbor Liaison Office, Box 7, Folder 1. Richardson at Long Beach to Stark, dated November 28, 1940.

25. Pearl Harbor Hearings, Part I, 319.

26. Pearl Harbor Hearings, Part V, 2195.

27. LoC Manuscript Division, Frank Knox Papers, Box 4, July-December

General Correspondence 1940 Folder. Ghormley to Knox, October 11, 1940.

28. *Honolulu Advertiser,* October 18, 1940, 1.

29. LoC Manuscript Division, John L. McCrea Papers, Box 1, Folder 5. Stark to Hart, October 22, 1940.

30. *Honolulu Advertiser,* October 27, 1940, 13. It actually was a very old article, apparently, only covering the first years of the bureau.

31. LoC, Dyer Papers, Box 9, Folder 6. "Notes Made While CinCUS."

32. The *Kiplinger Washington Letter,* circulated privately to businessmen, Saturday, October 19, 1940.

33. Richardson, *Treadmill,* 402.

34. *Honolulu Advertiser,* November 2, 1940, 9.

35. Ibid., 13, society page.

36. LoC Manuscript Division, William F. Halsey Papers, Box 2, General Correspondence, July-December 1940. Letter to Merritt T. Cooke from Halsey dated November 6, 1940, written on Fleet Air Detachment stationery, San Diego; and Halsey in San Diego to Associated Telephone Company in Long Beach, dated November 8, 1940.

37. *Honolulu Advertiser,* November 15, 1940, 9. The newspaper lists several Navy officers and wives who lived in the Gill Apartments.

38. *Honolulu Advertiser,* November 16, 1940, 15; November 27, 1940, 15.

39. *Honolulu Advertiser,* November 10, 1940, 7.

40. Ibid., November 4, 1940, 1. NHC, Operational Archives Division, Oral Interviews, Admiral George van Deurs, 366. He was quick to point out that Martin did not accept Bellinger's comments very easily.

41. *Honolulu Advertiser,* November 3, 1940, 6.

42. Ibid., 13.

43. Ibid., November 6, 1940, 3.

44. Ibid., November 10, 1940, editorial page.

45. LoC, Dyer Papers, Box 9, Folder 6. "Notes Made While CinCUS."

46. Ibid.

47. From USS *Augusta* 1940 activities as found on the Internet in 2003 at: http://www.internet-esq.com/ussaugusta/history/1940.htm.

48. *Honolulu Advertiser,* November 15, 1940, 3.

49. Ibid., November 16, 1940, 1.

50. Beigel, 65. Roosevelt declared November 21 to be Thanksgiving that year, hoping to assist the merchants of the country. Many simply celebrated it on the fourth Thursday as originally proclaimed by Abraham Lincoln. Some comments by sailors indicate they celebrated on November 28. After much confusion, especially for prescheduled football games and parades, and after reading thousands of letters of complaint and jest, Congress made the fourth Thursday official in 1941. LoC, Dyer Papers, Box 9, Folder 6. "Notes Made While CinCUS."

51. *Honolulu Advertiser,* December 2, 1940, 2.

52. Ibid., December 5, 1940, 1.

53. Ibid., 5.

54. Duane L. Whitlock, "Station C and Fleet Radio Unit Melbourne (FRUM-MEL) Revisited," presentation given to the third annual Cryptologic History Symposium at the National Security Agency on October 28, 1992. Copy in the

Whitlock Papers, Archives, University of Colorado at Boulder.

55. LoC, Dyer Papers, Box 9, Folder 6. "Notes Made While CinCUS."

56. *Honolulu Advertiser,* December 2, 1940, 2.

57. NHC Operational Archives, Oral Interviews, William R. Smedberg, #2-156.

58. LoC, Dyer Papers, Box 10-3. Hart to Richardson, December 15, 1940.

59. *Honolulu Advertiser,* December 17, 1940, 7.

60. Ibid., December 11, 1940, 1.

61. Ibid., December 12, 1940, 1.

62. Ibid., December 11, 1940, 5.

63. Ibid., December 17, 1940, 7.

64. LoC, Dyer Papers, Box 10, Folder 7. Notes on his book's chapter about CinCUS duty.

65. LoC, Dyer Papers, Box 9, Folder 6. "Notes Made While CinCUS."

66. USNI, Annapolis, Oral Interviews, Rear Admiral Raymond D. Tarbuck, #2-66.

67. NHC, Oral Interviews, Kent Melhorn, 62.

68. Pearl Harbor Hearings, Part I, 310.

69. *Honolulu Advertiser,* December 10, 1940, 5.

70. Ibid., December 8, 1940, 14.

71. Ibid., December 22, 1940, society page 4.

72. Most of Hewitt's World War II service was in and around the Mediterranean as commander of the Eighth Fleet. He led the invasion of Sicily, Salerno in Italy, and later southern France.

73. Evelyn Cherpak, ed., *Memoirs of Admiral H. Kent Hewitt* (Newport, RI: Naval War College Press, 2004), 110. He added that Kimmel kept up the same "indefatigable plan," but Hewitt somewhat contradicted his confidence in the preparations at Hawaii on page 109 by writing that antiaircraft artillery was parked at Schofield Barracks at the time of the Pearl Harbor attack in 1941, ammunition was still stored in caves, and projected battery positions had hardly been more than plotted on paper, most of these being Army assignments.

74. *Honolulu Advertiser,* December 24, 1940, 9.

75. Ibid., December 25, 1940, 1.

Chapter 21: War Plans Unrealistic

1. Richardson, *Treadmill,* 255.

2. Miller, 221.

3. U.S. Naval Station, Norfolk, Virginia. A building there was dedicated in Murphy's name in 1976.

4. Last Will and Testament of James O. Richardson, January 11, 1968. Signed by Vincent R. Murphy and attorney Lawrence C. Moore of 3503 30th NW, Washington, DC. It was filed with the District of Columbia Register of Wills, Peter J. McLaughlin, on May 2, 1974.

5. Pearl Harbor Hearings, Part I, 305.

6. NARA—College Park, Records of the Pearl Harbor Liaison Office, Box 7, Folder 1. Many of the Stark/Richardson letters of 1940 and early 1941 are located here, in photostat form, easier to research in one place than to plod through CNO and CinCUS files at NARA Washington. Plus, naval papers downtown go up to 1940, and then 1941 files are located in College Park.

7. Richardson, *Treadmill,* 278.

8. Harry W. Hill, Oral Interview for Columbia University, 178.

9. Miller, 221. Cooke was what Miller called a thruster. For some reason, Miller viewed Richardson as a defensivist, at the other end of the planning span of thought. However, he admitted in conversations he had not studied Richardson heavily.

10. Richardson, *Treadmill,* 112.

11. Telephone interview with Charlie Cooke of Sonoma, California, December 11, 2002. The son of Charles M. "Savvy" Cooke, Charlie says that his father did not have the same high opinion of Harry Hill.

12. A. J. Hill, *Under Pressure: The Final Voyage of Submarine S-Five* (New York: The Free Press, 2002).

13. Harry W. Hill, Oral Interview for Columbia University, 180.

14. Ibid.

15. Ibid., 181.

16. Ibid.

17. Ibid., 182.

18. Richardson, *Treadmill,* 286.

19. Ibid., 232.

20. Harry W. Hill, Oral Interview for Columbia University, 185.

21. Ibid., 183.

22. Richardson, *Treadmill,* 318. Richardson says Hill left in January, but Hill says he did not report for duty until March 7, 1940. See Harry W. Hill, Oral Interview for Columbia University, 185.

23. Pearl Harbor Hearings, Part XXVI, 268; or see Turner, 163.

24. Richardson, *Treadmill,* 286.

25. Ibid., 279-82.

26. Ibid., 280. Some of these had met in discussion with the General Board the previous week.

27. Richardson, *Treadmill,* 281.

28. Ibid., 282.

29. Ibid., 283.

30. Ibid. The Rainbow No. 1, WPL-42, can be found at NHD, CNO, 12 July 1940, Plan File.

31. Turner, 162.

32. Pearl Harbor Hearings, Part I, 309.

33. Richardson, *Treadmill,* 285.

34. Pearl Harbor Hearings, Part XIV, 935. Admiral Richardson letter to Stark, May 13, 1940.

35. Pearl Harbor Hearings, Part XIV, 938. Admiral Richardson letter to Stark, May 22, 1940.

36. Pearl Harbor Hearings, Part XIV, 935. Admiral Richardson letter to Stark, May 13, 1940; Part XIV, 938. Stark letter to Richardson, May 22, 1940.

37. Turner, 162.

38. Richardson, *Treadmill,* 398.

39. LoC, Dyer Papers, Box 9, Folder 6. "Notes Made While CinCUS." Knox called at 4:00 P.M.

40. Pearl Harbor Hearings, Part I, 305-6. Richardson, *Treadmill,* 400; Steely Collection, Richardson Research, Frank Knox File. Can also be found placed online by the FDR Library.

41. FDR Library, Safe Files, Box 4. Memorandum for the President from Secretary of the Navy, October 9, 1940. It could be viewed online in 2002 at: http://www.fdrlibrary.marist.edu/psf/box4/a46h02.html. Go to Navy Department 1934—Feb. 1942 Index. Click Secretary of the Navy—10/9/40.

42. Pearl Harbor Hearings, Part I, 311.

43. FDR Library, Safe Files, Box 4. Memorandum for the Secretary of the Navy, from The White House, October 10, 1940. It could be viewed online in 2002 at: http://www.fdrlibrary.marist.edu/psf/box4/t46h01.html. Go to Navy Department 1934—Feb. 1942 Index. Click FDR to the Navy—10/10/40.

44. Simpson, 63. Simpson says that after Knox asked for comments, Richardson "exploded." But, he bases his account of the meeting upon Richardson's book and Pearl Harbor Hearings, Part I, 305. Nowhere does Richardson mention he did anything like "explode."

45. Pearl Harbor Hearings, Part I, 305.

46. Simpson, 62.

47. Morgenstern, 59.

48. Pearl Harbor Hearings, Part I, 306.

49. LoC, Dyer Papers, Box 9, Folder 6. "Notes Made While CinCUS."

50. Morgenstern, 60. He wrote that even at his intuitive worst, Hitler never even engaged in such fantasies. Admirals did not go this far with statements about the president, though Stark did call detaching a naval group to the Philippines a "childish" idea from the State Department.

51. FDR Library, Safe Files, Box 4. U.S. Fleet Dispositions and Operations—October 11-1940, 1. It could be viewed online in 2002 at: http://www.fdrlibrary.marist.edu/psf/box4/t46I01.html. Steely Collection, Richardson Research, Burma Road File.

52. Miller, 262. Miller does not mention that the plan was to draw up a response to the reopening of the Burma Road, nor that Op-12 and Murphy worked all night. He called it a "stopgap" *Rainbow Three Plan,* a weak mixture of *Orange* and *Rainbow Two Plans.* By then, Stark was not warm to a Pacific war, knowing that Roosevelt would order a stronger Navy presence to the Atlantic at any time.

53. Richardson, *Treadmill,* 400. When Richardson was back on the USS *New Mexico* off San Pedro, he received orders from Stark to forward a copy of the plan to Admiral Hart. Pearl Harbor Hearings, Part I, 306. This was done on October 16, 1940.

54. Richardson, *Treadmill,* 401.

55. Pearl Harbor Hearings, Part I, 322.

56. FDR Library, Safe Files, Box 4. J. M. Reeves to Admiral Stark, 11/6/40. It could be viewed online in 2002 at: http://www.fdrlibrary.marist.edu/psf/box4/t46j02.html.

57. Interview by phone with the late Lee Somerville, Paris, Texas, stepnephew of Jessie Richardson Chambers, summer 2000.

58. *New York Times,* October 11, 1940, 1.

59. CinCUS, October 22, 1940, letter to CNO. Richardson, *Treadmill,* 288. Pearl Harbor Hearings, Part XIV, 963-64; Part XXXII, 79; Part XXXIII, 1190 (all of letter here); or, read it at the NARA—College Park, Records of the Pearl Harbor Liaison Office, Box 7, Folder 1; or in LoC, Dyer Papers, Box 9, Folder 7.

60. Richardson, *Treadmill,* 288.

61. LoC, Dyer Papers, Box 9, Folder 6. "Notes Made While CinCUS."

62. *Time,* Volume XXXVI, Number 1, July 1, 1940, 13. The crude rubber supply came from British Malaya and the Netherlands East Indies. From Indo-China came another 4.5 percent. America's supply of tin came mainly from the area also. NHC, Operational Archives Division, Oral Interviews, Henri Smith-Hutton, #24-278. Smith-Hutton said there was some strong protest from the American government, causing the Japanese Army to ask for assistance from their Navy.

63. Pearl Harbor Hearings, Part XXXIII, 1190-92, Richardson to Stark, CIN-CUS, serial 01705, October 22, 1940. Or, see Richardson, *Treadmill,* 292; or NARA—College Park, Records of the Pearl Harbor Liaison Office, Box 7, Folder 1.

64. *New York Times,* September 4, 1940, "Roosevelt Trades Destroyers for Sea Bases," front page. Also see middle of page, "Roosevelt Hails Gain of New Bases." The map designates the new bases under U.S. control.

65. LoC, Dyer Papers, Box 9, Folder 7. Richardson to Stark, War Plans, October 22, 1940. This statement is found on page 6.

66. Turner, 164.

67. Pearl Harbor Hearings, Part XXXII, 1011, "Narrative Statement of Evidence."

68. Pearl Harbor Hearings, Part XXVI, Hart Inquiry Proceedings, Thursday, April 6, 1944, 293.

69. Stillwell, "War Plans Under My Mattress" by Vice-Admiral John L. McCrea, 99.

70. Richardson, *Treadmill,* 292.

71. Miller, 261.

72. Pearl Harbor Hearings, Part I, 320.

73. LoC, Dyer Papers, Box 9, Folder 6. "Notes Made While CinCUS."

74. Pearl Harbor Hearings, Part XIV, 980. December 17, 1940, letter from CNO to CinCUS. Richardson, *Treadmill,* 294.

75. Richardson, *Treadmill,* 300. When France started to crumble and Italy jumped into the war, *Rainbow Four* was rushed to completion by the Joint Planning Committee and approved by the Joint Board on June 7, 1940. *Rainbow Four* went to President Roosevelt on June 13, 1940. A month later he sent it to his new secretaries of War and Navy. They returned it jointly to FDR on July 16, and the president approved it on August 14, 1940. The Navy did not complete a supporting plan. It was dropped in priority when the European War was stabilized in the fall of 1940.

76. NARA—College Park, Records of the Pearl Harbor Liaison Office, Box 9, Folder 2, War Plans. December 17, 1940, letter from Richardson to Stark.

77. Pearl Harbor Hearings, Part XXXII, 1011, "Narrative Statement of Evidence." Richardson, *Treadmill,* 295.

78. Pearl Harbor Hearings, Part XXVI, Hart Inquiry Proceedings, Thursday, April 6, 1944, 293.

79. Ibid.

80. LoC Manuscript Division, John L. McCrea Papers, Box 1, Folder 5. See Dyer letter, December 13, 1940.

81. LoC Manuscript Division, McCrea Papers, Box 2, Folder 1. Memo from McCrea to Stark, February 5, 1941.

82. LoC Manuscript Division, McCrea Papers, Box 2, Folder 1. McCrea from Cavite to Turner. Plane trouble and weather slowed the trip.

83. LoC Manuscript Division, McCrea Papers, Box 2, Folder 1. McCrea from Cavite to Turner. Purnell also read the memo sent to Hart from Richardson. Beard, 444. In a letter dated December 12, 1940, Stark authorized Hart to conduct staff discussions with the British and Dutch supreme commanders respecting war plans. They were to be secret.

84. Thomas C. Hart, Private Diary 1914-1952, microfilm, January 10, 1941, entry.

85. Stillwell, "War Plans Under My Mattress" by Vice-Admiral John L. McCrea, 100.

86. Thomas C. Hart, Private Diary 1914-1952, microfilm, January 12, 1941, entry.

87. Ibid., January 13, 1941, entry.

88. Pearl Harbor Hearings, Part XXVI, Hart Inquiry Proceedings, April 6, 1944, 293. LoC Manuscript Division, McCrea Papers, Box 2, Folder 1. Memo McCrea to Stark, dated February 5, 1941. Dates differ a bit from testimony, from Hart's diary and the memo.

89. NARA—College Park, Records of the Pearl Harbor Liaison Office, Box 16, Folder 16.

90. LoC Manuscript Division, McCrea Papers, Box 2, Folder 1. McCrea to Hart, February 13, 1941. Richardson and Murphy came in from the sea by destroyer and met McCrea that afternoon on Kimmel's flagship.

91. Pearl Harbor Hearings, Part XXVI, Hart Inquiry Proceedings, April 6, 1944, 293-94.

92. LoC Manuscript Division, McCrea Papers, Box 2, Folder 1. McCrea memo to Stark, February 5, 1941.

93. LoC Manuscript Division, McCrea Papers, Box 2, Folder 1. Memorandum for Admiral Richardson, dated January 27, 1941.

94. LoC Manuscript Division, McCrea Papers, Box 2, Folder 1. Page 12 of memo Hart to Richardson.

95. LoC Manuscript Division, McCrea Papers, Box 2, Folder 1. McCrea to F. C. Denebrink, dated February 3, 1941; McCrea to H. L. Grosskipf, same date; and to Captain Jessie B. Oldendorf, dated February 4, 1941.

96. LoC Manuscript Division, McCrea Papers, Box 2, Folder 1. McCrea to William M. Fechteler, February 4, 1941, and his memo to Stark detailing trip, February 5, 1941.

97. Pearl Harbor Hearings, Part XVII, 2475-76, Dispatch Number 212155 to CinCUS from CNO, January 22, 1941. Richardson, Treadmill, 299. NARA—College Park, Records of the Pearl Harbor Liaison Office, Box 1. A copy of

January 20 letter CinCUS to CNO, referring to the January 22 letter and a memo of November 12, 1940, to Knox.

98. LoC, Dyer Papers, Box 9, Folder 6. "Notes Made While CinCUS."

99. *New York Times,* September 28, 1940, "Japan Joins Axis Alliance Seen Aimed at U.S.," front page.

100. Robert A. Theobald, *The Final Secret of Pearl Harbor* (Old Greenwich, CN: Devin-Adair Company, 1954), 12.

101. Admiral William D. Leahy, *I Was There: The Personal Story of the Chief of Staff to Presidents Roosevelt and Truman Based on His Notes and Diaries Made at the Time* (New York: Whittlesey House, McGraw Hill Book Company, 1950), 7.

102. *New York Times,* July 26, 1940, "Embargo Put on Oil, Scrap Metal in License Order by Roosevelt," front page. The embargo would not take effect until October 18, 1940. It went into effect actually on October 16, 1940.

103. Testimony discussing points in this January 25, 1941, letter can be found in the Pearl Harbor Hearings, Part I, 368; Part IV, 1940; Part V, 2104, 2110, 2124; Part XIV, 993; Part XVI, 2147; Part XXII, 329; Part XXIII, 1135; Part XXXII, 654; Part XXXIII, 692, 1349; Part XXXVI, 368; Part XXXIX, 52; and Part XXXX, 75.

104. Pearl Harbor Hearings, Part XXXIII, 1349. Letter from CinCUS to CNO, January 25, 1942, serial 0129; or view it in the NARA—College Park, Records of the Pearl Harbor Liaison Office, Box 7, Folder 1.

105. NHC, Operational Archives Division, Oral Interviews, Admiral William R. Smedberg, 151. He says Admiral Charlie Wellborn actually explained many features to Stark, and worked many hours on the war plans.

106. CNO, November 12, 1940, memo "Plan Dog" to SECNAV, Plan File, NHD, 2. Richardson, *Treadmill,* 301. Mentioned in Pearl Harbor Hearings, Part XIV, 971.

107. Richardson, *Treadmill,* 303.

108. WPL-13, Change No. 6, March 26, 1937, Plan File, NHD, 17-17a. Richardson, *Treadmill,* 304.

109. Pearl Harbor Hearings, Part XXX, 1350. CinCUs, serial 0129, January 25, 1941, letter to CNO. Also see that letter in Part IV, 1940; Part XIV, 993; Part XVI, 2147, 2285; Part XXII, 329; Part XXIII, 1135; Part XXXII, 654; Part XXXIII, 692, 1349; Part XXXVI, 368; Part XXXIX, 62; Part XXXX, 75.

110. WPPac-46, 22.

111. Ibid., 26.

112. Richardson, *Treadmill,* 306.

Chapter 22: Patrol and Security of Fleet

1. Jack Fitch to Skipper Steely, August 30, 2003. Other than the worry, he said the summer was very touristy.

2. *Honolulu Advertiser,* October 27, 1940, 19.

3. Ibid., October 31, 1940, 8.

4. Pearl Harbor Hearings, Part XIV, 971.

5. Ibid., Part XV, 2189.

6. Richardson, *Treadmill,* 328.

7. Ibid., 405.

8. Ibid., 413.

9. LoC Manuscript Division, Frank Knox Papers, Box 4, July-December General Correspondence 1940 Folder. Knox to Ghormley, November 16, 1940. Letters across the Pacific took a month to deliver.

10. USNI, Annapolis, Oral Interviews, Vice-Admiral Charles A. Pownall, #1-50. When interviewed, Pownall was aware of Richardson's essay written at the War College, and was of the opinion that when the admiral discussed the fleet's positon with the president, Roosevelt had "dressed him down."

11. Paolo E. Coletta, *Patrick N.L. Bellinger and U.S. Naval Aviation* (Lanham, MD: University Press of America, 1987), 193.

12. Ibid., 212.

13. Dyer, "Reminiscences," 187.

14. NARA—College Park, Records of the Pearl Harbor Liaison Office, Box 16, Folder 1. Memorandum from John Ford Baecher to William D. Mitchell. Answers to questions asked Richardson about patrol statistics.

15. Coletta, 217. The letter is mentioned many times in the Pearl Harbor Hearings, some being in Part VIII, 3484; Part XVII, 2710; Part XXVI, 542-43; Part XXXII, 503, 681; Part XXXIII, 1186; Part XXXVI, 394.

16. Richardson, *Treadmill,* 356.

17. Dyer, "Reminiscences," 187, 211.

18. NHC, Operational Archives Division, Oral Interviews, Admiral George van Deurs, 359.

19. Ibid.

20. NHC Operational Archives, Oral Interviews, Bernard Max Strean, #2-60.

21. Richardson, *Treadmill,* 340.

22. NARA—College Park, Records of the Pearl Harbor Liaison Office, Box 16, Folder 1. Detailed patrol duties by Admiral W. L. Calhoun, commander base force, dated May 22, 1940.

23. Pearl Harbor Hearings, Part I, 272. Richardson, *Treadmill,* 341.

24. Richardson, *Treadmill,* 341.

25. Pearl Harbor Hearings, Part I, 273.

26. Richardson, *Treadmill,* 350-51.

27. NHC, Operational Archives Division, Oral Interviews, Admiral George van Deurs, 360.

28. Richardson, *Treadmill,* 353

29. Stillwell, 48.

30. Richardson, *Treadmill,* 286.

31. Pearl Harbor Hearings, Part I, 286. NARA—College Park, Records of the Pearl Harbor Liaison Office, Box 16, Folder 1. Memorandum for Admiral Colclough, dated December 5, 1945. No official Richardson orders were found in CinCUS records for air searches. By July 11, 1940, however, plans were extended and made more concrete.

32. Richardson, *Treadmill,* 354.

33. Ibid.

34. Ibid., 340; Pearl Harbor Hearings, Part IV, 1025.

35. Richardson, *Treadmill,* 358. He cites CinCUS, serial 0404, September

15, 1940, letter to COMBASEFOR; COMPATWINGTWO, serial 2786 of November 7, 1940, letter to COMSCOFOR. Dyer, "Reminiscences," 191, 212. Dyer says the Pat Wing Two files were destroyed after World War II. The Mechanicsburg depository became too full, and the Department of Defense made the decision that these were not that important. He found some of the records in the CinCUS file in the National Archives. See Pearl Harbor Hearings, Part I, 286, for more about the disposition of the patrol wing papers.

36. Richardson, *Treadmill*, 358.

37. Stillwell, 202.

38. Pearl Harbor Hearings, Part I, 338; Part VI, 2788; Part XIV, 975, 980 (much discussion; arrival date to CNO); and Part XXXX, 160.

39. Richardson, *Treadmill*, 359.

40. Captain Wyman H. Packard, *A Century of U.S. Naval Intelligence* (Washington, DC: Department of the Navy, a joint publication of the Office of Naval Intelligence and the Naval Historical Center, 1996), 20.

41. Beard, 485.

42. Pearl Harbor Hearings, Part XIV, 980.

43. Richardson, *Treadmill*, 419.

44. Ibid., 361, 365. Richardson writes that long-range patrols were basically stopped after December 5, 1940.

45. Richardson, *Treadmill*, 419.

46. Pearl Harbor Hearings, Part XXVI, Hart Inquiry Proceedings, 211. Question #48.

47. Pearl Harbor Hearings, Part I, 276 (in detail); Part XXVI, Hart Inquiry Proceedings, 13; Part XXXIX, 48.

48. LoC, Dyer Papers, Box 9, Folder 6. "Notes Made While CinCUS." The collection information and memo was given to Bloch to update from his end, and send on under his name.

49. Pearl Harbor Hearings, Part XXVI, Hart Inquiry Proceedings, 26; Letter from Richardson to Stark, sent January 7, 1941, from the Flagship USS *New Mexico*. Subject: Situation Concerning the Security of the Fleet, etc. CinCUS concurs with Bloch's basic letter.

50. Pearl Harbor Hearings, Part I, 277; or see NARA—College Park, Records of the Pearl Harbor Liaison Office, Box 7, Folder 1. Richardson to Stark, January 4, 1941; also, Bloch's report to Richardson, December 30, 1940.

51. NHC, Operational Archives Division, Oral Interviews, Admiral George van Deurs, 364.

52. Richardson, *Treadmill*, 364. He cited Husband E. Kimmel, *Admiral Kimmel's Story* (Chicago: Henry Regnery Company, 1955), 6.

53. Richardson, *Treadmill*, 361.

54. NHC, Operational Archives Division, Oral Interviews, Admiral William R. Smedberg, 150. "I don't think we followed up on all the lessons we could have learned from the Battle of Taranto," he commented.

55. USNI, Annapolis, Oral Interviews, Reminiscences of Mrs. Marc A. Mitscher and Mrs. Roy C. Smith, Jr., #2-153-154.

56. *Honolulu Star-Bulletin*, May 1, 1940, front page.

57. John Toland, *Infamy: Pearl Harbor and Its Aftermath* (New York: Berkley Books, 1982), 349. Joe F. Richardson was quoted by no others who wrote about Pearl Harbor.

58. Richardson, *Treadmill*, 363.

59. Pearl Harbor Hearings, Part I, 330.

Chapter 23: Just What Did Richardson Know?

1. Prange, *At Dawn We Slept*, 81.

2. Some sources say it was named "MAGIC" by William F. Friedman.

3. Robert B. Stinnett, *Day of Deceit: The Truth about FDR and Pearl Harbor* (New York: Touchstone, Simon & Schuster, 2000), 23.

4. LoC, Dyer Papers, Box 10-3. Stark to Richardson, November 19, 1940.

5. Edwin T. Layton with Captain Roger Pineau and John Costello, *"And I Was There:" Pearl Harbor and Midway—Breaking the Secrets* (New York: Morrow and Company, 1985), 100.

6. Richardson, *Treadmill*, 469.

7. David D. Lowman, *MAGIC: The Untold Story of U.S. Intelligence and the Evacuation of Japanese Residents from the West Coast during WWII* (Provo, UT: Athena Press, 2001), 123. Lowman says Ogawa was personally briefed by Yamamoto as early as February 1941 about the Pearl Harbor plans.

8. Theobald, 196.

9. Ladislas Farago, *The Broken Seal: "Operation Magic" and the Secret Road to Pearl Harbor* (New York: Random House, 1967), 139.

10. Ibid., 147.

11. *Honolulu Advertiser*, June 11, 1940, 2. He came as vice-consul replacing Binjiro Kudo.

12. Lowman, 126-40, or view on the Internet a listing of messages at: http://www.ibiblio.org/pha/timeline/Washington_v_Tokyo.html. Messages from Okuda in Honolulu to Gaimudaijin in Tokyo, #216, #232, and #234.

13. LoC Manuscript Division, John L. McCrea Papers, Box 2, Folder 1. See page 19 in his trip diary.

14. *Honolulu Advertiser*, November 10, 1940, 17. On board also was Senator R. O. Brewster, the congressman both Richardson and Zacharias would meet again in the Congressional Pearl Harbor Hearings of 1945-46. Zacharias is not listed as a passenger, but may have sailed under another name.

15. Zacharias, *Secret Missions*, 224-25. Four chapters could be found on the Internet in 2002 at: http://sandysq.gcinet.net/uss_salt_lake_city_ca25/secret-0.htm.

16. Zacharias Papers, on disk, but originals are in possession of son, Jerrold Zacharias, indexed as in PH-9, handwritten notes from November 9, 1940, to November 28, 1941. Zacharias, *Secret Missions*, 224.

17. "Pearl Harbor Revisited: United States Navy Communications Intelligence 1924-42," Department of the Navy, Naval Historical Center, Washington Navy Yard, Washington, DC. It was found on the Internet in 2002 at: http://www.history.navy.mil/books/comint/ComInt-4.html.

18. Zacharias, *Secret Missions*, 224.

19. NHC, Operational Archives, Oral Interviews, Edwin T. Layton, #1-66.

20. Layton, 38.

21. Ibid., 53.
22. Stinnett, 34. The author says that Roosevelt personally gave Anderson a promotion to rear admiral, and gave him the fleet assignment. See also Stillwell, "Unheeded Warnings," by Rear Admiral Arthur H. McCollum, 80.
23. Richardson, *Treadmill,* 201. Richardson quotes from Anderson's letter to Kimmel, dated February 13, 1941. Serial 096, Commander Battleships, W. S. Anderson.
24. *Honolulu Advertiser,* January 30, 1941.
25. Pearl Harbor Hearings, Part XVI, 2144. Stark to Kimmel, January 13, 1941. Also, see Anderson's oral history at Butler Library, Columbia University in New York City, 235. Read Stinnett, 34 and 329.
26. NARA—College Park, Records of the Pearl Harbor Liaison Office, Box 16, Folder 28. Memo for John F. Baecher from Earl E. Stone, chief of Navy communications.
27. NHC, Operational Archives, Oral Interviews, Arthur Howard McCollum, #7-304.
28. Stillwell, "Unheeded Warnings," by Rear Admiral Arthur H. McCollum, 80. Stinnett, 6.
29. Stinnett, 8. The entire book is based mainly upon this eight-action memorandum and how it might have been Roosevelt's method of drawing in the Japanese to an attack. McCollum draws no mention in Richardson's book.
30. Stillwell, "Unheeded Warnings," by Rear Admiral Arthur H. McCollum, 81. NHC, Operational Archives, Oral Interviews, Arthur Howard McCollum, #7-305.
31. NHC, Operational Archives, Oral Interviews, Edwin T. Layton, #1-45.
32. Lowman, 61. Cost of a machine was $684.65. Op-20-G and SIS in Washington had two each; two were sent to the British; and one was sent to CAST at Corregidor. The one intended for Hawaii was diverted to the British. Lowman points out that even if Hawaii had had the machine during early December 1941, it might not have assisted that much. The Japanese consulate used J-19 and a code called PA-K2. However, the Navy in Hawaii could have easily read these codes, but were not privy to that assignment.
33. Prange, *At Dawn We Slept,* 82. He and his collaborators thought that the machine went to the Navy Yard at Cavite in April 1941, and was then transferred over to Corregidor in August. More recent information says it came in January 1941 to Corregidor. See Theobald, 36. He thinks the machine went to the Sixteenth Naval District in the Philippines in April of 1941, but he gives no footnote. LoC, Dyer Papers, Box 10, Folder 4. Leigh Noyes testimony in Naval Inquiry, Pearl Harbor Hearings, Volume X, 4714-15. Admiral Noyes can't even remember, saying, "I had the approval from Admiral Stark to send it to Cavite," adding they could decipher diplomatic traffic and send it to Honolulu. "I should say that about March of 1941 one machine became available, and it was decided to send it to Cavite." The decision, he said, was to use it at Cavite "because it was the best listening post for us." He said he discussed it with Stark and Ingersoll, then backtracked and added, "I think with Admiral Stark."
34. Theobald, 37.
35. NHC, Operational Archives, Oral Interviews, Edwin T. Layton, #1-47.
36. Ibid., #1-49.

37. *Honolulu Advertiser,* November 21, 1940, editorial page; January 31, 1941, 2.

38. *Honolulu Advertiser,* February 1, 1941.

39. Ibid., January 31, 1941, 2. NHC, Operational Archives Division, Oral Interviews, Henri Smith-Hutton, #10-118. A Japanese ceremony in honor of Emperor Hirohito's birthday was bombed that April. It was in Shanghai's Hingkew Park before 5,000 Japanese soldiers. It killed the top military official in China, blew off Ambassador Mamoru Shigemitsu's leg, and took out the eye of Admiral Nomura.

40. NHC, Operational Archives, Oral Interviews, William Joseph Sebald, #2-153.

41. *Tokyo Gazette,* March 1941. The speech was on the Internet in 2003 at: http://www.ibiblio.org/pha/timeline/410121awp.html.

42. Stillwell, 277. NHC, Operational Archives, Oral Interviews, Edwin T. Layton, #1-66. Layton had tutored Nomura's godson in English.

43. *Honolulu Advertiser,* February 1, 1941.

44. Ibid., January 31, 1941, 2.

45. Richardson, *Treadmill,* 410.

46. *Honolulu Advertiser,* February 1, 1941, 3.

47. Zacharias, *Secret Missions,* 9.

48. H. R. Stark to E. M. Zacharias at Mare Island, February 17, 1941. Copy in Zacharias Papers, PH-17A, in possession of Jerrold Zacharias in 2003. Steely Collection, Nomura File.

49. Zacharias, *Secret Missons,* 225-28.

50. Messages from Okuda in Honolulu to Gaimudaijin (Foreign Minister) in Tokyo, #002, #003, #005, #011, #021, and #018; and from Grew to Washington, January 27, 1941. See Lowman, 126 and beyond. See Pearl Harbor Association Web site at: http://www.ibiblio.org/pha/timeline/Washington_v_Tokyo.html.

51. Grew to State Department, January 27, 1941, sent at 6:00 P.M. received in Washington at 6:38 A.M. Pearl Harbor Hearings, Part II, 580, 596, 720; Part XIV, 1042; Part XXI, 4584; Part XXXII, 630; Part XXXX, 522; or see Stinnett, 31 and 329. See also Theobald, 42. It is also in U.S. State Department Publication 1983, "Peace and War: United States Foreign Policy 1931-1941" (Washington, DC: U.S. Government Printing Office, 1943), 617-18. In Walter Millis, *This Is Pearl* (Westport, CN: Greenwood Press, 1947), he says that Stark sent the message on to Kimmel shortly after he took command. For more detail on the Peruvian envoy to Japan, Dr. Ricardo Rivera Schreiber, see Farago, 135.

52. Packard, 21.

53. Lowman, 62, 208.

54. CAST Report serial 301455, RG 38, Station US Papers, MMRB, National Archives II (College Park), or in Stinnett, 32 and 329.

55. David Kahn, "The Codebreakers: The Comprehensive History of Secret Communication from Ancient Times to the Internet," excerpt found on the Internet in 2003 at: http://www.wnyc.org/books/1622.

56. LoC Manuscript Division, Frank Knox Papers, Box 4, July-December General Correspondence 1940 Folder. Knox to Ghormley, November 16, 1940.

57. Lowman, 181.

58. Ibid., 58.

59. Ibid., 128. Message #043, January 30, 1941, Foreign Minister Yosuke Matsuoka to Koshi in Washington, translated February 7, 1941.

60. Lowman, 129-30. Message #044, January 30, 1941, Matsuoka to Koshi in Washington, translated February 7, 1941.

61. Lowman, 129. Message #056, Tokyo to Washington, Matsuoka to Koshi, February 5, 1941.

62. Office of Naval Intelligence Memo, February 12, 1941, 249. Or, read Lowman, 125, 249. Jules James was acting DNI at that time.

63. Farago, 154.

64. Lowman, 191-92. Though the messages were read, Morimura slipped away quietly into the future until a Japanese newspaper interviewed him in 1953.

65. Letter from McCollum to Layton, April 22, 1941, found in Pearl Harbor Congressional Hearings, Part X, 4845, or in Wohlstetter, 41. Actually, in Kimmel's first letter he began complaints, in this case that the Army air defense was inadequate. See Millis, 38.

66. Stinnett, 38; Millis, 39. Kimmel even traveled to Washington in July of 1941 to present some of his concerns.

Chapter 24: "They Can't Do That to Me!"

1. LoC, Dyer Papers, Box 9, Folder 6. "Notes Made While CinCUS." NHC Operational Archives, Oral Interviews, Bernhard Henry Bieri, #2-85.

2. *Honolulu Advertiser*, January 2, 1941, 11.

3. Dyer, "Reminiscences," 196. Admiral Eugene Farrell and Mrs. Walter Dean Short were so upset with that quote being placed in this publication that they cut off correspondence with the author. In Stillwell, *Air Raid*, 42, Dyer told this anecdote, and it is in 36-point headlines above the story. Dyer knew the admiral for more than fifty years and worked with him for hundreds of hours. The statement indicates nothing negative about Richardson. It does, however, emphasize the surprise and maybe the naivety he had at the time.

4. NHC, Operational Archives Division, Oral Interviews, Admiral William R. Smedberg, 146.

5. *Honolulu Advertiser*, January 2, 1941, 1. FDR Library, Memorandum for the President from Daniel J. Callaghan, and a longer one from Stark, dated August 14, 1940. Stark discussed the plans for Fleet Problem XXII, and alternatives in case of several scenarios. Roosevelt approved it at that time. It was to have been in the Pacific-Panama area.

6. USNI, Annapolis, Oral Interviews, Rear Admiral Charles Julian Wheeler, #4-234.

7. Short, 000237. She says the orders came on Christmas Eve.

8. Short, 000237, 000249.

9. Beard, 13-15.

10. Okuda in Honolulu to Gaimudaijin in Tokyo, January 7, 1941; Pearl Harbor Hearings Exhibit #2, Japanese messages concerning military installations, ship movements, etc.

11. *Honolulu Advertiser*, January 23, 1941, 3.

12. Ibid., January 9, 1941, 1.

13. Ibid., January 19, 1941, 7.

14. LoC, Dyer Papers, Box 9, Folder 6. "Notes Made While CinCUS."

15. Richardson, *Treadmill*, 417.

16. LoC, Dyer Papers, Box 10, Folder 8. Richardson to Peter Vischer, December 27, 1947.

17. Marie Jenkins Moore, "A History of Graham School, Paris, Texas, from 1853 through 1968" (Paris, TX: unpublished booklet, 1994), 4. She mentions that the Richardson home, built from wood taken from the First Methodist Church, and as old as 1853, was two-story and on the corner of current Fifth NW and West Cherry. It burned about 1907. Professor and Mrs. Richardson moved east to the other corner into a two-story house.

18. USNI, Annapolis, Oral Interviews, Reminiscences of Vice Admiral Charles A. Pownall and his wife, #1-101.

19. *Honolulu Advertiser,* February 1, 1941. Anderson had a knack for publicity, landing on the front page with a photo of him emerging from his quarters on the USS *West Virginia.*

20. Telephone interview between Skipper Steely and C. R. "Chris" Johnson, August 11, 2002.

21. NHC Operational Archives, Oral Interviews, Bernhard Henry Bieri, #2-85.

22. NHC, Oral Interviews, Kent Melhorn, 61.

23. Richardson, *Treadmill*, 420.

24. *Honolulu Advertiser,* January 19, 1941, military section photo page.

25. Telephone interview between Skipper Steely and Bob Curts, October 5, 2002.

26. Telephone interview between Skipper Steely and L. J. O'Brien, August 11, 2002.

27. Telephone interviews between Skipper Steely and C. R. "Chris" Johnson, August 11, 2002; October 1, 2002.

28. Dyer, "Reminiscences," 214.

29. *Honolulu Advertiser,* January 18, 1941, 5.

30. Ibid., February 1, 1941, 13.

31. Okuda in Honolulu to Gaimudaijin in Tokyo, January 16, 1941; Pearl Harbor Hearings, Exhibit #2. It said the USS *Pennsylvania* arrived back from the mainland on January 14, 1941.

32. *Honolulu Advertiser,* January 30, 1941, 2. This is a diagram of where all participates gathered.

33. *Honolulu Advertiser,* February 2, 1941. Photo on page 4.

34. Richardson, *Treadmill,* 449-50. *Honolulu Advertiser,* February 2, 1941, 10.

35. *Honolulu Advertiser,* January 25, 1941, 3.

36. Ibid., February 2, 1941, 10.

37. Ibid., January 25, 1941, 3.

38. Ibid., February 4, 1941, 2.

39. Ibid., February 2, 1941, society page.

40. Ibid.

41. Information on the Internet in 2007 at: http://www.imdb.com/title/tt0032477/. It was released at Christmas 1940.

42. *Honolulu Advertiser,* February 6, 1941, 4.

43. Ibid., February 3, 1941, 7.

44. Ibid., February 9, 1941, society page.

45. Ibid., February 8, 1941, 7.

46. Henry C. Clausen and Bruce Lee, *Pearl Harbor: Final Judgement* (Cambridge, MA: Da Capo Press, Perseus Book Group, 1992), 185.

47. Ibid., 184-87. Herron said that from what he learned through back-channel reports from his friends left on Hawaii, Isabel Short would frequently call her husband on busy days and complain vehemently about life in general. Short would then put on his jacket, abandon the office, and go home to placate his wife. Herron apparently did not write this assertion down anywhere, just verbally related it to Clausen. It is refuted and doubted by those close to Short in 1941.

48. *Honolulu Advertiser,* February 6, 1941, 4.

49. Short, 000263.

50. Ibid., 000250. She offers an entirely opposite view of the Hawaiian assignment from what Herron told Henry C. Clausen later.

51. *Honolulu Advertiser,* February 9, 1941, society page 4.

52. Ibid., February 8, 1941, 7.

53. Stinnett, photo section, which shows a photo of Isabel pinning on the new rank.

54. *Honolulu Advertiser,* February 8, 1941, 1; Stinnett, picture section after page 208.

55. Michael Gannon, *Pearl Harbor Betrayed: The True Story of a Man and a Nation under Attack* (New York: John McCrae Book, Owl Book, Henry Holt and Company, 2001), 15. Gannon says he found out the couples resided together from a Husband E. Kimmel statement in his rough draft of a statement given to the Congressional Pearl Harbor Hearing in 1946. The draft is in the Kimmel Papers at the University of Wyoming.

56. Short, 000251.

57. *Honolulu Advertiser,* February 11, 1941.

58. Richardson, *Treadmill,* 417.

59. *Honolulu Advertiser,* January 14, 1941, 7.

60. Zacharias, *Secret Missions,* 400. Zacharias, partially as a result of his service as aide-de-camp to the Japanese Imperial Highnesses in 1931, was elevated to a propaganda scheme in 1945.

61. LoC, Dyer Papers, Box 9, Folder 6. Memo for General Board, handwritten.

62. Ibid.

63. Letter from Clareda Purser of Karnes City, Texas, to Skipper Steely, September 18, 2001. She read the Richardson/Dyer book for the first time in 2001, and realized that someone had pulled a fast one on her in 1941.

Chapter 25: Duties Back in Washington

1. *Paris News,* February 2, 1941; September 16, 1945, 10.

2. LoC, Dyer Papers, Box 10, Folder 2. Knox to Richardson, change of duty, January 22, 1941.

3. LoC, Dyer Papers, Box 10, Folder 2. This source notes that he arrived in Washington, DC, on March 23, 1941, by car, at his own expense. See note attached to Knox orders, which somewhat details trip for reimbursement purposes.

4. Richardson, *Treadmill,* 424. See also LoC, Dyer Papers, Box 9, Folder 6.

Memo for General Board, handwritten. This version has Knox saying, "Oh, your courage was not questioned, and some day the President will send for you and have a talk."

5. Pearl Harbor Hearings, Part I, 268-69, 310.

6. Richardson, *Treadmill*, 424.

7. Ibid., 436; Pearl Harbor Hearings, Part I, 339-40.

8. Richardson, *Treadmill*, 436; Pearl Harbor Hearings, Part I, 339-40.

9. LoC Dyer Papers, Box 10, Folder 2. Knox to Richardson, dated March 25, 1941.

10. *New York Daily News,* April 9, 1941.

11. LoC Manuscript Division, Emory Land Papers, John G. Norris, *Navy Magazine,* February, 1969, 30, 32.

12. LoC, Dyer Papers, Box 9, Folder 7. Report dated September 26, 1941.

13. LoC, Bloch Papers, Box 3, Harold R. Stark File. Bloch to Stark, February 23, 1942. He noted that FDR had given him a vote of confidence, just as he did at the Naval Gun Factory two years earlier, then sent him to Hawaii.

14. LoC Manuscript Division, Ernest J. King Papers, Box 4, 1940-42 Orders to Duty Folder. Knox to King, December 20, 1941, and King to Stark, December 30, 1941.

15. LoC Manuscript Division, Ernest J. King Papers, Box 4, 1940-42 Orders to Duty Folder. King to Stark, December 30, 1941.

16. Simpson, 125.

17. LoC, Dyer Papers, Box 10-3. Milliken to Knox, February 20, 1942.

18. LoC, Bloch Papers, Box 3, Correspondence 1939-42, Richardson File. Richardson to Bloch, February 18, 1942.

19. LoC, Dyer Papers, Box 10, Folder 2. January 28, 1942, orders. Richardson went to Los Angeles on February 8 and returned on February 17, 1942.

20. Richardson, *Treadmill*, 442.

21. Ibid.; see also LoC, Dyer Papers, Box 9, Folder 7. Reorganization order dated March 12, 1942.

22. USNI, Annapolis, Oral Interviews, Vice-Admiral Ruthven E. Libby, #4-228-229.

23. Simpson, 126. Stark suggested that he take a London position as head of the naval command there.

24. LoC Manuscript Division, Ernest J. King Papers, Box 4, 1940-42 Orders to Duty Folder. Chief BuNav to King, March 19, 1942, the announcement that the president made the appointment, with commission attached. King lived near the observatory and CNO residence, at 2919 43rd Street NW, a place he purchased in 1933.

25. LoC, Dyer Papers, Box 9, Folder 7. Knox to Richardson, July 3, 1941. Francis E. M. Whiting, Ralph E. Davison, Joseph W. Knighton, and Richardson attended the first meeting.

26. Richardson, *Treadmill*, 442.

27. Ibid., 443.

Chapter 26: A Permanent Job or Two for Richardson

1. LoC, Dyer Papers, Box 10, Folder 2. Orders to detach from General Board, dated May 25, 1942.

2. LoC, Dyer Papers, Box 10, Folder 2. Randall Jacobs to Richardson, September 9, 1942.

3. Richardson, *Treadmill*, 457; also see LoC, Dyer Papers, Box 9, Folder 7. Knox letter dated September 23, 1942. Richardson was placed into retirement on October 1, 1942, and again on December 15, 1945. See Box 10, Folder 2. Forrestal to Richardson, saying "well done."

4. Richardson, *Treadmill*, 457. This is a 151-page summary of events, but the most valuable part is the 698 pages of documents attached, with index. It can be found in downloadable format at: http://www.ibiblio.org/pha/paw/index.html.

5. Turner, 177. Pearl Harbor Hearings, Part IV, 1938.

6. Richardson, *Treadmill*, 458.

7. LoC, Dyer Papers, Box 10, Folder 8. Peter Vischer to Richardson, January 18, 1948.

8. Richardson, *Treadmill*, 460.

9. Ibid.

10. Ibid., 471. Favorite words of Susan Richardson, teacher and mother to two families in her lifetime.

11. LoC, Dyer Papers, Box 9, Folder 3. John O'Donnell, "Capital Stuff," *New York Daily News,* December 8, 1942.

12. Herman S. Wolk, *The Struggle for Air Force Independence 1943-1947* (Washington, DC: Air Force History and Museums Program, 1997), 9. See also LoC, Dyer Papers, Box 9, Folder 7. Secretary of Navy Frank Knox order designating Richardson to head committee to study organization of postwar military departments, dated April 21, 1944; and Box 10, Folder 2. May 31, 1944. Orders from Forrestal for additional duty. Most committee records can be found at NARA—College Park, in RG 218-040 (1112143), Boxes 20-23.

13. Brigadier General W. T. Tompkins to the Deputy Chief-of-staff, U.S. Army, June 19, 1944. Obtained from NARA at College Park, Wilbert Mahoney, Modern Military Records, Textual Archives Services Division. October 8, 2003, letter to Skipper Steely. Office of the Chief-of-staff, Records of War Department General and Special Staffs, Record Group 165. The committee was formed under directive JCS 749/7.

14. The Reminiscenses of Frederick Trubee Davison, 1951, page 255, in the Oral History Collection of Columbia University, New York.

15. Ibid., 260.

16. Ibid., 256.

17. NHC, Operational Archives, Oral Interviews, Malcolm F. Schoeffel, #5-243.

18. Telephone conversation of January 5, 2005, Steely and Smith.

19. Elmer F. Smith Collection, Sterling, Virginia 2005, logs and notes on Trip #13, Order Number SO, 258, Headquarters ATC, dated October 27, 1944.

20. LoC, Dyer Papers, Box 10, Folder 7. Notes on book chapter about unification. In Folder 2 is the exact itinerary, dated November 20, 1944. Smith Collection, Sterling, Virginia 2005, logs and notes on Trip #13.

21. NHC, Operational Archives, Oral Interviews, Malcolm F. Schoeffel, #5-246.

22. Omar N. Bradley and Clay Blair, *A General's Life: An Autobiography by General of the Army Omar N. Bradley* (New York: Simon and Schuster, 1983),

323. For the office move to Versailles, see Stephen E. Ambrose, *Eisenhower: Soldier, General of the Army, President-elect, 1890-1952* vol. 1 (New York: Simon and Schuster, 1984), 351. "Too many temptations to go nightclubbing" in Paris, he said.

23. Harry Cecil Butcher, *My Three Years with Eisenhower: The Personal Diary of Harry C. Butcher* (New York: Simon and Schuster, 1946), xiii, 3, 690. See also Alfred D. Chandler, Jr., ed., and Stephen E. Ambrose, assoc. ed., *The Papers of Dwight David Eisenhower: The War Years* vol. 4 (Baltimore: Johns Hopkins University Press, 1970), 2266 (Letter 2084). Documents on the Richardson Special Board can be found, among several places, in the OPD 320, Case 78 file.

24. The Reminiscenses of Frederick Trubee Davison, 1951, page 259, in the Oral History Collection of Columbia University, New York.

25. Butcher, 689.

26. Ibid., 691, 696.

27. NHC, Operational Archives, Oral Interviews, Malcolm F. Schoeffel, #5-247.

28. Hansen Papers, Box 37. Diary for November and December 1944.

29. The Reminiscenses of Frederick Trubee Davison, 1951, page 261, in the Oral History Collection of Columbia University, New York.

30. Ibid.

31. Though copilot Smith says only a couple of others accompanied the committee on the aircraft, General Clark's notes, taken by an aide, start with a list of those present. Reese, Cole, Theis, and Robinson appeared at this meeting, and most likely were with the "junket" the entire way. See The Citadel Archives and Museum, Mark W. Clark Papers, Box 65, Folder Diary Volume 8, Traversa, November 13, 1944.

32. The Citadel Archives and Museum, Mark W. Clark Papers, Box 65, Folder Diary Volume 8, Traversa, November 13, 1944. LoC, Dyer Papers, Box 10, Folder 7. Notes on book chapter about unification.

33. NHC, Operational Archives, Oral Interviews, Malcolm F. Schoeffel, #5-248. NHC, Operational Archives, Oral Interviews, Malcolm F. Schoeffel, #5-249.

34. NHC, Operational Archives, Oral Interviews, Malcolm F. Schoeffel, #5-249.

35. Merrill Stickler, "John Lansing Callan 1886-1958," Glenn H. Curtiss Museum of Local History, Hammondsport, New York. His papers from the Naval Historical Center are now located in the Library of Congress Manuscript Division reading room. See also the Web site: http://www.earlyaviators.com/ecallan.htm.

36. Patrick Osborn, National Archives—College Park, to Skipper Steely by e-mail dated January 24, 2005. Record Group 218, Entry 1(UD), Boxes 20-23, about 3,000 pages of documentation about the creation of the Department of Defense. The Richardson committee work is partially here, including a Rome photo with these persons in it: Thomkins, George, Taylor, Richardson, Schoeffel, Yates, Cole, Reese, McDonnell, Davison, Steele, Robinson, Hoover, Theis, and Callan. Two Swiss guards flank the committee.

37. The Reminiscenses of Frederick Trubee Davison, 1951, page 257, in the Oral History Collection of Columbia University, New York.

38. USNI, Annapolis, Oral Interviews, Admiral Arleigh Burke, "A Study of OP-23 and Its Role in the Unification Debates of 1949," 15-355.

39. NHC, Operational Archives, Oral Interviews, Malcolm F. Schoeffel, #5-251. See also Elmer F. Smith Collection, Sterling, Virginia, Log Files and Notes, Trip 14, SO Number 280, Headquarters ATC, dated November 22, 1944.

40. Von Hardesty, *Air Force One* (San Diego: Tehabi Books, 2003), 34-45.

41. Telephone conversation between Steely and Smith, January 5, 2005.

42. NHC, Operational Archives, Oral Interviews, Malcolm F. Schoeffel, #5-251.

43. Weldon E. "Dusty" Rhodes, *Flying MacArthur* (College Station: Texas A&M University Press, 1987), 308. NHC, Operational Archives, Oral Interviews, Malcolm F. Schoeffel, #5-252. Schoeffel said that since it was an officers' club, the newsmen wrote that MacArthur was living in luxury while the GIs were in the rain. Water did seep down the walls, Schoeffel said. He and Davison were surely talking about two different locations.

44. LoC, Dyer Papers, Box 10, Folder 7. Notes on book chapter about unification.

45. MacArthur Memorial, City of Norfolk, copy of Douglas MacArthur daily schedule, Sunday, December 3, 1944, sent to Skipper Steely by Archivist James W. Zobel. It reveals that at twelve noon MacArthur met with Lindsay, Richardson, Schoeffel, Davison, Myers, Theis, Steele, and Craig. He met with no one else that afternoon. For more on the committee and meeting, see NARA, Record Group 30, Box 24, Folder 15, Sutherland Papers, General Correspondence, also located in MacArthur Memorial Archives. Sutherland was MacArthur's chief of staff at that time.

46. USS *Boyd* WWII Diary, Part 12 of 20, page 4. The Task Group returned to Ulithi, arriving on November 27. Could be found on the Internet in 2003 at: http://pages.cthome.net/ boyd544/Diary12.htm.

47. LoC Manuscript Division, William F. Halsey Papers, Box 2. War Diary Third Fleet, December 1944-February 1945.

48. The Reminiscenses of Frederick Trubee Davison, 1951, page 262, in the Oral History Collection of Columbia University, New York.

49. LoC, Dyer Papers, Box 10, Folder 2. Itinerary dated December 19, 1944.

50. Ibid. All dates are west longitude, with the times local.

51. Leahy, 287.

52. LoC Dyer Papers, Box 10, Folder 2. Itinerary dated February 16, 1945.

53. The Reminiscenses of Frederick Trubee Davison, 1951, page 265, in the Oral History Collection of Columbia University, New York.

54. An official copy of the report is numbered JSC 0030, "Memorandum Regarding the Origin and Activities of the Joint Chiefs of Staff Special Committee for the Reorganization of National Defense." It can be found in RG 30, Box 24, Folder 15, Sutherland Papers, General Correspondence, MacArthur Memorial Archives, Norfolk, Virginia, or at NARA—College Park, Maryland.

55. Leahy, 118-19. Leahy explains some of the early war scuffles between the Navy air arm and the Army Air Corps.

56. NHC, Operational Archives, Oral Interviews, Malcolm F. Schoeffel, #5-256.

57. *Congressional Digest,* Washington, DC, December 1944, Volume 24, Number 12, 304, 306.

58. Wolk, 92. For a bit more precise summary read the Ferdinand Eberstadt *Report to Hon. James Forrestal on Unification of the War and Navy Departments and Postwar Organization for National Security* (Washington, DC: Government Printing Office, 1945), 190-92.

59. *Congressional Digest,* Washington, DC, December 1944, Volume 24, Number 12, 307, 309.

60. Ibid., 309.

61. The *Sacred Cow,* called now the "Birthplace of the U.S. Air Force," was not destroyed. It even had transport duties until 1961, when it was trucked to the U.S. Air Force Museum at Wright Patterson Air Force Base in Ohio. Restoration took ten years. Visitors can see the plane as it was when the Richardson committee used it.

62. Ambrose, *Eisenhower,* 1:443.

63. Admiral R. M. Brainard, "Report of the Navy Relief Society for the Year Ending December 31, 1945" (Room 0137, Navy Department, Washington, DC) This report says Richardson served from June 2, 1942, until May 10, 1945. The annual meeting was held at the headquarters, based at 2118 Massachusetts Avenue NW, Washington, DC.

64. LoC, Dyer Papers, Box 10-3. Richardson to Munro, April 3, 1945; see Folder 3.

Chapter 27: All the Many Investigations

1. Richardson, *Treadmill,* preface, x. He burned only the parts that carried comments he considered highly critical of officers and governmental officials.

2. Kimmel, 135.

3. Ibid., 136.

4. LoC Manuscript Division, Frank Knox Papers, Box 4, General Correspondence 1941. Knox to Mowrer, December 18, 1941.

5. Coletta, 280-81. See Pearl Harbor Hearings, Part VIII, 3484; Part XXVI, 542; and Part XXXII, 503.

6. Theobald, 154. The stenographic staff working for the commission was inexperienced and made many mistakes and omissions. Theobald and Kimmel worked two days and nights restoring his testimony as best they could.

7. Neil M. Johnson, editor and interviewer, Truman Presidential Museum and Library, Louis Truman Oral Interview, December 7, 1991, 60-67. Found on the Internet in 2003 at: http://www.trumanlibrary.org/oralhist/trumanl.htm.

8. Ibid., 67-68.

9. Wildenberg, 263-64.

10. The Standley portion is on pages 135-45 of the 1955 Kimmel book, but was found online in 2006 at: http://www.rooseveltmyth.com/KimmelStory/.

11. Telephone conversation with Rear Admiral Leslie J. O'Brien, August 11, 2002. "Obie said he sent some files to Washington to help Kimmel there."

12. Kimmel, 139.

13. Richardson, *Treadmill,* 455.

14. Kimmel, 165.

15. Ibid., 166.

16. Richardson , *Treadmill,* 455. The exact quote is: "It is my firm belief that, when the President realized the extent of the damage done by the attack on Pearl Harbor, he lost his nerve and lost his head, and ordered the convening of the Roberts Commission, believing that he could best protect his own position by focusing public attention on Pearl Harbor." Richardson gave an idea of what he thought should have followed the attack, including the quick release of Kimmel and Short and immediate replacements.

17. Kimmel, 139. Standley told Knox the same thing, but added that, despite the vicious attack, "I have never seen the Fleet in a higher state of efficiency." Richardson, *Treadmill,* 455.

18. Richardson, *Treadmill,* 454.

19. Short, 000267.

20. Stinnett, 382. See Pearl Harbor Hearings, Part XXXII, 283.

21. Short, 000251.

22. Ibid., 000255.

23. Kimmel, 141. Standley said of this story, "A messenger boy was on his way to Fort Shafter with the message when the Japanese struck. The message was finally decoded and delivered to General Short at 3 P.M., December 7th." The exact trail of the message is described in Stinnett, 380. See also Pearl Harbor Hearings, Part IX, 4404.

24. Short, 000259.

25. USNI, Annapolis, Oral Interviews, Vice Admiral Ruthven E. Libby, #4-230. Libby's statements are overly emotional, clash with Isabel's statements, and are factually unfounded at times. He thought the various investigations were all "snow jobs;" that Stark was no more to blame than Marshall; that the Army was to blame for not defending properly; that Short was not on good terms with Kimmel; that Kimmel agreed to base the fleet at Pearl Harbor; and that Kimmel could have taken the fleet from the base if he wanted.

26. Richardson, *Treadmill,* 451.

27. NHC, Operational Archives, Oral Interviews, Kemp Tolley, #4-494.

28. Short, 000261. *Dallas Morning News,* December 25, 2003. George Elliott, Jr., obituary, "Pearl Harbor Alarm Dismissed." Elliott and Joseph Lockard, both privates, had been on radar duty since 4:00 A.M. at Kahuku Point on the northern tip of Oahu, familiarizing themselves with the new equipment. Elliott saw a huge blip, 137 miles due north. He called into the Fort Shafter information center, and Lieutenant Kermit Tyler, who was on the job for only the second time, mentioned that they must be the B-17s. In fact, the setup was so new that even had he wanted to sound an alarm, no telephone system was in place to do so. In ten minutes the blip disappeared behind Oahu's mountains. Up until his death, Elliott was frustrated that his warning was not investigated and reported to Pearl Harbor. "They could have [gotten] at least two planes in the air," his son quoted him as saying for years. See Pearl Harbor Hearings, Part XXXIX, 1095-1105. See Exhibits 143, 145, 146.

29. Short, 000262.

30. LoC Manuscript Division, Frank Knox Papers, Box 4, General Correspondence. Knox to Ted Roosevelt, December 18, 1941. Roosevelt was at headquarters, Twentieth Infantry, Fort Devons, Massachusetts.

31. LoC Manuscript Division, Frank Knox Papers, Box 4, General Correspondence, December 23, 1941.

32. Short, 000268.

33. Beard, 225. Also, *New York Times,* February 8, 1942.

34. LoC, Bloch Papers, Box 3, Correspondence 1939-42, Richardson File. Richardson to Bloch, February 18, 1942. Richardson said he had always thought the two Pearl Harbor commanders would be retired upon their own application, not knowing at the time that Marshall had coerced Short. Richardson thought there would be no further action on the matter.

35. Toland, 45. He cites from the Thomas Kimmel Collection.

36. Beard, 225.

37. Short, 000269.

38. Ibid., 000270.

39. NARA—College Park, Records of the Pearl Harbor Liaison Office, Box 23, Folder 27. Admiral O. S. Colclough began with an attempt to file felony charges against Safford for writing a memo to Kramer.

40. Toland, 95. He cites the interview with Hanify.

41. Simpson, 260.

42. Ibid., 265.

43. Ibid., 263.

44. *Congressional Record,* August 21, 1944, A3958.

45. Pearl Harbor Hearings, Part XXXIX, October 19, 1944, 297-322.

46. Simpson, 266.

47. Ibid., 254.

48. *Congressional Record,* August 21, 1944, A3958.

49. For a deeper treatment of speeches by Scott and Harness, see Beard, 276-81.

50. LoC, Dyer Papers, Box 9, Folder 7.

51. NARA—College Park, Records of the Pearl Harbor Liasion Office. Several officers, including Baecher, had been assisting Richardson and others prior to the November establishment of the Liaison Office.

52. *New York Daily News,* November 19, 1945, found in Rosendahl Collection at the University of Texas-Dallas.

53. Simpson, 272.

54. LoC, Dyer Papers, Box 10-3. Staton to Richardson, November 21, 1945.

55. LoC, Dyer Papers, Box 10-3. From Laguna Beach to Richardson, November 21, 1945, 4:38 P.M.

56. LoC, Dyer Papers, Box 10-3. Roper to Richardson, November 21, 1945.

57. LoC, Dyer Papers, Box 10-3. Hunter to Richardson, November 21, 1945.

58. LoC, Dyer Papers, Box 10-3. W. W. Smith to Richardson, November 25, 1945.

59. LoC, Dyer Papers, Box 10-3. Pearson to Richardson, November 26, 1945. He mentioned that another 1918 shipmate, Roland B. Burnham, visited and felt the same way.

60. LoC, Dyer Papers, Box 10-3. Starr to Richardson, November 26, 1945.

61. LoC, Dyer Papers, Box 10-3. Homer of the A. H. DeFriest Company to Richardson, November 29, 1945.

62. LoC, Dyer Papers, Box 10-3. Joe F. Richardson to Family, November 30, 1945. Joe obtained the job, and went on to help write more than thirty-five episodes of *The Lone Ranger,* and some episodes of shows such as *Sky King, Sheena, Queen of the Jungle,* and many others. He died in 1994.

63. Leahy, 2-3.

64. LoC Manuscript Division, William D. Leahy Papers, Box 13. Page 207 of "I Was There" manuscript. Also see his book, *I Was There,* 62.

65. *Chicago Sun,* November 22, 1945. A copy can be found in the LoC, Dyer Papers, Box 9, Folder 3.

66. Constantine Brown, "Leahy: Grand Old American," *Washington Evening Star,* July 21, 1959. This article written at the time of Leahy's death has many errors.

67. See Grinberg Worldwide Images for a tape of several Richardson events on film, including small portions of the Pearl Harbor Hearings testimony of Leahy, Hull, and Welles.

68. LoC, Dyer Papers, Box 10, Folder 2. Forrestal to Richardson, December 14, 1945. "You take with you the Navy's 'well done,'" the secretary of the Navy wrote.

69. Simpson, 274. See also NHC Operational Archives, Oral Interviews, Kemp Tolley, #4-491. He states that Knox thought Stark was at the White House in the wee hours of December 7 along with Tolley, Hopkins, Stimson, a couple of others, and the president. Tolley then said, "Of course, we all know that Admiral Stark was at the theatre that night before Pearl Harbor, that Roosevelt tried to get in touch with him and when he found he was at the theatre he deferred and said, 'I don't want to have him paged because that will cause a flap.'" He left word for Stark to call him after returning home. Tolley assumed that when Stark called, Roosevelt told him to come to the White House immediately. Tolley thought that Marshall was there too, or that was what Knox related. However, Tolley also thought the group knew from overflights of the Japanese Fleet that it was on its way to Malaya.

70. Beard, 532. Beard says Safford last saw the "winds execute message" on December 14, 1941, when he collected papers with Commander Kramer and turned them over for use as evidence before the Roberts Commission. Roberts said he never saw that or any "*MAGIC*" messages, and if they had been given to him, he would not have read them. See page 383. Or, see Pearl Harbor Hearings, Part XXXIX, 225, 229; Part XII, Exhibit 1, 361; Part III, 523.

71. Short, 000274.

72. Kimmel, 142. Standley wrote almost the same thing, confused that Marshall would take the June 17, 1940, alert so seriously and not follow up on the November 27, 1941, message in the same manner.

73. Short, 000275.

74. *The War Warning to the Army:*

Negotiations with Japanese appear to be terminated to all practical purposes with only the barest possibilities that the Japanese Government might come back and offer to continue. Japanese future action unpredictable, but hostile action possible at any moment. If hostilities cannot, repeat cannot, be avoided, the U.S. desires that Japan commit the first overt act. This policy should not, repeat not, be construed as restricting you to a course of action that might jeopardize your defense. Prior to Japanese hostile action you are directed to undertake such reconnaissance and other measures as you deem necessary, but these measures should be carried out so as not, repeat not, to alarm the civil population or disclose intent. Report measures taken. Should hostilities occur, you will carry out tasks assigned in *Rainbow Five* as far as they pertain to Japan. Limit dissemination of this highly secret information to minimum essential officers.

See Stinnett, 292, for an image of the original.

75. The testimony of General Short is found in Pearl Harbor Hearings, Part VII, 2921-3231.

76. *The War Warning to the Navy:*

CNO to CinPAC, November 27, 1941—This despatch [*sic*] is to be considered a war warning. Negotiations with Japan looking toward stabilization of conditions in the Pacific have ceased and an aggressive move by Japan is expected within the next few days. The number and equipment of Japanese troops and the organization of the naval task forces indicates an amphibious expedition [probably—*marked out*] against either the Philippines [Thai—*handwritten in*] or Kra Peninsula or possibly Borneo. Execute an appropriate defensive deployment preparatory to carrying out the tasks assigned in *WPL 46.* Inform district and army authorities. A similar warning is being sent by War Department. Inform naval district and Army authorities. SPENAVO [London] inform British. [Continental districts, Guam, Samoa directed to take appropriate measure against sabotage—*handwritten in*]. [*WPL 46* was the war plan commonly called *Rainbow Five.*]

See copy of original in Stinnett, 293.

77. Telephone interview with Rear Admiral Leslie J. O'Brien, August 11, 2002.

78. Short, 000277.

79. Ibid., 000273.

80. USNI, Annapolis, Oral Interviews, Vice-Admiral Ruthven E. Libby, #4-230.

81. Short, 000280.

82. Ibid., 000281.

83. Ibid., 000282.

84. Theobald, 171.

85. Richardson, *Treadmill,* 461.

86. LoC, Dyer Papers, Box 10, Folder 4, note of fable. Story reprinted with the permission of Tamiko and Marcia Toland.

87. Captain M. E. Watters to Skipper Steely, March 18, 1999. Watters was replying for Under Secretary of Defense Rudy de Leon, who replaced Dr. Edwin Dorn. Dorn compiled yet another report on the questions. Watters was at that time in the office responsible for officer promotion policies. He did admit that each submission or question sent to his attention "bring[s] insights to this piece

of history." Dr. Dorn, ironically, had a connection also to Paris, Texas. He roomed in college with a graduate of Paris High School, Gary O'Connor.

88. *Dallas Morning News,* December 7, 2000.

89. Kimmel, 145.

90. USNI, Annapolis, Oral Interviews, Vice-Admiral Ruthven E. Libby, #4-232-233.

91. LoC, Dyer Papers, Box 10, Folder 4. Undated letter probably written about late 1946 or early 1947 to *The Atlantic Monthly,* but never mailed.

Chapter 28: The Navy's Last Assignment

1. The University of New Mexico General Library Center for Southwest Research, Collection number MSS 413 BC, is one place outside Washington, DC, where the Japanese War Crime Tribunal Documents can be studied. The library's index to its holdings could be found on the Internet in 2003 at: http://elibrary.unm.edu/oanm/NmU/nmu1%23mss413bc/. Also see LoC, Dyer Papers, Box 10, Folder 2. Orders for recall to active duty, June 12, 1946; Louis Denfeld to Richardson, July 13, 1946.

2. National Personnel Records Center, St. Louis, Missouri. James O. Richardson personnel records file. Letter and copies sent to Skipper Steely from Gloria J. Torrence, August 30, 2002. His transcript record does not show that he was recalled to active service in 1946. However, in his book, *On the Treadmill,* 441, he mentions that his final retirement was on January 2, 1947, after duty in Japan.

3. Philip R. Piccigallo, *The Japanese On Trial: Allied War Crimes Operation in the East 1945-1951* (Austin: University of Texas Press, 1979), 17. This is a good summary of the Hirohito treatment.

4. Arnold C. Brackman, *The Other Nurenberg: The Untold Story of the Tokyo War Crimes Trials* (New York: William Morrow and Company, Inc., 1987), 54. Keenan was a member of FDR's White House inner circle, very influential with the president's decision making. He is never mentioned by Richardson in *Treadmill.* Keenan went to Brown, and then Harvard Law School.

5. Brackman, 55.

6. Kazuo Chiba, "Close Encounters of An Early Kind," found on the Internet in 2002 at: http://www.insightjapan.com/encounters.html.

7. Walter Lee Riley, "The International Military Tribunal for the Far East and the Law of the Tribunal as Revealed by the Judgment and the Concurring and Dissenting Opinions" (Dissertation at the University of Washington, 1947), 10. Seventeen nations formed the United Nations War Crimes Commission, first meeting in October 1943. Also, see University of Virginia Law Library, MSS93-4, Papers of Roy L. Morgan (Charlottesville, Virginia). Morgan, a Duke and Virginia graduate, lived in Greensboro, North Carolina, but worked prior to the war for the FBI. He represented the United States during the 1942 detention of 1,200 Japanese, German, and Italian diplomats at The Homestead in Hot Springs, Virginia, and at The Greenbrier in West Virginia.

8. B. V. A. Röling, *The Tokyo Trial and Beyond: Reflections of a Peacemonger,* ed. Antonio Cassese (Cambridge, MA: Polity Press, Blackwell Publishers, 1993), 31.

9. Richard H. Minear, *Victor's Justice—The War Crimes Trial* (Princeton, NJ: Princeton University Press, 1971), 211.

10. Riley, 62.

11. *Charter of the International Military Tribunal of the Far East in the Trial of the Japanese War Criminals* (Washington, DC: Department of State, 1948), 39-44. Or, see on the Internet The Avalon Project at Yale Law School, at: http://www.yale.edu/lawweb/avalon/imtfech.htm.

12. Röling, 28. Initially there were nine judges; then two, one from the Philippines and one from India, were added.

13. William Flood Webb was a judge in Queensland. He died on August 11, 1972. Röling, 30. Röling says that Webb was not elected, but was nominated by MacArthur.

14. Röling, 23.

15. Ibid., 52.

16. Brackman, 81.

17. Proceedings, International Military Tribunal for the Far East 1946-1948 (IMTFE), Court House of the Tribunal, War Ministry Building, Tokyo, Japan, November 25, 1946, 11175-76. (Shelf Number 10609, Reel #9 on microfilm.)

18. Ibid., 11176. Also, see LoC, Dyer Papers, Box 9, Folder 7. Letter to Richardson designating him to War Crimes duty.

19. LoC, Dyer Papers, Box 10, Folder 2. W. L. Taylor to Richardson, July 26, 1945, Pan American Airways to Hawaii. Also, J. H. Lowell to Richardson, July 31, 1945.

20. Röling, 79.

21. Morgenstern, *Pearl Harbor: The Story of the Secret War.* Röling obtained much of his Pearl Harbor attack knowledge outside the trial from reading this work.

22. Solis Horwitz, "The Tokyo Trial," *International Conciliation,* Number 465 (Carnegie Endowment for International Peace, November 1950), 581.

23. Riley, 76.

24. Ibid., 60. Riley felt it was well done. A secretariat coordinated the process, but was under a military officer.

25. J. A. Appleman, *Military Tribunals and International Crimes* (Indianapolis: Bobs-Merrill Company, 1954), 240-41. Röling, 30. Röling called Webb arrogant and dictatorial.

26. Riley, 65. Also see Horwitz, 489. Röling, 37. At first the defendants only had Japanese counsel, but after much confusion, each was allowed one American lawyer. Only Kingoro Hashimoto refused American help.

27. Riley, 56. This badgering between Webb and Logan was on July 10, 1946. Proceedings, International Military Tribunal for the Far East 1946-1948 (IMTFE), Court House of the Tribunal, War Ministry Building, Tokyo, Japan, November 25, 1946, 2,225-26. (Shelf Number 10609, Reel #9 on microfilm.)

28. Riley, 67, does not have him listed.

29. LoC, Dyer Papers, Box 10, Folder 2. Schedule of expenses and itinerary, September 24, 1946. Went from Hawaii to Kwajalein by government air, to Guam, to Tokyo.

30. LoC, Dyer Papers, Box 10, Folder 7. Notes on book chapter about the

Tokyo trials. His notes say he stayed at the Hotel Fuysa, or Fujia.

31. LoC, Dyer Papers, Box 10, Folder 4. Paul J. Mueller, major general, Chief-of-staff, US Army Forces Pacific, to Richardson, IPS Section, SCAP, dated September 12, 1946; see also CinPAC-POA to ComNAVJAP, dated September 12, 1946. A flag plane was sent from Honolulu that day for Tokyo to pick up Richardson. There was space for nine other passengers; see also Major General E. M. Almond, assistant Chief-of-staff, G-1, to John B. Cooley, adjutant general, September 12, 1946. Preliminary work and preparation for Richardson testimony is completed. Richardson arrived back in Washington on September 24. See also Box 2, Lowell to Richardson, completed paperwork dated September 15, 1946; and see schedule of expenses, September 24, 1946.

32. LoC, Dyer Papers, Box 10, Folder 2. Schedule of expenses and itinerary, December 3, 1946. He left Washington on November 4 at 10:50 P.M. on a government airplane.

33. Minear, 3.

34. Brackman, 89.

35. Piccigallo, 18. Piccigallo says there were 102 witnesses and affidavits from 1,200, with an additional 1,000 documents placed into evidence. Riley, 57. He says there were 3,915 exhibits not copied in the record, some of which Richardson produced only to see denied.

36. Minear, 5. See also Riley, 77. Röling, 52. He says there were 4,836 documents or exhibits.

37. Röling, 52.

38. Research on the testimony and proceedings of the IMTFE can be done either on the microfilm roles at NARA or by reading *The Tokyo War Crime Trials* (Herndon, CT: Garland Publishing Company, 1981), ISBN 082404755-9. Richardson's testimony in that collection is in volume 5. On microfilm, the Richardson presentation is on Shelf 10609, Reel #9, pages 11, 137-12, 478. Richardson's testimony is on pages 11, 166-11302.

39. Proceedings, IMTFE, Tokyo, Japan, November 25, 1946, 11137. (Shelf Number 10609, Reel #9 on microfilm). Brackman, 70. Pal's wife became ill during the trial; therefore he was gone at several times.

40. The papers of Joseph W. Ballantine are located at the Hoover Institution, Stanford University.

41. Brackman, 211.

42. Proceedings, IMTFE, Tokyo, Japan, November 25, 1946, 11165. (Shelf Number 10609, Reel #9 on microfilm.)

43. Ibid., 11172.

44. Ibid., 11175.

45. Ibid., 11176-77.

46. Ibid., 11178.

47. Ibid., 11179.

48. Richardson, *Treadmill,* 17.

49. Italy also refused to sign the March 25, 1936, document. That left the United States, Great Britain, and France as the signatories.

50. Proceedings, IMTFE, Tokyo, Japan, November 25, 1946, 11183. (Shelf Number 10609, Reel #9 on microfilm.)

51. Richardson, *Treadmill*, 25.

52. London Conference 1930. Found on the Internet in 2002 at: http://www.warships1.com/W-NRO/INRO_London_Treaty_1930.htm. Article 10: "Within one month after the date of laying down and the date of completion respectively of each vessel of war, other than capital ships, aircraft carriers and the vessels exempt from limitation under Article 8, laid down or completed by or for them after the coming into force of the present Treaty, the High Contracting Parties shall communicate to each of the other High Contracting Parties . . ."

53. Japan received the German Islands in the North Pacific as Class C mandates, meaning they were a long way from gaining independence. See League of Nations Charter, Article 22, *Papers Relating to the Foreign Relations of the United States 1922,* Department of State Publication in two volumes (Washington, DC: Government Printing Office, 1938) found on the Internet in 2008 at: http://www.yale.edu/lawweb/avalon/leagcov.htm.

54. Miller, 105. For several pages he described the islands and atolls.

55. The Avalon Project at the Yale Law School, Treaty Between the United States of America, the British Empire, France, and Japan, Signed at Washington on December 13, 1921. Found on the Internet in 2002 at: http://www.yale.edu/lawweb/avalon/diplomacy/forrel/1922v1/tr1921.htm#art1.

56. Proceedings, IMTFE, Tokyo, Japan, November 25, 1946, 11192. (Shelf Number 10609, Reel #9 on microfilm.)

57. Ibid., 11193.

58. Ibid., 11195. The Curts statement was presented to the court as Exhibit #1252.

59. Proceedings, IMTFE, Tokyo, Japan, November 25, 1946, 11198. (Shelf Number 10609, Reel #9 on microfilm.) A good summary of what Yamamoto and Nagumo did after leaving the Pearl Harbor attack is found in Prange, *At Dawn We Slept,* 573. Two carriers and their forces broke off on December 16 to attack Wake Island five days later. Nagumo continued toward home, arriving on December 23 in Hiroshima Bay. Yamamoto was already there, in the *Nagato.*

60. Proceedings, IMTFE, Tokyo, Japan, November 25, 1946, 11203. (Shelf Number 10609, Reel #9 on microfilm.)

61. Gannon, 190.

62. Stinnett, 111.

63. Richardson presented the messages in a book, labeled as Exhibit #1254. He presented other documents and maps as Exhibits #1254-A and #1255.

64. Proceedings, IMTFE, Tokyo, Japan, November 25, 1946, 11206. (Shelf Number 10609, Reel #9 on microfilm.)

65. Ibid., 11207.

66. Stinnett, 111.

67. Pearl Harbor Hearings, Part XXXVI, 464.

68. Stinnett, 106.

69. Layton, 244. Also, Prange, *At Dawn We Slept,* 357. The Japanese used MacKay Radio for their traffic in November, and at other times, so not all messages were captured.

70. Prange, *At Dawn We Slept,* 443.

71. Proceedings, IMTFE, Tokyo, Japan, November 25, 1946, 11209. (Shelf Number 10609, Reel #9 on microfilm.)

72. Ibid., 11210.

73. Ibid., 11211.

74. Mary Ann Phillips, *Fletcher Warren Reporting for Duty, Sir* (Austin, TX: Nortex Press, 2006), 66.

75. Gannon, 197. Gannon does not mention the RCA involvement.

76. NHC, Operational Archives, Oral Interviews, Arthur Howard McCollum, #8-388.

77. Proceedings, IMTFE, Tokyo, Japan, November 25, 1946, 11213. (Shelf Number 10609, Reel #9 on microfilm.) These were Exhibits #1259 and #1260.

78. Lowman, 201. The entire message is retyped here with locations added. It was not translated until December 11, 1941.

79. Stillwell, 254, "Pearl Harbor Aftermath," by Captain Wilfred J. Holmes.

80. University of Hawaii, The Otto Kuehn Family Papers, Dr. Bernhard L. Hormann, Collector. The papers were assembled by a Dr. Hormann, professor of sociology at the University of Hawaii. Dr. Hormann provided a home for the two sons of Otto and Freidel Kuehn during at least part of the time the Kuehns lived in incarceration on Sand Island. Dr. Hormann donated the papers to the Hawaii War Records Depository in 1981. The Otto Kuehn Family Papers in Hawaii in the War Records Depository contain three parts plus an introductory essay by Dr. Hormann.

81. Proceedings, IMTFE, Tokyo, Japan, November 25, 1946, 11214. (Shelf Number 10609, Reel #9 on microfilm.)

82. Not translated until December 11, 1941.

83. Proceedings, IMTFE, Tokyo, Japan, November 25, 1946, 11220. (Shelf Number 10609, Reel #9 on microfilm.)

84. Ibid., 11216.

85. Ibid. A copy is in the NARA—College Park, Records of the Pearl Harbor Liaison Office, Box 15, Folder 32.

86. Stinnett, 113.

87. Proceedings, IMTFE, Tokyo, Japan, November 25, 1946, 11223. (Shelf Number 10609, Reel #9 on microfilm.)

88. Ibid., 11225. A copy is in the NARA—College Park, Records of the Pearl Harbor Liaison Office, Box 15, Folder 32.

89. NARA—College Park, Records of the Pearl Harbor Liaison Office, Box 15, Folder 32. John Ford Baecher attached these to a memorandum to a Major Correa, dated October 17, 1945. He noted that Safford thought either (labeled Message #253 and #254) could have been decrypted in less than ninety minutes.

90. Clausen and Lee, 207. Also, see Stinnett, 108.

91. These messages to Tokyo from Honolulu are found in the Exhibits of the Joint Congressional Hearings, Exhibit #2, Japanese messages concerning military installations, ship movements, etc. The Grew message can be found in "Peace and War: United States Foreign Policy 1931-1941" (Washington, DC: United States Government Printing Office, 1943), 196. Also, could be seen on the Internet in 2002 at: http://www.ncsociety.net/pha/timeline/410127apw.html;

and in 2006 at: http://ibiblio.org/pha/timeline/Magic.html or http://www.ibib lio.org/pha/paw/index.html.

92. Proceedings, IMTFE, Tokyo, Japan, November 25, 1946, 11228. (Shelf Number 10609, Reel #9 on microfilm.)

93. Ibid.

94. Proceedings, IMTFE, Tokyo, Japan, October 25, 1946, 7,989. (Shelf Number 10609, Reel #6 on microfilm.) It was originally Research Report #13, dated December 1, 1945, called "Japan's Decision to Fight," published by the General Quarters, SCAP. The Russians were interested in a section discussing a secret operation dated November 1, 1942. See page 7,990.

95. Proceedings, IMTFE, Tokyo, Japan, November 25, 1946, 11230. (Shelf Number 10609, Reel #9 on microfilm.)

96. Ibid., 11233.

97. Proceedings, IMTFE, Tokyo, Japan, November 25, 1946, 11236. (Shelf Number 10609, Reel #9 on microfilm.)

98. Ibid., 11239.

99. Ibid., 11240.

100. Ibid., 11242.

101. Ibid., 11243.

102. Ibid.

103. Ibid., 11244.

104. Ibid., 11248.

105. Ibid., 11251.

106. Röling, 30. Röling said the French judge lacked social abilities too, but that even Russian General I. M. Zaryanow, through interpreters, would carry on pretty lively discussions at lunch.

107. Duane Schultz, *The Doolittle Raid* (New York: St. Martin's Press, 1988), 264-65.

108. Proceedings, IMTFE, Tokyo, Japan, November 25, 1946, 11253. (Shelf Number 10609, Reel #9 on microfilm.)

109. Ibid., 11258.

110. Ibid., 11259.

111. Ibid., 11261.

112. United States Navy, "A Brief History of Aircraft Carriers—USS Hornet (CV 8)," found at this Internet site in 2002: http://www.chinfo.navy.mil/nav palib/ships/carriers/histories/cv08-hornet/cv08-hornet.html.

113. Proceedings, IMTFE, Tokyo, Japan, November 25, 1946, page 11266. (Shelf Number 10609, Reel #9 on microfilm.)

114. Ibid., 11267. *Ranger,* 82; *Yorktown,* 72; *Wasp,* 72; *Saratoga,* 90; *Lexington,* 90; and *Enterprise,* 90.

115. Proceedings, IMTFE, Tokyo, Japan, November 25, 1946, 11269. (Shelf Number 10609, Reel #9 on microfilm.)

116. Ibid., 11169.

117. Ibid., 11274.

118. Richardson, *Treadmill,* 32, 34, 56, 116, 120, 398, 435, 463.

119. Proceedings, IMTFE, Tokyo, Japan, November 25, 1946, 11275. (Shelf Number 10609, Reel #9 on microfilm.)

120. "Japan Attacks the Philippines, MacArthur Abandons His Troops." The Web site of the Pacific War Historical Society. Found on the Internet in 2008 at: http://www.users.bigpond.com/pacificwar/gatheringstorm/Philippines/Philindex.html.

Read also about all the *Orange* and *Rainbow* plans in Miller, *War Plan Orange*.

121. Proceedings, IMTFE, Tokyo, Japan, November 25, 1946, 11277. (Shelf Number 10609, Reel #9 on microfilm.)

122. Ibid., 11281.

123. Ibid.

124. Ibid., 11282.

125. Ibid., 11286.

126. Ibid., 11289.

127. Brackman, 236.

128. Mark R. Peattie, *Hoover Essay: A Historian Looks at the Pacific War* (Stanford, CA: Leland Stanford Junior University, 1995), 7; or see Mark R. Peattie and David C. Evans, *Kaigun: Strategy, Tactics, and Technology in the Imperial Japanese Navy 1887-1941* (Annapolis, MD: Naval Institute Press, 1997).

129. Umberto Eco, "The Alpha: Pearl Harbor, December 1941," a paper found on the Internet in 2002 at a Web site created by Tim Lanzendorfer called The Pacific War: The U.S. Navy. Address is http://www.microworks.net/pacific/special/history1.htm.

130. Proceedings, IMTFE, Tokyo, Japan, November 25, 1946, 11292. (Shelf Number 10609, Reel #9 on microfilm.)

131. Ibid., 11295.

132. Ibid., 11296.

133. Ibid., 11218, 11298. The star on the boat, and the Roman numeral III location, indicated which series of signals to be used in the code. The star boat was to be anchored in Lanikai Bay. See Theobald, 119.

134. Proceedings, IMTFE, Tokyo, Japan, November 25, 1946, 11299. (Shelf Number 10609, Reel #9 on microfilm.)

135. Ibid., 11300.

136. Richardson's memory was a bit off, since the USS *Langley* was converted to a sea tender and reclassified on April 27, 1937. She was at Pearl Harbor in mid-July of 1938, but he probably saw her again in 1939 when he again went to sea. His description is correct, and there was no way she could have been compared to a carrier in 1941.

137. Proceedings, IMTFE, Tokyo, Japan, November 25, 1946, 11301. (Shelf Number 10609, Reel #9 on microfilm.)

138. Minear, 26.

139. LoC, Dyer Papers, Box 10, Folder 2. He spent the night of November 29 in Pearl Harbor, and arrived home on December 3 at noon.

140. LoC, Dyer Papers, Box 10, Folder 2. J. L. McCrea to Richardson, December 22, 1946.

141. LoC, Dyer Papers, Box 10, Folder 4. Forrestal to Richardson, January 13, 1947.

Chapter 29: Richardson Finally Free to Raise Roses

1. Conversation with Betty Carney Taussig of Annapolis, Maryland, August 2003, confirms the story. Also, conversation with next-door neighbor at 2701 35th Place NW, Guinevere Griest, held by phone in September 2002.

2. Phone conversation with Guinevere Griest, September 24, 2002.

3. Phone conversation with Emily Short of Las Cruces, New Mexico, August 25, 2001.

4. Letter from Emily Lee Short Thrasher of Vienna, Virginia, August 25, 2002.

5. Conversations with Elizabeth Wingo Banks and a letter from Duncan, Oklahoma, dated March 19, 2002.

6. *Tulia Herald*, October 27, 1955. This article includes what was most likely the last photo taken of the two together. They could have passed for twins.

7. Richardson, *Treadmill*, 471.

8. *Paris News*, December 23, 1994. Rear Admiral Eugene H. Farrell, "Admiral Richardson was a true Texas gentleman."

9. Letter from Clareda Chambers Purser to Skipper Steely, March 10, 1999.

10. Arlington National Cemetery, Interment Records. See letter from Phyllis B. White to Skipper Steely, September 5, 2003. Short was buried there on September 7, 1949, in Lot #1091. Isabel was placed there on April 12, 1984. Her records say the site is Grave Number 1091, Lot 7, in Section 30. See Grid #U37.3, Run #819. She was born on October 19, 1893, and died in Washington, DC, on April 10, 1984. Hines Rinaldi of Silver Spring, Maryland, was the funeral director. Short's official separation from the Army was on February 28, 1942.

11. Toland, 77. NHC, Operational Archives, Oral Interviews, Arthur H. McCollum, #18-792. An east wind is usually followed by rain, coming across from Japan with the warm current.

12. Prange, *Pearl Harbor: The Verdict of History*, 265. Also see Chapter 19 for a long discussion on "East Wind Rain"; John Prados, *Combined Fleet Decoded: The Secret History of American Intelligence and the Japanese Navy in World War II* (New York: Random House, 1995), 168.

13. NHC, Operational Archives, Oral Interviews, Arthur H. McCollum, #18-792.

14. NARA—College Park, Records of the Pearl Harbor Liaison Office, Box 4, Folder 5. Safford to Kramer-San, December 22, 1943, and January 22, 1944. By March Kimmel also wrote Kramer, then with Halsey in the South Pacific, asking similar questions. Kimmel was just realizing that another story was lurking in the background, mostly unreleased up until then in an attempt to keep the decrypting ability secret.

15. Zacharias, *Secret Missions*, 254. While Zacharias felt a winds code message would have added little to what was already known, he thought that an execute order surely would have come later. But, he said that by 1946 too much importance was put into finding this message.

16. *Washington Post*, May 18, 1973.

17. Conversation with Donald Goldstein by phone, fall of 2002. E-mail from Goldstein to Steely, October 10, 2002. "His wife was a real problem."

18. William S. White, "Navy Denies It Got 'Winds' Message Tipping Off War."

New York Times, December 14, 1945. Pearl Harbor Hearings, Part IV, 2034.

19. E-mail from Ned Kimmel to Skipper Steely, October 10, 2002.

20. Telephone conversation between Skipper Steely and David Richmond, October 1, 2001.

21. Richardson, *Treadmill,* 469.

22. Ibid., 424.

23. Theobald, 23.

24. *Dallas Morning News,* March 31, 1954.

25. LoC, Dyer Papers, Box 10, Folder 4. Standley to Richardson, April 24, 1954. Also, newspaper column called "Fair Enough" by Westbrook Pegler in Box 9, Folder 3.

26. LoC, Bloch Papers, Box 3, Richardson File 1939-42. Bloch to Richardson, March 3, 1942.

27. Pearl Harbor Hearings, Part XXVI, 205-12. Testimony taken in the Hart Inquiry.

28. Pearl Harbor Hearings, Part X, 4829-72 and 4877-4909; Part XXVI (Hart Inquiry Proceedings), 225-37, specifically question #16; Part XXVIII, 1582, before the Army Board; Part XXXVI, 164, before the Hewitt Investigation. He also testified before the Roberts Commission and the Navy Court and gave a memo to Clausen.

29. Pearl Harbor Hearings, Part XXVI, Hart Inquiry Proceedings, 152.

30. Betty Carney Taussig, *A Warrior for Freedom,* 212.

31. Coletta, 351.

32. Richardson, *Treadmill,* vi-vii.

33. Dyer, "Reminiscences," 204.

34. NHC, Oral Interviews, Kent Melhorn, 66.

35. FDR Library. Grace G. Tully to Admiral James O. Richardson, September 13, 1948.

36. FDR Library. J. O. Richardson to Miss Tully, September 30, 1948.

37. FDR Library. Miss Tully to Admiral J. O. Richardson, October 21, 1948.

38. FDR Library. J. O. Richardson to Miss Tully, November 2, 1948.

39. FDR Library, November 23, 1948. Notes typed by Grace G. Tully about her meeting with Admiral Richardson.

40. LoC, Dyer Papers, Box 9, Folder 6. Miss Tully was not the only one turned down by Richardson. E. M. Eller, director of Naval History, wrote on July 19, 1963, asking him if he would place his papers with the Department of the Navy's center.

41. LoC, Dyer Papers, Box 10, Folder 4. Land to Richardson, January 6, 1953; June 8, 1953. Twenty-one members were alive.

42. Richardson, *Treadmill,* x.

43. Ibid., 447.

44. *Paris News,* December 23, 1994. Admiral Eugene Farrell writes that "only when he was terminally ill did he [Richardson] authorize the publication of his memoirs."

Chapter 30: 40-40-20

1. Dyer, "Reminiscences," 215.

2. LoC, Dyer Papers, Box 10, Folder 4. Heffernan to Richardson, April 18, 1956.

3. LoC, Dyer Papers, Box 10, Folder 4. Richardson to Director of Naval History, May 9, 1956. The paperwork changing this stipulation was in a letter from Richardson to the Director of Naval History, Navy Operations, Navy Department, dated May 19, 1971, when he was ninety-three, but still in fair health though the Griest sisters who lived next door say he did not move outside the house those last years. His signature was still solid. He was the seventh oldest graduate of the Naval Academy at that time, and the last of the Class of 1902.

Bibliography

I. Primary Sources

Archives and Collections

Air Force, U.S. Museum at Wright Patterson in Ohio.

Annual Reports of the Secretary of the Navy.

Arlington National Cemetery, Arlington, Virginia.

Army Military History Center. Carlisle, Pennsylvania.

    Charles B. Hansen Papers.

Army Center of Military History. Washington, DC.

Avalon Project at the Yale Law School. On the Internet in 2002 at: http://www.yale.edu/lawweb/avalon/diplomacy/forrel/1922v1/tr1921.htm#art1.

Chan Robles Virtual Law Library.

    Philippine Law Statutes and Codes.

        The Philippine Independence Act.

Citadel Archives and Museum.

    Mark W. Clark Papers.

Coles, Robert L. History Room. Glen Cove, New York.

    F. Trubee Davison Papers (1921-1931).

Colorado, University of, at Boulder. Archives.

    Whitlock Papers.

Columbia University Library and Archives. New York, New York.

    Oral History Office:

        Hill, Harry W. Oral History Office. (Copy in NHC)

        Land, Emory S. Oral History Office. (Copy in NHC)

        Trubee, Davison, F. Oral History Office.

Curtiss, Glenn H. Museum of Local History.

Eisenhower, Dwight David, Library.

    Oral Interview with Sue Sarafian Jeh.

Hawaii, University of. Honolulu, Hawaii.

    The Otto Kuehn Family Papers, Dr. Bernhard L. Hormann, Collector.

Hoover, Herbert, Presidential Library. West Branch, Iowa.

Hoover Institution on War, Revolution and Peace, Stanford University. Stanford, California.

    Ballantine, Joseph W. Papers of.

    Radford, Arthur W. Collection.

    Short, Isabel Dean. "The General's Lady" (unpublished manuscript), General Walter C. Short Collection.

Library of Congress, Washington, DC.

    Manuscript Division, Papers of:

Bloch, Claude C.
Callan, John Lansing.
Dyer, George W.
Halsey, William F.
King, Ernest J.
Knox, Frank.
Land, Emory.
Leahy, William D.
McCrea, John L.
Pratt, William V.
Wright, Jerauld.
Yarnell, Harry.
MacArthur Memorial Museum Archives. Norfolk, Virginia.
MacArthur Office Diary.
Sutherland Papers.
Military Academy United States. West Point, New York.
Association of Graduates Archives.
Mississippi Department of Archives and History. Jackson, Mississippi.
Leigh, R. H. Papers.
National Archives and Records Administration, Washington, DC & College Park, Maryland.
General Board Subject Files.
Joint Basic War Plan Orange, 21 Feb. 38, JB 325, ser. 618.
Records of the Office of the Chief of Naval Operations, RG-38.
Records of Office of Naval Records and Library, RG-45.
Records of the Secretary of the Navy, RG-80.
General Correspondence 1926-1940.
Records of the Pearl Harbor Liaison Office.
USS *Panay* Correspondence.
Records of War Department General and Special Staffs, RG-165.
Records of the Department of Defense, RG-218.
Joint Chiefs of Staff.
Joint Chiefs of Staff, Special Committee for the Reorganization of National Defense. Richardson Committee.
Records of the U.S. Fleet, RG 313.
CinCUS Files 1939, 1940.
Ship Records:
USS *Chaumont* Deck Log.
USS *Itasca* radio transcripts reports.
USS *New Mexico* Log Book.
National Cryptologic Museum Foundation. Fort George G. Meade, Maryland.
National Personnel Records Center, St. Louis, Missouri.
Richardson, James O. Personnel records file.
Naval Historical Center. Washington Navy Yard, Washington, DC.
Operational Archives:
Manuscript Collection:
Oral Interviews Collection and Index Cards:

Bernhard Henry Bieri.

Felix L. Johnson.

Stephen Jurika.

Edwin T. Layton.

Arthur Howard McCollum.

Kent Melhorn.

Joseph J. Rochefort.

Malcolm F. Schoeffel.

William R. Smedberg.

Henry Smith-Hutton.

Bernard Max Strean.

Kemp Tolley.

George van Deurs.

Officer Biographical Files.

Online Library of Selected Images.

Photographic Section:

Richardson, Admiral J. O. Photographs.

Richardson, May Fenet. Photographs.

Publications:

Packard, Captain Wyman H. *A Century of U.S. Naval Intelligence,* 1996.

Naval, United States, Institute Archives and Library. Annapolis, Maryland.

Oral Interviews Collection:

Burke, Arleigh.

Edwards Sr., Frederick A.

Hustvedt, Olaf M.

Layton, Edwin T.

Libby, Ruthven E.

Mitscher Mrs. Marc A. and Smith, Jr., Mrs. Roy C.

Mustin, Lloyd M.

Pownall, Charles A.

Ramage, James D.

Tabuck, Raymond D.

Wheeler, Charles Julian.

Wylie, Jr., Joseph Caldwell.

Naval War College. Newport, Rhode Island.

Historical Collection:

Student Thesis, RG-13.

Papers Written by James O. Richardson.

Navy, U.S., Court of Inquiry.

Report of USS *Panay* Attack.

New Mexico, The University of. General Library Center for Southwest Research.

Japanese War Crime Tribunal Documents.

Purdue University of.

Earhart Special Collection.

Rigdon Collection, Henderson Library, Georgia Southern University.

Roosevelt Franklin Delano, Library. Hyde Park, NewYork.

Day by Day—The Pare Lorentz Chronology.
E-mails from Bob Parks, researcher, archivist.
Office of Social Entertainment.
Oral Histories and Interviews:
    Freidel, Frank. Interview with Admiral Joe Taussig.
Roosevelt Presidential Press Conferences.
Safe Files.
Secretary's File.
Various Correspondence Files.
Truman Presidential Museum and Library.
    Johnson, Neil M. (editor and interviewer):
        Truman, Louis. Oral Interview, December 7, 1991.
    Taylor, Myron C. Papers of.
Virginia, University of. Charlottesville, Virginia.
    Miller Center of History.
        White House Tapes.
    Law Library.
        Papers of Roy L. Morgan.
Royal Archives. London, England.
Schuylkill.com Archives.
Southern Historical Collection #3554. University of North Carolina. Chapel Hill.
    Hardison, Osborne Bennett. Papers.
UCLA Special Collections Department.
    Masbir, Sidney F. Papers, 1942-1960.Young Research Library.
Western Kentucky University Archives.
Yukon Archives. Whitehorse, Yukon, Canada.

Public Documents

150th Combat Engineering Battalion, November 1944, Report of the. Found on
    the Internet in 2003 at: http://www.150th.com/ reports/nov44.htm.
1880 Federal Census. Lamar County, Texas.
*Annual Register, U.S. Naval Academy, Annapolis, Maryland, 57th Academic
    Year.* Washington, DC: Government Printing Office, 1901.
Annual Reports of the Navy Department.
Army, U.S. Information School. Pamphlet No. 4, *Pillars of Peace: Documents
    Pertaining to American Interest in Establishing a Lasting World Peace:
    January 1941-February 1946.* Carlisle Barracks, Pennsylvania: Book
    Department, May 1946.
Charter of the International Military Tribunal of the Far East in the Trial of the
    Japanese War Criminals. Washington, DC: Department of State, 1948.
City Council Minutes. Paris, Texas.
Congressional Digest. Washington, DC, U.S. Congress, 1944.
    "American Troops in Siberia, July 22, 1919." 66th Congressional Document,
        First Session, Number 60, Senate. U.S Congress. Washington, DC.
Court of Federal Claims. United States.
    Achenbach, Marcia Fee, et al., Plaintiffs, The United States, Defendant. App. 6, 415.
Court of Inquiry Report.
    U.S. *Panay* Attack. U.S. Congress.

Deed Records. Lamar County, Texas.
District of Columbia. Washington, DC, City Records.
    Deed Records.
    Office of the Chief Financial Officer, Taxpayer Service Center.
    Probate Files.
        Register of Wills.
            Last Will and Testament of James O. Richardson.
Dorn Report to Deputy Secretary of Defense. Washington, DC, 1995.
    Dorn, Edwin. "Advancement of Rear Admiral Kimmell and
        Major General Short on the Retired List." Office of the Under
        Secretary of Defense for Personnel and Readiness.
Lamar County, Texas. Commissioners Court Minute Book 4 (1885-1889).
Lamar County. Deed Books.
Lamar County. Marriage License Books.
Lamar County, Texas. Probate Records.
League of Nations Charter.
Naval Affairs, U.S. Senate Committee on. April 22, 1940.
Naval Operations, Office of the Chief of. Naval History Division, *Dictionary of
    American Naval Fighting Ships.* Washington, DC.
Navy Marine Corps Relief Society. "History of the Navy Relief Society,"
    Alexandria, Virginia: March 1979.
Navy U.S. First Quarter Fiscal Employment Schedule, CinCUS, 1940, 1941.
*Pearl Harbor Attack: Hearings Before the Joint Committee on the Investigation
    of the Pearl Harbor Attack.* United States Government Printing Office, U.S.
    Congress. Washington, DC, 1946, Held before the Congress of the United
    States, 79th Congress First Session.
    Army Pearl Harbor Board.
    Clarke Investigation.
    Clausen Investigation.
    Hart Inquiry Proceedings.
    Hewitt Inquiry Proceedings.
    Navy Court of Inquiry.
    Roberts Commission Hearings.
Proceedings, International Military Tribunal for the Far East 1946-1948. Court
    House of the Tribunal, War Ministry Building. Tokyo, Japan.
Purdue University Libraries. West Lafayette, Indiana.
    George Putnam Collection of Amelia Earhart Papers.
Secretary of Defense:
    Cole, Alice C., Goldberg, Dr. Alfred, Tucker, Samuel A., and Winnacker,
        Rudolph A. *The Department of Defense: Documents on Establishment
        and Organization 1944-1978.* Washington, DC: Historical Office,
        1978.
Reports of the Navy Relief Society 1942-1945. Anderson House, Navy
    Department. Washington, DC.
Navy Marine Corps Relief Society Annual Reports, Alexandria, Virginia.
Senate, U.S. Committee of Naval Affairs.
State, U.S. Department of. Papers Relating to the Foreign Relations of the
    United States 1922.

State Department Publications:
"Peace and War: United States Foreign Policy 1931-1941." U.S. Government Printing Office, Washington, DC, 1943.
Wilson, Woodrow. War Messages, 65th Congress, 1st Session, Senate Document 5, Serial Number 7264, Washington, DC, 1917.

Unpublished Documents, Theses, and Dissertations

Dancer, Mattie Epperson. "Improvement of Instruction in the Rural Schools of Lamar County." Dallas, Texas. SMU masters thesis, ca. 1940.
Hart, Admiral Thomas C. Diary.
Mayock, Tom. "FDR: Pacific Warlord." Unpublished manuscript found on Internet in 2003 at: http://users.erols.com/tomtud/ index.html.
Smith, Elmer F. Collection, Sterling, Virginia, 2005.
Logs and notes, 1944.
Steely Collection.
Gee Library Archives. Commerce, Texas.
Genealogy Society of Lamar County Library Files, Steely Section.
Paris, Texas, Personal Files.
Swearingen, Jake Floyd. "History of Public Education in Lamar County." Austin, Texas: Masters thesis at the University of Texas, August, 1935.
Zacharias, Ellis M. Papers.

Interviews

Banks, Elizabeth Wingo. Duncan, Oklahoma.
Cooke, Charlie.
Curts, Bob.
Duncan, Evan. Washington, DC. By phone.
Fitch, Jack. By phone.
Goldstein, Donald. Pittsburg, Pennsylvania. By phone, e-mails.
Griest, Guinevere. Washington, DC.
Johnson, C. R. "Chris."
Kepper, Charles F. By phone.
O'Brien, Admiral Leslie J. By phone.
Purser, Clareda Chambers. By phone, e-mails.
Rich, Doris L. By phone.
Richmond, David.
Short, Emily. By phone.
Slany, Dr. William Z. Washington, DC. By phone.
Somerville, Lee.
Smith, Elmer F.
Taussig, Betty Carney. Annapolis, Maryland.
Trubee, Daniel. New York City. By phone.
Truman, General Louis.
Vlach, Jim

Movie Clips and Videos

Gettyimages.

Grinberg Worldwide Images.

Historic Films.

II. Secondary Sources

Books and Articles

Abbazia, Patrick. *Mr. Roosevelt's Navy: The Private War of the U.S. Atlantic Fleet 1939-1942.* Annapolis, MD: Naval Institute Press, 1975.

Albion, Robert G. and Robert Howe Connery. *Forrestal and the Navy.* New York: Columbia University Press, 1962.

Ambrose, Stephen E. *Eisenhower: Soldier, General of the Army, President-elect, 1890-1952.* Simon and Schuster: New York, 1984.

Anderson, Charles R. *Day of Lightning, Years of Scorn.* Annapolis, MD: Naval Institute Press, 2005.

Appleman, J. A. *Military Tribunals and International Crimes.* Indianapolis, IN: Bobs-Merrill Company, 1954.

Armstrong, Alan. *Preemptive Strike: The Secret Plan That Would Have Prevented the Attack on Pearl Harbor.* Guilford, MA: Lyons Press, 2006.

Astor, Gerald. *The Greatest War: Americans in Combat 1941-1945.* Novato, CA: Presidio Press, 1999.

Bailey, Beth and David Farber. *The First Strange Place: Alchemy of Race and Sex in World War II Hawaii.* Baltimore: Johns Hopkins University Press, 1994.

Barlow, Jeffrey G. *Revolt of the Admirals: The Fight for Naval Aviation 1945-1950.* Washington, DC: Naval Historical Center, 1994.

Beard, Charles A. *President Roosevelt and the Coming of War 1941.* New Haven, CT: Yale University Press, 1948.

Beigel, Harvey M. *Battleship Country: The Battle Fleet at San Pedro—Long Beach, California 1919-1940.* Missoula, MT: Pictorial Histories Publishing Company, 1983.

Blumenon, Martin. *Patton: The Man Behind the Legend 1884-1945.* New York: William Morrow and Company Inc., 1985.

Brackman, Arnold C. *The Other Nuremberg: The Untold Story of the Tokyo War Crimes Trials.* New York: William Morrow and Company, Inc., 1987.

Bradford, Sarah. *The Reluctant King: The Life and Reign of George VI 1895-1952.* New York: St. Martin's Press, 1989.

Bradley, John H. and Jack W. Dice. Ed. Thomas E. Griss. *The Second World War: Asia and the Pacific.* Wayne, NJ: Avery Publishing Group, Inc., 1989.

Bradley, Omar N. and Clay Blair. *A General's Life: An Autobiography by General of the Army Omar N. Bradley.* New York: Simon and Schuster, 1983.

Brothers, Ron, ed. *Old City Cemetery: Lamar County, Texas.* Paris, TX: Genealogy Society of Lamar County, 2001.

Brown, Anthony Cave. *The Last Hero: Wild Bill Donovan.* New York: Times Books, 1982.

Buell, Thomas B. *Master of Sea Power: A Biography of Fleet Admiral Ernest J. King.* Boston: Little Brown, 1980.

Burke, John. *Winged Legend: The Life of Amelia Earhart.* New York: Berkley Publishing Corporation and G. P. Putnam's Sons, 1970.

Burns, James MacGregor. *Roosevelt: The Lion and the Fox.* New York: 1956; reprint Harvest Books, 2002.

Butcher, Harry C. *My Three Years with Eisenhower: The Personal Diary of Captain Harry C. Butcher, USNR, Naval Aide to General Eisenhower 1942-1945.* New York: Simon Schuster, 1946.

Chamberlain, Rudolph W. *There Is No Truce.* New York: Macmillan, 1935.

Chandler, Alfred, ed., and Louis Galambos, assoc. ed. *The Papers of Dwight David Eisenhower,* vols. 6-9. Baltimore: Johns Hopkins University Press, 1979.

Chang, Iris. *The Rape of Nanking.* New York: Basic Books, a subsidiary of Perseus Books, 1997.

Chapman, Sally Putnam. *Whistled Like A Bird: The Untold Story of Dorothy Putnam, George Putnam and Amelia Earhart.* New York: Warner Books, Inc., 1997.

Cherpak, Evelyn, ed. *Memoirs of Admiral H. Kent Hewitt.* Newport, RI: Naval War College Press, 2004.

Chiba, Kazuo. "Close Encounters of an Early Kind," found on the Internet in 2002 at: http://www.insightjapan.com/encounters. html.

Clausen, Henry C. and Bruce Lee. *Pearl Harbor: Final Judgement.* Cambridge, MA: Da Capo Press, Perseus Book Group, 1992.

Coletta, Paolo E. *Patrick N.L. Bellinger and U.S. Naval Aviation.* Lanham, MD: University Press of America, 1987.

Costello, John. *The Pacific War.* New York: Rawson, Wade Publishers, 1981.

Cox, David. "US prisoners claim Roosevelt left them in Philippines deliberately," found on the Internet in 2003 at: http://why-ar.com/news/2002/07/30/prison er.html.

Cruttwell, Charles Robert Mowbray Fraser. *A History of the Great War 1914-1918.* Oxford: The Clarendon Press, 1936; reprint Chicago: 1991.

Cullum, Brevet Major General George W. *Biographical Register of the Officers and Graduates of the U.S. Military Academy at West Point, New York Since Its Establishment in 1802,* vols. 2, 3. Chicago: 1930.

Daugherty, Leo J. "Away All Boats: The Army-Navy Maneuvers of 1925." *Joint Force Quarterly* (Autumn/Winter, 1998-1999).

D'Este, Carlo. *Patton: A Genius for War.* New York: Harper Collins Publishers, 1995.

Dohoney, E. L., Sr. *An Average American.* Paris, TX: Privately published, ca. 1900.

Dower, John W. *War Without Mercy: Race and Power in the Pacific War.* New York: Panthelon, 1986.

Doyle, William. *Inside the Oval Office: The White House Tapes from FDR to Clinton.* New York: Kodansha International, 2002.

Dunlop, Richard. *Donovan: America's Master Spy.* New York: Rand McNally and Company, 1982.

Eberstadt, Ferdinand. *Unification of the War and Navy Departments and Post War Organization for National Security.* Washington, DC: GPO, 1945.

Farago, Ladislas. *The Broken Seal: Operation Magic and the Secret Road to Pearl Harbor.* New York: Random House, 1967.

Fleming, Thomas. *The New Dealers' War: FDR and the War within World War II.* New York: Basic Books, Perseus Books Group, 2001.

Ford, Corey. *Donovan of OSS.* Boston: Little, Brown and Company, 1970.

Gannon, Michael. *Pearl Harbor Betrayed: The True Story of a Man and a Nation under Attack.* New York: John McCrae Book, Owl Book., Henry Holt and Company, 2001.

Gilbert, Martin. *The First World War: A Complete History.* New York: Holt, 1994.

Goldstein, Donald M. *The Pearl Harbor Papers.* Ed. Katherine V. Dillon. Dulles, VA: Brassey's, 1993.

Goolrick, William K. and Ogden Tanner. *The Battle of the Bulge.* New York: Time-Life Books, 1979.

Hagan, Kenneth J. "The Critic Within in Naval History," *Naval History Magazine.* Annapolis, MD: December 1998.

Hammond, James W. Jr., *The Treaty Navy: The Story of the U.S. Naval Service Between the World Wars.* Victoria, Canada: Wesley Press, Trafford Publishing, 2001.

Hanlon, Michael E., ed. "Doughboy Center: The Story of the American Expeditionary Forces, The Story of the American Polar Bears A.E.F. Northern Russia." See at the Great War Society Web site: http://www.world-war1.com/dbc/p_bears.htm.

Hardesty, Von. *Air Force One.* San Diego, CA: Tehabi Books, 2003.

Hatch, Alden. *Franklin D. Roosevelt: An Informal Biography.* New York: Holt, 1947.

Hayes, John D. "Admiral Joseph Mason Reeves, Part II—1931-1948, *Naval War College Review,* Volume XXIV, Number 5 (January 1972); Volume XXIII, Number 3 (November 1970).

Heller, Milton F. Jr. *The Presidents' Doctor: An Insider's View of Three First Families.* New York: Vantage Press, 2000.

Hicks, Robert E. "All Paris Is Talking about Otto Richardson, Who Grew Up to be Commander-in-Chief of U.S. Fleet," *Fort Worth Star-Telegram,* Sunday, February 18, 1940.

Hill, A. J. *Under Pressure: The Final Voyage of Submarine S-Five.* New York: The Free Press, 2002.

Horwitz, Solis. "The Tokyo Trial," *International Conciliation.* Number 465. Carnegie Endowment for International Peace, 1950. Found on the Internet in 2008 at: http://books.google.com/books?id=DDu5li473rsC&pg=PR37&lpg=PR37&dq=international+conciliation+number&source=web&ots=F2R4vHAr GF&sig=BzBB3AlWJ81p_UrAg332CwTPCwQ.

Ickes, Harold L. *The Secret Diary of Harold L. Ickes: The Inside Struggle,* vol. 2. New York: Simon and Schuster, 1954.

James, Dorris Clayton. *Years of MacArthur,* vol. 2. New York: Houghton Mifflin, 1975.

Jasper, Joy Waldron, James P. Delgado, and Jim Adams. *The USS Arizona.* New York: Truman Tally Books, St. Martin's Press, 2001.

Jurika, Stephen Jr., ed. *Pearl Harbor to Vietnam: The Memoirs of Admiral Arthur W. Radford* . Stanford, CA: Hoover Institution Press, 1980.

Key, David M. Jr., *Admiral Jerauld Wright: Warrior Among Diplomats.* Manhattan, KS: Sunflower University Press, 2001.

Kimmel, Husband E. *Admiral Kimmel's Story.* Chicago: Henry Regnery Company, 1955.

Komatsu, Keiichiro. *Origins of the Pacific War and the Importance of Magic.* New York: St. Martin's Press, 1999.

Krepinevich, Andrew. "Transforming to Victory: The U.S. Navy, Carrier Aviation, and Preparing for War in the Pacific." Cambridge, MA: Olin Institute, 2000.

Lane, Mary Claunch, ed. *The 1870 Lamar County, Texas Federal Census.* Paris, TX: 1993.

Laughery, John. *The Other Side of Silence: Men's Lives and Gay Identities—A Twentieth Century History.* New York: Owl Books, 1999.

Layton, Edwin T., with Roger Pineau and John Costello. *"And I Was There:" Pearl Harbor and Midway—Breaking the Secrets.* New York: William Morrow, 1985.

Leahy, Admiral William D. *I Was There: The Personal Story of the Chief of Staff to Presidents Roosevelt and Truman Based on His Notes and Diaries Made at the Time.* New York: Whittlesey House, McGraw Hill Book Company, 1950.

Leon, Philip W. *Bullies and Cowards: The West Point Hazing Scandal, 1898-1901.* Westport, CT: Greenwood Press, 1999.

Lovell, Mary S. *The Sound of Wings: The Life of Amelia Earhart.* New York: St. Martin's Press, 1989.

Lowe, R. Stanley. *Wyoming's Great Admiral: Emory Scott Land.* Casper, WY: Privately published, 1998.

Lowman, David D. *Magic: The Untold Story of U.S. Intelligence and the Evacuation of Japanese Residents from the West Coast During WWII.* Provo, UT: Athena Press, 2001.

MacDonald, Scot. "Evolution of Aircraft Carriers: Last of the Fleet Problems." *Naval Aviation News.* Washington, DC: Government Printing Department, 1964. Found on the Internet in 2008 at: http://www.history.navy.mil/branches/car-toc.htm.

Mallory, J. R. *Some Mallorys and Bells.* Greenville, TX: Texas Printing Company, 1950.

Manchester, William. *American Caesar: Douglas MacArthur 1880-1964.* New York: Dell Publishing Company, 1978.

Manning, Ethel. "Admiral Boone, Healer of Presidents," found on the Internet in 2002 at: http://archives.pottsville.com/archives/2000/Nov/13/E425921A.htlm.

Marolda, Edward J., ed. *FDR and the U.S. Navy.* New York: Palgrave Macmillan, 1998. From a presentation by Ronald H. Spector titled "Josephus Daniels, Franklin Roosevelt, and the Reinvention of the Naval Enlisted Man."

Marshall, S. L. A. *The American Heritage History of World War I.* New York: The American Heritage Publishing Company, 1964.

Massie, Robert K. *Dreadnought: Britain, German and the Coming of the Great War.* New York: Ballantine Books, 1991.

McFarland, Stephen L. *A Concise History of the Air Force.* Washington, DC: Department of the Air Force, 1997.

Miller, Edward S. *War Plan Orange: The U.S. Strategy to Defeat Japan 1897-1945.* Annapolis, MD: Naval Institute Press, 1991.

Mills, Betsy, ed. *Loose Leaves of the History of Lamar County.* Paris, TX: Genealogy Society of Lamar County, 1995.

Minear, R. H. *Victor's Justice—The War Crimes Trial.* Princeton, NJ: Princeton University Press, 1971.

Moore, Joel R., Harry H. Mead, and Lewis E. Jahns. *The History of the American Expedition Fighting the Bolsheviki: Campaigning in North Russia 1918-1919.* Detroit, MI: Topping-Sonders Company, 1920, republished by Polar Bear Publishers.

Morgan, Ted. *FDR: A Biography.* New York: Simon & Schuster, 1985.

Morgenstern, George. *Pearl Harbor: The Story of the Secret War.* New York: Devin-Adair Publishers, 1947.

Morison, Samuel Eliot. "Did Roosevelt Start the War?" *The Atlantic Monthly,* Volume 182, 91, 7.

———*History of the United States Naval Operations in World War II.* 15 vols. Boston: Little Brown, 1947-1962.

Murphy, Lawrence R. *Perverts by Official Order.* Binghampton, NY: Haworth Press, 1988.

Nalty, Bernard C., ed. *Winged Shield, Winged Sword: A History of the United States Air Force.* vol. 1. Washington, DC: Air Force History and Museums Project, 1997.

Neville, Alexander White. *History of Lamar County.* Paris, TX: North Texas Publishing Company, 1937.

Nichols, David, ed. *Ernie's War: The Best of Ernie Pyle's World War II Dispatches.* New York: Random House, Inc., 1986.

Noble, Dennis. *The Eagle and the Dragon: The United States Military in China.* Westport, CT: Greenwood Press, 1990.

O'Connor, Richard. *London: A Biography.* New York: Little Brown, Inc., 1964.

Ogilvie, Craig, ed. "William Ogilvie: Gentleman of the Yukon." *Ogilvie Kith and Kin.* Volume 19, Number 1. Batesville, AR: September 2000.

Ogilvie, William. *Early Days on the Yukon & the Story of Its Gold Finds.* New York: 1974 reprint. Digital reproduction at: http://www.nosracines.ca /e/toc.aspx?id=2959.

Peattie, Mark R. *Hoover Essay: A Historian Looks at the Pacific War.* Stanford, CA: Leland Stanford Junior University, 1995.

Perez, Robert C. and Edward F. Willett. *Clarence Dillon: Wall Street Enigma.* New York: Rowman & Littlefield Publishers, Inc, 1995.

Phillips, Mary Ann. *Fletcher Warren Reporting for Duty, Sir.* Austin, TX: Nortex Press, 2006.

Piccigallo, Philip R. *The Japanese On Trial: Allied War Crimes Operation in the East 1945-1951.* Austin: University of Texas Press, 1979.

Potter, E. B. *Admiral Arleigh Burke.* New York: Random House, 1990.

Prange, Gordon W., in collaboration with Donald M. Goldstein and Katherine V. Dillon. *At Dawn We Slept*. New York: McGraw-Hill, 1981; reprint New York: Penquin Books, 1983.

———*Pearl Harbor: The Verdict of History*. New York: McGraw-Hill Book Company, 1985.

Pratt, Fletcher. "They Called Her 'The Swayback Maru,'" *Saga Magazine* (June 1956, Part 1).

Pye, Anne Briscoe and Nancy Shea. *The Navy Wife*. New York: Harper and Brothers, 1942.

Ralfalko, Frank J., ed. Federation of American Scientists, *Counterintelligence Reader* (National Counterintelligence Center, I.) On the Internet at: http://fas.org/irp/ops/ci/docs/ci1/.

Rhodes, Weldon E. "Dusty." *Flying MacArthur*. College Station: Texas A&M University Press, 1987.

Rich, Doris L. *A Biography of Amelia Earhart*. Washington, DC: Smithsonian Institution Press, 1989.

Richardson, James O., Assistant to the Chief of Naval Operations, "Organization of the Navy Department," speech given to the Army Industrial College, Washington, DC, December 9, 1937.

———*On the Treadmill to Pearl Harbor: The Memoirs of Admiral James O. Richardson as Told to George C. Dyer*. Washington, DC: Department of the Navy, 1973.

Riley, Walter Lee. "The International Military Tribunal for the Far East and the Law of the Tribunal as Revealed by the Judgment and the Concurring and Dissenting Opinions." Seattle, WA: Dissertation at the University of Washington, 1947.

Rodman, Hugh. *Yarns of a Kentucky Admiral*. London: Martin Hopkinson Ltd, 1929.

Röling, B. V. A. *The Tokyo Trail and Beyond: Reflections of a Peacemonger*. Ed., Antonio Cassese. Cambridge, MA: Polity Press, Blackwell Publishers, 1993.

Safford, Laurance F. and J. N. Wenger. *U.S. Naval Communications Intelligence*. Laguna Hills, CA: Aegean Park Press, 1994.

Safford, Laurance F. with Cameron A. Warren and Robert A. Payne. *Earhart's Flight into Yesterday: The Facts without the Fiction*. McLean, VA: Paladwr Press, 2003.

Schaffer, Ronald. "General Stanley D. Embick: Military Dissenter," *Military Affairs,* vol. 37, October 1973.

Schultz, Duane. *The Doolittle Raid*. New York: St. Martin's Press, 1988.

Schwoebel, Richard L. *Explosion aboard the IOWA*. Annapolis, MD: Naval Institute Press, 1999.

Simpson, B. Mitchell III. *Admiral Harold R. Stark: Architect of Victory 1939-1945*. Columbia: University of South Carolina Press, 1989.

Sinclair, Andrew. *Jack: A Biography of Jack London*. New York: Harper & Row, 1977.

Spector, Ronald H. *Eagle against the Sun: The American War with Japan*. New York: The Free Press, Macmillan, Inc., 1985.

———*Professors of War: The Naval War College and the Development of the Naval Profession*. Newport, RI, 1977; reprint Honolulu, HI: University Press of the Pacific, 2005.

Spelts, Carl. "A Nebraskan in the Navy in WW II," *Buffalo Tails* (Vol. 25, No. 2). Buffalo County, Nebraska, March-April, 2002. Nebraska Historical Society.

Standley, William B. and Arthur Agerton. *Admiral Ambassador to Russia.* Chicago: Henry Regnery Company, 1955.

Steely, Skipper and Frances Ellis. *First Church of Paris.* Wolfe City, TX: Wright Press, 1985.

Steely, Skipper, ed. *The Paris, Texas Scrapbook.* Paris, TX: Compiled by Betsy Mills and the Lamar County Genealogical Society, 1997.

Steinberg, Alfred. *Sam Rayburn.* New York: Hawthorn Books, 1975.

Steinberg, Rafael. *Return to the Philippines.* New York: Time-Life Books, Inc., 1979.

Stillwell, Paul, ed. *Air Raid: Pearl Harbor! Recollections of a Day of Infamy.* Annapolis, MD: Naval Institute Press, 1981.

Stinnett, Robert B. *Day of Deceit: The Truth about FDR and Pearl Harbor.* New York: Touchstone, Simon and Schuster, 2000.

Taussig, Betty Carney. *A Warrior for Freedom.* Manhattan, KS: Sunflower University Press, 1995.

Taussig, Captain J. K., "Prison 'Graduates' Not Welcome," *Army and Navy Journal,* January 10, 1920.

Theobald, Robert A. *The Final Secret of Pearl Harbor.* New York: Devin-Adair Company, 1954.

Thorpe, Elliott R. *East Wind, Rain.* Boston, MA: Gambit Incorporated, 1969.

Toland, John. *Infamy: Pearl Harbor and Its Aftermath.* New York: Berkley Books, 1982.

Tolley, Kemp. *Yangtze Patrol: The U.S. Navy in China.* Annapolis, MD: Naval Institute Press, 1971.

Trivizo, Gil. *A History of the Office of Naval Intelligence, 1882-1942,* found on the Internet in 2008 at: http://odh.trevizo.org/oni.html.

Tuchman, Barbara W. *Stillwell and the American Experience in China 1911-45.* New York: Macmillan Company, 1971; reprint New York: Grove Press, 2001.

Turner, Richmond Kelly. *The Amphibians Came to Conquer: The Story of Admiral Richmond Kelly Turner.* Ed., George C. Dyer. Washington, DC: U.S. Government Printing Office, 1972.

Tute, Warren. *The Deadly Stroke.* New York: Coward, McCann & Geoghegan, Inc., 1973.

Victor, George. *The Pearl Harbor Myth: Rethinking the Unthinkable.* Washington, DC: Potomac Books, 2007.

Vlahos, Michael. *The Blue Sword: The Naval War College and the American Mission 1919-1944.* Newport, RI: Naval War College Press, 1980.

Ward, Geoffrey C. *A First-Class Temperament: The Emergence of Franklin Roosevelt.* New York: Harper and Row, 1989.

Warwick, Christopher. *King George VI & Queen Elizabeth.* London: Beaufort Books, August 1985.

Watson, Mark. *Chief of Staff: Prewar Plans and Preparations,* in subseries *The War Department,* Office of the Chief of Military History, Department of the Army series *The United States Army in World War II.* Washington DC: Government Printing Office, 1950.

Webb, Walter Prescott. *Handbook of Texas I, II and Supplement.* Austin: Texas State Historical Association, 1973. Found online in 2008 at: http://www.tshaon line.org/.

Wheeler, Keith. *The Road to Tokyo.* New York: Time-Books Inc., 1979.

Whitlock, Duane L. "Station C and Fleet Radio Unit Melbourne (FRUMMEL) Revisited," presentation given to the third annual Crypotologic History Symposium at the National Security Agency on October 28, 1992.

Wildenberg, Thomas. *All the Factors of Victory: Admiral Joseph Mason Reeves and the Origins of Carrier Airpower.* Washington, DC: Brassey's Inc., 2003.

Wilhelm, Maria. *The Man Who Watched the Rising Sun: The Story of Admiral Ellis M. Zacharias.* New York: Franklin Watts Inc., 1967.

Wohlstetter, Roberta. *Pearl Harbor: Warning and Decision.* Stanford, CA: Stanford University Press, 1962.

Wolk, Herman S. "Arnold, Eisenhower and Norstad: The Fight for Air Independence," a paper found on the Internet in 2003 at: www.airforcehistory. hq.af.mil/Publications/golden/03.pdf.

———*The Struggle for Air Force Independence 1943-1947.* Washington, DC: Air Force History and Museums Program, 1997.

Wright, Michael, ed. *Reader's Digest Illustrated History of World War II.* New York: 1989.

Zacharias, Captain Ellis M. *Secret Missions: The Story of an Intelligence Officer.* New York: G. P. Putnam, 1946.

Internet Sources

A History of the Office of Naval Intelligence 1882-1942, "The Japanese Mandated Islands," found on the Internet in 2002 at: http://www.geocities.com/furry logic2/oni5.html

Avalon Projected at Yale Law School, found on the Internet at: http://www.yale. edu/lawweb/avalon/imtfech.htm

DANFS Online.
   http://www.hazegray.org/danfs

General History Subjects:
   http://www.chanrobles.com/tydingsmcduffieact.htm
   http://www.ibiblio.org/lia/president/EisenhowerLibrary/oral_histories/Jehl_ Sue-Sarafian.html
   http://www.villariviera.net/
   http://www.womanpilot.com/
   http://www.globalsecurity.org/military/world/naval-arms-control-1930.htm
   http://tighar.org/Projects/Earhart/AEoverview.html
   http://www.multied.com/navy/cruiser/Augusta.html
   http://www.trumanlibrary.org/oralhist/trumanl.htm
   http://www.nadn.navy.mil/VirtualTour/150years/
   http://www.talesofoldchina.com/shanghai/
   http://www.history.navy.mil/faqs/faq72-5.htm#anchor426903
   http://toto.lib.unca.edu/findingaids/mss/ashe/history.html

Kahn, David. "The Codebreakers: The Comprehensive History of Secret

Communication from Ancient Times to the Internet." http://www.wnyc.org/books/1622

Lamar County GenWeb Site. Lamar County Cemetery Records. http://www.rootsweb.com/~txlamar/cemetery/1cemmain.htm

Microsoft® Encarta® Online Encyclopedia 2000, at: http://encarta.msn.com

Naval Historical Center, Internet site at:
http://www.history.navy.mil/photos/sh-usn/usnsh-m
http://www.history.navy.mil/faqs/faq36-2.htm

Pearl Harbor subject:
http://polyticks.com/bbma/friendly_fire.htm
http://www.csbaonline.org/4Publications/Archive/A.20000000.Transforming_to_Vi/A.20000000.Transforming_to_Vi.htm
http://www.arlingtoncemetery.net/aradford.htm
http://www.transpect.com/japan_diary/#a23
http://www.fdrlibrary.marist.edu/psf/box4/t46h01.html
http://www.vectorsite.net/index.html
http://www.ibiblio.org/pha/timeline/Washington_v_Tokyo.html
http://www.ww2pacific.com
http://anthonydamato.law.northwestern.edu/WWII/Complaint%2013%20FINAL.htm
http://www.geocities.com/scs028a/index.html
http://www.navy.mil
http://elibrary.unm.edu/oanm/NmU/nmu1%23mss413bc/
http://navysite.de/ffg/FFG31.HTM#top
http://www.ukans.edu/~kansite/ww_one/naval/n0000000.htm
http://www.marxists.org/history/ussr/foreign/author/chicherin.htm
http://navysite.de/navy/facts.htm
http://www.vpnavy.com/vt5_history.html
http://www.internet-esq.com/ussaugusta/history/1928-31.htm
http://pages.cthome.net/boyd544/Diary12.htm
http://www.chinfo.navy.mil/navpalib/ships/battleships/wyoming/bb32-wyo.html
http://groups.yahoo.com/group/PBY/message/9010?source=1
http://www.indiana.edu/~easc/security_issues/unitedstates/vesailles_treaty.pdf
http://www.fbi.gov/page2/feb05/kuehn022105.htm
http://mywebpages.comcast.net/wgoffeney/Case/usscase.htm
http://www.airgroup4.com/book/indx/index33.htm
http://www.chinfo.navy.mil/navpalib/ships/carriers/histories/cv08-hornet/cv08-hornet.html
http://www.fdrlibrary.marist.edu/psf/box4/t46j02.html
http://www.hazegray.org/danfs/auxil/ad11.htm
http://www.history.navy.mil/photos/images/h77000/h770821.htm
http://www.history.navy.mil/sources/ms/mdah.htm
http://www.arlingtoncemetery.net/rhleigh.htm
http://www.ussarizona.org/survivors/vlach/index.html

http://www.ibiblio.org/hyperwar/USN/ships/dafs/DD/dd363.html

http://www.homeofheroes.com/news/archives/2002_1109_ boone.html

http://www.microworks.net/pacific/bases/btnb_online/ulithi.htm

http://www.warships1.com/

http://www.microworks.net/pacific/special/history1.htm

http://www.milhist.net/usaaf/mto44b.html

http://www.ncsociety.net/pha/timeline/410127apw.html

http://ibiblio.org/pha/timeline/Magic.html

http://www.revise.it/reviseit/EssayLab/Eb2.asp?eID=21

http://www.senate.gov/pagelayout/art/a_three_sections_with_teasers/art_hist _home.htm

http://www.users.bigpond.com/pacificwar/gatheringstorm/Philippines/Phil overview. htmlhttp://www.yale.edu/lawweb/avalon/wwii/cairo.htm

"Pearl Harbor Revisited: United States Navy Communications Intelligence 1924-42," found on the Internet in 2002 at: http://www.history.navy.mil/books/ comint/ComInt-4.html

Zwick, Jim, ed., "Anti-Imperialism in the United States, 1898-1935," found at http://www.boondocksnet.com/ail98-35.html

III. Periodicals

Advertiser, Honolulu

Advocate, Paris (Texas)

Army and Navy Journal

Army and Navy Register

Atlantic Monthly

Call-Bulletin, San Francisco

Colliers

Daily Globe, St. Louis

Daily News, New York

Evening Star, Washington

Gazette, Tokyo

Herald, Tulia (Texas)

Holland's Magazine of the South

Inquirer, Philadelphia

Keystone (yearbook, USS *Pennsylvania*)

Kiplinger Washington Letter

Literary Digest

Lucky Bag (yearbook, United States Naval Academy)

Manchester Guardian (United Kingdom)

Methodist Visitor (Dallas, Texas)

Morning News, Dallas

News, Charlotte (North Carolina)

News, Paris (Texas)

News-Pilot, San Pedro (California)

Newsweek

Owl (yearbook, Paris, Texas, High School)
Post, Washington
Post-Dispatch, St. Louis
Press-Telegram, Long Beach (California)
Proceedings (Annapolis, Maryland)
Relevance: Quarterly Journal of the Great War Society (Moscow, Idaho)
Saturday Evening Post
Star, Washington
Star-Bulletin, Honolulu
Star-Telegram, Fort Worth
Sun, Chicago
Time
Times, Los Angeles
Times, New York
Woman Pilot (magazine)
World-Telegram, New York

Index